The Nazi Germany Sourcebook

The Nazi Germany Sourcebook is an exciting new collection of documents on the origins, rise, course and consequences of National Socialism, the Third Reich, the Second World War, and the Holocaust. Packed full of both official and private papers from the perspectives of perpetrators and victims, these sources offer a revealing insight into why Nazism came into being, its extraordinary popularity in the 1930s, how it affected the lives of people, and what it means to us today.

This carefully edited series of 148 documents, drawn from 1850 to 2000, covers the pre-history and aftermath of Nazism. Sources include legislative and diplomatic records, minutes of meetings, speeches and manifestoes, personal diaries and eyewitness accounts. Each document is preceded by a brief critical analysis that also provides the historical context in which it was written. Organized into seven chapters, *The Nazi Germany Sourcebook* focuses on key areas of study, helping students to understand and critically evaluate this extraordinary historical episode:

- The ideological roots of Nazism, and the First World War
- The Weimar Republic
- The consolidation of Nazi power
- Hitler's motives, aims and preparation for war
- The Second World War
- The Holocaust
- The Cold War and recent historical debates.

The Nazi Germany Sourcebook contains numerous documents that have never before been published in English, and some documents, such as Goebbels' 1941 diaries that have only recently been discovered. This up-to-date collection of primary sources provides fascinating reading for anyone interested in this historical phenomenon.

Roderick Stackelberg is Robert K. and Ann J. Powers Professor of the Humanities at Gonzaga University. He is the author of *Hitler's Germany: Origins, Interpretations, Legacies* (1999). **Sally A. Winkle** is Professor of German Language and Literature and Director of Women's Studies at Eastern Washington University. She is the author of *Woman as Bourgeois Feminine Ideal* (1988).

The Nazi Germany Sourcebook

AN ANTHOLOGY OF TEXTS

Roderick Stackelberg
and
Sally A. Winkle

London and New York

First published 2002
by Routledge
I I New Fetter Lane, London EC4P 4EE

Simultaneously published in the USA and Canada
by Routledge
29 West 35th Street, New York, NY 10001

Routledge is an imprint of the Taylor & Francis Group

Typeset in Baskerville and Gill Sans by Bookcraft Ltd, Stroud, Gloucestershire
Printed and bound in Great Britain by TJ International Ltd, Padstow, Cornwall

British Library Cataloguing in Publication Data
A catalogue record for this book is available from the British Library

Library of Congress Cataloging in Publication Data
The Nazi Germany sourcebook: an anthology of texts/Roderick Stackelberg and
Sally A. Winkle.
p. cm.
Includes bibliographical references and index.
1. National socialism–History–Sources. 2. Germany–History–1933–1945–Sources.
3. Nationalism–Germany–History–Sources.
I. Stackelberg, Roderick. II. Winkle, Sally Anne.
DD256.5 .N359 2002
943'.086–dc21   2001051082

ISBN 0–415–22213–3 (hbk)
ISBN 0–415–22214–1 (pbk)

Contents

Illustrations

Maps

Tables

Plates
after page xxxi

Documents

THE GERMAN EMPIRE AND THE FIRST WORLD WAR

THE WEIMAR REPUBLIC, 1919–33

THE THIRD REICH: THE CONSOLIDATION OF NAZI RULE, 1933–35

THE THIRD REICH: THE ROAD TO WAR, 1936–39

THE SECOND WORLD WAR, 1939–45

THE HOLOCAUST

THE AFTERMATH OF NAZISM AND THE HISTORIANS' DEBATE

Note

† Denotes an original footnote to a document.

Authors' acknowledgements

The editors and publishers are grateful to the following for permission to reproduce copyright material:

To Stiebner Verlag, Munich, for permission to reprint extracts from H. S. Chamberlain's *Foundations of the Nineteenth Century*, the correspondence between Chamberlain and Wilhelm II, and Chamberlain's letter to Hitler.

To W. W. Norton for permission to reprint excerpts from Fritz Fischer's *Germany's Aims in the First World War*.

To University of Texas Press for permission to reprint "The Russian Jewish Revolution" by Alfred Rosenberg and "Draft of a Comprehensive Program of National Socialism" by Gregor Strasser.

To the Kommission für Geschichte des Parlamentarismus und der politischen Parteien in Bonn for permission to reprint the proclamation of Director General Wolfgang Kapp.

To the Estate of George Grosz and Visual Artists and Galleries Association, Inc., for permission to reproduce George Grosz' "The Pimps of Death" and reprint extracts from *George Grosz: An Autobiography*.

To Viking Penguin, a division of Penguin Putnam, Inc., and to Williams Verlag AG, Zurich, for permission to reprint excerpts from *The World of Yesterday* by Stefan Zweig.

To Houghton Mifflin for permission to reprint extracts Adolf Hitler's *Mein Kampf.*

To Dietz Verlag, Berlin, for permission to translate extracts from *Gesichte und Geschichte* by Lea Grundig, *Zur Geschichte der deutschen Arbeiterbewegung* by Walter Ulbricht, and *Im Kampf um die einige Deutsche Demokratische Republik* by Otto Grotewohl.

To Cordula Schacht for permission to reprint excerpts from Goebbels' diaries.

To E. S. Mittler & Sohn, Hamburg, for permission to reprint excerpts from *Aufbau einer Nation* by Hermann Goering.

To Paul Zsolnay Verlag Gesellschaft M. B. H., Vienna, for permission to translate excerpts from *Denn heute gehört uns Deutschland: Persönliches und politisches Tagebuch von der Machtergreifung bis zum 31. Dezember 1935* by Erich Ebermayer.

To Fischer Taschenbuch Verlag GmbH, Frankfurt am Main, for permission to translate excerpts from *Eine Handvoll Staub* by Lina Haag.

To the William L. Shirer Literary Trust for permission to reprint excerpts from *Berlin Diary* by William L. Shirer.

To R. Oldenbourg Verlag, Munich, for permission to translate extracts from *General Ludwig Beck: Studien und Dokumente zur politisch-militärischen Vorstellungswelt und Tätigkeit des Generalstabschefs des deutschen Heeres 1933–38.*

To Simon & Schuster for permission to reprint extracts from *The Rise and Fall of the Third Reich* by William L. Shirer.

To University Press of New England for permission to reprint excerpts from *The White Rose: Munich 1942–1943* by Inge Aicher-Scholl.

To Heinrich Hugendubel Verlag, Munich, for permission to translate excerpts from *Namen die keiner mehr nennt* by Marion Gräfin Dönhoff.

To the Verlagsgesellschaft mbH & Co in Cologne for permission to translate and reprint "The Diary of Erika S., Hamburg, 1944–1945".

To the Institute of Contemporary History and Wiener Library Limited, London, for permission to translate "Bericht Elfriede Loew" by Elfriede Loew.

To Kluwer Academic Publishers for permission to reprint "Farewell Letters from Tarnopol" in *In the Name of the People: Perpetrators of Genocide in the Reflection of their Post-war Prosecution in West Germany* by Dick de Mildt.

To Professor Joseph Walk, Jerusalem, for permission to translate excerpts from *Mit meinen Augen: Botschaft einer Auschwitz-Überlebenden* by Lucie Begov.

To Deutsche Verlags-Anstalt GmbH, Munich, for permission to translate excerpts from Konrad Adenauer, *Reden 1917–1967*, edited by Hans-Peter Schwartz.

To Viking Penguin, a division of Penguin Putnam, Inc., for permission to reprint excerpts from Willy Brandt, *My Life in Politics*, translated by Anthea Bell.

To Piper Verlag GmbH, Munich, for permission to translate and reprint "Geschichte in einem geschichtslosen Land" by Michael Stürmer, "Vergangenheit die nicht vergehen will" by Ernst Nolte, and "Eine Art Schadensabwicklung: Die apologetischen Tendenzen in der deutschen Zeitgeschichtsschreibung" by Jürgen Habermas.

To Beacon Press for permission to reprint "Reappraisal and Repression: The Third Reich in West German Historical Consciousness" by Hans Mommsen in *Reworking the Past: Hitler, the Holocaust, and the Historians' Debate*, edited by Peter Baldwin.

To the Interior Ministry of the Federal Republic of Germany for permission to translate "Bericht des Bundes-Innenministeriums: Rechtsextremistische Gewalttaten 1992."

To Zeitverlag, Hamburg, publishers of *Die Zeit*, for permission to translate "Ganz normal rechts: Zu Besuch an sächsischen Schulen" by Toralf Staud.

To the Centre for the Study of Cartoons and Caricature, University of Kent, Canterbury CT2 7NU, Kent, for supplying Plate 7.

While the editors and publisher have made every effort to contact all copyright holders of material used in this volume, they would be grateful to hear from any they were unable to contact.

Chronology

This chronology makes no claim to completeness. It is designed to assist readers in placing the documents in this book in historical context.

1871	January	Unification of Germany and founding of German Empire under Chancellor Otto von Bismarck.
1875		Founding of Socialist Workers' Party.
1878		Bismarck's anti-socialist Laws passed by Reichstag. Court Chaplain Adolf Stoecker founds anti-Semitic Christian Social Workers' Party.
1879		Austro-German Dual Alliance.
1888	June	Wilhelm II becomes kaiser.
1889	20 April	Adolf Hitler born in Braunau am Inn in Austria.
1890	March	Bismarck dismissed. Anti-socialist laws repealed.
1891		Socialist Party, renamed Social Democratic Party (SPD), adopts Marxist program. Formation of Pan-German League. Formation of Franco-Russian alliance.
1898		German naval construction program.
1899		Publication of Houston Stewart Chamberlain's *Foundations of the Nineteenth Century*.
1907	August	Formation of Triple Entente (Britain, France, Russia).
1908	5 October	Crisis precipitated by Austrian annexation of Bosnia.
1911	July	Crisis precipitated by dispatch of German gunboat to Agadir in French-controlled Morocco. SPD opposes German action.
1912	January	SPD gains 25 percent of seats and becomes largest party in the Reichstag.
1914	28 June	Heir to the Austrian throne assassinated in Sarajevo.
	28 July	Austria-Hungary declares war on Serbia.
	1 August	Germany declares war on Russia.
	3 August	Germany declares war on France.
	4 August	Britain declares war on Germany.
	10 September	Schlieffen Plan fails after German defeat at the Battle of the Marne.
1915	April	Germans introduce use of poison gas on the Western front.
	May	Italy enters the war against Germany and Austria-Hungary.
1916	August	Field Marshall Paul von Hindenburg appointed Commander-in-Chief of German forces with General Erich Ludendorff as his Chief of Staff.
1917	31 January	Germany resumes unlimited submarine warfare.
	16 March	Czar Nicholas II abdicates after a week of revolutionary turbulence.
	6 April	US declares war on Germany.
	July	SPD supports Peace Resolution in Reichstag. High Command ousts Chancellor Theodor von Bethmann-Hollweg from office.
	7 November	Bolsheviks under Vladimir Ilyich Lenin seize power in Russia.
	8 November	Lenin issues Peace Decree.
	16 December	Russian armistice with Germany.
1918	February	German troops seize Kiev and advance on Petrograd.
	14 March	Peace treaty between Russia and Germany signed at Brest-Litovsk.

	31 March	Germans mount final offensive in West.
	May	Civil war in Russia with Allies supporting the counter-revolution.
	July	German offensive halted in West.
	October	Germany sues for peace.
	3 November	Revolt of German sailors in Kiel.
	7 November	Revolution in Bavaria.
	9 November	Abdication of Kaiser Wilhelm II. Proclamation of German Republic.
	11 November	German government emissaries sign armistice at Compiègne ending First World War.
1919	January	Spartacus uprising is crushed in Berlin.
	February	National Constitutional Assembly convenes in Weimar. Friedrich Ebert elected President.
	23 March	Benito Mussolini organizes new fascism movement in Italy.
	May	Soviet regime crushed in Bavaria.
	28 June	Signing of Treaty of Versailles.
	31 July	Adoption of Weimar Constitution.
	12 September	Hitler joins the German Workers' Party in Munich.
1920	24 February	German Workers' Party adopts "25-point Program."
	March	Kapp Putsch attempt in Berlin.
	6 October	Armistice with Poland ends Russian Civil War.
1921	29 July	Hitler becomes chairman of renamed National Socialist German Workers' Party (NSDAP)
1922	30 October	Mussolini asked to form a new government in Italy after threatening a "March on Rome."
1923	11 January	French army occupies industrial Ruhr.
	27 January	First Nazi Party Congress in Munich.
	June	The "Great Inflation" in Germany.
	12 August	Gustav Stresemann becomes German chancellor and ends policy of passive resistance to the French.
	20 October	Under dictator Gustav von Kahr, Bavaria breaks relations with central government in Berlin.
	9 November	Hitler and Ludendorff launch Beer Hall Putsch in Munich.
	15 November	Introduction of new currency ends Great Inflation.
1924	1 April	Hitler sentenced to five years in prison for high treason with eligibility for parole in six months.
	20 December	Hitler released from prison.
1925	27 February	Hitler reorganizes NSDAP.
	25 April	Hindenburg elected German President.
	July	Publication of first volume of *Mein Kampf*.
	9 November	Formation of NSDAP protection squad (SS).
1926	January	Hitler rejects any modification to "25-point Program."
1927	10 March	Speaking ban on Hitler lifted in Prussia.
1928	20 May	Nazis receive only 2.6 percent of the vote in Reichstag elections.
1929	24 October	Start of stock market crash in New York.
1930	16 July	Chancellor Heinrich Brüning rules by decree under Article 48 of the Weimar Constitution.
	14 September	Nazis become second-largest party in the Reichstag with 18.3 percent of the vote.
1931	October	Hitler joins Nationalists (DNVP) in giant Harzburg Front rally.
1932	7 January	Chancellor Brüning declares Germany will not resume reparations.
	27 January	Hitler gains enthusiastic reception by industrialists in Düsseldorf.
	10 April	Hindenburg reelected President in run-off against Hitler.
	13 April	Brüning prohibits paramilitary units from marching in public.
	30 May	Brüning resigns as chancellor and is replaced by Franz von Papen.
	16 June	Ban on Nazi storm troopers lifted.
	20 July	Papen removes SPD prime minister in Prussia and declares martial law.
	31 July	Nazis double their strength and become largest party in Reichstag with 37.4 percent of the vote.

	13 August	Hitler refuses post of vice-chancellor in Papen's government.
	30 August	Hermann Goering elected president of Reichstag.
	November	Transit strike paralyzes Berlin.
	6 November	Nazis lose 35 seats in Reichstag election, while Communists continue to gain.
	2 December	General Kurt von Schleicher named German chancellor.
1933	30 January	Hitler appointed chancellor with Papen as vice-chancellor.
	27 February	Fire destroys Reichstag.
	28 February	Hitler suspends basic civil liberties.
	5 March	Nazis win 43.9 percent of Reichstag vote and form a majority with the Nationalists.
	20 March	Nazis open first official concentration camp in Dachau near Munich.
	23 March	Reichstag passes Enabling Act giving Hitler full dictatorial power.
	31 March	Beginning of Gleichschaltung of the states.
	1 April	Nazis organize one-day boycott of Jewish businesses.
	7 April	Removal of Jews, Communists, Social Democrats and other political opponents from the Civil Service.
	2 May	Dissolution of labor unions and formation of German Labor Front (DAF).
	10 May	Public burning of "un-German" books.
	14 July	Nazis become only legal party. Nazis pass sterilization law to prevent "genetically diseased offspring."
	20 July	Concordat between German Reich and the Vatican.
	22 September	Creation of German Chamber of Culture.
	14 October	Germany leaves League of Nations and disarmament conference.
1934	26 January	Non-aggression pact with Poland.
	17 June	Papen's Marburg speech.
	30 June	Over 120 persons killed in purge of Ernst Roehm and the SA.
	25 July	Austrian Nazis fail in attempt to gain power.
	2 August	Death of President Hindenburg. Hitler takes over presidency while retaining title of chancellor.
1935	13 January	90.8 percent vote in favor of reunion with Germany in Saar plebiscite.
	16 March	Hitler announces introduction of universal military training in defiance of Versailles Treaty.
	18 June	Anglo-German Naval Treaty.
	15 September	Nuremberg racial laws deprive Jews of rights.
	28 October	Mussolini's armies invade Ethiopia.
1936	7 March	Nazis enter Rhineland.
	17 June	Heinrich Himmler named head of Reich police.
	31 July	Right-wing forces under Francisco Franco start civil war against Spanish Republic.
	1 August	Hitler opens Olympic Games in Berlin.
	9 September	Announcement of Four-Year Plan.
	13 September	Founding of Lebensborn agency for aid to single mothers.
	25 October	Creation of "Axis" through Italo-German treaty.
	25 November	German–Japanese Anti-Comintern Pact.
	1 December	Membership in Hitler Youth made compulsory.
1937	14 March	Papal encyclical on "The Church in Germany."
	5 November	Hitler outlines his plans for expansion in "Hossbach Memorandum."
	6 November	Italy accedes to Anti-Comintern Pact.
	19 November	Lord Halifax visits Germany to seek British–German agreement.
1938	4 February	Hitler assumes direct control of armed forces through creation of new High Command (OKW).
	12 March	German troops enter Austria.
	10 April	More than 99 percent of voters in Germany and Austria approve the Austrian Anschluss.
	18 August	Resignation of Army Chief of Staff Ludwig Beck.
	29 September	Munich Agreement transfers Sudetenland from Czechoslovakia to Germany.

	9 November	Kristallnacht pogrom against German Jews.
1939	27 February	Britain recognizes Franco's regime in Spain.
	15 March	Nazis occupy Prague in violation of Munich Agreement and establish Protectorate of Bohemia and Moravia.
	1 April	Prime Minister Neville Chamberlain pledges to support Poland militarily against threats to her sovereignty. Germany renounces Anglo-German Naval Treaty and Non-Aggression Treaty with Poland.
	22 May	Italy and Germany sign Pact of Steel.
	2 August	Albert Einstein writes to President Roosevelt suggesting feasibility of atomic bomb.
	16 August	Germany demands Danzig (Gdansk) from Poland.
	22 August	France and Britain reaffirm pledge of aid to Poland.
	23 August	Nazi–Soviet Non-Aggression Treaty signed, with secret protocol dividing Eastern Europe into spheres of influence.
	1 September	Germans invade Poland.
	3 September	Britain and France declare war on Germany.
	27 September	Warsaw surrenders. SS Main Office for Reich Security (RSHA) established in Berlin under Reinhard Heydrich.
	October	Hitler authorizes euthanasia program.
	October 6	Britain and France reject Hitler's offer of peace in return for acceptance of conquest of Poland.
1940	21 February	Construction of concentration camp at Auschwitz.
	9 April	Germans occupy Denmark and invade Norway.
	10 May	Germans launch attack on France and Benelux countries. Winston Churchill replaces Chamberlain as prime minister.
	4 June	Allied expeditionary force evacuated from Dunkirk.
	10 June	Italy declares war on Britain and France.
	22 June	French sign armistice in Compiègne.
	22 July	British reject Hitler's peace proposal.
	September	Standoff in Battle of Britain forces postponement of plans to invade Britain.
	27 September	Signing of Italo–German–Japanese Tripartite Pact.
	October	Hitler unsuccessful in persuading Vichy France and Franco's Spain from joining war against Britain.
	28 October	Italians invade Greece.
	12 November	Soviet Foreign Minister Vyacheslav Molotov visits Hitler in Berlin.
	18 December	Hitler authorizes plans for Operation Barbarossa, the invasion of the USSR.
1941	6 April	Germans invade Yugoslavia and Greece.
	22 June	German troops invade the Soviet Union. Einsatzgruppen begin extermination of Jews.
	17 July	New Ministry for the Occupied Eastern Territories established under Alfred Rosenberg.
	31 July	Heydrich instructed to draw up plan for general solution of Jewish Question in Europe.
	14 August	Churchill and Roosevelt sign Atlantic Charter.
	27 August	German troops take Smolensk, 200 miles from Moscow.
	4 September	Leningrad surrounded.
	19 September	Jews in Germany forced to wear yellow Star of David.
	5 December	Soviets launch counterattack at Moscow.
	7 December	Japanese attack on Pearl Harbor.
	8 December	Gassing of Jews in mobile gas vans at Chelmno begins.
	11 December	Germany and Italy declare war on the US.
	19 December	Field Marshal Walther von Brauchitsch dismissed as Commander of the Army. Hitler assumes operational command of the army.
1942	20 January	Wannsee Conference to coordinate Final Solution of Jewish Question.
	22 June	Beginning of deportation of Jews from Warsaw Ghetto to Treblinka.
	September	German troops reach Stalingrad.
	31 October	British counteroffensive forces Rommel's Africa Corps to retreat at El Alamein in Egypt.

	8 November	Anglo-American landing in North Africa.
	11 November	Germans occupy Vichy France.
	23 November	Soviets encircle German Sixth Army in Stalingrad.
1943	15 January	Roosevelt and Churchill announce policy of "unconditional surrender" at Casablanca Conference.
	31 January	Surrender of the German Sixth Army at Stalingrad.
	18 February	"White Rose" student resistance leaders arrested. Goebbels announces "total war" at mass rally in Berlin.
	19 April	Start of Warsaw Ghetto uprising.
	12 May	Surrender of Africa Corps at Tunis.
	16 May	Warsaw Ghetto uprising suppressed and ghetto destroyed.
	10 July	Allies land in Sicily.
	13 July	German defeat in the Battle of Kursk.
	25 July	Mussolini deposed by Fascist Grand Council.
	24 August	Himmler becomes Reich Interior Minister.
	3 September	Italy signs armistice with Allies.
	25 September	Soviets retake Smolensk.
	13 October	Italy declares war on Germany.
1944	19 March	German troops occupy Hungary. Beginning of roundup of Hungarian Jews under personal direction of Adolf Eichmann.
	4 June	Allied forces enter Rome.
	6 June	D-Day: Allied invasion of Normandy.
	22 June	Opening of Soviet summer offensive.
	20 July	German military revolt fails.
	1 August	Start of uprising of Polish Home Army.
	18 August	Red Army reaches German borders in East Prussia.
	25 August	Liberation of Paris.
	15 September	Anglo-American forces reach German borders in West.
	3 October	Surrender of Polish Home Army in Warsaw.
	November	End of gassing operations at Auschwitz.
	16 December	German counterattack in the Battle of the Bulge in the Ardennes.
1945	27 January	Liberation of Auschwitz by Red Army troops.
	11 February	Big Three (Roosevelt, Stalin, Churchill) meet at Yalta in the Crimea and decide on temporary division of Germany into occupation zones after the war.
	14 February	Allied planes devastate Dresden.
	8 March	American troops cross Rhine River at Remagen.
	28 April	Mussolini killed by partisans in Milan.
	30 April	Hitler commits suicide in his bunker in Berlin.
	8 May	Germans surrender unconditionally.
	23 May	Hitler's successor Karl Doenitz and other government leaders arrested
	July–August	Potsdam Conference confirms formation of Allied Control Council to govern Germany from Berlin.
	2 September	Japan signs unconditional surrender.
	20 November	Beginning of Nuremberg War Crimes trials.
1946	16 October	Execution of Nazi war criminals at Nuremberg.
1947	1 Jan.	American and British zones of occupation combined into "Bizonia."
	5 June	Secretary of State George Marshall announces European Recovery Program.
1948	21 March	Soviets walk out of Allied Control Council in protest against failure to create central German government.
	25 June	Soviets blockade Western land access to Berlin to protest introduction of new Western currency and creation of separate West German state. Allies mount airlift.
1949	12 May	End of Berlin blockade.
	23 May	Establishment of Federal Republic of Germany (FRG).
	15 September	Konrad Adenauer becomes first chancellor of FRG.
	12 October	Establishment of German Democratic Republic (GDR) with Walter Ulbricht as head of the Socialist Unity Party (SED).

1952	10 September	The FRG and Israel sign agreement providing restitution payments to Jewish people.
1955	5 May	Paris Agreements give FRG full sovereignty with authority to rearm, without nuclear, biological, or chemical weapons.
	14 May	Soviet Union forms Warsaw Pact in response to German rearmament and membership in NATO.
	15 May	Austrian State Treaty ends occupation.
	September	Adenauer visits Moscow to open diplomatic relations between the FRG and USSR and to secure the return of remaining German POWs.
1956	17 August	Communist Party outlawed in FRG.
1961	11 April	Beginning of Eichmann trial in Jerusalem.
	13 August	Construction of Berlin Wall separating East and West Berlin.
1967	2 June	The killing of a student by a policeman at a demonstration against the Shah of Iran in Berlin precipitates militant student protests.
1969	21 October	Willy Brandt (SPD) is elected chancellor.
1970	7 December	Brandt signs treaty of reconciliation with Poland and kneels at memorial to the victims of the Warsaw Ghetto uprising.
1971	3 May	Walter Ulbricht replaced by Erich Honecker as First Secretary of the SED.
1972	17 May	The West German parliament ratifies treaty recognizing the GDR as a separate state within the German nation.
	3 June	Four-Power Accord recognizes special status of West Berlin.
1977	18 October	Leaders of the terrorist Red Army Fraction (RAF) commit suicide in prison.
1982	1 October	No-confidence vote leads to replacement of Chancellor Helmut Schmidt (SPD) by Helmut Kohl of the conservative Christian Democratic Union (CDU).
1985	5 May	US President Ronald Reagan joins Chancellor Kohl for a controversial ceremony at the military cemetery in Bitburg as an act of conciliation on the 40th anniversary of the end of the Second World War.
1986–87		Historian Ernst Nolte's revisionism precipitates bitter historians' dispute (*Historikerstreit*) on the place of National Socialism in German history.
1989	9 November	Opening of the Berlin Wall.
1990	18 March	Elections in the GDR bring the CDU to power.
	18 May	The FRG and GDR sign a treaty to unite Germany under the West German constitution.
	12 September	Four victor powers and two German states sign a treaty conferring full sovereignty on a united Germany and renouncing all German territorial claims arising from the Second World War.
	3 October	Reunification of Germany with its capital in Berlin.

Preface

This book is a collection of documents and source materials of various kinds on Nazi Germany. It provides a historical survey of the Nazi era, its pre-history, and its aftermath through the primary sources that are the building blocks of history. The book is probably most useful when read alongside a detailed narrative history, such as *Hitler's Germany: Origins, Interpretations, Legacies* (Routledge, 1999). It can, however, stand on its own, as the introductory materials and commentaries do provide a narrative and analytic framework to help readers make sense of the various documents.

While concentrating on the period from 1918 to 1945, the book contains relevant documents spanning the period from the mid-nineteenth century to the end of the twentieth. Many of the documents in this collection have not been published in English before. We have checked previously translated selections against the German originals as well to ensure their accuracy. Wherever possible we have tried to maintain the integrity of each selection by citing significant portions and avoiding excessively truncated texts.

Many people have been most helpful to us in completing this ambitious project. Both Eastern Washington University and Gonzaga University provided significant institutional support that ranged from funding faxes, copying expenses, and telephone costs to granting the professional leaves necessary for us to complete this anthology. The travel and supply budget of the Powers Chair at Gonzaga University funded travel to libraries and archives that would otherwise not have been possible. Many staff members from both universities contributed to the preparation of this book. From Eastern Washington University we wish to especially thank Judy McMillan, Graphic Designer in University Graphics, for map design; Judith L. Lee as well as the staff at the Interlibrary Loan Office for their tireless efforts in finding obscure books from distant libraries; and Vickie Roig of the Department of Modern Languages and Literatures for secretarial support. We also wish to thank the staff at the Gonzaga University Faculty Services, including Nancy Masingale, Sandy Hank, Fawn Gass, Dana Lartz, Janet Cannon, Paulette Fowler, and Gloria Strong for much-appreciated assistance in printing, duplicating, and faxing materials. We trust that many generations of students will benefit from the combined efforts of the many people who helped to shape this volume.

Finally, we wish to express our appreciation to our son Emmet for patiently putting up with the inevitable disruptions that accompany such a time-consuming project.

Roderick Stackelberg
Sally A. Winkle
Spokane, WA
September 2001

Introduction

The more Nazi Germany and the Holocaust recede in time, the more present they seem to be in our historical memory. In May 2001, on the 56th anniversary of the end of the Second World War, the German news-weekly *Der Spiegel* launched a 20-part series entitled, "Hitler's Long Shadow: The Presence of the Past." "The past is ever-present," the editors wrote: "when the Constitutional Court considers the prohibition of the [radical right wing] NPD, when German soldiers again go to war [in Kosovo], or when physician-assisted suicide is discussed."[1] The memory of Nazism and the Holocaust continues to affect many aspects of public life in Germany, and in other countries as well. And yet surveys in various countries have shown that significant segments of the public, especially younger people, are surprisingly ignorant of what National Socialism was all about. And though there is general agreement on the perfidy of Nazism, there is no firm consensus even among historians about its causes or its meaning. Indeed, the question seems more pressing than ever: how could such an event have occurred? And what lessons, if any, can we derive from this outbreak of savagery in what we had come to think of as the "civilized world?"

This collection of primary texts presumes to make some contribution to answering these questions. The principal criterion we have used in selecting documents is that they will help us to understand the origins, characteristics, and consequences of Nazism. There are documents of many types, including official papers, public addresses, diplomatic records, and ideological or propagandistic tracts, but also eyewitness accounts and personal experiences. If the former give a traditional view of history from the top, the latter provide an equally useful but often neglected historical perspective from below. Although the focus of the collection is on the actions and motives of the perpetrators, we have included selections describing the cruel plight of victims as well.

In picking out documents we have tried to choose representative examples that offer insights into the nature of Nazism and its effects. Some documents, such as the Nazi program (Doc. 2.6) are well-known; others, such as the Goebbels diary segments only recently discovered in Soviet archives (Doc. 5.20) are new. Many of the documents are published here in English for the first time. Most of the previously published selections have been carefully checked against the German originals to remove any inaccuracies in translation. With some exceptions where a thematic grouping seemed most helpful (for example, Docs. 4.17 and 4.18 on the friction between church and state), the 148 documents are organized chronologically, thus providing a consistent historical narrative. But primary documents, like facts, are only the building blocks of history. It is not until they are interpreted that they enable us to accurately reconstruct the history of the times. To be useful they must be read with a critical eye. They must be assessed for their truthfulness, the purpose for which they were written, and the interests they serve. The introductions to each chapter and each document provide the historical context in which these documents first appeared and some analysis of their content and significance.

This book differs from earlier collections of source material on Nazism in providing selections not just from the Weimar period and the Third Reich, but from earlier and later periods as well. The essay by Richard Wagner that opens the collection was first published in 1850; the last selection, a newspaper account of hostility to foreigners in East Germany, was written in 2000. The wide scope of the book reflects our conviction that the Nazi experience cannot be adequately understood without some examination of its long-term roots or its after-effects in public policy and memory. It must be borne in mind, however, that history is always contingent and open-ended, and the patterns in history that we can detect with the benefit of hindsight do not mean that these patterns were inevitable from the start or that history could not have taken an entirely different course at any given time. The identification of continuities is not intended to imply that Nazism was a necessary result of German history; it is only intended to facilitate understanding of how this extraordinary historical episode came about. The documents of the pre- and post-Nazi era thus serve not only as a record of the past but also as an admonition that it is within our power to determine our history and avoid the pitfalls of the past.

Although National Socialism was part of the broader twentieth-century European movement of fascism, its peculiarly radical features and the reasons for its triumph in Germany cannot be fully understood without some examination of nineteenth and early twentieth-century German history (see Chapter 1). The First World War was the essential precondition for the rise of European fascism, a movement dedicated to national regeneration through the destruction of democracy and socialism and the revival in modernized form of the authoritarian and militaristic values of the past. The constitutional weaknesses and lack of democracy of the German Empire founded by Otto von Bismarck in 1871 would not have culminated in the rise of Nazism if the First World War had not provided the necessary conditions. The war and the revolutions that came in its wake and, above all, German defeat had the effect of propelling the grievances, policies, ideas, and values of the marginalized pre-war radical right into the post-war conservative mainstream. If the German Empire had enjoyed a peaceful development it is unlikely that the extreme nationalism and anti-Semitism of the pre-war radical fringe would have been so widely embraced by "respectable" conservatives after the war.

The Weimar Republic that followed the war labored under severe handicaps from the start (see Chapter 2). Germans almost unanimously viewed the Versailles Treaty as terribly unjust. The fact that a democratic government had signed the treaty, even if under duress, did not commend democracy to Germans as a system that was likely to effectively represent German national interests. Many Germans also considered democracy incapable of defending Germany from a socialist movement emboldened by the Communist revolution in Russia and sustained by the economic deprivations brought on by war and the continuing Allied blockade. The Weimar government was weakened by the lack of support of many left-wing workers and intellectuals who saw liberal democracy as a barrier to establishing a socialist economy in Germany. Animus against the willingness of the moderate left to meet Allied demands and to renounce German imperial ambitions provided the driving force behind the radical-right organizations that were formed to counter left-wing (and supposedly "Jewish") pacifism, internationalism, and democracy after the war.

One of the many right-wing groups established after the war and dedicated to the overthrow of the Weimar government, the restoration of an authoritarian system, and a reversal of the results of the war was the Munich-based National Socialist German Workers' Party (NSDAP). It had the advantage of finding in Adolf Hitler (1889–1945) a fanatically determined leader with considerable rhetorical and organizational skills. Hitler failed, however, in his first attempt to achieve power through a "march on Berlin" in November 1923. He thought he could duplicate Benito Mussolini's (1883–1945) success in gaining the support of the Italian elites for his "march on Rome" in October 1922. German army leader Hans von Seeckt (1866–1936), however, withheld his support for the "Hitler Putsch," possibly because the Weimar government had shown its mettle by authorizing him to unseat democratically constituted Communist–Social Democratic governments in the central German states of Saxony and Thuringia a month earlier. Hitler had not yet gained the mass following that would make him indispensable to the conservative campaign against democracy ten years hence.

Hitler learned from this experience that the support of the conservative elites was essential to a successful seizure of power. The Great Depression of the early 1930s provided the opportunity to replace the moribund Weimar Republic with an authoritarian nationalist regime. The depression polarized German voters and made them receptive to promises of radical solutions to the economic crisis. The Communists called for the nationalization of industry and agriculture, while the Nazis demanded a revival of the nation's military power. Germany's economic elites supported the right for fear of a redistribution of property and wealth.

The Nazis' electoral success in September 1930 contributed to the virtual demise of parliamentary process in the closing years of the republic. The governments of Heinrich Brüning (1885–1970), Franz von Papen (1879–1969), and General Kurt von Schleicher (1882–1934) ruled Germany by decree under powers granted to the president, General Paul von Hindenburg (1847–1934), by the Weimar constitution. As the Nazis gained in electoral strength, reaching a peak of 37.1 percent of the vote in July 1932, conservatives increasingly came to realize that an authoritarian government with popular support was only possible through the inclusion of Hitler in a nationalist government. Hitler, however, refused to enter any government except as chancellor, with all the powers that went with that office. It was the fateful decision of conservative leaders, especially Hindenburg and Papen, to finally submit to these terms that elevated Hitler to the chancellorship on 30 January 1933 and spelled the end of the Weimar Republic.

Hitler's accession to power had a bandwagon effect as nationalist, conservative, and centrist groupings of all kinds fell in behind Hitler's "Government of National Concentration" (see Chapter 3). Middle-class Germans, from whose ranks Hitler had drawn most of his electoral support, overwhelmingly welcomed the end of democratic divisiveness and supported the ruthless Nazi crackdown on the left. It was the Catholic Center Party that provided the crucial votes to give Hitler full dictatorial powers in March 1933 in exchange for a guarantee of the Church's institutional independence. Through the process of *Gleichschaltung* (synchronization or coordination) the Nazis were able to gain full control of the civil service, the professions, the press, and the arts and entertainment business. State parliaments, the labor unions, and rival political parties were suppressed or dissolved themselves under the pressure of public opinion or Nazi sanctions.

The chief source of the Nazis' popularity was the promise of a true *Volksgemeinschaft*, a unified national community in which the liberal rights of the individual and the socialist claims of the underclasses were subordinated to the higher good of the nation as a whole. In practice this did not mean a more egalitarian society, but only the purging of diversity and dissent. The psychological rewards of membership in a superior racial and national community compensated for the failure to effect any real change in the distribution of wealth and property. The Nazis' massive public works projects and deficit financing did, however, contribute to economic recovery and thus to popular support for the regime.

The major victims of *Gleichschaltung* were political dissidents and Jews. In keeping with a long tradition of anti-Semitism in Europe, the Nazis blamed Jews for national disunity, economic dislocations, and political subversion. That Jews were the agents of moral and political sedition was an article of faith in the creed of Aryan, Nordic, and German supremacists. The official policy was to exclude Jews from all public offices and positions of influence in the private sector. The Nazis hoped to force Jews to leave Germany by depriving them of a chance to make a living. In the so-called Nuremberg Laws of 1935 the Nazis established an apartheid system that deprived Jews of full German citizenship and barred them from marrying or having sexual relations with non-Jewish Germans. Their extrusion from the economy proceeded more slowly, however, for fear of the economic repercussions that an abrupt closure of all Jewish businesses would have entailed. "Aryanization" of Jewish businesses did not become mandatory until late 1938, following the officially-sanctioned turn to violence in the November Pogrom of that year.

In the eyes of the general public the greatest benefit of national unity was the strength it would bring to Germany in the international arena. Germans overwhelmingly supported Hitler's decision to leave the League of Nations and rebuild the nation's armed forces. This also endeared Hitler to army leaders, who pressured him to eliminate the SA as a potential rival military organization. By summarily executing SA leader Ernst Roehm (1887–1934) and his leading associates in June 1934, Hitler signalled his intention of keeping the SA firmly under Nazi party control. Military leaders responded by giving him full support when he assumed the presidential title of Commander-in-Chief after Hindenburg's death in August 1934. In March 1935 Hitler announced the reintroduction of universal military training in open violation of the Versailles Treaty.

What most of the German public did not realize is that Hitler was consciously and deliberately planning to go to war with a target date of 1942–43 (see Chapter 4). His ultimate goal was not just the reversal of the results of the First World War or the restoration of Germany's 1914 borders, goals that most of the German public shared. Already in *Mein Kampf* he had announced Germany's need for *Lebensraum* to be gained at the expense of "Russia and its border states" (Doc. 2.15). His militant opposition to Soviet Communism was one reason conservative British and French leaders were so ready to submit to Hitler's territorial demands in the policy known as "appeasement." Hitler relied on deception and bluff to gain at least tacit Western acceptance of his remilitarization of the Rhineland in 1936, the annexation of Austria in March 1938, and the forced cession of the Sudetenland by Czechoslovakia in the Munich Agreements of September 1938. Nor did the Allies do anything to prevent Hitler's establishment of the "Protectorate of Bohemia and Moravia" on former Czech territory in March 1939. This brazen violation of the Munich Agreements, however, prompted the British government to change course and abandon the appeasement policy.

By this time Hitler was prepared to launch his war of expansion in the east even in the face of British and French opposition. The purpose of the Non-Aggression Pact with the Soviet Union in August 1939 was not to make peace with communism, but to create the conditions for a successful war against the Western powers, should they decide to intervene to stop the German conquest of Poland. Hitler was nothing if not an opportunist, and he prided himself in his ability to isolate his opponents and destroy them one by one. Despite the misgivings of some of his senior military leaders, Hitler was determined to take advantage of the "weakness of will" that British and French leaders had previously displayed and of American isolationism, the strong opposition to renewed American involvement in European wars.

Hitler seems to have sensed that when he gave the orders for the attack on Poland in late August 1939 he had in fact launched a war that would eventually involve all the world powers (see Chapter 5). After that fateful decision he was never fully in control of events again. The conquest of Poland was easy, but if he really believed that the West would accept the German victory and make peace, he was soon to be disabused of that notion. Even the triumphant German blitzkrieg against the Benelux countries and France in the spring of 1940 could not persuade the British, now under the leadership of Winston Churchill (1874–1965), to end the war. As in the case of Napoleon in the previous century, Hitler's defeat in the Second World War can ultimately be traced to his inability to force Britain to come to terms. Britain, aided by its dominions, was the only major power officially at war with Nazi Germany at the height of German power from 22 June 1940 to 22 June 1941.

An attempt to invade the British Isles became unfeasible after the failure of the Luftwaffe to gain control of the air in the so-called Battle of Britain in the summer and fall of 1940. A successful campaign to defeat Britain in the Mediterranean and the Near East was compromised by Spanish dictator Francisco Franco's (1892–1975) reluctance to go beyond formal expressions of support for the fascist cause. Nor was the Soviet Union willing to take a more active role in the war than as supplier of Germany's food and raw material needs. In this situation Hitler was forced to change his priorities. Rather than waiting to launch his long-planned war of expansion against the Soviet Union until after the end of the war in the West, he now decided to invade the Soviet Union even before Britain had made peace. Hitler hoped that a rapid conquest of the USSR would finally force Britain to come to terms. Even if it did not, control of European Russia would give Germany an ideal position from which to face the coming showdown with the Anglo-American powers. On Hitler's express orders, the war against the Soviet Union was to be fought without regard for international conventions on the treatment of civilians and prisoners of war. The Nazis' draconian policies had the effect, however, of stiffening Soviet resistance and alienating anti-communist national minorities like the Ukrainian and Baltic peoples, many of whom who had originally greeted the German invaders as liberators.

To deter American entry into the war in Europe, Hitler and Mussolini formed a military alliance with Japan, which, like the fascist powers in Europe, was pursuing the goal of national expansion. The Japanese attack on Pearl Harbor on 7 December 1941 boosted German morale at a time when the campaign to take Moscow had bogged down in the outskirts of the city. Three days after Pearl Harbor Hitler declared war against the US, thus fulfilling his pledge to Japan and formalizing the naval conflict that was already well under way in the Atlantic at the time. As Hitler had foreseen, the German war of expansion had turned into a second world war, but not according to a timetable of Hitler's choosing.

German expansion reached its peak in November 1942 when the Wehrmacht stood on the verge of completing its conquest of the city of Stalingrad on the Volga River and General Erwin Rommel's small but effective Africa Corps advanced to within 60 miles of the city of Alexandria in Egypt. Almost simultaneous developments on both fronts, however, changed the course of the war. A powerful Soviet counterattack encircled an entire German army in the city of Stalingrad and, after some of the most bitter house-to-house fighting in the history of warfare, forced it to surrender on 1 February 1943. General Bernard Montgomery's counterattack at El Alamein halted Rommel's advance into Egypt in November 1942, and in the same month a successful Anglo-American landing in North Africa brought American ground troops into the orbit of the European theater for the first time. Despite Hitler's dismissal of this invasion as an irrelevant diversion more than a thousand miles away (see Doc. 5.22), active American participation in the war meant that German defeat was now only a matter of time.

The Wehrmacht managed to mount another short-lived offensive in Soviet Russia in the summer of 1943; but after defeat in the Battle of Kursk in July 1943, the largest tank battle in the history of warfare, the Wehrmacht was no longer capable of sustained offensive operations. Italy fell in September 1943. The greatest blow of all occurred on 6 June 1944 when the Allies successfully landed an invasion force on the northern coast of France. The prospects of total ruin prompted dissident German officers to belatedly try to oust the Nazi regime. The failure of their attempt to assassinate Hitler on 20 July 1944 prolonged the war and almost doubled the number of German war casualties. After fanatical resistance the Germans finally submitted to the Allied terms of unconditional surrender on 8 May 1945, a week after Hitler's suicide in his bunker under the ruined Reich Chancellery in Berlin.

The Nazis had failed in their megalomanic attempt to conquer the Soviet Union and establish a New Order in Europe ruled by the supposedly superior German race. One aspect of that New Order was the elimination of the Jewish population of Europe. This goal the Nazis were determined to achieve even in defeat (see Chapter 6). Whether the physical destruction of the Jews was always part of the Nazi leadership's master-plan or whether they resorted to this drastic "final solution" only when the alternatives of expulsion and resettlement in isolated territories were no longer available cannot be definitively determined. Certainly it is hard to imagine how genocide on such a scale could have been carried out without the cover of war and its ever-present specter of death. But the logic of Nazi anti-Semitism entailed total destruction as the ultimate option if all else failed. To render German society and areas under German control *judenfrei* (free of Jews) was a central Nazi aim from the start. Total war provided the conditions for total destruction.

The war enabled the Nazis to put their murderous schemes into practice. Jews in occupied territories, especially in Poland, were confined in ghettos under inhuman conditions in 1939–40 to make their labor and resources available for German use and to create living space for Germans and for Poles expelled from the portions of Poland annexed to the Reich. Under the leadership of Heinrich Himmler (1900–45) and Reinhard Heydrich (1904–42), the SS made plans with the Wehrmacht in March and April 1941 to exterminate the Soviet Jews who fell into German hands in the course of the invasion of the Soviet Union. SS killing squads (*Einsatzkommandos*) followed the front-line troops to execute communist officials and Jews under the guise of combatting partisans. While only men were originally targeted for death, within a few weeks the SS was killing women and children as well.

At the height of the German campaign in Russia in July and August 1941, SS officials prepared plans for the systematic murder of *all* European Jews, the so-called "final solution." They benefited from the experience and expertise acquired in the so-called "Aktion T-4," the "euthanasia" of disabled people that began shortly after the start of the war in September 1939. Many of the leading SS officials responsible for the T-4 program were transferred to occupied Poland to assume command of advance planning, gassing experiments, and other preparations for the "final solution" in fall 1941. They appear to have gotten Hitler's explicit approval for industrial mass murder by October 1941, the month in which all emigration of Jews from areas under German control was prohibited. The entry of the US into the war in December 1941 may have removed the final barrier to implementation of the "final solution" (see Doc. 5.20).

While shooting operations continued throughout the war, most of the victims of the Holocaust were killed at special sites established in occupied Poland (see Table 6.1). They were killed by gas, either carbon monoxide or the pesticide Cyclon B, in large chambers disguised as shower rooms, a technology pioneered in the euthanasia program. Under plans and arrangements drawn up by Adolf Eichmann (1906–62), the official in charge of Jewish affairs at Gestapo headquarters in Berlin, Jews were systematically deported from the ghettos and camps throughout Europe to the extermination sites in Poland. Close to a million Jews were killed at the largest of these camps, Auschwitz-Birkenau, from early 1942 to the ending of gassing operations in November 1944. Thousands more died on death marches in the closing days of the war. Best estimates place the number of Jews killed at the extermination sites at approximately three million. Another one and a half million died by shooting operations throughout eastern Europe, and close to the same number died of disease, starvation, and abuse in the ghettos and concentration camps scattered throughout the areas under German control. The vibrant Jewish culture of pre-war Europe was effectively destroyed as tens of thousands of traumatized survivors, officially referred to as "displaced persons," had little choice after the war but to emigrate to Palestine, the United States, or other destinations overseas rather than to return to their lost ancestral homes.

Major war criminals were tried and convicted at Nuremberg in 1945–46, but the "denazification" process intended to prevent former Nazis from returning to positions of power and influence in German society turned instead into a process of rehabilitating former members of the Nazi party or affiliated organizations (see Chapter 7). The most important reason for this was the emerging cold war between the Western powers and the Soviet Union as a result of their very different economic and political systems. The 1945 Yalta and Potsdam agreements called for a unified Germany with its capital in Berlin. Contrary to original plans to maintain the German economy at a subsistence level, however, a situation that tended to generate support for communism among the economically deprived underclasses and threatened to spread communist influence throughout Germany, the Western Allies decided in 1946 to revive the economy in their own occupation zones and create a separate West German state. The ultimate beneficiaries of this initiative were former Nazis whose services were now valued on both sides of the "Iron Curtain" to facilitate the smooth functioning of institutions in the West and East German states founded in 1949. Former Nazis were particularly visible in positions of influence in the Western Federal Republic of Germany (FRG), where a constitutional provision permitted thousands of former Nazis not under indictment for war crimes to reclaim their positions in the civil service without penalty or prejudice.

While the terrible destruction of the war and the revelations of Nazi atrocities thoroughly discredited Nazi ideology, the Cold War facilitated the reintegration of former Nazis into both East and West German societies, provided they were willing to pledge their allegiance to the new systems they now served. Anti-communism provided the ideological medium that permitted West German rearmament and integration into the Western military alliance (NATO) in 1955. In the communist German Democratic Republic (GDR), on the other hand, anti-fascism became the official legitimating ideology. The leaders of the ruling Socialist Unity Party (SED) derived their moral authority from their record of active resistance to Nazism both within and outside the Third Reich. The need to resist fascism even provided the ideological justification for the erection of the Berlin Wall in 1961. While it was officially described as a protective wall against fascism, its true purpose was to prevent the migration of East Germans to the more prosperous and democratic West.

The different social and political values in East and West inevitably determined their respective interpretations of Nazism. While East German historians continued to attribute Nazism to the corruptions of capitalism, thereby incriminating the Federal Republic as at least potentially fascist, Western historians tended to favor the totalitarianism interpretation. By defining Nazism as the suppression of individual rights by a criminal clique of leaders, totalitarianism theory imputed to the communist GDR a close resemblance to the authoritarian structures of the Third Reich. Both sides vigorously repudiated anti-Semitism but, whereas the Federal Republic acknowledged the specificity of Jewish suffering and made restitution payments to survivors of the Holocaust, GDR officials subsumed Jewish victimhood under the larger category of anti-fascist resistance and de-emphasized the specifically Jewish nature of the Holocaust.

Underlying both Cold War-inspired interpretations, however, was agreement on the principle that Nazism and the Holocaust represented absolute evil. That consensus came under attack in West Germany in the conservative 1980s, thus precipitating the bitter *Historikerstreit* (historians' debate) of 1986–87. Conservative historians, determined to reverse the leftward political trends of the 1960s and 1970s, challenged the notion that Nazi atrocities, including the Holocaust, were any worse or even any different than the communist Gulag. Their objective was to restore German national pride by downplaying the significance or the abnormality of Nazism in the larger context of German and world history. That debate continued in the 1990s amidst disturbing signs of the revival of right radicalism in the wake of the communist collapse. While the radical right has no realistic chance of achieving political power in a reunified Germany, where Nazism and anti-Semitism remain heavily stigmatized, the increase of skinhead and neo-Nazi violence against foreigners and the reluctance of right-of-center parties and politicians to take vigorous action against it has given rise to growing concern in Germany's progressive community (see Doc. 7.15).

The legacy of Nazism is ubiquitous and ever-present, yet hard to pin down in precise terms. History teaches many lessons, and it is rarely unequivocally clear what lesson or lessons are applicable to a given situation. History may repeat itself, but it never does so under exactly the same conditions as before. Sometimes historical lessons are over-learned, which seemed to have been the case, for instance, in the "appeasement" policy of the 1930s, an overreaction to the perceived failure of governmental leaders to rely on diplomacy to resolve their national conflicts in July 1914. The failure of the appeasement policy led, in turn, to what some critics believe to have been an excessive reluctance on the part of the Western powers to negotiate differences with the Soviet Union after the war. If there is one indisputable lesson, however, that the history of Nazism seems to teach, it is of the terrible destructiveness of the values of the "radical right." The study of National Socialism may serve as an object lesson of the dangers inherent in doctrines of national and racial supremacy. If this documentary history of Nazism helps to increase public awareness of this danger, one of its main purposes will have been accomplished.

Plate 1   25-year-old Adolf Hitler at a rally proclaiming mobilization in front of the Theatiner Church in Munich at the start of the First World War, 2 August 1914. The lion's head at the left is on one of the statues in front of the *Feldherrnhalle*, the Soldiers' Memorial Hall where Hitler's putsch attempt on 9 November 1923 would come to an end. (Ullstein 11387,01)

Plate 2   "The Pimps of Death" (1919). Caricature by Georg Grosz (© Estate of Georg Grosz/Licensed by VAGA, New York, NY)

Plate 3 Children playing with worthless paper currency in 1923, the year of the great inflation (see Doc. 2.11). (Ullstein 461863,02)

Plate 4 Members of the government on their way to the Garrison Church in Potsdam on 21 March 1933 (see Doc. 3.7). Front center, Chancellor Adolf Hitler and Vice-Chancellor Franz von Papen. (Ullstein 41259,02)

Plate 5   Chancellor Hitler paying homage to President Paul von Hindenburg on the "Day of Potsdam," 21 March 1933. (Ullstein 21027,08)

Plate 6   *Eintopf*-Sunday in front of City Hall in Berlin in 1936. The banner across the entrance reads: "Here *Eintopf* (stew) will be eaten!" The difference in cost between a one-dish meal and the usual elaborate Sunday dinner was supposed to go to charity. In the background an SA band provides music. (Ullstein 229473,01)

Plate 7   Low cartoon of Stalin and Hitler bowing to each other. (*Evening Standard* (1939))

Plate 8   German Führer Adolf Hitler waves to crowds watched by Italy's leader Benito Mussolini, Rome, 28 May 1938. (©Popperfoto)

Plate 9 German soldiers tearing down border posts at the start of the invasion of Poland, 1 September 1939. (Ullstein 16277,07)

Plate 10 Hitler at the signing of the armistice in Compiègne after the fall of France on 22 June 1940 (see Doc. 5.4). (Süddeutscher Verlag)

Plate 11   A Wehrmacht soldier observes a burning village in the German invasion of the Soviet Union, July 1941. (Ullstein, 67745,05)

Plate 12   The deportation of Jews from the Warsaw Ghetto by SS units at the start of the Warsaw Ghetto Uprising, April 1943. This photo was included in the "Stroop Report" filed after the suppression of the uprising on 16 May 1943 (see Doc. 6.13). (Ullstein 3022,06)

Plate 13   The railway ramp at Auschwitz where selections occurred.

Plate 14   *Trümmerfrauen* (women cleaning up rubble) in Berlin in early 1946. The slogan in old German script on the handcart reads: *Das kann doch einen Schipper nicht erschüttern* ("even this can't get a shoveler down"). (Ullstein 28947,01)

Plate 15 Social Democratic Chancellor Willy Brandt kneels in front of the memorial to the victims of the Warsaw Ghetto Uprising on an official visit to Poland on 7 December 1970. This gesture provided a moving testimonial of German contrition (see Doc. 7.9). (Ullstein 74538,03)

Plate 16 President Ronald and Nancy Reagan and Christian Democratic Chancellor Helmut and Hannelore Kohl visit the military cemetery in Bitburg on 5 May 1985 in an official commemoration of the 40th anniversary of the end of the Second World War. The visit was controversial because it was the burial site not only of Wehrmacht soldiers but of soldiers of the SS. (Ullstein – Lothar Kucharz 26762,02)

1

The German Empire and the First World War

The political and ideological roots of National Socialism can be traced back to the increasingly desperate rearguard campaign against the modernizing trends of the nineteenth century. These included the social and economic consequences of industrialization, democratization, liberalization, rationalization, urbanization, and secularization. Anti-Semitism, an indicator of anti-modernism, had a long tradition in the predominantly Christian culture of Europe. Christian anti-Semites associated Jews with self-seeking materialism and commercialism. Unencumbered by Christian self-restraint, Jews allegedly pursued worldly gain by practices Christians considered immoral.

Growing nationalism in the second half of the nineteenth century was the major source of modern anti-Semitism. The ethnic difference of Jews and their adamance in maintaining a separate Jewish identity offended nationalists who considered ethnic homogeneity the basic precondition for a strong nation. Nationalists resented the growing cultural and political influence of Jews after their emancipation in the course of the nineteenth century. Richard Wagner's polemical essay, "Judaism in Music" (Doc. 1.1), provides an example of both traditional and modern nationalist prejudices.

The intensification of anti-Semitism in the late nineteenth century was also linked to the conservative backlash against middle-class liberalism and working-class Social Democracy. The Jewish community overwhelmingly supported the parties of the left, and Jews assumed leadership roles in both the Progressive and Social Democratic Parties. Pastor Adolf Stoecker attempted to wean workers from allegiance to the Social Democratic Party through a revival of Christianity and appeals to resentment against liberals and Jews (Doc. 1.2).

The tensions in German society provoked by the growth of the labor movement and the Social Democratic Party (SPD) were reflected in a surge of nationalism, militarism, and imperialism among the middle classes and government leaders under Kaiser Wilhelm II in the 1890s. The historian Heinrich von Treitschke was one of many publicists whose works idealized the nation and its heroic martial values (Doc. 1.3). Jewish "materialism" served as the foil to German "idealism" in Houston Stewart Chamberlain's widely-read *Foundations of the Nineteenth Century* (Doc. 1.4). Chamberlain, a trained botanist and self-proclaimed Christian, helped make racial anti-Semitism respectable among educated Germans. His influence even extended to the royal family, as his extensive correspondence with Wilhelm II attests (Doc. 1.5).

The movement of "national opposition" to the government's allegedly too moderate domestic and foreign policies reached a preliminary climax after the SPD became the largest party represented in the Reichstag in the elections of 1912. The leader of the Pan-

German League, Heinrich Class, called for an expansionist foreign policy, suppression of the SPD, and reversal of Jewish emancipation (Doc. 1.6). His program reads like an early blueprint for Nazi policies. By putting a premium on national unity and making dissent equivalent to treason, an aggressive foreign policy was closely linked to defense of the authoritarian system at home. Military leaders and wide sectors of the elite came to believe not only that war against France and Russia was inevitable, but also that it would have a meliorative effect on Germany's inner political dissension (Doc. 1.7). To weaken the left and pursue an aggressive foreign policy, however, seemed to require suppression of the liberalizing influence of the Jews (Doc. 1.8).

The excessive influence of military planners on German policy-making was revealed in the so-called Schlieffen Plan, put into effect upon the outbreak of war in 1914 (Doc. 1.9). The regime's expansionist aims were revealed in Chancellor Bethmann-Hollweg's "September Program" (Doc. 1.10), which was not, however, made public at the time. The First World War further radicalized the ideology of Germanic supremacy, which contrasted creative German "culture" to commercial Western "civilization" and the heroic "ideas of 1914" to the materialistic "ideas of 1789" (Docs. 1.11, 1.12, and 1.13).

As the war dragged on without resolution and war weariness grew, liberal and Social Democratic pressures for a compromise peace and internal reforms reemerged in strength. The determination of the left was boosted as well by the Russian revolutions of 1917. In response to the challenge of the left, the German High Command, which remained committed to victory, supported the formation of the German Fatherland Party in 1917 (Doc. 1.14). This mobilization of the right in defense of German imperialist aims presaged the even greater mobilization of the right to reverse the political and military results of the war after German defeat and the fall of the Empire in November 1918.

Anti-Semitism in Germany

Anti-Semitism has a 2,000-year history in Europe. The origins of the stereotype of Jews as immoral materialists can be traced to the unwillingness of Jews to give up their religion in favor of world-renouncing Christianity. That stereotype persisted throughout the Middle Ages and was by no means confined to Germany. Anti-Semitism took on particularly intolerant forms in countries in which Christianity formed the official state religion. Although Jews who converted to Christianity could frequently escape persecution, there was a racist dimension in the widespread assumption that Jews were inherently selfish and sinful. The growth of nationalism led to intensified anti-Semitism in nineteenth-century Europe, particularly in Germany, as the international Jewish diaspora increasingly served as the foil against which nationalists defined German identity. Anti-Semitic publicists contrasted Jewish materialism and commercialism to the creativity of German idealist culture.

The great composer Richard Wagner (1813–83) first published the essay below under the pseudonym R. Freigedank ("free thought") in a music journal in 1850 and reissued it as a pamphlet under his own name in 1869, the year that Jews gained full civil rights in the North-German Confederation. Wagner also disseminated anti-Semitism in the journal that he founded for his circle of followers, the *Bayreuther Blätter*. Driven, it would appear, in part by envy of the success of his contemporary, Giacomo Meyerbeer (1791–1864), Wagner was also reacting to the increasing commercialization of art in the era of free-market industrial capitalism. He attributed this commodification of cultural works to the influence of the Jews after their emancipation from the restrictions that had kept them from full participation in German culture and society in the past. Wagner claimed that the "Jewish" spirit of profit and sensuality was corrupting the arts and undermining the creativity of selfless German artists pursuing their ideal visions at the cost of personal comfort or gain. He called for a national regeneration by purging the arts and society of "Jewish" materialism. Convinced of the superiority of his own art, he saw no contradiction in demanding state support for a national theater to stage his grand operatic works.

Wagner was one of the more influential of the many German publicists whose anti-Semitism derived from and contributed to their opposition to liberalizing changes in the second half of the nineteenth century. This essay repeats the recurrent stereotypes of Jews as an alien, deracinated, money-oriented people without any roots in the soil or the culture of their host nation.

1.1 Richard Wagner, "Judaism in Music," 1850

... According to the present state of world affairs the Jew is already far more than emancipated: he rules, and will rule as long as money remains the power as a result of which all our activities and doings lose their force. That the historical misery of the Jews and the rapacious coarseness of Christian Germanic rulers were themselves responsible for handing the sons of Israel this power need not be elaborated here. But we do need to examine more closely the causes for why it is impossible to further develop the natural, the necessary, and the truly beautiful on the foundation of the present state of the arts without a total transformation of this foundation; and why this has now also placed control of the public aesthetic taste of our times into the busy hands of the Jews ...

It is not necessary to establish that modern art is judaized; it is immediately apparent and confirms itself to our senses all by itself. It would require a far too extensive treatment to try to explain this phenomenon from the character of the history of our art itself. If, however, we believe that emancipation from the spirit of Jewry is necessary, we must above all recognize the importance of examining what forces we can muster for this struggle of liberation. We cannot gain knowledge of these forces from an abstract definition of that phenomenon, but only by becoming familiar with the nature of our inherent, involuntary feeling, which expresses itself as an instinctive aversion to the Jewish character: this irrepressible feeling, if we are quite honest with ourselves, must make clear to us what it is that we hate in that character. What we know for certain we can confront. By merely exposing it we may hope to drive the demon from the field, on which it is able to hold its own only under the cloak of darkness that we good-natured humanists have ourselves thrown over it to make its sight less repugnant.

The Jew who, as we all know, has a God all to himself, sticks out in ordinary life first of all by his external appearance, which has something alien to whatever particular European nationality we may belong. Involuntarily, we wish to have nothing in common with a person of such an appearance. Up to now this no doubt redounded to his disadvantage, but in the modern age we cannot fail to recognize that he feels quite good with this disadvantage. In view of his successes, he may even regard his difference from us as a distinction. Ignoring the moral side of this disagreeable game of nature, we wish here only to point out that in respect to art, this exterior can never conceivably be an object of artistic representation. When the plastic arts wish to represent the Jew, they generally draw their model from the imagination, either discreetly ennobling or leaving out altogether those traits that characterize Jewish appearance in ordinary life. Never does the Jew stray on to the theatrical stage; exceptions to this are so rare in number and unusual in kind as to confirm the rule.

We cannot think of any ancient or modern character, whether hero or lover, as performed by a Jew without inevitably feeling the ludicrous inappropriateness of such a performance. This is very important: a person whose appearance we have to consider unqualified for artistic representation – not on account of his individual personality but on account of his type – must be considered unfit for any artistic expression whatsoever of pure human character.

… The Jew speaks the language of the nation in which he lives from generation to generation, but he speaks it only as a foreigner … In general, the fact that the Jew speaks the modern European languages only as acquired, not as native languages, excludes him from all capability of expressing himself in them independently and in accordance with his inner character. A language – its expression and development – is not the work of individuals, but of a historical community. Only he who has grown up without self-consciousness within that community takes part in its creations. The Jew, however, stood outside such a community, alone with his Jehovah in a dispersed and rootless tribe, with all development out of its own resources denied to it; even its peculiar (Hebrew) language has only remained as a dead language. To write genuine poetry in a foreign language has been impossible up to now, even for the greatest genius. But our entire European civilization and art has remained a foreign language to the Jews. For he has not taken part in the advancement of the latter nor in the development of the former; rather the unfortunate and homeless Jew has, at best, merely looked on coldly and with hostility. In such language or such art the Jew can only copy and imitate, but cannot write real poetry or create true art.

The purely sensual expression of Jewish language revolts us in particular … But, if the defects of language described above make the Jew quite incapable of all artistic expression of feeling through the medium of speech, it follows that he must be far less capable of such expression through the medium of song. Song is speech intensified by passion; music is the language of passion. If the Jew intensifies his language – in which he may demonstrate ridiculous emotionalism but never artistic passion – to the point of making music, he becomes entirely unbearable. Everything that irritated us in his speech or his outward appearance repels us entirely in his music, insofar as we are not spellbound by the utter ridiculousness of this experience. In song, the most vivid and irrefutably truest expression of personal feeling, we are naturally most aware of the revolting peculiarity of the Jewish nature; in whatever field of art we might consider the Jews as capable, it can never be in the field of music …

Source: Richard Wagner, *Gesammelte Schriften*, Vol. XII, ed. by Julius Kapp
(Leipzig: Hesse & Becker Verlag, 1914), pp. 9–15.
Translated by Rod Stackelberg

The suppression of Social Democracy

German Chancellor Otto von Bismarck's main domestic goal from the late 1870s to his dismissal by Kaiser Wilhelm II in 1890 was to weaken liberalism and suppress the recently founded Social Democratic Party (SPD), the party that represented the working class in the German Empire. Bismarck's anti-socialist law of 1878 restricted the right of the SPD to organize, publish, and meet. Socialists were still allowed to become candidates in parliamentary elections, however, and the percentage of SPD votes in Reichstag elections continued to increase despite the restrictions to which the party was subjected. In the 1880s Bismarck also attempted to gain worker allegiance through a state-sponsored pension plan and health insurance system. A variety of right-wing political activists sought to lure workers into the nationalist camp through religious, anti-liberal, and anti-Semitic appeals.

Adolf Stoecker (1835–1909), Chaplain to Kaiser Wilhelm's Court, founded the Christian Social Workers' Party in 1878 (renamed the Christian Social Party in 1881) for the purpose of weaning workers from their allegiance to socialism and converting them to monarchism through nationalist and religious appeals. The constituency he attracted, however, were mainly lower-middle-class artisans and tradesmen, hostile to both laissez-faire liberalism (because it favored big business) and the socialist labor movement. The following excerpt from a speech Stoecker delivered in Berlin in 1880 reflects the growing conservative concern about the "social question" (the disaffection of wage-earning workers), which threatened the stability of the imperial system. He denounced Social Democracy as the product of the excessive materialism and secularism of the modern age. His speech offers a typical example of how moralistic appeals could be used to serve conservative political ends. At the same time, however, he painted a surprisingly forth-right picture of the misery that attracted so many workers to socialism. His indictment of liberalism and individualism enjoyed particular resonance in the years of economic recession following the financial crash of 1873. Stoecker called for a revival of Christianity to combat the liberal, democratic, and socialist threats. Although he did not mention Jews in this particular selection, Stoecker and many of his fellow conservatives blamed the corruption of traditional values and the growth of left-wing movements on the influence of the Jews. In 1892 he lent his considerable prestige to the successful campaign to introduce anti-Semitic planks in the Conservative Party platform. His movement was one of the first attempts to use nationalism and religion to combat socialism.

1.2 Adolf Stoecker, speech on the social question, 1880

Of the stirring questions that are currently of general concern the social question is certainly the most stirring ... We in Germany have particular reason to pay attention to this movement and not to allow any of its phases to escape us. Nihilism in the east, the Commune in the west, the whole great revolutionary movement in Germany all show that we are in fact, as the phrase so often goes, on volcanic ground[1] ...

With respect to Social Democracy two different kinds of erroneous conceptions are prevalent. One group of economists see Social Democracy as something quite harmless, as a system of social reforms aimed at achieving the welfare of one's neighbors. They forget the immoral tendencies connected with it and the war against Christianity that is bound up with it, and – attracted by the intellectual energy of the Social Democratic Party, by its dedication,

---

1   Stoecker is here referring to the Nihilist movement in Russia, the Paris Commune of 1871, and the growth of the SPD in Germany.

and by its willingness to make sacrifices – they have almost nothing but good things to say of the movement. This conception is certainly wrong. Social Democracy is not just a movement for social reforms; as it portrays itself in Germany and as it has portrayed itself for decades in pamphlets, books, and assemblies it is a new conception of the world – a conception which once it has taken hold of people pries them away from Christianity, patriotism, and German morality, separates them from the ethical foundations of our life and directs them down a road which, in my opionion, can and will lead only to an abyss.

But on the other hand it is equally an error to say that Social Democracy is a product of idle heads, mean dispositions, and evil agitators. For it is not this either. To be sure, the easiest way of disposing of this deep-rooted popular movement would be to place the entire blame for it on a few ambitious, unpatriotic individuals. But in fact the affairs of mankind do not occur in this way. A movement that bites so deeply, that attracts such a large number of of German men, and also German women, in such a short time, that operates so persistently that it has to be dealt with by legislation contrary to modern ideas, such a movement is a product neither of idle minds, nor of chance, nor of foolishness, such a movement must have a source which it is our task and our duty to discover ...

I begin with a sketch of the phenomenon "Social Democracy" which is so much feared. Its parents are the *Zeitgeist* and poverty. It was born of ethical brutalization, religious defections, economic injustice, and misery. The last point must not be overlooked. There really is social injustice and poverty; it is to be found everywhere, we have it before us in Berlin. Injustice manifests itself in the indiscipline of the capitalists and in wages which are both meagre and insecure; over the last five years misery has made a frightful impact on the artisans and workers – and it is these who are predominant in the Social Democratic movement – and continues to agitate deeply among them. This point of view must be kept firmly in mind; without it it is impossible to evaluate Social Democracy correctly. We should not be impressed either with single examples of high wages or of wastefulness among workers; these examples are valid but they prove nothing and cannot change the general and permanent state of affairs ... The wages of our workers in some regions of our country are exceedingly small ... Another aspect of our current crises is, however, occupying a place almost more important for the workers than insufficient wages. In the last few years I have frequently had the opportunity to hear the complaints and cries of distress of workers, particularly of right-minded workers who are still attached to the Church, to the ethical foundations of our national life, to their country; and one thing became very clear to me and that is the complete insecurity of their existence. For four or five years thousands, sometimes tens of thousands of workers have been unemployed for months at a time. No one comes so close to the misery of the people as we clergy; I assure you that we have found countless families in Berlin who, during the period of unemployment, had pawned everything, who possessed nothing except a table, a couple of chairs, and perhaps a bed of straw on which to lie down ... Such conditions have to be faced squarely, their origins must be discovered, and they must be remedied. They are caused by the present form of business life, by large industry in combination with free competition, by the alternation of boom and bust which occur at ever shorter intervals and which harm no one more than the working class ... If such conditions were really unavoidable, if all the misery among the workers and artisans were inevitable, then we could in fact give no other advice to those who suffer from them than passive resignation. But this is not the situation. On the contrary, for the most part it is human and visible sins and follies which produce and increase the difficulties at the roots of our social conditions. It is true that one ought to be tolerant of sins against society, too, to work calmly and steadily toward eliminating abuses instead of immediately rebelling. But there is only one power that prevents us from grumbling while at the same time inspiring us to action: and that is religion. Unfortunately, this power has been broken among our people. For decades the learned and the ignorant, newspapers and books, lectures and assemblies have vied with each other to deprive people of the Bible and to cast the clergy and the church into contempt. We must not be surprised if people say: There is no hope, no salvation, no comfort for us there; you have taken heaven from us, now give us the earth! The atmosphere in which our workers live is not an ideal atmosphere; I do not think that I exaggerate if I say that the *Zeitgeist* is saturated with materialistic ideas ... Materialism makes people selfish and bad. The poor workers, the small artisans nowadays are well aware of this. They are abandoned and lost; they confront nothing but selfishness, therefore they also give up ethical ideas, they become bitter and they turn into enemies of present society. And often their poverty must be contrasted with a senseless luxury on the part of the propertied classes, excessive wealth which has not always been acquired entirely honestly or honorably. We in Berlin have witnessed the worship of the golden calf at its most extreme ... Is it surprising, then, that in the hearts of the poor and in the minds of thoughtful workers the idea should appear: Is property which has been won dishonestly holy property? Property carries with it heavy duties, wealth carries with it heavy responsibilities. If property abandons the foundations on which it rests; if it ignores the commands of God and the obligation to love one's neighbor, then it is itself conjuring up the dangers of revolt. I think that our whole social edifice is based on the respect that the property-less and uneducated feel toward the upper classes, and this presupposes above all that property honestly acquired shall be used nobly, charitably, and kindly, not only for one's own pleasure and advantage but also for the good of one's fellow men, for curing the ills of others, and for generous participation in all the great occasions of community life. There are many rich persons among our people who have no idea at all of this conception of wealth, and it is their ignorance, lack of conscience, and refusal to do their duty that is above all responsible for the social question ...

What is needed is a great conversion, a thoroughgoing reestablishment of the Christian conception of the world, of a lively respect for the ethical and religious foundations of our people, if the damage that has already been done is to be repaired. Specifically the Christian spirit must once again inspire the whole nation and not just the so-called "lower classes." What is needed is a general renaissance. I am frank to say that the opinion that moral laws and articles of religious faith are meant only for the lower classes is an opinion which has neither any chance of success nor any claim to respect. Religious truth is for everyone, for the philosopher at his lectern as much as for the artisan in his workshop; moral laws are valid for all, as much for those who dispose of millions as for the very poorest. First of all our people must be made to understand that everyone must accept the principles to which the German people owes its history, the principles of a clear, strong, Christian conception of the world ...

Socialism, however, has a very serious side to it; it is a very understandable contrast against exaggerated individualism. The liberal economic system has proclaimed the unlimited freedom of the individual ... In this way the chasm appears which separates the upper ten thousand from the great mass of impoverished and decaying people. The bridge that crosses this chasm is already narrow and fragile. If things go on as they are, then the chasm will become ever deeper and the possibility of rising out of poverty to prosperity ever smaller. But that is perhaps one of the most important motives in the Social Democratic movement, that those without property confront a future on earth which is often completely hopeless.

In the light of this the social conception has something to be said for it. For socialism does not mean only the idea of converting all private property into state property, but it contains as well the demand that business life should be made over into something social and organic. And it is my conviction that we shall overcome the dangers of the socialist system only if we come to grips with its justifiable elements, that we can deal with the socialist fantasy of abolishing private property only if we take up very seriously two ideas of socialism. One: to cast economic life once more in an organic form, and two: to narrow the gap between rich and poor ...

Let us therefore do what we can to meet the great dangers that lie in the social movement. I think that we must see Social Democracy as something that has emerged from the far-reaching destruction of our material, ethical, and religious life; we must see it as the scourge that God uses to bring us out of this worthless materialistic conception of the world which menaces our highest values, our German fatherland, and our German future ...

It is no longer enough to give the propertyless classes alms out of pity. We must help them out of love and justice to obtain everything that they have a right to ask, and we must do this in the living spirit of Christianity and of patriotism. It is this goal that has been before me in founding the Christian Social Workers' Party. I turn now to sketching for you briefly what I understand by this term. I know no other that is so suitable to indicate and to solve all the problems of the social question as this one. "Christian" means belief in the Trinity, in a providential world order, in peace, and in joy in the Holy Ghost. It includes all the virtues that the people need in economic life and all the duties that both employers and employees must perform. "Social" means fraternal and communal. It directs us to the slogan: one for all, and all for one; to the inner spirit it adds the external form of economic life that must be present if business life is to prosper. Both words taken together provide the internal and external conditions of fruitful human activity.

Source: *Germany in the Age of Bismarck*, ed. by **W. M. Simon**
(London: George Allen & Unwin, 1968), pp. 196–200

Nationalism and militarism

The historian Heinrich von Treitschke (1834–96), whose works celebrated the greatness of the Prussian tradition, was one of the most influential publicists of nationalism, authoritarianism, and an aggressive foreign policy in the German Empire. His career trajectory, from liberal supporter of German unification to staunch supporter of Bismarck and finally to conservative ideologue, mirrored the general growth of radical nationalism among the educated and propertied classes in imperial Germany. Thousands of students flocked to his lectures at the University of Berlin. The following selection, published posthumously, is taken from one of his lectures on politics. Treitschke's defense of the redemptive and regenerative value of war attests to the ease with which nationalism, militarism, and statism could be reconciled with Germany's idealist cultural tradition. In juxtaposing Germany's heroic martial values of discipline and self-sacrifice to the materialistic merchant mentality of England, Treitschke expressed the anti-British feeling that accompanied Germany's challenge to British predominance in the 1890s and anticipated one of the main German propaganda themes of the First World War. Like most nationalists, he also attacked socialists, ultramontanist Catholics, and Jews, most notoriously in his oft-cited slogan, "The Jews are our misfortune."

1.3 Heinrich von Treitschke, "The Aim of the State," 1897

... Here it is very obvious that the first task of the state is a twofold one: it is, as we have seen, power in an external direction and the regulation of justice internally; its fundamental functions must therefore be the organization of the army and the administration of the law, in order to protect the community of its citizens from external attack, and to keep them within bounds internally ...

The second essential function of the state is to make war. That we have so long failed to appreciate this, is a proof how effeminate the science of the state as treated by the hands of civilians had finally become. In our century, since Clausewitz, this sentimental conception has disappeared;[2] but its place has been taken by a narrowly materialistic one, which looks upon man, after the manner of Manchesterdom, as a two-legged being whose destiny is to buy cheap and to sell dear. That this conception is also very unfavorable to war is explainable; only after the experiences of our last wars did a healthy view of the state and its warlike power gradually emerge again. Without war there would be no state at all. All the states known to us have arisen through wars; the protection of its citizens by arms remains the first and essential task of the state. And so war will last till the end of history, as long as there is a plural number of states. That it could ever be otherwise is neither to be deduced from the laws of thought or from human nature, nor in any way desirable. The blind worshippers of perpetual peace commit the error of thought that they isolate the state or dream of a world-state, which we have already recognized as something irrational.

Since it is, further, impossible, as we have already seen, even to picture to oneself a higher judge above states, which are sovereign by their nature, the condition of war cannot be imagined away out of the world. It is a favorite fashion of our time to hold up England as especially inclined to peace. But England is always making war; there has been hardly a moment in modern history in which she had not to fight somewhere. The great advances of mankind in civilization can only be entirely realized, in face of the resistance of barbarism and unreason, by the sword. And even among the civilized peoples war remains the form of litigation by which the claims of states are enforced. The proofs which are led in these dreadful international lawsuits are more compelling than the proofs in any civil lawsuit. How often did we seek to convince the small states theoretically that only Prussia could assume the leadership in Germany; the really convincing proof we were obliged to furnish on the battlefields in Bohemia and on the Main.[3] War is also an element that unites nations, not one that only separates them: It does not only bring nations together as enemies; they also learn through it to know and respect one another in their particular idiosyncrasies.

We must, of course, also remember in our consideration of war that it does not always appear as a divine judgement; here, too, there are transient successes, but the life of nations is reckoned by centuries. We can only obtain the final verdict by the survey of long epochs. A state like the Prussian, which by the qualities of its people was always freer and more rational internally than the French, might indeed, because of transient enervation, come near to destruction, but it was able again to remember its inner nature and maintain its superiority. One must say in the

2   General Karl von Clausewitz (1770–1831) was the author of the classic study, *On War* (1833), in which he maintained that war was the continuation of politics by other means.
3   Treitschke is here referring to the Austro-Prussian War of 1866, which led to the unification of northern and central Germany under Prussia.

most decided manner: "War is the only remedy for ailing nations." The moment the state calls: "Myself and my existence are now at stake!" social self-seeking must fall back and every party hate be silent. The individual must forget his own ego and feel himself a member of the whole; he must recognize what a nothing his life is in comparison with the general welfare. In that very point lies the loftiness of war, that the small man disappears entirely before the great thought of the state; the sacrifice of fellow-countrymen for one another is nowhere so splendidly exhibited as in war. In such days the chaff is separated from the wheat …

It is precisely political idealism that demands wars, while materialism condemns them. What a perversion of morality to wish to eliminate heroism from humanity! It is the heroes of a nation who are the figures that delight and inspire youthful minds; and among authors it is those whose words ring like the sound of trumpets whom as boys and youths we most admire. He who does not delight in them is too cowardly to bear arms himself for the fatherland. All reference to Christianity in this case is perverse. The Bible says explicitly that the powers that be shall bear the sword, and it also says: "Greater love hath no man than this, that a man lay down his life for his friends." Those who declaim this nonsense of a perpetual peace do not understand the Aryan peoples; the Aryan peoples are above all things brave. They have always been men enough to protect with the sword what they had won by the spirit …

We must not consider all these things by the light of the reading-lamp alone; to the historian who lives in the world of will it is immediately clear that the demand for a perpetual peace is thoroughly reactionary; he sees that with war all movement, all growth, must be struck out of history. It has always been the tired, unintelligent, and enervated periods that have played with the dream of perpetual peace … However, it is not worth the trouble to discuss this matter further; the living God will see to it that war constantly returns as a dreadful medicine for the human race.

With all this it is not our intention to deny that with the progress of civilization wars must become fewer and shorter. All civilization aims at making human life more harmonious. Just as the abrupt alternation of sensualism and asceticism, which is characteristic of the Middle Ages, is no longer natural to the men of today, so does war, which connotes a complete breach with the everyday life, appear for that very reason so dreadful to us. The more refined man perceives, indeed, that he must kill hostile opponents, whose bravery he esteems highly; he feels that the majesty of war consists in the very fact that murder is done in this case without passion; therefore the struggle costs him much more self-conquest than it does the barbarian.

And the economic ravages of war are also much greater with civilized nations than with barbarians. A war nowadays may have stern, fearful consequences, especially through the destruction of the ingenious credit system. If it were ever to happen that a conqueror entered London, the effect would be simply appalling. There meet the threads of the credit of millions, and a conqueror of Napoleon's ruthlessness could cause ravages there of which we have as yet not the slightest conception. From the natural horror men have for the shedding of blood, from the size and quality of modern armies, it necessarily follows that wars must become fewer and shorter, for it is impossible to see how the burdens of a great war can be borne for any prolonged period under present conditions in the world. But it is a fallacy to infer from this that they could ever cease altogether. They cannot and should not cease, so long as the state is sovereign and confronts other sovereign states.

Source: *Selections From Treitschke's Lectures on Politics*, trsl. by Adam L. Gowans
(New York: Frederick A. Stokes Co., 1914), pp. 21–6

Racial anti-Semitism

The fear among conservatives and radical nationalists that the assimilation of Jews into German society would only increase their influence and strengthen the left was one of the factors that led to the growing vogue of racial anti-Semitism in the 1880s and 1890s. Another factor was that after the Darwinian revolution in biology, racialists who emphasized hereditary selection could claim a spurious scientific objectivity and thus evade the charge of religious bigotry. Houston Stewart Chamberlain (1855–1927), an expatriate English aristocrat who married one of Richard Wagner's daughters, became the most important publicist of racial theory, Germanic supremacy, and anti-Semitism in Germany. His books enjoyed a wide readership among the educated public in the Wilhelmian Empire. His widely acclaimed *Foundations of the Nineteenth Century*, from which these excerpts are taken, was first published in 1899 and went through 28 editions by 1942. A confidant of Wilhelm II, with whom he corresponded for over twenty years (see Doc. 1.5), and an early supporter of Hitler (see Doc. 2.12), Chamberlain personified the ideological link between the Second Empire and the Third Reich.

The *Foundations* was a political tract disguised as history and anthropology. Reasonable in tone and fitted out with all the trappings of a learned treatise, it celebrated the creativity and idealism of the Germanic peoples now supposedly threatened by the growing influence of the "Jewish" spirit of selfishness and materialism. It provided a sophisticated rationale for monarchical conservatism against the challenges of liberalism, socialism, and democracy. The fact that the growth of these egalitarian movements coincided with Jewish emancipation in the course of the nineteenth century allowed ideologues like Chamberlain to link the growth of democracy with the rise of the Jews.

Chamberlain was by no means the first publicist to attribute the growth of democracy to racial degeneration. A host of French aristocratic racialists, of whom the best known was probably Arthur Comte de Gobineau (1816–82), explained the fall of the *ancien régime* in the French Revolution as the result of racial intermixing that destroyed the original purity of the "Aryan" race. Their ideas, however, had more resonance in monarchical Germany than in republican France. It must be borne in mind that in the nineteenth and early twentieth centuries "race" was the favored term for what today would be designated "ethnicity." Chamberlain, too, assumed that the strength of a race or ethnic group was determined by its purity (hence his grudging admiration for the Jewish proscription of marriage outside the group). Trained as a botanist, Chamberlain provided scholarly-sounding arguments for his contention that the key to history was to be found in racial biology. Yet Chamberlain also considered himself a devout Protestant, and his works, replete with biblical quotations, attest to the easy overlap of religious and racial anti-Semitism at the turn of the century. His book issued a call for racial regeneration and religious revival, both to be achieved by excluding Jews. While he helped to make racial anti-Semitism respectable, his racial determinism was somewhat moderated by the idealist notion of the primacy of spirit over matter. In Hitler's Germany he would be officially celebrated as the "seer of the Third Reich."

1.4 Houston Stewart Chamberlain: *Foundations of the Nineteenth Century*, 1899

SACREDNESS OF PURE RACE

… Race, as it arises and maintains itself in space and time, might be compared to the so-called range of power of a magnet. If a magnet be brought near to a heap of iron filings, they assume definite directions, so that a figure is formed with a clearly marked centre, from which lines radiate in all directions; the nearer we bring the magnet the more distinct and more mathematical does the figure become; very few pieces have placed themselves in exactly the same direction, but all have united into a practical and at the same time ideal unity by the possession of a common centre, and by the fact that the relative position of each individual to all the others is not arbitrary but obedient to a fixed law. It has ceased to be a heap, it has become a form. In the same way a human race, a genuine nation, is distinguished from a mere congeries of men. The character of the race becoming more and more pronounced by pure breeding is like the approach of the magnet. The individual members of the nation may have ever so different qualities, the direction of their activities may be utterly divergent, yet together they form a molded unity, and the power – or let us say rather the importance – of every individual is multiplied a thousandfold by his organic connection with countless others …

THE JEWISH QUESTION

Had I been writing a hundred years ago, I should hardly have felt compelled at this point to devote a special chapter to the entrance of the Jews into Western history. Of course the share they had in the rise of Christianity, on account of the peculiar and absolutely un-Aryan spirit which they instilled into it, would have deserved our full attention, as well as also the economic part which they played in all Christian countries; but an occasional mention of these things would have sufficed; anything more would have been superfluous. Herder wrote at that time: "Jewish history takes up more room in our history and more attention than it probably deserves in itself."[4] In the meantime, however, a great change has taken place: The Jews play in Europe, and wherever European influence extends, a different part today from that which they played a hundred years ago; as Viktor Hehn expresses it, we live today in a "Jewish age;"[5] we may think what we like about the past history of the Jews, their present history actually takes up so much room in our own history that we cannot possibly refuse to notice them. Herder in spite of his outspoken humanism had expressed the opinion that "the Jewish people is and remains in Europe an Asiatic people alien to our part of the world, bound to that old law which it received in a distant climate, and which according to its own confession it cannot do away with."[6] Quite correct. But this alien people, ever-lastingly alien, because – as Herder well remarks – it is indissolubly bound to an alien law that is hostile to all

---

4   Johann Gottfried von Herder (1744–1803), a romanticist who believed in the uniqueness of all national cultures, was the author of *Outlines of a Philosophy of the History of Man* (1784–1791).

5   † *Gedanken über Goethe*, 3rd edn., p. 40. The passage as it stands reads, "From the day of Goethe's death, the 22nd March, 1832, Börne dated the freedom of Germany. In reality, however, one epoch was with that day closed and the Jewish age in which we live began."

6   † *Bekehrung der Juden*. Abschnitt 7 of the *Untersuchungen des vergangenen Jahrhunderts zur Beförderung eines geistigen Reiches*.

other peoples – this alien people has become precisely in the course of the nineteenth century a disproportionately important and in many spheres actually dominant constituent of our life. Even a hundred years ago that same witness had sadly to confess that the "ruder nations of Europe" were "willing slaves of Jewish usury;" today he could say the same of by far the greatest part of the civilized world. The possession of money in itself is, however, of least account; our governments, our law, our science, our commerce, our literature, our art ... practically all branches of our life have become more or less willing slaves of the Jews, and drag the feudal fetter if not yet on two, at least on one leg. In the meantime the "alien" element emphasized by Herder has become more and more prominent; a hundred years ago it was rather indistinctly and vaguely felt; now it has asserted and proved itself, and so forced itself on the attention of even the most inattentive. The Indo-European, moved by ideal motives, opened the gates in friendship: The Jew rushed in like an enemy, stormed all positions and planted the flag of his, to us, alien nature – I will not say on the ruins, but on the breaches of our genuine individuality.

Are we for that reason to revile the Jews? That would be as ignoble as it is unworthy and senseless. The Jews deserve admiration, for they have acted with absolute consistency according to the logic and truth of their own individuality, and never for a moment have they allowed themselves to forget the sacredness of physical laws because of foolish humanitarian day-dreams which they shared only when such a policy was to their advantage. Consider with what mastery they use the law of blood to extend their power: The principal stem remains spotless, not a drop of strange blood comes in; as it stands in the *Torah*, "A bastard shall not enter into the congregation of the Lord; even to his tenth generation shall he not enter into the congregation of the Lord" (*Deuteronomy* xxiii, 2); in the meantime, however, thousands of side branches are cut off and employed to infect the Indo-Europeans with Jewish blood. If that were to go on for a few centuries, there would be in Europe only one single people of pure race, that of the Jews, all the rest would be a herd of pseudo-Hebraic mestizos, a people beyond all doubt degenerate physically, mentally, and morally ... [Renan] demonstrates that culture could have no future unless Christian religion should move farther away from the spirit of Judaism and the "Indo-European genius" assert itself more and more in every domain.[7] That mixture then undoubtedly signifies a degeneration: Degeneration of the Jew, whose character is much too alien, firm, and strong to be quickened and ennobled by Germanic blood, degeneration of the European who can naturally only lose by crossing with an "inferior typoe" – or, as I should prefer to say, with so different a type. While the mixture is taking place, the great chief stem of the pure unmixed Jews remains unimpaired. When Napoleon, at the beginning of the nineteenth century, dissatisfied that the Jews, in spite of their emancipation, should remain in proud isolation, angry with them for continuing to devour with their shameful usury the whole of his Alsace, although every career was now open to them, sent an ultimatum to the council of their elders demanding the unreserved fusion of the Jews with the rest of the nation – the delegates of the French Jews adopted all the articles prescribed but one, namely, that which aimed at absolute freedom of marriage with Christians. Their daughters might marry outside the Israelite people, but not their sons; the dictator of Europe had to yield. This is the admirable law by which real Judaism was

7   The French philosopher Ernest Renan (1823–1892) was the author of the controversial *The Life of Jesus* (1863).

founded. Indeed, the law in its strictest form forbids marriage altogether between Jews and non-Jews …

My object has been at once and by the shortest way to meet the objection – which unfortunately is still to be expected from many sides – that there is no "Jewish Question," from which would follow that the entrance of the Jews into our history had no significance. Others, again, talk of religion: it is a question, they say, of religious differences only. Whoever says this overlooks the fact that there would be no Jewish religion if there were no Jewish nation. But there is one. The Jewish nomocracy (that is, rule of law) unites the Jews, no matter how scattered they may be over all the lands of the world, into a firm, uniform, and absolutely political organism in which community of blood testifies to a common past and gives a guarantee for a common future. Though it has many elements not purely Jewish in the narrower sense of the word, yet the power of this blood, united with the incomparable power of the Jewish idea, is so great that these alien elements have long ago been assimilated; for nearly two thousand years have passed since the time when the Jews gave up their temporary inclination to proselytising. Of course, I must, as I showed in the preceding chapter, distinguish between Jews of noble and less noble birth; but what binds together the incompatible parts is (apart from gradual fusing) the tenacity of life which their national idea possesses. This national idea culminates in the unshakable confidence in the universal empire of the Jews, which Jehovah promised. "Simple people who have been born Christians" (as Auerbach expresses it in his sketch of Spinoza's life)[8] fancy that the Jews have given up that hope, but they are very wrong; for "the existence of Judaism depends upon the clinging to the Messianic hope," as one of the very moderate and liberal Jews lately wrote.[9] The whole Jewish religion is in fact founded on this hope. The Jewish faith in God, that which can and may be called "religion" in their case, for it has become since the source of a fine morality, is a part of this national idea, not *vice versa*. To assert that there is a Jewish religion but no Jewish nation is simply nonsense …

THE ALIEN PEOPLE

… We certainly do the Jews no injustice when we say that the revelation of Christ is simply something incomprehensible and hateful to them. Although he apparently sprang from their midst, he embodies nevertheless the negation of their whole nature – a matter in which the Jews are far more sensitive than we. This clear demonstration of the deep cleft that separates us Europeans from the Jew is by no means given in order to let religious prejudice with its dangerous bias settle the matter, but because I think that the perception of two so fundamentally different natures reveals a real gulf; it is well to look once into this gulf, so that on other occasions, where the two sides seem likely to unite each other, we may not be blind to the deep abyss which separates them …

---

8   The German-Jewish writer Berthold Auerbach (1812-1882) wrote a celebrated biography of the philosopher Baruch Spinoza (1632-1677).

9   † Skreinka: *Entwicklungsgeschichte der jüdisachen Dogmen*, p. 75.

JUDAISM

There are no good and bad men, at least for us, but only before God, for the word "good" refers to a moral estimation, and this again depends on a knowledge of motive, which can never be revealed. "Who can know the heart?" was the cry of Jeremiah (xvii, 9)[10]. On the other hand there are certainly good and bad races, for here we have to deal with physical relations, general laws of organic nature, which have been experimentally investigated – relations in which, in contrast to those mentioned above figures provide irrefutable proofs – relations concerning which the history of humanity offers us abundant informa-tion. And scarcely less manifest are the leading ideas. In reference to race these must in the first place be looked upon as a consequence; but one should not underestimate this inner, invisible anatomy, this purely spiritual dolichocephaly and brachycephaly, which as cause also has a wide range of influence. Hence it is that every strong nation has so much power of assimilation. The entrance into a new union in the first place changes not a fibre of the physical structure, and only very slowly, in the course of generations, affects the blood; but ideas have a more rapid effect, because they direct the whole personality almost at once into new channels. And the Jewish national idea seems to exercise a particularly strong influence, perhaps for the very reason that in this case the nation exists merely as an idea and never, from the beginning of Judaism, was it a "normal" nation, but above all, a thought, a hope … Are we to suppose that the Jewish national idea has not the force of other national ideas? On the contrary, it is more powerful, as I have shown, than any other, and transforms men to its own image. One does not need to have the authentic Hittite nose to be a Jew; the term Jew rather denotes a special way of thinking and feeling. A man can very soon become a Jew without being an Israelite; often he needs only to have frequent intercourse with Jews, to read Jewish newspapers, to accustom himself to Jewish philosophy, literature, and art. On the other hand, it is senseless to call an Israelite a "Jew," though his descent is beyond question, If he has succeeded in throwing off the fetters of Ezra and Nehemiah, and if the law of Moses has no place in his brain, and contempt of others no place in his heart. "What a prospect it would be," cries Herder, "to see the Jews purely humanized in their way of thinking!"[11] But a purely humanized Jew is no longer a Jew because, by renouncing the idea of Judaism, he *ipso facto* has left that nationality, which is composed and held together by a complex of conceptions, by a "faith." With the apostle Paul we must learn that "he is not a Jew who is one outwardly, but he is a Jew who is one inwardly" (Rom. ii, 28–29) …

FREEDOM AND LOYALTY

Let us attempt a glance into the depths of the soul. What are the specific intellectual and moral characteristics of this Germanic race? Certain anthropologists would fain teach us that all races are equally gifted; we point to history and answer: that is a lie! The races of mankind are markedly different in the nature and also in the extent of their gifts, and the Germanic

10   † As Kant in his *Critique of Pure Reason* says (in explaining the cosmological idea of freedom): "The real morality of actions (merit and guilt) remains quite concealed from us, even in the case of our own conduct."

11   † *Adrastea* 7, Stück V., Abschnitt "Fortsetzung."

races belong to the most highly gifted group usually termed Aryan. Is this human family united and uniform by bonds of blood? Do these stems really all spring from the same root? I do not know and I do not much care; no affinity binds more closely than elective affinity, and in this sense the Indo-European Aryans certainly form a family … For freedom is by no means an abstract thing, to which every human being has fundamentally a claim; a right to freedom must evidently depend upon capacity for it, and this again presupposes physical and intellectual power. One may make the assertion that even the mere conception of freedom is quite unknown to most men. Do we not see the *homo syriacus* develop just as well and as happily in the position of slave as of master? Do the Chinese not show us another example of the same nature? Do not all historians tell us that the Semites and half-Semites, in spite of their great intelligence, never succeeded in founding a state that lasted, and that because every one always endeavored to grasp all power for himself, thus showing that their capabilities were limited to despotism and anarchy, the two opposites of freedom? And here we see at once what great gifts a man must have in order that one may say of him, he is "by nature free," for the first condition of this is the power of creating. Only a state-building race can be free; the gifts which make the individual an artist and philosopher are essentially the same as those which, spread through the whole mass as instinct, found states and give to the individual that which hitherto had remained unknown to all nature: the idea of freedom …

The fundamental and common "Aryan" capacity of free creative power had to be supplemented by another quality, the incomparable and altogether peculiar Germanic loyalty (*Treue*). If that intellectual and physical development which leads to the idea of freedom and which produces on the one hand art, philosophy, science, on the other constitutions (as well as all the phenomena of culture which this word implies), is common to the ancient Greeks and Romans as well as to the Germanic peoples, so also is the extravagant conception of loyalty a specific characteristic of the Germanic … This loyalty to a master chosen of their own free will is the most prominent feature in the Germanic character; from it we can tell whether pure Germanic blood flows in the veins or not …

Source: Houston Stewart Chamberlain, *Foundations of the Nineteenth Century*, Vol. I, trsl. by John Lees (1910; Rpr. New York: Howard Fertig, 1977), pp. 319–20, 329–32, 334–5, 338, 490–2, 542–5

Germanic supremacy

The following correspondence between Chamberlain and Kaiser Wilhelm II provides telling evidence of the highly favorable reception that Chamberlain's writings enjoyed among the conservative German elite. It also reveals the political ambitions that underlay the apparently apolitical notion of Germany's cultural world mission. Chamberlain's exaggerated Germanophilia may be typical of the ideological fervor of a convert, but it also reflects the sense of superiority of German nationalists and clearly struck a sympathetic chord in the Kaiser. Their shared hostility to Catholicism was rooted partly in Protestant fundamentalism but, more important, in the fear that the allegiance of German Catholics to nationalist goals would be weakened by the influence of the Church. This fear of political Catholicism was paralleled by fears that workers' allegiance to their nation might be weakened by allegiance to their class. Chamberlain's reference to "planned organization down to the minutest detail" as the key to German power prefigured the coming fascist state in which all political dissent would be suppressed.

1.5a Houston Stewart Chamberlain, letter to Kaiser Wilhelm II, 13 November 1901

... Your Majesty and all your subjects were born in a holy place; most of them, it is true, do not suspect it because they take it for granted – like the rays of the life-giving sun. I, however, had to follow a long and difficult path before I espied the holy shrine from afar, and it took many more years of hard work before I was able to ascend its steps. That is why I can only look back in horror at my past; because even though I had what one calls a happy childhood, for a man of my character there could be no true happiness outside of Germandom. I shudder to think how late in life I came into contact with the German language; I might easily not have learnt it at all. For it is my innermost belief – gained through years of study, gained in those sacred hours when the soul wrestles with divine wisdom, like Jacob with the angel – that the moral and spiritual salvation of mankind depends on things German. In that "moral world order" of which Your Majesty often spoke at Liebenberg, the German element presently forms the crux, *le pivot central*. It is the German language which proves this incontestably; for science, philosophy, and religion can today make no step forward except in the German language. From the existence of this language we learn something which is not always apparent in everyday life: that the highest qualities are united in this people, higher than may be found anywhere else. Language and the national soul condition one another; each grows out of the other; so long as both remain alive and linked together, the plant will continue to flower. In the case of the Romance peoples, both are dead; in the case of the other Germanics (I am thinking especially of England), the two have for some time been growing apart, with the result that the language is becoming ever more silent (that is, turning into a mere medium for communicating practical matters and losing all its inventiveness) and the soul is consequently shedding its flights and is simply dragging itself along on its belly like a worm. And since the German soul is bound indissolubly to the German language, it follows that the future progress of mankind is bound to a powerful Germany stretching far across the earth and preserving and imposing upon others the sacred heritage of its language. The actual *Realpolitik* of the German Reich, which surely cannot be really sober and matter of fact, therefore must be – at least in my view – quite distinct from the policies pursued by other countries. From the point of view of the moral world order, the Anglo-Saxon has forfeited his heritage – I speak not of today but look centuries ahead; the Russian is only the latest embodiment of the eternal empire of Tamburlain, and if one were to deprive it of its German dynasty, nothing would remain but a decaying *matière brute*; today God relies only on the Germans. That is the knowledge, the certain truth, which has filled my soul for years; in its service I have sacrificed my peace, for it I shall live and die ... My struggle – inspired not by hatred of Semites but by love of the Germanics – against the caustic poison of Judaism, my struggle against ultramontanism, against materialism; my attempt to transform the doctrine of transcendental knowledge from a possession of an academic cast into the possession of every educated German; my desire to divest religion of its Syrian–Egyptian rags, so as to enable the pure power of faith to unite us where the thoughtless repetition of slavish superstitions now only divides us; and later – if I live to see the day – the complete transformation of our conception of the life-problem so that our natural sciences will suddenly and for the first time find themselves in harmony with our German philosophy and religion, so giving us a true *Weltanschauung* at last ... all this means for me fighting and creating in the service of Germandom. For verily, the issues at stake are of great import, and if the creator of the moral world order has chosen the Germans as his instruments, then they must submerge themselves completely in the pursuance of this God-given duty. And if "things German" are, as I said above, the central pivot on which the future of man's spirit depends, then the present moment, the present century – and I mean it – is the central pivot of world history. The issue now is: to make or to mar.

There are times when history is, so to speak, woven ... according to a fairly well-established pattern; but then come times when the threads for a new tapestry must be introduced, when the nature of the cloth and the pattern to be woven have to be determined, and care taken to ensure a purposeful procedure. We find ourselves in such a time today. The creation of the German Reich was not a beginning but an end. Now there will either be a "new course" (as Your Majesty recently remarked) or else nothing at all; and in the latter instance Germany will have failed and will move slowly towards its downfall, to be overtaken and drowned in the waves of a Yankee-ized Anglo-Saxondom and a tartarized Slavdom. This is the moment when the future is being decided ...

On the other hand, how could a man like myself possibly study history without concluding that the future of the German cause is bound up with the Hohenzollern dynasty? How could one possibly observe the present political chaos of the Reich with its Reichstag without feeling that one's hopes could be based only on the dynasty? True, the entire German people with its incomparable language is the source of that strength without which the Hohenzollerns would themselves be nothing; but political salvation cannot be achieved by the people. In this extremely difficult world situation the House of Hohenzollern is the only trump card held by the German people. Only planned organization down to the minutest detail, and not – as with the Anglo-Saxons – the untrammelled liberty of the atomized individual, can help Germany to victory. Political freedom for the masses is a spent force; by using the principle of organization, however, Germany can achieve anything – anything! In this respect she has no equal. And at the head of this organization stands, as the foremost German of them all, the King of Prussia.

1.5b Kaiser Wilhelm's reply, 31 December 1901

My dear Mr. Chamberlain,

Unhappily you are completely correct in saying at the start of your compelling and gripping letter that you assume I know nothing about the "Upanishads" and other Indo-Aryan books, nor about the beautiful sayings of the wise men concerning rulers, which are contained therein. I openly admit my ignorance and beg for mercy! Here you have me at a disadvantage! But in the early 1870s there was no one, certainly among my teachers, who had the slightest knowledge of such matters! ... We had to wade through 1000 pages of grammar, we applied the rules, and attacked everything from Phidias to Demosthenes, from Pericles to Alexander, and even our dear great Homer, with a magnifying glass and scalpel! And throughout all these hundreds of surgical operations which I had to carry out upon the products of the Hellenes so as to get a "classical education," my heart rebelled and the lively feeling for harmony which I possess cried out: "Surely this is not, this cannot be, what we need from Hellas for the advancement of Germandom!" And this immediately after and still under the overpowering impression of the 1870 war, of the victories of my father and grandfather! They had forged the German Reich, and I felt instinctively that we boys needed another type of preparation if we were to continue the good work in the new Reich. Our severely depressed youth had need of a liberator like yourself! Someone who revealed the Indo-Aryan sources to us. But no one knew them!

And consequently all that massive primeval Aryan-Germanic feeling which lay slumbering within me had to fight its own way gradually to the fore. It came into open conflict with "traditional wisdom," expressed itself frequently in a bizarre form, frequently without form at all, because it was more like a dark sentiment stirring in my subconscious and trying to break free. Then you come along – with one magic stroke you bring order into confusion, light into darkness, aims for which we can strive and work, explanations for things which we sensed only darkly, paths which must be followed for the salvation of the Germans and thus for the salvation of mankind! You sing in high praise of things German and above all of our magnificent language and you cry out impressively to the Germanic: "Forget your quarrels and pettiness; your task on earth is: to be God's instrument for the spreading of His culture, His teaching! Hence deepen, raise, cultivate your language and through it science, enlightenment, and faith!" That was liberation! So! And now you know, my dear Mr. Chamberlain, what was going on in my mind when I felt your hand in mine!

Allow me to thank you for this precious jewel which you sent me in the form of a letter! Who am I, that you thank me? Surely only a poor child who tries to be a good instrument for our lord God up there ...

Truly, let us thank Him up there, that He still looks with such, such favor upon our Germans; for God sent your book to the German people and you personally to me, that is a firm belief which no one can destroy in me. You were chosen by Him to be my ally, and I shall thank Him eternally that He did so. For your powerful language grips people and forces them to think and naturally also to fight, to attack! What harm will it do! The German sleepy-head is waking up, and that is a good thing, then he will be on the look-out and will achieve something; and once he has begun to work he will achieve more than anyone else. His science in his own language is a gigantic weapon, and he must be reminded of this constantly! For "Reason" – i.e. common sense – and "Science" are our most dangerous weapons, especially in the fight against the deadly power of "ubiquitous" Rome. Once the Germanic Catholics have been led by you into the open conflict between Germanics and the Catholics, that is "Romans," then they will be "awakened" and will "perceive" that which the father confessors are trying to hide from them – that they are being kept in degrading subjection to "Rome" as an instrument against "Germany." Therefore *Eritis sicut deus, scientes bonum et malum.*" It is now possible to perceive a movement in this direction, and your book is being widely bought in such circles, praise God!

I first read your wonderful letter myself, and then I read it out to all the people gathered around my Christmas table. All ranks and generations listened in silence and were deeply moved. The Kaiserin sends you her sincere thanks and best wishes!

And now I wish God's blessing and the grace of our Savior upon my comrade-in-arms and ally in the struggle for the Germanic peoples against Rome, Jerusalem, etc. The feeling that we are fighting for an absolutely good, divine cause is our guarantee of victory! ...

Wilhelm II R

Source: Houston Stewart Chamberlain, *Briefe und Briefwechsel mit Kaiser Wilhelm II*, Vol. II (Munich: Bruckmann, 1928), pp. 137ff. English version in J. C. G. Röhl, *From Bismarck to Hitler: The Problem of Continuity in German History* (New York: Barnes & Noble, 1970), pp. 43–8

Pan-Germanism

The revocation of the Anti-Socialist Law after Bismarck's dismissal by the young Kaiser Wilhelm II in 1890 marked something of a turning point in the history of the German Empire. As the Social Democratic Party (SPD), founded in 1875, gained increasing support among workers, Wilhelm II's governments increasingly sought to channel public energies into a more aggressive foreign policy (*Weltpolitik*). In the 1890s numerous patriotic societies and right-wing pressure groups, such as the Pan-German League, the German League, the Agrarian League, the Naval League, the Eastern Marches Association, and the Colonial Society advocated *Weltpolitik* and publicized nationalist demands. Among the most radical of these was the Pan-German League whose goal was the consolidation of all ethnic Germans around the world. After the turn of the century the Pan-German League adopted an increasingly oppositional stance toward the government, calling for stronger leadership and attacking the Kaiser for his allegedly too moderate policies. Backed by Ruhr industrialists, the Pan-German League exercised considerably greater influence, particularly in the war years (1914–18), than its relatively small membership, which never exceeded 23,000, would suggest. The Pan-German League was not formally dissolved until 1939, when its goal of creating a greater German Reich was officially proclaimed to have been achieved.

The following selections are taken from an influential pamphlet published anonymously in the immediate aftermath of the Reichstag election of 1912, in which the SPD won 30 percent of the popular vote and for the first time gained the largest number of seats in the Reichstag as well. The author of the pamphlet, entitled *If I Were the Kaiser*, was Heinrich Class (1860–1954), head of the Pan-German League from 1908 on. His pamphlet expressed the frustration of radical nationalists with the government's failure to take sufficiently stringent action against the growing danger of liberalism, socialism, and democracy, all of which Class blamed on excessive Jewish influence. Class demanded a monarchical dictatorship to combat the left. In the absence of a willing and able monarch, another dictator would have to be found. Class' extremist policy proposals anticipated the post-war National Socialist program, particularly in calling for the suppression of the SPD, expulsion of their leaders, a ban on Jewish immigration, and restrictions on the rights of Jews, explicitly defined in racial terms. His pamphlet, 25,000 copies of which were circulated before the war, was reissued after the war with an addendum in which Class praised Adolf Hitler and his young National Socialist German Workers' Party (NSDAP) for their passionate nationalism, vigorous anti-Marxism, and "full recognition of the Jewish danger."

1.6 Heinrich Class, "If I Were the Kaiser," 1912

WEAKNESS AND LACK OF SUCCESS OF FOREIGN POLICY

The disappointment that all sectors of the population, even Social Democrats, feel about the lack of success and futility of the foreign policy of the German Reich is the most important of all the general causes of the winter of German discontent, which now has already lasted for over 20 years. All states around us here in Europe, all states around the globe, in which the vital nerve of the state – the will to power – has not yet died, spread and expand their area of influence. Even states as internally unhealthy as France and Russia do this. Even states with such immeasurably large possessions as England and the North-American Union do this. Finally, even a state like France in which the population has begun to diminish does this, though it certainly has no need for further colonial territory. All of them expand; even a weak Spain defends itself and seeks to regain in Morocco what it lost against the United States[12]. Only the German Empire is supposedly "saturated" and rushes to announce its "political disinterest" as soon as a conflict breaks out anywhere in a country of importance to the civilized nations; only the German Empire is content just to demand that its economic interests be safeguarded.

But if any state has cause to concern itself with the expansion of its power, then it is the German Empire; for its population is rapidly increasing, its industry needs markets, its economy needs soil for the cultivation of tropical and subtropical raw materials of all kind, the acquisition of which has placed us in unacceptable dependence on others, to point to cotton as just one example ...

THE JEWS

... The carriers and teachers of the materialism that today is dominant are the Jews; its German-born supporters are dupes seduced and alienated from their inborn instincts.

Having achieved economic power these racially foreign guests on German soil spread into all areas of national life – a tragi-comic contradiction in itself – but because it was tolerated, it has become a historical fact. Publishing, theater, journalism were taken over; law, academia, medicine became special fields of Jewish activity and influence.

And according to the law of his being – no person can get out of their skin; this is valid too for everything that is racially inherited – the Jew remains a Jew in everything he undertakes. If he engages in politics, he can only do so as a Jew, i.e., without sense or understanding for self-integration, for subordination, without love for what has grown historically and organically. If he becomes a lawyer, he acts subversively, because his inborn notions of justice stand in contradiction to those to be found in written German law. He resorts to those Talmudic tricks that turn justice into injustice. If he pursues art, he lacks the inwardness that is the basis of every creative achievement. We know that the so-called German theater is almost completely in Jewish hands today. Only the few people who reflect on the fact that the performance of new works depends on the judgement of Jewish theater directors and their advisers, who decide whether a piece is worth staging, realize what this means for German artistic creativity. The judgement, coming from Jews, will correspond to the Jewish conception of what is stageworthy, and we can categorically state that many works for the stage emerging from good, German minds gather dust in the desks of poets, because they are found not to be stageworthy by critics of alien blood. "Sensationalism," however, is their measure of stageworthiness, and the German-born writer who wants to write for the stage has to change and write like a Jew ...

Even worse is the influence of the Jewish press, because it affects the popular masses directly day by day. Here the proverb applies: "Constant dropping wears away the stone." Jewry has seized hold of the press, and it can be said that only the press of the Center Party is at least for the main part free of its influence – otherwise, however, except for the few anti-Jewish papers, this is not true of any paper on German soil, not even the party newspapers of the extreme right. If a newspaper is not under Jewish ownership, or if the editors are not

12   A reference to the Spanish defeat in the Spanish–American War of 1898.

Jewish, then it is the advertising that determines the attitude of the paper – at least on all questions that concern Jewry.

Thousands of Jewish writers daily form our public opinion; in millions of printed pages their writings reach German readers – and this is supposed to be without effect?

Let me just mention the shameless activities of Jewish satiric journals, which live from sex, and from ridiculing marriage, the throne, and all those things that once had an important place in the consciousness of the people. I would draw particular attention to the deliberate deprecation of marriage. Much worse, because of its wider impact, is the influence of the Jewish daily press: *What do these people know of German freedom, which sets boundaries through voluntary restraint? What do they know of the necessary subordination of everyone? What is the fatherland and the state to these homeless and stateless people? What is military discipline to them? What is monarchy to them?*

The Jew is nowhere creative – in what we are accustomed to calling politics he is entirely barren. He has not passed the political test in history, for he has never founded a lasting state. Looking closely at the fate of the tribes that have lived in Palestine, one must doubt whether there was really ever a Jewish state.

In recognizing the political and moral influence of the Jewish component among non-Jewish host peoples, Count Gobineau has done the latter a service, which, rightly understood, ought to be seen as an act of rescue.[13] … With truly brilliant inspiration this Germanic seer looked into the past and revealed the true causes of the decline of ancient peoples: subversion through Jewish blood and Jewish mind.

No German-born person has the right arrogantly to shove the grand intellectual achievement of this great man aside. If someone does so anyway, he has already taken in the poison. The seriousness of Gobineau's admonition demands a hearing – when will the people in government listen?

Another non-German, H. St. Chamberlain, comes to similar conclusions as Gobineau – not to mention the great German-blooded analysts of Jewry from Luther to Treitschke. At the time it was joyful news to those who understood the core of the Jewish question that Kaiser Wilhelm II was an enthusiastic admirer of Chamberlain and that he distributed thousands of copies of *The Foundations of the Nineteenth Century.* And now? Has the Kaiser read and understood the book? How is it possible then that right afterwards he became a patron of the Jews, even more so than his uncle Edward,[14] by drawing newly-rich Jewish industrialists, bankers, and merchants into his social circle, bestowing aristocratic title on them, and even seeking their advice. One of the contradictions of this otherwise rich life – probably the worst one, the one fraught with greatest consequences!

Even if Gobineau's *Essai sur l'inégalité des races humaines* and Chamberlain's *Foundations* had never been written, among people educated in history there is no dispute that whatever the Jew may be suited for, he certainly is not suited for the political leadership and councillorship of his host people.

And now it is possible that the same people, who in their innocence had recently granted equal rights to the Jews living among them, may voluntarily submit to Jewish leadership! The role that such shallow and barren pseudo-Germans as Lasker and Bamberger were able to play in the first years of the new Reich is not so important – these were relatively still the best

---

13   The French racial theorist Count Arthur de Gobineau (1816–82), author of *On the Inequality of Human Races* (4 vols., 1853–55), exercised considerable influence in Germany, particularly on Richard Wagner and his followers.

14   A reference to Edward VII (1841–1910), who reigned as British king from 1901 to 1910.

years of Jewish activity.[15] But that with very minor exceptions the entire non-ultramontane and non-anti-Semitic press could fall into Jewish hands or at any rate under Jewish influence – is this not an outrage? ...

THE SOCIAL DEMOCRATIC PARTY

[After Bismarck's dismissal] the Kaiser personally took over the struggle against the Social Democrats. He declared that he would be able to deal with them alone, while among the liberal parties as well the talk of "overcoming them in the sphere of intellect" and "fighting them in the private sphere" found increasing numbers of supporters.

Instead of learning the lesson of the election of 1890,[16] namely that earlier defensive measures had not sufficed and were perhaps psychologically ineffective, all resistance was given up and the urban masses were abandoned to socialist incitement, which now could grow without restrictions. *One day the greatest reproach against the government of Wilhelm II and his chancellors after Bismarck will be that they did not fulfill their duty of defense against the SPD.* Thus the party of Bebel has become the strongest one in the German Reichstag with more than four million voters behind them.[17] ...

Whoever wants to gain the right point of view about the socialist danger for the Reich has to be clear about the fact that the mass poisoning of German voters would not even have been possible without the participation of Jewry. The true leaders of Social Democracy are Jews ... Under Jewish leadership the "German" Social Democrats, like their Austrian counterparts, are serious about their internationalism, while, e.g., the French, Italian, or Czech Social Democrats certainly are not.

The constitution of the Reich is seriously threatened by the Social Democrats – can they be surprised that on the other side the idea of changing this constitution comes up, even if that change points in a different direction than the worshippers of the masses demand?

EFFECTS OF UNIVERSAL AND EQUAL SUFFRAGE

Universal and equal suffrage has always been an untruth, as it presupposes an equality among people that can never be realized in practice. It is immoral in that it treats the worthy, the capable, the mature exactly as it treats the unworthy, the incapable, and the immature. Finally, it is unjust in that through the power of the masses – majority vote – it deprives the educated and propertied classes of their rights. It was acceptable only as long as the nationalist and state-supportive convictions of the unpropertied and uneducated counterbalanced

15   Ludwig Bamberger (1823–99) and Eduard Lasker (1829–84) were prominent liberals who participated in the Revolution of 1848, joined the National Liberal Party, and supported Bismarck's unification of Germany but opposed his illiberal domestic policies.

16   In the Reichstag election of 1890 the Social Democrats doubled their vote total over the previous election of 1887 despite the legal restrictions placed on the party by Bismarck in the Anti-Socialist Law of 1878. Wilhelm II thereupon decided to change course, repeal the Anti-Socialist Law, and try to gain worker support through tactical concessions. The SPD, however, continued to gain votes in every subsequent election until they became the largest party in the Reichstag in 1912.

17   August Bebel (1840–1913) was co-founder and long-time leader of the Social Democratic Party in Germany.

the contradictions inherent in universal suffrage. Up to then it could be said that love of fatherland held the dangers in check: With massive defection from the fatherland this balancing factor is lacking, and *universal and equal suffrage functions in an undisguisedly destructive way against the state, depriving all who want to defend the state of their rights* ... .

... In summary let me point out that *my proposal for reform is a unified whole that can be described as follows:*

Replacement of universal and equal suffrage by an appropriate class or corporatist voting franchise; the simultaneous conversion to a parliamentary system that recognizes the personal accomplishments of the educated and the propertied in the realm of political work ... .

STRUGGLE AGAINST REVOLUTION

... But what is to be done?

We ought to reach back to the draft of the Anti-Socialist Law that Bismarck put before the Reichstag in the year 1878 and allow it to become law without watering it down in the way favored by the parliament of that day. Accordingly, everything that serves to undermine the state and social order, or is suspected of doing so, would be prohibited. Associations, clubs, newspapers, and periodicals conforming to the above tendencies will not be tolerated. Moreover, all the preventive measures envisioned in the draft law of September 1878 would have to be introduced.[18]

But one must take a further step.

An out-and-out working-class party that stands on the foundation of the state, the nation, and the monarchy can be integrated into our public life, and can, perhaps, even be put to good use to rouse the conscience against any inclination toward exclusively "bourgeois policies." *But not a party that drives the masses toward anarchy, that has disowned its own nation, its own fatherland.*

An improvement of Social Democracy under Jewish leadership is not possible, nor is a gradual turning away from internationalism. It is therefore necessary to give the masses the opportunity to turn away from or put a stop to Social Democracy by freeing them from the current leadership: all Reichstag and state parliament deputies, all party officials, all editors and publishers of socialist newspapers, all leaders of socialist trade unions – *in short, all who stand in the service of the socialist movement are to be expelled from the German Empire.* The same applies, of course, to all anarchists.

One must not be sentimental in liberating the people from those who are driving it into decadence. Whoever declares that he does not belong to any nation – and that is what the "international" Social Democrat does –, whoever enjoys proclaiming his irreconcilable hostility towards state, society, and monarchy again and again, must not be surprised when these institutions finally lose patience. *Such an enemy of his fatherland will long ago have lost the right to be treated as an equal citizen with equal rights,* which just allows him to continue his destructive incitement of the people under the protection of the law. If he is now expelled from the fatherland he hates, nothing bad has happened to him, after all, according to his own opinion. Let him try his luck in the countries he has praised for their alleged true freedom – *let him be expelled from the German Reich from which he has divorced himself* ... .

---

18   A softened version of Bismarck's bill was passed by the Reichstag in October 1878. State and local governments were empowered to abolish socialist societies, dissolve meetings, and prohibit publications. Violators of the law were subject to fines, imprisonment, and expulsion.

REFORM OF PUBLIC LIFE

But we must not limit ourselves to these defensive measures. They lie in the realm of the state. At the same time, society must do all it can to win the masses back to the fatherland. Public interest associations will publish the most inexpensive daily papers in order to provide the people with detoxified reading material. In this way the gap left by the suppression of the socialist press will be filled. Large-scale national meetings must be inaugurated through which the best people from all walks of life and the professions will work together for reconcilia-tion. Festivals are to be put on for the people – in short, we must recover what was neglected in the years of economic growth following the founding of the Reich and then in the subse-quent years of embitterment.[19] We must take up the "struggle for the soul of the people," to paraphrase a nice slogan. The army administration will support civil society in these efforts, providing the opportunity for soldiers to hear lectures drawn from German history – in short, those who are capable of and called to such honorable service in city and country will do their best to smooth out the divisions that through ill will have escalated into implacable enmity.

It is possible, even probable, that by proceeding in such a way against the danger of socialism we will face a few difficult, restless years – that cannot be helped, and we have to get through them. But let's wait and see whether peace and unity does not return to German lands once the inciters of division have been removed and kept at a distance. But if we are to take up this struggle, we must be clear about one thing: *no half-measures, no weakness, no sentimentality* …

THE JEWS UNDER ALIEN LAW

A return to health in our national life, in all its branches – cultural, moral, political, and economic – and sustaining that recovered health is *only possible if Jewish influence is either completely expunged or rolled back to a bearable, harmless level.*

Let us be clear in discussing these necessities that the innocent must suffer along with the guilty. However painful it may be for the fair-minded German, it is better that a certain number of upstanding Jews suffer as a result of the guilt of their less worthy tribal comrades than that the whole German people is ruined through the poison of the latter. The failure of the good Jews, acting out of a feeling of racial community, to work for the prohibition of immigration from the east at the time of emancipation is now taking its toll.

Today, *the borders must be totally and unconditionally barred to any further Jewish immigration.* This is absolutely necessary, but it is no longer enough. Just as self-evidently, *foreign Jews who have not yet acquired citizenship rights must be speedily and unconditionally expelled, to the last man.* But even this is not enough.

Hard as it may be on the German sense of justice: *we must restrict the general rights of resi-dent Jews*, as sorry as every individual among us may be when the good are affected along with the bad. In such cases one has to keep one's eye on what is necessary and has to close one's heart to compassion …

We must demand that *resident Jews be placed under alien law.*

The first question is, *who is a Jew?* And this question must be answered with toughness. Religious faith may be regarded as the original determinant of Jewishness, but racial member-

---

19   The reference here is to the financial crash of 1873 and subsequent hardship.

ship must be considered, and even Jews who have turned away from their faith must be treated as Jews, along with descendants of mixed marriages, according to the old Germanic principle that offspring of such marriages follow the inferior bloodline. To be effective we need the following definition: *A Jew, according to the prospective Aliens Law, is anyone who belonged to a Jewish religious corporation as of 18 January 1871, as well as all the descendants of such persons who were Jews at that date, even when only one parent was or is Jewish* ... [20].

The weakness of the German defense against Jewry actually lies in the fact that just about everyone in public life knows one or more unobjectionable Jews. And that is what skews their thinking when they deal with the Jewish question, and it makes them compassionate and weak. This is understandable on a human level – but, when it is a question of the future of our people we have to cast off all weakness. ...

... Friends, see to it that the genuine heir to Bismarck finds assistants when he forms the Reich for the second time and begins his work with the motto:

Germany to the Germans –
To each German his own!

Source: Daniel Frymann [Heinrich Class], *Das Kaiserbuch: Politische Wahrheiten und Notwendigkeiten*, 7th edn. (Leipzig: Verlag von Theodor Weicher, 1925), pp. 4–5, 30–2, 38–40, 59–60, 62–4, 69–70, 72, 206.
Translated by Rod Stackelberg

The preventive-war mentality

The following selection is taken from General Friedrich von Bernhardi's book *Germany and the Next War* which was published in 1912 and became a best-seller. According to historian Fritz Fischer, Bernhardi's views accurately reflected official thinking. It offers an example of the preventive-war mentality of the German General Staff, an attitude that contributed to the outbreak of the First World War. In the minds of many of Germany's leaders war with Britain and France was ultimately unavoidable. Hence it was in Germany's interests to fight sooner rather than later, and under conditions of its own choosing. The German leadership was not prepared to accept the status quo in the international balance of power. Equally noteworthy, however, is Bernhardi's rejection of expansion in the East, where millions of Poles already lived under German rule. In this respect, at least, German territorial aims were expanded during the First World War and again under the Nazis, for whom the acquisition of African colonies was less important than the acquisition of *Lebensraum* in the east. For Bernhardi Germany's main enemy was Britain, for Hitler it would be Russia. Common to imperialists before both world wars, however, was the linkage of German power with German culture. According to Bernhardi, war was necessary to defend "spiritual and moral liberty, and the profound and lofty aspirations of German thought."

20   18 January 1871 was the date of the unification of Germany and the formation of the German Empire.

1.7 Friedrich von Bernhardi, "World Power or Downfall," 1912

Under these conditions the position of Germany is extraordinarily difficult. We not only require for the full material development of our nation, on a scale corresponding to its intellectual importance, an extended political basis, but ... we are compelled to obtain space for our increasing population and markets for our growing industries. But at every step which we take in this direction England will resolutely oppose us. English policy may not yet have made the definite decision to attack us; but it doubtless wishes, by all and every means, even the most extreme, to hinder every further expansion of German international influence and of German maritime power. The recognized political aims of England and the attitude of the English Government leave no doubt on this point. But if we were involved in a struggle with England, we can be quite sure that France would not neglect the opportunity of attacking our flank. Italy, with her extensive coastline, even if still a member of the Triple Alliance, will have to devote large forces to the defense of the coast to keep off the attacks of the Anglo-French Mediterranean Fleet, and would thus only be able to employ weaker forces against France. Austria would be paralyzed by Russia; against the latter we should have to leave forces in the east. We would thus have to fight out the struggle against France and England practically alone with a part of our army, perhaps with some support from Italy. It is in this double menace by sea and on the mainland of Europe that the grave danger of our political position lies, since all freedom of action is taken from us and all expansion barred.

Since the struggle is, as appears on a thorough investigation of the international question, necessary and inevitable, we must fight it out, cost what it may. Indeed, we are carrying it on at the present moment, though not with drawn swords, and only by peaceful means so far. On the one hand it is being waged by the competition in trade, industries, and warlike preparations; on the other hand, by diplomatic methods with which the rival states are fighting each other in every region where their interests clash.

With these methods it has been possible to maintain peace hitherto, but not without considerable loss of power and prestige. This apparently peaceful state of things must not deceive us, we are facing a hidden, but nonetheless formidable, crisis – perhaps the most momentous crisis in the history of the German nation.

We have fought in the last great wars for our national union and our position among the powers of Europe; we now must decide whether we wish to develop into and maintain a world empire, and procure for German spirit and German ideas that fitting recognition which has been hitherto withheld from them.

Have we the energy to aspire to that great goal? Are we prepared to make the sacrifices which such an effort will doubtless cost us? Or are we willing to recoil before the hostile forces, and sink step by step lower in our economic, political, and national importance? That is what is involved in our decision ...

We must make it quite clear to ourselves that there can be no standing still, no being satisfied for us, but only progress or retrogression, and that it is tantamount to retrogression when we are contented with our present place among the nations of Europe, while all our rivals are straining with desperate energy, even at the cost of our rights, to extend their power. The process of our decay would set in gradually and advance slowly so long as the struggle against us was waged with peaceful weapons; the living generation would, perhaps, be able to continue to exist in peace and comfort. But should a war be forced upon us by stronger enemies under conditions unfavorable to us, then, if our arms met with disaster, our political downfall would not be delayed, and we should rapidly sink down. The future of German nationality would be sacrificed, an independent German civilization would not long exist, and the blessings for which German blood has flowed in streams – spiritual and moral liberty, and the profound and lofty aspirations of German thought – would for long ages be lost to mankind.

If, as is right, we do not wish to assume the responsibility for such a catastrophe, we must have the courage to strive with every means to attain that increase of power which we are entitled to claim, even at the risk of a war with numerically superior foes.

Under the present conditions it is out of the question to attempt this by acquiring territory in Europe. The region in the east, where German colonists once settled, is lost to us, and could only be recovered from Russia by a long and victorious war, and would then be a perpetual incitement to renewed wars. So, again, the reannexation of the former South Prussia, which was united to Prussia on the second partition of Poland, would be a serious undertaking, on account of the Polish population.

Under these circumstances we must clearly try to strengthen our political power in other ways.

In the first place, our political position would be considerably consolidated if we could finally get rid of the standing danger that France will attack us on a favorable occasion, as soon as we find ourselves involved in complications elsewhere. In one way or another we must square our account with France if we wish for a free hand in our international policy. This is the first and foremost condition of a sound German policy, and since the hostility of France once and for all cannot be removed by peaceful overtures, the matter must be settled by force of arms. France must be so completely crushed that she can never again come across our path.

Source: Friedrich von Bernhardi, *Germany and the Next War*
(London: Edward Arnold, 1914), pp. 103–6

Reversing Jewish emancipation

Konstantin von Gebsattel, a retired general, sent the draft for a new constitution to the Crown Prince in October 1913, from which the following selection is taken. Like many of his fellow conservatives, Gebsattel was particularly worried by the outcome of the 1912 elections in which the SPD had for the first time become the largest party in the Reichstag. Gebsattel's call for legal restrictions on Jews reiterated a frequent demand of the nationalist right and anticipated the Nazi program. Jews were to be denied full citizenship and placed under alien law. It is worth noting, however, that Gebsattel opposed the total expulsion of Jews, because he feared that the loss of Jewish wealth and economic skills would weaken Germany and that their departure would strengthen Germany's potential enemies. His juxtaposition of German idealism with Jewish materialism echoed long-standing stereotypes of German and Jewish cultural and racial incompatibility. Note also his concern that Jewish influence on popular opinion would weaken Germany's military posture in the war that by this time many conservatives had come to view as inevitable.

1.8 Konstantin von Gebsattel, "The Jewish Question," 1913

I am not an anti-Semite. I know some Jews, particularly business people, whom I respect and admire. On the other hand one would be blinder than Hödur [the Nordic god of darkness] if one stubbornly refused to see that our entire life is dominated and endangered by the Jewish spirit: internal affairs by the press in Jewish hands, financial affairs by the great banks directed by Jews, legal affairs by the huge number of Jewish lawyers in the big cities, cultural affairs by the many Jewish university professors, and the almost exclusively Jewish theater directors and critics. The Jewish and Germanic spirits contradict each other like fire and water: the latter is deep, positive, and idealistic, the former superficial, negative, destructively critical, and materialistic. The danger threatening Germandom and thus also the German Reich is grave and immediate; the more dangerous because it is cleverly disguised because the Jewish press has succeeded in persuading a large section of the nation that anyone who fights against the excesses of Judaism is backward and inferior. I, on the other hand, maintain that anyone who fails to take up this struggle even for one day is avoiding his urgent duty in a cowardly way …

The Jews should be placed under the law pertaining to aliens and should remain the guests of the German people. Naturally they will be exempt from military service and will pay instead an army tax, which will perhaps be up to twice as high as the taxes paid by Germans. Obviously they will not be allowed to enter public service, to be judges, officials, university professors, lawyers, officers; they will, however, be allowed to become businessmen, directors of private banks, doctors. The acquisition of sizeable landed estates will also be forbidden to them, and here the borderline will have to be drawn very low. For quarrels among themselves one could perhaps give them their own courts, but for quarrels with Germanics, they will come before the normal courts, as in the case of criminal proceedings.

There is a danger that such laws might cause the Jews to emigrate to states where they hoped to receive equal treatment with Christians, or rather, where they hoped to seize the entire executive power for themselves. I am sincerely convinced that [Werner] Sombart is wrong when he declares that the expulsion of the Jews was the reason for the economic collapse of states in the Middle Ages, and I would point there rather to the Germanic prophet Count Gobineau. That German commerce does not need the Jews is proven by the Fuggers, the Welsers, and the Hanseatic League, none of which succumbed to Jewish influence. I also know of not one case where a Jew has achieved great things in industry. I do admit, however, that a total emigration of Jews would be undesirable, and that we should try to use their good qualities to our advantage. I also do not know whether the German Reich could withstand the great capital loss involved, which I estimate in billions. It would, in any case, be a travesty of justice if we were to permit our guests to take with them the great riches which they have only gained by being more commercially-minded and unscrupulous than their hosts, so doing great damage to the nation's prosperity. Any Jew wishing to emigrate must therefore leave the major share of his property to the state. It will therefore be necessary when the state of siege is proclaimed, to close the borders and the banks until the Jewish fortune has been assessed.

A mixing of Jewish and Germanic races is not desirable, but cannot be prevented. Baptism must not, however, change the status of the Jew and the Jewess, nor of their children … Not until there is not more than one-quarter of Jewish blood in the grandchildren should these be able to acquire the rights of the Germanics …

As the Jews are only guests and not citizens, they should not be allowed to participate in the discussions about the constitution, the rights of the citizen, etc. They must therefore be prohibited from editing and writing for newspapers, on pain of severe punishment. They will only be allowed to publish a fixed number of Jewish newspapers, specifically marked as such, solely about Jewish matters and devoid of all opinion and comment on affairs of state ...

May the man come soon who will lead us along this path ...

Source: Konstantin Freiherr von Gebsattel, "Gedanken über einen notwendigen Fortschritt in der inneren Entwicklung Deutschlands," *Deutsches Zentralarchiv, Potsdam, Alldeutscher Verband, 204.* English version in J. C. G. Röhl, *From Bismarck to Hitler: The Problem of Continuity in German History* (New York: Barnes & Noble, 1970), pp. 49–51

The Schlieffen Plan

German preparations and tactics in the early stages of the war that broke out in August 1914 were based on a plan drawn up under the auspices of Field Marshal Alfred von Schlieffen (1833–1913), Chief of the German General Staff from 1891 to 1905. The problem the Germans faced was a two-front war against the Franco-Russian alliance. The Schlieffen Plan called for the defeat of France within six weeks by a flanking movement through Belgium and Holland. This would make possible the transfer of the bulk of German forces to the east to confront the technologically backward Russians, who were expected to require at least six weeks to fully mobilize their forces. The violation of Belgium's internationally guaranteed neutrality made it possible for the British government to enter the war on the side of her allies with full public support.

The Schlieffen Plan is historically significant for three major reasons: First, it demonstrated the undue political influence of the German military, which viewed strategic problems in purely military terms, disregarding political factors. Second, it was based on unrealistic dreams of total victory, thus departing from earlier military plans based on the limited objective of defending Germany's borders and bringing about a favorable peace. And third, the need for pinpoint timing to insure the success of the plan blocked diplomatic initiatives for a negotiated solution to the crisis in July 1914. Once the Russians began mobilization to prevent an Austrian attack on Serbia, German military leaders insisted that the Schlieffen Plan be put into effect immediately, lest the six-week window of opportunity envisaged in the plan be lost. The Schlieffen Plan, however, underestimated the French capability of reinforcing their troops at the front by rail. In the Battle of the Marne in September 1914 the French halted the German offensive. War in the west degenerated into a terrible war of attrition that lasted for more than four years.

The following selection presents the observations of General Helmuth von Moltke (1848–1916), Schlieffen's successor as Chief of the General Staff from 1906 until his dismissal after the Battle of the Marne in September 1914. Moltke embraced the general premises of the Schlieffen Plan but changed it to preserve Dutch neutrality. For this he was widely blamed by nationalists after the war, who insisted that the Schlieffen Plan would have worked if it had been implemented as originally drawn up. The Germans would not make the same mistake in the Second World War when they launched their western offensive by invading France, Luxembourg, Belgium, and Holland simultaneously on 10 May 1940.

1.9 General Helmuth von Moltke, comments on the Schlieffen Plan

It may be safely assumed that the next war will be a war on two fronts. Of our enemies, France is the most dangerous and can prepare the most quickly. Accounts must be settled with her very soon after deployment. Should the defeat of the French be achieved quickly and decisively, it will also be possible to make forces available against Russia. I agree with the basic idea of opening the war with a strong offensive against France while initially remaining on the defensive with weak forces against Russia. If a quick decision is sought against France, the attack should not be directed exclusively against the strongly fortified eastern front of that country. If, as may be expected, the French army remains on the defensive behind that front, there is no chance of quickly breaking through; and even a break-through would expose the German army, or those sections which have made it, to flank attack from two sides. If one wants to meet the enemy in the open, the fortified frontier-line must be outflanked. This is only possible by means of an advance through Switzerland or Belgium. The first would encounter great difficulties and, because of the defense of the mountain roads, would take a long time. On the other hand a successful outflanking of the French fortifications would have the advantage of forcing the French army towards the north. An advance through Belgium would force the French back into their interior. Nevertheless it should be preferred, because there one can count on quicker progress. We can count on the somewhat inefficient Belgian forces being quickly scattered, unless the Belgian army should withdraw without a battle to Antwerp, which would then have to be sealed off.

It is important, of course, that for an advance through Belgium the right wing should be made as strong as possible. But I cannot agree that the envelopment demands the violation of Dutch neutrality in addition to Belgian. A hostile Holland at our back could have disastrous consequences for the advance of the German army to the west, particularly if England should use the violation of Belgian neutrality as a pretext for entering the war against us. A neutral Holland secures our rear, because if England declares war on us for violating Belgian neutrality she cannot herself violate Dutch neutrality. She cannot break the very law for whose sake she goes to war.

Furthermore it will be very important to have in Holland a country whose neutrality allows us to have imports and supplies. She must be the windpipe that enables us to breathe.

However awkward it may be, the advance through Belgium must therefore take place without the violation of Dutch territory. This will hardly be possible unless Liège is in our hands. The fortress must therefore be taken at once. I think it possible to take it by a *coup de main*. Its salient forts are so unfavorably sited that they do not overlook the intervening country and cannot dominate it. I have had a reconnaissance made of all roads running through them into the center of the town, *which has no ramparts*. An advance with several columns is possible without their being observed from the forts. Once our troops have entered the town I believe that the forts will not bombard it but will probably capitulate. Everything depends on meticulous preparation and surprise. The enterprise is only possible if the attack is made at once, before the areas between the forts are fortified. It must therefore be undertaken by standing troops immediately war is declared. The capture of a modern fortress by a *coup de main* would be something unprecedented in military history. But it can succeed and must be attempted, for the possession of Liège is the *sine qua non* of our advance. It is a bold venture whose accomplishment promises a great success. In any case the heaviest artillery must be at hand, so that in case of failure we can take the fortress by storm. I believe the absence of an inner rampart will deliver the fortress into our hands.

On the success of the *coup de main* depends our chance of making the advance through Belgium without infringing Dutch territory. The deployment and disposition of the army must be made accordingly.

B [Berlin?] 1911
[signed] v. M.

Source: Gerhard Ritter, *The Schlieffen Plan: Critique of a Myth*,
trsl. by Andrew and Eva Wilson (New York: Frederick A. Praeger, 1958), pp. 165–7

Expansionist war aims

The "September Program" was drawn up by Chancellor Theobald von Bethmann-Hollweg (1856–1921) on 9 September 1914, shortly before the German offensive in the west ground to a halt in the Battle of the Marne. At the time it seemed that a favorable peace settlement in the west was within easy grasp. The annexationist aims of the government were withheld from the public in order to retain the allegiance of the SPD, which had rejected a war of conquest as a condition of its support for war credits in the Reichstag. Central to the September Program was the formation of a *Mitteleuropa*, a central European federation under German economic and political domination. France was to be permanently weakened, Luxembourg annexed, and Holland and a rump Belgium turned into German satellite states. Bethmann-Hollweg also envisioned a German colonial empire in central Africa. Although conditions did not yet seem to warrant drawing up specific aims in the east, Bethmann is quoted a saying that "Russia must be thrust back as far as possible from Germany's eastern frontier and her domination over the non-Russian vassal peoples broken."[21]

1.10 Chancellor Bethmann's September Program, 1914

1 *France.* The military to decide whether we should demand cession of Belfort and western slopes of the Vosges, razing of fortresses and cession of coastal strip from Dunkirk to Boulogne.

The ore-field of Briey, which is necessary for the supply of ore for our industry, to be ceded in any case.

Further, a war indemnity, to be paid in installments; it must be high enough to prevent France from spending any considerable sums on armaments in the next 15–20 years.

Furthermore: a commercial treaty which makes France economically dependent on Germany, secures the French market for our exports, and makes it possible to exclude British commerce from France. This treaty must secure for us financial and industrial freedom of movement in France in such a fashion that German enterprises can no longer receive different treatment from French.

2 *Belgium.* Liège and Verviers to be attached to Prussia, a frontier strip of the province of Luxembourg to Luxembourg.

---

21   Fritz Fischer, *Germany's Aims in the First World War* (New York: W. W. Norton, 1967), p. 103.

Question whether Antwerp, with a corridor to Liège, should also be annexed remains open.

At any rate Belgium, even if allowed to continue to exist as a state, must be reduced to a vassal state, must allow us to occupy any militarily important ports, must place her coast at our disposal in military respects, must become economically a German province. Given such a solution, which offers the advantages of annexation without its inescapable domestic political disadvantages, French Flanders with Dunkirk, Calais and Boulogne, where most of the population is Flemish, can without danger be attached to this unaltered Belgium. The competent quarters will have to judge the military value of this position against England.

3   *Luxembourg.* Will become a German federal state and will receive a strip of the present Belgian province of Luxembourg and perhaps the corner of Longwy.

4   We must create a *central European economic association* through common customs treaties, to include France, Belgium, Holland, Denmark, Austria-Hungary, Poland [*sic*], and perhaps Italy, Sweden and Norway. This association will not have any common constitutional supreme authority and all its members will be formally equal, but in practice will be under German leadership and must stabilize Germany's economic dominance over Mitteleuropa.

5   *The question of colonial acquisitions*, where the first aim is the creation of a continuous Central African colonial empire, will be considered later, as will that of the aims to be realized *vis-à-vis* Russia.

6   A short provisional formula suitable for a possible preliminary peace to be found for a basis for the economic agreements to be concluded with France and Belgium.

7   *Holland.* It will have to be considered by what means and methods Holland can be brought into closer relationship with the German Empire.

In view of the Dutch character, this closer relationship must leave them free of any feeling of compulsion, must alter nothing in the Dutch way of life, and must also subject them to no new military obligations. Holland, then, must be left independent in externals, but be made internally dependent on us. Possibly one might consider an offensive and defensive alliance, to cover the colonies; in any case a close customs association, perhaps the cession of Antwerp to Holland in return for the right to keep a German garrison in the fortress of Antwerp and at the mouth of the Scheldt.

**Source: Fritz Fischer, *Germany's Aims in the First World War*
(New York: W. W. Norton, 1967), pp. 104–5**

German *Kultur* vs. Western *Zivilisation*

Not surprisingly, the war gave rise to exaggerated propaganda on all sides. While the Western powers attacked Germany for its militarism and authoritarianism, German publicists countered by condemning French rationalism and British commercialism. A famous example of this kind of propaganda was the 1915 pamphlet, *Händler und Helden* (Merchants and Heroes), excerpts from which are given below. Written by the economist Werner Sombart (1863–1941), author of *Modern Capitalism* (1902) and the more nationalistic *The Jews and Modern Capitalism* (1911), the pamphlet is interesting as a typical example of how the war radicalized the long-term German tendency to juxtapose its own cultural creativity to the merely civilizational progress of the West. Sombart contrasted Germany's heroic spirit of idealism and self-sacrifice to the materialistic "merchant mentality" of England, supposedly concerned only with economic advantage and practical utility. This sense of cultural and ethnic superiority, rooted in the nineteenth century and radicalized during the war, culminated in the extreme Germanic supremacism of the Nazi years. Sombart, who later sympathized with Nazism, also believed that territorial expansion to gain "living space" was part of Germany's geopolitical destiny.

1.11 Werner Sombart, *Merchants and Heroes*, 1915

THE ELEMENTS OF THE ENGLISH MIND

… Under "merchant mentality" I understand the world-view that approaches life with the question: what's in it for me? …

THE GERMAN SPIRIT

… German thinking and German feeling expresses itself in the first place in the unanimous rejection of all that even distantly approximates English or West European thinking and feeling. With inner aversion, with indignation, with outrage, with deep horror, the German spirit arose against the "ideas of the eighteenth century," which were of English origin. With determination every German thinker, but also every German who thought in the German way, has at all times rejected utilitarianism, eudemonism, all philosophies of utility, happiness, and pleasure: in this the hostile kinsmen *Schopenhauer* and *Hegel*, and *Fichte* and *Nietzsche*, the classicists and romanticists, the Potsdamers and Weimarians, the old and the new Germans, were united … [22].

And what do we oppose to the English merchant ideal? Is there something affirmative that we can find in all German *Weltanschauung*? I believe so. And if I were to express in one sentence what that is, I would name the old sailor's proverb that is chiseled over the entrance to the Sailors' Home in Bremen:

"Navigare necesse, vivere non est"[23]

"We do not need to live; but if we live, we have to do our damned duty." Or: "Man has to do his work as long as he lives." Or: "The individual life: the importance of working on the greater whole is our destiny." Or: "The well-being of men is of no concern if only it serves the cause" or however one wants to translate this proverb: the meaning is always the same. And whatever German man we may ask for his opinion: he will answer with the proverb that is chiseled above the Sailors' Home in Bremen …

---

22   Arthur Schopenhauer (1788–1860), G. W. F. Hegel (1770–1831), Johann Gottlieb Fichte (1762–1814), and Friedrich Nietzsche (1844–1900) were German philosophers whose ideas often clashed. Potsdam, the residence of the Hohenzollern dynasty, stood for the Prussian monarchical and military tradition; Weimar, the home of Germany's foremost poets, Johann Wolfgang von Goethe (1749–1832) and Friedrich Schiller (1759–1805), stood for Germany's cultural tradition.

23   "To sail is necessary, to live is not."

It is the most glorious feature of our German thinking that already here on earth we effect unification with the divinity, and we effect it not by killing off our flesh and our will, but by robust action and work. That the surrender of our self proceeds through the uninterrupted setting and completing of new tasks in active life. That gives our world-view its victorious strength, not to be overcome on this earth. That is why I call it a heroic world-view, and now the reader will see the point to which I have led him: *to be German means to be a hero*, and to the English merchant mentality we oppose a German heroism.

Merchant and hero: they form the two great opposites, the two poles of all human orientation on earth. The merchant, as we have seen, approaches life with the question: what can life give to me? He wants to take, wants to exchange as much as possible for as little as possible, because he wants to make a profitable deal with life. The result: he is poor. The hero approaches life with the question: what can I give to life? He wants to give, wants to expend himself, wants to sacrifice himself – without anything in return. The result: he is rich. The merchants speaks only of "rights," the hero only of duties ...

The virtues of the hero are opposite to those of the merchant: they are all positive, giving and awakening life, they are "generous virtues:" sacrificial courage, loyalty, lack of cunning, reverence, bravery, piety, obedience, goodness. They are warlike virtues, virtues that are fully developed in war and through war, just as all heroism only achieves its full greatness in war and through war ...

THE MISSION OF THE GERMAN PEOPLE

... We have to eradicate even the last vestiges of the old ideals of a progressive development of "humanity" from our soul. There is no "progress" to something higher from one peoples to another: we don't stand on a higher level of "progress" than the ancient Greeks, unless we think of progress as a purely technological concept. Rather, the divine spirit becomes effective in the various individual peoples, which "progress" within, i.e., perfect their own character, approach their own ideal, just as the individual can develop during his own lifetime by approaching in his natural existence the ideal person within. In every peoples a certain vital force strives for development and realizes the individuality of *this* people in its history. Individual peoples grow, flourish, and wilt like flowers in the garden of God: We can recognize all this as the sense of human development. And the idea of mankind, the idea of humanity, cannot be understood in its deepest meaning in any other way than that this idea achieves its highest and grandest effect in individual noble peoples.

These are then the respective representatives of the idea of God on earth: these are the chosen peoples. Those were the Greeks, those were the Jews. And the chosen people of our current age are the German people.

Why this is so, this little book is designed to show: because the German *Volk* commits itself to the heroic *Weltanschauung*, which alone manifests the idea of God on earth in this age.

Now we also understand why the other peoples persecute us with their hate: they don't understand us, but they feel our huge spiritual superiority. Thus the Jews were hated in antiquity, because the were the regents of God on earth, as long as only they had received the abstract idea of God into their spirit. And they proceeded with heads held high, with a contemptuous smile on their lips, looking down disparagingly from their proud height on the teeming throng of peoples of their age. They also closed themselves off to all alien being, out of concern that the holiness that they carried within could be besmirched by contact with unbelievers. In the same way the Greeks, in their best days, lived among the barbarians.

We Germans, too, should go through the world of our time in the same way, proud, heads held high, in the secure feeling of being God's people. Just as the German bird, the eagle, soars high over all animals on this earth, so the German must feel himself above all other peoples that surround him and that he sees in boundless depth below him.

But aristocracy has its obligations, and this is true here, too. The idea that we are the chosen people places formidable duties – and only duties – on us. We must above all maintain ourselves as a strong nation in the world. Not for world conquest do we set forth. Have no fear, dear neighbors: we are not going to consume you. What are we to do with such an indigestible mouthful? To conquer half-civilized or primitive peoples to fill them with German spirituality, that is not our desire either. Such "Germanization" is not possible. The Englishman can possibly colonize foreign peoples like this and fill them with his spirituality. After all, he doesn't have any. Unless it be the money-grubbing mentality. I can make any old person into a shopkeeper, and to spread English civilization is no great feat. The great "talent for colonization" attributed to the English is nothing but an expression of their spiritual poverty. To implant German culture in other peoples, who would want to try that? Heroism cannot be transplanted to any old place on earth like gas pipelines. We Germans will therefore always remain – by right! – bad colonizers. To accumulate foreign countries, as England does: that does not seem to us to be worth the effort. There is therefore no "expansionist tendency" at all in the new Germany. Without envy we leave that to England, which has this tendency like every department store: by right!

We want to be a strong German *Volk*, to be and remain a strong German state, and also to grow within organic limits. And if it is necessary that we expand our territorial possessions so that the people gain greater space to develop, we will take as much land as seems necessary to us. We will also plant our feet where it seems important to us for strategic reasons, to maintain our unassailable strength: we will therefore, if it is good for our position of global power, establish naval bases in Dover, in Malta, in Suez. Nothing more. We do not want to "expand" at all. For we have more important things to do. We have our own spiritual character to develop, to maintain the purity of the German soul, to make sure that the enemy, the merchant mentality, doesn't infiltrate our senses: not from outside and not from inside. But this is a powerful and responsible task. For we know what is at stake: Germany is the last dam against the muddy flood of commercialism that has either already swamped all other peoples or is about to do so without hindrance, because none of them is armed against the urgent danger by a heroic *Weltanschauung*, which alone, as we have seen, can guarantee rescue and protection ...

Source: Werner Sombart, *Händler und Helden. Patriotische Besinnungen*
(Munich: Duncker & Humblot, 1915), pp. 14, 55–7, 141–5.
Translated by Rod Stackelberg

The German idea of freedom

The English-born racial publicist Houston Stewart Chamberlain, who became one of Hitler's earliest supporters after the war, played an active role during the war by churning out pamphlets that were distributed by the hundreds of thousands to soldiers at the front.

The German government's efforts to use them in English translation for propaganda purposes in England and the US backfired when the British government issued an official version under the title *The Ravings of a Renegade*, from which the excerpt below is taken. Chamberlain's pamphlets are of historical interest, however, because they do convey with some accuracy the ideological consensus in Germany. Most educated Germans would have agreed that true freedom lay not in political rights but in voluntary submission to law and morality. They would have shared Chamberlain's sense of the superiority of German idealist culture over Western (or Jewish) materialism and commercialism. Chamberlain's notorious anti-Semitism, restrained for the sake of unity during the war, would reemerge with a vengeance in the wake of German defeat.

1.12 Houston Stewart Chamberlain, "German Liberty," 1915

The assertion that Germany's enemies are fighting for liberty against tyranny is to be found with striking frequency in official manifestos and newspaper articles. The opinion has long been circulated throughout the world that everywhere where Germany goes there is an end to all freedom. I have met serious men, scholars in England, for instance, who had warm sympathy for German science and literature, and yet believed that, politically, it would be a misfortune if Germany's influence were to increase in Europe, for it would mean the destruction of all liberty.

Now when I occasionally attempted, in oral disputes to support the contrary, that Germany had, for centuries, been the real and sole home of a liberty which tends to raise the human race and is alone worthy of the name, I never succeeded in rousing interest. The English and French, even the well-educated, do not reflect on the essence of liberty, on its peculiar function in the complicated organism of the human mind; for them it is purely a political idea which has been handed down through the ages; they always considered they had refuted me when they brought out as trumps that the German Imperial Chancellor was appointed and retained by the Emperor, and could remain in office in spite of the majority of the Reichstag. The essence of liberty is, therefore, to be able to overthrow chancellors. Whole books would be necessary to give real enlightenment on this subject – to destroy wrong ideas and replace them by correct ones. I will only make a few remarks and give a little food for reflection.

Let us ask first: In what does the far-famed English political liberty really consist? If one were to sum up the internal history of England, which, till 1688, was heroic and sanguinary, and later on Machiavellian and intriguing, in a single formula, it would be: History of a struggle between nobility and crown. Neither of these forces thought of liberty; each only sought to increase its power. When Cromwell appeared, both joined issue against the same man, and the sole course which would have been capable of founding true freedom in England. Afterwards the course, thanks to the insular position of the country, was very simple, and from it rose the English Parliament, which has been set up as an unattainable model till one is tired of hearing of it, and in which, until a few years ago, the Lower House was just as aristocratic as the Upper House. For a long time England has been led by an oligarchy, the king is a puppet. Up to the commencement of the nineteenth century the sovereign, if he possessed the necessary energy, had a say in the election of the Prime Minister; then he lost this prerogative, and the secret committee of the parliamentary oligarchy has since governed alone. The fiction of the two chief parties is still kept up, and the minority of the male population which enjoy the franchise still decide when the one shall be superseded by the other; but the leaders of both parties work under the same cover and keep at a distance all who might be inclined to restrict their power or the profits they derive. Offices are given only by the governing caste: the leader of the victorious party must be Prime Minister, and all other ministers are elected not, as one might presume, by the party, but by the secret committee; king and people have no say whatever in the matter. Discipline is severely maintained in the parties by the Whips; woe to any member who should dare to express his own opinion. The House of Commons has, it is true, assumed a slightly more democratic appearance in consequence of the extension of the franchise, which was first carried out by Disraeli and then by Gladstone;[24] but the system has remained unaltered; aristocracy is yielding to plutocracy. What the House has lost in gentility it has gained in power. The restriction of the freedom of speech, particularly by the introduction of the so-called "guillotine," which permits every debate to be broken off at a certain time and a vote to be taken at once, has transformed this pretended freest of all parliaments into a kind of machine, by means of which a small group of politicians rule and govern for seven years according to their own sweet will. The tyranny of this clique, which ... are not even afraid of indulging in shady financial transactions, was rendered complete when, two years ago, a decisive influence on the legislation was withdrawn from the Upper House. The veto right of the crown has long ago fallen into abeyance. And thus England is governed by a "convent," or rather a "conventicle." And that is called freedom!

... Not only is English industry and manufacture, the whole spirit of public life, blighted by this hatred of culture, but it also destroys the possibility of liberty. Liberty, we know since Kant, is an idea; no man is born free;[25] liberty must be acquired by each individual. Its accessories are an education and strengthening of the mind, a methodical uplifting above all with which it was originally endowed, until that liberation is attained which alone deserves the name of liberty. External liberty, if not preceded by internal liberty, is but license. The English understand by liberty the right to walk on the grass without being stopped by a policeman; that they are not restricted by military duties from setting out into the world in search of adventures; that they may leave school at an early age to act as clerk in a solicitor's office, and thus, without the troublesome compulsion of studying law, in a few years become a solicitor, etc., etc. On the other hand, the German may not walk on the grass; he may not arrange his life as it pleases him best; but he is obliged to sacrifice valuable years of youth and, later on, many holiday weeks to his Fatherland, and his life when the necessity arises. None of the higher professions are open to him unless he has acquired extensive general and specific knowledge. Is he, on this account less free than the Englishman? Does not the irresistible superiority of the German soldier lie in his moral qualities particularly? And what does this mean but that he acts of his own free will. He alone wishes what he is ordered to do, wishes it with his whole heart; the English, the French, the Russian soldier is ordered to do a thing which has no relation to his personal will; in the best of cases he only obeys a desire of destruction which, not natural to him, has been roused by a system of lies. And is it not their education that raises the German middle class above all other nations? This education is

---

24   Benjamin Disraeli (1804–81) and W. E. Gladstone (1809–98) were the most prominent British prime ministers of the last third of the nineteenth century.

25   The German philosopher Immanuel Kant (1724–1804) defined freedom as voluntary submission to moral law.

enforced upon them by the nation with relentless severity, and thanks to it the individual becomes a person capable of free judgement. Even the numerous trifling annoyances, what may be done and what may not be done, which, at first, are very irksome to us foreigners in Germany, are they not at bottom the result of general good order from which all profit? They may be exaggerated, but are, on the whole a good school of discipline and consideration of others. Martin Luther teaches: "The flesh should have no liberty;" on the contrary, every man should be "servant of all." And then he continues: "But in the spirit and in our conscience we are most free from all servitude; there we believe no man, there we trust no man, put confidence in no man, fear no man but solely Jesus Christ." I do not know if the present-day Englishmen consider Martin Luther a free man; the great majority, even among the educated, know, I am afraid as little about him as their king does about Goethe, probably no more than the name. And were I now to let Frederick the Great speak: "Without liberty there is no happiness," they would certainly object that he was a tyrant. We, on the other hand, experience how liberty is obtained. Liberty is no abstract quality, that hovers in the air, and for which one needs only to stretch out one's hand; that is mock liberty that is thus caught, a deceptive illusion that falling from the horn of Pandora vanishes into thin air.

German Freedom – real freedom – was conceived and created by Martin Luther, Frederick, Kant, Goethe, Wilhelm von Humboldt, Bismarck, and thousands of others, who each, according to his strength, trod in the steps of these great creators of freedom. An un-German liberty is no liberty …

Germany has attained this precious possession in the course of struggles – physical and mental – throughout centuries. This German freedom is an absolutely original product. Humanity has, up to the present, known nothing which resembles it. It stands incomparably higher than Hellenic liberty; besides, it is much more firmly founded than that ephemeral product which could resist neither the external enemy nor internal decay. Characteristic of German liberty is the conscious assertion of the whole. All individual parts of the empire preserve their independence and submit to be subjected to the whole. Thus, too, every man submits from infancy for the good of the whole. That is the first step to liberty.

This freedom, and only this, can hope for duration. For the first time in the history of the world, freedom, as an inclusive and continuous property, becomes possible. Let this, above all, be borne in mind. "Freedom is not license but truthfulness," says Richard Wagner. But how can a whole commonweal, a whole nation in its political structure and character be no longer arbitrary but truthful? The sublime spectacle which Germany in the war of 1914 offers, teaches us. Let that be compared with the trivial nonsense we hear from kings, ministers, orators, and poets. It is unnecessary to speak of the liberty Russia has to dispense; what liberty poor betrayed and ruined France can promise, the country of political corruption, of hollow words, needs as little explanation. England understands by liberty only the right of the mighty, and this right only for herself. Not a single spark of intellectual life has ever sprung from its immense colonial empire. The inhabitants are all only cattle-owners, slave-owners, merchandise accumulators, mine exploiters, and everywhere there reigns the absolute license of brutality which develops everywhere where it is not opposed by intellectual culture: that brutality which Rudyard Kipling, England's most popular poet, has the effrontery to claim as the highest power and greatest glory of England.

The continuance and development of freedom on earth depends on the victory of the German arms and on Germany's remaining true to itself after victory. And just as freedom in Germany, though at first only the dream and hope of a few God-favored men – and which even today can only be completely and consciously conceived by those who are favored by nature and circumstances – nevertheless gradually permeates the whole people, as we now experience it in this war, when millions immediately rush to arms, who could not have been called upon, therefore by their own free will. In this same manner German freedom will spread over all the world as far as the German language sounds. True freedom will form a better glue than jingoism. And the German language – the holy warden of these mysteries – no longer despised and soon forgotten by her own children in far-off lands, but everywhere fostered and developed, will found a universal Germanicism, and by degrees educate other nations, insofar as nature has granted them the capacity, to understand liberty and thus enter into its possession.

God grant this victory.

Source: *The Ravings of a Renegade: Being the War Essays of Houston Stewart Chamberlain,* trsl. by Charles H. Clarke (London: Jarrold and Sons, 1915), pp. 47–52, 56–63

The ideas of 1914 vs. the ideas of 1789

In the so-called "ideas of 1914" – national unity, organic hierarchy, order, duty, discipline, and subordination of individual welfare to the welfare of the nation as a whole – mainstream nationalism and the *Völkisch* extremism of such groups as the Pan-Germans merged. The phrase was coined in a speech by that title by the prominent theologian Ernst Troeltsch (1863–1923). The following selection is taken from his wartime essay on the uniqueness of German philosophical, aesthetic, and political culture. Troeltsch was a political moderate who would later support the Weimar Republic, and he in no way contributed to National Socialism. But his essay helps us to understand the wartime culture in which National Socialism had its roots. Troeltsch strongly supported the German war effort and genuinely believed that culture itself was at stake in the ideological conflict with the materialistic West. Nationalists after the war idealized the patriotic fervor and ideological unity of the early war years and sought to recapture it in a new popular authoritarian regime.

Stung by the Western declaration that this was a war for democracy, Troeltsch made a virtue out of Western accusations of German authoritarianism and militarism. Troeltsch's essay provides a good example of the deeply conservative, anti-political, anti-liberal, anti-democratic, and anti-progressive spirit of German political culture, reinforced and intensified by the ideological radicalization of war. He defended the leadership principle and the notion of the army as "the school of the nation." Typical, too, of German ideology is his definition of freedom not as liberal freedom *from* the state, but as national freedom *of* the state.

1.13 Ernst Troeltsch, "The Spirit of German Culture," 1916

... We Germans are first of all a monarchical peoples. To this we are driven not just by the ancient inherited masculine conviction of loyalty and trust, which today refers above all to the Kaiser as the bearer and symbol of German unity, but even more by the necessities of state. Only under monarchical leadership could and can the work of unification and development of a nation coming together under the most serious dangers be carried out. This was always the case and still is so today. All European powers became unitary states through monarchy. The exceptions of the United States and Australia prove nothing, as their development took place without neighboring states. The French Republic is just a mutation into republican forms of what the Bourbon and Napoleonic monarchies created, and France has often enough experienced friction between democracy and a military demanding monarchical leadership. A unified military force requires a unified, autonomous, and stable leadership, and only monarchy can guarantee this, no matter how much it may rely on the will of the people and the free consensus of national comrades. Furthermore: unified Germany includes the greatest social disparities, from the old Prussian landed aristocracy all the way to industrial workers and peasants; it is in transition from an agrarian to an industrial state and therefore particularly needs a leadership standing above all social conflicts – a leadership that seeks nothing for itself, but only to do justice to the interests of all as best as it is able. No parliamentary majority can achieve this. As great as the advantages of a parliamentary government may be for the identification and training of political talent and for the political maturity of a peoples, it is of dubious value for the unity of the military and political leadership in a young state. That is why the desire for a parliamentary government is not great in Germany, quite apart from the legal and historical difficulties of such a government in a federated state. No plutocracy, no committee of intellectuals, and no syndicate of labor unions could achieve what is necessary for us. Only the monarchy can achieve this, and that is why we are monarchically-minded whether out of emotion or through understanding ...

Closely related to this is the military character of the German state and people. This is rooted in the ancient Germanic, warlike character, which no aestheticism, no Puritanism, and no commercial philosophy has broken, and which is natural to our peasants. Even more it is rooted in our geographical and political situation, which gives us security against our neighbors only through overwhelming strength. For just this reason the last century has witnessed the extension of this military character in a thorough way. It differentiates Germanness from other Germanic peoples and with its essentially Prussian character it is also distinct from all older Germanness. It has united the sense of honor and the corporate spirit of the Frederician officer with the spirit of Scharnhorst's people's army; it has blended the ruling and organizational capability of Prussia with the ethical idealism of German education (*Bildung*) to such a degree that the one has grown into the other, and precisely from this union the extraordinary capability of the German career officer and of the German people's army results.[26] Like the monarchy, national unity is in the last analysis also based on the army. In the organism of the army all the ideal forces of education, science, and technology are absorbed, and this military organization in turn provides the model and the strength for the quite extraordinary organization of the German people, in which the initiative of the individual and the discipline of the whole are successfully united ...

That leads us to the last, most important, and most controversial matter: the German idea of freedom. In it the metaphysical and religious spirit meets the political needs of the young empire in a singular and, to be sure, sometimes contradictory way. In it, too, there is something of the special German spirit and of special German history. It is therefore, as all polemicists rightly feel and many accurately recognize, different from the French–Romanist and also the Anglo-Saxon ideas.

---

26   General Gerhard von Scharnhorst (1755–1813) introduced universal military service into the Prussian army after its defeat by Napoleon.

The French idea of freedom is based on the concepts of equality of all citizens in their contribution to the construction of the will of the whole. Theoretical constitutional constructions, which secure this *egalité* and *liberté* and occasionally set the imagination and passion of the people in motion, are the main thing, which does not in practice exclude the rule of plutocrats and lawyers. It is best in this context not even to speak of *fraternité*; it is still, according to the well-known words of Count Chamfort, *"un peu la fraternité de Cain et Abel."*[27] The English idea of freedom on the other hand, a mixture of Puritan and old Saxon-corporate ideas, is essentially the independence of the individual from the state; it is self-control, self-rule. It watches over state power through popular opinion; constitutional theory is less important, and it represents the independence of religion, convictions, and culture from the coercion of the state. Above all it puts into effect the dominance of the English citizen, which, as is recognized all over the world, imposes on the lower races the way of life suitable to them and reserves for himself his own way of life. The Englishman acts from his own insight into what is useful, on the basic principle of personal inviolability. That this freedom accords with the well-being of the state is a tenet of faith to him, which he substantiates puritanically by appeal to providence or rationally to evolution, but in any case considers self-evident ...

Our freedom will always be different from that of the Western nations. From olden times we have inherited a different idea of the relationship of the whole to the individual, and we see in human rights above all the duties. Free self-integration and at the same time dedication in subordinate and automatic activity: that is the core of our idea of freedom. Parliaments are necessary but not, in our eyes, the essence of freedom. The right to vote and popular participation in governments raise people to political maturity; but this is not the freedom that we mean either. German freedom will never be purely political, it will always be bound up with the idealist concept of duty and the Romantic concept of the personality. Even as a political concept it will always bear the sign of its essentially spiritual and cultural origin, just as the English concept bears the sign of the puritanical and the French of the revolutionary. And above all we do not want this freedom to be prescribed for us by the West-European and American doctrine, which doesn't even shrink from the nonsense of wanting to liberate us from our "oppression" in this war. Here our own future tasks lie. In a victorious Germany the freedom of the nation will reach fruition, and this freedom will be German, not French and not English and most certainly not Russian.

If from this height one once again imagines all the features we have discussed as fused in the unity of life, we will have accurately drawn the spirit of German culture and its contrast to the cultures of our opponents. After all, our opponents for their part do not portray us very differently, only with reversed and unfriendly valuation. It would be childish to want to decide between these opposites with a simple dogmatic ruling. The great national cultures all have their advantages and liabilities, and the earth has room for all. In this connection let me just point to one result of the German idea of freedom. It doesn't, like the French, have the rationalist compulsion to impose itself on all people as the only scientifically possible idea; nor does it, like the English, have the supposedly moral compulsion to tie all civilization to the rule of English institutions. It has no urge to world dominance, neither materially, nor spiritually. It means the freedom of individual peoples living next to each other, who must not destroy their respective developmental possibilities, or stereotype them in the name of some law, whatever kind it may be. In this sense we believe that we are the ones who are fighting for the true and genuine progress of mankind, which violates no one and gives everyone freedom ...

---

27 Sebastién Chamfort (c. 1741–94) was a writer who was killed in the French Revolution.

So we fight first of all for life and the future. But our political life as a great power does at the same time also signify an idea that fills us with inexhaustible confidence: the world principle of the freedom of the different national spirits and the development of our fatherland to the full measure of its cultural powers.

Source: Ernst Troeltsch, "Der Geist der deutschen Kultur," in *Deutschland und der Weltkrieg*, ed. by Otto Hintze *et. al.* (Leipzig: B. G. Teubner, 1916), pp. 74–7, 95–9.
Translated by Rod Stackelberg

Mobilizing the Nationalist Right

As it became increasingly clear that the German High Command under Generals Paul von Hindenburg (1847–1934) and Erich Ludendorff (1865–1937) remained committed to an annexationist peace despite the military stalemate in the west, left-wing and liberal dissent against government policy reemerged. The High Command's decision to drop all restrictions on submarine warfare drew the US into the war in April 1917. A month earlier revolution in Russia had overthrown the czar and brought to power a liberal government (which would in turn be overthrown by the communist revolution in November 1917). The combination of war weariness, government intransigence, and the example of the Russian Revolution led to increasing demands for a compromise peace in Germany. The radical left under Karl Liebknecht (1871–1919) and Rosa Luxemburg (1870–1919), founders of the German Communist Party (KPD) at the end of the war, called for social revolution and were imprisoned until October 1918. In July 1917 the SPD, liberals, and the Catholic Center Party combined to pass a resolution in the Reichstag calling on the government to negotiate a compromise peace.

The response of the government, now fully controlled by the High Command, was to replace Bethmann-Hollweg by a more amenable chancellor, further reduce the power of the Reichstag, and organize a nationalist party to support an annexationist peace. The Fatherland Party was founded in September 1917 under the leadership of Grand Admiral Alfred von Tirpitz (1849–1932) and the monarchist Wolfgang Kapp (1858–1922), both of whom would actively oppose the Republic after the war. The purpose of this new *Völkisch* party was to provide a popular base for the government's annexationist policies, demonstrated again in the Treaty of Brest-Litovsk, which was imposed by the High Command on the newly-established Soviet Russian regime in March 1918. The growing opposition of the left and the mobilization of the right ended the tenuous *Burgfrieden* ("peace in the castle") of the early war years and led to the reemergence of political polarization at the end of the war. The nationalist right accused the dissident left of undermining the war effort and preparing German surrender. The Fatherland Party's hopes of creating a nationalist movement above the partisan fray presaged similar ambitions by the Nazis after the war.

1.14 Founding Proclamation of the German Fatherland Party, 2 September 1917

Broad sectors of the German nation do not agree with the position of the current Reichstag majority on the most vital issues facing the fatherland. They see the attempt to provoke quarrels over constitutional questions and to focus public attention on them just now, when the fate of the Empire is at stake, as a threat to the fatherland and as providing aid to our enemies, even if unintended. They believe that the Reichstag, which was elected before the war, no longer represents the will of the German people.

Who doesn't yearn for peace with all his heart! But weak-kneed peace rallies only delay peace. Our enemies, intent on the destruction of Germany, see these rallies merely as the collapse of German strength. And this at a time when, according to the testimony of our Hindenburg, we are in a better military position than ever before. If we assure the enemy that he can have an honorable compromise peace at any time, he has everything to gain and nothing to lose by continuing the war.

After the developments of the past our government is in a dilemma. Without the strong support of the people the government alone cannot master the situation. For a strong imperial policy the government needs a strong instrument. Such an instrument must be a large Peoples' Party supported by broad-based patriotic groups.

Partisan efforts to achieve political power must not fragment the German Empire at this time; an unshakable will, intent only on the victory of the fatherland must unite it! With grateful reverence for our unforgettable beloved first Kaiser and his Iron Chancellor, who united the German peoples, and mindful of the titanic fight against the destructive partisan spirit that Otto von Bismarck condemned in blazing words before God and history, we East Prussian men signing below have founded the German Fatherland Party. Faithful to the traditions of our forefathers, we establish this party in order to protect and shield the German fatherland from the original evil of divisiveness and partisanship in this the greatest and gravest hour of German history.

The German Fatherland Party aims to unite all patriotic forces without regard to their partisan political positions. The Party consists of patriotically-minded individuals and associations. It intends to be a buttress and support for a powerful Imperial Government which knows how to read the signs of the time not in weak-willed surrender to internal and external forces, but in German steadfastness and indestructible faith in victory! ...

We do not want any internal dissension! In our internal disputes we Germans too easily forget the war. The enemy does not forget it for a moment! Those Germans united in the German Fatherland Party pledge to work with all our might to make sure that internal discord ceases until the conclusion of peace. However the individual citizen may feel about domestic policy disputes, all policy decisions are to be reserved for the period following the war. Then our brave men will be home from the battlefield and can participate in the internal improvement of the Empire. Now victory is the only thing that matters!

Source: *Deutscher Geschichtskalender*, ed. by Friedrich Purlitz. Jg. 33, Vol. 2,1. (Leipzig: Meiner, 1917), pp. 514 ff.
Translated by Sally Winkle

2

The Weimar Republic, 1919–33

In August 1918 the High Command abruptly informed civilian members of the government that the war was lost and instructed them to sue for peace. In order to obtain more favorable terms the High Command authorized the reorganization of the government into a parliamentary regime. Although General Ludendorff later regretted this move, the momentum to end the war and introduce democratic reforms could no longer be stopped. In early November strikes and revolts broke out all over the country (Doc. 2.1). Kaiser Wilhelm II was persuaded to abdicate on November 9. The last wartime chancellor, Prince Max von Baden, turned the reins of government over to the Social Democratic Party (SPD) (Doc. 2.2). On 11 November 1918 the armistice ending the First World War was signed, stipulating the demobilization of the German army and its withdrawal from occupied areas in France and Belgium.

All over Germany, however, nationalist, *völkisch*, and radical right-wing groups formed to resist the new Republic and suppress revolutionary or democratic change. Anti-Semitism, muted for the sake of unity during the war, emerged with a vengeance, as nationalists blamed defeat and revolution on the alleged pacifism and sedition of Jews and "Marxists." The spectre of communism, established in Russia in 1918, provoked a violent counter-movement on the right that was as yet disorganized and disunited. Refugees from the Russian Revolution and the civil war that raged between "Whites" and "Reds" from 1918 to 1921 helped to shape the Nazi world view. The typically radical right-wing linkage of Jews with communism, already presaged in the notorious forgery of the tsarist secret police in 1912, "The Protocols of the Elders of Zion," reemerged in force in right-wing propaganda following the First World War (Doc. 2.3).

The punitive terms of the Versailles Treaty (Doc. 2.4), forcing Germans to accept full responsibility for the war, rallied popular support to the right, which hoped to reverse the results of the treaty at the earliest opportunity. Nationalists regarded the democratic constitution adopted at Weimar in the same month (Doc. 2.5) as a major obstacle to their hopes of restoring a strong authoritarian Reich. Opposition to Versailles and the Weimar Republic drew disgruntled nationalists to the many new *völkisch* organizations, one of which was the National Socialist German Workers' Party (NSDAP) in Munich. In February 1920, under Hitler's leadership, it announced its militantly nationalistic, anti-democratic, and anti-Semitic "25-point program" (Doc. 2.6).

The first serious attempt of the nationalist right to overthrow the government by force occurred in the Kapp Putsch of March 1920 (Doc. 2.7). The putsch was supported by the so-called Free Corps, volunteer units made up of soldiers discharged from the regular army under the terms of the armistice and the Treaty of Versailles. These units had been employed by the SPD-dominated government to suppress the uprisings sponsored by the newly formed German Communist Party (KPD). Now the Free Corps turned on the government itself. The Kapp Putsch received at least the tacit support of the regular army, the Reichswehr, whose leaders were unsympathetic to the "pacifist," "democratic," and allegedly "socialist" Republic. The putsch attempt nonetheless failed after several days because workers and civil servants heeded the government's call for a general strike.

Thus from the start the Weimar Republic was a highly polarized society (Doc. 2.8). A stream of publications poured forth from the presses of the nationalist right, calling for the regeneration of the demoralized German *Volk* through eugenics, racial purification, and the restoration of a powerful "Third Reich," cleansed of the politically disruptive elements of the left who had supposedly stabbed the German army in the back in the First World War (Docs. 2.9 and 2.10). The French occupation of the industrial heartland of the Ruhr Valley to enforce German reparations payments in 1923 set the stage for hyperinflation (Doc. 2.11) and a renewed right-wing attempt to seize power. This was Hitler's notorious "Beer Hall Putsch" of November 1923, which received the support of prominent former monarchists (Doc. 2.12), including General Ludendorff, who was slated to head the army in the new regime the putschists wished to establish. Although the putsch failed, as Reichswehr leaders remained loyal to a Weimar government that showed no reluctance to crack down on the radical left, Hitler's "idealistic" motives persuaded the nationalist judges at his trial for high treason in Munich to impose the minimum sentence permitted by law (Doc. 2.13).

Some Nazis under the leadership of Gregor Strasser sought to expand on the "25-Point Program" of 1920 by spelling out the party's social and economic goals in more detail (Doc. 2.14). Their plans for a corporatist state, however, were thwarted by Hitler, who countermanded all efforts to change the party program, in order to retain his own freedom of action as Führer. As he made clear in his autobiographical manifesto *Mein Kampf* (Doc. 2.15), Hitler's goal was not social reform, but rather the creation of a racially and ideologically homogeneous dictatorship that would lead the German nation to world power and the conquest of *Lebensraum* in the east. Hitler's movement remained marginal, however, during the most prosperous phase of the Weimar Republic from 1925 to 1929.

The Great Depression that followed the stock market crash on Wall Street in October 1929 undermined the tenuous stability of the Weimar regime and created the opportunity for the enemies of the Republic to destroy the parliamentary form of government. One reason for the weakness of the Republic was the bitter rift between Communists and Social Democrats on the left, which prevented the possiblity of a united front against the radical right (Doc. 2.16). The terrible deprivations of the Great Depression (Doc. 2.17) polarized the nation and attracted growing numbers to the extremes of the political spectrum. In the Reichstag election of 1930 (see Table 2.1) the Communists gained votes at the expense of the SPD, but on the right the NSDAP made even more spectacular gains, winning 95 more seats than in the 1928 election.

After the 1930 elections the parliamentary process became virtually defunct as Chancellor Heinrich Brüning and his successors governed by decree under the emergency powers granted to the president, the monarchist Paul von Hindenburg, by Article 48 of the Weimar constitution. To conservatives hoping to replace the Weimar constitution with an authoritarian regime the Nazis now became an attractive partner because of their mass appeal (Doc. 2.18). Hitler did his best to allay lingering conservative fears that the Nazis would carry out a social revolution if and when they came to power (Doc. 2.19).

Impressed by the Nazis' continuing electoral strength, which reached a peak of over 37 percent of the vote in July 1932, Brüning's successor Franz von Papen did his best to persuade the Nazis to join his government and thereby gain the mass support that he lacked. Papen's overthrow of the elected SPD-led state government in Prussia in July 1932, under the pretext that the Prussian government was unable to control the street battles between Communists and Nazis, struck a lethal blow to defenders of the Republic (Doc. 2.20). Papen openly sought to create an authoritarian system (Doc. 2.21), but remained reluctant to turn over full power to Hitler, who in turn refused to accept a subordinate role in a conservative government.

Although some prominent conservatives, such as future Economics Minister Hjalmar Schacht, continued to express support for Hitler (Doc. 2.22), Hitler's movement might well have been checked if Hindenburg, Papen, and their conservative advisers had remained firm in their resolve not to turn over full power to Hitler. Hitler's "all-or-nothing" strategy, criticized by Strasser and others in the party, seemed to backfire in the Reichstag election of November 1932, when the Nazis lost over two million votes. Strasser feared that the Nazis had reached the limits of their popular vote and that the party would lose its following if it refused to enter a coalition government. Head of the Reichswehr General Kurt von Schleicher, who replaced Papen as chancellor in December 1932, hoped to persuade Strasser to enter his government as vice-chancellor, but Hitler adamantly opposed any compromise, and in a bitter show-down with Strasser the Führer prevailed. Future Propaganda Minister Joseph Goebbels recorded the conflict and the sense of crisis in the party in his diary (Doc. 2.23). Would the Nazis ever gain power under Hitler's uncompromising strategy? The Nazis were rescued from their impasse, however, by conservatives who feared that the potential dissolution of the NSDAP would lead to further Communist gains and/or the restoration of the detested parliamentary system. In January 1933 Papen conspired with Hitler to form a "Government of National Concentration" with Hitler as chancellor of a conservative-dominated cabinet. Assured by Papen that conservatives would be able to control the Nazis, Hindenburg accepted a Hitler government. With the indispensable help of conservatives, Hitler had achieved his goal of gaining power by legal means.

The 1918–19 Revolution

With the war winding down and Allied armies now firmly in command on the Western front, revolutionary upheavals spread to various areas of Germany. In Kiel, the main German naval port, revolutionary sailors took power several days before the armistice was signed on 11 November 1918. The immediate cause for their mutiny was the suicidal order from the Naval High Command to put to sea for a final attack on the far superior British navy. The following proclamation by the revolutionaries captures their overly optimistic hopes that the end of the war would lead to a full-scale reform of Imperial German society. Although the revolution in Kiel was soon suppressed, it and similar temporarily successful uprisings across Germany enabled right-wingers to assert that the German armed forces had been stabbed in the back by socialists and democrats. Veterans returning from the front would be organized into so-called "Free Corps" to continue the war at home against the "enemy on the left."

2.1 Proclamation of the Workers' and Soldiers' Council in Kiel, 7 November 1918

Political power lies in our hands.

A provisional provincial government will be formed, which will construct a new order in cooperation with the existing authorities.

Our goal is a free, social people's republic. Where workers' and soldiers' councils do not yet exist, we call on the population of the city and the countryside to follow our example and close ranks behind the new people's government and support its work for the public welfare.

Our main task at first will be to secure peace and to heal the damages of war.

Issues that go beyond the limits of provincial administration remain of course, as before, subject to state and national legislation. We are willing to work in traditional ways with the entire civil service insofar as it subordinates itself to the new course.

We are determined to meet any resistance with all public powers available to us.

Citizens of Schleswig-Holstein! An old democratic dream of freedom and unity, for which many of our best members fought and suffered, will now become reality in new and superior ways.

Kiel, the 7th November 1918
The Workers' and Soldiers' Council

Source: *Zur Geschichte der Kieler Arbeiterbewegung* (Kiel: Gesellschaft für Kieler Stadtgeschichte, 1983). Translated by Rod Stackelberg

The SPD takes power, 1918

On 9 November 1918, the day of the Kaiser's abdication and the proclamation of the republic, the last chancellor of the Imperial Government, Prince Max von Baden (1827–1929), simply handed over the reins of government to the leader of the majority Social Democratic Party (SPD), Friedrich Ebert (1871–1925). Ebert persuaded the leader of the more radical Independent Social Democrats (USPD), Hugo Haase (1863–1919), to join him in forming a provisional government with equal representation from the two parties of the left. The USPD, most of whose members would ultimately join the German Communist Party (KPD) after its formation in 1919, had split off from the "majority Social Democrats" in 1917 on the issue of ending the war. Their post-war cooperation did not last long. In early 1919 the USPD members pulled out of the provisional government, because Ebert and the "majority Social Democrats" seemed determined to suppress the revolutionary uprisings that had broken out all over Germany and seemed reluctant to follow up on promises of extensive reforms. The following statement, issued by the newly-formed provisional government, reflects the optimism and reformist ardor with which a seemingly united left proclaimed the new republic. Only six weeks later, however, the rifts between moderates and radicals had become virtually unbridgeable. This rift was to haunt the Weimar Republic and weaken its defenders in their struggle against the radical right.

2.2 Proclamation of the Council of People's Representatives to the German People, 12 November 1918

To the German People!

The government that has emerged from the revolution, whose political leadership is purely socialist, sets itself the task of realizing the socialist program. It now announces the following with the force of law:

1　The state of siege is rescinded.
2　The rights of association and demonstration is subject to no restrictions, not even for civil servants and public employees.
3　There will be no censorship. Censorship of the theatre is abolished.
4　There will be freedom of opinion in speech and publication.
5　Freedom of religion is guaranteed. No one may be forced to participate in any religious activity.
6　Amnesty is granted for all political crimes. Cases resulting from any such crimes will be dismissed.
7　The law of national service is rescinded with the exception of provisions relating to the conciliation of conflicts.
8　The rules governing relations between servants and masters are rescinded, as well as the special laws affecting rural laborers.
9　The worker protection laws that were rescinded at the start of the war are hereby reinstated.

Further social and political decrees will be issued in the near future. At the latest on 1 January 1919 the eight-hour maximum work day will come into effect. The government will do what it can to insure sufficient job opportunities. A decree for compensation for the unemployed has been prepared. The burdens will be distributed to the national, state, and communal governments.

In the area of health insurance compulsory insurance will be extended beyond the present limit of 2,500 marks.

The housing shortage will be combatted by the provision of new housing.

The government will work towards the provision of a sufficient food supply.

The government will maintain orderly production and will defend property against the intervention of private individuals as well as protecting individual freedom and security.

All elections to public bodies are from now on to be held by equal, secret, direct, and universal vote on the basis of proportional representation of all men and women at least 20 years of age.

This voting system will also apply to the constitutional assembly, about which further directives will soon be issued.

Berlin, 12 November 1918
Ebert; Haase; Scheidemann;
Landsberg; Dittmann; Barth

Source: *Reichsgesetzblatt* 1918, p. 130. Translated by Rod Stackelberg

Anti-Semitism and anti-communism

The following selection by Alfred Rosenberg (1893–1946), editor of the Nazi Party newspaper *Völkischer Beobachter* from 1921, head of all "Intellectual and Ideological Education" of the Party from 1934, and Minister for the conquered territories in the Soviet Union from 1941, was published in the journal *Auf Gut Deutsch* (In Good German), in February 1919. The founder and editor of this right-wing, anti-Semitic journal was Dietrich Eckart (1868–1923), to whom Hitler would later dedicate the second volume of *Mein Kampf*. At the time of this article Germany was still in revolutionary turmoil and the Russian civil war was still raging, precipitated by Allied-supported attempts to overthrow the newly established Communist government. Rosenberg was a Baltic German who experienced the Russian Revolution at first hand before escaping to Germany. Disgruntled Russian and Baltic German emigrés, who had been loyal to the Russian Empire in the First World War but lost their property and their livelihood in the revolution, had considerable influence in the Nazi Party and helped to shape Hitler's world view. Rosenberg helped to convince Hitler that the Communist revolution was part of a Jewish plot to gain world power. Note that in the minds of anti-Semites like Rosenberg and Hitler Jewish capitalists and Jewish communists were working toward the same goal. The notion of "Jewish Bolshevism" remained a staple in Nazi propaganda; the alleged danger it posed to Western Civilization would later be used to justify war against the Soviet Union.

2.3 Alfred Rosenberg, "The Russian-Jewish Revolution," February 1919

"Does it not occur to you that the Jews, even without your help, are citizens of a state mightier and more powerful than any of yours, and that if you give them in addition citizenship in your own states, they will trample your other citizens under foot?" With this warning, based on deep historic insight, [Johann Gottlieb] *Fichte* addressed the German nation a hundred years ago. His words were in vain: ignoring the potential force possessed by a homogeneous race, bemused by the slogans of human equality, all parliaments adopted the dogma of infinite toleration. Tolerance toward the alien, the hostile and the aggressive was seen as a highly humanitarian achievement, but was, as the history of the nineteenth and especially of our present century shows, merely an ever greater abandoning of ourselves.

The gullible European has only too credulously listened to these temptations, sung to the lyrics of the sirens' song – freedom, justice, brotherhood. The fruits of this subversion are apparent today. They are so nakedly apparent that even the most unbiased person, a person who has no idea of the necessary historical relationships, must become aware that he has placed his confidence in crafty and glib leaders, who intended, not his good, but the *destruction of all laboriously acquired civilization, all culture*. The proof, grown to a bloody reality, can be found in the Russian Revolution, which has been passed over in silence by the liberal or Jewish papers, in striking contrast to their other doings. And during the war the newspapers of the right suppressed the clear facts of the matter, in order to protect their "inner front." This resoluteness came too late; in Germany too the Jews had become the leading enemies of the Germanic ideal.

Let us turn to the *facts* of the Russian revolution.

There can be no doubt that the entire Russian people longed for the end of tsarist rule. Anyone who has witnessed this form of government must acknowledge that it discouraged by every means any kind of independent activity – economic, communal, or intellectual, that the rule of a rotten civil service was a repressive one. Thus all of Russia felt as if relieved from a nightmare when the news of the fall of the tsar spread from the Baltic to the Pacific. The suppressed self-confidence of the citizen reappeared everywhere with a vigor which one would never have believed possible, and the leaders had every reason to look ahead optimistically and to hope to be able peacefully to solve their new problems.

But soon *centrifugal* forces set in *in the form of the soldiers' soviets*!!

The soldiers, who during March of 1917 had all promised to continue the war in Russia's defense until victory, came under the influence of manipulative agitators who aimed at aggravating discord and loosening discipline. The soldiers' soviets and the workers were first led by a couple of Georgians, Chkheidze and Tseretelli, who thought the time had come to apply socialism to politics, although they set aside economic and social demands. But very soon they were pushed aside, pushed aside by *Jews*, who flocked from all corners of Russia and from abroad. By energetic agitation, aimed at the egotism of each individual, they soon managed to be popular with the mob.

Taking note of the strong and widespread mood, they at first pretended to be moderates; thus the party spokesmen and representatives [M.I.] *Bernstein-Kogau*, [Mark] *Liber*, [Fedor] *Dan*, and [Abram] *Götz* acted faithful to the state, but secretly hindered the government, in the name of freedom, from taking steps against the rapidly growing Bolshevist movement.

The soul of this movement was the well-known [Lev] *Bronstein*, alias *Trotsky*, a Jew from the Ekaterinoslav Province, and his blood brother [Grigorii] *Apfelbaum*, called *Zinoviev*. The Jewish spirit, with all its energy, fastened on to these two, together with the Russo-Tatar [V.I.] Lenin. In the streets, in the barracks and military hospitals, in meetings and at the front, it was the Jews who promised peace, freedom, and bread to everybody, demanded a general *fraternization with the Germans*. In short, tried to disorganize the state with deliberate lies.

In July 1917, the Kronstadt sailors, led by the infamous [Simon] Roschal, a Jewish student from the technical college of Riga, tried to overthrow the [Alexander] Kerensky administration. The revolt failed and the Bolshevist leaders, the Jews Bronstein (Trotsky), [Lev] Rosenblum (pseud. Kamenev), [Alexandra] Kollontai and others, were taken prisoners. But not for long. Thanks to the energy of Liber and Dan they were released by the weak Kerensky. Dan and Liber, of course, justified their demand in the name of freedom. *After all, the Bolshevists had only fought for their ideals, and these convictions ought to be honored!* Which goes to show that it is good to have one's brothers at work in many parties.

Now the agitation began in earnest. The soldiers were told that they were too tired to go on with this war, that the slaughter had to end, and so forth. Their moral resistance had of course been worn down by three years of war and so it is no wonder that they yielded to the seductions of peace and threw away their arms when they were supposed to attack. Kerensky (by the way no Jew) wavered between his socialist principles and the national will; his hysterical speeches did not succeed in stemming the attrition, and in October 1917 a soldiers' congress appealed to all the armies, over the heads of their governments, to lay down their arms.

The history of this congress is informative and typical. It was supposed to discuss all social and political questions, but most of the Russian armies, in the face of the threatening military situation, refused to engage in political disputes for the time being. This hindered the zealous Bolshevists not at all: they gathered all their representatives together, the Jew [Nikolai]

Abraham (Krylenko) took the chair and, incompetent and unauthorized, issued proclamations and decrees *in the name of the entire Russian army*, in the name of the *entire Russian people*. The attempt of Kerensky to suppress this impudence failed miserably: the Petersburg garrison, demoralized by idleness and provided with money by a mysterious source (people were sure it was *German*, since the Jew Fürstenberg-Genezky had evidently transferred large sums from Stockholm to the Petersburg Soldiers' Soviet), sided with its patrons and overthrew the last Russian government in the beginning of November 1917. It is also characteristic that during the last sessions of the constituent assembly no Russian spoke against the government, *only Jews*.

In this way the victory of the Bolshevists was decided, and now the Jews showed no restraint. They removed their masks and established an almost purely Jewish "Russian" government.

Lenin is the *only non-Jew* among the peoples' commissars; he is, so to speak, the Russian storefront of a Jewish business. Who were the others? The names to be given here will completely reveal a *rule of Jews* which can no longer be denied.

Commissar for War and Foreign Affairs is the above-mentioned Bronstein (Trotsky), the soul of the red terror; Commissar for Culture, Lunacharsky; Commissar for Education, Mrs. Kollontai; Commissar for Trade, Bronsky; Commissar for Justice, Steinberg; Commissar for Defense against Counterrevolution [the CHEKA], the monster Moses Uritzky. In his interrogation prison in the notorious Gorokhovaya Nr. 2, thousands were incarcerated and murdered without trial. Ensign Abraham (Krylenko) became commander in chief of all armies; after he became involved in a too embarrassing scandal he was replaced by the Jew Posern. President of the Petersburg Workers' and Soldiers' Soviet is Apfelbaum (Zinoviev), of the Moscow Workers' and Soldiers' Soviet, Smidovitch. The peace delegates in Brest-Litovsk were Bronstein (Trotsky), Joffe, and Karakhan, and were, except for the typists, Jewish. The first political courier to London (he probably brought his blood brothers good news!) was the Jew Mr. Holtzmann, and as representatives of the Soviet government in all countries Jews sprang up like mushrooms after the rain. In Bern the name of the "Russian" ambassador is Dr. Schlowsky (he and his entire staff were fired the other day); in Christiana, Beitler; in Stockholm, Voronsky; Mr. Rosenblum (Kamenev) is delegated to Vienna, as is the notorious Mr. Joffe to Berlin.

The negotiations on the agreements which were to supplement Brest-Litovsk were directed "on the Russian side" by the above-mentioned Voronsky, to whom were attached about twelve Jews and Jewesses and two or three Latvians.

In addition there are the great agitators of the Bolshevist newspapers, Messrs. Nakhamkes (pseudonym Steklov), Lurie (Larin), Stlyansky, and Sobelsohn (Radek).

In the name of humanity they demanded freedom of speech and abolition of capital punishment. But scarcely had they come to power when there began a censorship such as even the darkest Tsardom had *never* known. Capital punishment was used in practice everywhere and then also "legally" reintroduced. Under the banner of brotherhood and peace they had attracted the naive masses; immediately they began inciting furious hatred against everything "bourgeois" and soon introduced *systematic massacre* and civil war, if one can so describe this one-sided slaughter. The entire Russian intelligentsia which had for decades toiled for the well-being of the Russian people, to the point of the gallows or exile, were simply killed wherever they could be found. Kokoshkin and Shingarev, lying critically ill in the hospital, were treacherously murdered. The murderers, of course, remain unpunished. Not everything can be treated here in detail; but whatever was known of honest Russiandom was *mercilessly executed*.

Because it did not want to submit to the Bolshevists, the National Assembly, the hope for many years of all Russian patriots, was abruptly dispersed by the Red Guard in the name of freedom, and now the true Russian stands helplessly at the grave of his plundered fatherland.

The workers and soldiers have been driven so far that there is *no going back for them any more*, they are the slavish creatures of a tough Jewry which has burned all its bridges. The true core of the Red Army is absolutely reliable; the other enlisted men are kept under a terrible discipline.

Enlistment happens in the following way: A commissar comes into a village and announces the call to arms of all men from the age of twenty to about forty. If this announcement is not absolutely obeyed, a so-called punitive expedition appears and shoots down the entire village including women and children. Since this has been done mercilessly many times, the people who are called up appear to the very last man. In such a way and by this alone, the Jewish government holds on, for it knows well: the hatred, still weak, of the unarmed population could become terrible if precautions are not taken daily. According to the figures given by *Pravda* ("Truth"), the "official" paper, more than 13,000 "counterrevolutionaries" have been shot to death in the last three months.

But one can observe, and all recent news confirms it, that the hatred against the Jews in Russia is constantly spreading, despite all terror. The most tenderhearted and tolerant Russians are now as full of this hatred as a tsarist bureaucrat used to be. If the present government falls no Jew will remain alive in Russia; one can say with certainty that what is not killed will be driven out. Where to? The Poles are already keeping them at bay, and so they will all come into old Germany, where we love the Jews so much and keep the warmest seats ready for them!

Source: Alfred Rosenberg, "The Russian-Jewish Revolution," in *Nazi Ideology before 1933: A Documentation*, intr. and trsl. by Barbara Miller Lane and Leila J. Rupp (Austin and London: University of Texas Press, 1978), pp. 12–16

The dictated peace, 1919

Virtually all Germans, whatever their politics, considered the Versailles Treaty a travesty of justice. They felt betrayed by the Allied promise to negotiate a peace on the basis of Woodrow Wilson's "Fourteen Points," which called among other things for open diplomacy, freedom of the seas, and national self-determination. Revulsion against Versailles proved to be one of the major sources of popular support for the right, which was committed to its reversal. The treaty became a major liability to defenders of the Republic. Representatives of the first Weimar government were forced to sign the treaty in June 1919 under the threat of Allied sanctions, including continuation of the economic blockade. Germans opposed the loss of territory, the restrictions on their military, and the economic reparations imposed on Germany. Their greatest contempt was reserved for Article 231, the so-called "War Guilt Clause," which pinned the blame for the war squarely on the German government. The Versailles Treaty thus became a major factor in the right-wing campaign to replace the Weimar Republic with a more powerful and authoritarian form of government.

The treaty, which ran to hundreds of pages, included as its first part the covenant of the League of Nations, based on a proposal by President Wilson. The United States

Senate never ratified the treaty, however, thus weakening both the League and the treaty, although the US, in a separate agreement with Germany, retained the "rights and advantages stipulated in that Treaty for the benefit of the United States." Relevant extracts from the treaty are reprinted below. Note that one purpose of the military provisions was to insure that the Reichswehr would not be used for the training of a large reserve force. The trial of the former Kaiser called for in Article 227 was never held, as the Netherlands refused the Allied extradition request. Nonetheless, the call for penalties in Part VII contributed to the virtually unanimous rejection of the treaty by the German public.

2.4 The Treaty of Versailles, 28 June 1919

PART III: POLITICAL CLAUSES FOR EUROPE

SECTION III. LEFT BANK OF THE RHINE

Article 42: Germany is forbidden to maintain or construct any fortifications either on the left bank of the Rhine or on the right bank to the west of a line drawn 50 kilometres to the East of the Rhine.

SECTION IV. SAAR BASIN

Article 45: As compensation for the destruction of the coal mines in the north of France and as part payment towards the total reparation due from Germany for the damage resulting from the war, Germany cedes to France in full and absolute possession, with exclusive rights to exploitation, unencumbered and free from all debts and charges of any kind, the coal mines situated in the Saar Basin.

SECTION VI. AUSTRIA

Article 80: Germany acknowledges and will respect strictly the independence of Austria within the frontiers which may be fixed in a treaty between that State and the Principal Allied and Associated Powers; she agrees that this independence shall be inalienable, except with the consent of the Council of the League of Nations.

SECTION VII. CZECHO-SLOVAK STATE

Article 82: The old frontier as it existed on August 3, 1914, between Austria-Hungary and the German Empire will constitute the frontier between Germany and the Czecho-Slovak State.

SECTION VIII. POLAND

Article 87: Germany, in conformity with the action already taken by the Allied and Associated Powers, recognizes the complete independence of Poland, and renounces in her favor all rights and title over the territory [ceded by Germany] ...

Article 100: Germany renounces in favor of the Principal Allied and Associated Powers all rights and title over the territory comprised within the following limits ...

Article 102: The Principal Allied and Associated Powers undertake to establish the town of Danzig, together with the rest of the territory described in Article 100, as a Free City. It will be placed under the protection of the League of Nations.

PART IV: GERMAN RIGHTS AND INTERESTS OUTSIDE GERMANY

SECTION I. GERMAN COLONIES

Article 119: Germany renounces in favor of the Principal Allied and Associated Powers all her rights and titles over her oversea possessions.

PART V: MILITARY, NAVAL AND AIR CLAUSES

In order to render possible the initiation of a general limitation of the armaments of all nations, Germany undertakes strictly to observe the military, naval and air clauses which follow.

SECTION I. MILITARY CLAUSES

CHAPTER I. EFFECTIVES AND CADRES OF THE GERMAN ARMY

Article 159: The German military forces shall be demobilized and reduced as prescribed hereinafter.

Article 160: 1) By a date which must not be later than March 31, 1920, the German Army must not comprise more than seven divisions of infantry and three divisions of cavalry.

After that date the total number of effectives in the Army of the States constituting Germany must not exceed one hundred thousand men, including officers and establishments of depots. The Army shall be devoted exclusively to the maintenance of order within the territory and to the control of the frontiers.

The total effective strength of officers, including the personnel of staffs, whatever their composition, must not exceed four thousand ...

CHAPTER III. RECRUITING AND MILITARY TRAINING

Article 173: Universal compulsory military service shall be abolished in Germany.

The German Army may only be constituted and recruited by means of voluntary enlistment.

Article 174: The period of enlistment for non-commissioned officers and privates must be twelve consecutive years ...

Article 175: The officers who are retained in the Army must undertake the obligation to serve in it up to the age of forty-five years at least. Officers newly appointed must undertake to serve on the active list for twenty-five consecutive years at least.

Officers who have previously belonged to any formations whatever in the Army, and who are not retained in the units allowed to be maintained, must not take part in any military exercise whether theoretical or practical, and will not be under any military obligations whatever ...

Article 177: Educational establishments, the universities, societies of discharged soldiers, shooting or touring clubs and, generally speaking, associations of every description, whatever the age of their members, must not occupy themselves with any military matters ...
Article 178: All measures of mobilization or appertaining to mobilization are forbidden.

In no case must formations, administrative services or General Staffs include supplementary cadres ...

CHAPTER IV. FORTIFICATIONS

Article 180: All fortified works, fortresses and field works situated in German territory to the west of a line drawn fifty kilometres to the east of the Rhine shall be disarmed and dismantled ...

SECTION II. NAVAL CLAUSES

Article 181: After the expiration of a period of two months from the coming into force of the present Treaty the German naval forces in commission must not exceed:

- 6 battleships of the *Deutschland* or *Lothringen* type,
- 6 light cruisers,
- 12 destroyers,
- 12 torpedo boats,
- or an equal number of ships constructed to replace them as provided in Article 190.
- No submarines are to be included.

All other warships, except where there is provision to the contrary in the present Treaty, must be placed in reserve or devoted to commercial purposes ...
Article 183: After the expiration of a period of two months from the coming into force of the present Treaty, the total personnel of the German Navy, including the manning of the fleet, coast defences, signal stations, administration and other land services, must not exceed fifteen thousand, including officers and men of all grades and corps.

The total strength of officers and warrant officers must not exceed fifteen hundred.

Within two months from the coming into force of the present Treaty the personnel in excess of the above strength shall be demobilized ...

SECTION III. AIR CLAUSES

Article 198: The armed forces of Germany must not include any military or naval air forces ...
Article 199: Within two months from the coming into force of the present Treaty the personnel of air forces on the rolls of the German land and sea forces shall be demobilized ...

PART VII: PENALTIES

Article 227: The Allied and Associated Powers publicly arraign William II of Hohenzollern, formerly German Emperor, for a supreme offense against international morality and the sanctity of treaties.

A special tribunal will be constituted to try the accused, thereby assuring him the guarantees essential to the right of defense. It will be composed of five judges, one appointed by each of the following Powers: namely, the United States of America, Great Britain, France, Italy, and Japan.

In its decision the tribunal will be guided by the highest motives of international policy, with a view to vindicating the solemn obligations of international undertakings and the validity of international morality. It will be its duty to fix the punishment which it considers should be imposed.

The Allied and Associated Powers will address a request to the Government of the Netherlands for the surrender to them of the ex-Emperor in order that he may be put on trial.

Article 228: The German Government recognizes the right of the Allied and Associated Powers to bring before military tribunals persons accused of having committed acts in violation of the laws and customs of war. Such persons shall, if found guilty, be sentenced to punishments laid down by law. This provision will apply notwithstanding any proceedings or prosecution before a tribunal in Germany or in the territory of her allies.

The German Government shall hand over to the Allied and Associated Powers, or to such one of them as shall so request, all persons accused of having committed an act in violation of the laws and customs of war, who are specified either by name or by the rank, office, or employment which they held under the German authorities.

Article 229: Persons guilty of criminal acts against the nationals of one of the Allied and Associated Powers will be brought before the military tribunals of that Power ...

Article 230: The German Government undertakes to furnish all documents and information of every kind, the production of which may be considered necessary to ensure the full knowledge of the incriminating acts, the discovery of offenders and the just appreciation of responsibility.

PART VIII: REPARATION

SECTION I. GENERAL PROVISIONS

Article 231: The Allied and Associated Governments affirm and Germany accepts the responsibility of Germany and her allies for causing all the loss and damage to which the Allied and Associated Governments and their nationals have been subjects as a consequence of the war imposed upon them by the aggression of Germany and her allies.

Article 232: The Allied and Associated Governments recognize that the resources of Germany are not adequate, after taking into account permanent diminutions of such resources which will result from other provisions of the present Treaty, to make complete reparation for all such loss and damage.

The Allied and Associated Governments, however, require, and Germany undertakes that she will make compensation for all damage done to the civilian population of the Allied and Associated Powers and to their property during the period of the belligerency of each as an Allied or Associated Power against Germany by such aggression by land, by sea and from the air, and in general all damage as defined in Annex I hereto ...

Article 233: The amount of the above damage for which compensation is to be made by Germany shall be determined by an Inter-Allied Commission, to be called the Reparation Commission and constituted in the form and with the powers set forth hereunder and in Annexes 2 to 7 inclusive hereto.

This Commission shall consider the claims and give to the German Government a just opportunity to be heard ...

Article 235: In order to enable the Allied and Associated Powers to proceed at once in the restoration of their industrial and economic life, pending the full determination of their claims, Germany shall pay in such installments and in such manner (whether in gold, commodities, ships, securities or otherwise) as the Reparation Commission may fix, during 1919, 1920 and the first four months of 1921, the equivalent of 20,000,000,000 gold marks. Out of this sum the expenses of the armies of occupation subsequent to the Armistice of November 11, 1918, shall first be met, and such supplies of food and raw materials as may be judged by the Governments of the Principal Allied and Associated Powers to be essential to enable Germany to meet her obligations for reparation may also, with the approval of the said Governments, be paid for out of the above sum. The balance shall be reckoned towards liquidation of the amounts due for reparation ...

Source: *Treaty of Peace With Germany* (Washington DC: Government Printing Office, 1919)

The Liberal Weimar Constitution, 1919

The Weimar constitution, named after the small city in central Germany where the National Assembly (the constitutional convention) met in 1919, called for a true parliamentary regime in which the head of government, the chancellor, was responsible to the Reichstag (the German parliament) and could remain in office only if his government enjoyed majority support. The upper house of parliament, the Reichsrat, was made up of representatives of the German states. The representational office of president held only limited powers, much like those of the head of state in a limited monarchy. However, under Article 48 of the constitution, the President was granted temporary power to rule by decree and suspend civil liberties in times of crisis. It was this article that was repeatedly invoked by Hindenburg at the request of his chancellors in the political impasse after 1930. Thus an article designed to strengthen the parliamentary form of government in an emergency became an instrument for circumventing the parliamentary process and weakening the Reichstag.

A number of the constitution's provisions, including those guaranteeing civil liberties, were similar to the provisions of the failed 1848 constitution. Note, however, that the provision for the Anschluss of Austria at least implicitly contradicted the pledge to respect Austrian independence in the Treaty of Versailles. Although the constitution disappointed many delegates of the left, who had hoped not just for political, but also social reform, its liberal and democratic provisions were anathema to the nationalist and authoritarian right. Their efforts to overthrow the constitutional Republic and establish or restore a dictatorial form of government finally succeeded when Adolf Hitler was appointed chancellor in January 1933.

2.5 The Constitution of the German Reich, 11 August 1919

The German people, united in all their racial elements and inspired by the will to renew and strengthen their Reich in liberty and justice, to preserve peace at home and abroad, and to promote social progress, have established the following constitution.

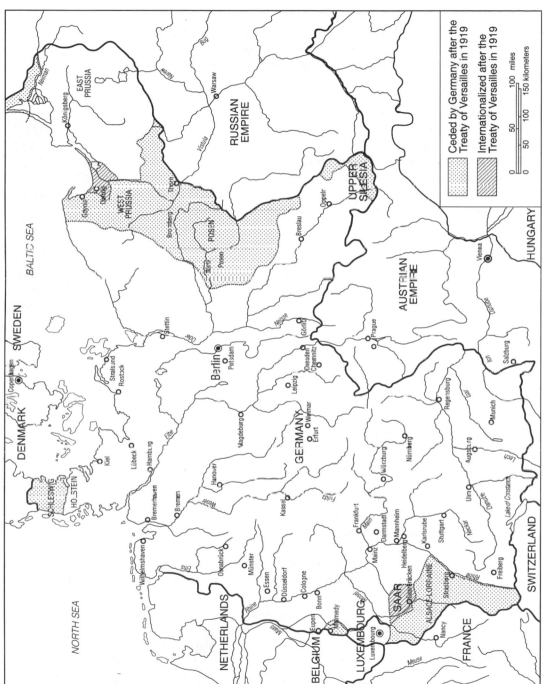

Map 1　The German Empire 1871–1919, showing territorial losses following the First World War

FIRST PART: STRUCTURE AND FUNCTION OF THE REICH

FIRST CHAPTER: REICH AND STATES

Article 1: The German Reich is a republic. Political authority emanates from the people.
Article 2: The territory of the Reich consists of the territories of the German member states. Other territories can be incorporated into the Reich by law if their inhabitants desire it by right of self-determination.
Article 3: The Reich colors are black, red, and gold. The merchant flag is black, white, and red, with the Reich colors in the upper inside corner.
Article 4: The generally accepted rules of international law are to be considered as binding components of the law of the German Reich …
Article 17: Every state [of the Reich] must have a republican constitution. The representatives of the people must be elected by universal, equal, direct, and secret suffrage of all German citizens, both men and women, in accordance with the principles of proportional representation. The government of the state must enjoy the confidence of the people's representatives …

SECOND CHAPTER: THE REICHSTAG

Article 20: The Reichstag is composed of the delegates of the German people.
Article 21: The delegates represent the whole people. They are subject only to their own conscience and are not bound by any instructions.
Article 22: The delegates are elected by universal, equal, direct, and secret suffrage by men and women over twenty years of age, according to the principle of proportional representation. Election day must be a Sunday or a public holiday.
Article 23: The Reichstag is elected for four years. New elections must take place at the latest on the sixtieth day after this term has run its course.
    The Reichstag convenes for the first time at the latest on the thirtieth day following the election …
Article 25: The Reich President can dissolve the Reichstag, but only once for the same cause. New elections will take place at the latest on the sixtieth day after dissolution …

THIRD CHAPTER: THE REICH PRESIDENT AND THE REICH GOVERNMENT

Article 41: The Reich President is elected by the whole German people. Every German who has completed his thirty-fifth year is eligible for election …
Article 43: The term of the Reich President is seven years. Reelection is permissible …
Article 46: The Reich President appoints and dismisses officials of the Reich and officers as long as no other provisions are adopted by law. He can allow the right of appointment and dismissal to be exercised by other offices.
Article 47: The Reich President is commander in chief of all the armed forces of the Reich.
Article 48: If any state does not fulfill the duties imposed upon it by the constitution or the laws of the Reich, the Reich President may enforce such duties with the aid of the armed forces.
    In the event that public order and security are seriously disturbed or threatened, the Reich President may take the measures necessary for their restoration, intervening, if necessary, with the aid of the armed forces. For this purpose he may temporarily suspend, wholly or in part, the basic rights laid down in Articles 114, 115, 117, 118, 123, 124, and 153. The Reich President

must without delay inform the Reichstag of all measures taken under Paragraph 1 or Paragraph 2 of this Article. These measures may be rescinded on demand of the Reichstag …

Article 50: All orders and decrees of the Reich President, including those relating to the armed forces, must, in order to be valid, be countersigned by the Reich Chancellor or by the appropriate Reich minister. Responsibility is assumed through the countersignature …

Article 52: The government of the Reich shall consist of the Reich Chancellor and the Reich ministers.

Article 53: The Reich Chancellor and, on his recommendation, the Reich ministers, are appointed and dismissed by the Reich President.

Article 54: The Reich Chancellor and the Reich ministers require for the exercise of their office the confidence of the Reichstag. Any one of them must resign if the Reichstag by formal resolution withdraws its confidence.

Article 55: The Reich Chancellor presides over the government of the Reich and conducts its affairs according to the rules of procedure laid down by the government of the Reich and approved by the Reich President.

Article 56: The Reich Chancellor determines the political program of the Reich and assumes responsibility to the Reichstag. Within this general policy each Reich minister conducts independently the office entrusted to him and is held individually responsible to the Reichstag …

FOURTH CHAPTER: THE REICHSRAT (REICH COUNCIL)

Article 60: A Reichsrat is formed to give the German sates representation in the law-making and administration of the Reich.

Article 61: Each state has at least one vote in the Reichsrat. In the case of the larger states one vote shall be assigned for every million inhabitants … No single state shall have more than two fifths of the total number of votes …

German Austria, after its union with the German Reich, shall be entitled to participate in the Reichsrat with the number of votes proportionate to its population. Until then the representatives of German Austria may take part in the deliberations.

Article 63: The states shall be represented in the Reichsrat by members of their governments …

FIFTH CHAPTER: REICH LEGISLATION

Article 73: A law of the Reichstag must be submitted to popular referendum before its proclamation, if the Reich President, within one month of its passage, so decides …

Article 76: The constitution may be amended by law, but acts amending the constitution can only take effect if two-thirds of the legal number of members are present and at least two-thirds of those present consent …

SECOND PART: FUNDAMENTAL RIGHTS AND DUTIES OF THE GERMANS

FIRST CHAPTER: THE INDIVIDUAL

Article 109: All Germans are equal before the law. Men and women have the same fundamental civil rights and duties. Public legal privileges or disadvantages of birth or of rank are abolished. Titles of nobility shall be regarded merely as part of the name and may no longer be bestowed. Titles may only be bestowed when they indicate an office or profession;

academic degrees are not affected hereby. Orders and decorations shall not be conferred by the state. No German shall accept titles or orders from a foreign government …

Article 114: Personal liberty is inviolable. Curtailment or deprivation of personal liberty by a public authority is permissible only by authority of law.

Persons who have been deprived of their liberty must be informed at the latest on the following day by whose authority and for what reasons they have been held. They shall receive the opportunity without delay of submitting objections to their deprivation of liberty.

Article 115: The home of every German is his sanctuary and is inviolable. Exceptions are permitted only by authority of law …

Article 117: The secrecy of letters and all postal, telegraph, and telephone communications is inviolable. Exceptions are inadmissible except by national law.

Article 118: Every German has the right, within the limits of the general laws, to express his opinion freely by word, in writing, in print, in picture form, or in any other way … Censorship is forbidden …

SECOND CHAPTER: THE GENERAL WELFARE

Article 123: All Germans have the right to assemble peacefully and unarmed without giving notice and without special permission …

Article 124: All Germans have the right to form associations and societies for purposes not contrary to the criminal law …

Article 126: Every German has the right to petition …

THIRD CHAPTER: RELIGION AND RELIGIOUS ASSOCIATIONS

Article 135: All inhabitants of the Reich enjoy full religious freedom and freedom of conscience. The free exercise of religion is guaranteed by the Constitution and is under public protection …

Article 137: There is no state church …

FOURTH CHAPTER: EDUCATION AND THE SCHOOLS

Article 142: Art, science, and the teaching thereof are free …

Article 143 The education of the young is to be provided for by means of public institutions. The Reich, states, and municipalities shall cooperate in their establishment …

FIFTH CHAPTER: ECONOMIC LIFE

Article 151: The regulation of economic life must be compatible with the principles of justice, with the aim of attaining humane conditions of existence for all. Within these limits the economic liberty of the individual is assured …

Article 152: Freedom of contract prevails in accordance with the laws. Usury is prohibited. Legal transactions contra bonos mores are invalid.

Article 153: The right of private property is guaranteed by the Constitution … Expropriation of property may take place only … by due process of law …

Article 159: Freedom of association for the preservation and promotion of labor and economic conditions is guaranteed to everyone and to all vocations. All agreements and measures attempting to restrict or restrain this freedom are unlawful …

Article 161: For the maintenance of health and capacity to work, for the protection of maternity, and for provision against the economic consequences of age, infirmity, and the vicissitudes of life, The Reich shall organize a comprehensive system of insurance ...

Article 165: Workers and employees are called upon to cooperate, on an equal footing, with employers in regulating wages and the conditions of work, as well as in the general development of productive forces ...

Article 181: The German people have drawn up and adopted this constitution through their National Assembly. It comes into force with the date of its proclamation.

Schwarzburg, August 11, 1919.

The Reich President: Ebert;

The Reich Cabinet: Bauer; Erzberger; Hermann Müller; Dr. David; Noske; Schmidt; Schlicke; Giesberts; Dr. Mayer; Dr. Bell

Source: *Reichsgesetzblatt* 1919, pp. 1383ff

The Nazi Party program, 1920

This 25-point program was proclaimed on 24 February 1920 at a public meeting in Munich of the German Workers' Party. Under Hitler's leadership the party changed its name to the National Socialist German Workers' Party (*Nationalsozialistische deutsche Arbeiterpartei*, or NSDAP) later that year. The program, drawn up by Gottfried Feder (1883–1941), was designed to appeal not only to small proprietors, the traditional constituency for the radical right because of their opposition to both socialism and an unregulated free market, but also to industrial workers in an effort to wean them from their allegiance to social democracy and communism. The economic demands of points 11 through 17 have a distinctly anti-capitalist thrust, reflecting both the shift of political discourse to the left in the immediate post-war period and the desire of the Nazis to match the promises of the left-wing parties. The contradictions in the program resulted from the fact that the party bitterly rejected the internationalist left but sought to appeal to the left's constituency. In 1928 Hitler issued a declaration that Point 17, the call for land reform, did not represent a threat to private property but was directed only against Jewish land speculators.

Anti-Semitism allowed the Nazis to channel anti-capitalist sentiment into conservative channels by blaming Jews for all economic distress. Points 3 through 9 were specifically directed against Jews and resembled the demands made by the Pan-German League and other radical anti-Semites before the war. In contrast to their economic promises, the anti-Semitic provisions of the program were enacted into law when the Nazis came into power in 1933.

The major appeal of the program lay in its promise of *Volksgemeinschaft*, a homogeneous, unified national community in which the common (or national) interest was supposed to take precedence over class- and self-interest. It thus offered a nationalist alternative to class-based socialism and individualistic liberalism that was particularly attractive to members of the lower middle class who felt threatened both by big business and by the labor movement. It also appealed to conservatives because it promised a strong state that would purge society of its disruptive left-wing elements.

Although in 1925 some Nazis, headed by Gregor Strasser (1892–1934), wanted to expand the program to include specific proposals for a corporative state (see Doc. 2.14),

Hitler refused to countenance any changes to the 25-points. He did not want to commit himself to any specific social changes (other than the exclusion of Jews). He viewed the program merely as an instrument to draw popular support. To serve that purpose it had to be couched in general terms and appeal to various sectors of society. He also believed that constant repetition of a few basic issues – whether grounded in fact or not – was the best way to gain mass support. A program not subject to alteration or debate also gave him maximum freedom of action in choosing what policies to pursue.

2.6 The program of the NSDAP

The Program of the German Workers' Party is limited as to period. The leaders have no intention, once the aims announced in it have been achieved, of setting up fresh ones, merely in order artificially to increase the discontent of the masses, and so ensure the continued existence of the party.

1 We demand the union of all Germans to form a Greater Germany on the basis of the right of self-determination enjoyed by nations.
2 We demand equality of rights for the German people in its dealings with other nations and abrogation of the peace treaties of Versailles and Saint-Germain.
3 We demand land and territory (colonies) for the sustenance of our people and for settling our excess population.
4 None but members of the nation may be citizens of the state. None but those of German blood, whatever their creed, may be members of the nation. No Jew therefore may be a member of the nation.
5 Anyone who is not a citizen of the state may live in Germany only as a guest and must be regarded as being subject to legislation governing aliens.
6 The right to determine the leadership and laws of the state is to be enjoyed by citizens alone. We demand therefore that all public offices, of whatever kind, whether national, regional, or local, shall be filled only by citizens. We oppose the corrupting parliamentary practice of filling posts merely with a view to party considerations and without reference to character or ability.
7 We demand that the state shall make it its first duty to provide the opportunity for a livelihood and way of life for citizens. If it is not possible to sustain the entire population of the state, foreign nationals (non-citizens) are to be expelled from the Reich.
8 Any further immigration of non-citizens is to be prevented. We demand that all non-Germans, who have immigrated to Germany since 2 August 1914, be forced immediately to leave the Reich.
9 All citizens must have equal rights and obligations.
10 The first obligation of every citizen must be to work with his mind or with his body. The activities of the individual may not clash with the interests of the whole, but must proceed within the framework of the community and be for the general good.
We therefore demand:
11 Abolition of incomes unearned by work.
Abolition of the Slavery of Interest
12 In view of the enormous sacrifice of life and property demanded of a people by every war, personal enrichment through a war must be regarded as a crime against the nation. Therefore we demand the total confiscation of all war profits.

13 We demand nationalization of all businesses that have previously been formed into trusts.
14 We demand a division of profits of large businesses.
15 We demand a generous extension of old-age benefits.
16 We demand creation and maintenance of a healthy middle class (*Mittelstand*), immediate communalization of large department stores and their lease at low cost to small firms, and that utmost consideration be given to all small firms in contracts with the state, district, or municipality.
17 We demand a land reform suitable to our national needs, provision of a law for expropriating without compensation land for public purposes; abolition of interest on land loans, and prevention of all speculation in land.
18 We demand struggle without consideration against those whose activities are injurious to the common interest. Common criminals against the nation, usurers, profiteers, etc., are to be punished with death, whatever their creed or race.
19 We demand that the Roman Law, which serves a materialistic world order, be replaced by a German common law.
20 The state is to be responsible for a fundamental reconstruction of our whole national education program, to enable every capable and industrious German to obtain higher education and subsequently advancement into leading positions. The curriculum of all educational establishments must be brought into line with the requirements of practical life. Comprehension of the concept of the state must be the school objective (civic education [*Staatsbürgerkunde*]), as early as the beginning of understanding in the pupil. We demand education of the gifted children of poor parents, whatever their class or occupation, at the expense of the state.
21 The state must see to raising the standard of health in the nation by protecting mothers and infants, prohibiting child labor, increasing physical fitness by obligatory gymnastics and sports, and by extensive support of clubs engaged in the physical development of the young.
22 We demand abolition of a mercenary army and formation of a national army.
23 We demand legal opposition to *conscious* political lies and their dissemination through the press. In order to facilitate creation of a German national press we demand:

(a) that all editors and employees of newspapers appearing in the German language must be members of the race;
(b) that non-German newspapers may be published only with special permission from the state. These may not be printed in the German language;
(c) that non-Germans shall be prohibited by law from any financial interest in or influence on German newspapers, and that the penalty for violation of the law shall be closing of any such newspaper and immediate deportation of the non-German concerned.

Publications which infringe on the national welfare are to be prohibited. We demand legal prosecution of all artistic and literary forms that have a destructive effect on our life as a nation, and the closing of organizations which contravene the requirements mentioned above.

24 We demand freedom of religion for all religious denominations in the state so long as they do not endanger it and do not oppose the moral feelings of the German race.

The Party as such stands for positive Christianity, without binding itself confessionally to any one denomination. It combats the Jewish-materialistic spirit within us and around us, and is convinced that a lasting recovery of our nation can only succeed from *within* on the principle:

The general interest before self-interest

25   That the foregoing may be realized, we demand the formation of a strong central power in the Reich; unlimited authority of the central parliament over the entire Reich and its organizations, and the formation of corporate and occupational chambers for the execution of the Reich laws in the various states of the confederation.

The leaders of the party promise, if necessary by sacrificing their own lives, to secure fulfillment of the foregoing points.

EXPLANATION, 1928

Adolf Hitler proclaimed the following explanation of this program on 13 April 1928:

Regarding the false interpretation of Point 17 of the Program of the NSDAP on the part of our opponents, the following definition is necessary:

> Since the NSDAP stands on the platform of private ownership, it follows that the passage 'expropriation of land without compensation' concerns only the creation of legal means of expropriating, if necessary, land which has been illegally acquired or is not administered in the interests of the national good. This is directed primarily against the Jewish land-speculation companies.

Source: Office of the US Chief of Counsel for Prosecution of Axis Criminality,
***Nazi Conspiracy and Aggression*, Vol. IV**
(Washington DC: US Government Printing Office, 1946), pp. 208–11 [Doc. 1708-PS]

The Kapp Putsch, 13 March 1920

The first post-war government, dominated by the SPD, encouraged the creation of so-called Free Corps, volunteer units made up of demobilized soldiers, in order to help the government suppress revolution from the radical left. These Free Corps units, however, had no sympathy for democracy and only waited for the opportunity to turn their weapons against the government they were supposed to defend. The Kapp Putsch, precipitated in March 1920 by the threatened dissolution of some Free Corps units in accordance with the Versailles Treaty, provided that opportunity. The putsch was led by the general in charge of army and Free Corps units in Berlin, Walther von Lüttwitz (1859–1942), in collusion with the conservative civil servant and former leader of the Fatherland Party (see Doc.1.14), Wolfgang Kapp (1858–1922), who was to become chancellor under the new regime. As the Reichswehr (the regular army) refused to intervene to stop the putsch, the Ebert government was forced to seek temporary refuge in the southern German city of Stuttgart. The putsch, however, collapsed after four days in the face of a general strike.

The following appeal was distributed as a leaflet on the day of the putsch. It attests to the hope and expectation of many conservatives that a strong authoritarian government would soon be restored in the recently defeated nation. Although Kapp's statement is less extreme than the Nazi Program issued a month earlier (note, for instance, Kapp's reluctant acceptance of the Versailles Treaty and the absence of any overt anti-Semitism), the similarity of purpose is nonetheless unmistakable and helps to explain why the soil was so fertile for the growth of the radical right in the early years of the Republic. While both conservatives and right-wing extremists sought to integrate disaffected workers in the national community, the former were not nearly as convincing in their anti-capitalist, anti-establishment rhetoric as the latter. Although Kapp denied any reactionary motives, it seems clear that his eventual goal was a restoration of the monarchy. Thus his defiant rejection of the Republican colors – black, gold, and red – in favor of the imperial colors of black, white, and red (which would also become the colors of the Nazi swastika flag).

2.7 Proclamation of Director General Wolfgang Kapp as Chancellor of the Reich

Empire and nation are in grave danger. We are speedily approaching the total collapse of the state and legal system. The people only vaguely sense the coming disaster. Prices soar without stopping. Misery is growing. Famine threatens. Corruption, usury, racketeering, and crime show up with ever greater audacity. The ineffective government, lacking authority and tied to corruption, is not capable of mastering the danger. Away with a government in which an Erzberger[1] is the leading spirit!

Militant Bolshevism threatens us with devastation and violation from the east. Is this government capable of fending it off? How will we avoid external and internal collapse?

Only by reestablishing the authority of a strong state. What concept should lead us in this endeavor?

Nothing reactionary, instead a further free development of the German state, restoration of order, and the sanctity of law. Duty and conscience are to reign again in German lands. German honor and honesty are to be restored.

The National Assembly, continuing to govern without a mandate, has declared itself to be permanent. In violation of the constitution it is postponing elections until the autumn. Instead of protecting the constitution it recently issued with such ceremony, a tyrannical party government already wants to deprive the nation of the important basic right of electing the president.

The chance to save Germany is disappearing; that is why there is no other way left but a government of action.

What are the tasks facing the new government?

The government will put into effect the peace treaty while preserving the honor of the German people and their ability to live and work, insofar as it is possible and does not involve self-destruction.

The government will restore on a constitutional confederative basis the federal states' fiscal and tax sovereignty, which they need to fulfill their cultural responsibilities independently.

The government will guarantee the war bonds as a just return for faithfully fulfilled patriotic duty and initiate their prompt repayment.

The government will levy appropriate taxes on rural and municipal property in order to reconstruct the state. After serious governmental collapse it has always been landed property that has had to make sacrifices for reconstruction. The government expects that it will once again fulfill its patriotic duty.

The government will however, give economic freedom back to landed property, so that it will be in a position to make such sacrifices. This alone will result in an increase in produc-

---

1   Matthias Erzberger (1875–1921), a member of the Center Party, introduced a peace resolution in the Reichstag in 1917 and was one of the signatories of the armistice on 11 November 1918.

tion and public revenues. At the same time it will be our main concern to provide people of lesser means and those on fixed salaries with food at affordable prices.

The government will suppress strikes and sabotage without mercy. Let each man peacefully go about his work. Everyone who is happy to work is assured of our vigorous protection; a strike is betrayal of the nation, the fatherland, and the future.

The government will involve the working class to a great degree in preparation and active cooperation beside the other professional and vocational classes for the purpose of economic reorganization. This will not be a one-sided capitalism, but rather it will protect German workers from the harsh fate of international domination by big business, and the government hopes through these measures to put an end to the working classes' hostility toward the state.

The government will amend existing insurance legislation with a provision for workers' right to self-determination.

The government will issue a homestead law for town and country that will make it easier for every German to gain access to landed property and property in general.

The government will help the civil service, which has been neglected at all levels since the November days, to attain its rights once again and will look after its interests in every respect. In exchange the government demands of its civil servants the old spirit of loyal fulfillment of duty in the service of the common good.

The government will view it as their most sacred duty to guarantee disabled veterans and the surviving dependents of fallen soldiers the full amount of their well-deserved pensions.

The government will to the best of its ability provide for the armed forces who are presently protecting the fatherland and their dependents and will offer them every protection against personal and economic boycotts. The same is true for temporary volunteers and the members of the home guard, the security service, the police, and the emergency repair service.

The government will guarantee the freedom of the churches and will reestablish national and religious education.

Attempts to separate from the *Reich* will be dealt with as high treason according to martial law. We are strong enough not to have to begin our rule with arrests and other violent measures. But we will strike down any revolt against the new order with ruthless determination.

We will not rule according to theories, but according to the practical needs of the state and the nation as a whole. According to the best German tradition the state must stand above all the struggles of occupational groups and parties. The state is the impartial judge in the current struggle between capital and labor. We reject every class preference, whether for the right or the left. We recognize only German citizens. Every German citizen who in this difficult hour gives to the fatherland what belongs to the fatherland can count on us.

Let each person do his duty! Today work is the most noble duty for everyone. Germany is to be a moral working community!

The colors of the German Republic are black–white–red!

Reich Chancellor: Kapp

**Source: Johannes Erger, *Der Kapp-Lüttwitz Putsch: Ein Beitrag zur deutschen Innenpolitik, 1920–21* (Düsseldorf: Droste, 1967), pp. 324–6. Reprinted by permission of the Kommission für Geschichte des Parlamentarismus und der politischen Parteien in Bonn.
Translated by Sally Winkle**

The Weimar Republic in the early 1920s

George Grosz (1893–1959) was one of the most provocative artists in Germany in the Weimar years and played an important role in the Dada movement from 1917 to 1920. His paintings, drawings, and cartoons brilliantly caricatured the powerful nationalist elites of German society: industrialists, bankers, military officers, judges, teachers, and churchmen. His acerbic political satire led to confrontations with the authorities and criminal prosecution. Grosz emigrated from Germany in January 1933, just prior to Hitler's appointment as chancellor. His autobiography was first published in German in 1946 under the title *A Little Yes and a Big No*. It described the disaffection of left-wing writers and artists from a Weimar establishment that failed to enact lasting reforms. The passages excerpted here depict the chaotic conditions following the First World War and the bitter political conflicts and social divisions that characterized the early years of the Weimar Republic. They also convey the sense of foreboding with which many supporters of the Republic viewed the political developments of the time.

2.8 George Grosz, *Autobiography*

Even the capital of our new German Republic was like a bubbling cauldron. You could not see who was heating the cauldron; you could merely see it merrily bubbling, and you could feel the heat increasing. There were speakers on every street corner and songs of hatred everywhere. Everybody was hated: the Jews, the capitalists, the gentry, the communists, the military, the landlords, the workers, the unemployed, the "Black *Reichswehr*,"[2] the [Allied] control commissions, the politicians, the department stores, and again the Jews. It was a real orgy of incitement, and the Republic was so weak that you hardly took notice of it. All this had to end with an awful crash.

It was a completely negative world, with gaily colored froth on top that many people mistook for the true, the happy Germany before the eruption of the new barbarism. Foreigners who visited us at that time were easily fooled by the apparent light-hearted, whirring fun on the surface, by the nightlife and the so-called freedom and flowering of the arts. But that was really nothing more than froth. Right under that short-lived, lively surface of the shimmering swamp were fratricide and general discord, and regiments were being formed for the final reckoning. Germany seemed to be splitting into two parts that hated each other, as in the saga of the Nibelungs. And we knew all that; or at least we had forebodings.

Postwar Berlin: noise, rumors, shouting, political slogans – what will happen now? Everybody can say whatever he wishes, so everybody talks about riots and strikes, about martial law and impending political takeover. [Matthias] Erzberger, who negotiated and signed the German peace treaty, is assassinated by members of a "patriotic" society. [Karl] Liebknecht is murdered by a soldier, "Red Rosa" Luxemburg is thrown into a canal.[3] Those in power do nothing. [Friedrich] Ebert[4] has his beard trimmed and exchanges his democratic worker's cap for a top-hat; he now looks more like a Chairman of the Board, and dresses accordingly.

---

2   The "Black *Reichswehr*" was a military formation secretly organized by the army (the *Reichswehr*) in the early 1920s to circumvent the limits placed on Germany's military forces by the Versailles Treaty. It enrolled approximately 20,000 volunteers in 1923.

3   Karl Liebknecht (1871–1919) and Rosa Luxemburg (1870–1919), founders of the German Communist Party (KPD) after the war, were killed in captivity during the failed Spartacus uprising in January 1919.

Privy councilor [Otto] Meissner,[5] the Master of Ceremonies of the Republic, tries to fill the shoes of his illustrious predecessors and avoid too many proletarian mistakes. Nasty jokes circulate about him. The little man takes his revenge, as he feels no power above him.

Yes, there was freedom of speech. But people had been used to marching for years, so they simply went on marching, albeit less straight, less smartly than before. For years they had obeyed orders; now they went on marching, but nobody gave orders ... yet. They had to march because they knew they must fall into line. But what they missed was the sharp voice of command. They simply did not know what to do with the freedom for which they had ardently yearned. Everyone had his own political opinion, a mixture of fear, envy, and hope, but what use was that without leadership? The unions? They sufficed no longer. The grumbling became increasingly threatening, finally dangerous. As no one felt guilty – a whole people never does – everyone looked for a scapegoat, and harmless old ditties about Jews suddenly had the odor of a pogrom.

Not only young people marched through the streets. There were many who could not get over the defeat. Others were unable to find their way back into the working world they had left. That world had disappeared or was disappearing, and actual work was hard to find, even by those who were eager to work. Berlin was teeming with the unemployed. To pacify them, they were given games instead of work. Out of every 100 persons, 80 lived from government unemployment benefits.

**Source: *George Grosz: An Autobiography*, trsl. by Nora Hodges
(Berkeley: University of California Press 1998), pp. 149–150**

Euthanasia and eugenics

The eugenic "racial hygiene" movement in Germany, founded in 1905, sought to strengthen the German nation and race in its Darwinian competition with other peoples. It viewed modern medicine and democratic, humanitarian values as contrary to natural selection, because they enabled the weak and the sick to survive. In the aftermath of defeat in the First World War, German nationalists increasingly looked to racial hygiene as a potential source of national regeneration. Already during the war, as shortages increased, mental patients had been allowed to die through reduced diets, and the medical facilities of mental hospitals had been made available to treat the casualties of war. Euthanasia, eugenics, and other measures aimed at purifying the German race entered the public discussion in the Weimar era to a greater degree than had been the case before the war.

In 1920 the lawyer Karl Binding and the psychiatrist Alfred Hoche published the pamphlet, *Permitting the Destruction of Unworthy Life*, excerpts from which are presented in the first selection below. The two authors stressed the high cost of keeping mentally defective and incurably ill patients in public institutions. They viewed involuntary euthanasia, forced sterilization, and other eugenic measures not as a regression to

---

4   Friedrich Ebert (1871–1925), head of the majority Social Democratic Party (SPD), was the first president of the Weimar Republic from 1919 to his death in 1925.
5   Otto Meissner (1880–1953) was a leading civil servant from 1911 to 1945. He continued as chief of the presidential chancellery under Hitler.

barbarism but as progress toward a better world. In the second selection below, an extract from the most widely used textbook on racial heredity in Weimar Germany, the racial publicist Fritz Lenz (1887–1976) deployed biological determinism as a weapon both against the environmentalism of Marxism and the faith in the generative power of purely spiritual values of religious movements. The selection makes clear, however, how much easier it was to reconcile racial biology to the "idealism" of the latter than to the "materialism" of the former. In Hitler's Germany the eugenic movement would gain full governmental and institutional support. Combined with anti-Semitism, the ideology of racial hygiene eventually led to the Holocaust.

2.9a Karl Binding and Alfred Hoche, *Permitting the Destruction of Unworthy Life*, 1920

KARL BINDING, "LEGAL EXPLANATION"

... Are there human lives which have so completely lost the attribute of legal status that their continuation has permanently lost all value, both for the bearer of that life and for society?

Merely asking this question is enough to raise an uneasy feeling in anyone who is accustomed to assessing the value of individual life for the bearer and for the social whole. It hurts him to see how wastefully we handle the most valuable lives (filled with and sustained by the strongest will to live and the greatest vital power), and how much labor power, patience, and capital investment we squander (often totally uselessly) just to preserve lives not worth living – until nature, often pitilessly late, removes the last possibility of their continuation.

Reflect simultaneously on a battlefield strewn with thousands of dead youths, or a mine in which methane gas has trapped hundreds of energetic workers; compare this with our mental hospitals, with their caring for their living inmates. One will be deeply shaken by the strident clash between the sacrifice of the finest flower of humanity in its full measure on the one side, and by the meticulous care shown to existences which are not just absolutely worthless but even of negative value, on the other.

It is impossible to doubt that there are living people to whom death would be a release, and whose death would simultaneously free society and the state from carrying a burden which serves no conceivable purpose, except that of providing an example of the greatest unselfishness. And because there actually are human lives, in whose preservation no rational being could ever again take any interest, the legal order is now confronted by the fateful question: Is it our duty actively to advocate for this life's asocial continuance (particularly by the fullest application of criminal law), or to permit its destruction under specific conditions? One could also state the question legislatively, like this: Does the energetic preservation of such life deserve preference, as an example of the general unassailability of life? Or does permitting its termination, which frees everyone involved, seem the lesser evil? ...

So far as I can see, the people who are to be considered here fall into two primary groups with a third intervening in between.

1   *The first group is composed of those irretrievably lost as a result of illness or injury, who, fully understanding their situation, possess and have somehow expressed their urgent wish for release. ...*

>   *But I cannot find the least reason – legally, socially, ethically, or religiously – not to permit those requested to do so to kill such hopeless cases who urgently demand death; indeed I consider this permission to be simply a duty of legal mercy, a mercy which also asserts itself in many other forms).* ...

2   The second group consists of incurable idiots, no matter whether they are so congenitally or have (like paralytics) become so in the final stage of suffering. *They have the will neither to live nor to die. So, in their case, there is no valid consent to be killed; but, on the other hand, the act encounters no will to live which must be broken.* Their life is completely without purpose, but they do not experience it as unbearable. They are a fearfully heavy burden both for their families and for society. Their death does not create the least loss, except perhaps in the feelings of the mother or a faithful nurse. Since they require extensive care, *they occasion the development of a profession devoted to providing years and decades of care for absolutely valueless lives.* It is undeniable that this is an incredible absurdity and a misuse, for unworthy ends, of life"s powers.

>   *Again, I find no grounds – legally, socially, ethically, or religiously – for not permitting the killing of these people, who are the fearsome counter-image of true humanity, and who arouse horror in nearly everyone who meets them* (naturally, not in everyone)! In times of higher morality – in our times all heroism has been lost – these poor souls would surely have been freed from themselves officially. But who today, in our enervated age, compels himself to acknowledge this necessity, and hence this justification? ...

3   I have mentioned a middle group, and *I find it in those mentally sound people who, through some event like a very severe, doubtlessly fatal wound, have become unconscious and who, if they should ever again rouse from their comatose state, would waken to nameless suffering.* ...

>   I do not believe that a standard procedure can be created for managing this group of killings. Cases will occur in which killing seems actually fully justified; but it can also happen that the agent, in the belief that he acted correctly, acted precipitously. Then he would never be guilty of premeditated murder but rather of negligent manslaughter. The possibility must be left open of letting killings which are later recognized as having been unjustified go unpunished. ...

DR. ALFRED HOCHE, "MEDICAL EXPLANATION"

... Thus, economically speaking, these same *complete idiots*, who most perfectly fulfill all the criteria for complete mental death, are also the *ones whose existence weighs most heavily on the community.*

In part, this burden is financial and can be readily calculated by inventorying annual institutional budgets. I have allowed myself to take up the task of collecting materials bearing on this question by surveying all relevant German institutions, and thereby I have discovered that the average yearly (per head) cost for maintaining idiots has till now been thirteen hundred marks. If we calculate the total number of idiots presently cared for in German institutions, we arrive at a rough estimate of twenty to thirty thousand. If we assume an average life expectancy of fifty years for individual cases, it is easy to estimate what *incredible capital* is withdrawn from the nation's wealth for food, clothing, and heating – for an unproductive purpose.

And this still does not represent the real burden by any means.

The institutions which provide care for idiots are unavailable for other purposes. To the extent that private institutions are involved in such care, we must calculate the return on our investment. A caretaking staff of many thousands must be withdrawn from beneficial work for this totally fruitless endeavor. It is painful to think that whole generations of caretakers grow old next to these empty human shells, not a few of whom live seventy years or more.

In the prosperous times of the past, the question of whether one could justify making all necessary provision for such dead-weight existences was not pressing. But now things have changed, and we must take it up seriously. Our situation resembles that of participants in a difficult expedition: the greatest possible fitness of every one is the inescapable condition of the endeavor's success, and there is no room for half-strength, quarter-strength, or eighth-strength members. For a long time, the task for us Germans will be the most highly intensified integration of all possibilities – the liberation of every available power for productive ends. Fulfilling this task is opposed by the modern efforts to maintain (as much as possible) every kind of weakling and to devote care and protection to all those who (even if they are certainly not mentally dead) are constitutionally less valuable elements. These efforts have their particular importance through the fact that, so far, preventing these defective people from *reproducing* has not been possible and has not even been seriously attempted. ...

The next issue to explore is whether the selection of these lives, which have *finally* become worthless for the individual and for society, can be accomplished with such certainty that mistakes and errors can be *excluded*.

This concern can only arise among lay people. For physicians, there is not the slightest question that this selection can be carried out with one hundred percent certainty and, indeed, with a much higher degree of certainty than can be found in deciding about the mental health or illness of convicted criminals.

For physicians, there are many indisputable, scientifically established criteria by which the *impossibility of recovery* for mentally dead people can be recognized. This is even truer since the condition of mental death beginning in earliest youth is of the first importance for our discussion.

Naturally, no doctor would conclude with certainty that a two- or three-year-old was suffering permanent mental death. But, *even in childhood*, the moment comes when this prediction can be made without doubt ...

Goethe originated the model for how important human questions evolve. He saw them as spiral. The core of this model is the fact that at regular intervals a spiral line rising in a particular direction perpetually returns to the *same position* relative to the axis crossing it but *each time a step higher*.

Eventually, this image will be apparent even in connection with the cultural question we have been discussing. There was a time, now considered barbaric, in which eliminating those who were born unfit for life, or who later became so, was taken for granted. Then came the phase, continuing into the present, in which, finally, preserving every existence, no matter how worthless, stood as the highest moral value. A new age will arrive – operating with a higher morality and with great sacrifice – which will actually give up the requirements of an exaggerated humanism and overvaluation of mere existence. I know that, in general, these opinions will not even be received with understanding, let alone agreement. But this prospect should not keep anyone from speaking out, particularly a person who, after more than an average lifetime of serving humanity's medical needs, has earned the right to be heard on the general problems of humanity.

Source: Karl Binding and Alfred Hoche, *Permitting the Destruction of Unworthy Life: Its Extent and Form*, trsl. by Walter E. Wright and Patrick G. Derr, in *Issues in Law and Medicine*, VIII, 2 (1992), 246–50, 260–61, 264–5

2.9b Fritz Lenz, "Psychological Differences Between the Leading Races of Mankind," 1921

... *Of course the heredity factors of race are not the only causes of great cultural achievements. All civilization, all achievement, is the outcome of a collaboration of racial endowments and environment.* Racial biologists must guard against being as one-sided as are those who preach the supreme importance of environment. For a long time, now, practical persons have been concerned to know how the differences between human beings and the differences between civilizations have arisen. Rousseau believed that the decisive cause was to be found in differences in private property. This view has secured its clearest and most developed expression in what is known as the "materialist conception (or interpretation) of history" of Karl Marx and his followers, which still has numerous adherents today. In contraposition to this "materialist" doctrine there has, likewise since the eighteenth century, come into vogue the "idealist" or "spiritualist" conception or interpretation, according to which spiritual or mental achievements and ideals are the real motive forces of civilization. But the champions of the "idealist" doctrine no less than the champions of the "materialist" doctrine overlook or positively deny that race is of any importance to civilization. Although the "materialists" and the "idealists" constitute rival factions, engaged in fierce mutual conflict, they are in truth warring brethren, being children of one father, Lamarck.[6] "Materialism" is substantially identical with that variety of Lamarckism which is known as "mechano-Lamarckism." According to this doctrine, all the differences between living beings, their adaptation and their evolution, are the outcome of the "direct influence" of environment. "Idealism," in its turn, in great measure coincides with "psycho-Lamarckism," a doctrine which ascribes the evolution of living creatures to mental forces, proclaiming that "the mind makes the body." The "materialists" tell us that the main differences consist in the differences between the educated and the uneducated. But the champions of these conflicting views regard the differences between human beings as bridgeable and eradicable. The "materialists" (the Marxists) teach that as soon as private property has been abolished, and as soon as the economic differences between human beings have disappeared, all persons will become good and noble; the "idealists" dream of a general ennoblement of the human race by the inward appropriation of spiritual ideals, and especially, of the idealist doctrine. Biologically, these two doctrines are equally untenable. The inequalities among human beings are mainly dependent upon the hereditary equipment, and this cannot be transformed in any simple way either by material or by spiritual influences. In the individual it cannot be changed at all, and in the race it can only be changed by selection. That contention, which shatters illusions, is regarded by the warring brethren as pessimistic, and they therefore join forces and make common cause against the biologists. The "idealists" declare that the biological view is "materialistic," which it is not; and the "materialists" often stigmatize it as high-flown idealism, which equally it is not. The modern biological outlook is fundamentally new, is something to which the old classifications and catchwords are inapplicable; and in its essential nature it is not pessimistic, for it, and it alone, points the way towards the renovation and stable advance of mankind and human civilization.

---

6   The French naturalist Jean Baptiste de Lamarck (1744–1829) believed that acquired characteristics could be inherited by future generations. Charles Darwin (1809–82) later discovered that evolution proceeds by natural selection, whereby those organisms most successful in adapting to their environment enjoy the reproductive success necessary to pass on their traits to their offspring.

The individualist conception of civilization is only a variety of the idealist. Inasmuch as the individualists place great individuals in the foreground, they recognize, indeed, that civilization has not been simply created by the masses, and also that it has not been created by economic conditions alone; but they usually overlook the fact that the creative energy of great individuals is the expression of their hereditary equipment, is the outcome of race.

An organic conception of civilization must, indeed, give due weight to the conditions which are so one-sidedly emphasized by the "materialists," on the one hand, and the "idealists," on the other; but it must, as against materialists and idealists alike, insist that race, or in more general terms the hereditary equipment, is the first and indispensable condition of all civilization. The Nordic thinker Kant, to whom the modern "idealists" especially appeal, was himself careful to avoid overestimating the importance of environmental influences, insisting that "the inborn character is formed by the mingling of the blood in man, and the acquired and artificial character is only the outcome thereof." The recognition that race is the substratum of all civilization must not, however, lead any one to feel that membership in a superior race is a sort of comfortable couch on which he can go to sleep. For that reason I must not conclude my account of the mental peculiarities of the races without expressly insisting that the biological heritage of the mind is no more imperishable than the biological heritage of the body. If we continue to squander that biological mental heritage as we have been squandering it during the last few decades, it will not be many generations before we cease to be the superiors of the Mongols. Our ethnological studies must lead us, not to arrogance, but to action – to eugenics.

**Source: Erwin Baur, Eugen Fischer, and Fritz Lenz, _Human Heredity_,
trsl. by Eden and Cedar Paul (New York: Macmillan, 1931), pp. 697–9**

The Conservative Revolution

To understand why Hitler's Third Reich gained the support of so many non-Jewish German intellectuals, some familiarity with the so-called "Conservative Revolution" is indispensable. This post-war intellectual movement echoed many of the ideas of the pre-war nationalist right. The conservative intellectuals of the 1920s were aware, however, that there was no turning back the clock to the failed monarchy of the past. Appalled by German defeat in the war and by the liberal and social democratic "November Revolution," right-wing publicists called not for an end to revolution but for its redirection into conservative and nationalist channels. A revolutionary upheaval was needed to end Germany's subservience to Western values and institutions and to establish a distinctly German socialism – a solidarity based on common membership in the German _Volk_ or race.

The following selections are taken from what was perhaps the single most important book of the Conservative Revolution: _The Third Reich_ by Arthur Moeller van den Bruck (1876–1925). First published in 1923, it was reissued in 1930 and exercised considerable influence as the movement for a "German revolution" gained strength. In the early stages of the Nazi regime, Moeller as well as Chamberlain and other radical nationalists were celebrated as "heralds of the Third Reich." Moeller shared with Chamberlain the conviction that German idealist culture was far superior to shallow Western (and Jewish) materialism.

The concept of a "Third Reich" had roots in medieval mysticism, but it also referred to the hoped-for successor regime to the Holy Roman Empire and the Bismarckian-

Wilhelminian Reich. The number three was particularly valued in the mystical tradition for its symbolic conciliation of opposites. Thus the Third Reich was envisioned as a unified, distinctively German national community in which the partisan divisions of Western parliamentarism, liberal individualism, and class-based socialism had been overcome.

Although the Conservative Revolution was primarily an intellectual movement, their exhortation to Germans not to lose themselves in philosophical dreams but to realize their dreams through politics played into Nazi hands. On the one hand conservative intellectuals celebrated the apolitical nature of German history, culture, and character; on the other hand, they worried that this typically German (and conservative) aversion to politics gave a fatal advantage to the supposedly politicized and partisan left. Hence they were ready to support a movement like National Socialism that was ready, if necessary, to achieve nationalist and conservative objectives by the unavoidably ruthless means of political struggle. There was much overlap in the programs of National Socialism and the Conservative Revolution, not least the hope of solving the problem of class divisions in the realm of consciousness rather than, as communists and socialists advocated, in material reality. Embittered by the failure of the Hitler–Ludendorff putsch (see Doc. 2.13) and the apparent stabilization of the Weimar regime, Moeller committed suicide in 1925.

2.10 Arthur Moeller van den Bruck, *Germany's Third Empire*, 1923

PREFATORY LETTER

Instead of government by party we offer the ideal of the THIRD EMPIRE. It is an old German conception and a great one. It arose when our First Empire fell; it was early quickened by the thought of a millennium; but its underlying thought has always been a future which should be not the end of all things but the dawn of a German Age in which the German People would for the first time fulfill their destiny on earth.

In the years that followed the collapse of our Second Empire, we have had experience of Germans; we have seen that the nation's worst enemy is herself: her trustfulness, her casualness, her credulity, her inborn, fate-fraught, apparently unshakable, optimism. The German people were scarcely defeated – as never a people was defeated before in history – than the mood asserted itself: "We shall come up again all right!" We heard German fools saying: "We have no fears for Germany!" We saw German dreamers nod their heads in assent: "Nothing can happen to me!"

We must be careful to remember that the thought of the Third Empire is a philosophical idea; that the conception which the words "Third Empire" arouse – and the book that bears the title – are misty, indeterminate, charged with feeling; not of this world but of the next. Germans are only too prone to abandon themselves to self-deception. The thought of a THIRD EMPIRE might well be the most fatal of all the illusions to which they have ever yielded; it would be thoroughly German if they contented themselves with day-dreaming about it. Germany might perish of her Third Empire dream.

Let us be perfectly explicit: the thought of the Third Empire – to which we must cling as our last and highest philosophy – can only bear fruit if it is translated into concrete reality. It must quit the world of dreams and step into the political world. It must be as realist as the problem of our constitutional and national life; it must be as skeptical and pessimistic as beseems the times.

There are Germans who assure us that the Empire which rose out of the ruins on the Ninth of November is already the Third Empire, democratic, republican, logically complete.[7] These are our opportunists and eudaemonists. There are other Germans who confess their disappointment but trust to the "reasonableness" of history. These are our rationalists and pacifists. They all draw their conclusions from the premises of their party-political or utopian wishes, but not from the premises of the reality which surrounds us. They will not realize that we are a fettered and maltreated nation, perhaps on the very verge of dissolution. Our reality implies the triumph of all the nations of the earth over the German nation; the primacy in our country of parliamentarism after the western model – and party rule. If the THIRD EMPIRE is to put an end to strife it will not be born in a peace of philosophic dreaming. The THIRD EMPIRE will be an empire of organization in the midst of European chaos. The occupation of the Ruhr and its consequences worked a change in the minds of men.[8] It was the first thing that made the nation think. It opened up the possibility of liberation for a betrayed people. It seemed about to put an end to the "policy of fulfillment" which had been merely party politics disguised as foreign policy. It threw us back on our own power of decision. It restored our will. Parliamentarism has become an institution of our public life, whose chief function would appear to be – in the name of the people – to enfeeble all political demands and all national passions.

When the Revolution overwhelmed the War, burying all prospects and all hopes, we asked ourselves the inner meaning of these events. Amidst all the insanity we found a meaning in the thought that the German nation would be driven into becoming politically-minded: now, at last, belatedly.

We said to ourselves then that this war was going to be our education.

Today we ask in despair: Has it, in fact, been so?

In bitterness we venture to hope: It will prove to have been so. ...

1. REVOLUTIONARY

... The revolutionaries of 1918 lost the War of 1914 because their revolution was not a German revolution. They thought they had done all that was required of them when they imitated what the West had done before. They were far indeed from grasping, as the Russian revolutionaries had done – more and more clearly with each passing year – that a people's revolution must be a national revolution, and acting consistently with this in mind.

The German revolutionaries made the German Revolution a Western-parliamentary one, a constitutional and political revolution on the English and French model. But centuries have passed since 1689 and 1789. Meantime the West has accustomed itself to liberalism. Liberalism has taught the West to turn its principles into tactics to deceive the people. The West dubs this "democracy," though it has become evident enough how ill men thrive on a political diet of Liberty, Equality, and Fraternity.

---

7   9 November 1918, two days before the armistice, was the date of the Kaiser's abdication and the establishment of the republic.

8   French and Belgian troops occupied the industrial area of the Ruhr to collect overdue reparations payments. The outrage of nationalists against the republican government's policy of "fulfillment" (instead of resistance) formed the context of Hitler's failed putsch attempt on 9 November 1923 (see Doc. 2.13).

Thus it came about that the German Revolution developed into a liberal revolution. The revolutionaries of 1918 called themselves socialists, yet they did not seek to prevent this development.

Socialism which grew up beneath and alongside liberalism, demands justice. But the German revolutionaries' fateful revolution did not realize justice between man and man, and had to look on while justice between nations was trampled under foot. We shall see that the fault lay in their socialism itself, which had always taken heed of classes, but never of nations. There can be no justice for men if there is not justice for nations first. For men can only live also.

The problems of socialism remain with us. They include the problem of a new world order which shall supersede the institutions of the nineteenth and twentieth centuries: democracy, liberalism, and parliamentarism, in an age of technical efficiency, of over-population, an age in which all participants lost the War.

We can only hope to solve this problem for Germany from a German starting-point, and perhaps in so doing we shall solve it also for Central Europe and the young states of Eastern Europe. If we cannot abjure our regrettable habit of thinking of the advantage of other nations before our own, we can take comfort in the thought that the solutions we arrive at will certainly benefit these other countries. But we must be prepared to find that there will be nations in the west who will offer the most strenuous opposition to any solution propounded by Germany, who will dispute with us every inch of the ground. In these intellectual matters, as in all others, we must be prepared to contest the ground. The revolutionary of today is the conservative of tomorrow. Let us not push the revolution further, but let us develop the ideas which were dormant in the revolution. Let us combine revolutionary and conservative ideas till we attain a set of conditions under which we can hope to live again.

Let us win the revolution!

What does that imply?

The revolution set the seal on our collapse; let it set the seal on our resurrection.

What does that imply?

We had reached a point in our history when a detour and a new path were necessary. The war was such a detour, so was the collapse which ended the war. Let the revolution prove to have been the opening up of a new path.

What does that imply?

There were problems in our history which would never have been soluble without a war and without a revolution. Let us make the war and the revolution the means of solving them. ...

III. LIBERAL

... Liberalism has undermined civilization, has destroyed religions, has ruined nations. Primitive peoples know no liberalism. The world for them is a simple place where one man shares with another. Instinctively they conceive existence as a struggle in which all those who belong in any way to one group must defend themselves against those who threaten them.

Great states have always held liberalism in check. When a great individual arose amongst them who gave the course of their history a new direction, they have been able to incorporate him into their tradition, to make his achievements contribute to their continuity.

Nations who had ceased to feel themselves a people, who had lost the state-instinct, gave liberalism its opportunity. The masses allowed an upper crust to form on the surface of the nation. Not the old natural aristocracy whose example had created the state; but a secondary stratum, a dangerous, irresponsible, ruthless, intermediate stratum which had thrust itself between. The result was the rule of a clique united only by self-interest who liked to style themselves the pick of the population, to conceal the fact that they consisted of immigrants and *nouveaux riches*, of freedmen and upstarts. They did not care whether their arrogance and new-won privilege was decked out with the conceptions of feudal or of radical ideology, though they preferred a delicate suggestion of aristocracy. But they found it most effective and successful to style themselves as democrats.

Liberalism was the ruin of Greece. The decay of Hellenic freedom was preceded by the rise of the liberal. He was begotten of Greek "enlightenment." From the philosophers' theory of the atom, the sophist drew the inference of the individual. Protagoras, the Sophist, was the founder of individualism and also the apostle of relativity. He proclaimed that: "Opposite propositions are equally true." Nothing immoral was intended. He meant that there are no general but only particular truths: according to the standpoint of the perceiver. But what happens when the same man has two standpoints? When he is ready to shift his standpoint as his advantage may dictate? This same Protagoras proclaimed that rhetoric could make the weaker case victorious. Still nothing immoral was intended. He meant that the better cause was sometimes the weaker and should then be helped to victory. But the practice soon arose of using rhetoric to make the worse cause victorious. It is no accident that the sophists were the first Greek philosophers to accept pay, and were the most highly paid. A materialist outlook leads always to a materialist mode of thought. This is very human: but true.

All this was hailed as progress: but it spelled decay. The same process continues: the disciples of reason, the apostles of enlightenment, the heralds of progress are usually in the first generation great idealists, high-principled men, convinced of the importance of their discoveries and of the benefit these confer on man. But no later than the second generation the peculiar and unholy connection betrays itself which exists between materialist philosophy and nihilist interpretation. As at the touch of a conjuror's wand the scientific theory of the atom reduces society to atoms …

V. PROLETARIAN

… The proletarian is a proletarian by his own desire.

It is not the machine, it is not the mechanization of industry, it is not the dependence of wages on capitalist production that makes a man a proletarian; it is the proletarian consciousness.

There was an assembly during the revolutionary year of 1919. In justification of the revolution and its prospects a proletarian contended that there are far more proletarians in Germany than is commonly supposed. "Ninety out of every hundred of us," he cried, "are proletarians!" Another interrupted: "But they don't want to be!" This contradiction sounds the death knell of the proletarian movement. There is a point after which it can gain no more recruits: there are people who *will not* be proletarians. The man who will not, supplies an answer to the question: Who is, and who is not, a proletarian?

The proletarian's philosophy of life is simple. Therein lies his strength. But his philosophy is also narrow, hidebound, elementary; it is inadequate, inexperienced, untried; it is without the idea of growth, without feeling for organization, without knowledge of the interrelationships of things. Therein lies its weakness, its impotence, and its hopelessness. The spell which binds the proletarian is the spell of birth. As men, as prehistoric men, if you like, we were all originally proletarians, who sat about naked on the bare ground. But a differentiation soon set in; inborn superiority asserted itself, and was inherited as outward privilege. The man who was not sufficiently developed to fit into this social structure as it developed remained at the bottom; he did not rise, he sank.

He was the proletarian. Proletarians multiplied and sought to assert themselves and to claim a share in the general progress. But only those succeeded in obtaining a share who wished to cease being proletarians. The proletariat is what remains at the bottom. The proletarian of today will succeed in obtaining such a share provided he does not shut himself out from the social organization, from the national organization; but he will succeed only in his children. The masses lift themselves by generations. This uplift is selection. The inertia of the mass remains. There always remains a proletariat. Socialism makes an attempt to hasten the raising process. Behind the fourth estate the fifth is seen advancing, dour and determined, and behind that the sixth, which is perhaps no longer a single enslaved class, but a whole nation which has been enslaved – with flags whose colors no man knows. There is always a proletariat.

Meanwhile the man who will not be a proletarian is differentiated from the other, by his inherited and acquired values which give him greater intellectual mobility and a wider outlook. The proletariat has not yet taken its share in the values which our forefathers bequeathed us and which distinguish more educated, more conscious men. These values existed before the proletariat came into a world it did not understand. The proletariat has no ancestors and no experience. It took over theories which uprooted idealists of other classes formulated to suit it. What is the past? It is not anything to eat! The proletariat sees the present only. According to what it feels to be its needs, it dreams of a more just future. It does not feel itself part of a community, but a body misused by society. It has its origin in overpopulation and thinks of itself as a superfluous, outcast section of humanity for whom there is no room on earth. So the proletarian demands a share not of the values of which he knows nothing – but of the goods which he sees in the possession of more privileged persons, of which he imagines himself to have been the creator.

The proletarian sees only his own, immediate, proletarian world; he is oblivious of the surrounding world which encompasses his and on which his is founded. His thought is keen – but short. He has no tradition of thinking. The more gifted man, who takes a share in the spiritual and intellectual values of a wider community, imbibes from these the strength to rise above class distinction, to extricate himself from the masses: To become the non-proletarian. The proletarian has no assurance that his sons or his sons' sons will remain proletarians; they may in the meantime have learned to find a place in the structure of society and be no longer in their own eyes proletarians. It is true that a revolution may hasten this process. In a revolution the will of the proletariat is directed to force, not power; but force is ephemeral, while power is enduring. Ultimately from a revolution there arises the man who is a proletarian and no conservative and who yet is constrained to act as a conservative: to conserve – in order to survive.

Creative conservatism is more vital in the political field than in any other. The proletariat had no political tradition. Its school had been the political party. The proletarian thinks only of the moment, he is a primitive and a materialist. But since no man can live wholly in the present, since even the most miserable of human beings yearns for some hope, the proletarian, with naive egotism, sees the future as a utopia specially reserved for him. Today a terrible reality is bringing home to him that he is living in a present of his own creation in which things, far from growing better, are growing every moment worse – and this because there were credulous people who imagined that all would now be well.

The conservative does not confine his thinking to economics, he takes account of the impulses and passions, the aims and ideals, which have gone to the making of history. His thought is not bounded in time. From all corners of the world and from all periods of history he garners the lessons which throw light on the present sufferings of his own people. The proletarian will only find salvation when he can rise to this supra-economic thought and concerns himself not with building up a proletarian world, but with finding a niche for the proletariat in the historic world.

The proletariat has a right to a recognized and stable position in a society dependent on industrial enterprise and proletarian labor, but it has no right to the arrogant position of power which the socialist parties would have liked to seize for it during the revolutionary upheaval. The more modest position is of vastly greater value; it is more genuine, justified and enduring.

All the world over, proletarian thought is taking on a more intellectual and spiritual color. In proportion as it does so, the proletarian ceases to be a proletarian. The working classes are taking their place as a part of the nation. This movement is contemporaneous with a conservative counter-movement. It is beginning to dawn on the working classes of the oppressed and unjustly-treated nations, that the social problem will never be solved until the national problem is solved, until the peoples have regained their freedom.

It is still possible that our first revolution may be followed by a second: that a communist revolution will follow in the social democrat revolution; a world revolution on the state revolution. But this second revolution would only precipitate the conservative counter-movement which would try to neutralize the disintegration and restore the cohesion necessary to the life of men and peoples unless indeed the complete dissolution of European civilization lies ahead: which we cannot know, but for which we must be prepared.

The man who is prepared for all eventualities is the conservative. It is not his role to despair when others despair; he is there to stand the test when others fail.

The conservative is always prepared to make a new beginning. ...

THE THIRD EMPIRE

... German nationalism is the champion of the Final Empire: ever promised, never fulfilled.

It is the peculiar prerogative of the German people for which other peoples vie with us. In the World War the peoples fought against the Empire-for-the-sake-of-the-empire, the Empire-for-the-sake-of-world-hegemony, in which we claimed our very material share. Each of these nations wanted an empire of its own: a sphere and empire of Latin or Anglo-Saxon or Pan-Slav thought. They annihilated our material empire. They still tremble before its political shadow.

But they had to leave our Empire standing. There is only ONE EMPIRE, as there is only ONE CHURCH. Anything else that claims the title may be a state or a community or a sect. There exists only THE EMPIRE.

German nationalism fights for the possible Empire. The German nationalist today as a German remains for ever a mystic; as a politician he has turned skeptic.

He knows that nations can only realize the idea committed to their charge in proportion as they maintain themselves and assert themselves in history.

The German nationalist is in no danger of falling under the spell of ideology for the sake of ideology. He sees through the humbug of the fine words with which the peoples who conquered us ascribed a world mission to themselves. He knows that within the radius of these peoples' civilization, which they so complacently describe as Western, humanity has not risen but has sunk.

In the midst of this sinking world, which is the victorious world of today, the German seeks his salvation. He seeks to preserve those imperishable values, which are imperishable in their own right. He seeks to secure their permanence in the world by recapturing the rank to which their defenders are entitled. At the same time he is fighting for the cause of Europe, for every European influence that radiates from Germany as the center of Europe.

We are not thinking of the Europe of today which is too contemptible to have any value. We are thinking of the Europe of yesterday and whatever thereof may be salvaged for tomorrow. We are thinking of the Germany of all time, the Germany of a two-thousand-year past, the Germany of an eternal present which dwells in the spirit, but must be secured in reality and can only so be politically secured.

The ape and tiger in man are threatening. The shadow of Africa falls across Europe. It is our task to be guardians on the threshold of values.

Source: Arthur Moeller van den Bruck, *Germany's Third Empire*, trsl. by E. O. Lorimer (New York: Howard Fertig, 1971), pp. 13–15, 37–8, 91–2, 161–5, 263–4

Hyperinflation, 1923

In this excerpt from Stefan Zweig's 1943 autobiography, the Austrian author describes his experience of the great inflation in Germany in 1923. Inflation had plagued the German economy because of pent-up consumer demand and reparations payments in kind ever since the end of the First World War, but it reached unprecedented proportions in the summer of 1923. In January of that year the French occupied the Ruhr industrial region to enforce German reparations shipments. The German government countered by calling on public employees to refuse to cooperate with the French. To finance this passive resistance the government resorted to printing currency that soon led to galloping inflation. The exchange rate went from 7.43 marks to the dollar in November 1918 to 7,589 marks to the dollar at the end of 1922. It declined precipitously in 1923 and reached a low of 4.2 trillion to one in November, the month that Hitler launched his "Beer Hall Putsch." By that time the new government under Gustav Stresemann (1878–1929) had called a halt to passive resistance. The currency was stabilized with international cooperation, and after the defeat of the Hitler Putsch (Doc. 2.13) the Weimar Republic entered a temporary phase of relative stability that lasted until the onset of the Great Depression in 1930.

The hyperinflation of 1923, however, left lasting scars. It impoverished millions of ordinary Germans with savings accounts while enriching businesses and wealthier people who held their assets in real property. The memory of this trauma in the public consciousness contributed to the policies that would later intensify the *deflation* of the 1930s. Because holders of foreign currency enjoyed privileges unavailable to ordinary Germans, the inflation undoubtedly exacerbated xenophobia as well. Most damaging of all were its long-term political effects. It further undermined public confidence in liberal institutions and gave added legitimacy to anti-republican forces. While Hitler failed to gain power in the Great Inflation, memories of its devastating impact on German society contributed to his popular support in the Great Depression.

2.11 Stefan Zweig, *The World of Yesterday*

Abruptly the mark plunged down, never to stop until it had reached the fantastic figures of madness, the millions, the billions and trillions. Now the real witches' sabbath of inflation started, against which our Austrian inflation with its absurd enough ratio of 15,000 old to 1 of new currency had been shabby child's play. To describe it in detail, with its incredibilities, would take a whole book and to readers of today it would seem like a fairy tale. I have known days when I had to pay fifty thousand marks for a newspaper in the morning and a hundred thousand in the evening; whoever had foreign currency to exchange did so from hour to hour, because at four o'clock he would get a better rate than at three, and at five o'clock he would get much more than he had got an hour earlier. For instance, I sent a manuscript to my publisher on which I had worked for a year; to be on the safe side I asked for an advance payment of royalties on ten thousand copies. By the time the check was deposited, it hardly paid the postage I had put on the parcel a week before; on street cars one paid in millions, trucks carried the paper money from the Reichsbank to the other banks, and a fortnight later one found hundred thousand mark notes in the gutter; a beggar had thrown them away contemptuously. A pair of shoe laces cost more than a shoe had once cost; no, more than a fashionable shoe store with two thousand pairs of shoes had cost before; to repair a broken window cost more than the whole house had formerly cost, a book more than the printer's shop with a hundred presses. For a hundred dollars one could buy rows of six-story houses on the Kurfürstendamm, and factories were to be had for the old equivalent of a wheel-barrow. Some adolescent boys who had found a case of soap forgotten in the harbor disported themselves for months in cars and lived like kings, selling a cake every day, while their parents, formerly well-to-do, slunk about like beggars. Messenger boys established foreign exchange businesses and speculated in currencies of all lands. Towering over all of them was the gigantic figure of the super-profiteer Stinnes.[9] Expanding his credit and in thus exploiting the mark he bought whatever was for sale, coal mines and ships, factories and stocks, castles and country estates, actually for nothing because every payment, every promise became equal to naught. Soon a quarter of Germany was in his hands, and perversely, the masses, who in Germany always become intoxicated at a success that they can see with their eyes, cheered him as a genius. The unemployed stood around by the thousands and shook their fists at the profiteers and foreigners in their luxurious cars who bought whole rows of streets like a box of matches; everyone who could read and write traded, speculated, and profited and had a secret sense that they were deceiving themselves and were being deceived by a hidden force which brought about this chaos deliberately in order to liberate the State from its debts and obligations.

Source: Stefan Zweig, *The World of Yesterday*, trsl. by Helmut Ripperger
(New York: Viking Press, 1943), pp. 311–313. Used by permission of Viking Penguin,
a division of Penguin Putnam, Inc. From the original German text,
(c) 1976 Williams Verlag AG, Zurich/Atrium Press Ltd, London

9   Hugo Stinnes (1870–1924) was an industrialist who took advantage of the inflationary situation to build what was for a time the largest industrial conglomerate in Germany.

Monarchist support for Hitler

The following letter from the prominent racial theorist and Wagnerian publicist, Houston Stewart Chamberlain (see Docs.1.4 and 1.5), to the aspiring *völkisch* politician Adolf Hitler was sent only a month before Hitler launched his "Beer Hall Putsch" on 9 November 1923. Hitler had paid his respects to the ailing Chamberlain in Bayreuth on 6 October 1923. Chamberlain personified the transition that so many conservatives made from monarchism to fascism after the First World War. His letter gives some indication of the profound effect that Hitler was capable of exercising on like-minded people. It also attests to Hitler's success in appearing to stand above politics as the unifier of his people. Encouragement of the kind he received from Chamberlain and other monarchists may well have helped to persuade Hitler that his putsch attempt would succeed.

2.12 Houston Stewart Chamberlain, Letter to Hitler, 7 October 1923

Most respected and dear Herr Hitler,

You have every right not to expect this surprise attack, since you have seen with your own eyes how difficult it is for me to speak. But I cannot resist the urge to say a few words to you. I regard this as an entirely unilateral act, however – i.e. I do not expect an answer from you.

I have been thinking why it should have been you of all people – you who are so successful at awakening people from their sleep and lethargy – who recently gave me a longer and more refreshing sleep than I have had since that fateful day in August 1914 when I was smitten with this treacherous illness. Now I believe I understand that precisely this is the essence of your being: the true awakener is simultaneously the bestower of peace.

You are not at all, as you were described to me, a fanatic. I would rather describe you as the direct opposite of a fanatic. The fanatic makes people into hotheads, you warm people's hearts. The fanatic wants to talk people into something, you want to convince them, only to convince them – and that is why you succeed. In fact, I would also describe you as the opposite of a politician – in the ordinary sense of the word – for the root of all politics is membership in a party, whereas in your case all parties disappear, devoured by the heat of your love for the fatherland. It was, in my opinion, the misfortune of our great Bismarck, that he ... became a little too involved in politics. May you be spared this lot! ...

I constantly ask myself whether the lack of political instinct of which the German is so widely accused may not be a symptom of a much deeper talent for state-building. At any rate the German's organizational talent is unsurpassed (see Kiaochow!)[10] and his scientific ability is second to none: it is on this that I have based my hopes in my essay *Political Ideals*. It should be the ideal of politics to have *none*. But this non-politics would have to be frankly admitted and forced upon the world through the exercise of power. Nothing will be achieved so long as the parliamentary system obtains; for this the Germans have, God knows, not a spark of talent! I regard its continued existence as the greatest misfortune; it can lead only again and again into the mire and ruin all plans for restoring the health and the prestige of the fatherland.

However, this is a digression, for I only wanted to speak of you. That you gave me peace is connected very much with your eyes and the motions of your hands. Your eyes seize people

---

10   The reference is to the German naval colony of Kiaochow in China, which Germany was forced to surrender after the First World War.

and hold them fast, as if with hands, and you have the singular habit of addressing yourself to one particular member of your audience at any one moment – I noticed this to be completely characteristic. As for your hands, they are so expressive in their movements that they are like eyes in this respect. It is hardly surprising that a man like that can give peace to a poor suffering spirit!

Especially when he is dedicated to the service of the fatherland.

My faith in Germandom has not wavered for a moment, though my hopes were – I confess – at a low ebb. With one stroke you have transformed the state of my soul. That Germany, in the hour of her greatest need, brings forth a Hitler – that is proof of her vitality ... that the magnificent Ludendorff openly supports you and your movement: What wonderful confirmation!

I could go untroubled to sleep, and there was no need for me to have woken up. May God protect you!

Source: Houston Stewart Chamberlain, *Briefe, 1882–1924, und Briefwechsel mit Kaiser Wilhelm II*, Vol. I (Munich: F. Bruckmann, 1928), pp. 124–6.
[Röhl, *From Bismarck to Hitler*, pp. 52–3]

The Beer Hall Putsch, 1923

The purpose of Hitler's failed "Beer Hall Putsch" in Munich on 8 and 9 November 1923 was to overthrow the Weimar Constitution and replace it with an authoritarian regime. Modelling his coup attempt on Mussolini's "March on Rome" of the year before, a successful bluff, Hitler thought he could count on the support of German conservatives, especially the dictatorial ruler of the state of Bavaria, Gustav von Kahr (1862–1934). Against the wishes of the national government in Berlin, Kahr had not only permitted but encouraged the activities of the radical right in Bavaria. Such prominent conservatives as General Erich Ludendorff (1865–1937), the chief of staff of the German Army in the First World War, were to have leading roles in the government Hitler hoped to establish. Kahr thought better of his alliance with Hitler, however, and ordered the Munich police to suppress the putsch attempt. In the ensuing shoot-out sixteen Nazis and three policemen were killed. Although Kahr had no sympathy for the Weimar system, he was reluctant to support an obviously illegal venture that did not command full army support. Hitler had not yet gained the millions of followers that would make him so indispensable to conservatives ten years hence. Kahr became a victim of Hitler's revenge in the "blood purge" of 30 June 1934 (see Doc. 3.21).

The following selection is an extract from Hitler's testimony at his trial. Posing as an unselfish patriot, he insisted that an attempt to overthrow a government that had signed the armistice in November 1918 and the Versailles Treaty in 1919 could never be considered treason. He pointed out that the highest Bavarian officials had originally been part of the conspiracy. He justified his putsch attempt by the danger of the spread of Marxism. Hitler understood that his appeal to conservatives lay in his willingness to use ruthless measures against the left. He knew that he could count on the sympathy of the court, which gave him the minimum penalty allowed by law. Sentenced to five years, he was released after serving only eight months. In prison he wrote his book, *Mein Kampf*. After his release he resolved to seek power legally and constitutionally in order to avoid a similar debacle in the future.

2.13 Hitler's speech in his own defense, 1924

Hitler: May it please the Court!

... Replacing the person by the cipher, energy by mass, the Marxist movement is destroying the foundation of all human cultural life. Wherever this movement breaks through, it must destroy human culture. The future of Germany means: destruction of Marxism. Either Marxism poisons the people, their Germany is ruined, or the poison is going to be eliminated – then Germany can recover again, not before that. For us, Germany will be saved on the day on which the last Marxist has either been converted or broken ...

We will fight spiritually for one who is willing to fight with the weapons of the spirit; we have the fist for the one who is willing to fight with the fist.

When we recognized that the territory of the Ruhr would be lost, our movement arrived at a big point of discord with the bourgeois world. The National Socialist movement recognized clearly that the territory of the Ruhr would be lost if the people would not wake up from its lethargy. World politics are not made with the olive branch, but with the sword. But the Reich too must be governed by National Socialists ...

But our movement has not been founded to gain seats in parliament and daily attendance fees; our movement was founded to turn Germany's fate in her twelfth hour ...

As we had declared at numerous public meetings that our leaders would not, like those of the Communists did, stand in the rear in the critical hours, our leaders marched in front. On [General Erich] Ludendorff's right side Dr. [Friedrich] Weber marched, on his left, I and [Max von] Scheubner-Richter and the other gentlemen. We were permitted to pass by the cordon of troops blocking the Ludwig Bridge. They were deeply moved; among them were men who wept bitter tears. People who had attached themselves to the columns yelled from the rear that the men should be knocked down. We yelled that there was no reason to harm these people. We marched on to the Marienplatz. The rifles were not loaded. The enthusiasm was indescribable. I had to tell myself: The people are behind us, they no longer can be consoled by ridiculous resolutions. The *Volk* want a reckoning with the November criminals, as far as it still has a sense of honor and human dignity and not for slavery. In front of the Royal Residence a weak police cordon let us pass through. Then there was a short hesitation in front, and a shot was fired. I had the impression that it was no pistol shot but a rifle or carbine bullet. Shortly afterwards a volley was fired. I had the feeling that a bullet struck in my left side. Scheubner-Richter fell, I with him. At this occasion my arm was dislocated and I suffered another injury while falling.

I only was down for a few seconds and tried at once to get up. Another shot was fired, out of the little street to the rear of the Preysing Palace. Around me there were bodies. In front of us were State Police, rifles cocked. Farther in the rear there were armored cars. My men were 70 to 80 meters in back of me. A big gentleman in a black overcoat was lying half covered on the ground, soiled with blood. I was convinced that he was Ludendorff. There were a few more shots fired from inside the Royal Residence and from the little street near the Preysing Palace and maybe also a few wild shots fired by our men. From the circle near the Rentenamt, I drove out of town. I intended to be driven back the same night ...

A few days later, at Uffing, we found out that I had suffered a fracture of the joint and a fracture of the collarbone. During those days I was all broken down by pains of body and soul, if only because I believed that Ludendorff was dead. I obtained the first newspapers at Landsberg. There I read the statement about a breach of my pledged word, that I had pledged my word to Herr von Kahr never to undertake anything without informing him, that I had given this pledge on the evening of November 6th. There I stood as a perfect scoundrel without honor. That is the lowest thing to do; that man, who worked together with us the whole time, stepped up with such lies against us now, when we could not defend ourselves and, to an extent, were broken down in spirit. I never gave such a pledge to Mr. von Kahr. I said, I am standing behind you loyally, I will do nothing against you. Finally I said: "If you are not going to make up your mind, then I will not consider myself obligated as far as my decisions are concerned." When this campaign of slander continued in the course of the next few days and one after the other was brought in to Landsberg [prison], whose only guilt was to have adhered to our movement, then I resolved to defend myself and to resist until the last breath. I did not enter this court to deny anything or to reject my responsibility. I protest against the attempt that Herr von Kriebel tries to assume the responsibility, be it only for the military preparations. I bear the responsibility all alone, but I declare one thing: I am no criminal because of that and I do not feel as if I were a criminal.

I cannot plead guilty, but I do confess the act. There is no such thing as high treason against the traitors of 1918. It is impossible that I should have committed high treason, for this cannot be implicit in the action of November 8th and 9th, but only in the intentions and the actions during all the previous months. But if I really should have committed high treason, then I am surprised not to see those gentlemen here at my side, against whom the prosecutor would be obliged to file indictments;[11] those who willed together with us the same action, discussed and prepared things down to the smallest detail, things which may be described in particular at a closed session later. I do not consider myself as a man who committed high treason, but as a German, who wanted the best for his people ...

Source: **Office of the US Chief of Counsel for Prosecution of Axis Criminality,**
Nazi Conspiracy and Aggression, **Vol. V**
(Washington DC: US Government Printing Office, 1946), pp. 73–4

Struggle for an expanded National Socialist program

This draft of a more detailed program than the Nazi Party's official "Twenty-five Point Program" (Doc. 2.6) was prepared under the leadership of Gregor Strasser (1892–1934) in 1925. Although Hitler countermanded its adoption to avoid any commitments to specific social and economic reforms and to keep full personal control of party policy, the draft is of interest as an indication of the kind of social and economic reforms that many idealistic Nazis favored, at least in the early years. This draft provides the most detailed record of what some party members understood under the term "German socialism." Striking are the many archaic features, such as the restoration of guilds, the special protections for small proprietors, especially farmers, and the establishment of vocational chambers, representatives of which would serve in a national parliament (the Reich Chamber of Corporations). The corporate state (*Ständestaat*), a

---

11   Hitler is here referring in particular to Kahr, General Otto von Lossow (commander of the Bavarian Reichswehr), and Colonel Hans Ritter von Seisser (chief of the Bavarian state police), all of whom had helped plan the putsch attempt with Hitler.

static and authoritarian model favored by fascist theorists as an alternative to liberal democracy and socialism, harked back to a time when society was divided into separate social orders (estates) and each social group was subject to its own specific legal code.

The Strasser program called for a strong executive, the Reich President, also referred to as "dictator." The fascist model of a "national dictatorship" was deliberately offered as an alternative to the communist "dictatorship of the proletariat." The program also contained some ostensibly socialist features designed to appeal to workers, such as the provision calling for state participation in the ownership of industry and the creation of agricultural cooperatives. Its demand for the division and redistribution of large estates was repudiated by Hitler, but its call for state protection for small hereditary holdings was actually put into law in 1933, though it failed to raise the standard of living of small farmers. While calling for the restoration of Germany's 1914 borders and its African colonies, the draft program also called for a European tariff and currency union. Its anti-Semitic provisions, however, did not differ from the original Nazi program.

A key factor in Hitler's success in suppressing the draft program was the defection of Strasser's close aide Joseph Goebbels (1897–1945) to Hitler's side. The future Propaganda Minister came to agree that Hitler's leadership offered the best chance of gaining power. The program was to remain unchanged. The Nazis relied on broad promises rather than specific plans to attract support across class lines. The revival of national power was given priority over social reform. With some reluctance, Strasser, too, accepted Hitler's opportunistic course. Strasser rose to become the organizational leader of the party before clashing with Hitler in 1932 on Hitler's risky but ultimately successful policy of refusing Nazi participation in government except on condition that he be appointed chancellor (see Doc. 2.23). For his opposition to Hitler's "all-or-nothing" strategy Strasser was killed in the "blood purge" of June 1934 (Doc. 3.21).

2.14 Gregor Strasser, draft of a Comprehensive Program of National Socialism, 1925

I. INTRODUCTION

(A nation is a community of fate, need, and bread!)

(a) In brief the disorder of conditions:

- in foreign policy
- in domestic policy
- in economic policy.

(b) Characterization of National Socialism as a wholly new, comprehensive view of political economy (a synthesis of a politically creative nationalism and of a socialism which guarantees the support and development of the individual).

(c) Prerequisite for carrying out this mighty project is the national dictatorship. Fateful and causal connection between the economic emancipation of German employees and the political emancipation of the German people.

II. FOREIGN POLICY

(a) Borders of 1914 ...
(b) Tariff union with Switzerland, Hungary, Denmark, Holland, and Luxemburg.
(c) Colonial empire in central Africa ...
(d) United States of Europe as a European league of nations with a uniform system of measure and currency. Preparation for a tariff union with France and the other European states ...

III. DOMESTIC POLICY

A. REICH

1 Levels of Office:

(a) Reich President with a seven-year term (first Reich President the dictator), with broad powers ... His specific functions:

 • designation of the presidents of the individual states,
 • appointments of ministers,
 • contracting of treaties, declaring of war and peace in cooperation with the ministry.

(b) Reich Ministry led by the Reichschancellor ...
(c) National Council, consists of the 12–14 presidents of the individual states and the leaders of the Reich Chamber of Corporations (the five chairmen of occupational chambers) under the chairmanship of the Reichspresident ...
(d) Reich Chamber of Corporations: consists of representatives of the individual Reich occupational chambers numbering 100; in addition 10 members named by the Reichspresident (representatives of the universities, of the Christian denominations, and otherwise outstanding individuals) ...

2 Administration: Division of the entire Reich territory into 12–14 states according to their particular historical traditions, with concomitant consideration of economic and religious affiliations ...

C. ELECTORAL SYSTEM

1 Reich President: National Council and Reich Chamber of Corporations each elect 5 candidates – the two groups of candidates need not be different from one another; the two bodies vote separately on the entire list. If a candidate receives more than half the votes in both bodies, he is elected ...

IV. ECONOMIC POLICY

A. AGRICULTURAL POLICY

1 Land and soil are the property of the nation! ...

2   Present-day properties, up to a size of 1,000 acres, may remain as hereditary holdings as long as there is a male heir in the family who is able and willing to carry on the hereditary obligations.

3   Holdings larger than 1,000 acres are to be divided into small holdings of 50 to 200 acres, after each man of German nationality who has been an agricultural laborer on the property has been compensated with 2 acres ...

6   No hereditary obligations can be sold or borrowed against ...

9   Mortgages are to be granted only by state loan offices set up by the Chamber of Agriculture in each state ...

B. INDUSTRIAL POLICY

1   All businesses which on a stated day in the past employed twenty or more employees are to be converted into joint stock companies.

2   The Reich Ministry of Economics divides industry into two groups:

  (a) Essential industries (key industries, armaments industries, banks, chemical and electrical industries)
  (b) Nonessential industries (finished goods industries, export industries, and all others)

3   For all joint stock companies, ownership of 51 percent of those in group 2.a will be turned over to the general public; 49 percent of those in group 2.b ...

4   The employees in each of these industrial enterprises are to be grouped in a works-union which will receive 10 percent of the stock of the company ...

C. TRADE AND SMALL BUSINESS POLICY

1   Those businesses or individuals who employ fewer than 20 are to be grouped by law in compulsory guilds.

2   Taxation of these self-governing bodies will take the form of a lump sum which the guilds themselves will divide and levy on their individual members ...

E. STRUCTURE AND CHARACTER OF THE CORPORATIONS

1   The various principal occupational groups are to be combined in regional, state, and Reich chambers ...

2   The following chambers are to be formed:

  (a) Chamber of Agriculture
  (b) Chamber of Industry and Trade
  (c) Chamber of Labor
  (d) Chamber of Civil Servants and Employees
  (e) Chamber of the Free Professions ...

8   Tasks of the Chamber of Corporations: The tasks of the regional chambers are of an administrative nature. Principal task is the observation and control of the effect of legal measures on economic life; the advising of officials, as well as the right to investigate complaints about the assessment of taxes ...

*F. DIVISION OF PRODUCTION (BASIC PRINCIPLE: SHORTEST POSSIBLE PATH BETWEEN
PRODUCER AND CONSUMER, WITH EXTENSIVE ELIMINATION OF FREE TRADE)*

1   Agriculture:

(a)   Compulsory combination of the farmers into local cooperatives, and of these cooperatives into regional cooperatives under the supervision of the Chamber of Agriculture

(b)   Prohibition of free sale of agricultural products; sale only to the cooperative

(c)   Combination of members of the finishing trades (butchers, millers, bakers, etc.) in
compulsory guilds

(d)   Conclusion of direct delivery contracts between these producers' cooperatives and
the guilds or large direct consumers' cooperatives ...

2   Industry: It is the task of the Reich Ministry of Economics to combine similar enterprises
into cartel organizations, but without using general legal compulsion. Continuous supervision of the modernity of the technical situation, with the possibility of closing down
unprofitable enterprises, is also the responsibility of the Reich Ministry of Economics,
because of joint ownership by the state.

V. CULTURAL POLICY

1   *JEWISH QUESTION*

(a)   All Jews who immigrated after 1 August 1914 are to be expelled within six months.

(b)   All individuals who have accepted the Mosaic religion (at any time) since 18 January
1871 and all former citizens descended from such individuals are to be declared
foreigners (Palestinians). In mixed ancestry the father is decisive ...

2   *CHURCH AND SCHOOL*

(a)   Protection and encouragement of the two Christian faiths by the state.

(b)   Denominational and nondenominational schools may coexist, but it will be enforced
that there is at least one nondenominational school in each locality ...

(d)   Attendance free at all schools, including the university; many study materials also free.

3   *PRESS*

(a)   Besides the previous *Reichsanzeiger*, an official Reich newsletter will appear; the
same in every state and in each district. Local officials may issue them also.

(b)   Official announcements will be permitted to appear only in these official newspapers.

(c)   Other private or self-supporting newspapers are free to appear.

(d)   Owners and editors must be citizens of the German Reich.

(e)   All articles must be signed by the author. (No immunity for members of parliament.)

4   *JUSTICE*

Far-reaching reform with conscious return to Germanic legal perceptions (man, not
things, the focal point). Basic principle is: few laws, but good ones, strictly enforced ...

VII. CONCLUSION (DRAWING TOGETHER AND REANALYSIS OF THE PROBLEMS)

1   *On the problem in foreign policy*: the organic arrangement and the powerful racial unification of the German nation in a greater German Empire; this greater German Empire as
the instigator of a central European customs union and as the dominant force in the
United States of Europe.
2   *On the domestic problem*: the division of authority between centralism and federalism
with the introduction of an organically structured system of corporations in the place of
an artificial parliamentarianism.
3   *On the economic problem*: the reconciliation of the rights of the general public with the
personal egoism which is rooted in human nature:

   (a)   In agriculture through realization of the idea of hereditary tenure
   (b)   In industry through far-reaching transfer of the ownership of the means of production to the general public; in both cases with maintenance of private enterprise and
with regard for the sense of property.

This powerful synthesis of chaotic, competitive political and economic forces, their utilization for the nation and for humanity, is Germany's predestined historical task.

**Source: Gregor Strasser, Joseph Goebbels, and others, "Draft of a Comprehensive
Program of National Socialism," in *Nazi Ideology before 1933: A Documentation*,
intr. and trsl. by Barbara Miller Lane and Leila J. Rupp (Austin and London: University of
Texas Press, 1978), pp. 83–7. Reprinted by permission of University of Texas Press**

Hitler's ideology: race, dictatorship, and German world power

Hitler wrote *Mein Kampf* (My Struggle) while in prison in 1924. The autobiographical
first volume was published in 1925. A second volume, from which the extracts below are
taken, appeared in 1926, setting forth his racial anti-Semitism and long-term imperialist goals with amazing candor. The thrust of his argument was that if Germany wished
to regain world power status, it would have to supplant the egalitarian philosophy of
Marxism (a codeword for social democracy) with the racial ideology of the *völkisch*
movement. Hitler viewed liberal or "bourgeois" democracy as merely a preliminary
stage to social democracy and finally a Red takeover. He claimed that National
Socialism was the only movement capable of effectively preventing communism.
Central to his *völkisch* ideology was the notion that communism was a doctrine invented
by Jews to eliminate national elites and facilitate Jewish world domination.

Hitler had no vision of domestic social reform other than the elimination of Jews
and all forms of diversity and dissent from German society, the creation of an authoritarian system based on race, and the preparation of the populace for war. All his
prescriptions for internal change were designed to achieve his major goal: the conquest
of *Lebensraum* in the east. He dismissed the restoration of the 1914 borders as an inadequate goal. Hitler viewed Communist Russia as Germany's primary target. He proposed
an alliance with Britain, a fellow Nordic people (temporarily dominated by Jews, in
Hitler's view), that would give Germany a free hand to crush the Soviet Union and gain
territory for German colonization. Although he always remained committed to the

goals so brazenly expounded in *Mein Kampf*, he was ultimately unable to persuade the British to go along with his expansionist scheme.

2.15 Adolf Hitler, *Mein Kampf*, 1926

[Karl Marx's] doctrine is a brief spiritual extract of the philosophy of life that is generally current today. And for this reason alone any struggle of our so-called bourgeois world against it is impossible, absurd in fact, since this bourgeois world is also essentially infected by these poisons, and worships a view of life which in general is distinguished from the Marxists only by degrees and personalities. The bourgeois world is Marxist, but believes in the possibility of the rule of certain groups of men (bourgeoisie), while Marxism itself systematically plans to hand the world over to the Jews.

In opposition to this, the *völkisch* view recognizes the importance of the racial subdivisions of mankind. In principle, it sees in the state only a means to an end, and it considers the preservation of the racial existence of men as its end. Thus, it by no means believes in the equality of all races, but along with their differences it also recognizes their superior and inferior nature, and feels itself obligated, through this knowledge, to promote the victory of the better and stronger, and demand the subordination of the inferior and weaker in accordance with the eternal will that dominates the universe. Thus, it is in agreement with the fundamentally aristocratic character of nature and it believes in the validity of this law down to the last individual. It recognizes not only the different value of the races but also the different value of individuals. From the mass it extracts the importance of individual personality, and thus, in contrast to the disorganizing effect of Marxism, it has an organizing effect. It believes in the necessity of idealizing mankind, in which it sees the only premise for the existence of humanity. But it cannot grant the right of existence to an ethical idea if this idea represents a danger to the racial life of the bearers of higher ethics, for in a hybridized and negrified world all conceptions of the humanly beautiful and sublime as well as conceptions of an idealized future of humanity would be lost forever.

… *The right to possess soil and territory can become a duty, if decline seems to threaten a great nation unless it extends its territory.* All the more so if what is involved is not some unimportant Negro people or other, but the German mother of all life, who has given the contemporary world its cultural imprint. *Germany will either be a world power or not exist at all.* To be a world power a nation must be large in size; this gives it its power, which gives life to its citizens.

We National Socialists consciously erase the foreign policy trend of our pre-war period and take up where the German nation stopped 600 years ago. We stop the endless German movement to the south and west, and turn our gaze toward the lands of the east. We terminate the colonial and trade policy of the pre-war period and proceed to the territorial policy of the future.

But if we talk about new soil and territory in Europe today, we have in mind primarily *Russia* and its border states. Fate itself seems to direct us toward the east. When Russia surrendered to Bolshevism, the Russian people were robbed of that intelligentsia that had theretofore produced and guaranteed the stability of the state. For the organization of a Russian state structure was not the result of the political talents of Russia's Slavs but rather the wonderful example of the state-building activities of the German element in a country of inferior race. Thus have innumerable mighty empires of the earth been created. Inferior nations, with German organizers and lords as their leaders, have more than once expanded into powerful states and have endured as long as the Germanic racial nucleus maintained itself. For centuries, Russia profited from this superior Germanic leadership nucleus. Today it is uprooted and obliterated. The Jew has replaced it. Impossible as it is for the Russians alone to shake off the yoke of the Jews by their own resources, it is equally impossible for the Jews to maintain their mighty empire in the long run. Jewry itself is not an organizing element but a ferment of decomposition. The Persian empire, once so powerful, is now ripe for collapse, and the end of Jewish domination in Russia will also be the end of the Russian state itself. We have been chosen by fate to witness a catastrophe that will be the most powerful confirmation of the *völkisch* theory of race.

Our task, the mission of the National Socialist movement, is to give our nation political insight and to make it see its future goal fulfilled, not by the intoxicating vigor of a new Alexandrian campaign but by the industrious labor of the German plow, which only needs to be given land conquered by the sword.

Source: Adolf Hitler, *Mein Kampf*, Vol. II
(New York: Reynal & Hitchcock, 1939), pp. 579–81, 950–53

The Communist threat

One factor in Hitler's successful rise to power was the genuine fear that militant communism inspired in the middle classes. The bitter division among the two working-class parties on the left, the militant Communists (KPD) and the reformist Social Democrats (SPD) also played into his hands. The rift had its roots in the Communist perception that SPD leaders were primarily responsible for the failure of left-wing revolutions in Germany after the war. The SPD, which consistently got about a quarter of the votes in Reichstag elections during the 1920s and participated in virtually every government coalition until 1930, was strongly identified with the Weimar Republic in the public mind. The KPD, on the other hand, sought to replace the parliamentary system with a Soviet style of government. In its opposition to the Weimar system, the KPD in effect made common cause with the Nazis.

The Communist (or Third) International (Comintern) was founded by Soviet Communists in 1919 to mobilize and direct the Communist movement and to distinguish its revolutionary aims from the reformist policies of the Socialist International (founded in 1889) after the war. In the late 1920s, parallelling the radicalization of Soviet policies when Stalin assumed full control of the USSR, the Comintern turned the main thrust of its propaganda against fellow-Marxists (Social Democrats and Trotskyists), whom they accused of paving the road to fascism. The following excerpt from the Comintern program is relevant both for its definition of fascism as the "terrorist dictatorship of big capital" and for its arguments linking social democracy to fascism. In directly engaging Nazis in street battles in the large cities, the KPD confronted Nazi efforts to recruit workers with far greater militancy than the SPD, but by rejecting democratic process the Communists made a unified opposition to Nazism impossible, thus contributing to the collapse of the Weimar Republic. This excerpt also illustrates the kind of revolutionary militancy that drove millions of middle-class Germans into the Nazi embrace in the Great Depression.

2.16 Program of the Communist International, 1929

THE WORLD WAR AND THE PROGRESS OF THE REVOLUTIONARY CRISIS

... The first attempts at revolutionary overthrow, which sprang from the acute crisis of capitalism (1918–21), ended in the victory and consolidation of the dictatorship of the proletariat in the USSR and in defeat of the proletariat in a number of other countries. These defeats were primarily due to the treacherous tactics of the social democratic and reformist trade union leaders, but they were also due to the fact that the majority of the working class had not yet accepted the lead of the Communists and that in a number of important countries Communist Parties had not yet been established at all. As a result of these defeats, which created the opportunity for intensifying the exploitation of the mass of the proletariat and the colonial peoples, and for severely depressing their standard of living, the bourgeoisie was able to achieve a partial stabilization of capitalist relations.

THE REVOLUTIONARY CRISIS AND COUNTER-REVOLUTIONARY SOCIAL DEMOCRACY

During the progress of the international revolution, the leading cadres of the social democratic parties and of the reformist trade unions on the one hand, and the militant capitalist organizations of the fascist type on the other, acquired special significance as a powerful counter-revolutionary force actively fighting against the revolution and actively supporting the partial stabilization of capitalism.

The war crisis of 1914–18 was accompanied by the *disgraceful collapse of the social democratic Second International.*[12] Acting in complete violation of the thesis of the "Communist Manifesto" written by Marx and Engels, that the proletariat has no fatherland under capitalism, and in complete violation of the Stuttgart and Basel Congresses,[13] the leaders of the social democratic parties in the various countries, with a few exceptions, voted for the war credits, came out definitely in defense of the imperialist "fatherland" (i.e., the state organizations for the imperialist bourgeoisie) and instead of combating the imperialist war, became its loyal soldiers, bards, and propagandists (social patriotism, which grew into social imperialism) ...

The principal function of social democracy at the present time is to disrupt the essential militant unity of the proletariat in its struggle against imperialism. In splitting and disrupting the united front of the proletarian struggle against capital, social democracy serves as the mainstay of imperialism in the working class. International social democracy of all shades; the Second International and its trade union branch, the Amsterdam Federation of Trade Unions, have thus become the last reserve of bourgeois society and its most reliable pillar of support.

12 The Second Socialist International was founded in 1889. The Third International, or Communist International, was founded in Moscow in March 1919.
13 The Socialist International adopted anti-war resolutions at congresses in Stuttgart in 1907 and in Basel in 1912, which were ignored by most socialist parties at the start of the war in 1914.

THE CRISIS OF CAPITALISM AND FASCISM

Side by side with social democracy, with whose aid the bourgeoisie suppresses the workers or lulls their class vigilance, stands fascism.

The epoch of imperialism, the sharpening of the class struggle and the growth of the elements of civil war – particularly after the imperialist war – led to the bankruptcy of parliamentarism. Hence, the adoption of "new" methods and forms of administration (for example, the system of inner cabinets, the formation of oligarchical groups, acting behind the scenes, the deterioration and falsification of the function of "popular representation," the restriction and annulment of "democratic liberties," etc.). Under certain special historical conditions, the progress of this bourgeois, imperialist, reactionary offensive assumes the form of fascism. These conditions are: instability of capitalist relationships; the existence of a considerable declassed social element; the pauperization of broad strata of the urban petty bourgeoisie and of the intelligentsia; discontent among the rural petty bourgeoisie, and, finally, the constant menace of mass proletarian action. In order to stabilize and perpetuate its rule, the bourgeoisie is compelled to an increasing degree to abandon the parliamentary system in favor of the fascist system, which is independent of inter-party arrangements and combinations. The fascist system is a system of direct dictatorship, ideo-logically masked by the "national idea" and representation of the "professions" (in reality, repre-sentation of the various groups of the ruling class). It is a system that resorts to a peculiar form of social demagogy (anti-Semitism, occasional sorties against usurers' capital, and gestures of impa-tience with the parliamentary "talking shop") in order to utilize the discontent of the petty bour-geoisie, the intellectuals, and other strata of society; it also resorts to corruption – the creation of a compact and well-paid hierarchy of fascist units, a party apparatus and a bureaucracy. At the same time, fascism strives to permeate the working class by recruiting the most backward strata of workers to its ranks, by playing upon their discontent, by taking advantage of the inaction of social democracy, etc. The principal aim of fascism is to destroy the revolutionary labor vanguard, i.e., the Communist Sections and leading units of the proletariat. The combination of social democracy, corruption, and active white terror, in conjunction with extreme imperialist aggres-sion in the sphere of foreign politics, are the characteristic features of fascism. In periods of acute crisis for the bourgeoisie, fascism resorts to anti-capitalist phraseology, but, after it has estab-lished itself at the helm of state, it casts aside its anti-capitalist rattle and discloses itself as a terrorist dictatorship of big capital.

The bourgeoisie resorts either to the method of fascism or to the method of coalition with social democracy according to the changes in the political situation; while social demo-cracy itself often plays a fascist role in periods when the situation is critical for capitalism.

In the process of development, social democracy reveals fascist tendencies which, however, does not prevent it, in other political situations, from acting as a sort of *Fronde* against the bourgeois government in the capacity of an opposition party.[14] The fascist method and the method of coalition with social democracy are not the methods usually employed in "normal" capitalist conditions; they are the symptoms of the general capitalist crisis, and are employed by the bourgeoisie in order to stem the advance of the revolution ...

Source: *Program of the Communist International*
(New York: Workers Library Publishers, 1929), pp. 18–23

---

14   The *Fronde* was an aristocratic rebellion against Louis XIV during his minority in the 1640s.

The Great Depression

Lea Langer Grundig and her husband Hans Grundig were artists in Dresden and were active in the German Communist Party in the 1920s and 1930s. Lea, born in 1906, was the youngest of three daughters of a Jewish merchant family in Dresden. She was arrested by the Gestapo in 1938, imprisoned, interrogated, and eventually ordered to leave for Palestine via Vienna in December 1939. Because of British restrictions on immigration Lea Grundig had to enter Palestine illegally in 1940. Lea Grundig returned from Israel to Dresden in 1948 and taught at the Dresden Academy of Art, where Hans Grundig became the first director. In 1964 she published her memoir, *Gesichte und Geschichte*, (Visions and History), which offers a personal perspective on the turbulent events of the Weimar Republic and the early Nazi years. The passages excerpted here describe the hopeless situation of the unemployed in Dresden and the appeal of socialism to impoverished workers during the Great Depression.

2.17 Lea Grundig, "Visions and History"

SIX MILLION UNEMPLOYED

The unemployed had to do a lot to get their benefits. They stood in endless lines in every kind of weather at the unemployment office on Materni Street, between Stern Square and Post Square.

There we stood and waited until it was our turn. The misery of years of unemployment had colored everyone the same shade of gray. Work qualifications, special abilities, skills and knowledge based on experience – these were all as outmoded as vanished snow. The radiance and color of particular occupations were lost in the gray of welfare misery. Endless conversations, discussions, resigned grumbling and cursing, simple, childish hopeful chatter, political arguments – all this was woven into the never-ending talk of those standing in line.

Unemployment became a tragedy for many. Not only because of the poverty that mutely sat at their table at all times. Not working, doing nothing, producing nothing – work that not only provided food, but also, despite all the harassment and drudgery, was satisfying, developed skills, and stimulated thinking; work, a human need – it was not available; and wherever it was lacking, decay, malaise, and despair set in.

An old carpenter chopped his table into pieces in his room, so he could painstakingly put it back together again. Thus he was able once again to do what had become essential to him.

Coal was expensive; people slept constantly. It was warm in bed and it was easier to sleep away the hunger. Strange customs emerged in some workers' tenements. They slept during the day but became mobile at night. They got together, pooled their unemployment pittance, and held pitiful parties with cheap schnapps and a gramophone. That's how people tried to drown out their misery.

Clothes were turned inside out, mended, continuously darned. Neither Hans nor I could buy a single piece of clothing – and it was the same for millions of people as it was for us. Everything we wore was given to us. ...

SOOTHSAYING AND TRUTH

The grim poverty, the hopelessness, the laws governing the crisis that were incomprehensible for many, all these made people ripe for "miracles". Sects shot out of the ground. Diviners of the stars or of coffee grounds, palm-readers, graphologists, speculators and swindlers, clairvoyants and miracle workers had a great time; they reaped rich harvests among the poor, who along with their poverty and idleness fell prey to foolishness.

Who was to blame? Where did this inconceivable misery come from? "The Jews are to blame!" they screamed in chorus. "The lost war!" "The Reds with their stab in the back!"

"Capitalism" said the Communists, and they were right. "Because a few own the machines and the factories and have them work only for their profit, without a plan, not according to real needs, and those who produce everything cannot buy anything, therefore the hungry have to watch while wheat is burned, milk is poured out, coffee is thrown away. Things have to be produced as they are really needed. All of life's necessities, all natural resources and machines have to belong to everyone. We must put an end to the exploitation, to labor for profit. And that is called socialism."

Socialism.

Like a great, solemn bell of ancient longing, that's how this word sounded. Sweet and full of hope, more than a legend, more than soothsaying ...

Socialism – that was the great dream, dreamed not by children and fools, but by warriors and seers.

They were not the worst, those who dreamed of socialism in those days.

We dreamed with open eyes, with sharpened hearing, and with a burning quest for the answer to the questions the suffering people asked.

Source: Lea Grundig, *Gesichte und Geschichte*, 10th edn. (Berlin: Dietz Verlag, 1984), pp. 99–100, 101–102. Reprinted by permission of Dietz Verlag. Translated by Sally Winkle

---

The "National Opposition"

On 11 October 1931 right-wing forces under the leadership of the industrialist and media tycoon Alfred Hugenberg (1865–1951) assembled in Bad Harzburg, a town in central Germany, to form a common front against the government of Heinrich Brüning (1885–1970) and the Weimar parliamentary system. Appointed Chancellor in March 1930 at the onset of the Great Depression, but unable to put together a majority coalition, Brüning called a special election in September 1930. The Nazis made huge gains and became the second-largest party in the Reichstag. Thereafter Brüning was forced to rely on the emergency powers granted to the President (Hindenburg) under Article 48 of the constitution (Doc. 2.5) in order to enact his program of unpopular austerity measures. Brüning provoked the wrath of nationalists and Nazis by refusing to work with them to establish a nationalist dictatorship, relying instead on the goodwill of the Social Democrats (SPD) to override no-confidence motions in the Reichstag. Although Brüning worked hard to lower Germany's reparations obligations and claimed to have favored an eventual restoration of the monarchy, nationalists viewed him as too loyal to the Weimar constitution and too weak to stand up to the West.

Table 2.1 Reichstag elections 1928–33

Party	20 May 1928			14 September 1930			31 July 1932			6 November 1932			5 March 1933		
	Total votes	%	No. deputies	Total votes	%	No. deputies	Total votes	%	No. deputies	Total votes	%	No. deputies	Total votes	%	No. deputies
No. eligible voters	41,224,700		491	42,957,700		577	44,226,800		608	44,373,700		584	44,685,800		647
No. valid votes cast	30,753,300	74.60		34,970,900	81.41		36,882,400	83.39		35,471,800	79.93		39,343,300	88.04	
Social Democrats (SPD)	9,153,000	29.8	153	8,577,700	24.5	143	7,959,700	21.6	133	7,248,000	20.4	121	7,181,600	18.3	120
Communist Party (KPD)	3,264,800	10.6	54	4,592,100	13.1	77	5,282,600	14.6	89	5,980,200	16.9	100	4,848,100	12.3	81
Center Party	3,712,200	12.1	62	4,127,900	11.8	68	4,589,300	12.5	75	4,230,600	11.9	70	4,424,900	11.7	74
Bavarian People's Party	945,600	3.0	16	1,059,100	3.0	19	1,192,700	3.2	22	1,094,600	3.1	20	1,073,600	2.7	18
Democrats (DDP)	1,505,700	4.9	25	1,322,400	3.8	20	371,800	1.0	4	336,500	1.0	2	334,200	0.8	5
People's Party (DVP)	2,679,700	8.7	45	1,578,200	4.5	30	436,000	1.2	7	661,800	1.9	11	432,300	1.1	2
Wirtschafts-partei	1,397,100	4.5	23	1,362,400	3.9	23	146,900	0.4	2	110,300	0.3	1	—	—	—
Nationalists (DNVP)	4,381,600	14.2	73	2,458,300	7.0	41	2,177,400	5.9	37	2,959,000	8.8	52	3,136,800	8.0	52

(continued next page)

Table 2.1 Reichstag elections 1928–33 (continued)

Party	20 May 1928			14 September 1930			31 July 1932			6 November 1932			5 March 1933		
	Total votes	%	No. deputies	Total votes	%	No. deputies	Total votes	%	No. deputies	Total votes	%	No. deputies	Total votes	%	No. deputies
Christlich-soz. Volksdienst	—	—	—	868,200	2.5	14	405,300	1.1	3	412,500	1.2	5	384,000	1.0	4
Landbund	199,500	0.6	3	194,000	0.5	3	96,900	0.2	2	105,200	0.3	2	83,800	0.2	1
Christlich-natl. Bauern u. Landvolk	581,800	1.8	10	1,108,700	3.0	19	90,600	0.2	1	46,400	0.1	—	—	—	—
Deutsch-Hannov. Partei	195,600	0.5	3	144,300	0.4	3	46,900	0.1	—	64,000	0.2	1	47,700	0.1	—
Deutsch Bauernpartei	481,300	1.5	8	339,600	1.0	6	137,100	0.3	2	149,000	0.4	3	114,000	0.3	2
National Socialists (NSDAP)	810,100	2.6	12	6,409,600	18.3	107	13,745,800	37.4	230	11,737,000	33.1	196	17,277,200	43.9	288
Other parties	1,445,300	4.8	4	1,073,500	3.1	4	342,500	0.9	4	749,200	2.2	—	136,646	0.3	—

For Hugenberg, head of the Nationalist Party of industrial and agrarian conservatives (DNVP), a major objective of the Harzburg Rally was to lure Hitler into partnership with the "traditional" right. Old-fashioned conservatives like Hugenberg with their narrow electoral constituency knew that they needed the Nazis' popular support to legitimize a nationalist dictatorship. Hitler, however, was careful not to identify himself too closely with the old elites for fear of alienating lower- and middle-class voters. Despite the similarity in their nationalist aims and values, rivalry between Hugenberg and Hitler was inevitable as both men aspired to the leadership of the national cause. Hugenberg was also suspicious of the economic radicalism of many of Hitler's followers.

The Harzburg Front anticipated the collaboration between Nazis and Nationalists that eventually led to the appointment of Hitler as head of a "Cabinet of National Concentration" in January 1933 (Doc. 3.1). Hugenberg would become Hitler's first Minister for Economics and Agriculture. Another prominent participant at the Harzburg rally, Franz Seldte (1882–1947), head of the leading veterans' organization *Stahlhelm*, became Hitler's Minister of Labor. Former Reichsbank president Hjalmar Schacht (1877–1970), whose speech at Bad Harzburg attracted national attention, served as Hitler's Finance Minister from 1934 to 1937. Much of Hitler's success in the waning years of the Weimar Republic was due to his skill in gaining and retaining the support of Germany's economic and military elites while at the same time effectively nurturing the revolutionary hopes of the disaffected rank and file.

2.18 Manifesto of the Harzburg Front, 11 October 1931

The national front, unified in its parties, associations, and organizations, and inspired with the will to take action jointly and in solidarity, issues the following declaration:

The National Opposition has been warning for years in vain against the failure of the government and the state apparatus in the face of Marxism's bloody reign of terror, continuing cultural Bolshevism, and the division of the nation through class warfare. The National Opposition has warned against the systematic exclusion of national forces from the governing of the state; against policies that go beyond the *Diktat* of Versailles in their political, economic, and military emasculation of Germany; against a policy that sacrifices the domestic economy in favor of global economic utopias; and against a policy of subservience to foreign nations, which has neither brought Germany equality of rights nor saved the conflicted east from military invasion.

Determined to protect our country from the chaos of Bolshevism and to save our polity from the maelstrom of economic bankruptcy through effective self-help, thereby helping the world to achieve real peace, we declare: We are ready to take responsibility in governments led by nationally-minded forces in the Reich and in Prussia. We will not spurn any hand offered to us in the spirit of truly honest collaboration. But we must refuse to support in any way the preservation of a false system and the continuation of false policies in the present government, which is merely posing as a nationally-minded government. Any government formed against the will of the united National Opposition will have to count us as opponents.

Thus we demand the immediate resignation of the governments of [Heinrich] Brüning and [Otto] Braun and the immediate lifting of the dictatorial powers of governments whose composition does not correspond with the will of the people and which can only remain in power with the help of emergency decrees. We demand an immediate new election of the outdated popular legislatures, especially in the Reich and in Prussia.

Fully conscious of the responsibility we herewith accept, we declare that during future unrest the organizations of the National Opposition will naturally defend the lives, property, residence, farm, and work-place of those who openly profess their loyalty to the nation, but we refuse to shed our blood to protect the current government and the system presently in power.

We demand the restitution of German military sovereignty and parity in arms.

We stand united in these demands. Anyone who wants to undermine our front will be repelled.

We beseech Reich President von Hindenburg, elected by us, to respond to the vehement urgings of millions of patriotic men and women, veterans of the front, and young people, and at long last to introduce a saving change of course by appointing a true national government. ...

> Source: *Ursachen und Folgen. Vom deutschen Zusammenbruch 1918 bis 1945 bis zur staatlichen Neuordnung Deutschlands in der Gegenwart. Eine Urkunden-und Dokumentensammlung zur Zeitgeschichte*, Vol. VIII, ed. by Herbert Michaelis and Ernst Schraepler with Günter Scheel (Berlin: Dokumentenverlag Dr. Herbert Wendlin, 1958–80), p. 365–6. Translated by Sally Winkle

Hitler and the industrialists

This two-and-a-half hour speech to German industrialists and businessmen is probably the most important speech Hitler gave before becoming chancellor a year later. It helped to overcome the skepticism of many members of the business and professional community about the putative socialism of the Nazi Party. The speech, later published as a pamphlet, was carefully constructed to appeal to the economic and political interests of his affluent and influential audience. Hitler emphasized the importance of personality, the distinction of the German nation, and the beneficence of struggle. His critique of democracy and praise of racial and political hierarchy struck a responsive chord. Study of this speech can help us to understand why so many members of Germany's conservative economic elite were prepared to accept Hitler's leadership despite his record and reputation as Jew-baiting rabble-rouser.

Hitler's major argument was that only the Nazis could prevent the eventual triumph of communism (Bolshevism) in Germany. Only the Nazis could provide the ideology (or *Weltanschauung*) to overcome the debilitating class conflict that Marxism had supposedly created, the Weimar multi-party "system" had fostered, and the depression had exacerbated. Only the Nazis, Hitler claimed, could restore unity to the nation, and the nation to its former greatness. Only the Nazis could hold democracy and its discontents in check. Hitler projected an optimistic attitude of self-reliance that closely corresponded to the entrepeneurial mindset of successful businessmen. They would readily have agreed with him that it was inconsistent and counterproductive to adhere to the "leadership principle," individual achievement and competition, and private property in the economy, but to favor democracy, the egalitarian principle, pacifism, and internationalism in politics. What democracy is to politics, Hitler warned, communism is to the economy.

The talk has an inspirational quality that enabled Hitler to evoke enthusiasm even among serious and level-headed people. Hitler took the line that Germany, with its inherent racial value, could solve the problems of the depression without depending on outside help. He portrayed the Nazi Party as motivated by idealism and faith, qualities that alone could save the nation from distributional conflicts and left-wing subversion. He also made frequent use of historical references, invoking the Thirty Years' War as an example of the perils of national disunity, and the outbreak of the First World War in August 1914 as an example of the unified national purpose that Germany would have to recapture if it wished to regain the power and prosperity it once had. His refusal, however, to blame Germany's troubles solely on the Versailles Treaty or the world economic crisis was directed against the government of Chancellor Brüning, who contended that German revival could be brought about simply by ending or reducing German reparations payments.

Hitler's speech is also noteworthy for what it did not contain. In deference to his hosts, a business group that included some Jews and persons of mixed ancestry, Hitler avoided any explicit denunciation of Jews. He knew that the anti-capitalist implications of rabble-rousing anti-Semitism would not endear him to "respectable" conservatives. He did not exercise similar restraint, however, in asserting the superiority of the "white race" and its right to colonial dominance. He apparently assumed that this was an uncontroversial point of view that most of his audience shared. Anti-Semitism was implied, on the other hand, in his reference to the "ferment of decomposition," a phrase first applied to the Jewish influence in the ancient Roman Empire by the great classical historian Theodor Mommsen.

2.19 Hitler's speech to the Industry Club in Düsseldorf, 27 January 1932

If today the National Socialist Movement is regarded among some circles in Germany as being hostile to business, I believe the reason for this view is that we adopted towards the events leading to our present position an attitude that differed from all the other organizations of any importance in our public life. Even now our outlook differs in many ways from that of our opponents.

Our conviction is that our present distress has its final and deepest cause not in general world events, which would from the outset more or less exclude any possibility for any one people to improve its conditions. If it were true that the cause of distress in Germany is to be found solely in a so-called world crisis from which none can escape … then we would have to describe Germany's future as hopeless. How can a state of affairs be altered for which no one is directly responsible? In my judgement the view that the world crisis is solely responsible must lead to a dangerous pessimism …

I am of the opinion that there is nothing that has been produced by the will of man that cannot in its turn be altered by another human will …

Assertions that a people's fate is solely determined by foreign powers have always formed the rationalizations of bad governments. Weak and bad governments have at all times used this argument in order to excuse and explain their own failure and that of their predecessors, the failure of their whole rigid and traditional mode of thought. Their plea has always been, "Anyone else in our position could not have done otherwise." For what could he begin to do with his people in the face of conditions that are fixed once and for all and have their roots in the world beyond Germany's frontiers – so long as he regards his people, too, as a factor whose value cannot change?

Against this conception I am the champion of another point of view: three factors essentially determine a people's political life.

First, the inner value of a people ... It is beyond question that certain traits of character, certain virtues, and certain vices always recur in peoples so long as their inner nature – their blood-conditioned composition – has not essentially altered. I can already trace the virtues and the vices of our German people in the writers of Rome just as clearly as I see them today. This inner value which determines the life of a people can be destroyed by nothing except a change in its blood-conditioned substance ... This is the great source of all hopes for a people's revival; it is this which justifies the belief that a people which in the course of thousands of years has furnished countless examples of the highest inner value cannot suddenly have lost overnight this inborn inherited value, but that one day this people will once again put this value into effect. If this were not the case, then the faith of millions of people in a better future – the mystic hope for a new Germany – would be incomprehensible. It would be incomprehensible how it was that this German people, at the end of the Thirty Years War, when its population had shrunk from 18 to 13½ million, could ever have once more formed the hope through work, through industry, and through ability, to rise again; how in this completely crushed people hundreds of thousands and finally millions should have been seized with the longing for a reformation of their state. This would have been inconceivable had it not been that in all these individuals, unconsciously, there was some trace of the conviction that there was present an essential value ... which always in the end had reappeared, and had always presented to the world the wonderful spectacle of a new revival of our people.

I said that this value can be corrupted. There are, however, two other closely related phenomena that we can time and again trace in periods of national decline: The one is that for the conception of the value of personality there is substituted a levelling idea of the supremacy of mere numbers – democracy. The other is the negation of the value of a people, the denial of any difference in the inborn capacity, the achievement, etc., of individual peoples. Thus both these phenomena condition one another or at least influence each other in the course of their development. Internationalism and democracy are inseparable conceptions. It is only logical that democracy, which within a people denies the special value of the individual and puts in its place a value which represents a sum – a purely numerical value – should proceed in precisely the same way in the life of peoples and should in that sphere result in internationalism. Broadly it is maintained: peoples have no inborn values, but at most there are perhaps temporary differences due to education; between Negroes, Aryans, Mongolians, and Redskins there is no essential difference in value. This view, which forms the basis of the whole international thought-world of today and finally is carried to such lengths that a Negro can preside over sessions of the League of Nations, leads necessarily to the point that within a people differences in value between the individual members of this people are similarly denied. Thereby of course every special capacity, every fundamental value of a people, can be rendered ineffective in practice. For the greatness of a people is the result not of the sum of all its achievements but in the last resort of the sum of its outstanding achievements ...

So it is only natural that when the capable intelligences of a nation, which are always in a minority, are regarded only as of the same value as all the rest, then genius, capacity, the value of personality are slowly subjected to the majority and this process is then falsely named the rule of the people. For this is not rule of the people, but in reality the rule of stupidity, of mediocrity, of half-heartedness, of cowardice, of weakness, and of inadequacy. Rule of the people means rather that a people should allow itself to be governed and led by its most capable individuals, those who are born to the task, and not that a chance majority which inevitably is unsuited to these tasks should be permitted to administer all spheres of life.

Thus democracy will in practice lead to the destruction of a people's true values. And this also serves to explain how it is that peoples with a great past, when they surrender themselves to the unlimited, democratic rule of the masses slowly lose their former position; for the outstanding achievements of individuals in all spheres of life are now rendered practically ineffective through the oppression of mere numbers. Thereby a people will gradually lose its importance not merely in the cultural and economic spheres but altogether; in a comparatively short time it will no longer retain its former value in the framework of nations. And that will also inevitably mean a change in its power to safeguard its own interests as against the rest of the world ...

And to this there must be added a third destructive factor: namely, after the denial of the value of personality and of the special value of a people, the view that life in this world does not have to be maintained through conflict. That is a conception which could perhaps be disregarded if it fixed itself only in the heads of individuals; yet it has appalling consequences, because it slowly poisons an entire people. It is not as if such general changes in people's ideological beliefs remained only on the surface or were a matter merely of intellectual interest. No, in the course of time they exercise a profound influence and affect all manifestations of a people's life.

Let me cite an example: you maintain, gentlemen, that the German economy must be constructed on the basis of private property. Now such a conception of private property can only be maintained in practice if it in some way appears to have a logical foundation. This conception must derive its ethical justification from the insight that this is what nature dictates. It cannot simply be upheld by saying: "It has always been so and therefore it must continue to be so." For in periods of great upheavals within states, of movements of peoples and changes in thought, institutions and systems cannot remain untouched merely because they have previously existed in this form ... And then I am bound to say that private property can be morally and ethically justified only if I admit that men's achievements are different ... Thus it must be admitted that in the economic sphere people are not of equal value or of equal importance in all branches from the start. But once this is admitted it is madness to say: In the economic sphere there are undoubtedly differences in value, but that is not true in the political sphere. It is absurd to build up economic life on the ideas of achievement, of the value of personality, and therefore in practice on the authority of personality, but in the political sphere to deny the authority of personality and to thrust into its place the law of the greater number – democracy. In that case there must gradually arise a cleavage between the economic and the political points of view; to bridge that cleavage an attempt will be made to assimilate the former point of view to the latter – indeed the attempt has been made, for this cleavage has not remained bare pale theory. The conception of the equality of values has already been raised to a system, not only in politics but in economics. And that not merely in abstract theory: No! This economic system is alive in gigantic organizations – in fact it has already gained control of a state that today rules over immense areas.

If the view is right that there are differences in human achievement, then it must also be true that the value of men in respect to the production of certain achievements is different. It is then absurd to grant the validity of this principle only in one sphere – the sphere of economic life and its leadership – and to refuse to acknowledge its validity in the sphere of the whole life-struggle of a people – the sphere of politics. Rather it is logical that if I recognize without qualification in the economic sphere that special achievements form the condition of all higher culture, then I must likewise give priority to special achievement and the authority of personality in the sphere of politics.

If, on the contrary, it is asserted – and that even by those engaged in business – that in the political sphere special abilities are not needed but that here an absolute equality in achievement reigns, then one day this same theory will be transferred from politics to economic life. But in the economic sphere communism is analogous to democracy in the political sphere. We find ourselves today in a period in which these two fundamental principles contend with each other in all contiguous spheres and are already intruding into economics.

… The conception of pacifism is logical if I assume a general equality amongst peoples and human beings. For in that case what sense is there in conflict? The conception of pacifism translated into practice and applied to all spheres must gradually lead to the destruction of the competitive instinct, to the destruction of the ambition for outstanding achievement. I cannot say: In politics we will be pacifists, we reject the idea that it is necessary to safeguard life through conflict – but in economics we want to remain keenly competitive. If I reject the idea of conflict as such, it is of no importance that for the time being that idea is still applied in the economic sphere. In the last analysis political decisions are decisive and determine achievement in every sphere. For fifty years you can build up the best economic system on the basis of the principle of achievement, for fifty years you may go on building factories, for fifty years you may amass wealth, and then in three years of mistaken political decisions you can destroy all the results of the work of these fifty years. ([Shouts of]Very true!)

To sum up: I see two diametrically opposed principles: the principle of democracy which, wherever it is put into practice, is the principle of destruction; and the principle of the authority of personality which I would call the principle of achievement, because whatever man has achieved up to now – all human civilization – is conceivable only if the supremacy of this principle is admitted.

… The situation which faces you today is not the consequence of a revelation of God's will, but the result of human weaknesses, of human mistakes, of men's false judgements. It is only natural that there must first be a change in these causes, that people must first be inwardly transformed, before one can count on any alteration in the situation.

That conclusion is evident if we look at the world today: We have a number of nations which through their inborn outstanding worth have fashioned for themselves a mode of life that stands in no relation to the life-space (Lebensraum) they inhabit in their densely populated settlements. We have the so-called white race which, since the collapse of ancient civilization, in the course of some thousand years has created for itself a privileged position in the world. But I am quite unable to understand this privileged position, the economic supremacy of the white race over the rest of the world, if I do not relate it closely to a political conception of supremacy that has been natural and unique to the white race for many centuries and has been maintained in its dealings with other peoples. Take any single area you like, take for example India. England did not conquer India by way of justice and of law, but rather without regard to the wishes, the views, or the notions of justice of the natives; and, when necessary, she has upheld this supremacy with the most brutal ruthlessness. Just in the same way Cortez or Pizarro annexed Central America and the northern states of South America, not on the basis of any right, but from the absolute inborn feeling of the superiority of the white race. The settlement of the North American continent is just as little the consequence of any superior right in any democratic or international sense; it was the consequence of a consciousness of right which was rooted solely in the conviction of the superiority and therefore of the right of the white race. If I think away this mindset, which in the course of the last three or four centuries has won the world for the white race, then the destiny of this race would in fact have been no different from that, say, of the Chinese: An immensely congested mass of human beings crowded upon an extraordinarily narrow territory, an over-population with all its unavoidable consequences. If fate allowed the white race to take a different path, that is only because this white race was convinced that it had the right to organize the rest of the world. It matters not what superficial disguises in individual cases this right may have assumed, in practice it was the exercise of an extraordinarily brutal right to dominate others (*Herrenrecht*). From this political conception was developed the basis for the economic annex-ation of the part of the world not inhabited by the white race.

... And as the last, most ominous phenomenon we regard the fact that, parallel with the gradual confusion in the thought of the white race in Europe, a *Weltanschauung* has seized on part of Europe and a great part of Asia which threatens to tear this continent out of the framework of international economic relations altogether – a phenomenon that today German statesmen still appear to pass over with an astonishing levity ... Cannot people see that a cleavage has already opened up in our midst, a cleavage not merely haunting the minds of a few persons, but forming today the ideological foundation of one of the greatest world powers? Can they not see that Bolshevism today is not merely a mob rioting in some of our streets in Germany, but is a conception of the world which is in the act of subjecting to itself the entire Asiatic continent, and which today in the form of a state stretches almost from our eastern frontier to Vladivostok?

The situation is represented in Germany as if it were merely a theory held by a few vision-aries or evil-minded individuals. No! A *Weltanschauung* has won over a state, and starting from this state it will gradually shatter the whole world and bring it down in ruins. Bolshevism, if its advance is not interrupted, will transform the world as completely as Chris-tianity once did. In three hundred years people will no longer say that it is a question of a new idea in formation. In three hundred years perhaps people will realize that it is a question almost of a new religion, though its basis is not that of Christianity. In three hundred years, if this movement develops further, people will see in Lenin not merely a revolutionary of the year 1917 but the founder of a new world doctrine, honored perhaps as is Buddha.

It is not as if this gigantic phenomenon could simply be thought away from the modern world. It is a reality and must inevitably destroy and overthrow one of the conditions for our continued existence as a white race ...

I know very well that gentlemen of the Reichswehr ministry and gentlemen representing German industry will object: We do not believe that the Soviets will ever be able to build up an industry that can really be capable of competing with us. Gentlemen, they could never build up such an industry if they were confined to the national resources of Bolshevik Russia. But this industry will be built up by elements of value drawn from the white peoples them-selves. It is nonsense to say that it is impossible to build up industry in Russia through forces supplied by other peoples – in the past it was possible through Germans to equip industry in Bohemia with all that was needed. And besides that: Old Russia was already in possession of some industries.

And if it be further stated that the methods of production will never be able to keep pace with our own – do not forget that a lower standard of living will fully compensate for any advantage that we perhaps possess in our method of production. (*Very true!*)

In any event – if European and American modes of thought remain as they are today – we shall find that Bolshevism will gradually spread over Asia. Thirty or fifty years, when it is a question of *Weltanschauungen*, count for nothing. Three hundred years after the death of Christ Christianity had only begun slowly to penetrate the whole of the south of Europe and it was seven hundred years later before it mastered the north of Europe. *Weltanschauungen* of this fundamental character can still display their absolute capacity for conquest five hundred years after their rise if they are not at the outset broken by the natural instinct of self-preservation of other peoples. But if this process continues only for another thirty, forty, or fifty years and our outlook still remains unchanged, it will not then, gentlemen, be possible to say "How does that concern our economic life?" ...

Gentlemen, we know from our own experience that, through spiritual confusion whose consequences you can in practice trace on every hand, Germany lost the war. Do you believe that when seven or eight million men have found themselves for ten or twenty years excluded from the national process of production [a reference to the unemployed], for these masses Bolshevism could appear as anything else than the logical theoretical (*weltanschaulich*) complement of their actual, practical economic situation? Do you really believe that the purely spiritual (*geistige*) side of this catastrophe can be overlooked without one day its transforming itself into bitter reality – the evil curse becoming the evil deed? ...

Here I would enter a protest against those who would simply sweep these facts aside by asserting that the Peace Treaty of Versailles is "according to the almost universal view" the cause of our misfortune. No, certainly not "according to the almost universal view," but rather only according to the view of those who share in the guilt of having concluded that treaty. (*Applause*)

The Peace Treaty of Versailles is itself only the consequence of our own gradual inner confusion and aberration of mind. We find ourselves – no one can doubt it – in a period in which the world is heading toward extraordinarily difficult and disruptive ideological conflicts. I cannot escape these conflicts by simply regretting them, by shrugging my shoulders and – without making clear to myself their causes – by saying "What we need is unity." These struggles are not caused merely by the ill-will of a few men; they have in the last analysis their deepest roots in the facts of race.

If Bolshevism is spreading today in Russia, this Bolshevism is fundamentally just as logical for Russia as csarism was before. It is a brutal regime over a people that cannot be held together as a state except through a brutal government. But if this view of the world gains a hold on us, too, then we must not forget that our people also is composed racially of the most varied elements and that therefore we have to see in the watchword "Proletarians of all countries, unite!" much more than a mere political battle-cry. It is in reality the expression of the will of men who in their essential character have in fact a certain kinship with analogous peoples on a low level of culture. Our people and our state, too, were once built up only through the exercise of the absolute right of the lord and the sense of lordship of the so-called Nordic people, the Aryan racial components that we still possess in our people today. Therefore whether we do or do not regain new political strength is just a question of regenerating the German people according to the laws of an iron logic. ...

In the life of peoples the strength which can be turned outwards depends upon the strength of a nation's internal organization, and that in its turn is dependent upon the firmness of views held in common on certain fundamental questions. What use is it for a government to publish a decree for the salvation of the economy, when the nation as the living object of that decree itself has two completely different attitudes towards the economy? One part says: The precondition for economics is private property; the other part maintains that private property is theft. Fifty percent declare for one principle and fifty percent for the other. ...

One half of the nation says: The traitor must be punished; the other half considers treason to be a duty. One half says: The nation must be defended with courage; the other half regards courage as idiotic. One half says: The basis of our morality is the religious life and the other half answers with scorn: The conception of a God has no basis in reality. Religions are but the opium of the people.

Do not think that once a people has come under the sway of these conflicts of *Weltanschauungen*, one can circumvent them by simply issuing emergency decrees; do not imagine that one need not adopt any attitude towards these conflicts because they are matters that do not concern economics, administrative affairs, or cultural life. Gentlemen, these conflicts strike at the power and strength of the nation as a whole. How is a people still to count for anything abroad when in the last resort fifty percent are inclined to Bolshevism and fifty percent are nationalists or anti-Bolshevists? It is quite conceivable to turn Germany into a Bolshevist state – it would be a catastrophe, but it is conceivable. It is also conceivable to build up Germany as a national state. But it is inconceivable that a strong and sound Germany can be created if fifty percent of its citizens are Bolshevist and fifty percent nationally-minded. (*Very true!*) From the solution of this problem we cannot escape! (*Loud applause.*)

... Germany once possessed – as the first condition for the organization of our people on a large scale – a *weltanschaulich* basis in our religion – Christianity. When this basis was shattered we see how the strength of the nation turned from external affairs to internal conflicts, since the nature of man from an inner necessity compels him, when the common *weltanschaulich* basis is lost or attacked, to seek a new common basis. These were the great periods of the civil wars, of the wars of religion, etc., struggles and disruptions during which either a nation finds a new *weltanschaulich* platform and on this can build itself up anew and then it can turn its force outwards, or else a people is split in two and falls into chaos. In Germany this process took its course in a truly classical form. The religious struggles meant that the whole force of Germany withdrew inwards – an absorption and exhaustion of this force internally – thereby automatically bringing with it a slowly increasing failure to react to great events of world-wide significance outside of Germany: to these events the people then remains completely unresponsive because of its own internal tensions pressing for resolution.

It is a mistake to say that world politics, the world situation alone, determined Germany's fate in the sixteenth century. No, our own internal condition at that time contributed to form that model of the world that later caused us so much suffering – the partition of the world without Germany.

This process is repeated in a second grand historical example: in place of the lost religious unity – for the two confessions are now ice-bound and neither can overcome the other – a new platform is discovered: the new conception of the state ... On this new platform Germany is once again united, and bit by bit through the consolidation of the Reich ... Germany permanently recovered her strength in foreign politics. This increase in strength led to those August days of 1914, an experience which we ourselves had the proud good fortune to share. A nation which seemed to have no internal differences and therefore could turn its united strength towards the world beyond its frontier! And scarcely four and a half years later we see the process once more take its backward course. Internal differences appear; they slowly grow larger and larger until gradually the nation's external strength is paralyzed. Domestic dissension again becomes paramount; finally there comes the collapse of November 1918. That means in fact simply that the German nation once more is spending its whole strength on its internal conflicts – towards the outside world it sinks back into complete lethargy and powerlessness.

But it would be a grave error to think that this process took place only during the days of November 1918. No, even in the period when Bismarck powerfully united Germany the *weltanschaulich* disintegration had begun. The *bourgeoisie* and proletarians stepped into the roles once played by Prussians, Bavarians, Württembergers, Saxons, Badeners, etc. In place of the disintegration into a number of conflicting states, a disintegration that had been overcome, there began a division into classes, the effects of which lead to precisely the same result ... Once more a mass of people running into millions solemnly declares that it prefers to enter into relations with people and organizations of similar views and conceptions to its own even though they belong to a foreign state, rather than with members of its own people who, though they are of the same blood, do not share its ideological outlook. This fact alone explains how it is that you can see today the red flag with the sickle and the hammer – the flag of an alien state – wave over Germany; that there are millions of men to whom one cannot say: You, too, are Germans – you, too, must defend Germany! If these men were ready to do so as they were in 1914, they would have to abandon their *Weltanschauung*, for it is quite absurd to think that in 1914 Marxism would have converted to the national cause. No! Intuitively recognizing this fact, the German working-man in 1914 deserted Marxism and turning against his leaders found his way to the nation. Marxism itself as conception and idea knows no German nation, knows no national state, but knows only the International! ...

One might have begun the process of regeneration in 1919 and then during the past eleven years Germany's external development would have taken a different course. For if the Peace Treaty could be presented in the form in which it was imposed upon us, then only because Germany at the time had ceased to be a factor that could exercise any influence whatever. (*Very true!*) And if this Peace Treaty in its application assumed the forms we know and experienced, then that, too, is only because in all these years Germany had no definite will of her own that could make itself felt. We therefore are not the victims of the treaties, but the treaties are the consequences of our own mistakes; and if I wish in any way to better the situation, then I must first change the value of the nation. I must above all recognize that it is not the primacy of foreign policy that can determine our actions in the domestic sphere; rather, the character of our actions in the domestic sphere is decisive for the character of our foreign policy successes ...

The essential thing is the formation of the political will of the nation as a whole: that is the starting-point for political action. If this formation of will is guaranteed in the sense of a readiness to fully participate in the attainment of national goals, then a government, supported by this common will, can also choose the ways that one day can lead to success. ...

If anyone today wishes to hurl against me as a National Socialist the most serious possible accusation, he says: "You want to force a decision in Germany by violence, and it is against this that we are bound to protest. You want to annihilate your political opponents in Germany one day. We on the other hand take our stand on the ground of the constitution, and we are bound to guarantee to all parties the right to exist." And to that I have only one reply: Translated into practice that means – you have a company. You have to lead that company against the enemy. Within the company there is complete liberty to form a coalition. (*Laughter.*) Fifty percent of the company have formed a coalition on the basis of love of the Fatherland and of protection of the Fatherland: the other fifty percent have formed a coalition on the basis of pacifism; they reject war on principle, they demand that freedom of conscience be inviolate, and declare that to be the highest, the sole good that we possess today. (*Laughter.*)

... With the body-politic as it is today one can no longer conduct any practical foreign policy. Or do you believe that with the Germany of today Bismarck would have been able to fulfill his historic mission or that the German Reich could have arisen from the present spiritual state?

... When I returned from the front in 1918 I found at home a state of affairs which, like all the others, I might simply have accepted as an accomplished fact ...

I was only a nameless German soldier, with a very small zinc identification number on my breast. But I came to realize that if a new body-politic was not formed within the nation starting from the smallest cell, a body-politic which could overcome the existing "ferments of decomposition," then the nation itself as a whole could never rise again ...

Events have proved that this reasoning was right in the end. For though even today there are many in Germany who believe that we National Socialists would not be capable of constructive work – they deceive themselves! If we did not exist, already today there would be no more *bourgeoisie* alive in Germany: the question Bolshevism or not Bolshevism would long ago have been decided! Take the weight of our gigantic organization – by far the greatest organization of new Germany – out of the scale of national fortunes and you will see that without us Bolshevism would already tip the balance – a fact of which the best proof is the attitude adopted towards us by Bolshevism. Personally I regard it as a great honor when Mr. Trotsky calls upon German Communists to act together with the Social Democrats at any price, since National Socialim must be regarded as the one real danger for Bolshevism.[15] That is for me all the greater honor as we have in twelve years built up our movement from nothing at all against the opposition of public opinion at the time, against the press, against capital, against business, against the administration, and against the state – in a word against everything. Today this movement cannot be destroyed. It is there: people must reckon with it, whether they like it or not. (*Loud applause.*) And I am convinced that for all those who still believe in a future for Germany it is clear what their attitude must be. For here they see before them an organization which does not merely preach the views that earlier in my speech I characterized as essential, but puts them into practice; an organization inspired to the highest degree by national sentiment, and constructed on the conception of an absolute authority of leadership in all spheres, at every stage – the sole party which among its members has completely overcome not only the conception of internationalism but also the idea of democracy; which in its entire organization acknowledges only the principles of responsibility, command, and obedience, and which therewith for the first time has introduced into the political life of Germany an organization numbering millions built up on the principle of achievement. Here is an organization that is filled with an indomitable aggressive spirit, an organization that, when a political opponent says "we regard your conduct as a provocation," for the first time does not see fit immediately to retire from the scene but brutally enforces its own will and hurls against the opponent the retort, "We fight today! We fight tomorrow! And if you regard our meeting today as a provocation we shall hold yet another one next week – until you have learned that it is no provocation when *German* Germany also professes its belief!" And when they say, "You must not come into the street" we go into the street in spite of them. And when they say, "Then we shall strike you," however many sacrifices they force upon us, this young Germany will always continue its marches, and one day it will completely reconquer the German street for the Germans. And when people cast in our teeth our intolerance, we proudly acknowledge it – yes, we have formed the inexorable decision to destroy Marxism in Germany down to its very last root. ...

15   Hitler here refers to Leon Trotsky's opposition to the Stalinist policy of attacking Social Democrats as "Social Fascists," a policy that prevented a united front against Nazism.

Today we stand at the turning-point of Germany's destiny. If the present development continues, Germany will one day of necessity land in Bolshevist chaos, but if this development is broken off, then our people will have to be taken into a school of iron discipline and gradually be freed from the prejudices of both camps. A hard schooling, but one we cannot escape!

If one thinks that one can preserve for all time the conceptions of "bourgeois" and "proletarian," then one will either preserve the weakness of Germany – which means our downfall – or one ushers in the victory of Bolshevism. If one refuses to surrender those conceptions, then in my judgement a resurrection of the German nation is no longer possible. The chalk line which *Weltanschauungen* have drawn for peoples in the history of the world already more than once has proved to be the death-line. Either we shall succeed in working out a body-politic hard as iron from this conglomerate of parties, associations, unions, and conceptions of the world, from this pride of rank and madness of class, or else, lacking this internal consolidation, Germany will fall into final ruin …

People say to me often: "You are only the drummer of national Germany!" And supposing that I were only the drummer? It would be a far more statesmanlike achievement today to drum once more into this German people a new faith than gradually to squander the one they have. (*Loud applause.*) … The more you bring back a people into the sphere of faith, of ideals, the more will it cease to regard material distress as the one and only thing that counts … Then you will understand how mighty is the force of an idea, of an ideal. Only thus can you comprehend how it is that in our movement today hundreds of thousands of young men are prepared to risk their lives to withstand our opponents.

I know quite well, gentlemen, that when National Socialists march through the streets and suddenly in the evening tumult and commotion arise, then the *bourgeois* draws back the curtain, looks out, and says: "Once more my night's rest is disturbed and I can not sleep. Why must the Nazis always be so provocative and run around at night?" Gentlemen, if everyone thought like that, then no one's sleep would be disturbed at night, it is true, but then the *bourgeois* today could not venture into the street. If everyone thought this way, if these young folk had no ideal to move them and drive them forward, then certainly they would gladly do without these nocturnal fights. But remember that it means sacrifice when today many hundred thousands of SA and SS men of the National Socialist Movement have to mount on their trucks every day, protect meetings, undertake marches, sacrifice themselves night after night and then come back in the grey dawn either to workshop and factory or as unemployed to take the pittance of the dole. It means sacrifice when from the little they possess they have to buy their uniforms, their shirts, their badges, yes, and even pay for their own fares – believe me, there is already in all this the force of an ideal, a great ideal! And if the whole German nation today had the same faith in its calling as these hundred thousands, if the whole nation possessed this idealism, Germany would stand differently in the eyes of the world than she stands now! (*Loud applause.*) For our situation in the world, so fatal in its effect for us, is only the result of our own underestimation of German strength. (*Very true!*) Only once we have again changed this fatal valuation of ourselves can Germany take advantage of the political possibilities which, if we look far enough into the future, can place German life once more upon a natural and secure basis: either new living space (*Lebensraum*) and the development of a great internal market or protection of German economic life against the outside world and utilization of all the concentrated strength of Germany …

And so in contrast to our official government I cannot see any hope for the resurrection of Germany if we regard the foreign policy of Germany as the primary factor: the primary necessity is the restoration of a sound, powerful, nationally-minded German body-politic. In order to realize this end I founded the National Socialist Movement thirteen years ago: This movement I have led for the last twelve years, and I hope that one day it will accomplish this task and that, as the finest result of its struggle, it will leave behind a German body-politic completely regenerated internally, intolerant of anyone who sins against the nation and its interests, intolerant against anyone who will not acknowledge its vital interests or who opposes them, intolerant and pitiless against anyone who attempts once more to destroy or subvert this body-politic, and yet ready for friendship and peace with anyone who has a wish for peace and friendship! (*Long and tumultuous applause.*)

Source: "**Vortrag Adolf Hitlers vor westdeutschen Wirtschaftlern im Industrie-Klub zu Düsseldorf**" (Munich: Franz Eher Verlag, 1932). [English: Norman H. Baynes, ed., *The Speeches of Adolf Hitler, April 1922–August 1939*, Vol. I (New York: Howard Fertig, 1969), pp. 777–8, 781–93, 797–800, 802–3, 805–6, 808–14, 816–17, 819, 821–9]

Papen's coup in Prussia, 1932

In July 1932 Chancellor Franz von Papen ordered the dismissal of the legally elected, SPD-dominated coalition government in the state of Prussia by the use of Article 48 of the Weimar constitution (Doc. 2.5). His pretext was the alleged failure of the Prussian government to contain the street disorders that Papen's own repeal of the Brüning government's ban on uniformed paramilitary formations in public had brought about. His real reason was to weaken the SPD and defenders of the parliamentary republic, who controlled the Prussian police.

There was a precedent for the use of Article 48 to supplant a legally elected state government. In October 1923 Chancellor Gustav Stresemann had invoked Article 48 to oust the legally elected Communist–SPD coalition government of the state of Saxony. However, Stresemann had immediately named a new state government to prevent the state from being governed by the national government, as leaders of the Reichswehr and other conservatives had wished. In contrast, the state of Prussia, which contained almost two-thirds of the German population and territory, was to be ruled by the national government from July 1932 on, thus eliminating a bulwark of parliamentary democracy in Germany. This action, taken six months before Hitler's appointment as Chancellor and approved by the supreme court of the Reich, represented an important stage in the destruction of the Weimar Republic.

2.20 Decree of the Reich President on the Restoration of Public Security and Order in Prussia, 20 July 1932

On the basis of Article 48, Sections 1 and 2, of the Reich Constitution, I decree the following measures for the purpose of restoring public safety and order in the territory of the state of Prussia:

1   For the period during which this decree is in force the Reich Chancellor is appointed Reich Commissioner for the state of Prussia. In this capacity he is empowered to dismiss

the members of the Prussian state cabinet from their offices. He is further empowered to assume the duties of the Prussian Prime Minister himself and to entrust the leadership of the Prussian ministries to other persons as Reich Commissioners.

The Reich Chancellor is empowered to exercise all the authority of the Prussian Prime Minister, and his appointees are empowered to exercise all the authority of the Prussian ministries to which they are appointed. The Reich Chancellor and the persons to whom he entrusts the leadership of the Prussian ministries exercise the authority of the Prussian state cabinet.

2   This decree takes effect on the day of its proclamation.

Neudeck and Berlin, 20 July 1932.

Reich President von Hindenburg
Reich Chancellor von Papen

Source: *Reichsgesetzblatt*, 1932 I, p. 377

Plans for an authoritarian constitution

By late 1932 the Weimar constitution, though formally still in effect, was no longer functioning as a parliamentary system. Chancellor Franz von Papen, like Brüning before him and General Kurt von Schleicher (1882–1934) and Hitler after him, exercised authority only by virtue of the emergency powers granted to the President (an office to which General Hindenburg had been reelected in April 1932) under Article 48 of the Weimar constitution. The only political parties still committed to democracy and parliamentary government were the Social Democrats (SPD) and, to a lesser extent, the Catholic Center Party. Together they represented only a little more than a third of the German electorate. A consensus was growing in Germany that the gridlocked parliamentary system would have to be replaced by an authoritarian regime. While the Communists, who increased their vote to 16 percent in the Reichstag elections of November 1932, wanted a dictatorship of the proletariat, conservatives and Nazis sought to establish a nationalist dictatorship.

In the speech excerpted below, Chancellor Papen advocated weakening the legislative powers of the Reichstag and strengthening the powers of the executive. Papen also obliquely defended his coup in Prussia (Doc. 2.20) by calling for the coordination of the Prussian state government with the national government in the new constitution, while deferring to Bavaria's traditional defense of states' rights. Papen's speech shows both the strength of conservative opposition to Weimar parliamentary democracy and the predicament that conservatives faced: They shared the Nazi goal of destroying the "Weimar system," but feared the radicalism and unpredictability of Nazi methods. They wanted to change the Weimar constitution, but were reluctant to turn power over to the Nazis. By their calls for national unity, an end to party politics, and the weakening of parliamentary democracy, conservatives like Papen in effect gave their stamp of approval to the Nazis' efforts to destroy the Weimar Republic. This speech clearly reveals Papen's distrust of Nazi extremism. But in the last analysis his distrust of democracy was stronger. In January 1933 he played a key role in persuading President Hindenburg to grant Hitler power. Papen himself took the post of vice-chancellor in Hitler's first cabinet and remained a faithful servant of the regime until the end of the war.

2.21 Speech by Chancellor Franz von Papen to Bavarian industrialists, 12 October 1932

... We want to create a powerful and nonpartisan state authority which will not become a plaything to be tossed about by political and social forces, but will stand above them unshakable as a *"rocher de bronce."*[16] The reform of the constitution must ensure that such a powerful and authoritarian government has the right relationship to the people.

The great basic laws contained in Part II of the Weimar Constitution are not to be undermined, but it is time to revitalize the forms of political life. The Reich government must gain more independence from the parties. Its existence must not be at the mercy of chance majorities. The relationship between government and the popular legislature must be regulated in such a way that the government rather than the parliament controls the authority of the state.

To counterbalance one-sided decisions by the Reichstag based on party interests, Germany needs a special First Chamber with clearly defined authority and strong legislative powers. Today the Reich President's power of decree, based on Article 48 of the Reich constitution, is the only remedy for the extreme parliamentary system and for the failure of the Reichstag. But as soon as normal stable conditions prevail once again, there will no longer be any reason to apply Article 48 in its present form.

The Reich government plans to carry out the constitutional reform in close consultation with the states. The historically received German state structures are not to be violated. The Reich government rejects any measure that leads to the direct or indirect disintegration of Prussia. As conceived by the Reich government, reform of the Reich cannot be based on dissolution of the state structure of Prussia, erosion of the unity developed in the course of a long history, or surrender of the East–West linkage.

Prussia's continued existence as a legally unified entity is regarded as a self-evident requirement not only by Prussia; it could also be viewed by the other states as a safeguard against the mediatization of non-Prussian states. The main emphasis of the reform must be the elimination of the dualism between the Reich and Prussia, which is also deplored by the Bavarian government. ...

In conjunction with the establishment of an organic connection between the Reich and Prussia, it will be quite possible to grant the remaining states the constitutional autonomy that particularly the Bavarian government has sought.

Even the territorial autonomy eliminated by Article 18 of the Weimar Constitution can be restored to viable states. ... The Reich government will complete the draft of the constitution so that it will be ready when the new Reichstag convenes. ...

The current claim that I, the chancellor, prevented National Socialism from taking governmental responsibility is a falsification of history. Herr Hitler did not accept the offer

---

16   "Rocher de bronce" – a reference to a phrase used by King Frederick William I of Prussia (1657–1713) to describe the statue-like motionlessness of his soldiers.

of 13 August of a share of power in the Reich and in Prussia, which would have assured the NSDAP decisive influence in the government, because he believed, as the leader of a movement with 230 seats in parliament, that he had to lay claim to the position of chancellor. He made this claim based on his party's principle of "totality" and "exclusivity." The insistence of the NSDAP that they had not demanded full power, but had been ready to give other men outside of the movement a role in the government, is therefore another false representation of the facts which it is my the duty to correct. Would such a concession have changed anything in their claim to exclusive leadership? It is well known that the Reich President, who alone has the right to appoint the chancellor, rejected this claim to totality. There cannot be any doubt why he rejected it. It certainly is not a question of personal aversion to the movement's leader, because the Reich President stands heads and shoulders above such considerations. The motives shaping the decision of the head of state were solely based on principle.

The essential element of every conservative world view is that it is anchored in the divine order of things. That is also its fundamental difference from the doctrine followed by the NSDAP. Their principle of "exclusivity," of the political "all or nothing," and their mystical messianic belief in their powerfully eloquent Führer as the only one called to preside over our destiny gives the party the character of a political religion. And it is precisely here that I see the insurmountable difference between a conservative politics based on religion and a National Socialist religion based on politics. ...

At its inauguration the Reich government proclaimed the unification of all truly nationally-minded forces as its highest goal in domestic politics. That goal remains unswervingly in place – it must remain so – for Germany's sake – even if the paths today lead in different directions. Nothing can thwart confidence in the revival of the nation more than the instability of political conditions, or governments that are merely driftwood on the waves of the party, vulnerable to every current. This kind of state administration by party arithmetics is finished in the eyes of the people. ...

Source: *Ursachen und Folgen. Vom deutschen Zusammenbruch 1918 bis zur staatlichen Neuordnung in der Gegenwart. Eine Urkunden- und Dokumentensammlung zur Zeitgeschichte,* Vol. VIII, ed. by Herbert Michaelis and Ernst Schraepler with Günter Scheel (Berlin: Dokumentenverlag Dr. Herbert Wendler, 1958), pp. 657 ff. Translated by Sally Winkle

Conservative support for Hitler

One of the factors in Hitler's rise to power was his ability to attract increasing support among the economic elites who had previously feared the "socialist" leanings of many of the rank and file in the Nazi Party. One of these influential supporters was Dr. Hjalmar Schacht (1877–1970), president of the Reichsbank from 1923 until 1929, when he resigned in protest against what he regarded as the excessively compliant attitude of the government toward reparations. In 1931 he was one of the main organizers of the so-called Harzburg Front, an effort by nationalists to create a strong movement in partnership with the Nazis against the Brüning government and the parliamentary system (see Doc. 2.18).

The first letter reprinted here was written shortly after Hindenburg's refusal to name Hitler chancellor in August 1932 despite the fact that the Nazis had emerged as the strongest party in the July Reichstag elections. It is interesting to note that Schacht advised Hitler not to put forth any specific economic proposals, a strategy that was quite in keeping with Hitler's efforts to appeal to a diverse constituency. After the November election, in which the Nazis lost two million votes but remained the largest party (see Doc. 2.23), Schacht wrote again to express his support for Hitler's continuing refusal to enter the government in any capacity other than chancellor. Schacht also helped to overcome Hindenburg's misgivings about appointing Hitler chancellor in January 1933. For his steadfast support Schacht was restored to his post as president of the Reichsbank (from 1933 to 1939) and as Minister of Economics from 1934 to 1937. His market-oriented policies, however, eventually brought him into conflict with the Nazis' "Four-Year Plan" to prepare Germany for war and led to his resignation from both posts (see Doc. 4.3).

2.22 Letters from Hjalmar Schacht to Hitler, 1932

I   The President of the Reichsbank (in retirement) Dr. Hjalmar Schacht   29 August 1932

Dear Herr Hitler,

I hope that you will allow me to use this form of addressing you, as the only purpose of my letter is to assure you of my unchanging sympathy in these times of great trials. I realize that you are not in need of consolation. The rise to a total of 14 million votes cast for you, the perfidious counterblow by the other – theoretically stronger – side, and the loss of the votes of political profiteers, all these are things which could not seriously surprise you. But what you could perhaps do with in these days is a word of most sincere sympathy. Your movement is carried internally by so strong a truth and necessity that victory in one form or another cannot elude you for long. During the time of the rise of your movement you did not let yourself be led astray by false gods. I am firmly convinced that now, when you are forced into a position of defense for a short time, you will like-wise resist the temptation of an alliance with false idols. If you remain the man that you are, then success cannot elude you.

You know that I do not intend to give you any tactical advice, as I admit absolutely to your superiority in this field. But perhaps as an economist I may say this: if possible, do *not* put forward any detailed economic program. There is no such program on which 14 millions could agree. Economic policy is not a factor for building up a party, but at best collects interest. Moreover, economic measures vary with time and circumstances. It merely depends on the spirit out of which they are born. Let this spirit be the deciding factor.

Wherever my work may take me to in the near future, even if you should see me one day *within* the fortress – you can always count on me as your reliable assistant.

I felt the need of writing the above to you, as in our time so few understand that every-thing depends on inner strength.

With a vigorous "Heil"
[signed] Hjalmar Schacht

2   The President of the Reichsbank (retired) Dr. Hjalmar Schacht   12 November 1932

Dear Herr Hitler,

Permit me to congratulate you on the firm stand you took immediately after the election. I have no doubt that the present development of things can only lead to your becoming chancellor. It seems as if our attempt to collect a number of signatures from business circles for this purpose was not altogether in vain, although I believe that heavy industry will hardly participate, for it rightfully bears its name "heavy industry" on account of its sluggishness.

I hope that in the next few days and weeks the slight difficulties which necessarily appear in the course of the propaganda campaign will not be so great as to provide the opponents with a reason for justified indignation. The stronger your internal position, the more dignified can be your fight. The more conditions develop in your favor, the more you can renounce personal attacks.

I am quite confident that the present system is certainly doomed to disintegration.

With the German salute,

yours very truly,

[signed] Hjalmar Schacht

Source: Office of the US Chief of Counsel for Prosecution of Axis Criminality,
Nazi Conspiracy and Aggression, **Vol. VII (Washington DC:**
US Government Printing Office, 1946), pp. 512–14 [Docs. EC–456 and EC–457]

Hitler takes power

In the Reichstag election on 6 November 1932, the last one before Hitler's appointment as chancellor, the Nazis lost more than two million votes from their high of 37.4 percent in July 1932. This electoral setback, though it left the Nazis with a comfortable plurality of 33.1 percent of the total vote, was widely interpreted as a repudiation of Hitler's refusal to enter into any coalition government except as chancellor. On 13 August 1932 President Hindenburg had emphatically rejected Hitler's request to head the government for fear that it would lead to a Nazi dictatorship. Hitler was also unwilling or unable to meet the terms of the Catholic Center Party for a coalition government with a parliamentary majority. Chancellor Franz von Papen, unable to gain a parliamentary majority himself without Nazi support, had thereupon dissolved the Reichstag and called for new elections, hoping to capitalize on incipient opposition in the Nazi ranks against Hitler's seemingly self-defeating, all-or-nothing strategy. In a desperate effort to increase or at least maintain their voting strength among Berlin's large working class, the Nazis supported a Communist-initiated strike of Berlin transit workers just before the November election. This tactic, too, backfired, and their electoral setback left the Party demoralized, divided, and in financial difficulties.

The following selections from the diary of Joseph Goebbels attest to the sense of crisis in the Nazi Party following the November election. Some Party members and SA leaders, headed by the second most powerful Nazi official, Reich Organization Leader Gregor Strasser, called for an end to Hitler's all-or-nothing strategy. They feared further electoral reversals (as actually occurred in state elections in Thuringia in early December 1932) if the Nazis continued to insist on full power rather than accepting a share of power. General Kurt von Schleicher, who replaced Papen as Chancellor on 2 December 1932, hoped to entice Strasser into his cabinet as vice-chancellor, thereby substantially strengthening his popular base (and possibly splitting the Nazi Party). Hitler, strongly supported by Goebbels and other Nazi leaders, adamantly opposed this move and ultimately prevailed. Strasser resigned his Party offices and went on a prolonged vacation before his final break with Hitler in January 1933.

Schleicher's inability to build a viable coalition with Nazi support (as well as his proposal to redistribute the lands of bankrupt *Junker* estates) finally persuaded Hindenburg to drop his opposition to Hitler, thus vindicating Hitler's all-or-nothing strategy at a time when the Nazis seemed to have reached a dead end. Papen played a key role in this unhappy development by agreeing to enter a Hitler cabinet as vice-chancellor. On 30 January 1933 the new government took power.

In 1934 Goebbels published an embellished version of his diary, translated into English under the title, *My Part in Germany's Fight.*[17] The selections below, however, are taken from his original diary, which give a more unvarnished version of events.

2.23 Excerpts from Goebbels' diary, November 1932–January 1933

---

6 NOVEMBER 1932

Contrary to all expectations, there is a strong voter turnout. It is taking place under totally changed circumstances in Berlin. The means of mass transit are at rest [due to the strike of transit workers], and the whole population is flooding through the streets. The day passes in extraordinary tension. In the evening we sit with a few guests at home and wait for the results. They are not as bad as the pessimists had feared: but it is still a strain to listen to the radio. Every new report brings a new defeat. In the end we have lost thirty-four seats. The Center Party took some losses as well, the Nationalists gained a bit, the Social Democrats lost a bit. Voter participation went down. The Communists made strong gains; that was to be expected. A reactionary government is always the pacemaker for Bolshevism. We have suffered a setback. The reasons: August 13, for which the masses don't yet have a sufficient understanding, and the unconscionable exploitation by Nationalist Party propaganda of our initial contacts with the Center. Neither circumstance is our own fault. We need not reproach ourselves for either one. We now face difficult struggles that will require sacrifices. The main thing is to maintain the Party. The organization must be reinforced and its spirit must be raised. The series of mistakes and shortcomings that have crept in must be stopped. But we must not lose sight of the fact that hardly ten percent of the people stand behind the present government. It therefore cannot hold up. Change of some kind will have to occur. I expound our view in an article on the subject, "A Chancellor Without a People." It speaks out very sharply against the government. I am right there at hand to make sure that the depressed mood in the Party does not spread too much. It is admirable how firmly and cheerfully the whole Party leadership conducts itself. There are no signs of weakness or pessimism. We have overcome other crises, we shall also manage this crisis. As the result of

---

17   Dr. Joseph Goebbels, *My Part in Germany's Fight,* trsl. by Dr. Kurt Fiedler (1940; rept. New York: Howard Fertig, 1979).

the election defeat, the prospects for a successful end to the transit strike have, of course, been greatly reduced. The Social Democrats have betrayed it. As a cat can't stop hunting for mice, Marxism can't stop back-stabbing. The red functionaries may be triumphant today, but their laughter will soon expire. What is unpopular today will be popular tomorrow. We must only stand fast, not give in, and insist that we are right.

8 NOVEMBER 1932

Yesterday: a lousy mood in the district. I arouse the district leaders, the SA leaders, and the transit people. Everything is ready for the fight again. Hitler's appeal: fight on. Papen must go! ... Transit strike is breaking up. It has become hopeless. Jump off! Worked some more at home. [Berlin SA leader Count Wolf Heinrich von] Helldorf came to report. SA in good form. Lots of anger, worry, and drudgery. In the evening studied the district press. Everywhere our defeat. No self-deception! ...

9 NOVEMBER 1933

Yesterday: conferred with Hitler for a long time. He is quite determined to fight. No conciliation. Onward! Papen must go. No compromises. The reactionaries will be amazed. We don't do things halfway. From Berlin there are reports: Papen wants to make concessions. Poor madman! To Hitler in his apartment. He is furious at Strasser. I can believe it. Strasser always sabotages ... Hitler philosophizes. About the right of the stronger. All very good and very well thought out. A fabulous man! For him I would allow myself to be drawn and quartered. He reads a lot and knows a lot. An eminent mind. At the end I read one of his letters from the front out loud. Fabulous. The Hitler of today. Almost unchanged. The first National Socialist ... We will remain hard. If only that fat Strasser doesn't act stupidly. He is so disloyal ...

10 NOVEMBER 1932

The situation is so confused that one sees almost no way out. If it goes on like this the government will bring the whole nation to the dogs. The bourgeois press is playing the guessing game. Reasonable journalists do now seem gradually to see that the situation is not as rosy for the reactionaries as they had imagined before the election. Now the great and probably the last great test of nerves begins. If we pass this test, we will take power.

11 NOVEMBER 1932

I accept a report about the financial state of the Berlin organization. It is quite desperate. Only low tide, debts, and obligations, along with the complete impossibility of coming up with funds in larger amounts after this defeat ... From an intermediary to the government I learn that the [Papen] cabinet is beginning to crack. Opposition to Papen has become very strong. We are advised to remain hard and not to initiate any negotiations. This is superfluous advice as we didn't think otherwise even for a second. We must now launch our attacks on the Communists more scathingly. During the strike we came into unpleasant but unavoidable contact with them. Now we have to again keep our distance. It is also important that we don't give way to illusions and stumble into a second August 13th. We must not get drawn into any more verbal negotiations at all. What we have in writing we can take home without qualms. But the Führer is so secure in his use of tactical means that no one need have any fear about this ...

4 DECEMBER 1932

General Schleicher has completed his cabinet. Not a single outstanding mind is among them. I give this cabinet at most two months. I speak before the [NSDAP] office holders in Karlshorst. They are again in excellent spirits. The Führer has returned to Berlin. We visit him in the Kaiserhof [Hotel] in the afternoon. He had a consultation with Dr. [Hjalmar] Schacht; he is as always on our side. In Thuringia we again had losses. Nor did we throw ourselves into this operation with full zeal. Strasser, for instance, didn't speak at all. This defeat comes at a very inopportune time. There must be no more elections in the future in which we lose even a single vote.

5 DECEMBER 1932

... In the Kaiserhof we have an extensive conference with the Führer. We confer about our attitude toward the Schleicher cabinet. Strasser takes the position that Schleicher has to be tolerated.[18] The Führer has fierce clashes with him. Strasser as always in recent times portrays the situation of the Party in the blackest colors. But even if that were the case, one must not surrender to the resignation of the masses. By accident we learn of the true reason for Strasser's policy of sabotage: Saturday evening he had a conference with General Schleicher in the course of which the General offered him the post of vice-chancellor. Strasser not only did not rule out this offer, but made known his decision to set up his own list of candidates if there are new elections. This is therefore perfidious betrayal of the Führer and the Party. This is not unexpected, I have never believed anything else. We are now just waiting for the moment that he also makes his betrayal public. In difficult crises of nerves a man proves himself through deeds; whoever folds now only proves thereby that he is not called to greatness. Crucial decisions always depend more on character than brains. Strasser tries everything to draw those present at the Führer conference over to his side. All, however, stand so firmly on the side of the Führer that there can be no question of this. Finally he delivers to the Führer Schleicher's threat: If we don't tolerate his cabinet, he would again dissolve the Reichstag. Once again we formulate the conditions under which there is a possibility of giving [Schleicher] an extension of time: Amnesty, social improvements, the right to self-defense, and the freedom to demonstrate, along with a total adjournment of the Reichstag. Meeting of our parliamentary fraction: The Führer speaks very sharply on the spreading addiction to compromise. There can be no question of giving in. It is not about his person, but about the honor and prestige of the Party. Whoever now acts treacherously only proves thereby that he hasn't understood the greatness of our movement. Strasser's features grow visibly more rigid. The fraction itself is of course unanimously in favor of a

---

18   Strasser is here proposing that the Nazis not attempt to oust the Schleicher government by supporting a vote of no confidence.

consistent continuation of the struggle. Only for the time being dissolution of the Reichstag is to be avoided, if possible, as we do not now have good prospects [in a new election] ...

9 DECEMBER 1932

... Call from the Kaiserhof: come immediately. It is 2 a.m. Röhm and Himmler also there. Article in the *Tägliche Rundschau*. Strasser the great man ... Hitler is to be set aside. Strasser officially on vacation. His letter to Hitler is the height of Jesuitical sophistry. We confer: First, the whole apparatus of the Reich Organization Leader is to be dismantled. Hitler takes over the Organization leadership himself with [Robert] Ley as chief of staff. I get Education of the People [*Volksbildung*] ... Agriculture will be independent. Hitler says, if the Party falls apart, I will end it all with my pistol in three minutes ...

10 DECEMBER 1932

... Strasser to Munich. But without any following. He lost all along the line ...

Source: *Die Tagebücher von Joseph Goebbels: Sämtliche Fragmente*,
ed. by Elke Fröhlich, Pt. I, Vol. 2 (Munich: K. G. Saur, 1987), pp. 272–5, 277, 292–3, 298–9.
Translated by Rod Stackelberg

3

The Third Reich

The consolidation of Nazi rule, 1933–35

One day after Hitler's appointment as chancellor he issued an optimistic proclamation to the people in the name of his new government (Doc. 3.1). Its conservative, revivalist, law-and-order tenor was designed to appeal to the millions of Germans who blamed the parliamentary system, partisan politics, and the Marxist left for the gridlock in national politics. To members of the military and industrial elites Hitler revealed his long-term aims (Docs. 3.2 and 3.3): Destruction of the parliamentary system, suppression of the left, creation of a national dictatorship, rearmament, reversal of the Versailles treaty, and preparations for war, should that become necessary to meet Germany's supposedly legitimate need for more territory.

The new regime called for new elections on 5 March 1933 in the hopes of using its incumbency and the machinery of state to obtain the two-thirds majority required to legally change the constitution. The Nazis also launched a campaign of violent persecution against political opponents on the left, particularly leaders and functionaries of the Communist and Social Democratic Parties (Doc. 3.4). The fire that destroyed the interior of the Reichstag building in Berlin on the night of 27 February 1933, in the last week of the election campaign, gave the Nazis the opportunity to suspend civil liberties and and repress the Communist opposition under full legal cover (Doc. 3.5). Hermann Goering, as Minister of the Interior in the state of Prussia, authorized the deputization of SA and SS personnel (Doc. 3.6). Yet despite all the resources at their command, the Nazis failed to obtain even a simple majority of the vote in the last election of 5 March 1933 (see Table 2.1).

While cracking down ruthlessly on the left, the regime made every effort to project an image of respectability, never more so than on the so-called "Day of Potsdam." On the occasion of the first meeting of the newly-elected Reichstag on 21 March 1933, the government mounted an impressive ceremony to symbolize the continuity in values and purposes between the Prussian monarchical tradition and the new Nazi regime (Doc. 3.7). Three days later the Reichstag passed the so-called Enabling Act (Doc. 3.8), granting Hitler full dictatorial powers and relieving him of the need to get Hindenburg's approval for legislation, as he was legally compelled to do while ruling under Article 48 of the constitution. The arrest of the 81 elected Communist delegates and the support of the Catholic Center Party (in return for a guarantee of independence for the Church) gave Hitler the necessary two-thirds majority to establish his dictatorship in quasi-legal fashion.

Jews were among the first victims of Nazi persecution, much of it random and unauthorized violence on the part of the SA. To provide a more controlled outlet for SA hooligans, the regime authorized an economic boycott of Jewish enterprises on 1 April 1933 (Doc. 3.9). The official boycott was limited to one day to avoid foreign retaliation as well as excessive disruption of the economy. Party members, however, continued their boycott and brought pressure to bear on Jewish proprietors to sell their businesses to "Aryans" below market prices. So numerous were the victims of Nazi persecution that the regime authorized the construction of concentration camps under SS control. The first of these was opened in the Munich suburb of Dachau in March 1933 (Doc. 3.10). Additional large-scale camps were opened at Sachsenhausen near Berlin in 1936 and at Buchenwald near Weimar in 1937. Although the announced purpose of the camps was to ensure public safety and "reeducate" political prisoners, inmates were in fact subjected to the arbitrary brutality of vicious SS guards (Doc. 3.11).

Jews, Marxists, and liberal dissidents were the primary victims of *Gleichschaltung*, the process of bringing all organizations and institutions in Germany under Nazi control. The proclaimed goal of *Gleichschaltung* was the creation of a harmonious *Volksgemeinschaft* (people's community) freed of all ethnic diversity or political dissent. The "Civil Service Law" (Doc. 3.12) contained the notorious "Aryan paragraph," according to which any person with one or more "non-Aryan" (i.e., Jewish) grandparents was dismissed from public employment. As a consequence German universities lost some of their top scientists and scholars, most of whom emigrated to Britain or the United States. An officially sponsored "book burning" in May 1933 was meant to symbolize the "purification" of German intellectual life. To further "purify" the German race, the Nazis introduced eugenic legislation in the form of enforced sterilization of the mentally handicapped and other supposedly genetically transmitted conditions like alcoholism, criminality, or vagrancy (Doc. 3.14).

The "Aryan paragraph" was applied, often voluntarily, in the private sector as well, as professional organizations of lawyers, doctors, and other vocations jumped on the Nazi bandwagon and purged their memberships of Jews and critics of the "national awakening." One day after the Nazis had coopted the traditional Mayday labor rallies, the independent labor unions were suppressed and replaced by a Nazi-run German Labor Front under Robert Ley (Doc. 3.13). The arts and the press were subjected to the censorship and control of the newly-established Ministry of Propaganda and Enlightenment, headed by the *Gauleiter* (district leader) of Berlin, Joseph Goebbels (Docs. 3.16 and 3.17). State governments were put under the control of the Reich, and governmental offices under the control of the party. The proudly proclaimed "unity of party and state" (Doc. 3.18), however, often concealed the ongoing rivalry between various office-holders about functions and jurisdictions that was so characteristic of the Nazi system. New opportunities for ambitious members of the party to expand their personal power generated conflicts and disputes that often reduced the administrative efficiency of the regime.

The process of *Gleichschaltung* had its limits. The churches, for instance, resisted control by the party or the state. To preserve their independence in religious matters, however, they were forced to renounce all anti-Nazi political activity. The Vatican signed a Concordat with the Nazi regime that in effect exchanged the right of political participation and dissent for a Nazi pledge to respect the institutional independence of the Church (Doc. 3.15). The Nazis sought to control the Protestant churches in Germany both by backing the nationalist faction, the "German Christians," and by supporting the movement for a nationwide Reich Evangelical Church (thus unifying the administratively separate churches of the individual German states). Their efforts, however, to intervene in internal church governance met with strong resistance from the newly-formed Confessing Church (Doc. 3.19).

By and large the conservative elites willingly cooperated with the Nazis in the *Gleichschaltung* of German society, and even members of the Confessing Church for the most part favored the Nazi aims of establishing strong government, reviving German power, suppressing left-wing opposition, and reducing the influence of the Jews. But some conservatives remained suspicious of the radical anti-establishmentarian practices and potential of the SA, many of whom openly proclaimed the need for a "second revolution" to displace non-Nazi office-holders and reward loyal lower-class Nazis. Vice-Chancellor Franz von Papen gave voice to conservative misgivings in a speech at Marburg University in June 1934 (Doc. 3.20). Military leaders were also suspicious of the ambitions of SA leader Ernst Roehm, who had proposed upgrading the SA into the official fighting force of the nation. Hitler, who needed the continued support of conservatives and the military to stabilize his dictatorship and achieve his foreign policy aims, decided to act. In the night of 30 June 1934 he dispatched SS units to arrest and execute SA leaders, including Roehm himself. His Minister of Justice provided retroactive legalization of the purge (Doc. 3.21). Gratified military leaders reciprocated by backing Hitler's assumption of the presidential title of Commander-in-Chief after Hindenburg's death in August 1934 and by introducing a loyalty oath to the Führer in the armed forces (Doc. 3.22). Hindenburg's testament provides eloquent testimony of the complicity of the conservative elite in the Nazi consolidation of power (Doc. 3.23).

Despite the openly anti-Semitic policies of the regime and the brutality inflicted on dissidents, Hitler's popularity grew. Nazi public works and construction programs helped pull the nation out of depression. His successful defiance of the West in rejecting disarmament negotiations and leaving the League of Nations in October 1933 boosted German national pride. The American reporter William Shirer recorded the public adulation Hitler enjoyed at the carefully orchestrated annual party rally in Nuremberg in September 1934 (Doc. 3.24). Hitler was popular even among women, notwithstanding the Nazis' male supremacist ideology (Doc. 3.25). Many women shared the traditional view of a natural separation of men's and women's spheres and appreciated the high status and public support that the regime bestowed upon child-bearing and child-rearing.

In early 1935 the coal-rich Saar voted to return from French to German rule. In March 1935 Hitler felt strong enough to openly announce German rearmament in defiance of the Versailles Treaty. The British response was to negotiate a naval treaty allowing the Germans to build a far larger navy than was permitted by Versailles. Emboldened by foreign policy successes, the Nazis now also moved to legally segregate Jews through the so-called Nuremberg Laws, passed by a special session of the Reichstag at the annual party rally in September 1935 (Doc. 3.26). The long-term right-wing goal of reversing the results of Jewish emancipation was finally realized.

Proclamation of the "Government of National Concentration"

This official proclamation of the government that took power on 30 January 1933 was read by Hitler in a radio address to the German people. It struck a conservative, revivalist, anti-communist tone designed to elicit maximum support among the German public. It was signed by all the members of Hitler's cabinet, in which the Nazis were outnumbered by traditional conservatives like Vice-Chancellor Franz von Papen, Minister of Economics Alfred Hugenberg, and Foreign Minister Konstantin von Neurath (1873–1956). Of the twelve signatories, only three – Hitler, Hermann Goering (Minister without Portfolio and Deputy Reich Commissioner for Prussia), and Minister of the Interior Wilhelm Frick (1877–1946) – were members of the NSDAP. Many Germans believed that the responsibilities of power would moderate the Nazis' aims and methods. A majority of Germans supported Hitler's call for unity and shared his goals of restoring the German economy, reviving Germany's military power, and raising Germany's standing in the world. Most Germans also agreed with his assessment that communists were mainly responsible for the terrible rifts in German society. The government's proclamation helped to prepare the public for the elimination of a parliamentary system that a growing number of Germans regarded as too permissive, divisive, and ineffective. Although the Nazis themselves did not command an electoral majority, there was a growing consensus for a more unified and authoritarian form of government than the failed Weimar system.

3.1 Proclamation of the Reich Government to the German People, 1 February 1933

More than fourteen years have passed since that ill-fated day when, deluded by promises at home and abroad, the German *Volk* forgot the most treasured values of our past, the Reich, its honor and its freedom, and thus lost everything. Since those days of betrayal, the Almighty has withheld his blessing from our *Volk*. Dissension and hatred broke out among us. Millions of the best German men and women from all walks of life watched in profound distress as the unity of the nation disintegrated and dissolved in a tangle of egotistical political opinions, economic interests, and ideological differences. As so often in our history, the portrait of Germany has been one of heartbreaking disunity since this day of revolution. We did not receive the equality and fraternity promised to us, but we did lose our liberty. For the disintegration of the unity of spirit and will of our *Volk* internally was followed by the decline of its political standing in the world ...

The insane notion of victor and vanquished has destroyed the trust between nations and thereby also the world economy. But the misery of our *Volk* is dreadful! The misery of millions of unemployed, starving proletarians in industry is being followed by the impoverishment of the entire *Mittelstand* and artisan vocations.[1] If this disintegration ultimately also engulfs the German peasants, we will be confronted by a catastrophe of incalculable dimensions. For not only will this mean the end of a Reich, but also of a two-thousand-year-old inheritance of the highest and loftiest values of human culture and civilization. The signs of disintegration are all around us. With unprecedented will and violence, Communists attempt with insane methods to poison and demoralize the shaken and uprooted *Volk* ...

Fourteen years of Marxism have ruined Germany. One year of Bolshevism would destroy Germany. The presently richest and most beautiful cultural areas of the world would be turned into chaos and a heap of ruins. Even the suffering of the last decade and a half would not compare with the misery of a Europe in whose heart the red flag of destruction had been raised. May the thousands of wounded and countless dead that this internal war has already cost serve as a warning signal against the coming storm. In these hours of overwhelming concern for the existence and future of the German nation, the aged leader of the World War appealed to us men in the national parties and organizations to fight under him once more as we had at the front, this time at home, in unity and loyalty, for the salvation of the

---

1   *Mittelstand* is the German designation for the lower middle class of small proprietors, shopkeepers, and tradesmen who, along with small-scale farmers ("peasants"), formed a high proportion of the Nazis' electoral constituency.

Reich. As the venerable Reich President has extended his hand to us to work together, we, the national leaders, vow to God, our conscience, and our *Volk* that we shall resolutely and steadfastly fulfill the task thus entrusted to us as the national government.

The situation we have inherited is a terrible one. The task we must fulfill is the most difficult one posed to German statesmen within living memory. But our confidence is unbounded, for we believe in our people and their imperishable values. Peasants, workers, and the middle classes must all join together to provide the building blocks for the new Reich. The national government regards as its first and foremost task to restore the unity of spirit and will of our *Volk*. It will preserve and defend the foundation upon which the strength of our nation rests. It will extend its firm protection to Christianity as the basis of our moral system, and to the family as the nucleus of our *Volk* and state. It will restore to our *Volk*, beyond the divisions of rank and class, its consciousness of national and political unity and the duties this entails. It will make reverence for our great past and pride in our ancient traditions the foundation for the education of German youth. In this way it will declare a merciless war against spiritual, political, and cultural nihilism. Germany must not and will not sink into anarchistic communism. In place of turbulent instincts it will again raise national discipline to the guiding principle of our life. In doing so, the government will devote careful attention to those institutions that constitute the true guarantors of the power and strength of our nation …

If Germany is to experience this political and economic revival and conscientiously fulfill its obligations towards other nations, one decisive step is required: overcoming the Communist subversion of Germany. We, the men of this government, feel ourselves responsible to German history for the reconstruction of an orderly body-politic and thus for finally overcoming the insanity of class and class conflict. It is not a single class that we envision, but rather the German *Volk*, its millions of peasants, bourgeois, and workers, who will either together overcome the problems of these times or succumb to them together. Full of resolve and true to our oath, we are determined – in view of the present Reichstag's inability to support this work – to entrust this task, to which we are committed, to the German *Volk* itself.

Reich President Field Marshal von Hindenburg has summoned us with the order to give our nation the opportunity to regain its strength through unity. We therefore now appeal to the German people to take part in this act of reconciliation. The government of the national resurgence wants to work, and it will work. It was not responsible for leading the German nation into ruin for fourteen years, but it wants to lead the nation back to the top. It is determined to make good in four years the damage done in fourteen years. But it cannot make the work of reconstruction dependent upon the approval of those who are to blame for the collapse. The Marxist parties and their fellow travellers have had fourteen years to prove their ability. The result is a heap of rubble. Now, German people, give us four years, and then pass judgment on us! True to the order of the Field Marshal, let us begin. May almighty God look mercifully upon our work, lead our will on the right path, bless us with insight, and reward us with the trust of our people. For we are not fighting for ourselves, but for Germany!

Adolf Hitler; v. Papen; Baron v. Neurath; Dr. Frick;
Count Schwerin v. Krosigk; Dr. Hugenberg; Seldte;
Dr. Gürtner; v. Blomberg; Eltz v. Rübenach; Göring; Dr. Gereke

Source: *Völkischer Beobachter*, 2 February 1933. Translated by Rod Stackelberg

Hitler and the army

On the evening of 3 February 1933, three days after the new government took power, the Chief of the Army Command, General Kurt von Hammerstein-Equord (1878–1943), invited the new chancellor to dinner at his home to introduce him to leading Reichswehr officers and to give him an opportunity to outline his political goals. One of the guests, General Liebmann, summarized Hitler's main points in the following notes. Hitler assured the Reichswehr officers of his intention to eradicate pacifism, Marxism, and democracy in Germany and to build up the armed forces at the earliest opportunity through the reintro- duction of universal military service. As the latter goal was also the principal objective of the Reichswehr, Hitler could be sure of a sympathetic hearing. In contrast to his public pronouncements, in which he rarely acknowledged his expansionist goals, Hitler felt no need to conceal his ultimate goal of acquisition of *Lebensraum* from his generals.

Hitler's reference to the army as "the most socialist institution" gives some insight into what the Nazis understood under the concept of socialism. The Nazis' notion of socialism bore some resemblance to the "Prussian socialism" of discipline, duty, and service advocated by such theorists of the "conservative revolution" as Oswald Spengler. Interesting, too, is Hitler's call to the army to remain non-partisan. This, of course, in no way excluded support for the Nazi party, as the Nazis themselves claimed to constitute a popular movement "above party politics," a claim they would soon enforce by banning all opposition parties.

Hitler assured the generals that the SA (including the still miniscule SS) were a purely political force and constituted no threat to the army's status as the nation's offi- cial armed force. Army leaders would remain unconvinced, however, until the "night of long knives" on 30 June 1934, when Hitler purged the SA leadership in part to retain the good will of army leaders (Doc. 3.21). Most army leaders enthusiastically shared the Nazis' political goals. Hammerstein, who had already opposed the Kapp–Lüttwitz Putsch in 1920 (Doc. 2.7), was not one of them, however, and his skepticism led to his removal as army chief in January 1934.

3.2 Hitler's remarks on his political goals to army and navy commanders, 3 February 1933

Goal of all policies: Regaining political power. The whole state must be directed toward this goal (all ministries!)

1   *Domestic policy.* Complete reversal of the present domestic political situation in Germany. Refusal to tolerate any attitude contrary to this aim (pacifism!). Those who can not be converted must be broken. Extermination of Marxism root and branch. Conversion of youth and of the whole people to the idea that only struggle can save us and that everything else must be subordinated to this idea. (Achieved in the millions of the Nazi movement. It will grow.) Training of youth and strengthening of the will to fight by all means. Death penalty for high treason. Tightest authoritarian state leadership. Elimination of the cancer of democracy!

2   *Foreign policy.* Struggle against Versailles. Equality of rights in Geneva;[2] but useless if people do not have the will to fight. Concern for allies.

3   *The economy!* The farmer must be saved! Settlement policy! Further increase of exports useless. The capacity of the world is limited, and there is over-production everywhere. Settlement offers the only possibility of again employing part of the army of unemployed.

But time is needed, and radical improvement [is] not to be expected since living space too small for German people.

4 *Building up the armed forces* is the most important prerequisite for achieving the goal of regaining political power. Universal military service must be reintroduced. But beforehand the state leadership must ensure that the men subject to military service are not, even before their entry, poisoned by pacifism, Marxism, Bolshevism, or fall victim to this poison after their service.

How should political power be used when it has been gained? Impossible to say at this point. Perhaps fighting for new export possibilities, perhaps – and probably better – the conquest of new living space in the east and its ruthless Germanization. Certain that only through political power and struggle the present economic conditions can be changed. The only things that can take place now – settlement – [are] stopgap measures.

Armed forces most important and most socialist institution of the state. They must stay unpolitical and non-partisan. The internal struggle not their affair but that of the Nazi organizations. Differently than in Italy, no fusion of army and SA intended. – Most dangerous time is during the reconstruction of the army. It will show whether or not France has *statesmen*; if so, they will not leave us time but will attack us (presumably with eastern satellites).

Source: Thilo Vogelsang, "Neue Dokumente zur Geschichte der Reichswehr," *Vierteljahrshefte für Zeitgeschichte* 2 (1954), pp. 434–5. Translated by Rod Stackelberg

Hitler and the industrialists

Hitler decided that the optimal course to full power was to hold one more election, in which, with the full resources of the government at their disposal, the Nazis could reasonably expect to gain a majority, perhaps even the two-thirds majority required to legally abrogate the Weimar constitution. The election was scheduled for March 5. On February 20 Hitler met with leading industrialists to gain their support for the upcoming campaign. He repeated the argument he had already made in his famous Industry Club speech in January 1932 (Doc. 2.19) that majority rule was incompatible with private enterprise. Only ideological unity, he asserted, could provide the condition for full economic development. Liberalism led to democracy, and democracy would lead to communism, unless this pernicious retrogression were halted by the strong-armed methods against the left that the Nazis were ready to employ. Hitler found a receptive audience among the industrialists, who contributed some 3 million marks to the party coffers. Contrary to Hitler's expectations, however, the Nazis were able to gain only 43 percent of the vote in the March elections.

2   The reference is to the disarmament conference at which Germany demanded parity in arms with France and Britain.

3.3 Hitler's speech to leading industrialists, 20 February 1933

With the year 1918 a whole system collapsed. That it had to come about was often predicted, as much by economic leaders as especially by *Geheimrat* Kirdorf.[3] The revolution which the year 1918 brought us was only conditional. In any case it did not bring about a revolution such as in Russia, but only a new school of thought, which slowly initiated the dissolution of the existing order. Bismarck's statement: "Liberalism is the pacemaker of Social Democracy" is now scientifically established and proven for us. A given school of thought – thought direction – can unsuspectedly lead towards the dissolution of the foundation of the state. In our country also, a new direction of thought had gained ground which slowly led to internal disruption and became the pacemaker of Bolshevism.

Private enterprise cannot be maintained in the age of democracy; it is conceivable only if the people have a sound idea of authority and personality. Everything positive, good, and valuable that has been achieved in the world in the field of economics and culture is solely attributable to the importance of personality. When, however, the defense of the existing order, its political administration, is left to a majority, it will go irretrievably under. All the worldly goods that we possess we owe to the struggle of the select few. If we had the present conditions in the Middle Ages, the foundations of our German Reich would never have been laid. The same mentality that was the basis for obtaining these values must be used to preserve these values. All values that made up the height of our culture originated from an entirely different mentality than that which seized its administration since 1918.

... Our people has not yet sufficiently recognized that there are two souls struggling for it. Our entire life is based upon common agreements. The smallest example of this is the family, and it leads on up to the state. It is an impossibility that part of the people recognizes private ownership while another part denies it. Such a struggle splits people. The struggle lasts until one side emerges victorious. When a man deserts his unit he can be punished. When, however, 15 percent to 20 percent disregard their oath of allegiance, the unit must fail as a military instrument. The same applies to a state; if 15 percent of the people deny the state as a permanent recognized social order, no sound system can be set up for the general public. Therefore, it is impossible to maintain culture, art, religion, and science, if a large percentage of the nation refuses to abide by the thoughts which created such a culture ...

No two ideologies can continuously live alongside one another. in such struggles the strength of a people eats itself completely up internally and therefore cannot act externally. It does not rest. This condition of attrition lasts until one party emerges victorious or the state itself dissolves, whereby a people loses its place in history. We live in such times now, when the die must be cast, and when we must decide whether we want to adopt a form of life that supports the state or to have communism. The latter is also thinkable. It is often being said that communism is the last step of humanity. I believe the very opposite; it is the origin of human development. It represents the most primitive form of human life. The deeper one delves into nature the more alike becomes its achievements, they become as in communism more and more homogeneous. The communist principle does not hold water. It is not by chance that one person accomplishes more than the other. The principle of private ownership ... is rooted in this fact.

---

3   Coal and steel magnate Emil Kirdorf (1847–1938), a long-time member of the Pan-German movement, was one of the first industrialists to join the Nazi Party in the 1920s.

The course that we have to take is clearly indicated. It is, however, not enough to say: We do not want communism in our economy. If we continue on our old political course, then we shall perish. We have fully experienced in the past years that economics and politics cannot be separated. The political conduct of the struggle is the primary decisive factor. Therefore, politically clear conditions must be reached ...

As I lay in the hospital in 1918 I experienced the revolution in Bavaria. From the very beginning I saw it as a crisis in the development of the German people, as a period of transition. Life always tears up humanity. It is therefore the noblest task of a leader to find ideals that are stronger than the factors that pull the people apart. I recognized even while in the hospital that one had to search for new ideas conducive to reconstruction. I found them in nationalism, in the value of personality, in the denial of reconciliation between nations, in the strength and power of individual personality. On this basis I tried to reach an understanding between two souls struggling with one another within the German people. The struggle that I undertook was so much harder because it was conducted during a time when the law for the protection of the weak and decadent held true, a law under which every nation is doomed to perish ...

For 40 years we have experienced a continuous growth of Social Democracy. Bismarck said shortly before he retired: "If this keeps up, Marx must remain victorious."

The creative and decomposing forces in a people always fight against one another. In this struggle one side always gains ever greater heights than the other, and therefore I have been following the development of Social Democracy with steadily growing concern and said to myself, we must come to a decision. I have repeatedly taken the occasion to point out to responsible people what dangers were threatening the German people. Time and again it was argued, amongst others by von Seeckt, that at the present time this would mean civil war.[4] And when a few years ago the number of socialist seats went back a little, I was told triumphantly: "Look here, the danger is already over." They always comforted themselves with the hope that the socialist movement would slow down by itself. The danger, however, cannot be overcome by such means. Human beings are nothing so little as equal, and if human beings are not led, they drop back into the most primitive ancient state. It was this perception that moved me to found a new nationalist movement, which after 14 years of struggle has become a leading force in the German Reich. We must not forget that all the benefits of culture must be introduced more or less with an iron fist, just as once upon a time the farmers were forced to plant potatoes. For all this, however, courage and iron will and perseverance are essential.

... Two fronts have thus shaped themselves that put us to the choice: Either Marxism in its purest form or the other side. One cannot assume the point of view and say: The other side will gradually break through again. When I wanted to act, I was advised to wait a while. But I did not agree to such tolerance. With the very same courage with which we have gone to work to make up for what has been sinned during the last 14 years, we have withstood all attempts to move us off the right course. We have turned down the offer of the Catholic Center Party to tolerate us.[5] Hugenberg has too small a movement.[6] He has only considerably

4   General Hans von Seeckt (1866–1936), Commander in Chief of the Reichswehr from 1920–26, withheld military support from the Hitler Putsch in 1923.

5   The Center Party's toleration of a Hitler regime in the Reichstag would have enabled Hitler to form a parliamentary government (a government with a parliamentary majority), but Hitler rejected such a coalition because he wanted to rule with full dictatorial powers.

slowed down our development.[7] We must first gain complete power if we want to crush the other side completely. While still gaining power one should not start the struggle against the opponent. Only when one knows that one has reached the pinnacle of power, that there is no further possible upward development, should one strike. In Prussia we must gain another 10 seats and in the Reich proper another 33. That is not impossible if we throw in all our strength. Then only begins the second action against Communism.

Now we stand before the last election. Regardless of the outcome there will be no retreat, even if the coming election does not bring about a decision. One way or another, if the election does not decide, the decision must be brought about even by other means. I have intervened in order to give the people once more the chance to decide their fate by themselves. ... The question of restoration of the Wehrmacht will not be decided at Geneva, but in Germany, when we have gained internal strength through internal peace.[8] There will, however, be no internal peace until Marxism is eliminated. Here lies the decision that we must meet, hard as the struggle might be. I put my life into this struggle day after day as do all those who joined me in this struggle. There are only two possibilities, either to crowd back the opponent on constitutional grounds, and for this purpose once more we have this election, or a struggle will be conducted with other weapons, which may demand greater sacrifices. I would like to see them avoided. I hope the German people thus recognize the greatness of the hour. It shall decide over the next 10 or probably even 100 years. It will become a turning point in German history, to which I pledge myself with glowing energy.

Source: Office of the US Chief of Counsel for Prosecution of Axis Criminality,
Nazi Conspiracy and Aggression, **Vol. VI**
(Washington DC: US Government Printing Office, 1946), pp. 1080–84 [Doc. D–203]

Nazi persecution of political opponents, 1933

Although the Nazis had gained power legally, their takeover was accompanied by a wave of terror against the left, particularly Communist and Social Democratic activists. Rudolf Diels (1900–57) was a career official in the Prussian police who was retained by Goering (as Prussian Interior Minister) to head the Prussian Gestapo (Secret State Police) when it was founded on 26 April 1933. Diels describes the extra-legal violence of the SA, which began as soon as Hitler took power. Violence was escalated after the Reichstag Fire Decree (Doc. 3.5) suspended legal protections for people charged with political crimes. Goering had SA members deputized as auxiliary members of the Prussian police to give their violence legal cover. A favorite device for the arrest of political opponents who had committed no crime was "protective custody." Diels estimated the number of political opponents murdered from March to October 1933 at between 500 and 700.

Diels was eventually relieved of his post (he was named to the highest governing office in the city of Cologne) when Heinrich Himmler assumed control of the Prussian

---

6   Alfred Hugenberg's Nationalist Party had less than 10 percent of the vote in the 1932 elections, not enough to form a parliamentary majority with the Nazis.

7   By syphoning off votes that would otherwise have gone to the Nazis.

8   The reference is to the Geneva Disarmament Conference, from which the Germans withdrew in October 1933.

police in 1934 and incorporated the Gestapo into the SS. The Gestapo continued to employ professional policemen who were willing to cooperate with the Nazis in achieving their political aims. Diels, who became a witness for the prosecution at the Nuremberg trials after the war, claimed that he was dismissed for failing to arrest and eliminate Gregor Strasser and General Kurt von Schleicher, both of whom were murdered in the "Blood Purge" of 30 June 1934 (Doc. 3.21). This selection is taken from the record of the US prosecutors.

3.4 Affidavit of Rudolf Diels

I, Rudolf Diels, being duly sworn, declare:

When Hitler came into power on 30 January 1933 I was chief of the political police in Berlin. On 26 April 1933 Goering founded the secret state police, and I was nominated as deputy leader of the Gestapo. Most of my orders were given to me personally by Goering. Goering told me my main task was to eliminate political opponents of National Socialism and Hitler. The most important task was the fight against communism.

Because of the interference of the SA and because of the whole revolutionary development during the course of 1933, all police forces, including the Gestapo, had to work mostly as a normalizing and legalizing agent, and had to fight more strongly against SA excesses than against the communists themselves. This condition changed completely at the beginning of 1934. The extra-legal arrests by the SA were annulled again toward the end of 1933, and the Gestapo started to investigate the cases of people still in prison under protective custody to see if they could be accused of high treason. These intentions were interrupted when [Heinrich] Himmler was made the chief of the entire Prussian police and [Reinhard] Heydrich Chief of the Gestapo. Himmler immediately started the reorganization of the police as he had already done in the other states. In the field of the political police he introduced the SD in Prussia, a purely SS organization which Goering had not permitted so far.[9] The Gestapo was now extended over all of Germany, and Heydrich discharged radically the old officials and replaced them with reliable Nazis and SS officers. He started immediately to make up for what in his opinion had been neglected; he again filled up the jails and concentration camps and organized the purge of 30 June 1934. From now on the Gestapo was responsible for all deprivations of freedom and breaches of law and killings in the political field which took place without court verdict. Of primary importance among these was the shooting of numerous persons who had been committed to jails by the courts and then shot supposedly because of resistance. Many such cases were at that time published in the papers. For people guilty of immorality such illegal shootings became the rule. As for deprivation of freedom, there was no legal reason any more for protective custody orders after 1934, which had still been the case before that date, since from 1934 on the power of the totalitarian state was so stabilized that the arrest of a person for his own protection was only an excuse for arbitrary arrest – without court verdict and without legal measures for him. The terroristic measures, which led to the development of the pure force system and punished to an increasing degree each

---

9   SD was the acronym for *Sicherheitsdienst* (Security Service, the SS agency for the collection of internal intelligence headed by Reinhard Heydrich (1904–42). The SD later took over the functions of foreign intelligence as well.

critical remark and each impulse of freedom with the concentration camp, took on more and more arbitrary and cruel forms. The Gestapo became the symbol of the regime of force. Fear of it ruled everybody, especially because of the tortures connected with the arrests.

From the events which caused me to tender my resignation I recognized that the Gestapo was developing as the willing executor not only of Hitler's orders but also of his wishes. Hitler had ordered me to the Obersalzberg in January 1934 and told me in the presence of Goering that some "traitors" had to disappear. From his words I had to infer the order to remove Strassor (Gregor), [Kurt von] Schleicher, and other persons. Since I had not done anything to execute this order for about a week, Goering informed me that he would accept my resignation, which had already been tendered earlier, and that he wanted to subordinate the Prussian police to Himmler and Heydrich. The above-named persons [Strasser and Schleicher] and many others were killed on 30 June 1934.

Source: Office of the US Chief of Counsel for Prosecution of Axis Criminality, *Nazi Conspiracy and Aggression*, Vol. V (Washington DC: US Government Printing Office, 1946), pp. 205–6

The Reichstag Fire Decree

In the night from February 27 to 28, less than a month after Hitler's accession to the office of chancellor, the majestic Reichstag building in Berlin, the site of the German parliament, was burned and badly damaged. Whether the arsonist, a young Dutchman who had at one time belonged to the Communist Party, acted alone or whether he received assistance, presumably from the Nazis, has never been conclusively determined. Hitler's new government took full advantage of the event to crack down on Communists and the left in general. Portraying the fire as a signal for a Communist uprising, the government issued a decree suspending the basic civil liberties guaranteed by the constitution (Doc. 2.5) and introducing and extending the death penalty for a variety of political crimes.

The so-called Reichstag Fire Decree was never repealed. Its effect was to create a permanent state of emergency that served as the legal basis of the Nazi police state. It was used to arrest and frequently execute leading Communist officials. Conveniently, it allowed the Nazis to arrest Communist candidates in the Reichstag election held on March 5, less than a week after the fire. The arrest of all 81 elected Communist Party members (most under the pretext of "protective custody") made possible the two-thirds majority the Nazis needed to pass the Enabling Act. Although the Reichstag Fire Decree was proclaimed "as a defensive measure against Communist acts of violence," it was applied by the government and the courts against the SPD and the democratic left as well. On the basis of this decree SPD publications were suppressed. Left-wing opposition of any kind to the regime was branded as contributing to Communist subversion. The Reichstag Fire Decree in effect freed the police from all restrictions and gave the regime the legal weapon to prosecute dissent.

3.5 Decree of the Reich President for the Protection of the People and State, 28 February 1933

On the basis of Article 48, Section 2, of the German constitution, the following is decreed as a defensive measure against Communist acts of violence endangering the state:

1   Articles 114, 115, 117, 118, 123, 124, and 153 of the Constitution of the German Reich are suspended until further notice. Thus, restrictions to personal liberty, on the right of free expression of opinion, including freedom of the press, on the right of assembly and the right of association, and violations of the privacy of postal, telegraphic, and telephonic communications, and warrants for house-searches, orders for confiscations as well as restrictions on property, are also permissible beyond the legal limits otherwise prescribed.

2   If in a state the measures necessary for the restoration of public security and order are not taken, the Reich Government may temporarily take over the powers of the highest state authority. ...

5   The crimes which under the Criminal Code are punishable with penitentiary for life are to be punished with death: i.e., in Sections 81 (high treason), 229 (poisoning), 306 (arson), 311 (explosion), 312 (flooding), 315, Paragraph 2 (damage to railway facilities), 324 (public endangerment through poison).

Insofar as a more severe punishment has not been previously provided for, the following are punishable with death or with life imprisonment or with imprisonment not to exceed 15 years:

1   Anyone who undertakes to kill the Reich President or a member or a commissioner of the Reich Government or of a state government, or provokes to such a killing, or agrees to commit it, or accepts such an offer, or conspires with another for such a murder;

2   Anyone who under Section 115, Paragraph 2 of the Criminal Code (serious rioting) or of Section 125, Paragraph 2 of the Criminal Code (serious disturbance of the peace) commits these crimes with arms or cooperates deliberately and intentionally with an armed person;

3   Anyone who commits a kidnapping under Section 239 of the Criminal Code with the intention of making use of the kidnapped person as a hostage in the political struggle. This decree enters in force on the day of its promulgation.

Berlin, 28 February 1933
The Reich President: von Hindenburg
The Reich Chancellor: Adolf Hitler
The Reich Minister of the Interior: Frick
The Reich Minister of Justice: Dr. Gürtner

Source: *Reichsgesetzblatt* 1933, I, p. 83

Repression of the Left

The following selection is taken from a pamphlet by Hermann Goering (1893–1946) in which he describes his purge of the police and creation of the Gestapo (Secret State Police) in his capacity as Prussian Interior Minister in Hitler's first cabinet. The pamphlet was written in late 1933 and published in both an English and German edition in 1934. (The following selection is a translation of the version that was read by the German public.) Its purpose was to defend the brutal methods employed by the Nazis in their repression of the left in the first year of their regime, methods that were criticized not just by observers abroad, but by many moderate Germans as well (before such criticisms became too dangerous). Goering also felt the need to disavow his widely suspected involvement in the fire that destroyed the Reichstag on 28 February 1933, giving the Nazis a convenient pretext to suspend civil liberties in the closing stages of the election campaign (Doc. 3.5). A mentally retarded Dutch Communist was arrested and executed for setting the fire, but the Nazis did not have enough evidence to persuade a German court to convict the German Communist Party or the Communist International of involvement.

This selection provides a stark example of how the Nazis exploited popular fears of communism and yearnings for "law and order." Indeed, one of the keys to the Nazis' success in rapidly consolidating their rule was the sympathy and support they could count on among rank-and-file police officers, many of whom felt that the governments of the Weimar Republic had imposed excessive restrictions on their use of force. The Gestapo was formed out of the political police that had previously served the SPD government in the state of Prussia (see Doc. 3.4). Goering, whose main duties involved heading both the air force and, after 1936, the economy (see Doc. 4.3), turned over control of the police to Heinrich Himmler (1900–45) and the SS in 1934. In 1939 Goering was designated by Hitler as his successor in case of his death (Doc. 5.1).

This pamphlet was also intended to counter what the Nazis called the "atrocity propaganda" from abroad. Central to the Nazi mindset was the linkage they made between communism and the Jews (see Docs. 2.3 and 6.3), and the threat of communist subversion served as the primary rationale for the brutal persecution of Jews. The apocalyptic language of the extermination of "subhumanity" that Goering here directs against the Communist "plague" was the same kind of language that the Nazis would later direct against the Jewish people as a whole.

3.6 Hermann Goering, *Reconstruction of a Nation*

THE REORGANIZATION OF THE POLICE

I had taken on a grave responsibility. An enormous amount of work lay before me. It was quite clear to me that I could make little use of the existing system, but would have to make sweeping changes. To begin with, it seemed to me that I had to gain firm control over the regular and political police. Here is where I made the first major personnel changes. Of the 32 chiefs of the regular police I removed 22. Hundreds of inspectors and thousands of police sergeants were removed in the following months. New men were brought in, and everywhere they were chosen from the great manpower pool of the SA. It was important to instill a completely new spirit in the police.

Previously, the police had been degraded to the role of whipping boy of the republic, in part because they used force, but also because all responsibility for the use of force was placed on minor officials while leading officials were too cowardly to defend their subordinates. All of that has now changed. Proper authority has now been restored. In just a few weeks one could see how the morale of the police changed, how they became more confident and proud. Gradually the embittered police began once again to become valuable and useful officers, who, though they had not enjoyed any military training, did possess the old soldierly virtues. Duty, loyalty, obedience, and, above all, unconditional allegiance to the National Socialist state and to the new Germany were the traits that were called for. Younger or more seasoned officers who in the past had not given in to the Republic were given preferential promotion to responsible positions.

... As an outward manifestation of the newly revived sense of honor I forbade the police to carry night sticks. I could not reconcile my conception of an officer with the practice of running around beating up people with night sticks. A police officer resorts to violence only in an extreme emergency, and then he must draw his revolver and use it ruthlessly to protect the people and the state. But, up to now, when a police officer had to fire in self-defense, he was subjected to criminal proceedings, and the usual result was punishment and humiliation. No wonder, then, that the police no longer dared to act in a brave and resolute manner, but used their night sticks to work off their frustrations wherever they believed they could do so without danger ...

I gave strictest orders that the police should devote themselves energetically to vanquishing enemies of the state. In one of my first meetings in Dortmund I said that in the future only one man would bear responsibility in Prussia, and that I was that man. Whoever did his duty, whoever obeyed my orders, whoever proceeded ruthlessly against enemies of the state, and whoever used his revolver when attacked could be sure of my protection. Whoever, on the other hand, avoided a fight in a cowardly manner, whoever pretended not to have seen anything, whoever hesitated to use his weapon, would have to count on being speedily dismissed by me. At that time I declared in front of thousands of national comrades that every bullet fired by a police officer was a bullet fired by me personally. If you call that murder, then I am the murderer. I ordered it, I stand behind it, and I do not hesitate to take responsibility for it.

Whoever sees the Prussian police today, after three-quarters of a year under our control, will not recognize them as the police trained by Mr. Severing.[10] In a few months we succeeded – because the core of the police was so excellent – in making the Prussian police into an instrument that gives the state a feeling of security, but that also gives the police the proud feeling of being the first and sharpest weapon of the state. The replacement of the ugly uniforms and introduction of new flags has raised the self-esteem of the officers. The new oath to the flag has a different meaning for them, and its fulfillment has become a sacred duty.

THE ORGANIZATION OF THE SECRET STATE POLICE

Conditions in the secret state police were dismal indeed. Everywhere I found agents of the Social Democrats, these creatures of Mr. Severing. These men formed the notorious Division I-A, the political police. Under the circumstances I could make no use of them whatsoever. Bracht,[11] my predecessor, had already removed some of the worst elements. But now I

10   Carl Severing (1875–1952), a leading member of the Social Democratic Party, was Goering's predecessor as Prussian Interior Minister.

had to make a clean sweep. For weeks I personally undertook the work of reorganization, and finally it was my personal decision to create the Secret State Police Office. This instrument, so much feared by our enemies, is the principal reason why in Germany and Prussia there is today no Marxist or Communist menace. Ignoring seniority, I put the most able men into the Secret State Police Office and put it under one of the most able young officials. Daily I am again and again convinced that I chose the right men. The job that the Office Chief [Rudolf] Diels and his men did will always remain one of the principal achievements of the first year of German recovery.

The SA and SS actively supported my efforts. Without their help I would never have been able to master our enemies so quickly. Since then I have once again reorganized the secret police and put them under my direct command. By means of a network of offices around Germany, with Berlin as the headquarters, I am kept informed daily, even hourly, of everything that happens in the diverse regions of Prussia. The last hideout of the Communists is known to us, and no matter how often they change their tactics, or rename their couriers, within a few days they are again tracked down, registered, monitored, and broken up. We have had to proceed against the enemies of the state with total ruthlessness. It must not be forgotten that when we took over the government over 6 million people still supported the Communists and over 8 million people the Marxists [SPD], according to the Reichstag elections in March. Certainly these people were not all enemies of the state. The greater part, innumerable millions, were good Germans led astray by this insane world view, but also by the spinelessness and weakness of the middle-class parties. All the greater was the need to rescue these people from error and to lead them back into the national community. But it was just as necessary to proceed mercilessly against the deceivers, the agitators, and the leaders themselves. Thus concentration camps were established, in which we had first to intern thousands of officials of the Communist and Social Democratic Parties. It was only natural that certain excesses occurred in the beginning. Of course here and there innocents were also affected. Of course here and there a few beatings took place and brutal acts were committed. But measured against everything that preceded it, and against the greatness of the occasion, this German revolution for freedom was the most bloodless and most disciplined revolution in history.

DESTRUCTION OF MARXISM AND COMMUNISM

Every revolution is accompanied by some unpleasant and undesired phenomena. But when they are as few as they are here, and when the aim of the revolution is so completely achieved as here, no one has the right to get excited about them or even to discuss them.

But I totally reject the flood of the meanest and most outrageous slanders and atrocity stories that have been spread by creatures without honor or fatherland who have fled abroad. Hereby German Jewry has proven more conclusively than we could in our attacks and speeches how right we were in our defensive actions against them. The Jew is here in his element, concocting atrocity stories and similar lies. Here he could once again without risk, because in a foreign country, pour buckets of mud on the people and nation whose hospitality he enjoyed for many decades.

11 Fritz Bracht (1899–1945) was put in charge of the Prussian police after Chancellor Franz von Papen
     declared himself Reich Commissioner of Prussia on 20 July 1932.

The decent Jews have only these members of their own race to thank if we now treat them all alike. Let them send their protests to all the Jewish organizations abroad that have participated in the atrocity campaign. Our case against the Jews is not merely that they are disproportionately represented in the professions; it is not merely that they have made themselves the masters of finance capital; it is not merely that they have carried on usury and corruption on a vast scale, so vast that they have sucked off the lifeblood of their host nation; it is not merely that they are to blame for the crime of the inflation; and it is not merely that they have economically strangled their financially weaker German hosts. It was also the Jews who provided the Marxists and Communists with their principal leadership. They were also the ones who manned the editorial offices of the defamatory and subversive newspapers that besmirched everything that we Germans held sacred. They were also the ones who cynically distorted and ridiculed the words "German" and "national" and the concepts of honor and freedom, marriage and loyalty. No wonder that the German people at last were overcome by a righteous anger and were no longer willing to allow these parasites and oppressors to play the master. Only someone who has himself observed the role the Jews played in Germany and knows the Jewish behavior here can understand why things had to happen as they did. The Jewish question has not yet been fully solved. All that has happened up to now has been self-defense of the German people and reaction against the ruination brought upon us by the Jews. Seen in this light the revolution proceeded in a perfectly ordered and bloodless fashion, destroying what was old and decayed, and breaking ground for new and undefiled forces.

The Secret State Police have contributed much to the success of this revolution and to the fortification of its achievements.

In the midst of this work of reconstruction the great fire broke out in the high cupola and plenary hall of the Reichstag building. Criminals set this fire, sending the German Reichstag up in flames to thereby give the already moribund Communist Party a signal to make a last desperate attack before the Hitler government was firmly in the saddle. The fire was to be a signal to the Communists to unleash general terror, a general revolt, and civil war. That the fire did not have this desired result was not due to the noble motives of the Communists; Germany and the world owe this exclusively to the iron resolve and mailed fist of Adolf Hitler and his closest fellow fighters, who struck more rapidly than our enemies had counted on and more harshly than they could have suspected, crushing Communism once and for all with one blow.

In that night, as I gave the order for the arrest of 4,000 Communist officials, I knew that by dawn the Communists had lost a great battle. Now the task was to inform the people of the terrible danger that had threatened them. At last we got a look at the most secret Communist intentions and their organizations and goals. We saw with what criminal and ruthless methods this subhumanity intended to destroy a brave people and a proud Reich. I have been reproached for publishing old instructions as the Communist orders for civil war. Does anyone really believe that an order is less dangerous just because it was issued years earlier? Does anyone really believe that the burning of the Reichstag should be judged more leniently just because one could say that the Communists had already intended to do it many years ago?

When I am so often asked by bourgeois politicians today whether this extreme defensive action was necessary, whether the Communist danger was really so great, whether I did not over-react, I can only answer with amazement and contempt: "Yes, if you middle-class cowards no longer have to fear the Communist danger, if you escaped the horrors of a

Communist revolution, then this is not due to you or people like you, but due to men who recognized and eliminated the danger while you babbled your parlor Bolshevism."

If I am further accused of having the Reichstag fire set to gain a pretext to proceed against the Communists, I must reject this charge as grotesque and ridiculous. To proceed against Communism no special grounds were required. Their record of guilt was already so great, their crimes so immense, that in any case I was determined and ready to begin the ruthless war of extermination against this plague with all means at my disposal. On the contrary, as I already testified at the Reichstag fire trial, the fire, which forced me to act rapidly, was extremely inconvenient to me, as it forced me to act sooner than I had intended and to strike before I had completed all of my necessary preparations. I have no doubt whatsoever that the ideological originator and initiator of the fire was the Communist Party and that there must have been several perpetrators, of whom probably the stupidest and least competent one was captured. But it is not the incendiaries who were the crucial actors here, but rather their ideological progenitors, the ones who secretly pulled the strings; they are the true culprits and destroyers of the German people and their culture.

**Source: Hermann Goering, *Aufbau einer Nation*
(Berlin: E. S. Mittler & Sohn, 1934), pp. 83–9. Translated by Rod Stackelberg**

The "Day of Potsdam"

On 21 March 1933, the first day of spring, the new Hitler government staged an elaborate ceremony in Potsdam, the traditional residence of the Prussian kings. The ceremony was intended to symbolize the continuity between Prusso-German monarchism and the new Nazi-led regime. In the venerable Garrison Church, in front of the vault of Frederick the Great and the throne traditionally occupied by the kaiser, President Hindenburg called on the new government to overcome the selfishness and partisan divisions of the Weimar era and to lead the national renewal for a unified, free, and proud Germany. Hitler, in turn, extolled Hindenburg as the patron of the German "awakening" and as the symbol of the indestructible vitality of the German nation. In his diary (which was not published until 1959 and may therefore have been subjected to some later revision) the conservative German writer Erich Ebermayer captured the triumphalist mood of the day, but also the foreboding of isolated dissidents.

3.7 Erich Ebermayer, diary entry on the "Day of Potsdam," 21 March 1933

In the morning, broadcast of the ceremony in Potsdam on the radio. Everything is smooth, impressive, even exciting, at least for the masses. But we cannot and must not close our eyes either to what's happening here. Here today the marriage was successful, if not forever, then at least for a while, between the masses led by Hitler and the "spirit of Potsdam," the Prussian tradition, represented by Hindenburg.

What magnificent staging by the master director Goebbels! Hindenburg, the cabinet, and members of parliament ride from Berlin to Potsdam through a single, solid line of cheering millions. All of Berlin seems to be in the streets. The cabinet and members of parliament walk from the Nikolai Church to the Garrison Church. Bells pealing and cannons firing.

Hindenburg and Hitler enter the Garrison Church together. The radio announcer is moved almost to tears.

Then Hindenburg reads out his message. Simple, powerful, coming from an unpretentious soul and therefore likely to appeal to unpretentious souls. Merely the fact that here is a man who unites generations of German history, who fought in 1866, who was present at the crowning of the kaiser in 1871 in Versailles, who rose up to become a national hero from 1914 to 1918; whose popularity among our peculiar people was diminished neither by lost battles nor the lost world war; whom, on the contrary, the defeat actually raised to mythical transfiguration; who then as an old man once again and finally a second time took over the leadership of the empire, not out of vanity or lust for power, but without a doubt out of a Prussian sense of duty – he has achieved now, shortly before his death, the marriage of his world with the newly ascendant world represented by the Austrian corporal Hitler.

Then Hitler speaks. It cannot be denied: he has grown. Surprisingly for his opponents, the demagogue and party leader, the fanatic and rabble-rouser seems to be developing into a real statesman. So he is a genius after all, in whose enigmatic soul there are unsuspected and unprecedented possibilities? The government declaration stands out in its striking moderation. Not a word of hatred against opponents, not a word of racial ideology, no threats directed inside or outside of the country. Hitler only speaks about what they want. Preservation of the great tradition of our nation, stability of the government instead of constant vacillation, taking into consideration all the experiences in the life of the individual and the community that have proven to be useful for the well-being of the people throughout the millennia.

Hindenburg lays wreaths on the graves of the Prussian kings. The aged Field Marshal offers his hand to his corporal from the World War. The corporal bows low over the Field Marshal's hand. Canons thunder over Potsdam – over Germany.

No one can escape the emotion. Father is deeply impressed as well. Mother has tears in her eyes.

I silently leave the room, then the house, and go out into the woods. I must be alone.

In the evening a quiet hour with M. He is completely unmoved by the events of the day, as if enwrapped in a thick protective skin. He thinks it is all merely a rigged act; he does not for a moment waver in his instinctive aversion. "You'll see what will happen!" says the twenty-one year old.

I say nothing, ashamed and distressed.

Source: Erich Ebermayer, *Denn heute gehört uns Deutschland: Persönliches und politisches Tagebuch* (Hamburg and Vienna: Paul Zsolnay Verlag, 1959), pp. 45–7. Translated by Sally Winkle

The Enabling Act

The so-called Enabling Act formed the legal basis of Hitler's dictatorship. The law that abrogated the Weimar constitution and destroyed parliamentary democracy in Germany was given a typically euphemistic title. The necessary two-thirds majority required to change the constitution was achieved by barring elected Communist delegates from taking their seats in the Reichstag and by persuading the Catholic Center Party to support the law. There was some precedent for such a law as both the German People's

Party leader Gustav Stresemann (1878–1929) and his successor as chancellor, the Center Party leader Wilhelm Marx (1863–1946), had succeeded in gaining temporary legislative powers for their cabinets, though in more restricted form, in the Ruhr Crisis in 1923. The Enabling Act gave Hitler dictatorial powers for a period of four years and freed him from dependence not only on the Reichstag but also on the President, whose approval was needed for all legislation passed by decree under Article 48 of the Weimar constitution (Doc. 2.5). The Enabling Act was twice renewed by what had by then become a rubber-stamp Reichstag, and was extended indefinitely by Hitler's decree in 1941.

The Enabling Act passed by a vote of 444 to 94. Only the SPD voted against the law, despite intimidation and threats of retaliation by the Nazis. In negotiations preceding the passage of the law, Hitler made several concessions to gain the support of the Catholic Center, including a pledge to respect the continued existence of the constituent states, the Reichstag, an independent judiciary, and the presidency. Most importantly, Hitler pledged to respect the independence of the Church in Germany. His promise to negotiate a Concordat with the Vatican, a goal of Vatican policy since the 1920s, may have persuaded the Church hierarchy not to oppose the Enabling Act. Hitler's threat to declare a national emergency and rule without legal authorization may also have influenced the Center Party's fateful decision to support the Enabling Act.

3.8 Law to Remove the Distress of People and State, 24 March 1933

The Reichstag has resolved upon the following law which is promulgated herewith with approval of the Reichsrat [the council representing the individual states of the Reich] after it has been established that all the requirements of legislation for changing the constitution have been complied with.

ARTICLE 1

Laws for the Reich can be enacted by the Reich Cabinet as well as in accordance with the procedure provided by the Constitution of the Reich. This applies also to the laws referred to in article 85, paragraph 2, and in article 87 of the Constitution.

ARTICLE 2

The national laws enacted by the Reich Cabinet may deviate from the Constitution insofar as they do not affect the institution of the Reichstag or the Reichsrat as such. The powers of the Reich President will remain intact.

ARTICLE 3

The laws for the Reich enacted by the Reich Cabinet are issued by the Reich Chancellor and published in the *Reichsgesetzblatt*. They come into effect, unless otherwise specified, on the day following their publication. Articles 68 to 77 of the Constitution do not apply to the laws enacted by the Reich Cabinet.

ARTICLE 4

Treaties of the Reich with foreign countries relating to matters of national legislation do not require the approval of the bodies participating in the legislation. The Reich Cabinet is empowered to issue the necessary provisions for the execution of these treaties.

ARTICLE 5

This law will become effective on the day of its promulgation. It becomes invalid on 1 April 1937. Moreover it becomes invalid if the present Reich government should be replaced by another. Berlin, 24 March 1933

> The Reich President: von Hindenburg
> The Reich Chancellor: Adolf Hitler
> The Reich Minister of the Interior: Frick
> The Reich Minister of Foreign Affairs: Freiherr von Neurath
> The Reich Minister of Finance: Count Schwerin von Krosigk

> Source: *Reichsgesetzblatt*, 1933, I, p. 141

Persecution of the Jews

The widespread random attacks on Jews by SA and Nazi party members that accompanied the Nazi assumption of power resulted in adverse publicity, criticism by foreign governments, and efforts to organize boycotts of German imports to Britain, the US, and other countries. Under the pretext of punishing Jews for "atrocity propaganda," but in reality to provide a controlled outlet for party militants who wanted to force Jews out of Germany through violent action, the Nazi leadership called a one-day boycott of all Jewish enterprises on 1 April 1933. The SA was under orders not to enter the premises of Jewish businesses, however, or to destroy property. The direction of this action was entrusted to a "Committee for the Defense Against Jewish Atrocity and Boycott Propaganda" under the thuggish Julius Streicher (1885–1946), Gauleiter of Franconia and publisher of the anti-Semitic tabloid *Der Stürmer*. Streicher's public proclamation of the boycott held German Jews accountable for any boycott activity abroad. For a number of reasons the official boycott lasted only one day. The Nazis feared the chaotic consequences that might result from a sudden extrusion of Jews from German economic life. Industrial leaders also feared foreign retaliation against German exports. Public compliance with the boycott was sporadic at best. Unofficially, however, boycotts continued on the local level, and SA and party members were prohibited from patronizing Jewish businesses.

3.9 Julius Streicher, Appeal for the boycott of all Jewish enterprises, 31 March 1933

German national comrades! The ones who are guilty of this insane crime, this malicious atrocity propaganda and incitement to boycott, are the Jews in Germany. They have called on their racial comrades abroad to fight against the German people. They have transmitted the lies and calumnies abroad. Therefore the Reich leadership of the German movement for freedom have decided, in defense against criminal incitement, to impose a boycott of all Jewish shops, department stores, offices, etc., beginning on Saturday, 1 April 1933, at 10 a.m. We are calling on you, German women and men, to comply with this boycott. Do not buy in Jewish shops and department stores, do not go to Jewish lawyers, avoid Jewish physicians. Show the Jews that they cannot besmirch Germany and disparage its honor without punishment. Whoever acts against this appeal proves thereby that he stands on the side of Germany's enemies. Long live the honorable Field Marshal from the Great War, Reich President Paul v. Hindenburg! Long live the Führer and Reich Chancellor Adolf Hitler! Long live the German people and the holy German fatherland!

[signed] Streicher

Source: *Schulthess' europäischer Geschichtskalender. Neue Folge*, ed. by Ulrich Thürauf, Vol. 49 (Munich: Beck, 1933), p. 81. Translated by Rod Stackelberg

The concentration camps

The first official concentration camp to intern and "reeducate" political prisoners was established at Dachau near Munich in late March 1933. Even before this the SA had created its own extra-legal holding camps for political prisoners in various locations across Germany, most of which were dismantled in 1934. In the twelve years of Nazi rule the concentration camp system became the main instrument of Nazi terror. Two other major concentration camps established before the onset of the Second World War were Sachsenhausen near Berlin in 1936 and Buchenwald near Weimar in central Germany in 1937. There followed the opening of camps at Flossenbürg in northern Bavaria and Mauthausen in newly annexed Austria in 1938, and a camp for women at Ravensbrück, 50 miles north of Berlin, in April 1939.

Many of the prisoners assigned to the camps in the 1930s had been arrested under the pretext of "protective custody," which did not require any judicial proceeding. More than 26,000 persons, mostly Communists and Social Democrats, had already been arrested by the end of July 1933 under measures authorized by the Reichstag Fire Decree. Concentration camps were also used to intern clerical opponents, homosexuals, gypsies, common criminals, and "asocials," a category that allowed the Nazis considerable latitude in defining their victims. As Heinrich Himmler, the newly-appointed police commissioner in Munich in 1933, expanded his control of the police nationwide, the SS took control of the entire camp system. Eventually each of the major camps engendered numerous outside satellite camps in which the labor of inmates was exploited in construction, mining, and other industrial or agricultural work. Brutal treatment, inadequate food and clothing, and the spread of disease led to high mortality rates even before the start of the war.

During the war the camp system expanded exponentially until it included at least 22 major camps, more than 1,200 satellite camps, and thousands of smaller labor camps. With the implementation of the "Final Solution of the Jewish Question" in late 1941, killing centers for the systematic gassing of inmates were created in six camps in occupied Poland (see Docs. 6.9, 6.15, and 6.16). Hundreds of thousands of inmates from all over Europe were also forced into slave labor, used in medical experiments, or exploited in other ways. In the eyes of the world the concentration camps epitomized Nazi terror more than any other institution. The selection below is a news report of the establishment of the first concentration camp at Dachau.

3.10 "The Former Gunpowder Factory in Dachau a Concentration Camp for Political Prisoners," Dachauer Volksblatt, 6 April 1933

In a press conference on 20 March the Police Commissioner of Munich [Heinrich Himmler] made the following announcement: The first concentration camp will be opened on Wednesday near Dachau. It has a capacity of 5,000 people. All of the Communist functionaries and, insofar as necessary, the Reichsbanner and Marxist functionaries who threaten the security of the state will be assembled here.[12] Leaving individual Communist functionaries in the courthouse jails is not possible for the long term without putting too much strain on the apparatus of the state. On the other hand, it is not appropriate, either, to let them go free again. Isolated attempts we have made in this regard resulted in continued efforts by the functionaries to agitate and organize. We have taken these steps regardless of minor misgivings, in the conviction that our actions serve to reassure the national population and are in their interest. Police Commissioner Himmler further asserted that protective custody of individuals would not be continued any longer than necessary. But it is understandable that the unexpectedly large amount of evidence confiscated will take a long time to examine. The police will simply be delayed in this process if they are constantly being asked when this or that person in protective custody will be set free. The inaccuracy of rumors that are frequently spread about the treatment of persons in protective custody is shown by the fact that visits by a priest were freely granted to several persons in protective custody who wished them, such as Dr. Gerlich and Baron von Aretin.

On Wednesday, 22 March, the concentration camp at the former gunpowder factory received its first allocation of 200 inmates. The Dachau camp consists of over 20 one- to two-story stone buildings, each of which can hold 200 to 250 men. At first the occupancy of the camp will gradually increase to 2,500 men and will possibly be expanded to 5,000 men later. A labor service detachment recently prepared the barrack for the first 200 men and secured it for the time being with a barrier of triple barbed-wire. The first job of the camp inmates will be to restore the other stone buildings, which are very run-down. Once that is accomplished, they will be led out in small groups of about 50 men into the countryside, where extensive land cultivation projects wait to be implemented. Perhaps later some of the camp inmates will be offered the possibility of settling here. The guard unit will initially consist of a contingent of one hundred state police (Landespolizei), which is to be further reinforced by SA auxiliary police guards. Meals will be taken in the large dining hall of the former ammunition factory, which can hold up to 1,500 people. But cooking will be done in field kitchens. No visits are allowed at the Concentration Camp in Dachau.

Source: "'Die ehemalige Pulverfabrik in Dachau ein Konzentrationslager für politische Gefangene.' Ein Bericht des Dachauer Volksblatts," in Hitlers Machtergreifung. Vom Machtantritt Hitlers 30. Januar 1933 bis zur Besiegelung des Einparteienstaates 14. Juli 1933, ed. by Joseph and Ruth Becker (Munich: Deutscher Taschenbuch-Verlag, 1983), pp. 149ff. Translated by Sally Winkle

---

12   The Reichsbanner was the paramilitary organization of the SPD.

Concentration camp conditions in the 1930s

Lina Haag and her husband Alfred were members of the Communist Party arrested shortly after the Nazis came to power in 1933. Alfred Haag, a representative in the Württemberg state parliament, spent seven years in different concentration camps, including Dachau and Mauthausen, a camp opened by the Nazis in Austria after the *Anschluss* in 1938. Lina Haag was released in December 1933, but then arrested again in 1935 for refusing to provide the names of her former communist comrades to the Gestapo. She spent the following four and a half years in various prisons, ending up in the fortress of Lichtenburg that served as a concentration camp for women from 1937 to 1939. She was released in late 1938 and spent the war years as a physical therapist for wounded soldiers in Bavaria. Her husband was released in 1940 and conscripted into the army to serve on the eastern front. In 1944 Lina Haag began to write her recollections in the form of a letter to her husband, who at that time was missing in action. Alfred Haag returned from a Soviet prisoner of war camp in 1948. He served as chairman of the organization of Dachau camp survivors for many years.

Lina Haag's recollections, published under the title *Eine Handvoll Staub* (A Handful of Dust) in 1947, provide a first-hand account of the plight of political dissidents in Nazi Germany in the 1930s. The concentration camps were an integral part of the Nazi system of dominance not only as a means of punishment, but also as a deterrent to any form of political opposition. Political prisoners who had successfully undergone "reeducation" were sometimes released, but only on condition that they never mention their camp experiences to anyone. In the excerpts below Haag describes the military discipline, the dehumanization, and the arbitrary brutality to which inmates were subjected as a matter of course. Her bitterly ironic reflections on the psychology of the camp guards and the indifference of the general population are relevant to the current public debate on the complicity of ordinary Germans in Nazi atrocities.

3.11 Lina Haag, *A Handful of Dust*

We are brought to Lichtenburg. The Lichtenburg is the old fortress of Torgau, a massive medieval castle with many towers, wide courtyards, dark dungeons, and endless halls, a daunting gigantic structure with mighty walls. Not a bright castle ("lichte Burg"), it is the ideal concentration camp …

We are lined up in one of the courtyards. About thirty women: political prisoners, Jews, criminals, prostitutes, and Jehovah's Witnesses. Female guards from the SS circle us like gray wolves. I see this new ideal type of German woman for the first time. Some have blank faces and some have brutal looks, but they all have the same mean expression around their mouths. They pace back and forth with long strides and fluttering gray capes, their commanding voices ring shrilly across the court, and the large wolfhounds with them strain threateningly at their leashes. They are preposterous and terrifying, reminiscent of old sagas, merciless and probably even more dangerous than the brutal SS henchmen, because they are women. Are they women? I doubt it. They could only be unhuman creatures, creatures with gray dogs and with all the instincts, viciousness, and savagery of their dogs. Monsters. …

The inspections are the worst, or rather the days preceding them. Washing, brushing, scrubbing goes on for hours. Punishment rains down at the slightest infraction. We are bellowed at if there is a wrinkle in the bed sheet, or if a tablespoon is not lying straight in the locker. It's always the same show, no matter who comes. The door is shoved open; we jump up from our seats; the visitor comes in and shouts a cheerful greeting; enthusiasm glows in the eyes of the female warders; the visitor looks benevolently over at us; then he turns to Commandant Kögel with a silly remark, such as "A very nice room" or "They seem to be in good health." Of course Kögel happily agrees and repeatedly gives assurance that noone is subjected to hardships, which the visitor has never doubted. Then with an ebullient "Heil Hitler" he turns to go. The entourage respectfully makes way, eager hands throw open the door, and the visitor leaves.

Once even Himmler himself appears, in order to see his German reeducation project. He looks insignificant; we had visualized this Satan personified differently, but he is in good spirits and friendly, he laughs a lot and grants several early releases. Acts of mercy by a despot in a good mood. Even the so-called Women's Leader Scholtz-Klink[13] manages an inspection visit. She too is cheerful, friendly, enthusiastic, and happy that we are doing so well. She says she has a very special, a womanly understanding for us and for our situation, and to hear her talk, she almost envies us. She most likely will not visit the dark isolation cells nor will she observe a flogging. That probably would not interest her so much, although both are essential educational methods in this New German institution. The camp commandant assures her, too, that there are no hardships – we stand there and listen with fixed expressions. No one steps forward and says: No, that's not true; the truth is that we are beaten on the slightest pretext. For the beating we are tied naked to a wooden post, and Warder Mandel flogs us with a dog whip as long as she can keep it up. No one steps forward and says this. Because everyone wants to live . . .

Oh, dear husband, I always thought that after two years of solitary confinement nothing more in this world could frighten me, but I was wrong. I am terribly afraid of the beatings, of the dark cells in which women die so quickly, and of the dreaded chambers in which prisoners are interrogated by Gestapo officials. There are interrogations of the first, second, and third degrees. What cannot be found in this hellish place! Fear is torment enough; torment enough is the certainty that these things will happen to us one day. It is absolutely impossible to be here for years without disaster striking one day. It will come. One day it will come. Either through the denunciation of a "comrade," or because of the guard, or because a shoe string was not properly tied, or because the work wasn't adequate, or because of fishing a potato or bread crust out of the pigsty, or maybe once one has a crazy day and forgets that one is nothing, no more than a handful of dust, and one cries out the truth. We haven't gotten that far yet. We still stand there quietly and hear the Women's Leader of the German Reich praise the nice room and the cleanliness and the discipline of the inmates; we hear the oily voice of the camp commandant, who laughs flatteringly, and jovially asserts that there are no hardships, the same camp commandant who at times, when he feels like it, takes the whip into his own hands in order to relieve the overworked guard. As I said, we haven't gotten that far yet.

Then Thea is released. Very suddenly. I am happy for her. Anyone who gets out of here is granted the gift of life.

Now Doris Maase of the illegal Communist Party becomes the senior of the room. At the beginning it is not easy for her. Our station warden is a bitch: suspicious, vain, and guilty of

---

13   Gertrud Scholtz-Klink (1902–98) was the head of the main Nazi association for women.

favoritism. She wants to be respected and feared. Everyone is supposed to grovel before her. Those who do not prostrate themselves are shouted down. She talks or flatters some of us into submissiveness; the rest of us are beaten down. It all depends on her moods, her likes and dislikes. Anyone unlucky enough to be disliked by her can hardly be saved, and then only through the brilliant diplomacy of our Doris. She helps us a great deal. ...

Sometimes we ask one another whether there is no one outside who thinks of us and why no one speaks out against all this? What is happening here must have gradually leaked out. And not only here but in all the camps. Do all the released prisoners really keep silent once they are let out? Or do the petty conformists outside refuse to listen to them? Or don't the people hear them in the triumphalist celebrations of the nation?

Once again the "greatest statesman of all time" was right. The Sudetenland has returned home.[14] Without war. With all the blessings of the world. Is it any wonder, then, that on the outside they believe the Führer rather than prisoners released from concentration camps? If the world doesn't even protest the brutal annexation of foreign countries, is it likely to protest the beating of some poor working class woman who had perhaps protested that annexation? Why should the world protest at all, when even in Germany no one speaks out against this reign of terror? Why should anyone in Germany speak out against the inhumanity of a regime that has the blessing of the world? "It's no use, Doris" I say, "the Führer is always right, and we are poor wretches, completely forsaken wretches." ...

It does not even take a real denunciation; just a disparaging or dissatisfied comment from a guard is enough to have one sent to the hole. Not that we have no laws here. These are the moods of the camp commandant, the orders that he shouts across the prison yard. He has the revolver and the power over life and death. When he screams, everyone has to scramble, even the guards and all the she-wolves too, the dogs and us. When he strides across the courtyard, when he marches by the lines of fear and misery, hundreds of pairs of hate-filled eyes stare after him. A veritable cloud of hate envelops him. It almost seems to me as if he needs this hate as much as the air he breathes.

On Easter Sunday he personally whips three women. Our comrade Steffi is one of them. She had helped her boyfriend, a Jew, escape from Germany. She is beautiful, intelligent, and a good comrade. Soon after the whipping she dies. She could not take it. That is how the commandant of the Lichtenburg concentration camp celebrates Easter. By beating three naked women, tied to a wood post, until he is no longer able. Would anyone believe that outside of this place? Even if someone believed it, and maybe even told others, a Gestapo thumbnail on the tendons over the knuckle would be enough to make him forget everything as completely as if he had never heard anything. What am I saying, a Gestapo thumbnail – no, the merest threat is enough, and the people are silent. They are not only silent, they cheer, march, inform, and close ranks behind the Führer, just as the Führer wants. Threats constitute his political strategy, his foreign policy, and his domestic policy. Threats and fear, cruelty and cowardice, are the foundations of his state. They threaten us and they use us to threaten the people, as necessary. The petty police official threatens, and the Führer threatens. That's how they do it. Threats are the unifying bond that joins together the "people's community." Bond? No, chain. They have to be brutal and cruel, how else could they threaten? Behind every threat lies the concentration camp, an abyss of depravity, illegality, and criminality. The

14 This is a reference to the Czech crisis of 1938, in which Hitler claimed the German-populated border area, the Sudetenland (see Doc. 4.12).

citizens sense it. That's enough. For them to know more would be detrimental. Fear is to be inspired, not outrage. And fear it is that is inspired.

We could perhaps understand that the people outside are intimidated. But it is incomprehensible to us that there are so many sadists. Are they really sadists, criminals by nature, murderers? I don't think so, and neither does Doris. They are just respectable petty bourgeois conformists. Only they happen to be employed not in the tax office, but in the police office. They happen not to be municipal clerks, or meat packers, or office assistants, or construction workers, or accountants, but are instead Gestapo employees and SS men. They do not distinguish between good and evil; they simply do what they are ordered to do. They are not ordered to distinguish between good and evil, or between right and wrong, but to rid the state of enemies and destroy them. They do this with the same stubborn pedantry, the same German industriousness, and the same German thoroughness with which they would otherwise check tax returns or write minutes or butcher pigs. They whip a defenseless woman tied to a post with matter-of-fact earnestness and conscientiousness, fully convinced that in so doing they are serving the state or their Führer, which is the same to them. In the case of the whipping there may be some pleasure, but the essential factor is the German sense of duty, raised by a demon to the demonic. Thus the inscription on their belt buckle reads: "My honor is my loyalty."

I have looked into terrible hearts and minds, into hearts that besides monstrous cruelty contained a disposition always inclined to sentimentality, and into minds that seemed harmless and simple and good-natured, but still were the minds of diligent executioners. We find it dreadful and disturbing that Hitler's creatures are not recruited from an asocial element, but from the lower middle-class element of the people. They are not born sadists, nor professional criminals, nor impassioned murderers, but just small-minded middle-class conformists. Like everyone else. The same talent for organization that works on the outside to improve the people's physical fitness with goose-stepping and vitamin drops drives the mortality rates here in the concentration camps ever higher. Hardly a day passes in which a dead woman is not found in the dark cells. She is "found," although the day before the prisoners working in that section often have to take the clothes out of the cells of those who are to die that night. Naked, with shattered bones and bodies besmirched with blood, the dead women are lying on the floor. Some tried to hide under the plank beds or fled under the table in order to escape the fatal blows. Bent, beaten, petrified beings, who once had names, husbands, children, and homes, they lie there with impenetrable, fixed stares. That is the hell of the dark cells with their insane horrors. It is the end of the world. Honor to all those nameless women. Honor to them a thousand times.

Source: Lina Haag, *Eine Handvoll Staub: Widerstand einer Frau 1933–1945* (1947; rept. Frankfurt: Fischer Taschenbuch Verlag, 1995), pp. 107, 111–113, 117–119. Reprinted by permission of Fischer Taschenbuch Verlag GmbH.
Translated by Sally Winkle

The purge of the Civil Service

The so-called Civil Service Law, based on a draft prepared by the Prussian Interior Ministry in 1932, enabled the Nazis to gain full control of the civil service despite the fact that civil servants in Germany enjoyed the legal protection of guaranteed tenure in office except in cases of incompetence or other irregularities. The new law permitted dismissal of anyone solely on the grounds that they might not "without reservation at all times act in the interest of the national state" (Article 4). The law was aimed at political opponents of the left and at Jews. Article 3 introduced the notorious "Aryan Paragraph," which was subsequently widely applied in the private sector as well, especially the professions, even before this was required by law. The exceptions granted in paragraph (2) of Article 3 were repealed after President Hindenburg's death in August 1934.

A "non-Aryan" was defined by the Ministry of the Interior on 11 April 1933 as anyone with one or more Jewish grandparents. The term "non-Aryan" was dropped in later racial legislation, partly as a result of objections on the part of Japan. The Nuremberg Laws of September 1935 (Doc. 3.26) defined a "Jew" as anyone with three or four Jewish grandparents and created separate categories for persons of mixed descent.

The Civil Service Law was declared to be necessary because Marxists and Jews had supposedly undermined the professionalism of the civil service by bending it to their political ends in the Weimar era. Because of the scope of the public sector in Germany, which included all universities and schools, the Civil Service Law represented one of the most important instruments of *Gleichschaltung* – the process of "coordinating" all institutions. Under the pretense of creating unity of purpose, *Gleichschaltung* brought all aspects of German society under Nazi control. As a result of this law thousands of Jewish or dissident scientists, artists, scholars, and professional people were removed from their posts. Most Jewish scientists eventually emigrated, taking with them the skills and capabilities that helped the Allies to defeat Germany in the war.

3.12a Law for the Restoration of the Professional Civil Service, 7 April 1933

The Reich government has enacted the following law, which is hereby proclaimed:

ARTICLE 1

To restore a national, professional civil service and to simplify administration civil servants can be dismissed from office according to the following regulations, even if the necessary conditions required by current law do not exist ...

ARTICLE 2

1   Officials who entered the civil service after 9 November 1918 without possessing the required or usual training or other qualifications are to be dismissed from service. Their former salaries will be accorded them for a period of three months after their dismissal ...

ARTICLE 3

1   Officials who are of non-Aryan descent are to be retired; insofar as honorary officials are concerned, they are to be removed from official status.

2   Paragraph (1) does not apply to officials who have been civil servants since 1 August 1914, or who fought during the World War at the front for the German Reich or who fought for its allies or whose fathers or sons were killed in the World War. The Reich Minister of the Interior can permit further exceptions for officials abroad in consultation with the appropriate minister or the highest authorities of the federal states.

ARTICLE 4

Officials whose former political activity does not offer a guarantee that they will at all times without reservation act in the interest of the national state can be dismissed from service. For a period of three months after dismissal they are accorded their former salary. From this time on they receive three-quarters of their pension and corresponding survivors' benefits. ...

ARTICLE 17

1   The Reich Minister of the Interior will issue in agreement with the Reich Minister of Finance, the necessary regulations for the execution and carrying through of this law and the general administrative provisions.
2   If necessary the highest federal state authorities will issue supplementary regulations. In this matter they must confine themselves to the framework of the Reich regulations ... Berlin, 7 April 1933

> The Reich Chancellor: Adolf Hitler
> The Reich Minister of the Interior: Frick
> The Reich Minister of Finance: Count Schwerin von Krosigk

3.12b First Regulation for Administration of the Law for the Restoration of the Professional Civil Service, 11 April 1933

On the basis of Article 17 of the Law for the Restoration of the Professional Civil Service of 7 April 1933, the following regulation is issued:

I

TO ARTICLE 2

Unfit are all civil servants who belong to the Communist Party or Communist auxiliary or supplementary organizations. They are, therefore, to be discharged.

2

TO ARTICLE 3

1   A person is to be considered as non-Aryan who is descended from non-Aryans, especially Jewish parents or grandparents. This holds true even if only one parent or grand-

parent is of non-Aryan descent. This principle obtains especially if one parent or grandparent was of Jewish faith.

2   If a civil servant was not already a civil servant on 1 August 1914, he must prove that he is of Aryan descent, or that he fought at the front, or that he is the son or the father of a man killed during the World War. Proof must be given by submitting documents (birth certificate and marriage certificate of the parents, military papers).

3   If Aryan descent is doubtful, an opinion must be obtained from the expert on racial research commissioned by the Reich Minister of the Interior.

3

TO ARTICLE 4

1   In determining whether the conditions of Article 4, sentence 1) are given, the whole political career of the official is to be considered, particularly from 9 November 1918 on.

2   Every official is required on request to testify to the highest Reich or state authority as to what political party he has been a member of up to the present. Political parties in the sense of this definition include the *Reichsbanner* [paramilitary organization of the SPD], Black-Red-Gold [republican organization], the Republican Judges' Union, and the League for the Rights of Man ...
Berlin, 11 April 1933

The Reich Minister of the Interior: Frick
The Reich Minister of Finance: Count Schwerin von Krosigk

Source: *Reichsgesetzblatt*, 1933, I, pp. 175, 341

The *Gleichschaltung* of labor, 2 May 1933

Only a day after the Nazis had celebrated the international socialist holiday (May 1) as the "Day of National Labor," thus establishing it as a national holiday, the Nazis struck at the independent trade unions, which were closely affiliated with the SPD. (The Christian trade unions were subjected to *Gleichschaltung* shortly thereafter.) This action was taken without legal basis by the Nazi Party and its affiliated organizations. Legal authorization was only provided by the government after the fact. This became a typical *modus operandi* in the Third Reich. The free trade unions were replaced by a German Labor Front (*Deutsche Arbeitsfront* or DAF) under the direction of Party Organizational Leader Robert Ley (1890–1945). It was Ley who issued the directive for the take-over of the unions reprinted here. The purpose of the DAF was primarily to maintain labor peace through a combination of propaganda, social and recreational services for workers, and, if necessary, coercion.

3.13 NSDAP Order for the *Gleichschaltung* of the Free Labor Unions, 21 April 1933

Circular Letter Nr. 6/33

On Tuesday, 2 May 1933, the coordination action [*Gleichschaltungsaktion*] of the free trade unions begins.

The direction of the entire action lies in the hands of the Action Committee. ...

The essential part of the action is to be directed against the General German Trade Union Federation [*Allgemeiner Deutscher Gewerkschaftsbund* or ADGB] and the General Salaried Employees Federation [*Allgemeiner Freier Angestelltenbund* or AFA]. Anything beyond this that is dependent upon the free trade unions is left to the discretion of the Gauleiter's judgement.

The Gauleiters are responsible for the execution of the coordination action in the individual areas. The action is to be carried out by members of the National Socialist Factory Cell Organizations [*Nationalsozialistische Betriebszellenorganisation* or NSBO].

SA as well as SS are to be employed for the occupation of trade union properties and for taking into protective custody personalities concerned.

The Gauleiter is to proceed with his measures in closest cooperation with competent regional factory cell directors [*Gaubetriebszellenleiter*].

The action in Berlin will be conducted by the Action Committee itself.

In the Reich the following will be occupied:

The directing offices of the unions; the trade union houses and offices of the free trade unions; the Party houses of the Social Democratic Party of Germany insofar as trade unions are involved there; the branches and pay offices of the Bank for Workers, Employees, and Officials; the district committees of the General German Trade Union Federation and of the General Salaried Employees Federation; the local committees of the ADGB and of the AFA.

The following are to be taken into protective custody:

All trade union chairmen; the district Secretaries and the branch directors of the Bank for Workers, Employees, and Officials.

The chairmen of local committees as well as the employees of unions are not to be taken into protective custody but are to be induced to continue their work.

Exceptions are granted only with the permission of the Gauleiter.

The taking over of the independent trade unions must proceed in such a fashion that the workers and employees will not be given the feeling that this action is against them, but is, on the contrary, an action against a superannuated system which is not directed in conformity with the interests of the German nation. ...

As soon as possible mass assemblies are to be arranged free to all trade union members at which the meaning of the action is to be set forth, and it is to be explained that the rights of the workers and employees are being unequivocally guaranteed. ...

It is understood that this action is to proceed in a strongly disciplined fashion. The Gauleiters are responsible in this respect for holding the direction of the action firmly in hand.

Heil Hitler!

[signed] Dr. Robert Ley

Source: Office of the US Chief of Counsel for Prosecution of Axis Criminality, *Nazi Conspiracy and Aggression,* **Vol. III (Washington DC: US Government Printing Office, 1946), pp. 380–82 [Doc. 392-PS]**

Eugenic Sterilization Law

The Nazis were committed to strengthening the German "race" through eugenics, the science of improving a population group through selective breeding. The effort to gain public acceptance for eugenic practices had a long tradition not only in Germany (see Doc. 2.9) but in other countries as well (including the United States, where various states adopted compulsory sterilization laws in the early twentieth century). The Racial Hygiene movement in Germany was founded in 1905 and gained momentum in the 1920s after defeat in the First World War gave new impetus to any scheme that promised to "regenerate" the German *Volk*. Despite the opposition of the Roman Catholic Church, there was a growing public consensus that persons with hereditary illnesses or mental retardation should not be allowed to reproduce.

The following law, adopted in July 1933, led to the eventual sterilization of approximately 400,000 persons with hereditary illnesses or conditions presumed to be hereditary. The law was later expanded to include habitual criminals and other "asocials," a category that included persons on welfare or poor relief. The law included provisions for voluntary sterilization originally proposed in the state of Prussia in 1932. Its most important provisions, however, were for compulsory sterilization authorized by specially established Genetic Health Courts (*Erbgesundheitsgerichte*). This obsession with "purifying" the race eventually led to the "euthanasia" of mentally and physically handicapped persons, especially children, during the war (see Docs. 6.1 and 6.2) and contributed to the "Final Solution," the murder of the Jews (see Chapter 6).

3.14 Law for the Prevention of Genetically Diseased Offspring, 14 July 1933

The Reich Government has passed the following law, which is hereby announced:

PAR. I

1   Anyone who is suffering from a hereditary disease can be sterilized by a surgical operation if, according to the experiences of medical science, it is to be expected with great probability that his offspring will suffer from serious hereditary physical or mental defects.

2   Those who suffer from any of the following diseases are considered to be suffering from a hereditary disease within the meaning of this law:

(1) Mental deficiency from birth
(2) Schizophrenia
(3) Circular (manic-depressive) illness
(4) Hereditary epilepsy
(5) Hereditary St. Vitus' Dance (Huntington's Disease)
(6) Hereditary blindness
(7) Hereditary deafness
(8) Serious hereditary physical deformation.

3   Furthermore, persons suffering severely from alcoholism can be sterilized.

PAR. 2

1   The person to be sterilized has the right to make an application. If this person is incapaci-
tated or under tutelage because of mental deficiency or is not yet 18, the legal representative has the right to make an application but needs the consent of the court dealing
with matters of guardianship to do so. In other cases of limited capacity the application
needs the consent of the legal representative. If someone who has attained his or her
majority has received someone to look after his or her person, the consent of the latter
is necessary.

2   A certificate from a physician approved for the German Reich is to be attached to the
application, to the effect that the person to be sterilized has been informed of the nature
and results of sterilization.

3   The application can be withdrawn.

PAR. 3

Sterilization can also be applied for by the following:

1   The civil service physician

2   For the inmates of a sanatorium, hospital, nursing home, or prison, by the head thereof.

PAR. 4

The application is to be made to the office of the Genetic Health Court. ...

PAR. 12

1   Once the Court has made its final decision for sterilization it must be carried out even
against the will of the person to be sterilized. The civil service physician has to request
the necessary measures from the police authorities. Where other measures are insufficient, direct force may be used.

2   If facts that necessitate a renewed investigation of the case come out, the Genetic Health
Court must reopen the proceedings and suspend the sterilization. If the application was
refused, it is only permissible to reopen the case if new facts have arisen that justify sterilization. ...

PAR. 18

This law comes into force on 1 January 1934.
     Berlin, 14 July 1933

The Reich Chancellor: Adolf Hitler
The Reich Minister of Interior: Frick
The Reich Minister of Justice: Dr. Gürtner

Source: *Reichsgesetzblatt*, 1933, I, p. 529

The Concordat

One of Hitler's early successes was the signing of a Concordat with the Vatican under Pope Pius XI in July 1933. The Concordat gave his government international legitimacy, effectively eliminated the Center Party (the political party of Catholics in Germany that had supported the Weimar Republic), and assured him of the support of millions of German Catholics. Hitler also understood, like many dictators before him, that religion could be useful in strengthening loyalty to the state (see Articles 16 and 30).

The Vatican, which had unsuccessfully sought to negotiate a Concordat with the Weimar government, gained important benefits as well, especially the guarantee that the state would respect the independence of the Church and its role in elementary, secondary, and higher education. The Concordat also contained a secret appendix governing the role of priests and members of religious orders in the armed forces in case of the reintroduction of universal military service, which was prohibited under the Versailles Treaty.

In the negotiations, the Church was represented by the Papal nuncio in Germany, Cardinal Eugenio Pacelli (1876–1958), who became Pope Pius XII in 1939. The Nazi government was represented by the Catholic aristocrat, Vice-Chancellor Franz von Papen, who had been so instrumental in Hitler's accession to the chancellorship. Pacelli, who admired Germany and shared the Nazis' militant anti-communism, was anxious to conclude an agreement that would guarantee the self-administration of the German Church, ensure its continued public role, and strengthen the authority of the Vatican. The price the Nazis demanded was dissolution of the Center Party (despite the fact that it was this party that had given Hitler the necessary votes to pass the Enabling Act (Doc. 3.8). By agreeing to these terms the Church hierarchy in effect withdrew support from the many German Catholics ready to oppose the Nazis in the political realm. The Nazis could invoke the terms of the Concordat to justify their arrests of priests who criticized the regime. Strict compliance with the Concordat also meant that the Church would not openly criticize the anti-Semitic policies of the regime (see Doc. 4.9).

Article 31 confirming the right of the Church to operate organizations devoted exclusively to "charitable, cultural, or religious" pursuits gave rise to the greatest conflict between Church and state. Because no agreement could be reached on whether this included Catholic social and professional organizations, the determination of what organizations would fall under the purview of this article was postponed to a later date. The Nazis took advantage of this omission to forcibly dissolve Catholic youth groups in the late 1930s and to integrate their members in the Hitler Youth (Doc. 4.7).

3.15 Concordat between the Holy See and the German Reich, 20 July 1933

His Holiness Pope Pius XI and the President of the German Reich, moved by a common desire to consolidate and enhance the friendly relations existing between the Holy See and the German Reich, wish to regulate the relations between the Catholic Church and the State for the whole territory of the German Reich in a permanent manner and on a basis acceptable to both parties. They have decided to conclude a solemn agreement, which will supplement the

Concordats already concluded with certain individual German states, and will ensure for the remaining states fundamentally uniform treatment of their respective problems.

For this purpose His Holiness Pope Pius XI has appointed as his plenipotentiary His Eminence the Most Reverend Lord Cardinal Eugenio Pacelli, his Secretary of State. The President of the German Reich has appointed as plenipotentiary the Vice-Chancellor of the German Reich, Herr Franz von Papen. Having exchanged their respective credentials and found them to be in due and proper form, they have agreed to the following articles:

Article 1. The German Reich guarantees freedom of profession and public practice of the Catholic religion.

It acknowledges the right of the Catholic Church, within the limit of those laws which are applicable to all, to manage and regulate her own affairs independently, and, within the framework of her own competence, to publish laws and ordinances binding on her members.

Article 2. The Concordats concluded with Bavaria (1924), Prussia (1929), and Baden (1932) remain in force, and the rights and privileges of the Catholic Church recognized therein are secured unchanged within the territories of the states concerned. For the remaining states the agreements entered into in the present Concordat come into force in their entirety. These last are also binding for those states named above insofar as they affect matters not regulated by the regional Concordats or are complementary to the settlement already made.

In the future, regional Concordats with states of the German Reich will be concluded only with the agreement of the Reich Government.

Article 3. In order to foster good relations between the Holy See and the German Reich, an Apostolic Nuncio will reside in the capital of the German Reich and an Ambassador of the German Reich at the Holy See, as heretofore.

Article 4. In its relations and correspondence with the bishops, clergy, and other members of the Catholic Church in Germany, the Holy See enjoys full freedom. The same applies to the bishops and other diocesan officials in their dealings with the faithful in all matters belonging to their pastoral office.

Instructions, ordinances, Pastoral Letters, official diocesan gazettes, and other enactments regarding the spiritual direction of the faithful issued by the ecclesiastical authorities within the framework of their competence may be published without hindrance and brought to the notice of the faithful in the hitherto customary form.

[Articles 5 through 8 provide for state protection of clergy and free them from obligation to hold official offices not compatible with the provisions of Canon Law.]

Article 9. The clergy may not be required by judicial and other officials to give information concerning matters which have been entrusted to them while exercising the care of souls, and which therefore come within the obligation of pastoral secrecy.

Article 10. The wearing of clerical dress or of a religious habit on the part of lay persons, or of clerics or religious who have been forbidden to wear them by a final and valid injunction made by the competent ecclesiastical authority and officially communicated to the state authority, is liable to the same penalty on the part of the state as the misuse of military uniform.

Article 11. The present organization and demarcation of dioceses of the Catholic Church in the German Reich remains in force. Such rearrangements of a bishopric or of an ecclesiastical province or of other diocesan demarcations as shall seem advisable in the future, so far as they involve changes within the boundaries of a German state, remain subject to the agreement of the government of the state concerned. Rearrangements and alterations which extend beyond the boundaries of a German state require the agreement of the Reich government, to whom it shall be left to secure the consent of the regional government in question. The same applies to rearrangements or alterations of ecclesiastical provinces involving several German states. The foregoing conditions do not apply to such ecclesiastical boundaries as are laid down merely in the interests of local pastoral care.

In the case of any territorial reorganization within the German Reich, the Reich government will communicate with the Holy See with a view to rearrangement of the organization and demarcation of dioceses.

Article 12. Without prejudice to the provisions of Article 11, ecclesiastical offices may be freely constituted and changed, unless the expenditure of state funds is involved. The creation and alteration of parishes shall be carried out according to principles with which the diocesan bishops are agreed, and for which the Reich government will endeavor to secure uniform treatment as far as possible from the state governments.

[Article 13 guarantees legal rights in the civil domain to Catholic institutions.]

Article 14. As a matter of principle the Church retains the right to appoint freely to all Church offices and benefices without the cooperation of the state or of civil communities, insofar as other provisions have not been made in previous Concordats mentioned in Article 2 ... Furthermore, there is accord on the following points:

1   Catholic clerics who hold an ecclesiastical office in Germany or who exercise pastoral or educational functions must:

    (a) Be German citizens.
    (b) Have graduated from a German secondary school.
    (c) Have studied philosophy and theology for at least three years at a German public university, a German ecclesiastical college, or a papal college in Rome.

2   The Bull nominating Archbishops, Coadjutors *cum jure successionis*, or appointing a Praelatus nullius, will not be issued until the name of the appointee has been submitted to the governor (*Reichsstatthalter*) of the state concerned, and until it has been ascertained that no objections of a general political nature exist.

[Article 15 guarantees the freedom to religious orders and congregations in respect to their founding, pastoral activities, and administration.]

Article 16. Before bishops take possession of their dioceses they are to take a loyalty oath either to the governor (*Reichsstatthalter*) of the state concerned, or to the President of the Reich, according to the following formula:

> Before God and on the Holy Gospels I swear and promise, as becomes a bishop, loyalty to the German Reich and to the state of ____. I swear and promise to honor the legally constituted government and to cause the clergy of my diocese to honor it. In the performance of my spiritual office and in my solicitude for the welfare and the interests of the German Reich, I will endeavor to avoid all detrimental acts which might endanger it.

[Articles 17 and 18 guarantee the property rights of the Church. Article 19 provides for the maintenance of Catholic theological faculties at public universities. Article 20 confirms the right of the Church to establish seminaries for the training of clergy.]

Article 21. Catholic religious instruction in elementary, secondary, and vocational schools constitutes a regular portion of the curriculum, and is to be taught in accordance with the principles of the Catholic Church. In religious instruction, special care will be taken to inculcate patriotic, civic, and social consciousness and sense of duty in the spirit of the Christian Faith and the moral code, precisely as in the case of other subjects. The syllabus and the selection of textbooks for religious instruction will be arranged by consultative agreement with the ecclesiastical authorities, and these latter will be given the opportunity to investigate, in consultation with school authorities, whether pupils are receiving religious instruction in accordance with the teachings and requirements of the Church.

Article 22. With regard to the appointment of Catholic religious instructors, agreement will be arrived at as a result of mutual consultation on the part of the bishop and the government of the state concerned. Teachers who have been declared by the bishop unfit for the further exercise of their teaching functions, either on pedagogical grounds or by reason of their moral conduct, may not be employed for religious instruction so long as the problem remains.

Article 23. The retention of Catholic denominational schools and the establishment of new ones, is guaranteed. In all parishes in which parents or guardians request it, Catholic elementary schools will be established, provided that the number of pupils available appears to be sufficient for a school managed and administered in accordance with the standards prescribed by the state, due regard being given to the local conditions of school organizations.

Article 24. In all Catholic elementary schools only such teachers are to be employed as are members of the Catholic Church, and who guarantee to fulfill the special requirements of a Catholic school.

Within the framework of the general professional training of teachers, arrangements will be made which will secure the formation and training of Catholic teachers in accordance with the special requirements of Catholic denominational schools.

Article 25. Religious orders and congregations are entitled to establish and conduct private schools, subject to the general laws and ordinances governing education. Insofar as these schools follow the curriculum prescribed for public schools, those attending them acquire the same qualifications as those attending public schools.

The admission of members of religious orders or congregations to the teaching office, and their appointment to elementary, secondary, or advanced schools, are subject to the general conditions applicable to all.

Article 26. With the reservation that a more comprehensive regulation of the marriage laws may later take effect, it is understood that, except in cases of critical illness of one member of an engaged couple which does not permit a postponement, and in cases of great moral emergency (the presence of which must be confirmed by the proper ecclesiastical authority), the ecclesiastical marriage ceremony may precede the civil ceremony. In such cases the pastor is duty bound to notify the registry office without delay.

[Article 27 regulates the appointment and administration of military clergy. Article 28 provides for pastoral care in hospitals, prisons, and similar public institutions. Article 29 allows national minorities to use their native language in church services to the degree that German is permitted to German minorities in the corresponding foreign states.]

Article 30. On Sundays and Holy Days, special prayers, conforming to Church liturgy, will be offered during the principal Mass for the welfare of the German Reich and its people in all episcopal, parish, and convent churches and chapels of the German Reich.

Article 31. Those Catholic organizations and societies which pursue exclusively charitable, cultural, or religious ends, and, as such, are placed under the ecclesiastical authorities, will be protected in their institutions and activities.

Those Catholic organizations which to their religious, cultural, and charitable pursuits add others, such as social or professional interests, regardless whether they are integrated into public organizations, are to enjoy the protection of Article 31, Section 1, provided they guarantee to develop their activities outside all political parties.

It is reserved to the Reich government and the German episcopate, in joint agreement, to determine which organizations and associations come within the scope of this article.

Insofar as the Reich and its constituent states supervise sports and other youth organizations, care will be taken that it shall be possible for the members of such organizations regularly to practice their religious duties on Sundays and Holy days, and that they shall not be required to do anything not in harmony with their religious and moral convictions and obligations.

Article 32. In view of the special situation existing in Germany, and in view of the legislation guaranteed through this Concordat to safeguard the rights and privileges of the Roman Catholic Church in the Reich and its component states, the Holy See will issue regulations for the exclusion of clergy and members of religious orders from membership in political parties, and from engaging in work on their behalf.

Article 33. All matters relating to clerical persons or ecclesiastical affairs, which have not been treated of in the foregoing articles, will be regulated for the ecclesiastical sphere according to current Canon Law.

Should differences of opinion arise regarding the interpretation or execution of any of the articles of this Concordat, the Holy See and the German Reich will reach a friendly solution by mutual agreement.

Article 34. This Concordat, whose German and Italian texts shall have equal binding force, shall be ratified, and the certificates of ratification shall be exchanged, as soon as possible. It will be in force from the day of such exchange.

In witness hereof, the plenipotentiaries have signed this Concordat.

Signed in two original exemplars.

In the Vatican City, 20 July 1933

[signed] Eugenio, Cardinal Pacelli
[signed] Franz von Papen

SUPPLEMENTARY PROTOCOL

At the signing of the Concordat concluded today between the Holy See and the German Reich, the undersigned, being legitimately thereto empowered, have adjoined the following explanations which form an integral part of the Concordat itself.

IN RE

Article 3. The Apostolic Nuncio to the German Reich, in accordance with the exchange of notes between the Apostolic Nunciature in Berlin and the Reich Foreign Office on 11 and 27 March, respectively, shall be the Doyen of the Diplomatic Corps thereto accredited.

Article 13. It is understood that the Church retains the right to levy Church taxes.

Article 14, Par 2. It is understood that when objections of a general political nature exist, they shall be presented within the shortest possible time. If after twenty days such representations have not been made, the Holy See may be justified in assuming that no objections exist to the candidate in question. The names of the persons concerned will be kept confidential until the announcement of the appointment. No right of the state to assert a veto is to be derived from this article. ...

Article 29. Since the Reich government has seen its way to come to an agreement regarding non-German minorities, the Holy See declares – in accordance with the principles it has constantly maintained regarding the right to employ the vernacular in Church services, religious instruction, and the conduct of Church organizations – that it will bear in mind similar clauses protective of German minorities when concluding Concordats with other countries.

Article 31, Par. 4. The principles laid down in Article 31, Par. 4, hold good also for the Labor Service.

Article 32. It is understood that similar provisions regarding activity in party politics will be introduced by the Reich government for members of non-Catholic denominations.

The conduct, which has been made obligatory for the clergy and members of religious orders in Germany according to Article 32, does not involve any sort of limitation of official and prescribed preaching and interpretation of the dogmatic and moral doctrines and principles of the Church.

In the Vatican City, 20 July 1933

[signed] Eugenio, Cardinal Pacelli
[signed] Franz von Papen

APPENDIX

(The contracting parties agree to keep the appendix secret.)

In case of an alteration of the present German military system to include the introduction of universal military service, the conscription of priests and other members of the clergy or religious orders will be regulated in consultation with the Holy See according to the following general principles:

(a) Students of philosophy and theology in Church institutions who are preparing for priesthood are exempt from military service and preparatory training, except in the case of general mobilization.

(b) In case of general mobilization priests who are active in diocesan administration or pastoral ministry are exempt from military service ...

(c) Other priests, if they are declared fit, will enter the armed forces of the state to devote themselves to the pastoral care of the troops under the ecclesiastical jurisdiction of the army bishop, unless they are conscripted into medical service.

(d) Other clerics or members of religious orders who are not yet priests are to be assigned to the medical service ...

In the Vatican City, 20 July 1933

Eugenio, Cardinal Pacelli
Franz von Papen

Source: Department of State Publication 6545, *Documents on German Foreign Policy, 1918–1945*, Series C (1933–1937) *The Third Reich: First Phase*, Vol. I (Washington DC: US Government Printing Office, 1957), pp. 669–79 [Doc. 371]

The *Gleichschaltung* of the arts

In the process known as *Gleichschaltung* – the regimentation and synchronization of German society – the Nazis created ideologically monolithic umbrella organizations in all fields. The Reich Chamber of Culture (*Reichskulturkammer*) was founded in September 1933 under the leadership of Propaganda Minister Josef Goebbels as an instrument of ideological control. It was divided into seven separate chambers for the fine arts, literature, music, theatre, film, radio, and the press, respectively. These chambers served as means to enforce both racial homogeneity and ideological conformity in the cultural sphere. Membership was compulsory for any person active or employed in these fields. The following selection is taken from the 1937 Handbook of the Reich Chamber of Culture.

3.16 The nature and functions of the Reich Chamber of Fine Arts

The Reich Chamber of Creative Art was established as a professional body of public law on grounds of the law of the Reich Chamber of Culture. Membership in the Chamber is a prerequisite, for the members of the following professions, in practicing their professions:

Architects, interior decorators, horticulturists, sculptors, painters, engravers, commercial engravers, designers, fine art craftsmen, copyists, restorers of works of art, dealers in works of art and antiques, fine art publishers, dealers in prints.

The following must also be members of the Chamber: all artists' associations, art associations, associations of fine art craftsmen, institutes for creative art and their faculties.

The first problem confronting the Chamber following its establishment was to locate and organize all professionals required to join the Chamber and to unite them in an organization in conformity with the new principles. In the course of these measures all former associations which were backed by some interests were discontinued without exception, and each member obligated to become a member of the Reich Chamber without fail.

Source: Office of the US Chief of Counsel for Prosecution of Axis Criminality,
***Nazi Conspiracy and Aggression*, Vol. V**
(Washington DC: US Government Printing Office, 1946), p. 262 [Doc. 2529-PS]

The *Gleichschaltung* of the press

With this law the German press came under the direct control of Joseph Goebbels, who headed the Ministry for Public Enlightenment and Propaganda, newly established in March 1933. Censorship of the press was one of the key provisions of the Nazi program ever since 1920. As the left-wing press had been forced to cease publication long before, this law was directed against those liberal and independent publications that still were allowed to appear in fall 1933. The Editorial Law allowed the regime to control the press without necessarily changing its ownership, except in the case of newspapers or periodicals owned by Jews. Promulgation of this law followed the creation of the Reich Press Chamber on 22 September 1933, one of six chambers of the Reich Chamber of Culture (Doc. 3.16), through which Goebbels' ministry controlled the cultural life of the country. The use of the somewhat archaic term *Schriftleiter* (rather than the more usual *Redakteur*, derived from the French) to designate editors was symptomatic of the Nazis' efforts to purify the German language of foreign words and phrases.

3.17 Editorial Law, 4 October 1933

The Reich Government has enacted the following law, which is hereby published:

PART ONE: THE EDITORIAL PROFESSION

SECTION 1

Involvement in the shaping of the intellectual contents of the newspapers or political periodicals published in the Reich, whether through writing, news reporting, or illustration, or through appointment as chief editor, is a public function regulated as to professional duties and rights by the state through this law. Persons involved in this way are called editors (*Schriftleiter*). No one may call himself an editor who is not entitled to do so according to this law.

SECTION 2

1   Newspapers and periodicals are printed matter which appear in regular sequence at intervals of at most three months without limiting their circulation to a certain group of persons.
2   All reproductions of writings or illustrations, destined for dissemination, which are produced by means of a mass reproduction process are to be considered as printed matter.

SECTION 3

1   The provisions of this law relating to newspapers are valid also for political periodicals.
2   This law does not apply to official newspapers and periodicals.
3   The Reich Minister of Public Enlightenment and Propaganda will determine which periodicals are to considered political within the meaning of the law. In case the periodical affects a certain specialized field, he will make the decision in agreement with the Reich or state agency concerned.

SECTION 4

Involvement in the shaping of the intellectual contents of German newspapers is also given when it does not take place in the management of a newspaper, but in an establishment which supplies newspapers with intellectual contents (written word, news, or illustrations).

PART TWO: ADMISSION TO THE PROFESSION OF EDITOR

SECTION 5

Persons who can be editors are only those who

1   possess German citizenship;

2   have not lost their civic rights (*bürgerliche Ehrenrechte*) and the qualification to hold public office;
3   are of Aryan descent and are not married to a person of non-Aryan descent;
4   have completed their 21st year of age;
5   have the right to enter into contracts;
6   have been trained in the profession;
7   have the qualities which the task of exerting intellectual influence upon the public requires ...

SECTION 8

Admission to the editorial profession will be effected by entry upon application in the professional editors' list. The professional rosters are kept by the offices of the state associations (*Landesverbände*) of the German press. The registration will be authorized by the head of the state association. He must authorize the registration, if the requirements which are set forth in Section 5 are fulfilled. He has to reject it if the Reich Minister for Public Enlightenment and Propaganda raises objections ...

PART THREE: EXERCISE OF THE PROFESSION OF EDITOR

SECTION 12

By registration in the professional roster, the editor becomes entitled to practice his profession with German newspapers or with German enterprises of the kind described in Section 4. If he moves into the district of a different state association, he will be transferred to the respective professional roster without further examination.

SECTION 13

Editors are charged to treat the subjects they write about truthfully and to judge them according to the best of their knowledge.

SECTION 14

Editors are especially obligated to keep out of the newspapers anything which

1   is misleading to the public by mixing selfish interests with community interests;
2   tends to weaken the strength of the German Reich, in foreign relations or domestically; the sense of community of the German people; German defense capability, culture, or the economy; or offends the religious sentiments of others;
3   offends the honor and dignity of Germany;
4   illegally offends the honor or the well-being of another, hurts his reputation, or ridicules or disparages him;
5   is immoral for other reasons.

SECTION 15

Editors are bound to practice their profession conscientiously and by their conduct within or outside their profession prove themselves worthy of the respect that this profession demands ...

PART FOUR: LEGAL PROTECTION OF THE EDITORIAL PROFESSION

SECTION 22

The editorial group as a whole will watch over the fulfillment of duty on the part of individual professional colleagues and will look after their rights and their welfare.

SECTION 23

Editors are legally united in the Reich Association of the German Press (*Reichsverband der Deutschen Presse*). By virtue of his registration on the professional roster every editor belongs to it. By virtue of this law the Reich Association becomes a public corporation. It has its seat in Berlin ...

SECTION 26

The Reich Minister for Public Enlightenment and Propaganda will exercise supervision to ensure that the Reich Association fulfills tasks which have been assigned to it.

SECTION 27

1   Professional Courts (*Berufsgerichte*) will be established for the protection of the editorial profession.
2   Professional Courts of the first instance are the District Courts (*Bezirksgerichte*) of the press. The Professional Court of the second instance is the Press Court (*Pressegerichtshof*) in Berlin ...

SECTION 30

A publisher may dismiss an editor because of the views expressed by him in the newspaper only if they are in conflict with the public professional duties of the editor or if they contravene the agreed-upon guidelines. The Professional Court will, at the request of the editor, find whether the dismissal, in its opinion, is contrary to the provisions of the preceding sentence or amounts to an evasion of them. Legal proceedings before the regular courts, if any have been initiated, are to be deferred until the requested opinion has been obtained.

SECTION 31

1   An editor who fails in his public professional duties, as set forth in Sections 13 to 15, 19, 20, paragraph 3, commits a professional misdemeanor. In such a case the Professional Court may

(1)   warn the editor;

(2) punish him with a fine not exceeding the sum of one month's professional income;

(3) decree the removal of his name from the professional roster.

2   With his removal from the roster his license to practice the editorial profession and to call himself an editor is terminated.

3   The Professional Court may temporarily deny an editor, against whom proceedings have been initiated, the right to exercise his profession ...

SECTION 35

The Reich Minister for Public Enlightenment and Propaganda may decree the removal of an editor from the professional list independent of the proceedings of the Professional Court, if he deems it necessary for pressing reasons of public welfare ...

SECTION 47

The Reich Minister for Public Enlightenment and Propaganda will set the date on which this law becomes valid.

Berlin, 4 October 1933

The Reich Chancellor: Adolf Hitler

The Reich Minister for Public Enlightenment and Propaganda: Dr. Goebbels

Source: Office of the US Chief of Counsel for Prosecution of Axis Criminality,
***Nazi Conspiracy and Aggression*, Vol. IV**
(Washington DC: US Government Printing Office, 1946), pp. 709–17 [Doc. 2083-PS]

The unity of party and state

Although parallel offices of government and party existed throughout the Third Reich, the organs of government were increasingly subordinated to the organs of the Nazi party. An important stage in this process was the following law issued in December 1933, which gave cabinet status to the Führer's Deputy Rudolf Hess and the Chief of Staff of the SA (the cabinet status of the latter was revoked after the so-called "Roehm Putsch" in June 1934 [Doc.3.21]). Even if governmental and party offices remained formally separate, the effect of merging was usually achieved by appointing party officials to parallel offices in the government. The party also had its own system of courts for the adjudication of internal disputes or the prosecution of violations of law by its members.

3.18 Law to Secure the Unity of Party and State, I December 1933

The Reich Government has issued the following law which is announced herewith:

PAR. I

I   After the victory of the National Socialist revolution, the National Socialist German Workers' Party is the bearer of the concept of the German state and is inseparable from the state.

2   It is a corporation in public law. Its statutes will be determined by the Führer.

PAR. 2

The Deputy of the Führer and the Chief of Staff of the SA will become members of the Reich Government in order to insure close cooperation of the offices of the Party and SA with the public authorities.

PAR. 3

1   The members of the National Socialist German Workers' Party and the SA (including their subsidiary organizations), as the leading and driving force of the National Socialist state, will bear greater responsibility toward the Führer, the people, and the state.
2   In case they violate these duties, they will be subject to special jurisdiction by Party and state. ...

PAR. 8

The Reich Chancellor, as Führer of the National Socialist German Workers' Party and as the supreme commander of the SA will issue the regulations necessary for the execution and augmentation of this law, particularly with respect to the establishment and procedure of the jurisdiction of the Party and SA. He will determine the time at which the regulations concerning this jurisdiction will be effective.
Berlin, 1 December 1933

The Reich Chancellor: Adolf Hitler
The Reich Minister of the Interior: Frick

Source: *Reichsgesetzblatt*, 1933, I, p. 1916

The Church struggle

The Protestant Evangelical Church, the dominant church in Prussia, lacked the unity of the Catholic Church, as each German state had its own church organization. The Nazis sought to gain control of the Evangelical Church by putting it under a unified Church government. They seemed to have succeeded in this goal when Ludwig Müller (1883–1945), Hitler's plenipotentiary for Evangelical Church affairs, was elected Reich Bishop by a national synod in July 1933. He was strongly supported by the nationalist faction in the Evangelical Church, the "German Christians," who sought to create a specifically German national religion. Müller's rule was short-lived, however, as a majority of Evangelical clergy rallied to the so-called Confessing Church, a movement to defend the integrity of traditional Lutheran doctrine and to oppose the intervention of the state. Under the leadership of Martin Niemöller (1892–1984), who was imprisoned in 1937 and throughout the war, and Otto Dibelius (1880–1967), Bishop of Berlin-Brandenburg after the war, the Confessing Church issued a declaration in May 1934 rejecting the doctrines of the "German Christians" and denouncing state control. The famous Barmen Declaration, excerpts of which are given below, was not intended as a political protest, however. The Confessing Church was a religious movement to uphold traditional Lutheran doctrine, not a political movement of resistance to the Nazi state. The "Church Struggle" was primarily an internal contest between nationalists, who rejected the Old Testament and sought to introduce the "Aryan Paragraph" (see Doc. 3.12) into the Church, and traditionalists, who wished to preserve the separation of religion and politics. While the Confessing Church succeeded in warding off the challenge of the "German Christians," the vast majority of its membership remained loyal to the Nazi regime.

3.19 The Confessional Synod of the German Evangelical Church in Wuppertal-Barmen, 29–31 May 1934

THEOLOGICAL STATEMENT ON THE PRESENT SITUATION OF THE GERMAN EVANGELICAL CHURCH

We, the representatives of Lutheran, Reformed, and United Churches, of free synods, church assemblies, and congregational groupings, gathered together as the Confessing Synod of the German Evangelical Church, declare that we take as our common basis the German Evangelical Church as a federation of the German Confessing Churches. In this we are united by faith in the one Lord of a single, holy, universal, and apostolic church.

We declare before the membership of all evangelical churches in Germany that the unity of this faith and therefore also the unity of the German Evangelical Church is severely endangered. It is threatened through the ever more visible doctrine and conduct of the ruling Church party of the German Christians and the church regimen that they represent ...

In view of the havoc wrought in the Church and the disruption of the unity of the German Evangelical Church brought about by the false teachings of the German Christians and of the present Reich Church Government, we bear witness to the following evangelical truths:

1 "I am the way, the truth, and the life: no man cometh unto the Father but by me." (John 14, 6) "Verily, verily, I say unto you, He that entereth not by the door into the sheepfold, but climbeth up some other way, the same is a thief and a robber. I am the door; by me if any man enter in, he shall be saved." (John 10, 1, 9)

   Jesus Christ, as witnessed to us in Holy Scripture, is the one word of God to which we have to listen, trust, and obey in life and in death.

   We reject the false teaching that the church can and must recognize any other events, powers, personalities, and truths apart from and in addition to this one word of God as sources of its proclamation.

2 ... We reject the false teaching that there are areas of our life which are subject not to Jesus Christ, but to other lords, areas in which justification and sanctification through him are not needful.

3 ... We reject the false teaching that the church can let the form of its message and its polity be determined by its own inclinations or by the ideological or political views which happen to have the upper hand at the time ...

4 ... The various offices in the Church are not based on the dominance of one over the others, but on the performance of services entrusted to and prescribed by the entire Church community.

   We reject the false doctrine that the Church can or may give itself or allow itself to be given leaders invested with ruling functions apart from these services.

5   … We reject the false teaching that the state has the right or the power to exceed its own particular commission and become the sole and total authority in human life, thus fulfilling the vocation of the church as well.

   We reject the false doctrine that the Church, over and above its special commission, should and could appropriate the characteristics, the tasks, and the dignity of the state, thus itself becoming an organ of the state.

6   … We reject the false doctrine that the Church could in human hubris put the word and work of Christ in the service of some wishes, goals, or plans chosen on our own …

STATEMENT ON THE LEGAL POSITION OF THE CONFESSING SYNOD OF THE GERMAN EVANGELICAL CHURCH

1   The unalterable basis of the German Evangelical Church is the Gospel of Jesus Christ, witnessed to us in Holy Scripture and brought to light again in the Reformation confessions.

   The present Reich Church Government has departed from this unalterable basis and has committed countless breaches of the law and of the constitution. Thereby it has forfeited its right to be the legitimate leadership of the German Evangelical Church.

Source: Kurt Dietrich Schmidt, ed., *Die Bekenntnisse und grundsätzlichen Äusserungen zur Kirchenfrage,* **Vol. 2,** *Das Jahr 1934* **(Göttingen: Vandenhoeck & Ruprecht, 1935), pp. 92–5.**
Translated by Rod Stackelberg

Conservative criticism of the SA

The speech below was held by Vice-Chancellor Papen at the University of Marburg in June 1934. The man who had been so instrumental in the destruction of the Weimar Republic expressed the frustrations and disappointments of many conservatives about developments since Hitler's rise to power. The Nazi storm-troopers (SA) had grown into an organization with several million members. Many of the SA rank and file called for a "second revolution," a euphemism for the distribution of offices and spoils to Nazi Party members. Radicals in the SA, conditioned by the years of struggle for power to oppose the "establishment," had long been critical of Hitler's policy of cooperation with the elites. In Papen's Marburg speech conservatives struck back.

Papen's speech represents an attack on the socially radical aspects of National Socialism, not on Hitler or the idea of National Socialism. Papen was critical of excessive thought-control, anti-religious forces in the Nazi Party, the lack of deference for established law and traditional hierarchies, and the subordination of the state to the party. Once the left had been suppressed and an authoritarian system restored, conservatives saw no further need for mass mobilization or social change. The dynamic that the conservative elites had helped to unleash by bringing Hitler to power now threatened to engulf them as well. On the other hand, they certainly appreciated and supported the goals and accomplishments of the Nazi regime, especially the reestablishment of a unified national community. It was this unity and stability that seemed threatened by the radicalism and lawlessness embodied in the SA.

Papen's Marburg speech probably helped convince Hitler to move against the SA in the so-called "night of long knives" on 30 June 1934 (Doc. 3.21). Hitler had no sympathy for cautious conservatism but was pragmatic enough to realize that he had to retain conservative support for his regime. Many conservatives, possibly including Papen, still viewed the Nazi government as a transitional stage to the restoration of the monarchy. Hitler was particularly anxious to maintain the goodwill of the military leadership, who distrusted the ambitions of SA leader Ernst Roehm (1887–1934). Although there is no evidence that Roehm had any immediate plans to launch a putsch, he was known to covet the position of Minister of War for himself. By purging Roehm and about 100 of his closest associates, Hitler assured himself of continued military and conservative support. This would prove particularly useful when President Hindenburg died on 2 August 1934, giving Hitler the opportunity to become head of state as well as government.

Conservatives did not emerge unscathed from the Blood Purge, however. While Papen merely suffered the loss of his post as Vice-Chancellor, his assistants Herbert von Bose (1893–1934) and Edgar Jung (1894–1934), youthful representatives of the intellectual movement known as the "Conservative Revolution" (Doc. 2.10), were murdered by the SS. Jung, who had written Papen's Marburg speech, was best known for his 1927 book, *Die Herrschaft der Minderwertigen* (The Rule of Inferiors), a scathing attack on democracy and the Weimar Republic. Their deaths, and Papen's demotion, dramatically exposed the predicament of members of the "Conservative Revolution," who sympathized with the Nazi goals of authoritarian government and the revival of national power but disapproved of their radical methods and unruly mass following.

3.20 Vice-Chancellor Franz von Papen's speech at Marburg, 17 June 1934

… The events of the past one and one-half years have gripped the whole German people and affected them deeply. It seems almost like a dream that out of the valley of misery, hopelessness, hate, and fragmentation we have found our way back to a German national community. The horrendous tensions in which we have lived since the August days of 1914 have dissolved, and out of this discord the German soul has emerged once again, before which the glorious and yet so painful history of our people pass in review, from the sagas of the German heroes to the trenches of Verdun, and even to the street fights of our time.

An unknown soldier of the World War, who conquered the hearts of his countrymen with contagious energy and unshakable faith, has set this soul free. With his Field Marshall he has placed himself at the head of the nation, in order to turn a new page in the book of German destiny and to restore spiritual unity.

We have experienced this unity of spirit in the exhilaration of a thousand rallies, flags, and celebrations of a nation that has rediscovered itself. But now, as the enthusiasm has lessened and tough work on this project has become imperative, it has become clear that a reform process of such historical proportions also produces slag, from which it must be cleaned. …

The function of the press should be to inform the government where deficiencies have crept in, where corruption has settled, where serious mistakes are being made, where unsuitable men are in the wrong positions, and where transgressions are committed against the spirit of the German revolution. An anonymous or secret news service, no matter how well organized, can never be a substitute for this responsibility of the press. … If other countries claim that freedom has died in Germany, then the openness of my remarks should instruct them that the German government can afford to allow a discussion of the burning questions of the nation. The only ones who have earned the right to enter this debate, however, are those who have put themselves at the service of National Socialism and its efforts without reservation and have proven their loyalty. ...

If the liberal revolution of 1789 was the revolution of rationalism against religion, against attachment, so the counter-revolution taking place in the twentieth century can only be *conservative*, in the sense that it does not have a rationalizing and disintegrating effect, but once again places all of life under the natural law of Creation. That is presumably the reason why the cultural leader of the NSDAP, Alfred Rosenberg, spoke of a conservative revolution.

From this there emerge in the field of politics the following clear conclusions: The time of emancipation of the lowest social orders against the higher orders is past. This is not a matter of holding down a social class – that would be reactionary – but of preventing a class from arising, gaining the power of the state, and asserting a claim to totality. Every natural and divine order must thereby be lost; it threatens a permanent revolution ... The goal of the German Revolution, if it is to be a valid model for Europe, must therefore be the foundation of a natural social order that puts an end to the never-ending struggle for dominance. True dominance cannot be derived from one social order or class. The principle of popular sover-eignty has, however, always culminated in class rule. Therefore an anti-democratic revolu-tion can only be consummated by breaking with the principle of popular sovereignty and returning to natural and divine rule. ...

But once a revolution has been completed, the government represents only the people as a whole, and is never the champion of individual groups; otherwise it would have to fail in forming a national community ... It is not permissible, therefore, to dismiss the mind (*Geist*) with the catchword "intellectualism." Deficient or primitive intellect are not in themselves justification for war against intellectualism. And if today we sometimes complain about 150 percent Nazis, then we mean those intellectuals without substance, people who would like to deny the right of existence to scientists of world fame just because they are not Party members ...

The sentence, "men make history," has frequently been misunderstood as well. The Reich government is therefore right to criticize a false personality cult, which is the least Prussian kind of thing one can imagine. Great men are not made by propaganda, but rather grow through their deeds and are recognized by history. Even Byzantinism cannot delude us about the validity of these laws. Whoever speaks of Prussian tradition, therefore, should first of all think of silent and impersonal service, and last or not at all of reward and recognition. ...

I have so pointedly described the problems of the German Revolution and my attitude toward it, because talk of a second wave that will complete the revolution seems not to want to end. Whoever toys with such ideas should not conceal the fact that the one who threatens with the guillotine is the one who is most likely to come under the executioner's axe. Nor is it apparent to what this second wave is to lead. Have we gone through an anti-Marxist revo-lution in order to carry out a Marxist program? ...

No nation can afford a constant revolt from below if it wants to pass the test of history. The Movement must come to a standstill some day; at some time a stable social structure must emerge, maintained by an impartial judiciary and by an undisputed state authority. Nothing can be achieved through everlasting dynamics. Germany must not go adrift on uncharted seas toward unknown shores, with no one knowing when it will stop. History moves on its own; it is unnecessary to drive it on incessantly. If therefore the German revolu-tion should experience a second wave of new life, then not as a social revolution, but as the creative culmination of work already begun. The statesman is there to create standards; the state and the people are his only concerns. The state is the sole power and the last guarantor of something to which every citizen can lay claim: iron-clad justice. Therefore the state also cannot endure any dualism in the long term, and the success of the German Revolution and the future of our nation depend on whether a satisfactory solution can be found to the dualism between party and state.

The Government is well informed on all the self-interest, lack of character, want of truth, unchivalrous conduct, and arrogance trying to rear its head under cover of the German Revolution. It is also not deceived about the fact that the rich store of confidence bestowed upon it by the German people is threatened. If one wishes a close proximity to and a close connection with the people, one must not underestimate the good sense of the people; one must return their confidence and not constantly want to tell them what to do. The German people know that their situation is serious; they feel the economic distress; they are perfectly aware of the defects of many laws conditioned by the emergency; they have a discerning feeling for violence and injustice; they smile at clumsy attempts to deceive them with false optimism. No organization and no propaganda, no matter how good, will in the long run be able to retain trust. I have therefore viewed the wave of propaganda against the so-called petty critics differently from many others. Confidence and readiness to cooperate cannot be won by incitement, especially of youth, nor by threats against helpless segments of the people, but only by discussion with the people with trust on both sides. The people know that great sacrifices are expected from them. They will bear them and follow the Führer with unwavering loyalty, if they are allowed to have their part in the planning and in the work, if every word of criticism is not taken for ill will, and if despairing patriots are not branded as enemies of the state. ...

Source: *Trial of the Major War Criminals Before the International Military Tribunal,* Vol. XV (International Military Tribunal, 1949), pp. 544–557

Retroactive legalization of the Roehm Purge

In the night of 30 June 1934 Hitler authorized the SS (aided in some areas by regular army units) to liquidate the SA leadership. He was encouraged to do so by Himmler, Goering, and Goebbels, as well as the Reichswehr leadership, all of whom viewed Roehm as a dangerous rival. The Nazi leaders took the opportunity to liquidate others who had opposed or criticized Hitler in the past, including Gregor Strasser, General Kurt von Schleicher, Gustav von Kahr, and the Catholic publicist Erich Klausener. Papen escaped with his life, but the author of his Marburg speech, Edgar Jung, was shot (see Doc. 3.20). The exact number of victims has never been determined; they may have numbered in the hundreds. Hitler justified the purge as a necessary defense against a planned SA putsch, despite the fact that virtually the entire SA leadership was on furlough at the time. Nonetheless, wide sectors of the public approved of Hitler's actions, and President Hindenburg sent him a congratulatory telegram. The Ministry of Justice retroactively legalized the summary executions in the following decree.

3.21 Law Relating to National Emergency Defense Measures, 3 July 1934

The Reich Government has enacted the following law, which is hereby promulgated:

The measures taken on 30 June and 1 and 2 July 1934 to suppress attempts at treason and high treason are legal emergency measures in defense of the state.

Berlin, 3 July 1934

The Reich Chancellor: Adolf Hitler
The Reich Minister of the Interior: Frick
The Reich Minister of Justice: Dr. Gürtner

Source: *Reichsgesetzblatt*, 1934, I, p. 529

Loyalty oath of the armed forces to Hitler

This loyalty oath was initiated by leaders of the Reichswehr after Hitler combined the offices of President and Chancellor in his person following Hindenburg's death on 2 August 1934. In a reversion to a practice typical of absolutist monarchies of the past, officers and soldiers pledged loyalty to the Führer personally, not to the offices of president or chancellor as prescribed in the constitution. By introducing this oath army leaders expressed their appreciation to Hitler for his suppression of the SA as a potential rival to the military. The loyalty oath also reflected the common interest of the Reichswehr and the Nazi Party in the speedy introduction of universal military training and accelerated rearmament. Reichswehr leaders were well aware that they depended on the Nazi government and on Hitler's leadership and diplomacy to achieve these goals.

3.22 Oath of officials and soldiers of the Wehrmacht, 20 August 1934

The Reich Government has enacted the following law, which is hereby proclaimed:

ARTICLE 1

Civilian officials and soldiers of the Armed Forces must take an oath of service on entering the service.

ARTICLE 2

1　The oath of service of civilian officials will be:

I swear: I shall be loyal and obedient to Adolf Hitler, the Führer of the German Reich and people; respect the laws; and fulfill my official duties conscientiously, so help me God.

2　The oath of service of the soldiers of the Armed Forces will be:

I swear by God this sacred oath, that I will render unconditional obedience to Adolf Hitler, the Führer of the German Reich and people, supreme commander of the Armed Forces, and will be ready as a brave soldier to risk my life at any time for this oath. …

Berlin, 20 August 1934

> The Führer and Reich Chancellor: Adolf Hitler
> The Reich Minister of the Interior: Frick
> The Reich Minister of Defense: von Blomberg

Source: *Reichsgesetzblatt*, 1934, I, p. 785

Paul von Hindenburg, Political Testament

President Hindenburg's testament was published in the official National Socialist newspaper, *Völkischer Beobachter*, on 16 August 1934, two weeks after the popular war hero's death at the age of 86. His testament is noteworthy because it reflects the good-will of the old elites toward the Third Reich and their approval of its accomplishments and what they took to be its direction and its aims. Although Hindenburg was a monarchist who hoped for the eventual restoration of the Hohenzollern dynasty, he, too, believed in Germany's "world mission," the necessity of rearmament, and the reversal of Germany's defeat in the First World War. Particularly interesting is his apology for the role that he played as the president of the Weimar Republic in upholding a form of government he abhorred. This strategy was necessary, he wrote, to preserve German independence while Germany was still too weak to resist the threat of foreign intervention. He viewed Hitler's accession to power as the event that had unified Germany and would enable the nation to finally throw off the fetters of foreign oppression and reclaim its rightful place in the world. He ends by exhorting his countrymen to continue to participate in the national reconstruction initiated by the Nazis.

3.23 Hindenburg's Political Testament, August 1934

To the German nation and its Chancellor, my testament.

In 1919 I wrote in my message to the German nation: "We were at the end! Just like Siegfried under the cunning spear of the furious Hagen, our exhausted front collapsed. In vain we tried to drink new life from the perennial spring of inborn strength. It was our task now to save the remaining strength of our army for the coming reconstruction of the Fatherland. The present was lost. There remained now only hope – for the future!

"I understand the idea of escape from the world which obsessed many officers, in view of the collapse of all that was dear and true to them. The desire to know nothing more of a world where seething passions obscured the vital qualities of our nation, so that they could no longer be recognized, is humanly conceivable. And yet – but I must express it frankly, just as I think! Comrades of the once grand, proud German army! Can you speak of losing heart? Think of the men who more than a hundred years ago created for us a new Fatherland. Their religion was their faith in themselves and in the sanctity of their cause. They created the new Fatherland, basing it not on freak doctrinaire theories foreign to our nature, but building it up on the foundations of the free development of the framework and the principles of our own common weal! When it is able, Germany will take this path again.

"I have the firm conviction that now, as in those times, the links with our great rich past will be preserved, and, where they have been broken, will be restored. The old German spirit will again assert itself triumphantly, though only after it has been purged in the flames of suffering and passion.

"Our enemies knew the strength of this spirit; they admired and hated it in times of peace; they were astonished at it and feared it on the battlefields of the Great War. They sought to explain our strength to their peoples by using the empty word 'organization.' They were silent about the spirit that lived and moved behind the veil of this word. But in and with this spirit we will again courageously reconstruct our nation.

"Germany, the focus-point of so many of the inexhaustible values of human civilization and culture, will not go under so long as it retains faith in its historical world mission. I am confident that the depth and strength of thought of the best in our fatherland will succeed in blending new ideas with the precious treasures of former times, and from them will together forge lasting values for the welfare of our fatherland.

"This is the unshakable conviction with which I leave the bloody battlefield of international warfare. I have seen the heroic agony of my fatherland and never, never will I believe that it was its death agony.

"For the present our entire former constitution lies buried under the flood-tide raised by the storm of wild political passions and resounding phrases which has apparently destroyed all sacred traditions. But this flood-tide will subside. Then, from the eternally agitated sea of human life, will again emerge that rock to which the hope of our fathers clung, that rock upon which, nearly half a century ago, the future of our fatherland was, by our strength, confidently founded – the German Empire! When the national idea, the national consciousness, has again been raised, then, out of the Great War – on which no nation can look back with such legitimate pride and with such clear conscience as we – as well as out of the bitter severity of the present days, precious moral fruits will ripen for us. The blood of all those who have fallen in the faith of the greatness of the fatherland will not then have flowed in vain. In this assurance I lay down my pen and rely firmly on you – the youth of Germany."

I wrote these words in the darkest hours and in the conviction that I was fast approaching the close of a life spent in the service of the fatherland. Fate disposed otherwise for me. In the spring of 1925 a new chapter of my life was opened. Again I was wanted to cooperate in the destiny of my nation. Only my firm confidence in Germany's inexhaustible resources gave me the courage to accept the office of *Reichspräsident*. This firm belief lent me also the moral strength to fulfill unswervingly the duties of that difficult position.

The last chapter of my life has been for me, at the same time, the most difficult. Many have not understood me in these troubled times and have not comprehended that my only anxiety was to lead the distracted and discouraged German nation back to self-conscious unity.

I began and conducted the duties of my office in the consciousness that a preparatory period of complete renunciation was necessary in domestic and international politics. From the Easter message of the year 1925 – in which I exhorted the nation to the fear of God, to social justice, to internal peace and political sanity – onwards, I have not become tired of cultivating the inward unity of our nation and the self-consciousness of its best qualities. Moreover, I was conscious that the political constitution and form of government which were provided for the nation in the hour of its greatest distress and greatest weakness did not correspond with the needs and characteristics of our people. The time must arrive when this knowledge will become general. It therefore seemed my duty to rescue the country from the morass of external oppression and degradation, internal distress and disruption, without jeopardizing its existence, before this hour struck.

The guardian of the state, the Reichswehr, must be the symbol and firm support for this superstructure. On the Reichswehr, as a firm foundation, must rest the old Prussian virtues of self-realized dutifulness, of simplicity, and comradeship. The German Reichswehr had, after the collapse, cultivated the continuation of the high traditions of the old army in typical style. Always and at all times the Reichswehr must remain the pattern of state conduct, so that, unbiased by any internal political development, its lofty mission for the defense of the country may be maintained.

When I shall have returned to my comrades above, with whom I have fought on so many battlefields for the honor and glory of the nation, then I shall call to the younger generation:

"Show yourselves worthy of your ancestors, and never forget, if you would secure the peace and well-being of your native country, you must be prepared to give up everything for its peace and honor. Never forget that your deeds will one day become tradition."

The thanks of the Field Marshal of the World War and its Commander-in-Chief are due to all the men who have accomplished the construction and organization of the Reichswehr.

Internationally the German nation had to travel the road through a Gethsemane. A frightful treaty weighed heavily upon it, and through its increasingly evil effects threatened to bring about the collapse of our nation. For a long time the surrounding world did not understand that Germany must live, not only for its own sake, but also for the sake of Europe and as the standard-bearer of Western culture. Only step by step, without arousing an overwhelming resistance, were the fetters which bound us to be loosened. If many of my comrades at that time did not understand the difficulties that beset our path, history will certainly judge rightly, how severe, but also how necessary in the interests of the maintenance of German existence, was many a state act signed by me.

In harmony with the growing internal recovery and strengthening of the German nation, a progressive and – God willing – a generous contributon towards the solution of all troublesome European questions could be striven for and obtained, on the basis of its own national honor and dignity. I am thankful to Providence that, in the evening of my life, I have been allowed to see this hour of the nation's renewal of strength. I thank all those who, by unselfish devotion to the fatherland, have cooperated with me in the reconstruction of Germany. My Chancellor, Adolf Hitler, and his movement have together led the German nation above all professional and class distinctions, to internal unity – a decisive step of historical importance. I know that much remains to be done, and I desire with my whole heart that the act of reconciliation which embraces the entire German fatherland may be the forerunner of the act of national exaltation and national cooperation.

I depart from my German people in the full hope that what I longed for in the year 1919, and which was coming slowly to fruition in January 1933, may mature to the complete fulfillment and realization of the historical mission of our nation.

In this firm belief in the future of the fatherland, I close my eyes in peace.

Source: *Völkischer Beobachter*, 16 August 1934. J. W. Wheeler-Bennett, *Hindenburg, The Wooden Titan* (New York: Macmillan, 1967), pp. 470–3

The Nuremberg Party rally, September 1934

The week-long annual Nazi Party rallies in Nuremberg, officially described in 1938 as "the most German of all German cities," were intended to reinforce the enthusiasm of hundreds of thousands of party faithful and to spread the Nazi faith to the population at large. Not coincidentally, Nuremberg was the setting for Richard Wagner's most famous opera, *Die Meistersinger* (1867), a favorite of German nationalists, including Hitler. The site of the rallies on the outskirts of Nuremberg, particularly the enormous Zeppelin Meadow, was conspicuous for its monumental architecture and landscaping. The Nazis pioneered elaborate staging and lighting techniques to give the annual celebrations the character of sacred religious rituals with Hitler in the role of High Priest. The function of the ceremonies was to manufacture ecstacy and consensus, eliminate all reflective and critical consciousness, and instill in Germans a desire to submerge their individuality in a higher national cause.

This unifying function was particularly important at the 1934 rally, since it followed only two months after the bloody liquidation of the SA leadership. At the rally Hitler squelched all talk of a "second revolution" by proclaiming that there would be no more revolution in Germany for a thousand years. The documentary film of this rally made by Leni Riefenstahl under the title, *Triumph of the Will*, was widely shown throughout Germany and became one of the most successful Nazi propaganda vehicles. Rallies were held annually until 1938. The 1939 rally, planned to be longer and more spectacular than all the previous ones, was preempted by the outbreak of war one day before its scheduled opening. Party rallies were suspended during the war as the reality of sacrifice on the battlefield made its ritual incantation at Nuremberg superfluous. The following critical account of the 1934 rally is taken from the personal diary of the American radio and newspaper correspondent William Shirer, who wrote an important history of the Third Reich after the war.[15]

3.24 William L. Shirer, *Berlin Diary*

NUREMBERG, SEPTEMBER 4

Like a Roman emperor Hitler rode into this medieval town at sundown today past solid phalanxes of wildly cheering Nazis who packed the narrow streets that once saw Hans Sachs and the *Meistersinger*. Tens of thousands of Swastika flags blot out the Gothic beauties of the place, the faces of the old houses, the gabled roofs. The streets, hardly wider than alleys, are a sea of brown and black uniforms. I got my first glimpse of Hitler as he drove by our hotel, the Württemberger Hof, to his headquarters down the street at the Deutscher Hof, a favorite old hotel of his, which has been remodelled for him. He fumbled his cap with his left hand as he stood in his car acknowledging the delirious welcome with somewhat feeble Nazi salutes from his right arm. He was clad in a rather worn gaberdine trench-coat, his face had no particular expression at all – I expected it to be stronger – and for the life of me I could not quite comprehend what hidden springs he undoubtedly unloosed in the hysterical mob which was greeting

---

15   William L. Shirer, *The Rise and Fall of the Third Reich: A History of Nazi Germany* (New York: Simon & Schuster, 1960).

him so wildly. He does not stand before the crowd with that theatrical imperiousness which I have seen Mussolini use. I was glad to see that he did not poke out his chin and throw his head back as does the Duce nor make his eyes glassy – though there *is* something glassy in his eyes, the strongest thing in his face. He almost seemed to be affecting a modesty in his bearing. I doubt if it's genuine.

This evening at the beautiful old Rathaus Hitler formally opened this, the fourth party rally. He spoke for only three minutes, probably thinking to save his voice for the six big speeches he is scheduled to make during the next five days. Putzi Hanfstaengl, an immense, high-strung, incoherent clown who does not often fail to remind us that he is part American and graduated from Harvard, made the main speech of the day in his capacity of foreign press chief of the party.[16] Obviously trying to please his boss, he had the crust to ask us to "report on affairs in Germany without attempting to interpret them." "History alone," Putzi shouted, "can evaluate the events now taking place under Hitler." What he meant, and what Goebbels and Rosenberg mean, is that we should jump on the bandwagon of Nazi propaganda. I fear Putzi's words fell on deaf, if good-humored, ears among the American and British correspondents, who rather like him despite his clownish stupidity.

About ten o'clock tonight I got caught in a mob of ten thousand hysterics who jammed the moat in front of Hitler's hotel, shouting: "We want our Führer." I was a little shocked at the faces, especially those of the women, when Hitler finally appeared on the balcony for a moment. They reminded me of the crazed expressions I saw once in the back country of Louisiana on the faces of some Holy Rollers who were about to hit the trail. They looked up at him as if he were a Messiah, their faces transformed into something positively inhuman. If he had remained in sight for more than a few moments, I think many of the women would have swooned from excitement.

Later I pushed my way into the lobby of the Deutscher Hof. I recognized Julius Streicher, whom they call here the Uncrowned Czar of Franconia. In Berlin he is known more as the number-one Jew-baiter and editor of the vulgar and pornographic anti-Semitic sheet the *Stürmer*. His head was shaved and this seemed to augment the sadism of his face. As he walked about, he brandished a short whip.

SEPTEMBER 5

I'm beginning to comprehend, I think, some of the reasons for Hitler's astounding success. Borrowing a chapter from the Roman church, he is restoring pageantry and color and mysticism to the drab lives of twentieth-century Germans. This morning's opening meeting in the Luitpold Hall on the outskirts of Nuremberg was more than a gorgeous show; it also had something of the mysticism and religious fervor of an Easter or Christmas Mass in a great Gothic cathedral. The hall was a sea of brightly colored flags. Even Hitler's arrival was made dramatic. The band stopped playing. There was a hush over the thirty thousand people packed in the hall. Then the band struck up the Badenweiler March, a very catchy tune, and used only, I'm told, when Hitler makes his big entries. Hitler appeared in the back of the auditorium, and followed by his aides, Goering, Goebbels, Hess, Himmler, and the others, he

---

16   Ernst "Putzi" Hanfstaengl (1887–1975), who had studied in the US, served the NSDAP in various functions before losing favor and emigrating to London in 1937. An early backer of Hitler, he participated in the Beer Hall Putsch and hid Hitler in his home after it failed.

strode slowly down the long center aisle while thirty thousand hands were raised in salute. It is a ritual, the old-timers say, which is always followed. Then an immense symphony orchestra played Beethoven's Egmont Overture. Great Klieg lights played on the stage, where Hitler sat surrounded by a hundred party officials and officers of the army and navy. Behind them the "blood flag," the one carried down the streets of Munich in the ill-fated putsch. Behind this, four or five hundred SA standards. When the music was over, Rudolf Hess, Hitler's closest confidant, rose and slowly read the names of the Nazi "martyrs" – brown-shirts who had been killed in the struggle for power – a roll-call of the dead, and the thirty thousand seemed very moved.

In such an atmosphere no wonder, then, that every word dropped by Hitler seemed like an inspired Word from on high. Man's – or at least the German's – critical faculty is swept away at such moments, and every lie pronounced is accepted as high truth itself. It was while the crowd – all Nazi officials – were in this mood that the Führer's procla-mation was sprung on them. He did not read it himself. It was read by *Gauleiter* [Adolf] Wagner of Bavaria, who, curiously, has a voice and manner of speaking so like Hitler's that some of the correspondents who were listening back at the hotel on the radio thought it was Hitler.

As to the proclamation, it contained such statements as these, all wildly applauded as if they were new truths: "The German form of life is definitely determined for the next thou-sand years. For us, the nervous nineteenth century has finally ended. There will be no revolu-tion in Germany for the next one thousand years!"

Or: "Germany has done everything possible to assure world peace. If war comes to Europe it will come only because of Communist chaos." Later before a "*Kultur*" meeting he added: "Only brainless dwarfs cannot realize that Germany has been the breakwater against Communist floods which would have drowned Europe and its culture."

Hitler also referred to the fight now going on against his attempt to Nazify the Protestant church. "I am striving to unify it. I am convinced that Luther would have done the same and would have thought of unified Germany first and last."

SEPTEMBER 6

Hitler sprang his *Arbeitsdienst*, his Labor Service Corps, on the public for the first time today and it turned out to be a highly trained, semi-military group of fanatical Nazi youths.[17] Standing there in the early morning sunlight which sparkled on their shiny spades, fifty thousand of them, with the first thousand bared above the waist, suddenly made the German spectators go mad with joy when, without warning, they broke into a perfect goose-step. Now, the goose-step has always seemed to me to be an outlandish exhibition of the human being in his most undignified and stupid state, but I felt for the first time this morning what an inner chord it strikes in the strange soul of the German people. Spontane-ously they jumped up and shouted their applause. There was a ritual even for the Labor Service boys. They formed an immense *Sprechchor* – a chanting chorus – and with one voice

---

17   The *Reichsarbeitsdienst* (RAD), an organization under the purview of the Ministry of Interior, remained
      voluntary until 1935 (and for women until 1939). The term of service for youth between 18 and 25 was
      six months. Until the introduction of universal conscription in 1935, its purpose was mainly to carry out
      military training under the guise of labor service.

intoned such words as these: "We want one Leader! Nothing for us! Everything for Germany! *Heil Hitler!*" ...

SEPTEMBER 7

Another great pageant tonight. Two hundred thousand party officials packed in the Zeppelin Wiese with their twenty-one thousand flags unfurled in the searchlights like a forest of weird trees. "We are strong and will get stronger," Hitler shouted at them through the microphone, his words echoing across the hushed field from the loud-speakers. And there, in the flood-lit night, jammed together like sardines, in one mass formation, the little men of Germany who have made Nazism possible achieved the highest state of being the Germanic man knows: the shedding of their individual souls and minds – with the personal responsibilities and doubts and problems – until under the mystic lights and at the sound of the magic words of the Austrian they were merged completely in the Germanic herd. Later they recovered enough – fifteen thousand of them – to stage a torchlight parade through Nuremberg's ancient streets, Hitler taking the salute in front of the station across from our hotel. Von Papen arrived today and stood alone in a car behind Hitler tonight, the first public appearance he has made, I think, since he narrowly escaped being murdered by Goering on June 30. He did not look happy.

SEPTEMBER 9

Hitler faced his SA storm troopers today for the first time since the bloody purge. In a harangue to fifty thousand of them he "absolved" them from blame for the Roehm "revolt." There was considerable tension in the stadium and I noticed that Hitler's own SS bodyguard was drawn up in force in front of him, separating him from the mass of the brown-shirts. We wondered if just one of those fifty thousand brown-shirts wouldn't pull a revolver, but not one did. Viktor Lutze, Roehm's successor as chief of the SA, also spoke. He has a shrill, unpleasant voice, and the SA boys received him cooly, I thought. Hitler had in a few of the foreign correspondents for breakfast this morning, but I was not invited.

SEPTEMBER 10

Today the army had its day, fighting a very realistic sham battle in the Zeppelin Meadow. It is difficult to exaggerate the frenzy of the three hundred thousand German spectators when they saw their soldiers go into action, heard the thunder of the guns, and smelled the powder. I feel that all those Americans and English (among others) who thought that German militarism was merely a product of the Hohenzollerns – from Frederick the Great to Kaiser Wilhelm II – made a mistake. It is rather something deeply ingrained in all Germans. They acted today like children playing with tin soldiers. The Reichswehr "fought" today only with the "defensive" weapons allowed them by Versailles, but everybody knows they've got the rest – tanks, heavy artillery, and probably airplanes.
Later. – After seven days of almost ceaseless goose-stepping, speech-making, and pageantry, the party rally came to an end tonight. And though dead tired and rapidly developing a bad case of crowd-phobia, I'm glad I came. You have to go through one of these to understand

Hitler's hold on the people, to feel the dynamic in the movement he's unleashed and the sheer, disciplined strength the Germans possess. And now – as Hitler told the correspondents yesterday in explaining his technique – the half-million men who've been here during the week will go back to their towns and villages and preach the new gospel with new fanaticism. Shall sleep late tomorrow and take the night train back to Berlin.

Source: **William L. Shirer**, *Berlin Diary: The Journal of a Foreign Correspondent 1934–1941*
(New York: Alfred A. Knopf, 1941), pp. 16–23

Women in the Third Reich

One of the puzzles of Nazi Germany is the reasonably successful integration of women in a society committed to an ideology of male supremacy. Despite their openly anti-feminist policies the Nazis had little trouble gaining at least the tacit support of most German women. One reason may have been that the Nazis made every effort to endow the traditional role of women as mothers and homemakers with status and respect. Their view of women's natural role as loyal, devoted, self-sacrificing wives and mothers was not much different from the attitudes and theories that prevailed in Europe in the eighteenth and nineteenth centuries. The Nazis' opposition to women's emancipation was also shared by many conservative and religious groups in Germany both before and after 1933. The following speech by Hitler to the National Socialist Women's Organization at the annual Nazi Party rally in Nuremberg in September 1934 exemplifies both the typical Nazi attitude toward women and the kind of appeals they made to gain women's support. Hitler repeatedly stressed the importance of nature and providence in defining the character and responsibilities of men and women in the German *Volksgemeinschaft* (people's community).

Through laws restricting the number of women in higher education, barring women from serving in the civil service until the age of 35, and giving women financial incentives to give up their jobs to have children the Nazis sought to increase the German birthrate and restore a separation of spheres. According to the euphemistically named "Law to Combat Unemployment" in 1933, married couples received low interest loans on condition that the wife give up her job. The amount to be repaid was reduced by one-quarter after the birth of each child, provided that the parents could prove the child was racially "pure" and healthy. Other "family-friendly" legislation (always on condition that the families in question were "Aryan," i.e., non-Jewish) included child support payments, maternity benefits, state-supported birth clinics, and awards to women with four or more children. Female education was directed toward household management, homemaking skills, child-rearing, and motherhood training. In the second selection below, an excerpt from a 1936 anthology entitled *Mothers Who Give Us the Future*, a functionary of the National Socialist Women's Organization provides the rationale for Nazi policies toward women.

3.25a Hitler's speech to the National Socialist Women's Organization, September 1934

The feelings and above all the psychology of woman have always had a complementary effect on the mind of man.

If the spheres of activity in daily life have sometimes shifted between man and woman in a way not in accordance with nature, it was not because woman as woman was striving for power over man; rather it was because man was no longer in a position to completely fulfill his responsibilities. That is the wonderful thing about nature and providence: no conflict between the two sexes is possible as long as each party fulfills the task assigned to them by nature.

The phrase "women's liberation" is a phrase invented only by Jewish intellectualism, and its content is shaped by the same spirit. The German woman never needed to be emancipated in the really good times of German life. She possessed exactly the gifts that nature had perforce given her to manage and preserve, exactly as man in his good times never needed to fear that he would be forced out of his role in relation to woman.

His place was least of all threatened by woman. It was only when he himself was not certain about what his responsibility was that woman's eternal instinct for self-preservation and preservation of the people began to rebel. A change of roles not in accord with nature began with this rebellion, and it lasted until both sexes returned once again to the roles that an eternally wise providence assigned to them.

If one says that man's world is the state, man's world is his struggle, his readiness to act on behalf of the community, then one could perhaps say that the world of woman is a smaller one. For her world is her husband, her family, her children, and her home. But where would the larger world be if no one wanted to look after the smaller world? How could the larger world exist, if there were no one who would make the cares of the smaller world the content of their lives? No, the large world is founded on this small world! This large world cannot exist, if the small world is not stable. Providence assigned to woman the cares of a world that is particularly her own, and it is only on this that man's world can be shaped and constructed.

That is why these two worlds are never in conflict. They complement each other, they belong together, as man and woman belong together.

We feel it is not appropriate when woman forces her way into man's world, into his territory; instead we perceive it as natural when these two worlds remain separate. One world is characterized by strength of feeling, strength of the soul! The other world is characterized by strength of vision, toughness, determination, and willingness to act. In the former case this strength requires the willingness of woman to commit her life to preserve and increase the family unit; in the latter case this power requires from man the readiness to provide security.

Whatever sacrifices man makes in the struggles of his people, woman makes in the struggle for the preservation of her people in family units. What man offers in heroic courage on the battlefield, woman offers in ever patient devotion, in ever-patient suffering and endurance. Each child that she brings into the world is a battle that she wages for the existence of her people. Both man and woman must therefore value and respect each other, when they see that each accomplishes the task that nature and providence have ordained. Out of this separation of functions there will necessarily come mutual respect.

It is not true, as Jewish intellectualism maintains, that respect depends on overlapping spheres of activity of the sexes; instead respect requires that neither sex try to do what rightly is the task of the other. In the final analysis respect comes from each side knowing that the other is doing everything necessary to maintain the whole!

Thus woman was at all times the helper of man and because of this his most devoted friend, and man was at all times the guardian of his wife and therefore her best friend! And both saw in this way of life the common basis for the continued existence and preservation of all that they love. Woman is selfish in maintaining her small world so that man can take the role of protecting the larger world, and man is selfish in the maintenance of this larger world, for it is indivisibly connected with the other, smaller one. We will defend ourselves against an intellectualism of the most corrupt sort that would tear asunder what God has joined.

Woman, because she springs from the root of life, is also the most stable element in the preservation of a people.

In the last analysis she has the most infallible sense for what is necessary so that a race does not die out, because it is above all her children who will be the first to be affected by that misfortune.

Man is often psychologically too erratic to find his way immediately to these fundamental truths. Only in good time and with a good education will man come to know exactly what his responsibility is. For many years we National Socialists have therefore opposed bringing woman into political life, a life that in our eyes is unworthy of her. A woman once said to me: "You must see to it that women get into the parliament, because only they can ennoble it." "I do not believe," I replied, "that we should ennoble something inherently bad. And the woman who gets caught in this parliamentary machinery will not ennoble it; instead it will dishonor her. I do not want to leave something to woman that I intend to take away from men." My opponents believed that we would never win women for our movement. But we gained more women than all the other parties put together, and I know we would have won over the very last German woman if she had only had the opportunity to study the parliament and the degrading function of the women involved in it.

We have therefore included women in the struggle of the national community as nature and providence intended. Our women's movement is for us not a movement that inscribes on its banner a program of fighting against man, but instead it is a movement that embraces in its program the common struggle of woman together with man. For we have strengthened the new National Socialist *Volksgemeinschaft* precisely because millions of women became the most loyal, fanatical comrades-in-arms; women fighting for life together in the service of the common preservation of life; women fighters who in this struggle do not set their gaze on rights with which a Jewish intellectualism bedazzles them, but on duties which nature imposes on all of us in common.

If earlier the liberal intellectual women's movements included in their programs many, many points that started with the so-called intellect, the program of our National Socialist women's movement has actually only one single point, and this point is: the child, this tiny being which must be born and must thrive, for the child alone gives the entire life's struggle its meaning. For what purpose would we fight and struggle, if something did not come after us that could use what we acquire to its advantage and benefit and could hand it down to its heirs? What other reason is there for the whole human struggle? Why the worry and the sorrow? Only for an idea? Only for a theory? No, it would certainly not be worth going through this earthly valley of tears for that. The only thing that enables us to overcome all that is the view from the present into the future, from ourselves to the generation coming after us.

I spoke just a few minutes ago at the youth rally. It is glorious to look at this golden youth, and to know: they will become Germany when we no longer exist! They will preserve everything we have created and built. We are working for them. That is indeed the meaning of the whole struggle! And if we recognize this simplest and most succinct goal of nature, the work of both sexes will be settled of its own accord, logically and correctly, no longer in conflict, but in a common struggle for life as it really is.

You, my party comrades, stand here as leaders, organizers, and helpers in this struggle. You have accepted a magnificent responsibility. What we want to create in our nation as a whole is what you must establish and firmly support in the inner world. You must provide the inner psychological and emotional stability! You must complement man in this struggle that we are leading for our people's freedom, equality, honor, and peace, so that we can look to the future as fighters for our people!

Then strife and discord can never break out between the sexes; instead they will go through life hand in hand fighting together, just the way providence intended, and for the purpose that both sexes were created. Then the blessing of such work carried out together can not fail to appear. Then no insane struggle will flare up over theories, and man and woman will not quarrel because of false ideas; instead the blessing of the Almighty will accompany their joint fight for survival!

Source: *Der Kongress zu Nürnberg vom 5. bis 10. September 1934. Offizieller Bericht über den Verlauf des Reichsparteitages mit sämtlichen Reden* (Munich: F. Eher Verlag, 1935), pp. 169–172. **Translated by Sally Winkle**

3.25b Emilie Müller-Zadow, "Mothers who give us the future," 1936

There is a growing recognition that mothers carry the destiny of their people in their hands and that the success or ruin of the nation depends on their attitude toward the vocation of motherhood.

Nation and race are facts of creation, which we, too, are called upon to share in forming and preserving. Therefore a national leadership that respects and honors its mothers is on a sound and healthy path. ...

Of course a woman, simply because she is able to cook porridge, sew shirts, and grasp the basic rules of bringing up children, still in no way has the inner aptitude to be a mother, if she does not yet know how to fill her nursery with all the warmth, with the healthy, clean, strong, and cozy atmosphere necessary for growing children to become men and women capable "of ensuring the continued existence of their people." But we believe that in addition to succeeding externally, she cannot fail but succeed inwardly, either, if both of these conditions are fulfilled.

Motherhood training is not limited to any time period or age and is always a task for the long term; it is the seed of hope. It must be as close to nature, as full of life, and as many-sided as the young life that it serves. More than any other training, it has to be free of dogmas or of rigid formulas, forms, and methods. And yet it has to be "training", that is, it has to proceed consciously and be planned according to firm guidelines and clear principles.

For this reason it is only now, in the National Socialist state, that we can really speak of motherhood training. Much valuable education of mothers has already been done by different groups (mainly Christian) – a good deal of these experiences were incorporated into the present work. But if, despite all good intentions and the realization that time was pressing, this earlier educational work only remained fragmentary, that was because the conditions for large-scale, systematic, and standardized motherhood training were not yet established. These conditions were only created by the National Socialist world view and the unification of the people.

The place that Adolf Hitler assigns to woman in the Third Reich corresponds to her natural and divine destiny. Limits are being set for her, which earlier she had frequently violated in a barren desire to adopt masculine traits. The value and sanctity of goals now being set for her have been unrecognized and forgotten for a long time; and due respect is now being offered to her vocation as mother of the people, in which she can and should develop her rich emotions and spiritual strengths according to eternal laws. This wake-up call of National Socialism to women is one more indication that in Germany today it is not arbitrary laws that are being issued, but rather a nation is returning to essential, eternal rules of order.

It is therefore not at all surprising that the state and party claim the education of mothers as exclusively their task and insist that all training be carried out only by National Socialists and according to the principles of National Socialism. For the way a mother sees her child, how she cares for, teaches, and forms him, the principles that she instills in him, the attitude that she demands of him, all of this is crucial for the national health, for a German morality, and for the unified overall mind-set of the future nation.

Some think they can argue that the purely practical part of motherhood training – for example the care of newborns – is independent of politics and worldview and is not influenced by them. But this is only partially true. The following may serve as an example:

In the post-war period a real mania prevailed in clinics and institutions to keep premature babies or infants with the most serious hereditary diseases alive for a shorter or longer time in incubators and with the most sophisticated measures, even those babies whose chances for a full life every doctor judged as next to nothing. These experiments cost great amounts of the national wealth, while in the homes of the unemployed, normal children died from a lack of bare necessities. A complete change of opinion has occurred in this area, as now only the functional, realistic principles of the state are in force, a state that examines and treats the individual according to his value. So in the whole project of motherhood training there is scarcely a component whose basic orientation and objectives are not formed by National Socialism.

The training of German women for the calling of motherhood cannot be confined to the official courses which are offered for this purpose by the German Women's Organization,[18] nor can it be limited to the education of the nation's youth provided by the League of German Girls.[19] A complete educational development and permeation of the whole nation can only succeed if all responsible maternally-oriented women feel impelled to instruct and actively help their sisters. Indeed, this wholly personal, heartfelt concern for one another and communication from person to person cannot be matched in its effectiveness by any course-work. Experience does show, however, that the actions of the director of motherhood courses provide the stimulus for the emergence in the whole national community of this willingness to help and for its self-evident acceptance everywhere. A bond of trust connects the course participants very quickly, old barriers and prejudices fall away, and the gulf of class differences is bridged over. For in their concern for young life almost all mothers are alike. It is amazing to observe with what joy the course participants pass on their newly acquired knowledge and ability, especially in rural areas; or how they suddenly become fully aware of the obligation to let others as well

---

18   The German Women's Organization (*Deutsches Frauenwerk*) was formed by the Nazis in October 1933 for women who were not necessarily members of the Nazi Party or its women's affiliate, the *Nationalsozialistische Frauenschaft*. However, the leadership and hierarchical structure of both groups were largely the same. In February 1934 Gertrud Scholtz-Klink became the leader (*Reichsführerin*) of both organizations.

19   The League of German Girls (*Bund Deutscher Mädel*), the Hitler Youth organization for girls.

participate in the richness of their lives as mothers, which becomes apparent to them for the first time in the course, in all its seriousness and fullness.

Source: Emilie Müller-Zadow: "Schulung und Selbsterziehung"
(Training and Self-education), in *Mütter, die uns die Zukunft schenken* (Königsberg, 1936),
pp. 7–11. Translated by Sally Winkle

The Nuremberg Laws

The Nazis had long promised to exclude Jews from German society. Economic boycott (see Doc. 3.9), exclusion of Jews from the Civil Service (Doc. 3.12), and *Gleichschaltung* of the professions and the arts (Docs.3.16 and 3.17) were all directed toward this goal. The notorious "Aryan paragraph" of the Civil Service Law, the model for *Gleichschaltung*, had excluded "Non-Aryans," defined as anyone with one or more Jewish grandparents. The vagueness of the category of "Non-Aryans," which obviously included a great number of people who had no connection with the Jewish community, elicited increasing pressure from within the party to provide more specific and precise legislation on the role of Jews in Germany. The so-called Nuremberg Laws, passed by acclamation by the Reichstag convened for that purpose at the annual Nazi Party rally in 1935, constituted the official Nazi response. There were three separate laws: First, a law making the Nazi swastika the official national flag; second, a law defining German citizenship in a way that excluded Jews; and third, a law banning marriage and sexual intercourse between Germans and Jews. The Interior Ministry later issued amendments to the citizenship law defining who was a Jew (anyone descended from three or four grandparents) and creating separate categories for persons of mixed descent (so-called *Mischlinge*). The first of these amendments, issued in November 1935, is included here.

The Nuremberg Laws achieved what had been one of the main goals of the radical right in Germany for more than half a century: the reversal of Jewish emancipation (see Doc. 1.8). Jews in Germany once again became aliens in their own country. Nonetheless, because they gave legal status to Jews in Germany (as secondary citizens), the Nuremberg Laws had the paradoxical effect of giving Jews a certain sense of security. To mitigate the effect of the Nuremberg Laws on world opinion and to gain their acceptance by the German public, Nazi propaganda claimed, quite falsely, that the Nuremberg Laws marked the end of legal measures against Jews. The Reich Citizenship Law, in particular, provided the basis for later discriminatory legislation aimed at driving Jews out of Germany and isolating and segregating those who remained.

3.26a Reich Flag Law, 15 September 1935

The Reichstag has unanimously adopted the following law which is herewith promulgated:

ARTICLE I

The colors of the Reich are black, white, and red.

ARTICLE 2

The Reich and national flag is the swastika flag. It is also the merchant flag.

ARTICLE 3

The Führer and Reich Chancellor will designate the design of the Reich War Flag and the Reich Service Flag.

ARTICLE 4

The Reich Minister of the Interior will issue the necessary legal and administrative regulations for the execution and extension of this law insofar as they are not within the jurisdiction of the Minister of War.

ARTICLE 5

The law takes effect on the day of its promulgation.
    Nuremberg, 15 September 1935, at the Reich Party Rally of Freedom
                              The Führer and Reich Chancellor: Adolf Hitler
                                 The Reich Minister of the Interior: Frick
    The Reich Minister of War and Commander in Chief of the Wehrmacht: von Blomberg

3.26b Reich Citizenship Law, 15 September 1935

The Reichstag has adopted unanimously the following law, which is herewith promulgated.

ARTICLE 1

1   A subject of the State (*Staatsangehöriger*) is a person, who belongs to the protective union (*Schutzverband*) of the German Reich, and who therefore has particular obligations toward the Reich.
2   The status of the subject is acquired in accordance with the provisions of the Reich- and State Law of Citizenship.

ARTICLE 2

1   A citizen of the Reich (*Reichsbürger*) is only that subject, who is of German or kindred blood and who, through his conduct, shows that he is both willing and fit to serve faithfully the German people and Reich.
2   The right to citizenship is acquired by the granting of Reich citizenship papers.
3   Only the citizen of the Reich enjoys full political rights in accordance with the provision of the laws.

ARTICLE 3

The Reich Minister of the Interior in conjunction with the Deputy of the Führer will issue the necessary legal and administrative decrees for the carrying out and supplementing of this law. Nuremberg, 15 September 1935 at the Reich Party Rally of Freedom

The Führer and Reich Chancellor: Adolf Hitler

The Reich Minister of the Interior: Frick

The Reich Minister of War and Commander in Chief of the Wehrmacht: von Blomberg

3.26c First Regulation to the Reich Citizenship Law, 14 November 1935

On the basis of Article 3, Reich Citizenship Law of 15 September 1935, the following is ordered:

ARTICLE 1

1   Until further issue of regulations regarding citizenship papers, all subjects of German or kindred blood who possessed the right to vote in the Reichstag elections at the time the Citizenship Law came into effect shall, for the time being, possess the rights of Reich citizens. The same shall be true of those whom the Reich Minister of the Interior, in conjunction with the Deputy of the Führer, has given preliminary citizenship.
2   The Reich Minister of the Interior, in conjunction with the Deputy of the Führer, can withdraw the preliminary citizenship.

ARTICLE 2

1   The regulations in Article 1 are also valid for Reich subjects of mixed Jewish blood.
2   An individual of mixed Jewish blood is one who descended from one or two grandparents who were racially full Jews, insofar as that individual does not count as a Jew according to Article 5, paragraph 2. A grandparent shall be considered as full-blooded if he or she belonged to the Jewish religious community.

ARTICLE 3

Only the Reich citizen, as bearer of full political rights, exercises the right to vote in political affairs, and can hold a public office. The Reich Minister of the Interior, or any agency empowered by him, can make exceptions during the transition period, with regard to occupying public offices. The affairs of religious organizations will not be touched upon.

ARTICLE 4

1   A Jew cannot be a citizen of the Reich. He has no right to vote in political affairs; he cannot occupy a public office.

2   Jewish officials will retire as of 31 December 1935. If these officials served at the front in the World War, either for Germany or her allies, they will receive in full, until they reach the age limit, the pension to which they were entitled according to last received wages; they will, however, not advance in seniority. After reaching the age limit, their pension will be calculated anew, according to the last received salary, on the basis of which their pension was computed.
3   The affairs of religious organizations will not be affected.
4   The conditions of service of teachers in Jewish public schools remain unchanged until new regulations of the Jewish school systems are issued.

ARTICLE 5

1   A Jew is anyone who descended from at least three grandparents who were racially full Jews. Article 2, par. 2, second sentence will apply.
2   A Jew is also anyone who descended from two full Jewish parents, if: (a) he belonged to the Jewish religious community at the time this law was issued, or he joined the community later; (b) he was married to a Jewish person at the time the law was issued, or married one subsequently; (c) he is the offspring from a marriage with a Jew, in the definition of paragraph 1, which was contracted after the Law for the Protection of German Blood and Honor became effective; (d) he is the offspring of an extramarital relationship, with a Jew, in the definition of paragraph 1, and will be born out of wedlock after 31 July 1936.

ARTICLE 6

1   As far as requirements are concerned for the purity of blood as laid down in Reich law or in orders of the NSDAP and its echelons – not covered in Article 5 – they will not be affected.
2   Any other requirements for purity of blood, not covered in Article 5, can only be made with permission from the Reich Minister of the Interior and the Deputy of the Führer. If any such requirements have been made, they will be void as of 1 January 1936, if they have not been requested from the Reich Minister of the Interior in agreement with the Deputy of the Führer. These requests must be made from the Reich Minister of the Interior.

ARTICLE 7

The Führer and Reich Chancellor can grant exemptions from the regulations laid down in the law.
Berlin, 14 November 1935

The Führer and Reich Chancellor: Adolf Hitler
The Reich Minister of the Interior: Frick
The Deputy of the Führer: R. Hess (Reich
Minister without Porfolio

3.26d Law for the Protection of German Blood and Honor, 15 September 1935

Convinced of the truth that the purity of the German blood is the necessary condition for the continued existence of the German people, and animated by the inflexible determination to safeguard the German nation for all time, the Reichstag has unanimously decreed the following law, which is hereby announced:

#1   (1) Marriages between Jews and citizens of German or kindred blood are forbidden. Marriages concluded in defiance of this law are void, even if, for the purpose of evading this law, they are concluded abroad.

(2) Proceedings for annulment may be initiated only by the Public Prosecutor.

#2   Extra-marital intercourse between Jews and citizens of German or kindred blood is forbidden.

#3   Jews may not employ female citizens of German or kindred blood under the age of 45 in their households.

#4   (1) Jews are forbidden to hoist the Reich and national flag and to display the colors of the Reich.

(2) On the other hand, the display of the Jewish colors is permitted. The practice of this authorization is protected by the state.

#5   (1) Whoever acts contrary to the prohibition of #1 will be punished by penitentiary.

(2) The man who acts contrary to the prohibition of #2 will be punished by jail or penitentiary.

(3) Whoever acts contrary to the provisions of #3 or #4 will be punished by imprisonment up to one year and with a fine or with one of these penalties.

#6   The Reich Minister of the Interior in agreement with the Deputy of the Führer and the Reich Minister of Justice will issue the legal and administrative regulations necessary for the implementation and supplementation of this law.

#7   The law will become effective on the day after its promulgation; #3, however, will not become effective until 1 January 1936.

Nuremberg, 15 September 1935, on the day of the Reich Party Rally of Freedom

The Führer and Reich Chancellor: Adolf Hitler

The Reich Minister of the Interior: Frick

The Reich Minister of Justice: Dr. Gürtner

The Führer's Deputy: R. Hess, Reich Minister without Portfolio

Source: Office of the US Chief of Counsel for Prosecution of Axis Criminality,
Nazi Conspiracy and Aggression
(Washington DC: US Government Printing Office, 1946),
Vol. IV, pp. 7–10, 707, Vol. V, pp. 916–17 [Docs. 2079-PS, 1416-PS, 1417-PS, 3179-PS]

4

The Third Reich
The road to war, 1936–39

Hitler's foreign policy aims were to reverse the results of Versailles, create a greater German Reich through the incorporation of Austria and other ethnically German areas of Europe (including the Czech border territory of the Sudetenland), and to gain *Lebensraum* in the east, a project he realized could not be accomplished without war. Hence his first step was to extricate Germany from the commitment to disarmament it made in joining the League of Nations in 1926. In a plebiscite following German withdrawal from the League in October 1933, 95 percent of the voters gave the government their approval. Over 90 percent of the voters of the Saarland approved the return of this coal-rich territory to Germany in January 1935. Two months later, with the strong support of Reichswehr leaders, Hitler officially announced that Germany would reintroduce universal military training in defiance of the Versailles Treaty. The British, committed to a policy of appeasement (which at that time meant only "bringing about peace"), negotiated a naval treaty that allowed the Germans to ignore the restrictions of Versailles. Mussolini's Italy took advantage of the climate of appeasement by attacking Ethiopia in October 1935. German support for Italian aggression helped cement what Mussolini would call the German–Italian "Axis."

In March 1936 Hitler was ready to take his greatest gamble yet by sending a token force into the Rhineland, the left bank of the Rhine, which by treaty was supposed to remain demilitarized in perpetuity to prevent a renewed Franco-German conflict (Doc. 4.1). Hitler's rationale was the French ratification of a mutual assistance pact with the Soviet Union, negotiated after the German announcement of rearmament in March 1935. Hitler guessed rightly that the Western powers would protest but would do nothing to stop the remilitarization of the Rhineland. Western anti-communism and appeasement also left Germany and Italy free to intervene on the side of the fascist-supported rebellion of Francisco Franco (1892–1975) against the elected Popular Front government in Spain in July 1936. In September 1936 Hitler announced a new four-year plan, under Hermann Goering's direction, to make Germany economically self-sufficient and ready for war (Doc. 4.3). In November 1936 Germany moved closer to a formal alliance with expansionist Japan by signing the so-called Anti-Comintern Pact (Doc. 4.6).

On the home front, too, the Nazis prepared for war by enforcing ideological conformity, expanding the SS, and continuing their brutal repression of political dissent (see Docs. 4.2 and 4.8) while promoting pro-natal policies designed to enlarge the population of "pure-blooded" Germans (Docs. 4.4 and 4.5). The expansion of the Hitler Youth (Doc. 4.7) caused conflict with the Catholic Church, which unsuccessfully fought for the right to maintain its own independent youth organizations. Catholic frustrations with the failure of the regime to live up to the Concordat (Doc. 3.15) were expressed in Pius XI's encyclical "With Burning

Anxiety" in March 1937 (Doc. 4.9). This protest against Nazi neo-paganism added to Nazi mistrust of the Church (see Doc. 4.17) and underscored the incompatibility of Nazi and Christian ideology (Doc. 4.18). The Church, however, remained faithful to the commitment it had made in the Concordat not to engage in political criticism or resistance.

In November 1937 Hitler told his military commanders in strict confidence his plans for expansionist war in the east, to be launched, at the latest, by 1943 (Doc. 4.10). His immediate goals were the annexation of Austria and the destruction of Czechoslovakia. The skepticism of some army leaders about a policy that might lead to war against Britain and France before Germany was ready induced Hitler to take over the functions of Minister of War himself. A new High Command (*Oberkommando der Wehrmacht* or OKW) was formed in February 1938 under the leadership of Generals Wilhelm Keitel and Alfred Jodl to serve as the conduit for Hitler's orders to the armed forces (Doc. 4.11). The new command structure facilitated the takeover of Austria in the so-called *Anschluss* of March 1938. Shortly thereafter Hitler used the grievances of the German minority in Czechoslovakia, mostly concentrated in the border areas known as the Sudetenland, to threaten military action against the Czech state. Some German generals, including Army Chief of Staff Ludwig Beck, opposed his seemingly reckless policy (Doc. 4.12), but the Western surrender to Hitler's demands in the Munich Agreements of September 1938 removed all grounds for a possible military revolt. In any case, most German generals shared Hitler's general goals, while only opposing the reckless pace at which he sought to achieve them (Doc. 4.14).

Hitler's foreign policy successes may have contributed to a renewed escalation of anti-Jewish policies, which moved toward open violence in the party-sponsored pogrom of November 1938, euphemistically known as *Kristallnacht* (Doc. 4.13). Persecution of the Jews now reached truly draconic proportions. Through "Aryanization" – the compulsory sale of Jewish businesses to non-Jews – Jews were to be forced out of German economic life. By depriving Jews of their ability to make a living, the Nazis hoped to force them to emigrate. The effect of impoverishment, however, was to make it virtually impossible for many Jews to leave Germany (and Austria) or to meet the standard of financial self-support required for immigration to most countries. Only about half of the approximately 700,000 German and Austrian Jews were able to emigrate before the start of the war. In a militant speech on 30 January 1939, the sixth anniversary of his assumption of power, Hitler threatened to destroy the Jews in the case of another world war (Doc. 4.15).

Hitler hoped, but did not expect, to be able to fight an expansionist war in the east while maintaining the neutrality of Great Britain and France. The prospects of British and French neutrality were greatly reduced in March 1939 when Hitler seized what remained of the Czech state and established the "Protectorate of Bohemia and Moravia" and a Slovak satellite state in March 1939. This flagrant violation of the tenuous accord reached at Munich induced the British and French governments, under the pressure of outraged public opinion, to extend unconditional guarantees of support to Poland and Romania, the next likely targets of German and Italian aggression, respectively. Hitler now decided on military action against Poland and instructed his generals accordingly (Doc. 4.16). By August 1939 the Nazi leadership was firmly resolved on war (Doc. 4.19). To overcome the lingering fears of his generals about British and French intervention, Hitler summoned them to Berchtesgaden for lengthy harangues (Doc. 4.20). He pointed out that the impending non-aggression pact with the Soviet Union (Doc. 4.21) was likely to deter the Western powers from entering the war. If they did intervene, Hitler said, the Nazi–Soviet Pact made Germany immune to economic blockade and thus put the Germans in a far more favorable military position than in the First World War.

When Britain and France announced their intention of honoring their commitment to Poland despite the Nazi–Soviet Pact, Hitler postponed the target date for the invasion by a week to allow Goering to pursue diplomatic efforts designed to keep the Western powers out of the war. But neither President Franklin D. Roosevelt's last-minute mediation efforts (Doc. 4.22) nor Mussolini's decision to remain out of the conflict for the time being (Doc. 4.23) could dissuade Hitler from launching the attack. The German invasion of Poland on 1 September 1939 began what was to become the Second World War.

Remilitarization of the Rhineland

The French Parliament's ratification of a mutual assistance pact with the Soviet Union, negotiated a year earlier in response to German rearmament, served as the pretext for the German move into the Rhineland in March 1936. The Rhineland was to have remained as a permanently demilitarized buffer zone between Germany and France according to both the Versailles and Locarno treaties. Despite the misgivings of his generals, who realized that the West still enjoyed substantial military superiority, Hitler successfully gambled that France and England would not take military action to prevent his violation of legally binding international treaties.

The Rhineland occupation did not immediately change the existing balance of power, but it had important psychological and diplomatic ramifications, not least in increasing Germany's influence in neutral countries. Holland and Belgium refused to coordinate defensive measures with France or Britain for fear that they would be drawn into an eventual conflict. By invoking the Soviet threat Hitler could be sure of gaining sympathy among European conservatives who considered communism a greater danger than fascism. Hitler's successful defiance of the Western powers greatly increased his popularity at home.

4.1 Hitler's speech to the Reichstag, 7 March 1936

Men of the German Reichstag! France has replied to the repeated friendly offers and peaceful assurances made by Germany by infringing on the Rhine Pact through a military alliance with the Soviet Union, exclusively directed against Germany. In this manner, however, the Locarno Rhine Pact has lost its inner meaning and ceased in practice to exist. Consequently, Germany regards herself for her part as no longer bound by this dissolved treaty. The German Government is now constrained to face the new situation created by this alliance, a situation which is rendered more acute by the fact that the Franco-Soviet Treaty has been supplemented by a Treaty of Alliance between Czechoslovakia and the Soviet Union, exactly parallel in form. In accordance with the fundamental right of a nation to secure its frontiers and insure its possibilities of defense, the German Government has today restored the full and unrestricted sovereignty of Germany in the demilitarized zone of the Rhineland …

Source: Office of the US Chief of Counsel for Prosecution of Axis Criminality,
Nazi Conspiracy and Aggression, **Vol. IV**
(Washington DC: US Government Printing Office, 1946), pp. 994–5 [Doc. 2289-PS]

Nazi persecution of internal enemies

The main victims of Nazi persecution and terror were Jews and political opponents, especially the Communist and Social Democratic underground, which remained active in the 1930s despite massive repression (see Doc. 3.6). The brunt of the Nazi terror apparatus was unleashed against these alleged "enemies of the people and the state." But as the following selection shows, the Nazis also faced opposition from "politicized" ministers and priests. This form of protest was in some ways more difficult to combat because of the public support oppositional clergy often enjoyed. In the following article in the Nazi party newspaper *Völkischer Beobachter* in April 1936, Reinhard Heydrich (1904–42), as head of the Security Service (SD) the second-ranking official in the SS, attempted to mobilize public support for the Nazis' campaign of repression. His article attests to the potency of the churches' challenge to the "new paganism" of the Nazis and provides a typical example of how the Nazis sought to counter clerical opposition.

4.2 Reinhard Heydrich, "Fighting the Enemies of the State," 29 April 1936

… National Socialism, which led the movement's struggle for power on the basis of ideology, also breaks with the liberalist fight against enemies of the state. According to liberalist thinking, the government only fought against the subversive act and the subversive organization as the group responsible for this act.

For National Socialism it is these opponents' intellectual forces that are crucial; these we want to identify and strike. We know today that they are always the same ones: The Jew, the freemason, and the politicized cleric. Their goals are the same but their organizational forms adapt to what is legally possible at any given time.

So how does the enemy of the people function today? He tries to fight us by legal means, that is, disguised within the framework of the present realities. Always under the heading, "Everything for the National Socialist Reich," he attempts to use all his powers against us, yet without forming an organization that could be apprehended.

Jewry as such, of course, is now isolated as the Jewish race and Jewish people as a result of the Nuremberg Laws. A direct infusion of Jewish blood into the body of the *Volk* has thereby been averted. But the indirect Jewish intellectual influence has not been completely stopped by any means. In the first place many in academic and intellectual life unknowingly still carry the residues of Jewish, liberal, and Masonic infection. On the other hand, our own German history has shown us that the Jewish goal always remains the same: world dominance through a more or less visible Jewish elite. And if National Socialist policies make political conditions in Germany unsuitable for the attainment of this goal, the Jew will switch to economic and foreign policies. In economic affairs he has always been able to count on egotistical and traitorous elements as collaborators even in Germany. In foreign affairs the Jew works with those organizations that are already completely under his control, Bolshevism and the Masonic Lodges that are still operating freely abroad.

The Communist, whose core is drawn mainly from the ranks of international criminals and who fights with all the methods of modern technology, is especially dangerous, as he must also be regarded as a spy for Soviet Russia. This makes the anarchist criminal at the same time the most dangerous assailant against the elements of national defense.

Even in Germany the Masonic lodges were never more than auxiliary organizations of the Jews. Their purpose was very gradually and imperceptibly to transform the character and mind of the German according to Jewish ideas. With the exception of a few incorrigibles, all Germans now recognize the hostility of Jews, Communists, and Freemasons toward the state and the *Volk*, and they approve of their treatment with no holds barred as enemies of the state and the people. One still encounters a considerable lack of understanding, however, with respect to another enemy of the people and the state, the politicized church official.

The Führer and his followers have emphasized often enough that National Socialism believes in the one God, and this belief is obligatory for every German and National Socialist. Just how the German sees and imagines this God is a private matter for each German. Conversely, however, that also necessitated the elimination from politics of those forces who under the guise of religion pursued ecclesiastical world power and still pursue it today. A very large segment of the politicized priesthood – and the unpolitical segment is very small – has resorted to the old method of hypocritical deceit in order to reach these goals. Dolefully they bemoan the so-called new paganism. Apparently they don't want to see that this new paganism – when viewed in purely ecclesiastical terms – should probably be appraised as in essence nothing more than a reaction to the churches' inner manifestations of weakness. No, they prefer to identify new paganism with National Socialism in order to be able to combine the fight against this reaction to the churches with the fight against the National Socialist state. ...

Source: *Völkischer Beobachter*, North-German edition, 29 April 1936.
Translated by Sally Winkle

The Four-Year Plan

In the summer of 1936 Hitler faced a decision as to the further course of the German economy. His Economics Minister and head of the central Reich Bank, Hjalmar Schacht, cautioned against excessive deficit financing and advocated increased production for export and full integration into the world market as the optimal routes to national prosperity. Hitler was not willing, however, to slow down rearmament for economic reasons. In this memorandum he insisted that Germany must be both militarily and economically ready for war within four years. Once again the threat of Soviet communism served as the rationale for his decision. Only Germany, he insisted, had the necessary ideological solidarity and capacity for economic and military mobilization to win the unavoidable conflict with Soviet communism.

The Four-Year Plan was officially announced at the annual Party Rally in September. Goering was appointed to head the Plan with full powers to rule the economy by decree. The technical expertise to manage the plan was provided by the I. G. Farben cartel. As Hitler made clear in his memorandum, the goal of the plan was not to displace private industry, but to use state power to augment and assist private industry in the achievement of economic self-sufficiency (autarky). The state would only step in to carry out militarily important projects that private industry was unable or unwilling to undertake. Thus the state-owned Hermann Goering Works, founded in 1937, produced iron and steel from the low-grade ore that the steel industry rejected as unprofitable. Priority was also given to the production of synthetic products, especially fuel and rubber. As virtual economic czar from 1937 until Albert Speer (1905–81) took command of the war-time economy in 1942, Goering repeatedly clashed with Schacht, who resigned as Economics Minister in November 1937. Schacht was replaced by the more amenable Walther Funk (1890–1960), who also succeeded him as president of the Reich Bank in January 1939.

4.3 Hitler's Memorandum on the Four-Year Plan [Obersalzberg, August 1936]

THE POLITICAL SITUATION

Politics are the conduct and the course of the historical struggle for life of the peoples. The aim of these struggles is the assertion of existence. Even the idealistic ideological struggles [*Weltanschauungskämpfe*] have their ultimate cause and are most deeply motivated by nationally [*Völkisch*] determined purposes and aims of life. Religions and ideologies are, however, always able to impart particular harshness to struggles of this kind, and therefore also to give them great historical impressiveness. … Since the outbreak of the French Revolution, the world has been moving with ever increasing speed towards a new conflict, the most extreme solution to which is called Bolshevism, whose essence and aim, however, is solely the elimination of those strata of mankind which have hitherto provided the leadership, and their replacement by world-wide Jewry.

No state will be able to withdraw or even remain at a distance from this historical conflict. *Since Marxism, through its victory in Russia, has established one of the greatest empires in the world as a forward base for its future operations, this question has become a menacing one. Against a democratic world ideologically rent within itself stands a unified aggressive will founded upon an authoritarian ideology.* The means of military power available to this aggressive will are in the meantime increasing rapidly from year to year. One has only to compare the Red Army as it actually exists today with the assumptions of military men 10 or 15 years ago to realize the menacing extent of this development. Only consider the results of a further development over 10, 15, or 20 years and think what conditions will be like then!

Germany

Germany will, as always, have to be regarded as the focal point of the Western world in face of the Bolshevik attacks. I do not regard this as an agreeable mission but rather as a handicap and encumbrance upon our national life regrettably resulting from our position in Europe. We cannot, however, escape this destiny.

Our political situation results from the following:

Europe has at present only two states which can be regarded as standing firm in the face of Bolshevism: Germany and Italy. The other countries are either disintegrated through their democratic form of life, infected by Marxism, and thus likely themselves to collapse in the foreseeable future, or ruled by authoritarian governments whose sole strength lies in their military means of power; this means, however, that, being obliged to secure the existence of their leadership in face of their own peoples by means of the armed hand of the executive, they are unable to direct this armed hand outward for the preservation of their states. All these countries would be incapable of ever conducting a war against Soviet Russia with any prospects of success. In any case, apart from Germany and Italy, only Japan can be regarded as a power standing firm in the face of the world peril …

GERMANY'S DEFENSIVE CAPACITY

Germany's defensive capacity is based upon several factors. I would give pride of place to the intrinsic value of the German people *per se*. A German people with an impeccable political leadership, a firm ideology and a thorough military organization certainly constitutes the most valuable factor of resistance which the world of today can possess. Political leadership is ensured by the National Socialist Party; ideological solidarity has, since the victory of National Socialism, been introduced to a degree that had never previously been attained. It must be constantly deepened and hardened on the basis of this concept. This is the aim of the National Socialist education of our people.

Military development [*Auswertung*] is to be effected through the new army. *The extent and pace of the military development of our resources cannot be made too large or too rapid!* It is a capital error to think that there can be any argument on these points or any comparison with other vital necessities. However much the general pattern of life of a people ought to be a balanced one, it is nonetheless imperative that at particular times certain disturbances of the balance, to the detriment of other, less vital, tasks, must be adopted. *If we do not succeed in developing the German Wehrmacht within the shortest possible time into the first army in the world, in training, in the raising of units, in armaments, and, above all, in spiritual education as well, Germany will be lost!* The principle applies here that the omissions of peace-time months cannot be made good in centuries.

All other desires must therefore be unconditionally subordinated to this task. For this task is life and the preservation of life, and all other desires – however understandable they may be in other periods – are, by comparison, of no account or are even mortally dangerous and therefore to be rejected. Nor will posterity ever ask us by what methods or by what concepts, views, etc., which are valid today, we achieved the salvation of the nations, but only *whether* we achieved it. Nor would it one day be an excuse for our downfall were we to point to the measures, be they ever so well tried, which had nevertheless unfortunately caused that downfall.

GERMANY'S ECONOMIC POSITION

Just as the political movement among our people knows only one goal – to make good the claim to life of our people and Reich, that is to say to secure all the spiritual and other prerequisites for the self-assertion of our people – so too the economy has but this one purpose. The people do not live for the economy or for economic leaders or economic or financial theories; on the contrary, finance and economy, economic leaders and theories must all exclusively serve this struggle for self-assertion in which our people are engaged.

Germany's economic position is, however, in the briefest outline, as follows:

1 We are overpopulated and cannot feed ourselves from our own resources.
2 When our nation has 6 or 7 million unemployed, the food situation improves because these people are deficient in purchasing power …
3 But if a rise in employment fails to take place, then a higher percentage of the people must gradually be deducted from the body of our nation, as having become valueless through undernourishment …
4 Insofar as this consumption applies to articles of general use, it is possible to satisfy it to a *large* extent by increasing production …

5   It is, however, wholly pointless to keep on noting these facts, i.e., stating that we lack foodstuffs or raw materials; what is decisive is to take those measures which can bring about a *final* solution for the *future* and a *temporary* easing for the *transitional period*.

6   The final solution lies in extending the living space of our people and/or the sources of its raw materials and foodstuffs. It is the task of the political leadership one day to solve this problem.

7   The temporary easing can only be brought about within the framework of our present economy …

It is not sufficient merely to draw up, from time to time, raw material or foreign exchange balances, or to talk about the preparation of a war economy in time of peace; on the contrary, it is essential to ensure peacetime food supplies and above all those means for the conduct of a war which it is possible to make sure of by human energy and activity. And I therefore draw up the following program for a final solution of our vital needs.

1   Like the military and political rearmament and mobilization of our people, there must also be an economic one, and this must be effected in the same tempo, with the same determination, and, if need be, with the same ruthlessness as well.

      In future the interests of individual gentlemen can no longer be allowed to play any part in these matters. There is only one interest and that is the interest of the nation, and only one single view, which is that Germany must be brought politically and economically into a state of self-sufficiency.

2   For this purpose, in every sphere where it is possible to satisfy our needs through German production, foreign exchange must be saved in order that it can be applied to those requirements which can under no circumstances be supplied *except* by imports.

3   Accordingly, German fuel production must now be stepped up with the utmost speed and be brought to final completion within 18 months. This task must be attacked and carried out with the same determination as the waging of a war; for on its solution depends the conduct of the future war and not on the laying in of stocks of petroleum.

4   It is equally urgent that the mass production of synthetic rubber should be organized and secured. The contention that the processes are perhaps not yet fully determined and similar excuses must cease from now on. It is not a matter of discussing whether we want to wait any longer, for that would be losing time, and the hour of peril would take us all unaware. Above all it is not the task of state economic institutions to rack their brains over production methods. This has nothing to do with the Ministry of Economics. Either we possess today a private industry, in which case it is its task to rack its brains over production methods, or we believe that the determination of production methods is the task of the state, in which case we no longer need private industry.

5   The question of the cost of these raw materials is also quite irrelevant, since it is in any case better for us to produce in Germany more expensive tires which we can use than for us to sell [*sic – verkaufen*] theoretically cheap tires for which, however, the Ministry of Economics can allocate no foreign exchange and which, consequently cannot be used at all …

It is further necessary to increase the German production of iron to the utmost. The objection that we are not in a position to produce from the German iron ore, with a 26 percent content, as cheap a pig-iron as from the 45 percent Swedish ores, etc., is irrelevant because we are not in fact faced with the question of what we would *rather* do but only of what we *can* do. The objection, moreover, that in that event all the German blast furnaces would have to be converted is equally irrelevant; and, what is more, this is no concern of the Ministry of Economics. It is for the Ministry of Economics simply to set the national economic tasks, and it is for private industry to carry them out. But should private industry believe that it is not able to do this, then the National Socialist state will succeed in carrying out this task on its own. In any case, for a thousand years Germany had no foreign iron ores. Even before the war, more German iron ores were being processed than during the period of our worst decline. *Nevertheless, if we still have the possibility of importing cheap ores, well and good. But the future of the national economy and, above all, of the conduct of war, must not be dependent on this.*

It is further necessary to prohibit forthwith the distillation of alcohol from potatoes. Fuel must be obtained from the ground and not from potatoes. Instead, it is our duty to use any arable land that may become available, either for human or animal foodstuffs or for the cultivation of fibrous products.

It is further necessary for us to make our supplies of *industrial* fats independent of imports as rapidly as possible and to meet them from our coal. This task has been solved chemically and is actually crying out to be done. The German economy will either grasp the new economic tasks or else it will prove itself quite incompetent to survive in the modern age when a Soviet state is setting up a gigantic plan. *But in that case it will not be Germany who will go under, but, at most, a few industrialists.*

It is further necessary to increase Germany's output of other ores, *regardless of cost*, and in particular to increase the production of light metals to the utmost in order thereby to produce a substitute for certain other metals.

It is, finally, necessary for rearmament too to make use even now whenever possible of those materials which must and will replace high-grade metals in time of war. *It is better to consider and solve these problems in time of peace than to wait for the next war, and only then, in the midst of a multitude of tasks, to try to undertake these economic researches and methodical testings, too.*

In summary: I consider it necessary that now, with iron determination, 100 percent self-sufficiency should be attained in all those spheres where it is feasible, and not only should the national requirements in these most important raw materials be made independent of other countries but that we should also thus save the foreign exchange which in peacetime we require for our imports of foodstuffs. *Here I would emphasize that in these tasks I see the only true economic mobilization and not in the throttling of armament industries in peacetime in order to save and stockpile raw materials for war.* But I further consider it necessary to make an immediate investigation into the outstanding debts in foreign exchange owed to German business abroad. There is no doubt that the outstanding claims of German business are today quite enormous. Nor is there any doubt that behind this in some cases there lies concealed the contemptible desire to possess, whatever happens, certain reserves abroad which are thus withheld from the grasp of the domestic economy. I regard this as deliberate sabotage of our national self-assertion and of the defense of the Reich, and for this reason I consider it necessary for the Reichstag to pass the following two laws:

1 A law providing the death penalty for economic sabotage, and
2 a law making the whole of Jewry liable for all damage inflicted by individual specimens of this community of criminals upon the German economy, and thus upon the German people ...

Nearly four precious years have now gone by. There is no doubt that by now we could have been completely independent of foreign countries in the sphere of fuel supplies, rubber supplies, and partly also iron ore supplies. Just as we are now producing 700,000 or 800,000 tons of petroleum, we could be producing 3 million tons. Just as we are today manufacturing a few thousand tons of rubber, we could already be producing 70,000 or 80,000 tons per annum. Just as we have stepped up the production of iron ore from 2½ million tons to 7 million tons, so we could be processing 20 or 25 million tons of German iron ore, and if necessary even 30 million. There has been time enough in four years to discover what we cannot do. It is now necessary to state what we can do.

I thus set the following task:

1   The German army must be operational [*einsatzfähig*] within four years.
2   The German economy must be fit for war [*kriegsfähig*] within four years.

Source: **US Department of State Publication 8083,**
***Documents on German Foreign Policy 1918–1945,* Series C (1933–1935)**
***The Third Reich: First Phase,* Vol. V**
(Washington DC: US Government Printing Office, 1966), pp. 853–62 [Doc. 490]

Selective breeding

In the following selection, Himmler announced the founding of *Lebensborn* (well of life), an agency to care for unmarried mothers of good racial stock and their children. Although *Lebensborn* certainly incorporated the principle of selective breeding, as it enabled unmarried "Aryan" women to have children with a minimum of social stigma, it was not, as was once widely assumed, a "breeding farm" that made men available to women who wanted to have children. Nonetheless, in his announcement Himmler took the opportunity to once again remind SS men that it was their duty to have large families as part of the Nazi effort to increase the "Aryan" German population.

4.4 Founding of the organization "Lebensborn e.V.," 13 September 1936

As early as 13 December 1934 I wrote to all SS leaders and declared that we have fought in vain if political victory was not to be followed by victory of births of good blood. The question of multiplicity of children is not a private affair of the individual, but his duty towards his ancestors and our people.

The SS has taken the first step in this direction long ago with the engagement and marriage decree of December 1931. However, the existence of sound marriage is futile if it does not result in the creation of numerous descendants.

I expect that here, too, the SS and especially the SS leadership corps, will serve as guiding examples.

The minimum number of children for a good sound marriage is four. Should unfortunate circumstances deny a married couple their own children, then every SS leader should adopt racially and hereditarily valuable children, educate them in the spirit of National Socialism, and let them have education corresponding to their abilities.

The organization "Lebensborn e.V." serves the SS leaders in the selection and adoption of qualified children. The organization "Lebensborn e.V." is under my personal direction, is part of the Race and Settlement central bureau of the SS, and has the following obligations:

1   Support racially, biologically, and hereditarily valuable families with many children.
2   Place and care for racially and biologically and hereditarily valuable pregnant women, who, after thorough examination of their and the progenitor's families by the Race and Settlement central bureau of the SS, can be expected to produce equally valuable children.
3   Care for the children.
4   Care for the children's mothers.

It is the honorable duty of all leaders of the central bureau to become members of the organization "Lebensborn e.V.". The application for admission must be filed prior to 23 September 1936. ...

I shall personally keep myself informed of the success of my appeal.

Let me remind every SS leader once more that only sacrifices of a personal and material nature have brought us success in the times of struggle, and that the further construction of Germany, to last hundreds and thousands of years, will not be possible unless each and every one of us is ready to keep doing his share in the fulfillment of his obvious duty.

Reichsführer SS

[signed] H. Himmler

Source: Office of the US Chief of Counsel for Prosecution of Axis Criminality,
Nazi Conspiracy and Aggression, **Vol. V**
(Washington DC: US Government Printing Office, 1946), pp. 465–6 [Doc. 2825-PS]

The duty of the SS to beget children

Nazi pro-natalist policies reached something of a climax when early in the war Heinrich Himmler issued an order urging SS men to father children before leaving for the front and promising care for any children born out of wedlock. He encouraged women "of good blood" to become mothers of these soldiers' children as a "sacred duty."

4.5 SS Order for the entire SS and Police

Reichsführer SS and Chief of the German Police in the Reich Ministry of the Interior, Berlin, 28 October 1939

Every war causes the best blood to be shed. Many a victory of arms meant for a people at the same time a disastrous loss of living strength and blood. But unfortunately inevitable death of its best men, deplorable as that may be, is not the worst. Of much more disastrous consequences is the lack of those who were not begotten by the living during, and by the dead after the war.

The old saying that only those who have children can die in peace must again become an acknowledged truth in this war, especially for the SS. Only those who know that their kind, that all for which they and their ancestors have striven, is continued in their children, can die in peace. The possession most prized by the widow of a fallen soldier is always the child of the man whom she loved.

Though it may perhaps be considered an infraction of necessary social standards and convention in other times, German women and girls of good blood can fulfill a high obligation even out of wedlock by becoming mothers of children of soldiers going to the front, whose eventual return or death for Germany lies entirely in the hands of fate – not because of promiscuity, but because of the deepest sense of ethics. It is the sacred duty also of these men and women whose place has been determined by the state to be on the home front, to become parents of children again, especially now.

Let us never forget that the victory of the sword and of the spilled blood of our soldiers remains fruitless if it is not succeeded by the victory of the child and the colonizing of conquered soil.

In past wars, many a soldier has decided, out of a deep sense of responsibility, to beget no more children during the time of war, so as not to leave his wife and an additional child in want and distress in case of his death. You SS men need not have such worries; the following regulations eliminate them.

1   Special commissioners, personally appointed by me, shall be entrusted in the name of the Reich Führer with the guardianship of all legitimate and illegitimate children of good blood whose fathers were killed in action. We shall support these mothers and humanely assume the responsibility for the education and upbringing of these children so that no mother and widow need to have any material worries.

2   During the war the SS will care for all legitimate and illegitimate children begotten during the war and for pregnant mothers in cases of need and distress. After the war, the SS will gener-ously grant additional material aid should these fathers who return request so. SS men and you mothers of these children, the hope of Germany show that in your belief in the Führer and your willingness to do your share in the perpetuation of our blood and people, you are just as willing to continue the life of Germany as you have had the courage to fight and die for it.

The Reichsführer SS
[signed] H. Himmler

Source: Office of the US Chief of Counsel for Prosecution of Axis Criminality,
Nazi Conspiracy and Aggression, **Vol. V**
(Washington DC: US Government Printing Office, 1946), pp. 466–7 [Doc. 2825-PS]

The Anti-Comintern Pact

The Anti-Comintern Pact represented an important stage in the increasing convergence of interests between Germany and Japan. The Spanish Civil War, which broke out when Fran-cisco Franco's troops attacked the democratically elected Popular Front government in July 1936, gave the Nazis, who supported Franco, the opportunity and incentive to once again focus world attention on the Soviet threat. As the appeasement policy precluded Western support for the Spanish government, the Soviet Union became the only country to provide military aid to the beleaguered republic. Just as invocation of the communist threat had facilitated the Nazis' rise to power, so now invocation of the Soviet threat could serve as a convenient pretext for armament and aggression. The Nazis realized that anti-communism was their most effective propaganda weapon both at home and abroad. Japan, too, could use the alleged Soviet threat to justify its expansion into Manchuria.

On the anniversary of the signing of the pact in 1937 Italy became its third member. The three countries eventually entered into a military alliance, the Tripartite Pact (Doc. 5.7) of September 1940, directed primarily against the United States.

4.6 Treaty Between the Government of the Reich and the Imperial Government of Japan Regarding the common fight against the Communist International, 25 November 1936

The Government of the German Reich and the Imperial Japanese Government, recognizing that the aim of the Communist International, known as the Comintern, is to disintegrate and subdue existing states by all the means at its command; convinced that the toleration of interference by the Communist International in the internal affairs of the nations not only endangers their internal peace and social well-being, but is also a menace to the peace of the world; desirous of cooperating in the defense against Communist subversive activities; have agreed as follows:

ARTICLE 1

The High Contracting Powers agree to inform one another of the activities of the Communist International, to consult with one another on the necessary preventive measures, and to carry these through in close collaboration.

ARTICLE 2

The High Contracting Parties will jointly invite third states whose internal peace is threatened by the subversive activities of the Communist International to adopt defensive measures in the spirit of this agreement or to take part in the present agreement.

ARTICLE 3

The German as well as the Japanese text of the present agreement is to be deemed the original text. It comes into force on the day of signature and shall remain in force for a period of five years. Before the expiration of this period the High Contracting Parties will come to an understanding over the period of their cooperation.

In witness whereof the undersigned, being duly and properly authorized by their respective Governments, have signed this agreement and affixed their seals.

Done in duplicate at Berlin on November 25, 1936 – that is, November 25 of the 11th year of the Showa Period.

[signed] Joachim von Ribbentrop,
Extraordinary and Plenipotentiary Ambassador of the German Reich
[signed] Viscount Kintomo Mushakoji,
Imperial Japanese Extraordinary and Plenipotentiary Ambassador

Source: Office of the US Chief of Counsel for Prosecution of Axis Criminality,
***Nazi Conspiracy and Aggression*, Vol. V**
(Washington DC: US Government Printing Office, 1946), pp. 242–3 [Doc. 2508-PS]

The Hitler Youth

The origins of the Hitler Youth dated back to 1922 when it was formed as an organization for the recruitment of new members for the SA. After 1933 the Hitler Youth gradually absorbed most other youth groups until in 1936 it was granted a monopoly of youth organizations by the law reprinted below. This led to increasing conflict with the Catholic Church which by the Concordat signed in 1933 was permitted to sponsor organizations for purely religious, charitable, or cultural purposes. The Nazis, however, insisted that Catholic youth organizations served socialization purposes that did not fall under the protection of the Concordat.

It was not, however, until March 1939 that membership in the Hitler Youth became compulsory by law for all youth beginning with the cohort of ten-year-olds in 1940. Since members of Catholic youth organizations were excluded from the Hitler Youth, this in effect forced the dissolution of all Catholic youth groups. The organization for girls in the Hitler Youth was called the League of German Girls (*Bund Deutscher Mädel*) and was organized in the same way as its male counterpart (see Doc. 3.25). Although membership in the Hitler Youth grew from about 108,000 at the end of 1932 to close to 9 million in 1939, the Nazis never succeeded in forcing all young people into its ranks.

4.7 Law on the Hitler Youth, 1 December 1936

The future of the German nation depends on its youth. All German youth will therefore have to be prepared for its future duties.

Therefore, the Government of the Reich has prepared the following law which is published herewith:

ARTICLE 1

All German youth in the Reich will be organized within the Hitler Youth.

ARTICLE 2

Besides being reared in the family and school, German youth shall be educated physically, intellectually, and morally in the spirit of National Socialism to serve the people and community through the Hitler Youth.

ARTICLE 3

The task of educating the German youth through the Hitler Youth is being entrusted to the Reich Leader of German Youth in the NSDAP. He is the "Youth Leader of the German Reich." The position of his office is that of a higher governmental agency with its seat in Berlin, and he is directly responsible to the Führer and Chancellor of the Reich.

ARTICLE 4

All regulations necessary for the execution and extension of this law will be issued by the Führer and Chancellor of the Reich.

Berlin, 1 December 1936

The Führer and Chancellor of the Reich: Adolf Hitler

The Permanent Secretary and Chief of the Reich Chancellery: Dr. Lammers

Source: Office of the US Chief of Counsel for Prosecution of Axis Criminality,
Nazi Conspiracy and Aggression, **Vol. III**
(Washington DC: US Government Printing Office, 1946), pp. 972–3 [Doc. 1392-PS]

Himmler on the concentration camps

The following selection is taken from Heinrich Himmler's address to Wehrmacht soldiers as part of a course of political indoctrination in 1937. Himmler discussed the concentration camps established to imprison, punish, and "reeducate" political opponents of the regime. Himmler's sometimes defensive tone and his evident need to justify the camps attest to the unsavory reputation of the camps and their SS guards. These SS guards were incorporated into the notorious Death's Head Units in 1936. The Death's Head Units formed the core of the *Waffen-SS* (the military arm of the SS) after the start of the war in 1939.

Himmler evidently also wanted to prepare the military, and the German public, for the expansion of the camp system in war. After the first influx of political prisoners in 1933, most of whom were released before the end of the year, the camp population remained relatively stable at about 10,000 until late 1938, when increasing numbers of Jews were interned as Germany prepared for war. Himmler ended his address in typical fashion by invoking the myth of the Führer's infallible leadership in the coming racial struggle.

4.8 National political course for the armed forces, 15–23 January 1937

HIMMLER: ORGANIZATION AND OBLIGATIONS OF THE SS AND THE POLICE

... I now come to the Death's Head Units ... The Death's Head Units originated from the guard units of the concentration camps. In connection with these concentration camps, I should like to give some data. We have in Germany today the following concentration camps which, in my opinion, should increase rather than decrease in number for certain reasons:

(1) Dachau near Munich; (2) Sachsenhausen near Berlin, which is the former camp Esterwege in Emsland. I have dissolved this camp in Emsland upon the suggestion of Reich Labor Leader [Konstantin] Hierl, and the judiciary, who declared it was wrong to tell one person that service in the swamps to make land arable is an honor, and to say to another, by sending him there as a prisoner: "I'll teach you people what it means to get sent to the swamps." This is indeed illogical, and after half or three-quarters of a year, I dissolved the camp in Esterwege and transferred it to Sachsenhausen near Oranienburg. Then there is a

camp in Lichtenburg near Torgau, one in Sachsenburg near Chemnitz, besides a few smaller ones. The number of prisoners is about 8,000. I shall explain to you why we must have so many and still more camps. We once had a very efficiently organized German Communist Party (KPD). This KPD was crushed in the year 1933. A number of the functionaries went to foreign countries. Others were part of the very high number of protective custody prisoners in the year 1933. Because of my extensive knowledge of Bolshevism, I have always opposed the release of these people from the camps. It must be clear to us that the great mass of workmen are absolutely susceptible to National Socialism and the present form of the state as long as their way of thought has not been changed by the specifically indoctrinated, trained, and financially backed functionaries [of the KPD] ...

It would be extremely instructive for everyone – some members of the Wehrmacht were already able to do so – to inspect such a concentration camp. Once they have seen it, they are convinced of the fact that no one had been sent there unjustly; that it is the offal of criminals and freaks. No better demonstration of the laws of inheritance and race ... exists than such a concentration camp. There you can find people with hydrocephalus, people who are cross-eyed, deformed, half-Jewish, and a number of racially inferior subjects. All that is assembled there. Of course we distinguish between those inmates who are only there for a few months for the purpose of education, and those who are to stay for a very long time. On the whole, education consists of discipline, never of any kind of instruction on an ideological basis, for the prisoners have, for the most part, slave-like souls; and only very few people of real character can be found there. They would pretend to do all that would be asked of them, repeat all that is said in the *Völkischer Beobachter*, but in reality stay the same. The discipline thus squeezes order out of them. The order begins with these people living in clean barracks. Such a thing can really only be accomplished by us Germans; hardly another nation would be as humane as we are. The laundry is frequently changed. The people are taught to wash themselves twice daily, and to use a toothbrush with which most of them have been unfamiliar ... The concentration camps are guarded by these Death's Head Units. It is impossible to use exclusively married people for guard duty as has been suggested once, for no state can afford to do so. It is further necessary to keep the number of such guards for concentration camps – there are 3,500 men currently in Germany – at a relatively high level, for no form of service is as exacting and strenuous for troops as the guarding of crooks and criminals ...

In case of war, it must become clear to us that a considerable number of unreliable persons will have to be put here if we are to assure ourselves of the absence of highly disagreeable developments in case of war.

The prisoner guards were formerly members of the general SS. We gradually collected them into the so-called Death's Head Units. They are not arranged in companies, but in centuries (groups of 100) and have naturally also machine guns. In such camps there are two or three control towers, manned day and night with fully loaded machine guns, so that any attempt at a general uprising – a possibility for which we must always be prepared – can be immediately suppressed. The entire camp can be strafed from three towers ...

We must clearly recognize that an opponent in war is an opponent not only in a military but also in an ideological sense. When I speak here of opponents, I obviously mean our natural opponent, international Bolshevism, under Jewish–Masonic leadership. This Bolshevism, of course, has its supreme citadel in Russia. But this does not mean that there is danger of Bolshevist attack from Russia only. One must always reckon with this danger from wherever this Jewish Bolshevism has gained decisive influence for itself. The states or people under Jewish–Masonic–Bolshevist leadership, or at least strong influence, will of necessity be unfriendly toward Germany and will constitute a danger ...

Let us all clearly realize that the next decades do not signify any foreign political argument which Germany either can or cannot overcome, but they signify a fight of extermination of the above-mentioned subhuman opponents in the whole world who fight Germany, as the nuclear people of the Northern race; Germany, as nucleus of the German people; Germany, as bearer of the culture of mankind. They signify the existence or nonexistence of the white race of which we are the leading people. We have, of course, one conviction: we are lucky enough to be alive just at the time when once in 2,000 years an Adolf Hitler has been born, and we are convinced that we shall survive every danger in both good and bad times because we all hold together and because each one approaches his work with this conviction.

Source: Office of the US Chief of Counsel for Prosecution of Axis Criminality, *Nazi Conspiracy and Aggression*, Vol. IV (Washington DC: US Government Printing Office, 1946), pp. 624–34 [Doc. 1992-PS]

Catholic critique of Nazism

Tension between Church and state reached a head with the issuance of the encyclical, "With Burning Anxiety," by Pope Pius XI in March 1937. Although the Concordat (Doc. 3.15) gave the Church the right to publish and distribute encyclicals in Germany, the Nazi state sought to confiscate all published copies of this one and to prevent further dissemination. The encyclical, addressed to the clergy and laity in Germany, criticized the German government for failing to live up to its commitments under the Concordat. These included the right of the Church to sponsor denominational schools as well as organizations devoted to religious and charitable purposes. The failure of the Concordat to specify precisely what groups were to be included in this category (this task was left to future negotiations) gave the Nazis the opportunity to declare social and athletic organizations outside the protection of the Concordat. Catholic youth organizations were particularly affected by Nazi efforts to eliminate all competition to the Hitler Youth (see Doc. 4.7).

The encyclical also protested Nazi pressures on Catholics to leave the Church and join the Nazi-sponsored "German Faith Movement." Founded in July 1933, this movement was designed to lure members from both the Catholic and the Protestant churches in Germany. Although the Nazis had pledged in their program to support "positive Christianity," they disdained the humanitarian and egalitarian values of both the major denominations. Some leading Nazis, such as Heinrich Himmler and Alfred Rosenberg, unsuccessfully sought to introduce a neo-pagan cult based on the ancient Germanic tribal gods. The most important Nazi-backed religious movement was the "German Christians," a Protestant sect that sought to introduce racism into church doctrine and practice. It was successfully resisted, however, by the so-called "Confessing Church," which upheld traditional Lutheran doctrine and resisted all state and party efforts to intervene in the governance of the church (see Doc. 3.19).

While the papal encyclical firmly rejected racism or nationalism and defended the universalism of the Catholic faith, it failed to protest, or even to mention, the Nazis' discriminatory measures against the Jews. To have done so would have opened the Church to the charge of interfering in policy matters, a violation of the Church's commitment to renounce all political activity. In keeping with the Concordat, Pius XI was careful to confine his criticism of the state to spiritual and doctrinal matters. His aim was to discourage Catholic defections and to defend the independence of the Church against state intervention. The Nazis responded with a campaign of harassment, putting a number of priests on trial for alleged immorality, and seeking indirectly to undermine public confidence in the Church. They were careful, however, not to directly attack the Church for fear of losing the support of German Catholics, who constituted a third of the German population.

4.9 Pope Pius XI, Encyclical Letter, "The Church in Germany," 14 March 1937

1   With deep anxiety and increasing dismay, We have for some time past beheld the sufferings of the Church, and the steadily growing oppression of those men and women who, loyally professing their faith in thought and deed, have remained true to her amidst the people of that land to which St. Boniface once brought the light and glad tidings of Christ and the Kingdom of God.

2   This anxiety of Ours has not been lessened by the accurate reports dutifully brought to Us by the representatives of the most reverend episcopate, who came to visit at Our sick-bed. They related much that is consoling and edifying about the struggle for religion that is being waged by the faithful, and yet, despite their love for their people and their fatherland, with every possible attempt to reach a dispassionate judgement, they could not pass over much that is bitter and sad. After receiving their accounts, We could say in great thankfulness to God: "I have no greater grace than this, to hear that my children walk in truth."[1] But the frankness befitting Our responsible apostolic office, and the desire to place before your eyes and those of the entire Christian world the actual facts in all their gravity, require Us to add: A greater anxiety, a more bitter suffering in Our pastoral care, We have not, than to hear "many leave the way of truth."[2]

3   In the summer of 1933, Venerable Brethren, We accepted the offer made by the Government of the Reich to institute negotiations for a Concordat in connection with a proposal of the previous year, and to the satisfaction of you all brought them to a conclusion with a solemn agreement. In this We were guided by the solicitude incumbent on Us to safeguard the freedom of the Church in the exercise of her apostolic ministry in Germany and the salvation of the souls entrusted to her, and at the same time by the sincere wish of rendering an essential service to the progress and prosperity of the German people.

4   In spite of many serious misgivings at the time, We forced Ourselves to decide that We should not withhold Our consent. We wished to spare Our faithful sons and daughters in Germany, so far as was humanly possible, the anxiety and suffering which, in the given circumstances, We would certainly have otherwise had to expect. Through Our act We wished to prove to all, that seeking only Christ and the things of Christ, We do not refuse the hand of peace of Mother Church to anyone who does not himself reject it.

5   If the tree of peace which We planted with pure intention in German soil has not borne the fruit We desired in the interests of your people, no one in the wide world who has eyes to see and ears to hear can say today that the fault lies with the Church and her Head. The lessons of the past years make it clear where the responsibility lies. They disclose machinations that from the beginning had no other aim than a war of extermination. In the furrows where We labored

1   † III John, 1, 4.
2   † II Peter, 2, 3.

to plant the seeds of sincere peace, others were sowing – like the enemy of Holy Scripture –[3] the tares of distrust, of discord, hatred, calumny, of secret and open enmity against Christ and His Church, an enmity in principle, fed from a thousand springs and working with every means at its disposal. With them and only with them, as well as with their open and silent supporters, lies the responsibility that now, instead of the rainbow of peace, the storm-clouds of destructive religious conflicts are visible on the German horizon.

6　… Everyone in whose mind there is left the least perception of the truth, in whose heart there is a trace of feeling for justice, will then have to admit that in these grievous and eventful years after the signing of the Concordat, in every word and in every action of Ours, We have stood faithful to the terms of the agreement. But with amazement and deep aversion he will be obliged to admit that to change the meaning of the agreement, to evade the agreement, to empty the agreement of all its significance, and finally more or less openly to violate the agreement, has been made the unwritten law of conduct by the other party.

7　… Even today, when the open campaign waged against the denominational school guaranteed by the Concordat, when the nullification of the freedom of the vote for Catholics who should have the right to decide in the matter of education, shows the dreadful seriousness of the situation in a most important field of the Church's life and the unparalleled torment of conscience of believing Christians, Our pastoral care for the salvation of souls counsels Us not to leave unheeded even the slight prospects of return to a loyal adherence to a responsible agreement. In compliance with the prayers of the Most Reverend Episcopate, We shall not weary in the future also of pleading the cause of outraged right with the rulers of your people. Unconcerned with the success or failure of the day and obeying only Our conscience and in accordance with Our pastoral mission, We shall oppose an attitude of mind that seeks to stifle chartered right with open or covered violence.

8　The purpose of the present letter however, Venerable Brethren, is a different one. As you kindly visited Us as We lay on Our bed of sickness, so today We turn to you and through you to the Catholic faithful of Germany, who, like all suffering and oppressed children, are particularly close to the heart of the Common Father. In this hour, when their faith is being tried like pure gold in the fire of tribulation and concealed and open persecution, when they are surrounded by a thousand forms of organized bondage in matters of religion, when the lack of true information and absence of the customary means of defense weigh heavy on them, they have a double right to words of truth and spiritual comfort from him, to whose first predecessor the significant words of the Savior were spoken: "But I have prayed for thee, that thy faith fail not; and thou being once converted, confirm thy brethren."[4]

TRUE BELIEF IN GOD

9　Take care, Venerable Brethren, that first of all belief in God, the primary and irreplaceable foundation of all religion, be preserved true and unadulterated in German lands. He is not a believer in God who uses the words of God rhetorically but he who associates with the sacred word the true and worthy idea of God.

10　He who, in pantheistic vagueness, equates God with the universe, and identifies God with the world and the world with God does not belong to believers in God.

3　† Matthew, 13, 25.
4　† Luke, 22, 32.

11   He who replaces a personal God with a weird impersonal Fate supposedly according to ancient pre-Christian German concepts denies the wisdom and providence of God, that "reacheth from end to end mightily and ordereth all things sweetly"[5] and directs everything for the best. Such a one cannot claim to be numbered among those who believe in God.

12   He who takes the race, or the people, or the State, or the form of Government, the bearers of the power of the State or other fundamental elements of human society – which in the temporal order of things have an essential and honorable place – out of the system of their earthly valuation, and makes them the ultimate norm of all, even of religious values, and deifies them with an idolatrous worship, perverts and falsifies the order of things created and commanded by God. Such a one is far from true belief in God and a conception of life corresponding to true belief. ...

14   . . . Only superficial minds can lapse into the heresy of speaking of a national God, of a national religion; only such can make the mad attempt of trying to confine within the boundaries of a single people, within the narrow bloodstream of a single race, God the Creator of the world, the King and Lawgiver of all peoples before whose greatness all peoples are small as a drop of a bucket.[6] ...

TRUE BELIEF IN CHRIST

17   No belief in God will in the long run be preserved pure and genuine, if it is not supported by belief in Christ ...

20   The climax of revelation reached in the Gospel of Jesus Christ is definite, is obligatory for ever. This revelation knows no addition from the hand of man, above all, knows no substitution and no replacement by arbitrary "revelations" that certain speakers of the present day wish to derive from the myth of blood and race ...

TRUE BELIEF IN THE CHURCH

24   ... In your districts, Venerable Brethren, voices are raised in ever louder chorus urging men on to leave the Church. Among the spokesmen there are many who, by reason of their official position, seek to create the impression that leaving the Church, and the disloyalty to Christ the King which it entails, is a particularly convincing and meritorious form of profession of loyalty to the present State. With cloaked and with manifest methods of coercion, by intimidation, by holding out the prospect of economic, professional, civic and other advantages, the loyalty of Catholic officials to their faith is put under a pressure that is as unlawful as it is unworthy of human beings. All Our fatherly sympathy and deepest condolence We offer to those who pay so high a price for their fidelity to Christ and the Church ...

THE BELIEF IN THE PRIMACY

25   Belief in the Church will not be kept pure and genuine if it is not supported by belief in the primacy of the Bishop of Rome ...

5   † Wisdom, 8, 1.
6   † Is., 40, 15.

MORAL DOCTRINE AND MORAL ORDER

34   The moral conduct of mankind is grounded on faith in God kept true and pure. Every attempt to dislodge moral teaching and moral conduct from the rock of faith, and to build them on the unstable sands of human norms, sooner or later leads the individual and the community to moral destruction. The fool, who hath said in his heart, there is no God, will walk the ways of corruption.[7] The number of such fools, who today attempt to separate morality and religion, has become legion. They do not or will not see that by expelling confessional, i.e. clear and definite, Christianity from instruction and education, from the formation of social and public life, they are treading the ways of spiritual impoverishment and decline. No coercive power of the State, no mere earthly ideals, though they be high and noble in themselves, will be able in the long run to replace the final and decisive motives that come from belief in God and Christ. Take the moral support of the eternal and divine, of comforting and consoling belief in the Rewarder of all good and the Punisher of all evil, from those who are called on to make the greatest sacrifices, to surrender their petty self to the common weal, the result will be in countless instances not the acceptance, but the shirking, of duty. The conscientious observance of the ten commandments of God and the commandments of the Church – the latter are only the practical applications of the principles of the Gospel – is for every individual an incomparable schooling of systematic self-discipline, moral training and character formation – a schooling that demands much, but not too much ...

RECOGNITION OF THE NATURAL LAW

37   ... Conscientious parents, aware of their duty in the matter of education, have a primary and original right to determine the education of the children given to them by God in the spirit of the true faith and in agreement with its principles and ordinances. Laws or other regulations concerning schools that disregard the rights of parent guaranteed to them by the natural law, or by threat and violence nullify those rights, contradict the natural law and are utterly and essentially immoral ...

TO YOUTH

40   ... We know that many, very many, of you for the sake of loyalty to your religion and Church, for the sake of belonging to Church associations guaranteed by the Concordat, have borne and still endure bitter days of misunderstanding, of suspicion, of contempt, of denial of your patriotism, of manifold injury in your professional and social life ...

41   Today, when new perils and conflicts threaten, We say to this youth: "If anyone preach to you a gospel, besides that which you have received" at the knees of a pious mother, from the lips of a Catholic father, from the education of a teacher true to his God and his church, "let him be anathema."[8] If the State founds a State-Youth to which all are obliged to belong, then it is – without prejudice to the rights of Church associations – an

7   † Ps., 13, 1.
8   † Gal., 1, 9.

obvious, an inalienable right of the young men themselves, and of their parents responsible for them before God, to demand that this obligatory organization should be cleansed of all manifestations of a spirit hostile to Christianity and the Church, which, up to the recent past and even at the present moment, place Catholic parents in hopeless conflicts of conscience, since they cannot give to the State what is demanded in the name of the State without robbing God of what belongs to God.

42   No one has any intention of obstructing the youth of Germany on the road that is meant to bring them to the realization of true popular union, to the fostering of the love of freedom, to steadfast loyalty to the fatherland. What We object to, and what We must object to, is the intentional and systematically fomented opposition which is set up between these educational purposes and those of religion. Therefore we call out to youth: Sing your songs of freedom, but do not forget the freedom of the sons of God while singing them. Do not allow this noble freedom, for which there is no substitute, to pine away in the slave chains of sin and sensuality. He who sings the song of loyalty to his earthly country must not, in disloyalty to God, to his church, to his eternal country, become a deserter and a traitor. You are told a great deal about heroic greatness, in designed and false contrast to the humility and patience of the Gospel. Why is silence kept about the heroism of moral struggle? Why is it not told you that the preservation of baptismal innocence represents an heroic action which should be assured of the appreciation it deserves in the religious and moral sphere? A great deal is told you of human weaknesses in the history of the Church. Why is nothing said of the great deeds that accompany her on her way through the centuries, of the Saints she has produced, of the blessings which came from the living union between this Church and your people and enriched the culture of the west? You are told a great deal of the exercises of sport. Undertaken with discretion, the cult of physical fitness is a benefit for youth. But now so much time is devoted to it, in many cases, that no account is taken of the harmonious development of mind and body, of what is due to family life, of the commandment to keep holy the Lord's day. With a disregard bordering on indifference, the sacredness and peace that are in the best tradition of the German Sunday are taken from it. With confidence We expect from practising Catholic youth that, in the difficult circumstances of obligatory State organization, they will insist unflinchingly on their right to keep Sunday in a Christian manner, that in the cult of physical fitness they will not forget the interests of their immortal souls; that they will not allow themselves to be overcome by evil, but will strive to overcome evil by good;[9] that their highest and holiest ambition will be so to run the race towards immortal life as to achieve the crown of victory ...

TO THE FAITHFUL OF THE LAITY

51   ... He who searches the heart and reigns[10] is Our witness, that We have no more heartfelt wish than the restoration of a true peace between Church and State in Germany. But if, through no fault of Ours, there shall not be peace, the Church of God will defend her rights and liberties in the Name of the Almighty, Whose arm even today is not shortened. Trusting in Him "We cease not to pray and beg"[11] for you, the children of the Church, that the days

9   † Rom., 12, 21.
10   † Ps., 7, 10.

of anguish may be shortened and that you may be found true in the day of searching; and We pray also for the persecutors and oppressors; may the Father of all light and all mercy grant them an hour of enlightenment, such as was vouchsafed to Paul on the road to Damascus, for themselves and all those who with them have erred and err …

Given at the Vatican, on Passion Sunday, 14 March 1937.

PIUS PP. XI

Source: "The Church in Germany: Encyclical Letter of His Holiness, Pope Pius XI," Vatican Press Translation (Washington DC: National Catholic Welfare Conference, 1937), pp. 1–9, 11, 16–17, 21–2, 25–8, 35

Plans for eastward expansion

Hitler met with Minister of War Werner von Blomberg (1878–1946), the heads of the three branches of the armed forces, Army chief Werner von Fritsch (1880–1939), Navy chief Erich Raeder (1876–1960), and Air Force chief Hermann Goering, as well as Foreign Minister Konstantin von Neurath (1873–1956) on 5 November 1937 to outline his military plans in strict secrecy. The minutes of the meeting were taken by Hitler's adjutant, Colonel Friedrich von Hossbach. Hitler's comments are remarkable for their candor. At his trial in Nuremberg after the war Goering attempted to downplay the significance of this meeting by saying that its purpose was primarily to put pressure on Fritsch to expedite the army's lagging rearmament. Hitler outlined several scenarios, including a British–Italian war or a civil war in France, that would make possible the annexation of Austria and Czechoslovakia as early as 1938. To achieve favorable conditions he counseled prolongation of the war in Spain. If conditions did not warrant earlier action, however, Hitler was determined to launch a war of conquest no later than 1943 to 1945. His generals offered no objections other than to warn against a premature clash with the Western powers. Their caution may have led Hitler to remove Blomberg, Fritsch, and Neurath from their posts only three months later (see Doc. 4.11).

4.10 The Hossbach Memorandum, 5 November 1937

Notes on the Conference in the Reichskanzlei on 5 November 1937 from 1615–2030 hours. Present: The Führer and Reich Chancellor

The Reichsminister for War, Field Marshal v. Blomberg

The Commander in Chief of the Army, General v. Fritsch

The Commander in Chief of the Navy, Admiral Raeder

The Commander in Chief of the Airforce, General Goering

The Reich Minister for Foreign Affairs, Freiherr v. Neurath

Colonel Hossbach

The Führer stated initially that the subject matter of today's conference was of such importance, that its discussion would, in other countries, probably take place in Cabinet sessions.

11 † Coloss., 1, 9.

However, he, the Führer had decided not to discuss this matter in the larger circle of the Reich Cabinet just because of its importance. His statements to follow were the result of thorough deliberations and of the experiences of his four-and-a-half years in government; he wished to explain to those present his fundamental ideas on the possibilities and reqirements of developing our foreign policy, and he requested, in the interests of a long-term policy, that his statements be regarded, in the event of his death, as his last will and testament.

The Führer then stated:

The aim of German policy is the security and the preservation of the nation (*Volksmasse*), and its enlargement. It is therefore a question of space.

The German nation is composed of 85 million people, which, because of the density of settlement, form a homogeneous European racial body which cannot be found in any other country. This justifies the right to greater living space than is the case in any other country. If there is no political body in this region corresponding to the German racial body, then that is the consequence of several centuries of historical development, and should this political condition continue, it will represent the greatest danger to the preservation of the German people (*Volkstum*) at its present high level. It will be just as impossible to arrest the deterioration of the German element in Austria and Czechoslovakia as it will be to preserve the present state in Germany itself. Instead of growth there will be sterility, and as a consequence, tensions of a social nature will appear after a number of years ... The German future is therefore entirely dependent on the solution of the need for living space. Such a solution can be sought naturally only for a limited period, about one to three generations ...

[Hitler then discussed the possibility of achieving autarky–economic self-sufficiency. He concluded that "in the sphere of raw materials, only limited, but not total autarky can be attained" and "in the case of foods, the question of autarky must be answered with a definite NO."]

Participation in World Economy. There are limits to this which we are unable to transgress. The market fluctuations would be an obstacle to a secure foundation of the German position; international commercial agreements do not offer any guarantee for practical execution. It must be considered on principle that since the World War (1914–18) industrialization has taken place in countries which formerly exported food. We live in a period of economic empires, in which the tendency to colonize again approaches the condition which originally motivated colonization; in Japan and Italy economic motives are the bases of their will to expand. Economic need will also drive Germany to it. Countries outside the great economic empires have special difficulties in expanding economically.

The upward tendency of the world economy due to armament competition can never form a permanent basis for an economic settlement, and this latter is also hampered by the economic disruption caused by Bolshevism. Economic dependence is a pronounced military weakness of those states that base their existence on export. As our exports and imports are carried out over sea lanes ruled by Britain, it is more a question of security of transport rather than of foreign currency, and this explains our great weakness in our food situation in wartime. The only way out, and one which may seem like a dream, is the securing of greater living space, an endeavor which at all times has been the cause of the formation of states and of movements of nations. It is explicable that this tendency finds no interest in Geneva[12] and in satisfied states. Should the security of our food position be our foremost thought, then the space required for this can only be sought in Europe, but we will not copy liberal capitalist policies which rely on exploiting colonies.

---

12   Geneva was the site of the League of Nations.

It is not a case of conquering people, but of conquering agriculturally useful territory. It would also be more to the purpose to seek raw material-producing territory in Europe directly adjoining the Reich and not overseas, and this solution would have to be brought into effect in one or two generations. What would be required at a later date over and above this must be left to subsequent generations. The development of great world-wide national bodies is naturally a slow process and the German people, with its strong racial root, has for this purpose the most favorable foundations in the heart of the European continent. The history of all times – Roman Empire, British Empire – has proved that every space expansion can only be effected by breaking resistance and taking risks. Even setbacks are unavoidable: neither formerly nor today has space been found without an owner; the attacker always comes up against the proprietor.

The question for Germany is where the greatest possible gain could be made at lowest cost.

German politics must reckon with its two hateful enemies, England and France, to whom a strong German colossus in the center of Europe would be intolerable. Both these states would oppose a further strengthening of Germany, both in Europe and overseas, and in this opposition they would have the support of all parties ...

[Hitler next discussed the potential weaknesses of the British Empire as a result of independence movements in Ireland and India, the Japanese threat to British possessions in the Far East, and the Italian threat to British possessions in the Mediterranean. Hitler concluded "that the Empire cannot be held permanently by power politics by 45 million Britons, in spite of all the solidity of her ideals." France's position was more favorable, but "France is faced with difficulties of internal politics."]

The German question can be solved only by way of force, and this is never without risk. The battles of Frederick the Great for Silesia, and Bismarck's wars against Austria and France had been a tremendous risk, and the speed of Prussian action in 1870 had prevented Austria from participating in the war. If we place the decision to apply force with risk at the head of the following expositions, then we are left with the questions of "when" and "how." In this regard we have to decide on three different cases.

Case 1. Period 1943–45. After this we can only expect a change for the worse. The rearming of the Army, the Navy, and the Air Force, as well as the formation of the Officers' Corps, are practically concluded. Our material equipment and armaments are modern; with further delay the danger of their becoming out-of-date will increase. In particular the secrecy of "special weapons" cannot always be safeguarded. Enlistment of reserves would be limited to the current recruiting age groups and an addition from older untrained groups would be no longer available.

In comparison with the rearmament, which will have been carried out at that time by the other nations, we shall decrease in relative power. Should we not act until 1943–45, then, dependent on the absence of reserves, any year could bring about the food crisis, for the countering of which we do NOT possess the necessary foreign currency. This must be considered as a "point of weakness in the regime." Over and above that, the world will anticipate our action and will increase counter-measures yearly ...

What the actual position would be in the years 1943–45 no one knows today. It is certain, however, that we can wait no longer.

On the one side the large armed forces, with the necessity for securing their upkeep, the aging of the Nazi movement and of its leaders, and on the other side the prospect of a lowering of the standard of living and a drop in the birth rate, leaves us no other choice than to act. If the Führer is still living, then it will be his irrevocable decision to solve the German space problem no later than 1943–45. The necessity for action before 1943–45 will come under consideration in cases 2 and 3.

Case 2. Should the social tensions in France lead to an internal political crisis of such dimensions that it absorbs the French Army and thus renders it incapable for employment in war against Germany, then the time for action against Czechoslovakia has come.

Case 3. It would be equally possible to act against Czechoslovakia if France should be so tied up by a war against another state that it cannot "proceed" against Germany.

For the improvement of our military political position it must be our first aim, in every case of war, to conquer Czechoslovakia and Austria simultaneously, in order to remove any threat from the flanks in case of a possible advance westwards. In case of a conflict with France it would hardly be necessary to assume that Czechoslovakia would declare war on the same day as France. However, Czechoslovakia's desire to participate in the war will increase proportionally to the degree to which we are being weakened. Its actual participation could make itself felt by an attack on Silesia, either towards the North or the West.

Once Czechoslovakia is conquered – and a mutual frontier, Germany-Hungary, is obtained – then a neutral attitude by Poland in a German–French conflict could more easily be relied upon. Our agreements with Poland remain valid only as long as Germany's strength remains unshakeable; should Germany have any setbacks, then an attack by Poland against East Prussia, perhaps also against Pomerania, and Silesia, must be taken into account.

Assuming a development of the situation, which would lead to a planned attack on our part in the years 1943–45, then the behavior of France, Poland, and Russia would probably have to be judged in the following manner:

The Führer believes personally that in all probablility England and perhaps also France have already silently written off Czechoslovakia, and that they have got used to the idea that this question would one day be resolved by Germany. The difficulties in the British Empire and the prospect of being entangled in another long-drawn-out European War, were decisive factors in the non-participation of England in a war against Germany. The British attitude would certainly NOT remain without influence on France's attitude. An attack by France without British support is hardly probable given the prospect that its offensive would founder on our Western fortifications. Without England's support, it would also not be necessary to take into consideration a march by France through Belgium and Holland, and this would also not have to be reckoned with by us in case of a conflict with France, as in every case it would have as a consequence the enmity of Great Britain. Naturally, we should in every case have to bar our frontier during the operation of our attacks against Czechoslovakia and Austria. It must be taken into consideration here that Czechoslovakia's defense measures will increase in strength from year to year, and that a consolidation of the inner strength of the Austrian army will also be effected in the course of years. Although the population of Czechoslovakia is not a small one, the absorption of Czechoslovakia and Austria would nevertheless constitute the conquest of food for 5–6 million people, assuming that a compulsory emigration of 2 million from Czechoslovakia and of 1 million from Austria could be carried out. The annexation of the two states to Germany would constitute a considerable military and political relief, owing to shorter and better frontiers, the freeing of combat troops for other purposes, and the possibility of creating new armies up to a strength of about 12 divisions, representing a new division per 1 million population.

No opposition to the elimination of Czechoslovakia is expected on the part of Italy; however, what her attitude in the Austrian question would be cannot be judged today since it would depend largely on whether the Duce were still alive at the time.

The degree of surprise and the speed of our action would decide Poland's attitude. Poland will have little inclination to enter the war against a victorious Germany, with Russia in the rear.

Military participation by Russia must be countered by the speed of our operations; it is highly questionable whether a Russian intervention need be taken into consideration at all in view of Japan's attitude.

Should Case 2 occur – paralysis of France by a civil war – then the situation should be utilized *at any time* for operations against Czechoslovakia, as Germany's most dangerous enemy would be eliminated.

The Führer sees Case 3 looming nearer; it could develop from the existing tensions in the Mediterranean, and should it occur, he has firmly decided to make use of it any time, perhaps even as early as 1938.

Following recent experiences in the course of the events of the war in Spain, the Führer does not see an early end to hostilities there. Taking into consideration the time required for past offensives by Franco, a further three years duration of war is within the bounds of possibility. On the other hand, from the German point of view a 100 percent victory by Franco is not desirable; we are more interested in the continuation of the war and preservation of the tensions in the Mediterranean. Should Franco be in sole possession of the Spanish Peninsula it would mean the end of Italian intervention and the presence of Italy on the Balearic Isles. As our interests are directed towards continuing the war in Spain, it must be the task of our future policy to strengthen Italy in her fight to hold on to the Balearic Isles. However, a solidification of Italian positions on the Balearic Isles can not be tolerated either by France or by England and could lead to a war by France and England against Italy ...

If Germany uses this war to resolve the Czechoslovakian and Austrian questions, it must be assumed with high probability that England – being at war with Italy – would not decide to commence operations against Germany. Without British support a warlike action by France against Germany is not to be anticipated.

The date of our attack on Czechoslovakia and Austria must be made dependent on the course of the Italian–English–French war and would not occur at the same time as the commencement of the war involving these three states. Nor is the Führer thinking of military agreements with Italy, but rather he wishes in full independence to use this uniquely favorable opportunity to begin and carry out the campaign against Czechoslovakia. The attack on Czechoslovakia would have to take place with "the speed of lightning" (*blitzartig schnell*).

Field Marshal von Blomberg and General von Fritsch, in giving their estimate of the situation, repeatedly pointed out that England and France must not appear as our enemies, and they stated that the war with Italy would not bind the French army to such an extent that it would not be in a position to commence operations on our Western frontier with superior forces. General von Fritsch estimated the French forces which would presumably be employed on the Alpine frontier against Italy to be in the region of 20 divisions, so that a strong French superiority would still remain on our Western frontier. The French would, according to German reasoning, attempt to advance into the Rhineland. We should consider the lead that France would have in mobilization, and quite apart from the very small value of our then existing fortifications – which was pointed out particularly by Field Marshal von Blomberg – the four motorized divisions that had been planned for the West would be more or less incapable of movement. With regard to our offensive in a southeasterly direction, Field Marshal von Blomberg draws special attention to the strength of the Czechoslovakian fortifications, the building of which had assumed the character of a Maginot line and which would present extreme difficulties to our attack.

General von Fritsch mentioned that it was the purpose of a study which he had scheduled for this winter to investigate the possibilities of carrying out operations against Czechoslovakia with special consideration of the conquest of the Czechoslovakian system of fortifications; the General also stated that owing to the prevailing conditions he would have to relinquish his leave abroad, which was to begin on 10 November. This intention was countermanded by the Führer who gave as a reason that the possibility of the conflict was not to be regarded as being so imminent. In reply to the remark by the Minister for Foreign Affairs, that an Italian–English–French conflict was not as close as the Führer seemed to assume, the Führer stated that the date which appeared to him to be a possibility was summer 1938. In reply to statements by Field Marshal von Blomberg and General von Fritsch regarding England's and France's attitude, the Führer repeated his previous statements and said that he was convinced of Britain's non-participation and that consequently he did not believe that France would take military action against Germany. Should the Mediterranean conflict already mentioned lead to a general mobilization in Europe, then we should have to commence operations against Czechoslovakia immediately. If, however, the powers who are not participating in the war should declare their disinterestedness, then Germany would, for the time being, have to side with this attitude ...

The second part of the discussion concerned material armament questions.

(Signed) Hossbach

Source: Office of the US Chief of Counsel for Prosecution of Axis Criminality,
Nazi Conspiracy and Aggression, **Vol. III**
(Washington DC: U.S. Government Printing Office, 1946), pp. 295–305 [Doc. 386-PS]

Hitler takes control of the Wehrmacht

Sensing the reluctance of some leading generals to back his expansionist policy in the East for fear of a premature clash with Britain and France, Hitler took direct control of the Wehrmacht in early 1938. With Himmler's and Goering's connivance, he used the occasion of War Minister Werner von Blomberg's marriage to a former prostitute to oust him from office. The War Ministry was replaced by a new Supreme Command of the Wehrmacht (OKW) under the reliable and efficient administrator, General (later Field Marshal) Wilhelm Keitel (1882–1946), who served as a conduit for Hitler's wishes and orders to the Wehrmacht until the end of the war. At the same time the Chief of the Supreme Command of the Army (*Oberkommando des Heeres* or OKH), General Werner von Fritsch, was dismissed on trumped-up charges of consorting with a homosexual. Some 60 generals were retired or dismissed with the evident purpose of weeding out officers who might have some scruples about waging aggressive war. On 19 December 1941, two years after the start of the war, Hitler himself took over operational command of the army from Fritsch's successor, Field Marshal Walther von Brauchitsch (1881–1948), who was blamed for German reversals in the battle for Moscow.

4.11 Decree concerning the leadership of the armed forces, 4 February 1938

From now on, I take over directly the command of the whole Armed Forces.

The former Armed Forces Office in the Reich War Ministry will come directly under my command with all its tasks which it fulfilled under the jurisdiction of the Supreme Command of the Army (*Oberkommando des Heeres* [OKH]) and my military staff.

At the head of the staff of the Supreme Command of the Armed Forces (*Oberkommando der Wehrmacht* [OKW]) is the former Chief of the Armed Forces Office as "Chief of the Supreme Command of the Armed Forces." He is equal in rank to a Reich Minister.

At the same time, the Supreme Command (OKW) takes the responsibility for the affairs of the Reich Ministry of War, and by my order, the Chief of the Supreme Command of the Armed Forces exercises the authority formerly belonging to the Reich Minister.

It is the Supreme Command of the Armed Forces' duty to carry out in peacetime in accordance with my instructions, the preparation of the defense system of the Reich.

Berlin, 4 February 1938

The Führer and Reich Chancellor: Adolf Hitler

The Reich Minister and Chief of the Reich Chancellery: Dr. [Hans Heinrich] Lammers

The Chief of the Supreme Command of the Armed Forces: Keitel

Source: Office of the US Chief of Counsel for Prosecution of Axis Criminality,
***Nazi Conspiracy and Aggression*, Vol. III**
(Washington DC: US Government Printing Office, 1946), pp. 295–305 [Doc. 386-PS]

The Czech crisis

After the successful *Anschluss* of Austria in March 1938, Hitler set his sights on the destruction of Czechoslovakia, a country with a defensive alliance with France and the Soviet Union. His pretext for the dismemberment of Czechoslovakia was the growing discontent among the 3½ million ethnic Germans living in the Sudetenland, the area of Czechoslovakia bordering on Germany, Austria, and Poland. In May 1938 the first great war scare enveloped Europe as the Czechs mobilized their army to ward off the German threat. Fearing war with France and Britain, Hitler pulled back, but at the same time informed his military of his "unalterable decision to smash Czechoslovakia by military action in the near future."[13] It was in reaction to this threat of war that General Ludwig Beck (1880–1944), Chief of the Army General Staff, jotted down the following notes. He hoped to persuade fellow Army and Air Force leaders to oppose war against Czechoslovakia on the grounds that this would lead to a clash with the Western powers for which the German army was not yet prepared. Without the support of the military Hitler would be forced to give up or at least delay his plans. Beck also seems to have intended a more far-reaching action, if necessary, to quell the hard-liners in the party and the SS. Apparently he was hoping to save Hitler both from his hard-line advisers and from his own excessive ambitions. Receiving no encouragement, however, from General Walther von Brauchitsch, who had replaced the more cautious Werner von Fritsch as Army Commander in Chief in February 1938, Beck handed in his resignation on 18 August 1938.

British Prime Minister Neville Chamberlain's surrender to Hitler's demands in the Munich Agreement of 29 September 1938 ended the immediate threat of war. In March 1939, however, Hitler violated the agreement by seizing the Czech portion of Czechoslovakia and establishing the German Protectorate of Bohemia and Moravia.

---

13   Norman Rich, *Hitler's War Aims: Ideology, the Nazi State, and the Course of Expansion* (New York: W. W. Norton, 1973), p. 105.

Chamberlain responded by giving Poland an unconditional guarantee of military support in case of German attack. Hitler's refusal to be deterred by British and French warnings led to the outbreak of war on 1 September 1939. Beck, meanwhile, played an active role behind the scenes in organizing the military conspiracy that culminated in the unsuccessful attempt on Hitler's life on 20 July 1944 (see Doc. 5.27). Beck, who was slated to become head of state if the coup had succeeded, committed suicide at Army Headquarters in Berlin on the evening of July 20 1944.

4.12 Notes of Chief of the Army General Staff Ludwig Beck on the risks of war with Czechoslovakia, 16 July 1938

Apparently the Führer thinks a forcible solution to the Sudeten German question by invading Czechoslovakia is inevitable; his views are reinforced by an entourage of irresponsible, radical elements. Opinion is divided on Göring's position. Some believe he recognizes the gravity of the situation and is trying to have a moderating effect on the Führer. Others think he's playing a double game, as in the case of Blomberg and Fritsch, and that he'll flip-flop when he's in front of the Führer.[14]

All honest and serious German men in responsible national positions must see it as their mission and duty to use all conceivable means and methods to avert a war with Czechoslovakia, regardless of the consequences. Such a war must inevitably lead to a world war that would mean the end of Germany.

The highest ranking leaders of the Wehrmacht are the most befitting and capable for this task, since the Wehrmacht is the operational instrument of power for the national leadership in conducting a war.

At stake here are ultimate decisions for the survival of the nation; history will burden these leaders with guilt for shedding blood if they do not act according to their professional knowledge, their political understanding, and their conscience.

Their military obedience has its limits when their knowledge, their conscience, and their responsibility forbid them from carrying out a command.

If their recommendations and warnings are ignored in such a situation, it is their right and obligation to the nation and to history to resign their positions.

If they all act together with a unified will, it will be impossible to carry out an act of war. They will thus have saved their fatherland from the worst, from ruin.

There is a lack of greatness and recognition of duty when at such a time a high-ranking soldier regards his duties and tasks only within the limited framework of his military assignments, without awareness that his highest responsibility is to the nation as a whole.

Extraordinary times require extraordinary actions!

Other upstanding men in positions of national responsibility outside the Wehrmacht will join us on their way.

If people keep their eyes and ears open, if they do not deceive themselves with false statistics, if they do not live under the narcotic of ideology, they can only reach the conclusion that

---

14   Goering played a key role in the dismissal of Reichswehr Minister Werner von Blomberg (1878–1946) and Army Commander in Chief Werner von Fritsch (1880–1939) in February 1938 (see Doc. 4.11).

at this time we are not prepared for war militarily (leadership, training, and armaments), economically, or in public morale. ...

POSTSCRIPT ON 19 JULY 1938

If action in the form of a protest with all its consequences is decided upon and the outbreak of a war can thereby be prevented, the further step should be considered whether a conflict with the SS and the party bosses *must* be allowed to occur, since such a clash is essential for the restoration of a lawful state of affairs.

This is probably the last time that fate offers us the opportunity to liberate the German people and the Führer himself from the nightmare of a Cheka and from the manifestations of boss rule that are destroying the stability and well-being of the Reich through the mood of the people and that are leading to the revival of communism.[15]

In this regard the following points must be emphasized:

1   There can and must be no doubt that this fight is being waged *for* the Führer.
2   Honest and able men of the party must be informed of the gravity of the situation by means of an objective description; they must be convinced of the necessity of such a step and be won over to the cause. E.g., Gauleiter Wagner in Silesia, Governor Bürckel in Vienna.[16]

... Not even the faintest suspicion of a conspiracy must arise and yet the highest ranking military leaders must stand *united* behind this step. Supportive generals can also be found in the air force.

Brief, clear slogans:
For the Führer!
Against War!
Against the Party Bosses!
Peace with the Church!
Freedom of Expression!
An End to Cheka Methods!
Restore Law in the Reich!
Cut all Fees in Half!
No more building of Palaces!
Housing for Fellow Germans!
Prussian Simplicity and Cleanliness!

B[eck]

Source: Klaus-Jürgen Müller, *General Ludwig Beck. Studien und Dokumente zur politisch-militärischen Vorstellungswelt und Tätigkeit des Generalstabschefs des deutschen Heeres 1933–1938* (Boppard: Boldt, 1980), pp. 551–552, 554–556. Translated by Sally Winkle

15   The Cheka was an organization established in the Soviet Union in December 1917 to combat counter-revolutionary activities. It was superseded in 1922 by the GPU and later the NKVD.
16   Gauleiter Josef Wagner (1898–1945) was expelled from the party in 1942 and probably murdered by the Gestapo in April 1945. Gauleiter Josef Bürckel (1895–1944) committed suicide in September 1944.

The November Pogrom, 1938

With preparations for war in full swing by 1938, leading Nazis pressured for an escalation of measures to force Jews to emigrate. The SS, in particular, wanted to make sure that there would be no threat to internal unity in case of war. The Nazis launched a systematic campaign to deprive Jews of their means of livelihood and force them to leave. Jews were not, however, permitted to take any of their assets with them, thus making it more difficult for them to gain admission as refugees in other countries. In July 1938 Jews were barred by law from participation in numerous sectors of the economy. Jewish physicians and lawyers were prohibited from serving non-Jewish patients or clients. For purposes of easier identification, Jews who did not have recognizably Jewish first names were forced to add the middle names Sarah or Israel in August 1938. At the request of the Swiss government, a "J" was stamped into their passports in October 1938.

Persecution of the Jews culminated in unprecedented violence in the night of 9–10 November 1938. The assassination of a German diplomat in Paris two days earlier (he died on the 9th) provided the pretext for the Nazis to unleash the pogrom. Disguised as a spontaneous popular outburst, the assault on Jewish synagogues, businesses, and homes was organized and carried out by party members while the police and SS were instructed not to interfere except to prevent looting and the destruction of German property. The orders (below) issued by Gestapo chief Heinrich Müller (1900–45) and the chief of the Security Service (SD) Reinhard Heydrich clearly reveal the extent to which the pogrom was planned in advance.

Legislative action followed two days later under the authority of Hermann Goering, the virtual economic dictator of Germany as Commissioner of the Four-Year Plan. Jews were held responsible for the damage and assessed a collective fine of 1 billion Marks, collected by the Ministry of Finance from individuals in periodic installments based on their ability to pay. The most far-reaching result of the pogrom was mandatory "Aryanization" of all Jewish businesses and the total exclusion of Jews from German economic life. Jews were also barred from entering parks, forests, theaters, concerts, and cultural exhibits and from attending German schools.

In the wake of the pogrom about 30,000 Jewish men were interned in concentration camps with their release made conditional on proof of arrangements to emigrate. Emboldened by their successes in foreign policy and by Germany's growing military and economic strength, Nazi leaders apparently no longer felt they needed to take world opinion or foreign reactions into account (although foreign Jews were excluded from harassment by Heydrich's directive). Hitler's commitment to eastern expansion increased the likelihood of war in the near future and gave added urgency to the expulsion of the Jews, whose influence could be expected to weaken popular support for the war effort. While the official goal of the regime remained to force Jews to leave Germany, the turn to open, officially-sponsored violence in 1938 marked an important stage in the evolution of anti-Jewish policy toward systematic genocide in 1941 (see Chapter 6).

4.13a Orders issued to police by Gestapo Headquarters

To all state police offices and state police administrative offices. Berlin, 9. 11. 1938
   This teletype message is to be transmitted immediately in the most rapid way.

1   Actions against the Jews and in particular against their synagogues will occur in a short time in all of Germany. They are not to be hindered. However, it is to be made certain, in agreement with the ordinary police, that plundering and similar law-breaking will be held to a minimum.
2   Insofar as important archive material is present in the synagogues, it is to be secured by immediate measures.
3   The seizure of some 20 to 30 thousand Jews in the Reich is to be prepared. Wealthy Jews above all are to be chosen. More detailed directives will appear in the course of this night.
4   If in the course of this action Jews are found in possession of arms, the sharpest measures are to be employed. Special troops of the SS as well as the general SS can be drawn into the action. In any case the direction of the actions through the state police is to be assured by proper measures.

ADDENDA FOR STATE POLICE COLOGNE

In the synagogue of Cologne there is especially important material. This is to be made safe immediately by the quickest measures in agreement with the Security Services.

Gestapo: H. Müller

This teletype is secret.

Source: Office of the US Counsel for Prosecution of Axis Criminality,
***Nazi Conspiracy and Aggression*, Vol. III**
(Washington DC: US Government Printing Office, 1946), p. 277 [Doc. 374-PS]

4.13b Order of Chief of the Security Service (SD)

Teletype Message Munich, 10 November 1938, 1:20 a.m.
To all State Police Main Offices and Field Offices
To all SD Main and Sub-Sectors

SECRET

Urgent – to be submitted immediately to the Chief or his deputy

SUBJECT: MEASURES AGAINST JEWS TONIGHT

Because of the attempt on the life of von Rath, Legation Secretary in Paris, demonstrations against the Jews are to be expected in the entire Reich in the course of this night – from the 9th to the 10th of November 1938. For the handling of these actions the following directions are issued:

1   The chiefs of the State Police Offices or their deputies will immediately after receipt of this teletype message establish telephone contact with the political leadership offices – Gau Directorate or Kreis Directorate – within their region and arrange a conference about the handling of the demonstrations. The respective inspectors and commanders of the Order Police are to participate in the conference. In this conference the political leadership offices are to be informed that the German police have received the following directives

from the Reichsführer of the SS and the Chief of the German Police, which directives are to be conformed to by the political leadership offices in an appropriate manner:

(a) Only such measures may be taken which do not jeopardize German life or property (for instance, burning of synagogues only if there is no danger of fires for the neighborhood).
(b) Business establishments and homes of Jews may be destroyed but not looted. The police have been instructed to supervise the execution of these directives and to arrest looters.
(c) In business streets special care is to be taken that non-Jewish establishments will be safeguarded at all cost against damage.
(d) Subjects of foreign countries may not be molested even if they are Jews.

2   Under the provision that the directives given under No. 1 are being complied with, the demonstrations are not to be prevented but merely supervised regarding compliance with the directives.
3   Immediately after receipt of this teletype the archives of the Jewish communities are to be confiscated by the police, so that they will not be destroyed in the course of the demonstrations. Important in this respect is historically valuable material, not recent tax lists, etc. The archives are to be delivered to the respective SD Office.
4   The direction of the measures of the Security Police regarding the demonstrations against Jews is in the hands of the State Police Offices, in as much as the inspectors of the Security Police do not issue different directives. For the performance of the measures of the Security Police, officers of the criminal police as well as members of the SD, the special troops, and the SS may be used.
5   As soon as the events of this night permit the use of designated officers, as many Jews, particularly wealthy ones, as the local jails will hold are to be arrested in all districts. Initially only healthy male Jews, not too old, are to be arrested. After the arrests have been carried out the appropriate concentration camp is to be contacted immediately with a view to a quick transfer of the Jews to the camps. Special care is to be taken that Jews arrested on the basis of this directive will not be mistreated.
6   The content of this order is to be communicated to the respective inspectors and commanders of the Order Police and to the SD Main Sectors and the SD Sub-Sectors with the notification that these police measures have been issued by the Reichsführer of the SS and the Chief of the German Police. The Chief of the Order Police issues appropriate orders to the Fire Department Police. The Security Police and the Order Police are to work in closest coordination in the execution of these measures.

The receipt of this teletype is to be confirmed by the State Police Director or a deputy via teletype to the Secret State Police Office into the hands of SS Colonel [Standartenführer] Müller.

[signed] Heydrich, SS General [Gruppenführer]

Source: Office of the US Chief of Counsel for Prosecution of Axis Criminality,
Nazi Conspiracy and Aggression, **Vol. III**
(Washington DC: US Government Printing Office, 1946), pp. 545–7 [Doc. 765-PS]

4.13c Decree relating to the payment of a fine by the Jews of German nationality, 12 November 1938

The hostile attitude of Jewry towards the German people and Reich, an attitude which does not even shrink from committing cowardly murder, makes decisive defensive action and harsh atonement necessary. I order, therefore, by virtue of the decree concerning the execution of the Four Year Plan of 18 October 1936 as follows:

1   On the community of Jews in Germany the payment of a contribution of 1,000,000,000 Reichsmark to the German Reich is imposed.
2   Provisions for the implementation will be issued by the Reich Minister of Finance in agreement with the Reich ministers concerned.

Berlin, 12 November 1938

The Commissioner for the Four Year Plan
Goering, Field Marshal

Source: *Reichsgesetzblatt*, 1938, I, p. 1580

4.13d Order eliminating Jews from German economic life, 12 November 1938

On the basis of the Decree of 18 October 1936 for the execution of the Four Year Plan, the following is ordered:

ARTICLE 1

1   From 1 January 1939 operation of retail shops or mail order houses as well as independent handicrafts businesses is forbidden to Jews ...
2   Moreover from the same date it is forbidden to Jews to offer goods or services in markets of any kind, fairs, or exhibitions, or to advertise such or accept orders therefor.
3   Jewish shops operated in violation of this order will be closed by police ...

ARTICLE 2

1   No Jew can manage a firm according to the interpretation of the term "manager" under the Law for National Labor of 20 January 1934.
2   If a Jew is an executive in a business concern he may be dismissed with notice of six weeks. At expiration of this period all claims resulting from the employee's contract, especially claims for severance pay or pensions, become null and void.

ARTICLE 3

1   No Jew can be a member of a cooperative society.
2   Jewish members of cooperatives lose membership from 21 December 1938. No notice is necessary.

ARTICLE 4

The Reich Economic Minister in consultation with other Reich ministers whose competencies are involved are empowered to issue regulations required by this decree. They may permit exceptions insofar as this is necessary for the transfer of Jewish firms into non-Jewish hands, the liquidation of Jewish businesses, or in special cases to insure the availability of supplies. Berlin, 12 November 1938

The Commissioner for the Four Year Plan
Goering, Field Marshal

Source: *Reichsgesetzblatt* 1938, I, p. 1580

The German nationalist mindset

The following extract from a letter by former Army Commander in Chief Werner von Fritsch, written only a month after the *Kristallnacht* Pogrom, reveals the extent to which the goals of non-Nazi nationalists and Nazis overlapped. Although a year earlier he had cautioned Hitler about the risks of war against the Western powers (see Doc. 4.10), he clearly shared Hitler's belief that the restoration of German power required suppression of the left, subordination of the Catholic Church, and exclusion of the Jews. Fritsch, demoted to commander of an artillery regiment, was killed in the assault on Warsaw in September 1939.

4.14 Werner von Fritsch, letter, 11 December 1938

From: Freiherr v. Fritsch
To: Baronin Margot v. Schutzbar

Achterberg, 11 December 1938

My dear Baroness:

Many thanks for your two letters ... It is really peculiar that so many people should look to the future with increasing fears, in spite of the Führer's indisputable successes during the past years. Herr von Wiegand's letter interested me very much and I am returning it herewith. Unfortunately, I am afraid he is right when he speaks of the profound hate which is directed to us by a large part of the world.

Soon after the war I came to the conclusion that we should have to be victorious in three battles, if Germany were to become powerful again:

1   The battle against the working class – Hitler has won this.
2   Against the Catholic Church, perhaps better expressed against Ultramontanism, and
3   Against the Jews.

We are in the midst of these battles and the one against the Jews is the most difficult. I hope everyone realizes the intricacies of this campaign ...

[signed] Fritsch

Source: Office of the US Chief of Counsel for Prosecution of Axis Criminality,
***Nazi Conspiracy and Aggression*, Vol. IV**
(Washington DC: US Government Printing Office, 1946), p. 585 [Doc. 1947-PS]

Hitler threatens destruction of the Jews

On 30 January 1939 Hitler delivered his first major speech after the so-called *Reichskristallnacht* pogrom of 9 November 1938 (Doc.4.13), which resulted in the loss of dozens of Jewish lives and enormous damage to Jewish property. In this long speech Hitler addressed the strong criticisms directed against Germany by the world community as a result of the pogrom. This speech contained Hitler's notorious prediction that in case of war the Jews in Europe would be annihilated. Hitler hoped to use threats against the Jews as leverage to dissuade the Western powers from intervening to prevent German expansion to the east. Note also that Hitler was able to exploit for propaganda purposes the evident reluctance of other countries to accept an influx of indigent Jews. Germans were particularly receptive to Hitler's invocation of German suffering as a result of the post-First World War settlement.

4.15 Hitler's Reichstag speech, 30 January 1939

... The German nation has no feeling of hatred towards England, America, or France; all it wants is peace and quiet. But these other nations are continually being stirred up to hatred of Germany and the German people by Jewish and non-Jewish agitators. And so, should the warmongers achieve what they are aiming at, our own people would land in a situation for which they would be psychologically quite unprepared and which they would fail to grasp. I therefore consider it necessary that from now on our propaganda and our press always make it a point to answer these attacks, and above all bring them to the notice of the German people.

The German nation must know who the men are who want to bring about a war by hook or by crook. It is my conviction that these people are mistaken in their calculations, for when once National Socialist propaganda is directed toward answering the attacks, we shall succeed just as we succeeded inside Germany herself in overcoming, through the convincing power of our propaganda, the Jewish world-enemy. The nations will shortly realize that National Socialist Germany wants no enmity with other nations; that all the assertions as to our intended attacks on other nations are lies – lies born of morbid hysteria, or of a mania for self-aggrandizement on the part of certain politicians; but that in certain states these lies are being used by unscrupulous profiteers to salvage their own finances. That, above all, international Jewry is hoping in this way to satisfy its thirst for revenge and gain, but that on the other hand this is the grossest defamation that can be brought to bear against a great and peace-loving nation. Never, for instance, have German soldiers fought on American soil, unless it was in the cause of American independence and freedom; but American soldiers were brought to Europe to help strangle a great nation that was fighting for its freedom. Germany did not attack America, but America attacked Germany, and, as the Committee of Investigation of the American House of Representatives concluded: from purely capitalist motives, without any other cause. But there is one thing that everyone should realize: these attempts cannot influence Germany in the slightest as to the way in which she settles her Jewish problem.

On the contrary, in connection with the Jewish question I have this to say:

It is a shameful spectacle to see how the whole democratic world is oozing sympathy for the poor tormented Jewish people, but remains hard-hearted and obdurate when it comes to helping them – which is surely, in view of its attitude, an obvious duty. The arguments that are brought up as an excuse for not helping them actually speak for us Germans and Italians.

For this is what they say:

1   "We," that is the democracies, "are not in a position to take in the Jews." Yet in these empires there are not even ten people to the square kilometer. While Germany, with her 135 inhabitants to the square kilometer, is supposed to have room for them!
2   They assure us: We cannot take them unless Germany is prepared to allow them a certain amount of capital to bring with them as immigrants.

For hundreds of years Germany was good enough to receive these elements, although they possessed nothing except infectious political and physical diseases. What they possess today, they have to by far the largest extent gained at the cost of the less astute German nation by the most reprehensible manipulations.

Today we are merely paying this people what it deserves. When the German nation was, thanks to the inflation instigated and carried through by Jews, deprived of the entire savings which it had accumulated in years of honest work, when the rest of the world took away the German nation's foreign investments, when we were divested of the whole of our colonial possessions, these philanthropic considerations evidently carried little noticeable weight with democratic statesmen.

Today I can only assure these gentlemen that, thanks to the brutal education with which the democracies favored us for fifteen years, we are completely hardened to all attacks of sentiment. After more than eight hundred thousand children of the nation had died of hunger and undernourishment at the close of the war, we witnessed almost one million head of milking cows being driven away from us in accordance with the cruel paragraphs of a dictate which the humane democratic apostles of the world forced upon us as a peace treaty. We witnessed over one million German prisoners of war being retained in confinement for no reason at all for a whole year after the war was ended. We witnessed over one and a half million Germans being torn away from all that they possessed in the territories lying on our frontiers, and being whipped out with practically only what they wore on their backs. We had to endure having millions of our fellow countrymen torn from us without their consent, and without their being afforded the slightest possibility of existence. I could supplement these examples with dozens of the most cruel kind. For this reason we ask to be spared all sentimental talk.

The German nation does not wish its interests to be determined and controlled by any foreign nation. France to the French, England to the English, America to the Americans, and Germany to the Germans. We are resolved to prevent the settlement in our country of an alien people which was capable of snatching for itself all the leading positions in the land, and to oust it. For it is our will to educate our own nation for these leading positions. We have hundreds of thousands of very intelligent children of peasants and of the working classes. We shall have them educated – in fact we have already begun – and we wish that one day they, and not the representatives of an alien race, may hold the leading positions in the state together with our educated classes. Above all, German culture, as its name alone shows, is German and not Jewish, and therefore its management and care will be entrusted to members of our own nation. If the rest of the world cries out with a hypocritical mien against this barbaric expulsion from Germany of such an irreplaceable and culturally eminently valuable element, we can only be astonished at the conclusions they draw from this situation. For how thankful they must be that we are releasing these precious apostles of culture, and placing them at the disposal of the rest of the world. In accordance with their own declarations they cannot find a single reason to excuse themselves for refusing to receive this most valuable race in their own countries. Nor can I see a reason why the members of this race should be imposed upon the German nation, while in the states, which are so enthusiastic about these "splendid people," their settlement should suddenly be refused with every imaginable excuse. I think that the sooner this problem is solved, the better; for Europe cannot settle down until the Jewish question is cleared up.

It may very well be possible that sooner or later an agreement on this problem may be reached in Europe, even between those nations which otherwise do not so easily come together.

The world has sufficient space for settlements, but we must once and for all get rid of the opinion that the Jewish race was only created by God for the purpose of being in a certain percentage a parasite living on the body and the productive work of other nations. The Jewish race will have to adapt itself to sound constructive activity as other nations do, or sooner or later it will succumb to a crisis of an inconceivable magnitude.

One thing I should like to say on this day which may be memorable for others as well as for us Germans: In the course of my life I have very often been a prophet, and have usually been ridiculed for it. During the time of my struggle for power it was in the first instance the Jewish race which only received my prophecies with laughter when I said that I would one day take over the leadership of the state, and with it that of the whole nation, and that I would then among many other things settle the Jewish problem. Their laughter was uproarious, but I think that for some time now they have been laughing on the other side of their face.

Today I will once more be a prophet: If the international Jewish financiers in and outside Europe should succeed in plunging the nations once more into a world war, then the result will not be the Bolshevization of the earth, and thus the victory of Jewry, but the annihilation of the Jewish race in Europe!

For the time when the non-Jewish nations had no propaganda is at an end. National Socialist Germany and Fascist Italy have institutions which enable them when necessary to enlighten the world about the nature of a question of which many nations are instinctively conscious, but which they have not yet clearly thought out. At the moment the Jews in certain countries may be fomenting hatred under the protection of a press, of the film, of radio propaganda, of the theatre, of literature, etc., all of which they control. If this nation should once more succeed in inciting the millions which compose the nations into a conflict which is utterly senseless and only serves Jewish interests, then there will be revealed the effectiveness of an enlightenment which has completely routed the Jews in Germany in the space of a few years.

The nations are no longer willing to die on the battlefield so that this unstable international race may profiteer from a war or satisfy its Old Testament vengeance. The Jewish watchword "Workers of the world unite" will be conquered by a higher realization, namely "Workers of all classes and of all nations, recognize your common enemy!"

Source: *The Speeches of Adolf Hitler, April 1922–August 1939*,
ed. by Norman H. Baynes (New York: Howard Fertig, 1969), Vol. I, pp. 736–41

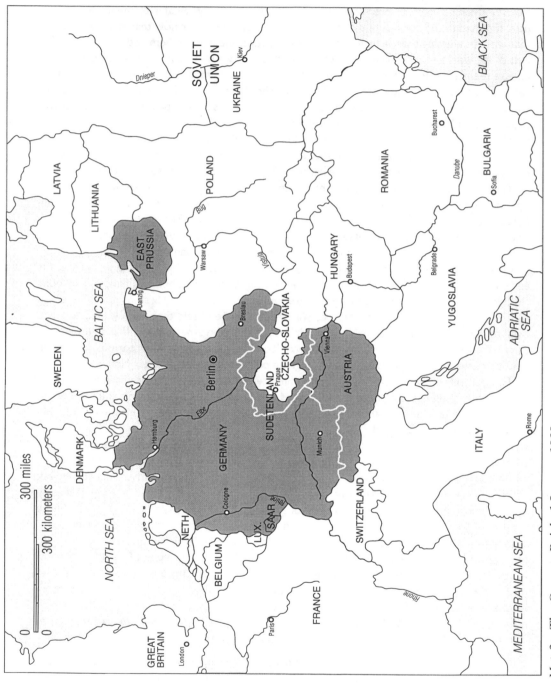

Map 2   The German Reich, 1 January 1939

Preparations for war against Poland

After the German occupation of Prague on 15 March 1939, in violation of the Munich Agreement, the British government abruptly abandoned the appeasement policy it had pursued in the Czech crisis. Britain extended an unconditional guarantee of support to Poland in case Germany should use force to gain its territorial demands. Members of Chamberlain's government had begun to realize that Hitler was aiming for more than merely a rectification of Versailles or the restoration of the 1914 German borders. Hitler responded to Britain's show of support for Poland by officially repudiating the non-aggression pact he had signed with Poland in 1934 and the naval treaty with Britain in 1935. On 11 April 1939 he gave the order to prepare an attack on Poland with a target date of 26 August. On 22 May he signed a formal military alliance (the Pact of Steel) with Italy to gain Italian support against France and England. To overcome Italian apprehensions he told them that war would not come before 1942–43.

One day later, on 23 May 1939, he summoned the heads of the three branches of the Wehrmacht and their chief aides to the Chancellery to inform them that war with Poland was likely to lead to war with the West and to give them some guidelines for preparing for this prospect. The minutes of the meeting were taken by Lt. Col. (and later General) Rudolf Schmundt, who had replaced Col. (later General) Friedrich Hossbach as his chief military adjutant in January 1939. Like the Hossbach Memorandum (Doc. 4.10), this document, though somewhat disjointed, reveals more of Hitler's true aims than his public speeches, which were always geared toward achieving maximum propagandistic effect. Hitler candidly admitted that the return of Danzig was not Germany's true objective in the struggle with Poland. The true objective was territorial expansion, to which England would regrettably, from Hitler's point of view, never agree. Hence war with England could not be avoided in the long run even if the Western powers stayed out of the war against Poland, and the military would have to prepare accordingly. Although he claimed to have learned valuable lessons from the failures of the First World War, Hitler apparently still believed that after the conquest of France Germany could defeat England by imposing a naval and air blockade.

4.16 Minutes of a conference on 23 May 1939

TOP SECRET

Place: The Führer's Office, New Reich Chancellery
Present: The Führer, Field Marshal Goering, Grand Admiral [Erich] Raeder, General [Walther] von Brauchitsch, General [Wilhelm] Keitel, General [Erhard] Milch, General [Franz] Halder, General [Karl Heinrich] Bodenschatz, Rear Admiral Schniewindt, Colonel [Hans] Jeschonnek, Colonel [Walter] Warlimont, Lieutenant Colonel [Rudolf] Schmundt, Captain Engel, Lieutenant Commander Albrecht, Captain von Below.

SUBJECT: INSTRUCTIONS ON THE POLITICAL SITUATION AND FUTURE AIMS

The Führer defined as the purpose of the conference:

I   Analysis of the situation.

2   Definition of the tasks for the Wehrmacht arising from the situation.
3   Clarification of the consequences of these tasks.
4   Ensuring the secrecy of all decisions and work resulting from these consequences.

Secrecy is the precondition for success.
The Führer's observations are paraphrased below:
Our present situation must be considered from two points of view:

I   The actual development of events from 1933 and 1939.
2   The permanent and unchanging situation in which Germany finds itself.

In the period 1933–1939 progress was made in all areas. Our military situation improved enormously.

Our situation in regard to the rest of the world has remained the same.

Germany had dropped from the circle of great powers. The balance of power had been effected without Germany's participation. This equilibrium is disturbed when Germany's demands for the necessities of life make themselves felt, and Germany reemerges as a great power. All demands are regarded as "encroachments."

The English are more afraid of dangers in the economic sphere than of the simple threat of force.

A mass of 80 million people has solved the ideological problems. So, too, must the economic problems be solved. No German can evade the creation of the necessary economic conditions for this. The solution of these problems demands courage. The principle by which one evades solving the problems by adapting oneself to circumstances is unacceptable. Circumstances must rather be adapted to aims. This is impossible without invasion of foreign states or attacks upon foreign property.

Living space proportionate to the size of the state is the basis of all power. One may refuse for a time to face the problem, but finally it is solved one way or another. The choice remains between ascent or decline. In 15 or 20 years we shall be compelled to find a solution. No German state can evade the question longer than that. We are at present in a state of patriotic fervor, which is shared by two other nations: Italy and Japan. ...

Poland will always be on the side of our adversaries. In spite of treaties of friendship, Poland has always had the secret intention of exploiting every opportunity to do us harm.

Danzig is not what it is about at all. It is a question of expanding our living space in the East and of securing our food supplies, as well as the settlement of the Baltic problem. Food supplies can be expected only from thinly populated areas. Over and above the natural fertility, thoroughgoing German cultivation will enormously increase the surplus.

Colonies: Beware of gifts of colonial territory. This does not solve the food problem. Remember – blockade.

If fate forces us into conflict with the West, possession of extensive areas in the east will be advantageous. We can rely even less on record harvests in time of war than in peace.

The population of non-German areas will perform no military service and will be available as a source of labor.

The Polish problem is inseparable from conflict with the West. Poland's internal power of resistance to Bolshevism is doubtful. Thus Poland is of doubtful value as a barrier against Russia. It is questionable whether military success in the West can be achieved quickly. Questionable, too, is the attitude of Poland.

The Polish government will not resist pressure from Russia. Poland sees danger in a German victory in the West and will attempt to rob us of victory. There is therefore no question of sparing Poland, and we are left with the decision to attack Poland at the first suitable opportunity.

We cannot expect a repetition of the Czech affair. There will be war. Our task is to isolate Poland. The success of this isolation will be decisive.

Therefore, the Führer must reserve the right to give the final order to attack. There must be no simultaneous conflict with the Western powers (France and England).

If it is not certain that a German-Polish conflict will not lead to war with the West, then the fight must be primarily against England and France.

Fundamental principle: Conflict with Poland – beginning with an attack on Poland – will only be successful if the Western Powers keep out of it. If this is impossible, then it will be better to attack in the West and to deal with Poland at the same time.

The isolation of Poland is a matter of skillful politics.

Japan is a weighty question. Even if at first for various reasons it showed little interest in collaborating with us, it is nevertheless in Japan's own interest to take the initiative in attacking Russia in good time.

Economic relations with Russia are possible only when political relations have improved. A cautious trend is apparent in press comment. It is not impossible that Russia will show itself to be disinterested in the destruction of Poland. Should Russia continue to oppose us, our relations with Japan may become closer. If there were an alliance of France, England, and Russia against Germany, Italy, and Japan, I would be constrained to attack England and France with a few annihilating blows.

The Führer doubts the possibility of a peaceful dispute with England. We must prepare ourselves for the conflict. England sees in our development the foundation of a hegemony which would weaken England. England is therefore our enemy, and the conflict with England will be a life-and-death struggle. What will the struggle be like?

England cannot finish off Germany and subjugate us with a few powerful blows. It is imperative for England that the war be brought as near to the Ruhr basin as possible. It will not be sparing with French blood (West Wall!!).[17] The possession of the Ruhr basin will determine the duration of our resistance.

The Dutch and Belgian air bases must be occupied by armed force. Declarations of neutrality must be ignored. If England and France intend the war between Germany and Poland to lead to a conflict, they will support Holland and Belgium in their neutrality and make them build fortifications in order finally to force them into cooperation.

Belgium and Holland will, albeit under protest, yield to pressure. Therefore, if England intends to intervene in the Polish war, we must occupy Holland with lightning speed. We must aim at securing a new defense line on Dutch soil up to the Zuider Sea. The war with England will be a life-and-death struggle.

The idea that we can get off cheaply is dangerous; there is no such possibility. We must then burn our bridges, and it is no longer a question of justice or injustice, but of life or death for 80 million people.

Question: Short or long war?

Every country's armed forces or government must aim for a short war. The government, however, must also be prepared for a war of 10 to 15 years' duration.

---

17   The West Wall (also known as the Siegfried Line) was constructed on the frontier with France in 1938–39.

History shows that people always believed that wars would be short. In 1914 the opinion still prevailed that it was impossible to finance a long war. Even today this idea still persists in many minds. But on the contrary, every state will hold out as long as possible unless it immediately suffers some grave weakening (e.g., the Ruhr basin). England has similar weaknesses. England knows that to lose a war will mean the end of its world power.

England is the driving force against Germany. Its strength lies in the following:

1   The British themselves are proud, courageous, tenacious, firm in resistance, and gifted as organizers. They know how to exploit every new development. They have the love of adventure and bravery of the Nordic race. Quality is lowered by dispersion. The cross-section of Germans is higher.
2   It is a world power in itself. It has been constant for 300 years. Extended by the acquisition of allies. This power is not merely something concrete, but must also be considered as a psychological force embracing the entire world. Add to this immeasurable wealth, with accompanying creditworthiness.
3   Geopolitical security and protection by strong sea power and a courageous air force.

England's weaknesses:

If in the World War we had two additional battleships and two cruisers, and if the Battle of Jutland had begun in the morning, the British fleet would have been defeated and England brought to its knees. It would have meant the end of the World War. It was formerly not enough to defeat the fleet; landings had to be made in order to defeat England. England could provide her own food supplies. Today that is no longer possible.

The moment England's food supply is cut she is forced to capitulate. The import of food and fuel depends on protection by the fleet.

Attack on England by air will not force England to capitulate in one day. But if the fleet is destroyed, immediate capitulation will be the result.

There is no doubt that a surprise attack can lead to a quick decision. It would be criminal, however, for the government to rely entirely on the element of surprise.

Experience has shown that surprise may be nullified by:

1   Betrayal to persons outside the circle of military experts.
2   Mere chance, which may cause the collapse of the whole enterprise.
3   Human incompetence.
4   Weather conditions.

The date for attack must be fixed well in advance. Beyond that time, however, the tension cannot be endured for long. It must be borne in mind that weather conditions can render any surprise intervention by navy and air force impossible.

In drawing up plans of attack these unfavorable conditions must be borne in mind.

1   An effort must be made to deal the enemy a significant or a final decisive blow right at the start. Considerations of right and wrong, or treaties, do not enter into the matter. This will only be possible if we are not involved in war with England on account of Poland.
2   In addition to plans for a surprise attack, preparations for a long war must be made, while opportunities for England on the continent are eliminated.

The army will have to hold positions essential to the navy and air force. If Holland and Belgium are successfully occupied and held, and if France is also defeated, the fundamental conditions for a successful war against England will have been secured.

England can then be blockaded at close range by the air force from western France while the navy with its submarines can extend the range of the blockade ...

The experience of the World War make the following strategic considerations imperative:

1   With a more powerful navy at the outbreak of the war, or a wheeling movement by the army towards the channel ports, the end would have been different.
2   A country cannot be defeated by an air force. It is impossible to attack all objectives simultaneously, and the lapse of time of a few minutes leaves time for defensive counter-measures.
3   The unrestricted use of all resources is essential.
4   Once the army, in cooperation with the air force and navy, has taken the most important positions, industrial production will cease to flow into the bottomless pit of the army's battles and can be diverted to benefit the air force and the navy.

The air force must therefore be capable of taking these positions. Systematic preparations for the attack must be made. Studies to this end are of the utmost importance. The aim will always be to force England to its knees. Any weapon is only of decisive importance in winning battles as long as the enemy does not possess it.

This applies to gas, submarines, and the air force. It would be true of the latter, for instance, as long as the English fleet had no available counter-measures; this will no longer be the case in 1940 and 1941. Against Poland, for example, tanks will be effective as the Polish army possesses no counter-measures.

Where effectiveness can no longer be definitively determined, its place must be taken by the elements of surprise and inspired deployment. That is the plan of attack.

[Hitler then gave some more specific instructions for how the plan of attack was to be drawn up by the general staff.]

We shall not be forced into a war, but we shall not be able to avoid one.

Secrecy is the decisive requirement for success. Our objective must be kept secret even from Italy or Japan ...

The close combination of the services for the study of the problem in its entirety is important ...

The staff must include men with great imaginative powers and the best technical knowledge, as well as officers of sober and skeptical judgement.

Working principles:

1   No one must be informed who does not have to know.
2   No one may learn more than he has to know.
3   When must the person concerned know at the latest? No one may know of a matter earlier than is necessary for him to know it.

At the request of Field Marshal Goering the Führer decrees that

(a)   the various services shall decide what construction is to be undertaken;
(b)   there shall be no alterations in the shipbuilding program;
(c)   the armaments programs are to be geared to 1943 or 1944.

Certified as correct for the record
[signed] Schmundt, Lt. Col.

Source: Office of the US Chief of Counsel for Prosecution of Axis Criminality,
Nazi Conspiracy and Aggression, Vol. VII
(Washington DC: US Government Printing Office, 1946), pp. 847–54 [Doc. L–79]

Friction with the churches

The troubled relationship between the churches and the Nazi party is illustrated by the following directive prohibiting party membership to members of or candidates for the clergy. The reason given is to avoid the appearance of favoring one denomination over another. Presumably, however, an equally important motive was to exclude clerical influence on the formation of party policy or the execution of party functions.

4.17 Party directive making clergy and theology students ineligible for Party membership, 14 July 1939

THE DEPUTY OF THE FÜHRER   MUNICH, 14 JULY 1939

SUBJECT: ADMISSION OF CLERGYMEN AND STUDENTS OF THEOLOGY INTO THE NSDAP

In my regulation No. 24/37, dated 9 February 1937, I decreed that in order to avoid the penetration of differences of an ecclesiastical–political nature into the movement and to avoid the suspicion of a one-sided attitude for or against an existing denomination, the admission of members of the clergy into the Party is to be avoided. It turned out that the nonadmission of members of the clergy into the Party is not sufficient for the purpose in question.

In his regulation No. 34/39, dated 10 May 1939, on the lifting of the restriction of memberships the Reich Treasurer of the NSDAP dealt with this experience by decreeing that clergymen, *as well as other fellow Germans who are also closely connected with the church*, cannot be admitted into the Party.

In addition to this I decree that in the future Party members who enter the clergy or who turn to the study of theology have to leave the Party. This decree does not affect those students who are matriculated mainly in other fields and only attend some lectures in theology without intending to become clergymen.

[signed] for Bormann

Source: Office of the US Chief of Counsel for Prosecution of Axis Criminality,
Nazi Conspiracy and Aggression, Vol. III
(Washington DC: US Government Printing Office, 1946), p. 606 [Doc. 840-PS]

Bormann on the incompatibility of National Socialism and Christianity

The Nazis' relationship with the churches was governed by practical considerations. Well over 90 percent of Germans, including most rank and file party members, remained formal members of either the Lutheran or Catholic churches. Therefore the Hitler state had to reach a compromise with the churches, based on a separation of spheres. While the state exercised restraint in legislating internal church affairs, the churches showed equal restraint in refraining from political opposition. Within the Nazi party leadership, however, there was strong anti-Christian sentiment and considerable frustration that both the Catholic Church in Germany and the Confessing Church, committed as it was to maintaining the integrity of Lutheran doctrine (see Doc. 3.19), resisted National Socialist teachings, especially on the importance of race. The Nazi goal of total ideological uniformity was bound to cause conflict with the churches, and it is virtually certain that the Nazis would have attempted to supplant Christian religion with their own quasi-religious *völkisch* ideology if they had won the war.

The start of the war created the conditions for the radicalization of the party's religious policies. The following letter by Martin Bormann (1900–45), at that time still Deputy Führer Rudolf Hess' (1894–1987) chief assistant, to Alfred Rosenberg in his capacity as "Representative of the Führer for the Supervision of all Spiritual and Worldview-related Schooling and Education of the NSDAP" reveals some of the differences within the party on the appropriate strategy to pursue toward organized religion. While Rosenberg, "Reich Bishop" Ludwig Müller, and Reich Minister for Church Affairs Hanns Kerrl (1887–1941) believed it was possible to fuse Christian with National Socialist principles in religious instruction in schools, Bormann vetoed such a fusion on the grounds that the differences between National Socialism and Christian doctrine were too great to be reconciled. Instead he proposed that the party develop its own materials for moral and religious instruction that would eventually replace the instruction presently provided by the churches. This strategy would presumably avoid open conflict with the churches while weaning German youth from Christianity without the use of force. Conflict with the churches was somewhat lessened, however, by the Nazis' frank acceptance of the instrumental uses of religion. Even Bormann believed that some form of moral education based on the Ten Commandments was necessary to insure obedience and order in the "People's Community." It was the humanitarian, not the disciplinary functions of Christianity that the Nazis rejected.

4.18 Letter of Martin Bormann to Alfred Rosenberg, 24 February 1940

SUBJECT: DIRECTIONS FOR RELIGIOUS INSTRUCTION

Dear Party Member Rosenberg:

The Deputy of the Führer has heard from different sources that Reich Bishop Müller says that he received a commission from you to work out directives for the teaching of religion in the schools.

I have not been able to examine the statements of Reich Bishop Müller as to their correctness. The question ... is, however, in my mind of such fundamental importance for the future ideological position of the party that I find it necessary to point out to you the serious objections I have in regard to such a commission.

The Ministry of Education of the Reich has repeatedly indicated its desire in the course of the past few years for formulating new guidelines for the teaching of religion which would also be acceptable to the NSDAP.

With your concurrence this request has repeatedly been refused by the Führer's Deputy. Just as your ministry did, so the Deputy of the Führer took this position on the assumption that it could not be the task of the party to give directions for the instruction of the teachings of the Christian religions.

Christianity and National Socialism are phenomena which originated from entirely different sources. Both differ so fundamentally that it will not be possible to construct a Christian doctrine that would be completely compatible with the point of view of National Socialist ideology, just as the communities of Christian faith would never be able to accept the ideology of National Socialism in its entirety. The issuing of National Socialist directions for the teaching of religious classes would, however, involve a synthesis of National Socialism and Christianity, which I find impossible.

If these directions should really be permeated by the spirit of National Socialism, some very fundamental articles of faith of the Christian doctrines could not be recognized. I am referring here to the position of the Christian churches on the race question, on the question of the destruction of "life not worthy of living," to their position on marriage, which advocates the celibacy of priests and the toleration and furtherance of orders, for monks and nuns, to the doctrine, contradictory to German feeling, of the immaculate conception of Mary, etc.

No matter how these directions may be formulated, in no case will they ever simultaneously find the approval of the churches and the party.

Furthermore, the denominations themselves cannot agree on the contents of Christian teachings. As far as Protestants are concerned, there are not only the followers of the Confessional Church in the Reich and the German Christians, but also the adherents of a doctrine, who are endeavoring to create a new Lutheran Christendom of a particular kind approximately in the shape which seems desirable to the Reich Minister for Church Affairs, party member [Hanns] Kerrl. The party would thus have to decide which of these directions of faith it would give preference, or if it should even decide for a fourth. I do not think it entirely impossible that the Reich Bishop may take this latter road, since according to his last publication he himself has already turned sharply away from conceptions that up to now have been part of the faith of the German Christians.

But if directions for religious instruction should ever be worked out, it will not be enough, to my mind, to make them for Protestants only; corresponding directions should also be worked out for Catholics. To draw up directions for the instruction of Catholic faith, the Reich Bishop is hardly the suitable person, and we would probably have to choose a Catholic. Of course the directions for both faiths would differ in fundamental questions; each, however, would lay claim to containing the truly authentic interpretation of Point 24 [pledging support for "positive Christianity"] of the party program.

By issuing directions nothing would therefore be improved in the present situation in church affairs. The fight between the faiths would be carried on in the old form and spread into the ranks of the party. Indeed, all Christian faiths and groups would attack state and party, because they had presumed to encroach on their own territory, that of teaching the Christian faith, and tried to reform it.

The churches cannot be conquered by a compromise between National Socialism and Christian teachings, but only through a new ideology whose coming you yourself have announced in your writings. Because of this conviction we have always been careful not to exert a reforming influence on Christian dogma in any form nor to exert any influence on church directives for religious instruction. In complete mutual agreement we have rejected the intention of the Reich

Minister for Church Affairs [Hanns Kerrl], who, over the objection of the party, has always tried anew to renew church life in the framework of National Socialist spirit by searching for a compromise between Christian teachings and the ideology of National Socialism ...

On the other hand, of course, I am also of the opinion that it is not possible to eliminate religious instruction in schools without replacing it with something better for the moral education of youth.

Religious instruction as given in schools today does not only comprise instruction in Christian doctrines, the teachings of the creation of the world and of the life hereafter; besides this, children also receive instructions in the Ten Commandments, which for most fellow Germans (*Volksgenossen*) to this day still remain the only directives for their moral behavior and for an orderly collective life in the people's community (*Volksgemeinschaft*). If this instruction is taken from children without replacing it with something better, the objection can be made – in my estimation not without reason – that, as many contend, the present degradation of youth is in part caused by the lack of religious instruction in schools.

What in my opinion is therefore necessary is the preparation of a short directive on a National Socialist code for living. For education in the party, especially in the Hitler Youth, we need a short directive on the ethical principles, to which each German boy and girl, who in time will become representatives of National Socialist Germany, must be educated. In such a directive, for instance, belong the law of bravery, the law against cowardice, the commandment of love for soulful nature, through which God makes himself apparent also in the animal and the plant, and the commandment to keep the blood pure; many principles belong here which are, for instance, also contained in the decalogue of the Old Testament, insofar as they can be regarded as moral principles in the lives of all peoples.

The publication of such a directive can and must only come out of our National Socialist conduct of life. Its commandments need to be explained by reference to a doctrine of faith about the creation of life and about life of the soul after death.

They can and must originate beyond any confessional discussions.

I take the publication of such a directive to be of utmost importance, because German boys and girls must once be told what they can and must do, and what is forbidden for them to do. I don't even think it is necessary to introduce this directive immediately into the schools as a text; it would be sufficient for the time being to introduce it into the party and its affiliates. Later it could also be taken over by the schools, just as the Catechism also was not created by the school boards but was first taught by the Church and later taken over by the schools.

As far as religious instruction in the schools is concerned, I do not think that anything has to be changed in the present situation. No fault can be found with any National Socialist teacher, who, after the unmistakably clear instructions of the Führer's Deputy, is ready to give school instructions in the Christian religion. For the contents of this instruction, however, the directives should still be binding which have in earlier years been made by the churches themselves ...

When some time later the proposed directive for a new German conduct of life, first to be used in the educational work of the party, will have found entry into the schools, it shall in no way supplant classes in religion. It may perhaps be used as a foundation for some classes in German and must have validity for all pupils, without consideration of their religious affiliations. Against such an educational procedure the churches could not object, either, because it would really be a matter of additional education that would take place alongside religious instruction and without any connection with it. On the contrary, the churches would have reason to be thankful to the state, because it is not satisfied with the very insufficient moral education based on the Ten Commandments, but is giving youth additional education that makes much higher demands on its moral conduct.

Parallel to this the desire of parents for instruction in the doctrines of faith may thus well go on. The stronger and more fertile our *positive* educational work in the schools is formulated, however, the more certain it is that instruction in religion will lose in importance.

When the youth that is now being educated according to our moral laws later have to decide if they are still willing to have their children brought up in the far inferior Christian doctrines, their decision will in most cases be negative ...

Heil Hitler!

[signed] M. Bormann

Source: Office of the US Chief of Counsel for Prosecution of Axis Criminality,
Nazi Conspiracy and Aggression, Vol. III
(Washington DC: US Government Printing Office, 1946), pp. 152–7 [Doc. 098-PS]

The Nazis decide on war

The following selection from the diary of Count Galeazzo Ciano di Cortellazzo (1903–44), Mussolini's son-in-law and Italian foreign minister, shows how determined the Nazi leadership was to go to war in August 1939. Ciano opposed Italy's entry into the war on the side of its German ally in 1939. He changed his mind under the impression of German military superiority, however, and supported Mussolini's decision for war in June 1940. Ciano also supported Italy's military expansion in the Balkans as a way to prevent German dominance of the area. He remained Italian foreign minister until February 1943. In July 1943, with the war now favoring the Allies, he voted with the majority in the Fascist Grand Council for Mussolini's ouster. For this "betrayal" he was tried and executed by Mussolini's German-backed rump regime in northern Italy in 1944.

4.19 Count Ciano's Diary, August 1939

11 AUGUST 1939

I have collected in the conference records verbal transcripts of my conversations with Ribbentrop and Hitler. Here I shall only note some impressions of a general nature. Ribbentrop is evasive every time I ask him for particulars of the forthcoming German action. He has a guilty conscience. He has lied too many times about German intentions towards Poland not to feel embarrassment now over what he must tell me and what he is preparing to do.

The will to fight is unalterable. He rejects any solution which might satisfy Germany and prevent the struggle. I am certain that even if the Germans were given everything they demanded, they would attack just the same, because they are possessed by the demon of destruction.

Our conversation sometimes takes a dramatic turn. I do not hesitate to speak my mind in the most brutal manner. But this doesn't shake him in the least. I realize how little weight this view carries in German opinion.

The atmosphere is icy. And the cold feeling between us is reflected in our followers. During dinner we do not exchange a word. We distrust each other. But I at least have a clear conscience. He does not.

12 AUGUST 1939

Hitler is very cordial, but he, too, is adamant and relentless in his decision. He speaks standing in the large drawing room of his house, in front of a table on which some maps are spread. He displays a thorough knowledge of military affairs. He speaks with great calm and becomes excited only when he advises us to deliver the coup de grâce to Yugoslavia as soon as possible.

I soon realize that there is nothing more to be done. Our arguments cannot serve to check him in the slightest. He keeps repeating that he will localize the conflict with Poland, but his affirmation that the great war must be fought while he and the Duce are still young leads me to believe that he is once again speaking in bad faith.

He has words of high praise for the Duce but listens in an uninterested and impersonal manner when I tell him of the trouble which a war will bring upon the Italian people. Fundamentally I feel that the alliance with us is useful to the Germans only for the number of forces we can divert from their fronts; nothing more. Our fate doesn't interest them. They know that the war will be decided by them, not by us. And at the end, they promise us a gift of charity.

13 AUGUST 1939

The second talk with Hitler is shorter, and I would say more concise. Even in his manner the man reveals more than he did yesterday his desire for immediate action. The parting is cordial, but reserved on both sides.

At the Palazzo Venezia I report to the Duce ...

The Duce's reactions are mixed. At first he agrees with me. Then he says that honor forces him to march with Germany. Finally, he admits that he wants his share of the booty in Croatia and Dalmatia.

Source: Office of the US Chief of Counsel for Prosecution of Axis Criminality,
***Nazi Conspiracy and Aggression*, Vol. V**
(Washington DC: US Government Printing Office, 1946), pp. 690–1 [Doc. 1987-PS]

Hitler's decision for war

On 22 August 1939, on the eve of the signing of the Nazi–Soviet Pact (Doc. 4.21), Hitler summoned his leading generals to his mountain retreat in Berchtesgaden to inform them of the imminent start of the war against Poland. His major concern was to allay their fears of a war on two fronts and to explain why the attack on Poland could be delayed no longer. He also had to offer some explanation of his pact with communist Russia, which many Nazis, not to mention his supporters in Italy, Japan, Spain, and the anti-communist states of Eastern Europe and the Balkans regarded as a betrayal of the fascist cause. The Nazi–Soviet Pact may have played a role in Mussolini's decision, communicated to Hitler three days later, not to join Hitler in war at this time (see Doc.

4.23). Hitler told his generals that he would have preferred to maintain good relations with Poland in order first to neutralize the Western threat (a strategy supported by Mussolini to eliminate Britain and France as rivals in the Mediterranean and North Africa) and then turn his war machine with full force towards the east. Hitler alleged that Poland's refusal to negotiate, reinforced by Britain's unconditional pledge of military support after the German occupation of Czechoslovakia in March 1939, left him no choice but to destroy Poland first. The time was right, he told his generals, because the weakness of Western leaders and the strength of the Axis leadership gave Germany an important advantage, which might not last. He pointed out that he himself might be assassinated at any time, thus depriving Germany of the necessary will and determination to achieve the territorial expansion supposedly so vital to the nation's future.

Hitler may have believed that the Nazi–Soviet Pact would persuade Britain and France to stay out of the war, all the more so as there was little they had done or could do in the way of direct military aid to Poland. But he told his generals that the risk of British and French participation had to be accepted. The pact with Stalin made Germany impervious to economic blockade and far less vulnerable than in the First World War. Hitler candidly admitted that his successes in Austria and Czechoslovakia had been achieved by bluff. Even more surprisingly, he also acknowledged that many Germans had opposed what they regarded as an excessively reckless policy. Hitler suspected that their opposition may have encouraged the British to stand firm. But now the time to test Germany's revived military power had come. Germany's foreign policy aims, he said, would be achieved one at a time.

Because Hitler still noted some reservations among his generals, he followed up his first speech with a second, more militant pep talk after lunch.

4.20a The Führer's speech to the Commanders-in-Chief of the Wehrmacht, 22 August 1939

I have called you together to give you a picture of the political situation in order that you may have insight into the individual elements on which I have based my decision to act and in order to strengthen your confidence.

After this we will discuss military details.

It was clear to me that a conflict with Poland had to come sooner or later. I had already made this decision in spring, but I thought that I would first turn against the West in a few years, and only afterwards against the East. But the sequence cannot be fixed. One cannot close one's eyes to threatening conditions, either. I wanted to establish an acceptable relationship with Poland in order to fight first against the West. But this plan, which was agreeable to me, could not be executed, since essential conditions have changed. It became clear to me, that Poland would attack us in case of a conflict with the West. Poland wants access to the sea. This further development became obvious after the occupation of the Memel region,[18] and it became clear to me that under certain circumstances a conflict with Poland could arise at an inopportune moment. I enumerate as reasons for this reflection:

18   The city of Memel, annexed by Lithuania after the First World War, was returned to Germany in March 1939.

First of all two personal factors:

My own personality and that of Mussolini.

Essentially it depends on me, my existence, because of my political activities. Then there is the fact that probably no one will ever again have the confidence of the whole German people as I do. There will probably never again be a man in the future with more authority than I have. My existence is therefore a factor of great value. But I can be eliminated at any time by a criminal or an idiot.

The second personal factor is the Duce. His existence is also decisive. If something happens to him, Italy's loyalty to the alliance will no longer be certain. The basic attitude of the Italian Court is against the Duce. Above all, the Court sees in the expansion of the empire a burden. The Duce is the man with the strongest nerves in Italy.

The third personal factor favorable for us is Franco. We can ask only benevolent neutrality from Spain. But this depends on Franco's personality. He guarantees a certain uniformity and steadiness of the present system in Spain. We must take into account the fact that Spain does not as yet have a Fascist party with our internal unity.

On the other side a negative picture as far as decisive personalities are concerned. There is no outstanding personality in England or France.

For us it is easy to make decisions. We have nothing to lose; we can only gain. Our economic situation is such, because of our austerity measures, that we can only hold out for a few more years. Goering can confirm this. We have no other choice, we must act. Our opponents risk much and can gain only a little. England's stake in a war is unimaginably great. Our enemies have leaders who are below average. No personalities. No masters, no men of action.

Besides the personal factors, the political situation is favorable for us; in the Mediterranean, rivalry among Italy, France, and England; in East Asia, tension between Japan and England; in the Middle East, tension that alarms the Muslim world.

The English Empire did not emerge from the last war strengthened. From a maritime point of view, nothing was achieved. Conflict between England and Ireland. The South African Union became more independent. Concessions had to be made to India. England is in great danger. Unhealthy industries. A British statesman can look into the future only with concern.

France's position has deteriorated, particularly in the Mediterranean.

Further favorable factors for us are these:

Since [Mussolini's invasion of] Albania there is an equilibrium of power in the Balkans.[19] Yugoslavia carries the germ of dissolution because of its internal situation. Romania did not grow stronger. It is open to attack and vulnerable. It is threatened by Hungary and Bulgaria. Since [Mustafa] Kemal's death, Turkey has been ruled by small minds, unsteady, weak men.[20]

All these fortunate circumstances will no longer prevail in two to three years. No one knows how long I shall live. Therefore better to have the conflict now.

The creation of Greater Germany was a great achievement politically, but militarily it was questionable, since it was achieved through a bluff by our political leadership. It is necessary to test the military. If at all possible, not by a general reckoning, but by the solution of individual tasks.

The relationship to Poland has become intolerable. My Polish policy hitherto was in contrast to the attitude of the people. My proposals to Poland (Danzig and the Corridor) were disrupted by England's intervention. Poland changed her tone toward us. The initiative

19 Mussolini occupied Albania in April 1939.
20 Mustafa Kemal (1881–1938), better known as Attatürk, led a nationalist rebellion that overthrew the Ottoman Sultanate in Turkey in 1922.

cannot be allowed to pass to the others. This time is more favorable than in two to three years. An attempt on my life or Mussolini's could change the situation to our disadvantage. One cannot eternally confront one another with cocked rifle. A compromise suggested to us would have required us to change our convictions and make agreeable gestures. They talked to us again in the language of Versailles. There was a danger of losing prestige. Now the probability is still great that the West will not interfere. We must accept the risk with relentless resolution. A politician must accept a risk as much as a military leader. We are facing the alternative to strike or to be destroyed with certainty sooner or later …

I have always accepted a great risk in the conviction that it may succeed.

Now it is also a great risk. Iron nerves. Iron resolution.

The following specific reasons strengthen me in my attitude: England and France have obligated themselves [to support Poland], neither is in a position to do so. There is no actual rearmament in England, just propaganda. It has done much damage that many disapproving Germans wrote and said to Englishmen after the solution of the Czech question: The Führer carried the day because you lost your nerve, because you capitulated too soon. This explains the present propaganda war. The English speak of a war of nerves. One element of this war of nerves is to claim an increase of armament. But how is the state of British rearmament in actual fact? The construction program of the navy for 1938 has not yet been fulfilled. Only mobilization of the reserve fleet. Purchase of fishing steamers. Considerable strengthening of the Navy will not occur before 1941 or 1942.

Little has been done on land. England will be able to send a maximum of three divisions to the continent. A little has been done for the air force, but it is only a beginning. Anti-aircraft defense is in its beginning stages. At the moment England has only 150 AA guns. The new AA gun has been ordered. It will take a long time until enough have been produced. Fire equipment is lacking. England is still vulnerable from the air. This can change in two to three years. At the moment the English air force has only 130,000 men, France 72,000 men, Poland 15,000 men. England does not want the conflict to break out for two or three years.

The following is characteristic for England. Poland wanted a loan from England for rearmament. England, however, only gave credit in order to make sure that Poland buys in England, although England cannot deliver. This means that England does not really want to support Poland. It won't risk 8 million pounds in Poland, although it put half a billion into China. England's position in the world is very precarious. It will not accept any risks.

France lacks men (decline of birth rate). Little has been done for rearmament. The artillery is antiquated. France did not want to enter on this adventure. The West has only two possibilities to fight against us:

1   Blockade: It will not be effective because of our autarky and because we have sources of aid in the east.
2   Attack from the west from the Maginot line: I consider this impossible.

Another possibility is the violation of Dutch, Belgian, and Swiss neutrality. I have no doubt that all these states as well as Scandinavia will defend their neutrality by all available means. England and France will not violate the neutrality of these countries. England, therefore, actually cannot help Poland. There remains an attack on Italy. A military attack is out of the question. No one is counting on a longer war. If [Army Commander in Chief] von Brauchitsch had told me that I would need four years to conquer Poland I would have replied: then it cannot be done. It is nonsense to say that England wants to wage a long war.

We will hold our position in the West until we have conquered Poland. We must be conscious of our great industrial productivity. It is much greater than in 1914–18.

The enemy had another hope, that Russia would become our enemy after the conquest of Poland. The enemy did not count on my great strength of resolve. Our enemies are little worms. I saw them in Munich.

I was convinced that Stalin would never accept the English offer. Russia has no interest in maintaining Poland, and Stalin knows that no matter whether his soldiers come out of a war victoriously or beaten, it would mean the end of his regime. [Soviet ambassador Maxim] Litvinov's replacement was decisive. I brought about the change toward Russia gradually. In connection with the commercial treaty we got into political dialogue. Proposal of a non-aggression pact. Then came a general proposal from Russia. Four days ago I took a special step, which led to Russia answering yesterday that she is ready to sign. The personal contact with Stalin is established. The day after tomorrow von Ribbentrop will conclude the treaty. Now Poland is in the position in which I wanted her.

We need not be afraid of a blockade. The East will supply us with grain, cattle, coal, lead, and zinc. It is a great goal, which demands great efforts. I am only afraid that at the last minute some pig (*Schweinehund*) will make a proposal for mediation.

The political aim is set further. A beginning has been made for the destruction of England's hegemony. The way is open for the soldiers, after I have made the political preparations.

Today's announcement of the non-aggression pact with Russia struck like a bombshell. The consequences cannot be overlooked. Stalin also said that this course will benefit both countries. The effect on Poland will be tremendous.

[Goering answers with thanks to the Fuhrer and the assurance that the armed forces will do their duty.]

Source: Office of the US Counsel for Prosecution of Axis Criminality,
***Nazi Conspiracy and Aggression*, Vol. III**
(Washington DC: US Government Printing Office, 1946), pp. 581–6 [Doc. 798-PS]

4.20b Second speech by the Führer on 22 August 1939

Things can also work out differently regarding England and France. It is impossible to prophesy with any certainty. I am expecting an embargo on trade, not a blockade, and furthermore that relations will be broken off. The most iron determination on our part. No shrinking back from anything. Everyone must hold the view that we have been determined to fight the Western powers right from the start. A life and death struggle. Germany has won every war when she was united. An inflexible, unflinching bearing, above all on the part of superiors, firm confidence, belief in victory, overcoming the past by becoming accustomed to the heaviest burdens. A long period of peace would not do us any good. It is therefore necessary to be prepared for anything. A manly bearing. It is not machines that fight each other, but men. We have the better men as regards quality. Spiritual factors are decisive. On the opposite side they are weaker men. The nation collapsed in 1918 because the spiritual prerequisites were insufficient. Frederick the Great only achieved final success by his fortitude.

The destruction of Poland has priority. The aim is to eliminate active forces, not to reach a definite line. Even if war breaks out in the West, the destruction of Poland remains the priority. A quick decision in view of the season.

I shall give a propagandist reason for starting the war, no matter whether it is plausible or not. The victor will not be asked afterwards whether he told the truth or not. When starting and waging a war it is not right that matters, but victory.

Close your hearts to pity. Act brutally. Eighty million people must obtain what is their right. Their existence must be made secure. The stronger man is right. The greatest harshness.

Swiftness in making decisions is necessary. Firm faith in the German soldier. Crises are due solely to leaders having lost their nerve.

First requirement: Advance up to the Vistula and the Narev. Our technical superiority will shatter the nerves of the Poles. Every newly formed active Polish force is to be destroyed again immediately. A continuous process of attrition.

New German frontier delimitation according to sound principles and possibly a protectorate as a buffer state. Military operations will not be influenced by these considerations. The wholesale destruction of Poland is the military objective. Speed is the chief thing. Pursuit until complete annihilation.

Conviction that the German Wehrmacht is equal to all demands. The order for the start of hostilities will be given later, probably Saturday morning.

Source: US Department of State Publication 6462,
Documents On German Foreign Policy 1918–1945, Series D (1937–1945), Vol. VII,
The Last Days of Peace (Washington DC: US Government Printing Office, 1956),
pp. 205–6 [Doc. 193]

The Nazi–Soviet Non-Aggression Pact

After the Munich Conference, to which the Soviet Union had not been invited despite its treaties of mutual assistance with France and Czechoslovakia, Stalin drew the logical conclusion: the Western powers were determined to avoid war with Germany. The Munich Agreements also effectively ended the mutual assistance pacts between the USSR, Czechoslovakia, and France. As a result the Soviets cautiously turned away from their policy of seeking collective security with the West, a policy they had been pursuing under Commissar for Foreign Affairs Maxim Litvinov (1876–1951) since 1934. The replacement of Litvinov, who was Jewish, by Vyacheslav Molotov (1890–1986) on 3 May 1939 sent the Germans a clear signal that Stalin was interested in coming to some kind of agreement to avoid war. In August 1939 Hitler seized the opportunity to sign a non-aggression treaty with the USSR in the hopes of thereby deterring Britain and France from fighting to defend Poland, but also to overcome the reluctance of the Army General Staff, which had informed him that the German army was not prepared to fight a war on two fronts.

Their mutual interest in partitioning Poland (the eastern portion of which was populated by a majority of Ukrainians and White Russians) provided the basis for a Nazi–Soviet understanding. The Non-Aggression Pact contained a secret protocol (not discovered by the Western powers until 1945) dividing eastern Europe into spheres of influence. On 28 September 1939, after the conquest of Poland, a further secret Treaty of Demarcation modified some of the terms of the secret protocol to the Non-Aggression Pact, notably by allotting Lithuania to the Soviets in return for additional Polish territory. The Nazi–Soviet Non-Aggression Pact set the stage for the German invasion of Poland on 1 September 1939.

4.21 Treaty between Germany and the Soviet Union, 23 August 1939

The Government of the German Reich and the Government of the Union of Soviet Socialist Republics, guided by the wish to strengthen the cause of peace between Germany and the USSR and starting from the basic provisions of the Treaty of Neutrality concluded between Germany and the USSR in April 1926, have reached the following agreement:

Article 1. The two contracting parties undertake to refrain from any act of violence, any aggressive action, or any attack against one another, whether alone or jointly with other powers.

Article 2. In case either of the contracting parties should become the object of warlike acts on the part of a third power, the other contracting party will not support that third power in any form.

Article 3. The governments of the two contracting parties will in the future continuously remain in contact with each other for consultation in order to inform each other about questions affecting their mutual interests.

Article 4. Neither of the two contracting parties will participate in any grouping of powers that is indirectly or directly aimed against the other party.

Article 5. Should disputes or conflicts arise between the contracting parties regarding questions of any kind, the two parties will clear away these disputes or conflicts solely by means of friendly exchanges of views or if necessary by arbitration commissions.

Article 6. The present Treaty is concluded for a period of ten years with the provision that unless one of the contracting parties renounces it one year before the end of this period the duration of the validity of this treaty is to be regarded as automatically prolonged for another five years.

Article 7. The present Treaty is to be ratified within the shortest possible time. The ratification documents are to be exchanged in Berlin. The Treaty becomes effective immediately upon signature.

SECRET ADDITIONAL PROTOCOL

On the occasion of the signature of the Non-Aggression Treaty between the German Reich and the Union of Soviet Socialist Republics, the undersigned plenipotentiaries of the two parties discussed in strictly confidential conversation the question of the delimitation of their respective spheres of interest in Eastern Europe. These conversations led to the following result:

1   In the event of a territorial and political transformation in the territories belonging to the Baltic states (Finland, Estonia, Latvia, Lithuania), the northern frontier of Lithuania shall represent the frontier of the spheres of interest both of Germany and the USSR. In this connection the interest of Lithuania in the Vilna territory is recognized by both parties.

2   In the event of a territorial and political transformation of the territories belonging to the Polish state, the spheres of interest of Germany and the USSR shall be bounded approximately by the line of the rivers Narev, Vistula, and San.

The question of whether the interests of both parties make the preservation of an independent Polish state seem desirable and how the frontiers of this state should be drawn can be definitively determined only in the course of further political developments.

In any case both governments will resolve this question by means of a friendly understanding.

3   With regard to south-eastern Europe, the Soviet side emphasizes its interest in Bessarabia. The German side declares complete political disinterest in these territories.

4   This Protocol will be treated by both parties as top secret.

Moscow, 23 August 1939

For the German Reich Government: v. Ribbentrop
With plenipotentiary authority of the Government of the USSR: W. Molotov

Source: US Department of State Publication 6462, *Documents of German Foreign Policy*
1918–1945*, Series D (1937–1945), Vol. VII, *The Last Days of Peace
(Washington DC: US Government Printing Office, 1956), pp. 245–6 [Doc. 228]

President Roosevelt's mediation efforts

US President Franklin D. Roosevelt (1882–1945) made a last-minute appeal to Hitler to negotiate a peaceful solution to the Polish crisis in late August 1939. Hitler did postpone the attack on Poland, originally scheduled for 26 August, to 1 September, not because of the American appeal, but because Britain made clear its intention to stand by Poland. By insisting on 30 August that Poland send an emissary with full plenipotentiary powers to Berlin within 24 hours, Hitler deliberately blocked negotiations that would very likely have led to some Polish territorial concessions. But for Hitler the war was not about Danzig or the Polish Corridor. It was about gaining *Lebensraum* and a free hand to establish a new order in Europe under German domination.

4.22a Message from President Roosevelt to Herr Hitler, 24 August 1939

In the message which I sent you on the 14th April, I stated that it appeared to be that the leaders of great nations had it in their power to liberate their peoples from the disaster that impended, but that, unless the effort were immediately made, and with goodwill on all sides, to find a peaceful and constructive solution of existing controversies, the crisis which the world was confronting must end in catastrophe. Today that catastrophe appears to be very near – at hand, indeed.

To the message which I sent you last April I have received no reply, but because my confident belief that the cause of world peace – which is the cause of humanity itself – rises above all other considerations I am again addressing myself to you, with the hope that the war which impends and the consequent disaster to all peoples may yet be averted.

I therefore urge with all earnestness – and I am likewise urging the President of the Republic of Poland – that the Governments of Germany and Poland agree by common accord to refrain from any positive act of hostility for a reasonable stipulated period, and that they agree, likewise by common accord, to solve the controversies which have arisen between them by one of the three following methods:

First, by direct negotiation;

Second, by the submission of these controversies to an impartial arbitration in which they can both have confidence; or

Third, that they agree to the solution of these controversies through the procedure of conciliation, selecting as a conciliator or moderator a national of one of the American Republics, which are all of them free from any connection with, or participation in, European political affairs.

Both Poland and Germany being sovereign Governments, it is understood, of course, that, upon resort to any one of the alternatives I suggest, each nation will agree to accord complete respect to the independence and territorial integrity of the other.

The people of the United States are as one in their opposition to policies of military conquest and domination. They are as one in rejecting the thesis that any ruler or any people possess the right to achieve their ends or objectives through the taking of action which will plunge countless of millions into war, and which will bring distress and suffering to every nation of the world, belligerent and neutral, when such ends and objectives, so far as they are just and reasonable, can be satisfied through the processes of peaceful negotiation or by resort to judicial arbitration.

I appeal to you in the name of the people of the United States, and I believe in the name of peace-loving men and women everywhere, to agree to a solution of the controversies existing between your Government and that of Poland through the adoption of one of the alternative methods I have proposed.

I need hardly reiterate that should the Governments of Germany and Poland be willing to solve their differences in the peaceful manner suggested, the Government of the United States still stands prepared to contribute its share to the solution of the problems which are endangering world peace in the form set forth in my message of the 14th April.

4.22b President Roosevelt's Second Appeal to Herr Hitler, 25 August 1939

I have this hour received from the President of Poland a reply to the message which I addressed to your Excellency and to him last night.

(The text of President Moscicki's reply is then given. President Roosevelt continues as follows):

Your Excellency has repeatedly publicly stated that the aims and objects sought by the German Reich were just and reasonable.

In his reply to my message the President of Poland has made it plain that the Polish Government is willing, upon the basis set forth in my message, to agree to solve the controversy which has arisen between the Republic of Poland and the German Reich by direct negotiation or the process of conciliation.

Countless human lives can yet be saved and hope may still be restored that the nations of the modern world may even now construct the foundation for a peaceful and happier relationship, if you and the Government of the German Reich will agree to the pacific means of settlement accepted by the Government of Poland. All the world prays that Germany, too, will accept.

Source: Office of the US Chief of Counsel for Prosecution of Axis Criminality, *Nazi Conspiracy and Aggression*, Vol. VIII (Washington DC: US Government Printing Office, 1946), pp. 475–7 [Doc. TC–72 Nos. 124 and 127]

Italy backs out

Hitler's Fascist ally Mussolini made it clear that while he supported the German cause, he was not ready to enter the war. Earlier discussions between German and Italian military leaders had been predicated on the assumption that war with the West, which Mussolini, too, considered inevitable at some point, would not come until 1942–43.

4.23 Telegram from the German Embassy in Rome to Ribbentrop, 27 August 1939

TOP SECRET

To: Reich Foreign Minister

As already announced by phone, I have transmitted the reply letter of Hitler to Duce in presence of Ciano at 0910 hours. The Duce will reply quickly and confirm that he will comply with Hitler's wishes 100%, and that he stands with him in complete solidarity. As far as the desired tying down of English–French forces is concerned, the military measures already taken by the Italians are above suitable to tie down, according to a conservative estimate, at least 300,000 opponents along the line Alps, Corsica, Tunisia …

The Duce then referred again, with emphasis, to his view, already aired yesterday, that he still believed in the possibility of reaching our goals without armed conflict. He therefore decided to mention that, also, in his intended letter to Hitler. It is probably so, that a delay of 3–4 years of the war with the Western powers, which in his opinion, too, is unavoidable, would change the prospects, for him as for us completely. Field Marshall Goering had talked to him about 4 years for us some time ago. And even in talks to him about Pariani–Keitel the latter had considered a period of several years necessary to bring us to the apex of military efficiency. But even a delay of several months would be a gain …

Source: **Office of the US Chief of Counsel for Prosecution of Axis Criminality,**
Nazi Conspiracy and Aggression, **Vol. V**
(Washington DC: US Government Printing Office, 1946), p. 452 [Doc. 2817-PS]

5

The Second World War, 1939–45

On 1 September 1939 Hitler told the German nation that since 5:45 that morning their armed forces had been "returning fire" against Poland (Doc. 5.1). A raid on a German border station was staged by SS men in Polish uniforms to give some credibility to Hitler's assertion that the Germans were acting in self-defense. Chamberlain's government issued an ultimatum to the Germans to halt their drive into Poland. When the ultimatum ran out on 3 September without a German response, Britain and France declared war (Doc. 5.2).

The well-planned German blitzkrieg swept through Poland, reaching Warsaw on 9 September. The Poles were no match for Germany's technologically superior forces. On 17 September the Soviets occupied the eastern half of Poland, the territory allotted to them in the secret protocol of the Nazi–Soviet Pact (Doc. 4.21). In October they also sent troops into the Baltic states, and in November launched the so-called "Winter War" against Finland to regain formerly Russian territory deemed necessary to the defense of Leningrad in case of war. It was not until late March 1940 that the vastly outnumbered Finns were forced to end the war on Soviet terms. The poor performance of the Red Army in the "Winter War" helped to persuade German military leaders that the Soviet Union was too weak to withstand a German attack.

The so-called "phony war" in the West, where British and French troops remained in a purely defensive posture, came to an end in spring 1940. In April the Germans invaded Denmark and Norway to preempt a possible Allied landing and secure the supply of iron ore from Sweden. On 10 May, without warning, the Wehrmacht launched simultaneous attacks on Holland, Belgium, Luxembourg, and France. Once again, German blitzkrieg tactics were crowned with success (see Doc. 5.3), although the British, now under Winston Churchill's (1874–1965) leadership, gained something of a moral victory by extricating their surrounded expeditionary forces from the beaches of Dunkirk in early June. Italy entered the war on the German side on June 10 to get in on some of the spoils. France surrendered on 22 June in a humiliating ceremony in the very same railroad car in Compiègne where the Germans had signed the armistice ending the First World War (Doc. 5.4). A collaborationist regime under the French hero of the First World War, Marshal Henri Philippe Pétain (1856–1951), was established with its capital at Vichy, while the Germans occupied the northern half and the western coastline of the country.

But Hitler's triumphant expectation that the British would now be forced to accept Germany's "generous" peace terms proved to be wrong (Doc. 5.5). Nor could the conditions for a successful invasion of the British Isles be obtained, as the *Luftwaffe* failed in its efforts to establish air supremacy over the Channel in the Battle of Britain in summer and fall 1940 (Doc. 5.6). Hitler weighed several military options to persuade Britain to make peace, but the potentially promising strategy of defeating Britain in the Mediterranean was impeded by the Spanish Caudillo Franco's refusal to be drawn into the war. Hitler was convinced that Britain would refuse to make peace as long as it could hope for American or Soviet intervention (see Doc. 5.6). To deter American entry into the war, Hitler formed a military alliance with Japan in the Tripartite Pact of September 1940 (Doc. 5.7). After some perfunctory, but unsuccessful, attempts in November 1940 to persuade the Soviet Union to actively join in the war against Britain, Hitler decided to attack the Soviet Union even before the end of the war in the west (Doc. 5.10).

The timing of "Operation Barbarossa" was determined by the need to eliminate Russia while Britain posed no offensive threat and the US was still officially neutral. The motives for war against the Soviet Union, however, were of much longer duration. Already in *Mein Kampf* (Doc. 2.15) Hitler had announced his long-term aim of acquiring *Lebensraum* in the east for the German people. He was also committed to the destruction of communism, which Nazi propaganda described as the means by which Jews hoped to gain world power (see Docs. 2.3 and 6.3). As early as December 1940 the American reporter William L. Shirer accurately predicted that Hitler's long-term plans included conquest of the Soviet Union (Doc. 5.9), which in turn would lead to war against the US. In his letter to Mussolini announcing the start of "Operation Barbarossa" Hitler acknowledged that the decision to attack Russia had made him "again feel spiritually free" (Doc. 5.13).

According to Nazi racial ideology, the effects of which occupied Poland had already experienced since 1939 (see Doc. 5.8), Slavic peoples were inferior to Germanics and suited primarily for physical labor. From the start, the war against the Soviet Union was planned as a war of extermination (Doc. 5.11) in which the traditional rules of warfare were to be ignored. Jews and Communist officials were targeted for mass murder in plans drawn up prior to the attack (see Docs. 5.12 and 6.6). Moscow and Leningrad were to be razed to the ground (Doc. 5.16). The Wehrmacht would play an active role in Nazi atrocities (Doc. 5.17).

Despite numerous warnings by British and American intelligence, dismissed by Stalin as Western efforts to provoke war with Germany, the Soviets were unprepared for the German invasion (Doc. 5.14). The surprise factor helped German troops make enormous gains in the early stages of the war. By November 1941 advance units of the Wehrmacht reached the outskirts of Moscow. But in early December, taking advantage of the fierce winter weather for which overconfident Wehrmacht leaders had failed to prepare, the Soviets launched a counter-attack that saved Moscow from German occupation.

The failure of Foreign Minister Ribbentrop's efforts to persuade Japan to enter the war against the Soviet Union (Doc. 5.15) made it all the more imperative to incite war between Japan and the United States. From the German point of view, the one eventuality to be prevented at all costs was a Japanese–American compromise that would free the US to increase its aid to Britain and the USSR or even to formally enter the war in Europe. To encourage Japan to attack the US, the Germans (and Italians) promised to join Japan in declaring war on the US. The German leadership reacted with elation to the news of the attack on Pearl Harbor on December 7 (Doc. 5.18 and 5.20). The German declaration of war on the US (Doc. 5.19) was made easier by the fact that it merely formalized an already existing naval war between the two powers in the Atlantic. The Nazi leadership, convinced of the weakness of democracy, shockingly underestimated the American will and capacity to fight a successful war.

Initiative and momentum lay with the Axis powers until the late summer of 1942. The turning-point in the war came in November 1942. The British Army halted

General Erwin Rommel's advance into Egypt at El Alamein, forcing the Africa Corps to retreat, and on November 8 American and British forces landed in Vichy-controlled French Morocco and Algeria. On that very day Hitler addressed the party faithful in Munich on the 19th anniversary of the 1923 putsch (Doc. 5.22). He put up a brave front, belittling the significance of the North African invasion, but it turned out to be his last major public speech. As the war turned against Germany he withdrew more and more from contact with the German public.

The worst news of all came in late November 1942, when Soviet forces succeeded in encircling the German Sixth Army in the strategically important city of Stalingrad on the Volga River. The Sixth Army, worn out by weeks of fierce fighting for control of the city, was doomed. Hitler refused to permit a breakout attempt, and efforts to relieve and resupply the encircled army failed. On 1 February 1943 the surviving remnants of the Sixth Army went into Soviet captivity. The Nazis' draconic occupation policies and treatment of Soviet prisoners of war, $3^{1}/_{2}$ million of whom died in German captivity, contributed to the failure of the Russian campaign (see Doc. 5.21). German authorities were unable or unwilling to capitalize on potential opposition to Soviet rule in the occupied territories. Instead of winning the battle for the hearts and minds of national minorities in the Soviet Union, German forces faced increasing attacks from Soviet partisans in the rear.

Propaganda Minister Josef Goebbels attempted to rally the German people behind the slogan of "total war" in an emotional speech in Berlin in February 1943 (Doc. 5.23), but the full mobilization of the German public was never achieved. The Nazis' own idealization of female domesticity worked against their efforts to enlist women in the workforce (see Doc. 5.25). Instead the Nazis relied on the forced labor of foreign workers, who numbered more than 7 million by 1944. Internally the Nazis tightened their grip, and all opposition or signs of defeatism were ruthlessly suppressed, as in the case of the courageous student group, the "White Rose," in Munich in early 1943 (Doc. 5.24). None of these measures could reverse the course of the war. Defeat in the battle of Kursk in July 1943, the relentless bombardment of German cities, the failure of the German submarine campaign in the Atlantic, and the surrender of Italy in September 1943 brought the war ever closer to home.

The success of the Allies' cross-channel invasion on 6 June 1944 (Doc. 5.26) finally induced a number of high-ranking military officers to try to overthrow the Nazi regime (Doc. 5.27). However, the bomb planted by Colonel Claus von Stauffenberg in Hitler's headquarters on 20 July 1944 failed to kill the Führer, and the revolt was quickly crushed. The war continued in undiminished intensity, finally encroaching on German territory itself at the end of 1944. Now it was Germans who were uprooted, especially in the east, where millions of Germans fled to escape the Soviet advance (see Doc. 5.28).

Hitler committed suicide in his bunker under the Chancellery in Berlin on 30 April 1945. His political testament (Doc. 5.29) showed no change of attitude or remorse for the destructive war he had unleashed. The formal German surrender followed on 8 May 1945 (Doc. 5.30). The fanatical Nazi determination to fight to the bitter end only magnified the totality of destruction and collapse. For most Germans the end of the war came as a relief. For the small minority of Nazi opponents it came as liberation (Doc. 5.31).

The invasion of Poland, 1 September 1939

Aware that the German public was not enthusiastic about war, Hitler attempted to justify the German invasion as a defensive reaction to Poland's incursions (which were actually staged by the Germans to gain public support for the war). He also accused Poland of refusing to negotiate a peaceful resolution of the crisis. But by insisting that the Polish government send a plenipotentiary to Berlin within 48 hours he had himself deliberately prevented the negotiations through which the British government still hoped to prevent war. He was determined to take advantage of the remaining few weeks of favorable weather to launch a war of conquest. The apparently modest war aims he outlined in his speech were designed both for domestic consumption and to deter the Western powers from intervening.

In this speech Hitler also gave his first public accounting for why he had signed the Nazi–Soviet Non-Aggression Pact (Doc. 4.21). This tactical quasi-alliance with his proclaimed arch-enemy shocked and dismayed anti-communists all over Europe (while also disillusioning many on the left who had been attracted to communism by its principled opposition to fascism). Hitler's speech was primarily intended to convince his listeners of the righteousness of the German cause. Although he hoped to confine the war to Poland, in keeping with his successful pre-war strategy of achieving his imperialistic aims one step at a time, several passages in his speech suggest that Hitler was quite aware that he had launched what would become a second world war. He even seems to have anticipated that he would not survive this war.

5.1 Hitler's Reichstag speech, 1 September 1939

Delegates, men of the German Reichstag!

For months we have been tormented by a problem once imposed upon us by the Dictate of Versailles and which, in its deterioration and escalation, has now become utterly intolerable. *Danzig was and is a German city! The Corridor was and is German!* All these territories owe their cultural development exclusively to the German people, without whom absolute barbarism would reign in these eastern territories. Danzig was separated from us! The Corridor was annexed by Poland! The German minorities living there were mistreated in the most cruel manner. Already during the years 1919–20 more than one million people of German blood were driven from their homes. As usual I have tried to change this intolerable state of affairs through proposals for a peaceful revision. It is a lie if it is claimed throughout the world that we ensure all our revisions only by applying pressure. There was ample opportunity for fifteen years before National Socialism assumed power to carry through revisions by means of a peaceful understanding. This was not done. In every single case did I then take the initiative, not once but many times, to bring forward proposals for the revision of absolutely intolerable conditions ...

One thing, however is impossible: to demand that a peaceful revision should be made of an intolerable state of affairs, and then obstinately refuse such a peaceful revision. It is equally impossible to assert that in such a situation to act on one's own initiative in making a revision is to violate a law. For us Germans the Dictate of Versailles is not a law. It does not work to force somebody at the point of a pistol and by threatening to starve millions of people into signing a document and afterwards proclaim that this document with its forced signature was a solemn law ...

Although I was deeply convinced that the Polish government – perhaps also because of its dependence on an unrestrained, wild military rabble – is not seriously interested in a real understanding, I nevertheless accepted a proposal by the British government for mediation. The latter proposed that it would not carry on negotiations itself but assured me that it would establish a direct contact between Poland and Germany in order to get talks going once more. I must state the following: I accepted this proposal. For these talks I drew up the fundamentals that are known to you! And then I and my government sat for two whole days waiting for the Polish government to make up its mind whether to finally dispatch a plenipotentiary or not! Until last night it had not sent any plenipotentiary but informed us through its ambassador that at present it was considering the question whether and to what extent it might be able to accept the British proposals. It would inform England of its decision.

Members of the Reichstag! If such treatment can be meted out to the German Reich and its head of state, and the German Reich and its head of state were to submit to such treatment, then the German nation would deserve no better than to disappear from the political scene! My proposals for peace and my endless patience must not be mistaken for weakness, much less for cowardice! Therefore, I have last night informed the British government that, things being as they are, I have found it impossible to detect any inclination on the part of the Polish government to enter into a really serious discussion with us.

Thus these proposals for mediation have failed, for in the meantime the answer to these proposals have been, first, the Polish order for general mobilization, and secondly, new grave atrocities. These incidents recurred again last night. After twenty-one frontier incidents had recently occurred, there were fourteen more last night, three of them very grave. *For that reason I have now decided to talk to Poland in the same language Poland has been using toward us for months.*

If there are statesmen in the West who declare that their interests are involved, I can only regret such a declaration; however, not for one single minute could that persuade me to deviate from the execution of my duties ...

I am happy to be able to inform you here of an event of special importance. You are aware that Russia and Germany are governed under two different doctrines. There was only one question that had to be cleared up: Germany has no intention of exporting its doctrine, and the minute Russia does not intend to export its own doctrine to Germany, I no longer see any reason why we should ever be opponents again! Both of us are agreed on this point: any struggle between our two people would only be of use to others. We therefore resolved to enter into an agreement that excludes any application of force between us in the future, obligates us to consult each other in certain European questions, makes economic cooperation possible, and above all makes sure that these two great powers don't exhaust their energies in fighting each other. Any attempt on the part of the Western powers to alter these facts will fail, and in this connection I should like to give the following assurance: this political decision signifies an enormous change for the future and is absolutely final!

I believe the whole German people will welcome this political attitude! In the World War, Russia and Germany fought each other and in the final analysis they both were the ones to suffer. That shall not happen a second time! The non-aggression and consultation pact, which already went into effect upon its signing, was yesterday ratified in Moscow and in Berlin. In Moscow the pact was welcomed just as you have welcomed it here. I approve of every word in the speech made by Mr. Molotov, the Russian Commissar for Foreign Affairs.

Our aims: I am determined:

First, to solve the question of Danzig; second, the question of the Corridor; and third to see to it that a change takes place in Germany's relations to Poland, which will insure a peaceful coexistence of the two powers. I am determined to fight until either the present Polish government is willing to effect this change or another Polish government is prepared to do so. I want to remove from the German frontiers the element of insecurity, the atmosphere which permanently resembles civil war. I shall see to it that peace on the eastern frontier is the same as it is on our other frontiers. I want to carry out the necessary actions in such a manner that they do not contradict the proposals that I made known to you here, members of the Reichstag, as my proposals to the rest of the world. That means I do not want to wage war against women and children. I have instructed my air force to limit their attacks to military objectives. However, if the enemy should conclude from this that he might get away with waging war in a different manner he will receive an answer that will knock him out of his wits!

Last night for the first time regular soldiers of the Polish Army fired shots on our territory. Since 5:45 a.m. we have been returning fire! From now on every bomb will be answered with another bomb! Whoever fights with poison gas will be fought with poison gas. Whoever disregards the rules of humane warfare can but expect us to do the same. I will carry on this fight, no matter against whom, until such a time as the safety of the Reich and its rights are secured!

For more than six years now I have been engaged in building up the German armed forces. During this period more than 90 billion Reichsmark were spent building up the Wehrmacht. Today ours are the best-equipped armed forces in the world, and they are far superior to those of 1914. My confidence in them can never be shaken.

If I call upon the Wehrmacht and if I ask sacrifices of the German people, and, if necessary, unlimited sacrifices, then I have the right to do so, for I myself am just as ready today as I was in the past to make every personal sacrifice. I don't ask anything of any German that I myself was not prepared to do at any moment for more than four years. There shall not be any deprivations for Germans in which I myself will not immediately share. From this moment on my whole life shall belong more than ever to my people. I now want to be nothing but the first soldier of the German Reich.

Thus I have once again put on the uniform which has always been the most sacred and dearest to me. I shall not put it aside until after victory – or I shall not live to see the end! Should anything happen to me in this war, my first successor will be Party member Goering. Should anything happen to Party member Goering, his successor will be Party member Hess. To these men as your leaders you would then owe the same absolute loyalty and obedience that you owe to me. In the event that something should also happen to Party member Hess, I will make legal provisions for the convocation of a senate, who shall then elect the worthiest, that is to say the most valiant, from their midst!

As a National Socialist and a German soldier I enter upon this fight with a stout heart! My whole life has been but one continuous struggle for my nation, for its resurrection, for Germany, and this whole struggle has been inspired by one single conviction: faith in this people! One word I have never known: capitulation. And if there is anybody who thinks that hard times are ahead of us I'd like him to recall the fact that at one time a Prussian king with a ridiculously small state confronted one of the greatest coalitions ever known and emerged victorious after three campaigns because he possessed that strong and firm faith which we, too, need in these times.[1] As for the rest of the world, I want to assure them: *a November 1918 shall never occur again in German history.* Just as I myself am prepared at any time to risk my life for my people and for Germany, I demand the same from everyone else!

Whoever believes he has a chance to evade this patriotic duty directly or indirectly shall perish. We will have nothing to do with traitors. We all are acting only in accordance with our old principle: our own life matters nothing; all that matters is that our people, that Germany shall live …

---

1   Hitler is referring to Frederick the Great who successfully fought a coalition of France, Austria, and Russia in the Seven Years' War (1756–63).

I conclude with the words with which I once started my struggle for power in the Reich. At that time I said: "If our will is so strong that it cannot be broken through any distress, then our will and our German steel will also be able to master and conquer distress." Germany – Sieg Heil!

Source: Office of the US Counsel for Prosecution of Axis Criminality,
Nazi Conspiracy and Aggression, Vol. IV
(Washington DC: US Government Printing Office, 1946), pp. 1026–33 [Doc. 2322-PS]

The British declaration of war

Hitler had delayed the attack on Poland until 1 September in the hopes of dissuading the Western powers from intervening. The British and French, however, made it clear that they would honor their guarantee to Poland. On 1 September the British government sent Germany an ultimatum calling on Germany to suspend all military operations against Poland within 24 hours. When Germany failed to respond, Foreign Secretary Lord Halifax sent the telegram below to the British ambassador to Germany, Neville Henderson. The reluctance of the British government to go to war is unmistakable.

5.2 Viscount Halifax to Sir Neville Henderson (Berlin), 3 September 1939

(Telegraphic)   Foreign Office, September 3, 1939, 5 a.m.

Please seek interview with Minister for Foreign Affairs at 9 a.m. today, Sunday, or, if he cannot see you then, arrange to convey at that time to representative of German Government the following communication:

In the communication which I had the honor to make to you on 1st September I informed you, on the instructions of His Majesty's Principal Secretary of State for Foreign Affairs, that unless the German Government were prepared to give assurances that the German Government had suspended all aggressive action against Poland and were prepared promptly to withdraw their forces from Polish territory, His Majesty's Government in the United Kingdom would, without hesitation, fulfil their obligations to Poland.

Although this communication was made more than twenty-four hours ago, no reply has been received but German attacks upon Poland have been continued and intensified. I have accordingly the honor to inform you that, unless not later than 11 a.m. British Summer Time, today 3rd September, satisfactory assurances to the above effect have been given by the German Government, and have reached his Majesty's Government in London, a state of war will exist between the two countries as from that hour.

If the assurances referred to in the above communication are received, you should inform me by any means at your disposal before 11 a.m. today, 3rd September. If no such assurance is received here at 11 a.m. we shall inform the German representative that a state of war exists as from that hour.

Source: Office of the US Chief of Counsel for Prosecution of Axis Criminality,
Nazi Conspiracy and Aggression, Vol. VIII
(Washington DC: US Government Printing Office, 1946), pp. 474–5 [Doc. TC–72, No. 118]

The campaign in the West, Spring 1940

Enjoying vast superiority in artillery, tanks, and aircraft, the German army swept through Poland, which surrendered in early October 1939. The French and the British remained in their defensive positions behind the Maginot line and made no move to relieve the Polish front. This "phony war" came to an end in April 1940. To ensure the continued shipment of iron ore from nominally neutral Sweden and to prevent the Allies from gaining a foothold in Scandinavia, Germany invaded Denmark and Norway on 9 April 1940. On 10 May 1940 the Wehrmacht unleashed the powerful offensive that led to the conquest of Holland, Belgium, Luxembourg, and France and the expulsion of British forces from the continent. Holland fell on 15 May and Belgium two weeks later. The Germans broke through the French lines in the Ardennes Forest and surrounded the British expeditionary force at Dunkirk. Before its fall on 4 June, however, the British were able to evacuate 338,000 British, French, and Belgian soldiers, thus preventing a complete disaster. Paris fell on 13 June and four days later the new French government under the aged hero of World War One, Marshal Henri-Philippe Pétain (1856–1951) sued for an armistice.

The following extracts from the private war diary of General Franz Halder (1884–1972), Chief of Staff of the Army from September 1938 to his dismissal in September 1942, offer a German perspective on the dramatic events of spring and summer 1940. Halder was the chief architect of German military success in Poland and the West. A number of his entries document Hitler's unwelcome interventions into army operations, although from Halder's point of view, at this stage of the war at least, these interventions occurred on the side of excessive caution. Halder, for instance, faults Hitler for halting the German drive on Dunkirk on 24 May 1940 and for his unwillingness to take risks in the final battle for France. That same caution was not evident in Hitler's grandiose geopolitical plans, however, as is apparent from Halder's report on the conference at the Führer's alpine retreat on 31 July 1940 (see Doc. 5.6). Halder's war diary was translated into English under the auspices of the American Military Government in Germany after the war.

5.3 The Halder War Diary, 1940

---

24 MAY 1940

ObdH [Commander in Chief of the Army General Walther von Brauchitsch] returns from OKW [High Command of the Wehrmacht]: Apparently again a very unpleasant interview with the Führer. At 2020 hours a new order is issued, cancelling yesterday's order and directing encirclement to be effected in area Dunkirk–Estaires–Lille–Roubaix–Ostend. The left wing, consisting of armor and motorized forces, which has no enemy before it, will so be stopped upon direct orders of the Führer! Finishing off the encircled enemy army is to be left to the Air Force!!

25 MAY 1940

The day starts off with one of those painful wrangles between ObdH and the Führer on the next moves in the encircling battle. The battle plan I had drafted called for Army Group A, by heavy frontal attacks, merely to hold the enemy, who is making a planned withdrawal, while

Army Group B, dealing with an enemy already whipped, cuts into his rear and delivers the decisive blow. This was to be accomplished by our armor. Now the political leadership has formed the idea that the decisive battle must not be fought on Flemish soil, but rather in Northern France. To camouflage this political goal, the assertion is made that Flanders, criss-crossed by a multitude of waterways, is unsuited for tank warfare. Accordingly, all tanks and motorized troops will have to be stopped on reaching the line St. Omer–Béthune.

This is a complete reversal of the plan. I wanted to make Army Group A the hammer and Army Group B the anvil in this operation. Now B will be the hammer and A the anvil. As Army Group B is confronted with a consolidated front, progress will be slow and casualties high. Because the Air Force, on which all hopes are pinned, is dependent on the weather.

This divergence of views results in a tug-of-war that costs more nerves than does the actual conduct of the operations. However, the battle will be won, one way or another.

6 JUNE 1940

The Führer thinks that changing the direction of the offensive, as proposed by me, is still too hazardous at this time. He wants to play absolutely safe. First he would like to have a sure hold of the Lorraine iron ore basin, so as to deprive France of her armament resources. After that he believes it would be time to consider a drive in westerly direction, probably having in mind a strong wing at the coast (Fourth Army).

There we have the same old story again. On top, there just isn't a spark of the spirit that would dare putting high stakes on a single throw. Instead, everything is done in cheap piece-meal fashion, but with the air that we don't have to rush at all. However, we can be pretty sure that before 36 or 48 hours are over, the ideas proposed by us today will be served right back to us in the form of a top-level directive.

21 JUNE 1940

2000 HOURS

ObdH [Brauchitsch] returns from Compiègne. He is deeply stirred. The French (the most likeable of whom was the army representative) had no warning that they would be handed the terms at the very site of the negotiations in 1918. They were apparently shaken by this arrangement and at first inclined to be sullen.

The Führer and ObdH were present only at the reading of the preamble. In the following negotiations, presided over by [General Wilhelm] Keitel, there seems to have been a great deal of wrangling, and ObdH is worried that the French might not accept.

I don't understand his apprehension. The French must accept and, with Pétain[2] at the helm, will do so. Moreover, our terms are so moderate that sheer common sense ought to make them accept.

French attempts to have our terms bracketed with those of the Italians[3], and to make accep-tance of our terms contingent on what the Italians demand, has of course been rejected by us. They

---

2   General Henri Pétain (1856–1951), hero of the French defense of Verdun in the First World War, became prime minister after the fall of Paris on 16 June 1940 and initiated negotiations with the Germans. On 10 July 1940 he was named head of state with dictatorial powers of the pro-German regime established in the unoccupied portion of France with its capital in Vichy.

have been given until tomorrow noon to accept. Aerial assault of Bordeaux has been authorized ...
Von Stülpnagel for supper.[4] We had a very pleasant chat.

22 JUNE 1940

The dominant event of the day is the conclusion of the Armistice with the French ...

Source: Office of the Chief of Counsel for War Crimes, *The Halder Diaries:*
The Private War Journals of General Franz Halder
(Nuremberg: Office of Military Government [US], 1948)

The fall of France, 22 June 1940

The spectacular German campaign in the West in the spring of 1940 marked Germany's greatest military success. The Franco-German armistice was signed on 22 June 1940 in the same railroad car in the French town of Compiègne in which the Germans had been forced to sign the armistice ending the First World War on 11 November 1918. This extraordinary reversal of German military fortunes was the greatest triumph of Hitler's career. American correspondent William Shirer was present and wrote the following dramatic eye-witness account in his personal diary.

5.4 William L. Shirer, *Berlin Diary*

PARIS, JUNE 21

On the exact spot in the little clearing in the Forest of Compiègne where at five a.m. on November 11, 1918 the armistice which ended the World War was signed, Adolf Hitler today handed *his* armistice terms to France. To make German revenge complete, the meeting of the German and French plenipotentiaries took place in Marshal Foch's private car, in which Foch laid down the armistice terms to Germany twenty-two years ago. Even the same table in the rickety old *wagon-lit* car was used. And through the windows we saw Hitler occupying the very seat on which Foch had sat at that table when he dictated the other armistice.

The humiliation of France, of the French, was complete. And yet in the preamble to the armistice terms Hitler told the French that he had not chosen this spot at Compiègne out of revenge; merely to right an old wrong. From the demeanor of the French delegates I gathered that they did not appreciate the difference.

The German terms we do not know yet. The preamble says the general basis for them is: (1) to prevent a resumption of the fighting; (2) to offer Germany complete guarantees for her

---

3   Italy had declared war on France and England on 10 June 1940. Italy and France signed a separate
     armistice on 24 June 1940.
4   General Carl Heinrich v. Stülpnagel (1886–1944) chaired the German Armistice Commission and was
     Commander in Chief of the German armies in France from February 1942 to July 1944. He was
     executed on 30 August 1944 in the wake of the failed 20 July 1944 military revolt against Hitler.

continuation of the war against Britain; (3) to create the foundations for a peace, the basis of which is to be the reparation of an injustice inflicted upon Germany by force. The third point seems to mean: revenge for the defeat of 1918.

... The armistice negotiations began at three fifteen p.m. A warm June sun beat down on the great elm and pine trees, and cast pleasant shadows on the wooded avenues as Hitler, with the German plenipotentiaries at his side, appeared. He alighted from his car in front of the French monument to Alsace-Lorraine which stands at the end of an avenue about two hundred yards from the clearing where the armistice car waits on exactly the same spot it occupied twenty-two years ago.

The Alsace-Lorraine statue, I noted, was covered with German war flags so that you could not see its sculptured work nor read its inscription. But I had seen it some years before – the large sword representing the sword of the Allies, and its point sticking into a large, limp eagle, representing the old Empire of the Kaiser. And the inscription underneath in French saying: "TO THE HEROIC SOLDIERS OF FRANCE ... DEFENDERS OF THE COUNTRY AND OF RIGHT ... GLORIOUS LIBERATORS OF ALSACE-LORRAINE."

Through my glasses I saw the Führer stop, glance at the monument, observe the Reich flags with their big Swastikas in the center. Then he strode slowly towards us, towards the little clearing in the woods. I observed his face. It was grave, solemn, yet brimming with revenge. There was also in it, as in his springy step, a note of the triumphant conqueror, the defier of the world. There was something else, difficult to describe, in his expression, a sort of scornful, inner joy at being present at this great reversal of fate – a reversal he himself had wrought.

Now he reaches the little opening in the woods. He pauses and looks slowly around. The clearing is in the form of a circle some two hundred yards in diameter and laid out like a park. Cypress trees line it all round – and behind them, the great elms and oaks of the forest. This has been one of France's national shrines for twenty-two years. From a discreet position on the perimeter of the circle we watch.

Hitler pauses, and gazes slowly around. In a group just behind him are the other German plenipotentiaries: Goering, grasping his field-marshal's baton in one hand. He wears the sky-blue uniform of the air force. All the Germans are in uniform, Hitler in a double-breasted grey uniform, with the Iron Cross hanging from his left breast pocket. Next to Goering are the two German army chiefs – General [Wilhelm] Keitel, chief of the Supreme Command, and General [Walther] von Brauchitsch, commander-in-chief of the German army. Both are just approaching sixty, but look younger, especially Keitel, who has a dapper appearance with his cap slightly cocked on one side.

Then there is Dr. [Erich] Raeder, Grand Admiral of the German Fleet, in his blue naval uniform and the invariable upturned collar which German naval officers usually wear. There are two non-military men in Hitler's suite – his Foreign Minister, Joachim von Ribbentrop, in the field-grey uniform of the Foreign Office; and Rudolf Hess, Hitler's deputy, in a grey party uniform.

The time is now three eighteen p.m. Hitler's personal flag is run up on a small standard in the center of the opening.

Also in the center is a great granite block which stands some three feet above the ground. Hitler, followed by the others, walks slowly over to it, steps up, and reads the inscription engraved in great high letters on that block. It says: "HERE ON THE ELEVENTH OF NOVEMBER 1918 SUCCUMBED THE CRIMINAL PRIDE OF THE GERMAN EMPIRE ... VANQUISHED BY THE FREE PEOPLES WHICH IT TRIED TO ENSLAVE."

Hitler reads it and Goering reads it. They all read it, standing there in the June sun and the silence. I look for the expression on Hitler's face. I am but fifty yards from him and see him through my glasses as though he were directly in front of me. I have seen that face many times at the great moments of his life. But today! It is afire with scorn, anger, hate, revenge, triumph. He steps off the monument and contrives to make even this gesture a masterpiece of contempt. He glances back at it, contemptuous, angry – angry, you almost feel, because he cannot wipe out the awful, provoking lettering with one sweep of his Prussian boot. He glances slowly around the clearing, and now, as his eyes meet ours, you grasp the depth of his hatred. But there is triumph there too – revengeful, triumphant hate. Suddenly, as though his face were not giving quite complete expression to his feelings, he throws his whole body into harmony with his mood. He swiftly snaps his hands on his hips, arches his shoulders, plants his feet wide apart. It is a magnificent gesture of defiance, of burning contempt for this place now and all that it has stood for in the twenty-two years since it witnessed the humbling of the German Empire.

Finally Hitler leads his party over to another granite stone, a smaller one fifty yards to one side. Here it was that the railroad car in which the German plenipotentiaries stayed during the 1918 armistice was placed – from November 8 to 11. Hitler merely glances at the inscription, which reads: "The German Plenipotentiaries." The stone itself, I notice, is set between a pair of rusty old railroad tracks, the ones on which the German car stood twenty-two years ago. Off to one side along the edge of the clearing is a large statue in white stone of Marshal Foch as he looked when he stepped out of the armistice car on the morning of November 11, 1918. Hitler skips it; does not appear to see it.

It is now three twenty-three p.m. and the Germans stride over to the armistice car. For a moment or two they stand in the sunlight outside the car, chatting. Then Hitler steps up into the car, followed by the others. We can see nicely through the car windows. Hitler takes the place occupied by Marshal Foch when the 1918 armistice terms were signed. The others spread themselves around him. Four chairs on the opposite side of the table from Hitler remain empty. The French have not yet appeared. But we do not wait long. Exactly at three thirty p.m. they alight from a car. They have flown up from Bordeaux to a near-by landing field. They too glance at the Alsace-Lorraine memorial, but it's a swift glance. Then they walk down the avenue flanked by three German officers. We see them now as they come into the sunlight of the clearing.

General [Charles] Huntziger, wearing a bleached khaki uniform, Air General Bergeret and Vice-Admiral Le Luc, both in dark blue uniforms, and then, almost buried in the uniforms, M. Noël, French Ambassador to Poland. The German guard of honor, drawn up at the entrance to the clearing, snaps to attention for the French as they pass, but it does not present arms.

It is a grave hour in the life of France. The Frenchmen keep their eyes straight ahead. Their faces are solemn, drawn. They are the picture of tragic dignity.

They walk stiffly to the car, where they are met by two German officers, Lieutenant-General Tippelskirch, Quartermaster General, and Colonel Thomas, chief of the Führer's headquarters. The Germans salute. The French salute. The atmosphere is what Europeans call "correct." There are salutes, but no handshakes.

Now we get our picture through the dusty windows of that old *wagon-lit* car. Hitler and the other German leaders rise as the French enter the drawing-room. Hitler gives the Nazi salute, the arm raised. Ribbentrop and Hess do the same. I cannot see M. Noël to notice whether he salutes or not.

Hitler, as far as we can see through the windows, does not say a word to the French or to anybody else. He nods to General Keitel at his side. We see General Keitel adjusting his papers. Then he starts to read. He is reading the preamble to the German armistice terms. The French sit there with marble-like faces and listen intently. Hitler and Goering glance at the green table-top.

The reading of the preamble lasts but a few minutes. Hitler, we soon observe, has no intention of remaining very long, of listening to the reading of the armistice terms themselves. At three forty-two p.m., twelve minutes after the French arrive, we see Hitler stand up, salute stiffly, and then stride out of the drawing-room, followed by Goering, Brauchitsch, Raeder, Hess, and Ribbentrop. The French, like figures of stone, remain at the green-topped table. General Keitel remains with them. He starts to read them the detailed conditions of the armistice.

Hitler and his aides stride down the avenue towards the Alsace-Lorraine monument, where their cars are waiting. As they pass the guard of honor, the German band strikes up the two national anthems, *Deutschland, Deutschland über Alles* and the *Horst Wessel* song. The whole ceremony in which Hitler has reached a new pinnacle in his meteoric career and Germany avenged the 1918 defeat is over in a quarter of an hour.

Source: **William L. Shirer,** *Berlin Diary: The Journal of a Foreign Correspondent 1934–1941*
(New York: Alfred A. Knopf, 1941), pp. 419–25

Hitler's peace offer, July 1940

On 19 July 1940, three days after issuing a top secret directive to prepare a landing operation against England, Hitler once again offered to make peace, just as he had after the successful completion of the Polish campaign on 6 October 1939. Hitler's terms had not changed: British acceptance of Germany's continental domination and the return of Germany's pre-war colonies. In return Hitler promised to respect the integrity of the British Empire.

Peace with Britain would allow Hitler to accomplish his primary goal, the conquest of Lebensraum in the east. At the time of Hitler's first peace offer in October 1939, Churchill, a member of the cabinet but not yet prime minister, made the acid but accurate comment that Germany had been free to choose the time for the beginning of the war, but Hitler was not free to choose the time for its end. In July 1940, despite the threat of a German invasion, the British were even less inclined to accept a settlement that would leave Hitler's Germany in complete control of Europe. It was not just the desire to avoid humiliation that stiffened British resolve, but the long-term danger to democracy all over the world from any settlement that left Hitler the master of Europe. Although Britain could not have defeated Nazi Germany without the United States and the Soviet Union, Churchill's refusal to negotiate a settlement on Hitler's terms in the spring or summer of 1940 prevented Hitler from winning the war and dramatically improving his prospects of achieving his expansionist goals.

Hitler himself seemed to be aware that the terms he was offering had virtually no prospects of being accepted. His speech was primarily intended for domestic consumption. Hitler took full advantage of the celebratory mood that had gripped the country since the fall of France. He began his speech by reviewing the injustices of Versailles, blaming the English and the French for the start of the war, and exultantly recounting the course of German military successes. He announced the promotion of no fewer than twelve generals to the rank of field marshal. Goering, the only active field marshal up to then, received the newly created rank of Reich Marshal. Hitler's seemingly generous offer of peace to Britain was delivered in his usual aggressive, sarcastic tone. His real intention was to prepare the German people for the coming Battle of Britain. To maintain German morale for what promised to be a longer war than most Germans had anticipated, Hitler had to make what at least to loyal Germans seemed like a good-faith effort at peace.

5.5 Hitler's Reichstag speech, 19 July 1940

… When Marshal Pétain offered to lay down French arms, he did not lay down arms that he still held, but ended a situation that every soldier could recognize as untenable. Only the blood-drenched dilettantism of a Mr. Churchill could fail to understand this or try to deny this in spite of better knowledge.

[Hitler then recounted in detail Germany's military successes up to that point.]

As I now come to the end of this purely military summation of events, truth compels me to state the historic fact that none of this would have been possible without the staunch attitude of the home front – or without, most importantly, the founding, the work, and the activities of the National Socialist Party.

In the year 1919, at the time of our greatest decline, the Party already proclaimed as its goal the reconstruction of a German people's army and has advocated this goal with fanatical determination for decades. Without the Party's work all the preconditions for the resurrection of the German Reich and thus the creation of a German Wehrmacht would have been lacking. Above all, the Party also gave the struggle its ideological (weltanschaulich) foundation. To our democratic opponents' senseless sacrifice of life for the interests of their plutocracies we juxtapose the defense of a socially-minded people's community (Volksgemeinschaft). The work of the Party has therefore resulted in the unity between front and home front that unfortunately was lacking in the World War.

[Hitler then announced honors and promotions for leading Party officials and Wehrmacht officers before proceeding to his "peace offer."]

Ever since there has been a National Socialist regime, its foreign policy program has contained two goals:

1 The achievement of a true understanding and friendship with Italy and,
2 the achievement of the same relationship with England.

You, my Party comrades, know that these objectives already motivated me 20 years ago just as much as they did later. I have dealt with and defended these ideas innumerable times in publications and in talks, as long as I myself was still in the opposition in the democratic Republic. As soon as the German people entrusted me with their leadership, I immediately tried to realize this oldest goal of National Socialist foreign policy in practice. Even today I am still saddened that despite all my efforts I did not succeed in bringing about the friendship with England that, I believe, would have been a blessing for both peoples. And especially as I did not succeed despite my persistent and sincere efforts.

[Hitler then described Germany's good relations with Italy.]

Men of the German Reichstag, if I now speak about the future, then I do not do so to boast or to brag. I can safely leave that to others who probably need to do so more, as for example Mr. Churchill. I would like, without any exaggeration, to give a picture of the situation as it is and as I see it.

The course of this war for the past six months has proved my conception to be right and the views of our opponents to be wrong.

When so-called English statesmen assure us that their country emerges stronger from every defeat and failure, then it is certainly not arrogance on my part when I hereby inform you that we have emerged strengthened from our successes.

[Hitler then discussed German advantages in weaponry, ammunition, raw materials, popular morale, and strategic situation, especially the friendship with Russia.]

England's hope, however, to alleviate its own situation by bringing about some new European crisis is a fallacy, insofar as Germany's relationship with Russia is concerned. Although the British statesmen see everything more slowly, they will yet come to understand this in the course of time.

It now is clear that in my speech on 6 October 1939 I correctly foretold the further development of this war. I assured you, my Deputies, that I could not for a moment doubt our victory. Unless one happens to see in defeats the signs and guarantees of final victory, I believe that developments up to now have proven me right. In spite of the fact that I was quite sure about these developments, I offered France and England my hand for an understanding at the time. You will still recall the answer I received. All my arguments on the nonsense of continuing this war, on the certainty that even in the most favorable case they would reap not victory, but casualties, were dismissed with mockery and disdain or simply ignored.

At that time I assured you that I feared, because of my peace offer, to be decried as a yellow-belly who did not want to fight any longer because he was not able to fight any longer. Exactly this happened. I do believe, however, that France – less the guilty statesmen than the people, of course – thinks differently about this October 6 today. What unspeakable misery has befallen this great country and people since then ...

From London I now only hear cries – not the cries of the masses, but of the politicians – to continue the war now all the more.

I do not know whether these politicians already have the right notion of what a continuation of this war will bring. They do declare that they will continue this war, and, if England goes to ruin as a result, they will continue it from Canada. I hardly believe that this means the people will be going to Canada; rather it will probably be the war profiteers who will retreat to Canada. The people, I believe, will have to remain in England. And they will surely view the war with different eyes than their so-called leaders in Canada.

Believe me, members of the Reichstag, I feel an inner disgust at this sort of unconscionable parliamentary destroyer of peoples and states. It almost hurts me that fate has chosen me to give a shove to what these people have brought to the point of falling. For my intention was not to wage war but to construct a new socially-minded state of the highest culture.

Every year of this war robs me of my work. And the ones who cause me to be robbed are ridiculous ciphers whom one can only call assembly-line products of nature, insofar as they do not derive some special distinction from their venal corruption.

Mr. Churchill has just declared again that he wants the war. About six weeks ago he began war in an arena in which he apparently believes he is particularly strong, the air war against the civilian population, albeit under the pretext of hitting so-called war-related objectives. Ever since Freiburg,[5] these objectives have been open cities, market places, peasant villages, residences, hospitals, schools, kindergartens and whatever else gets hit.

Up to now I have hardly responded. But this does not mean that this is our only possible response or will remain the only one.

I am quite aware of the fact that from our response, which will come at some time, nameless suffering and misfortune will descend upon people. Not on Mr. Churchill, of course, for he will surely be sitting in Canada, where the property and children of the leading war profiteers have already been brought. But for millions of other people great suffering will result. And Mr. Churchill should perhaps believe me just this once when I now make the following prophecy:

5   The southwestern city of Freiburg near the French border was bombed on 10 May 1940, possibly by German planes.

A great world empire will be destroyed, a world empire which it was never my intention to destroy or damage. But I am fully aware that the continuation of this war will only end with the complete destruction of one of the two warring parties. Mr. Churchill may believe that this will be Germany. I know it will be England.

At this hour I feel obligated by conscience to direct one more appeal of reason to England. I believe I am entitled to do this, because I am not asking for something as the vanquished but am speaking for reason as the victor. I see no reason that should compel us to continue this war.

I regret the sacrifices it will demand. I would like to avert them from my own people as well. I know that millions of German men and youths are aglow at the prospect of finally being able to fight the enemy, who for the second time has declared war on us without any reason …

Mr. Churchill might again dismiss my declaration with the yowl that this is just the offspring of my fear and my doubt about final victory. At any rate I will have relieved my conscience about the things to come …

Source: Deutsches Nachrichtenbüro, 19 July 1940.
Translated by Rod Stackelberg

The failure of Operation Sea Lion, Summer 1940

The fall of France marked the high point of German fortunes and Hitler's career. Germany appeared to have won the war. But Britain remained defiant. Winston Churchill (1874–1965), who had replaced Chamberlain as prime minister on 10 May, persuaded his war cabinet, including Chamberlain and the appeasement-minded Lord Halifax, not to accept Hitler's terms. With a peace settlement unattainable on German terms and a successful invasion of England dependent on control of the air, Hitler turned to another option: a surprise attack on the Soviet Union even before the end of the war against Britain. On 31 July 1940 he discussed this option with his leading generals, as recorded by General Halder below. Although Hitler had his doubts about the feasibility of an invasion of the British Isles, at this point he still hoped to end the war with Britain before launching the attack on Russia.

Throughout the summer of 1940 the air war known as the "Battle of Britain" raged. Failure of the German Air Force to establish air supremacy forced a suspension of plans to invade Britain, code-named "Operation Sea Lion," in early September. Halder's diary shows that army and navy leaders disagreed on the site, extent, and feasibility of the landing. The army was unwilling to risk a landing attempt without full control of the air or the sea. Halder was also critical of the passive role of the High Command (OKW) in planning the operation.

5.6 The Halder War Diary, 1940

31 JULY 1940

Führer:

(a) Stresses his skepticism regarding technical feasibility [of Operation Sea Lion]; however, satisfied with results produced by Navy.

(b) Emphasizes weather factor.
(c) Discusses enemy resources for counteraction. Our small Navy is only 15% of enemy's; 8% of enemy's destroyers; 10–12% of his motor torpedo boats. So we have nothing to bring into action against enemy surface attacks. That leaves mines (not 100% reliable), coastal artillery (good!) and Air Force.

　　In any decision we must bear in mind that we do not take risks for nothing.
(d) In the event that invasion does not take place, our action must be directed to eliminate all factors that let England hope for a change in the situation. To all intents and purposes, the war is won. France has stepped out of the set-up protecting British convoys. Italy is pinning down British forces.

　　Submarine and air warfare may bring about a final decision, but this may be one or two years off.

Britain's hope lies in Russia and the United States. If Russia drops out of the picture, America, too, is lost for Britain, because elimination of Russia would tremendously increase *Japan's power* in the Far East.

Russia is the Far Eastern sword of Britain and the United States pointed at Japan. Here, an evil wind is blowing for Britain. Japan, like Russia, has her program which she wants to carry through before the end of the war.

[Marginal note:] The Russian victory film on the Russo-Finnish War!

Russia is the factor on which Britain is relying the most. Something must have happened in London! The British were completely down; now they have perked up again. Intercepted telephone conversations. Russia is painfully shaken by the swift development of the Western European situation.

All that Russia has to do is to hint that it does not care to have a strong Germany, and the British will take hope, like one about to go under, that the situation will undergo a radical change within six or eight months.

With Russia smashed, Britain's last hope would be shattered. Germany then will be master of Europe and the Balkans.

Decision: Russia's destruction must therefore be made a part of this struggle. Spring 1941.

The sooner Russia is crushed, the better. Attack achieves its purpose only if Russian State can be shattered to its roots with one blow. Holding part of the country alone will not do. Standing still in the winter would be perilous. So it is better to wait a little longer, but with the resolute determination to eliminate Russia. This is necessary also because of situation on the Baltic Sea. It is awkward to have another major power there. If we start in May 1941, we would have five months to finish the job in. Tackling it this year would have been best, but unified action would be impossible at this time.

Objective is destruction of Russian manpower. Operation will be divided into three actions:

First thrust: Kiev and securing flank protection on Dnieper. Air Force will destroy river crossings. Odessa.

Second thrust: Baltic states and drive on Moscow.

Finally: Link-up of northern and southern prongs.

Later: Limited drive on Baku oil fields.

It will be seen later to what extent Finland and Turkey should be brought in.

Later: Ukraine, White Russia, Baltic states to us. Finland extended to the White Sea.

6 AUGUST 1940

[General] *v. Greiffenberg* – [Colonel] *v. Witzleben*: Discussion of points which have to be cleared up with Navy.

Information brought by von Witzleben shows that Navy insists on landing to be made on narrowest frontage.

Plans of this sort are undebatable because success of landing operation cannot be assured on so narrow a frontage.

Moreover, Navy asserts that inasmuch as weather conditions and postponement of large-scale Air Force operations have delayed start of mine sweeping, 15 Sep date for jump-off has already been jeopardized.

We have the paradoxical situation where the Navy is full of misgivings, the Air Force is very reluctant to tackle a mission which at the outset is exclusively its own, and OKW [Wehrmacht High Command], which for once has a real combined forces operation to direct, just plays dead. The only driving force in the whole situation comes from us, but alone we would not be able to swing it, either.

7 AUGUST 1940

Conference with OKM [Naval High Command]; [Admiral] Schniewind, [Admiral] Fricke, [General] Reinhardt.

Conference results merely in confirming the existence of irreconcilable differences between us. Navy maintains that landing is possible only on narrowest frontage, between Folkestone and Beachy Head, and feels confident of being able to assure a continuous shuttle service to the beach-head. However, this front would be too narrow for us, all the more so as it leads into a terrain that offers backbreaking obstacles to any swift advance. A landing between Folkestone and Ramsgate is held practicable by Navy only after coastal defenses have been rolled up from the landside. Navy opposes any westward extension of the assault front out of fear of Portsmouth and the British High Seas Fleet. There could be no adequate air defense against these threats.

In view of the limited transport resources, completion of the cross-Channel operation on a broader frontage would take 42 days, which is utterly prohibitive for us. Our views are diametrically opposed on that point. The issue must therefore be settled on higher level.

Source: **Office of the Chief of Counsel for War Crimes,** *The Halder Diaries: The Private War Journals of General Franz Halder* **(Nuremberg: Office of Military Government [US], 1948).**
German version: Generaloberst Halder, *Kriegstagebuch: Tägliche Aufzeichnungen des Chefs des Generalstabes des Heeres 1939–1942*, ed. by Hans-Adolf Jacobsen with Alfred Philippi, Vol. 1, *Vom Polenfeldzug bis zum Ende der Westoffensive* (14. 8. 1939–30. 6. 1940) (Stuttgart: W. Kohlhammer, 1962), pp. 318–19, 336–7, 366–7; Vol. 2, *Von der geplanten Landung in England bis zum Beginn des Ostfeldzuges* (1. 7. 1940–21. 6. 1941) (Stuttgart: W. Kohlhammer, 1963), pp. 48–50, 57–8

The Tripartite Pact

Through the Tripartite Pact Japan became the third member of the military alliance previously formed between Germany and Italy in the so-called Pact of Steel (May 1939). Under Article 3 the Tripartite Pact committed each of the signatory states to come to the aid of the other in case any one of them was attacked by a country not presently involved in the war. The pact was primarily designed to deter the United States from entering the war. Article 5 was added to assuage Soviet fears that the pact might be directed against them. After the Japanese attack on Pearl Harbor, Germany honored its commitment to Japan by declaring war on the US (Doc. 5.19), even though they were not technically obligated to do so under the terms of the Pact.

5.7 Three-power pact between Germany, Italy, and Japan, 27 September 1940

The governments of Germany, Italy, and Japan consider it as a condition precedent of a lasting peace that each nation be given its own proper place. They have therefore decided to stand together and to cooperate with one another in their efforts in Greater East Asia and in the regions of Europe wherein it is their prime purpose to establish and maintain a new order of things calculated to promote the prosperity and welfare of the peoples there. Furthermore, it is the desire of the three Governments to extend this cooperation to such nations in other parts of the world as are inclined to give their endeavors a direction similar to their own, in order that their aspirations towards world peace as the ultimate goal may thus be realized. Accordingly, the governments of Germany, Italy, and Japan have agreed as follows:

ARTICLE 1

Japan recognizes and respects the leadershp of Germany and Italy in the establishment of a new order in Europe.

ARTICLE 2

Germany and Italy recognize and respect the leadership of Japan in the establishment of a new order in Greater East Asia.

ARTICLE 3

Germany, Italy, and Japan agree to cooperate in their efforts on the aforesaid basis. They further undertake to assist one another with all political, economic, and military means, if one of the three contracting parties is attacked by a power at present not involved in the European war or in the Chinese–Japanese conflict.

ARTICLE 4

For the purpose of implementing the present pacts, joint technical commissions, the members of which are to be appointed by the governments of Germany, Italy, and Japan, will meet without delay.

ARTICLE 5

Germany, Italy, and Japan affirm that the aforesaid terms do not in any way affect the political status which exists at present between each of the three contracting parties and Soviet Russia.

ARTICLE 6

The present Pact shall come into force immediately upon signature and shall remain in force for ten years from the date of its coming into force.

At the proper time before expiration of the said term the high contracting parties shall, if one of them so requests, enter into negotiations for its renewal.

In faith whereof, the undersigned, duly authorized by their governments, have signed this pact and have hereunto apposed their seals.

Done in three original copies at Berlin, on the 27th day of September, 1940, in the XVIIIth year of the Fascist Era, corresponding to the 27th day of the 9th month of the 15th year of the Showa era.

Joachim von Ribbentrop
Ciano
[Signature of the Japanese Representative]

Source: Office of the US Chief of Counsel for Prosecution of Axis Criminality,
Nazi Conspiracy and Aggression, **Vol. V**
(Washington DC: US Government Printing Office, 1946), pp. 355–7 [Doc. 2643-PS]

Germanization of areas annexed from Poland

After the conquest of Poland substantial areas in the north and west were directly annexed to the Reich. These areas, which considerably exceeded the borders of the German Empire in 1914 and included some territory previously part of the Austro-Hungarian Empire, were called the Incorporated Eastern Territories to distinguish them from the remainder of occupied Poland, referred to as the General Government (*Generalgouvernement*). Nazi plans called for the expulsion of ethnic Poles from the Incorporated Territories into the *Generalgouvernement* to make way for the settlement of ethnic Germans, including those displaced from the Baltic states when these fell to the Soviets as a result of the Nazi–Soviet Non-Aggression Pact. The Incorporated Territories included many people of mixed ethnic descent. The Nazis tried to "re-Germanize" Poles of ethnically German background.

This task was superintended by SS chief Heinrich Himmler, whose many offices included that of Reich Commissioner for the Strengthening of German Ethnicity (*Reichskommissar für die Festigung deutschen Volkstums*). Under this program of "re-

Germanization" Polish children with Nordic traits were removed from their parents and brought up as Germans in German institutions. The Nazis' ultimate goal was a racially homogeneous German population ready to colonize and "Germanize" living space in the east conquered by the Wehrmacht. The following selection is taken from a publication of the Office of the Reich Commissioner for the Strengthening of German Ethnicity in December 1940, six months before the invasion of the Soviet Union.

5.8 Re-Germanization of lost German blood, December 1940

INTEGRATION OF POLES QUALIFIED FOR RE-GERMANIZATION

The removal of foreign races from the Incorporated Eastern Territories is one of the most essential goals to be accomplished in the German East. This is the chief *national political* task that has to be executed in the Incorporated Eastern Territories by the Reichsführer SS, Reich Commissioner for the Strengthening of the National Character of the German People. In solving this question, which is most closely connected with the ethnic problem in the Eastern Territories, the racial problem is of the utmost and decisive importance, next to the aspects of language, education, and confession. As necessary as it is, in the interest of a permanent solution for the German Eastern Territories, that the elements there of foreign descent should not be allowed to have or to take up their permanent residence there, so it is indispensable, too, that persons of German blood in these territories must be regained for the German nation, even if those of German blood are Polonized as far as their confession and language is concerned. Just from these people of German blood the former Polish state obtained those leaders who eventually showed a violently hostile attitude against their own German people, be it through delusion, be it through a desired or unconscious misconception of their ties of blood.

Therefore, it is an absolute *national political* necessity to comb out those of German blood in the Incorporated Eastern Territories and later also in the General Government and to return the lost German blood to its own German people. It is, perhaps, of secondary importance what kind of measures are to be taken against renegades. It is critical that at least their children do not devolve anymore to the Poles, but are brought up in a German environment. The re-Germanization, however, can under no circumstance be carried out in former Polish environments and can only be effected in the old German Reich or in the Ostmark [Austria].

Thus, there are the following two primary reasons that make the regaining of lost German blood an urgent necessity.

1   Prevention of a further increase of the Polish intelligentsia through families of German descent even if they are Polonized.
2   Increase of the population by racial elements desirable for the German nation, and the acquisition of ethno-biologically unobjectionable forces for the German reconstruction of agriculture and industry. The task of the re-Germanization of the last German blood has been embarked upon next within the framework of the evacuation of those Poles in

the Warthegau [Incorporated Territories] who had to make room for the resettlement of Baltic and Wolhynien-Germans.

Source: Office of the Chief of Counsel for Prosecution of Axis Criminality,
Nazi Conspiracy and Aggression, **Vol. V**
(Washington DC: US Government Printing Office, 1946), pp. 581–2 [Doc. 2915-PS]

Hitler's long-term plans: an American view, December 1940

Five days before leaving Germany for good, the strongly anti-Nazi American radio correspondent William L. Shirer reflected in his diary on the likelihood of a war between Nazi Germany and the US. With considerable prescience, given the fact that his book went to press in April 1941 and was published in June 1941, Shirer predicted both a German attack on Russia and a declaration of war against the US. In December 1940, shortly after his reelection to a third term, President Roosevelt moved toward greater American involvement on the side of Britain, but he had to proceed warily in view of strong isolationist sentiment in the US. American isolationism bore some resemblance to pre-war appeasement in Britain in that isolationists rejected any intervention that might involve the US in war with Nazi Germany.

5.9 William L. Shirer, *Berlin Diary*

DECEMBER 1, 1940

... There is one final question to be tackled in these rambling conclusions: does Hitler contemplate war with the United States? I have argued this question many hours with many Germans and not a few Americans here and have pondered it long and carefully. I am firmly convinced that he does contemplate it and that if he wins in Europe and Africa he will in the end launch it unless we are prepared to give up our way of life and adapt ourselves to a subservient place in his totalitarian scheme of things.

For to Hitler there will not be room in this small world for two great systems of life, government, and trade. For this reason I think he also will attack Russia, probably before he tackles the Americas.

It is not only a question of conflict between the totalitarian and democratic ways of life, but also between Pan-German imperialism, whose aim is world domination, and the fundamental urge of most of the other nations on the earth to live as they please – that is, free and independent.

And just as Hitler's Germany can never dominate the continent of Europe as long as Britain holds out, neither can it master the world as long as the United States stands unafraid in its path. It is a long-term fundamental conflict of dynamic forces. The clash is as inevitable as that of two planets hurtling inexorably through the heavens towards each other.

As a matter of fact, it may come sooner than almost all Americans at home imagine. An officer of the High Command somewhat shocked me the other day while we were discussing the matter. He said: "You think Roosevelt can pick the moment most advantageous to America and Britain for coming into the war. Did you ever stop to think that Hitler, a master at timing, may choose the moment for war with America – a moment which he thinks will give him the advantage?"

I must admit I never did.

As far as I can learn, Hitler and the High Command do not contemplate any such move within the next few months. They still hold that they can bring Britain to her knees before American aid becomes really effective. They talk now of winning the war by the middle of next summer, at the latest. But there are a few in high places who argue that if Hitler actually declares war (he hasn't *declared* any wars yet) against America, he can reap decided advantages. First, it would be the signal for widespread sabotage by thousands of Nazi agents from coast to coast, which would not only demoralize the United States but greatly reduce its shipments to Britain. Second, in case of an actual declaration of war, they argue, our army and especially our navy, alarmed at what Japan might do (according to the tripartite pact it would have to go to war against us), would hold all war supplies at home, supplies that otherwise would go to Britain. Third, they believe that there would be a great increase in American internal strife, with the isolationists blaming Roosevelt for the state of things, as they blamed him for the Three-Power pact. The third point obviously is false thinking, as a war declaration by Germany would destroy American isolationist sentiment in America in ten seconds.

The Lindberghs and their friends laugh at the idea of Germany ever being able to attack the United States.[6] The Germans welcome their laughter and hope more Americans will laugh, just as they encouraged the British friends of the Lindberghs to laugh off the very idea that Germany would ever turn on Britain.

How would Germany ever attack the United States? I have no authoritative information of German military plans. But I have heard Germans suggest the following possibilities:

If they get all or part of the British navy or have time to build in Europe's shipyards (whose total capacity is far beyond ours) a fairly strong navy, they would attempt to destroy in the Atlantic that part of our fleet which was not engaging the Japanese in the Pacific. This done, they could move an army and air force in stages across the North Atlantic, basing first on Iceland, then Greenland, then Labrador, then Newfoundland and thence down the Atlantic seaboard. As the bases were moved westward, the air armada would penetrate farther, first towards and then into the United States. This sounds fantastic, perhaps, but at the present time we have no great air force to oppose such a move.

Most Germans talk more convincingly of a move across the South Atlantic. They assume that Germany will have the French port of Dakar [in the French West African colony of Senegal] from which to jump off for South America. They assume too that the main United States fleet will be engaged in the Pacific. From Dakar to Brazil is a much shorter distance than from Hampton Roads [i.e., the US naval station at Norfolk, VA] to Brazil. A German naval force based on the African port could feasibly operate in Brazilian waters, but these waters are almost too far for an American fleet to be effective in. Transports could get there from Dakar before transports from America arrived. Fifth-column action by the hundreds of thousands of Germans in Brazil and Argentina would paralyze any defense

---

6   The aviator Charles A. Lindbergh (1902–74) was a leading member of the America First Committee, an isolationist group that sought to mobilize public opinion in the US against intervention in the European war. America Firsters did not see Nazi Germany as a threat to the US. The Committee, which opposed Roosevelt's pro-British policies, was disbanded after Pearl Harbor.

which those countries might try to put up. South America could thus, think these Germans, be taken fairly easily. And once in South America, they argue, the battle is won.

Source: William L. Shirer, *Berlin Diary: The Journal of a Foreign Correspondent 1934–1941*
(New York: Alfred A. Knopf, 1941), pp. 591–4

Plans for the invasion of the Soviet Union

After the failure of the Luftwaffe to achieve air superiority in the Battle of Britain, the Nazis were forced to suspend plans for the invasion of Britain. Hitler was also unsuccessful in his efforts to persuade Spain and/or the Soviet Union to actively join in the war against Britain. He then turned to his initial option, a surprise attack on his treaty partner, the Soviet Union (see Doc. 5.6). Although war against Soviet Russia had always been part of his long-range plan for conquest of *Lebensraum*, already announced in *Mein Kampf* (Doc. 2.15), his original intention was to first bring the war against Britain to a successful conclusion. In December 1940, against the better judgement of Navy chief Grand Admiral Erich Raeder (1876–1960), he decided to reverse these priorities. His decision was based on the expectation of a rapid victory over the USSR. This was the war Hitler had always wanted to fight. Elimination of Soviet power would achieve his most important goals: continental dominance, the conquest of territory for German settlement, and the destruction of communism. It would also greatly strengthen the German position in the struggle for world power with Britain and the United States.

5.10 Directive for Operation Barbarossa, 18 December 1940

SECRET

The Führer's Headquarters, 18 December 1940

The German Armed Forces must be prepared *to crush Soviet Russia in a quick campaign* before the end of the war against England (Operation Barbarossa).

For this purpose the *army* will have to employ all available units with the reservation that the occupied territories will have to be safeguarded against surprise attacks.

For the Eastern campaign the *air force* will have to free such strong forces for the support of the army that a rapid completion of the ground operations may be expected and that damage to the eastern German territories through enemy air attacks will be avoided as much as possible. This concentration of the main effort in the East is limited by the following reservation: That the entire battle and armament area dominated by us must remain sufficiently protected against enemy air attacks, and the attacks on England and especially the supplies for them must not be permitted to break down.

Concentration of the main effort of the *navy* remains unequivocally against England also during an Eastern campaign.

Should the occasion arise I will order the concentration of troops for action against Soviet Russia eight weeks before the intended commencement of operations.

Preparations requiring a longer time period are to begin presently – if they have not already done so – and are to be completed by 15 May 1941.

Great caution, however, is to be taken that the intention of an attack will not be recognized.

The preparations of the High Commands are to be made on the following basis:

I. GENERAL PURPOSE

The mass of the Russian army in western Russia is to be destroyed in bold operations by driving forward deep wedges with tanks, and the retreat of intact battle-ready troops into the wide spaces of Russia is to be prevented.

In quick pursuit a line is to be reached from where the Russian air force will no longer be able to attack German territory. The final goal of the operation is the protection from Asiatic Russia along the general line Volga–Archangelsk. If necessary, the last industrial area in the Urals left to Russia could be eliminated by the Luftwaffe.

In the course of these operations the Russian Baltic Sea fleet will quickly lose its bases and will then no longer be able to fight.

Effective intervention by the Russian air force is to be prevented through forceful blows at the start of operations.

II. PROBABLE ALLIES AND THEIR TASKS

1   On the flanks of our operation we can expect the active participation of *Romania* and *Finland* in the war against Soviet Russia.

In what form the armed forces of both countries will be subordinated to German command will be negotiated and arranged by the High Command of the Wehrmacht in due time.

2   It will be the task of Romania, together with the forces concentrated there, to pin down the opponent on the other side and, in addition, to render auxiliary services in the rear area.

3   Finland will cover the deployment of the German northern army group coming from Norway and will coordinate operations with them. Besides this, the task of eliminating [the Soviet base at] Hanko will fall to Finland.

4   It is probable that Swedish railways and roads will be available for the deployment of the German northern troops at the latest at the start of operations.

[Part III provides more detailed instructions on the conduct of operations against the Soviet Union.]

IV.

It must be clearly understood that all orders given by the commanders-in-chief on the basis of this directive are to be presented as *precautionary measures* in case Russia should change its present attitude toward us. The number of officers to be drafted for these preparations at an early time is to be kept as small as possible. Further collaborators are to be involved in the project as late as possible and only to the extent needed by each individual for his specific task. Otherwise, the danger exists that our preparations (the date of their going into effect not even having been fixed yet) will become known and thereby grave political and military disadvantages would result.

V.

I am expecting the reports of the commanders-in-chief on their further plans based on this directive.

The preparations planned by all branches of the Wehrmacht, as well as the projected time-line, are to be reported to me through the High Command.

[signed] Hitler

(Initialed by Keitel, Jodl, Warlimont, and v. Lossberg)

Source: Office of the US Chief of Counsel for Prosecution of Axis Criminality,
Nazi Conspiracy and Aggression, **Vol. III**
(Washington DC: US Government Printing Office, 1946), pp. 407–9 [Doc. 446-PS]

Plans for a war of extermination

In the following selection from his war diary Army Chief of Staff Franz Halder recorded Hitler's instructions to his generals on how he wished the campaign against the Soviet Union to be conducted. In contrast to the war in the west, in which the Germans adhered to the Geneva conventions on treatment of war prisoners, the war in the east was to be an ideological war fought with no holds barred.

5.11 The Halder War Diary, 1941

30 MARCH 1941

Meeting with *Führer*. ...

Clash of two ideologies. Crushing denunciation of Bolshevism, identified with asocial criminality. Bolshevism is an enormous danger for our future. We must forget the concept of comradeship between soldiers. A Communist is no comrade before nor after the battle. This is a war of extermination. If we do not grasp this, we shall still beat the enemy, but 30 years later we shall again have to fight the Communist foe. We do not wage war to preserve the enemy.

Future structure of states: Northern Russia goes to Finland. Protectorates: Baltic States, Ukraine, White Russia.

War against Russia: Extermination of the Bolshevist Commissars and of the Communist intelligentsia. The new states must be socialist, but without new intellectual classes of their own. Growth of a new intellectual class must be prevented. A primitive socialist intelligentsia is all that is needed. We must fight against the poison of subversion. This is no job for military courts. The individual troop commanders must know the issues at stake. They must be leaders in this fight. The troops must defend themselves with the methods with which they are attacked. Commissars and GPU [Soviet secret service] men are criminals and must be dealt with as such. This need not mean that the troops should get out of hand. Rather, the commander must give orders that express the common feelings of his men.

This war will be very different from the war in the West. In the East, harshness today means lenience in the future. Commanders must make the sacrifice of overcoming their personal scruples. [Marginal note:] Embody in ObdH [Army High Command] order.

Source: Office of the Chief of Counsel for War Crimes, *The Halder Diaries:*
The Private War Journals of General Franz Halder
(Nuremberg: Office of Military Government for Germany [US], 1948).
German version: Generaloberst Halder, *Kriegstagebuch*, Vol. 2,
Von der geplanten Landung in England bis zum Beginn des Ostfeldzuges [1. 7. 1940–21. 6. 1941,
ed. by Hans-Adolf Jacobsen (Stuttgart: W. Kohlhammer Verlag, 1963), pp. 336–7

The "Commissar Decree"

The war against the Soviet Union was planned from the start to be a racial and ideological war with no holds barred. The Commissar's Decree, signed for the Chief of the OKW Wilhelm Keitel by his subordinate, Major General Walter Warlimont (1894–1976), called for the immediate execution of all captured communist commissars, Soviet officers attached to troop units for the task of political indoctrination. The Nazis justified this violation of international law on the spurious grounds of preemptive self-defense: the Soviet Union had not signed the Geneva Convention on the treatment of prisoners of war and the Soviets could therefore be expected to kill and mistreat captured German soldiers. The Germans' draconian treatment of Soviet prisoners of war (see Doc. 5.21) – like their oppressive occupation policies – was self-defeating, however, as it encouraged fanatical Soviet resistance and invited retaliation against Germans who fell into Soviet hands. It is estimated that over 40 million people, four-fifths of them civilians, were killed in the savage war in the East.

5.12 The Commissar Decree, 6 June 1941

OKW Operations Staff/Section L (IV/Qu)   Führer H.Q. 6.6.41
No. 44822//41 TOP SECRET   [stamped] TOP SECRET
                                                By hand of officer only!

Further to the Führer decree of 14 May regarding the exercise of military jurisdiction in the area of "Barbarossa" ... , the attached document, "General Instructions on the Treatment of Political Commissars," is circulated herewith. You are requested to limit its distribution to the Commanders of Armies and Air Force and to arrange for its further oral communication to lower commands.

Chief of the High Command of the Wehrmacht (OKW)
[signed] Warlimont

INSTRUCTIONS ON THE TREATMENT OF POLITICAL COMMISSARS

In the struggle against Bolshevism, we must *not* assume that the enemy's conduct will be based on principles of humanity or of international law. In particular, hate-inspired, cruel, and inhuman treatment of prisoners can be expected on the part of *all ranks of political commissars*, who are the real leaders of resistance.

The attention of all units must be drawn to the following:

1   To show consideration to these elements during this struggle or to act in accordance with international rules of war is wrong and endangers both our own security and the rapid pacification of conquered territory.
2   Political Commissars have initiated barbaric, Asiatic methods of warfare. Consequently they will be dealt with *immediately* and with maximum severity. As a matter of principle they will be shot at once whether captured *during operations or otherwise showing resistance.*

The following regulations will apply:

I. THEATER OF OPERATIONS

1   Political commissars *who oppose our forces* will be treated in accordance with the decree on "The Exercise of Military Law in the Area of Barbarossa." This applies to every kind and rank of Commissar even if only suspected of resistance or sabotage or incitement to resist. In this connection see "General Instructions on the Conduct of Troops in Russia."
2   Political commissars *serving with enemy forces* are recognizable by their distinctive insignia – a red star interwoven with a hammer and sickle on the sleeve band (see details in "Armed Forces of the USSR" ...). On capture they will be immediately separated from other prisoners on the field of battle. This is essential to prevent them from influencing in any way the other prisoners. Commissars will not be treated as soldiers. The protection afforded by international law to prisoners of war will not apply in their case. After they have been segregated they will be liquidated.
3   *Political commissars* who are *neither guilty nor suspected of being guilty* of hostile actions will be initially exempt from the above measures. Only as our forces penetrate further into the country will it be possible to decide whether remaining officials should be allowed to stay where they are or whether they should be handed over to the *Sonderkommandos* [special units], who should where possible carry out the investigation themselves. In reaching a verdict of "guilty or not guilty," greater attention will be paid to the character and bearing of the commissar in question than to his offence, for which corroborative evidence may not be forthcoming.
4   Under 1. and 2. a short report (on a report form) on the case will be forwarded

    (a) by divisional units to divisional headquarters (Intelligence Section)
    (b) by units directly subordinate to a Corps, Army Group, or Armored Group to the Intelligence Section at Corps or higher headquarters.

5   None of the above measure must be allowed to interfere with operations. Systematic screening and cleansing operations by combat units will therefore not take place.

II. IN THE COMMUNICATIONS ZONE

Commissars who are apprehended in the rear areas for acting in a suspicious manner will be handed over to the *Einsatzgruppen* or *Einsatzkommandos* of the SD.

III. MODIFICATION OF GENERAL AND REGIMENTAL COURTS MARTIAL

General and regimental courts martial will not be responsible for carrying out the measures in Sections I and II.

[The distribution list for the High Command of the Army (OKH) follows.]

**Source: Doc. NOKW–1076 (*Anatomie des SS-Staates*, Vol. 2, ed. by Martin Broszat,
Hans-Adolf Jacobsen, and Helmut Krausnick [Munich: Deutscher Taschenbuchverlag, 1967],
pp. 188–91 [originally published Olten: Walter-Verlag, 1965].
(English translation: H. Krausnick, Hans Buchheim, M. Broszat, H-A Jacobsen,
Anatomy of the SS State, trsl. by Richard Barry, Marian Jackson, and Dorothy Long
[New York: Walker & Co., 1968], pp. 532–4)**

Hitler's motives for the attack on the Soviet Union

The invasion of the Soviet Union, originally set for May 1941, was delayed until 22 June because of the need to pacify the Balkans before the start of the eastern campaign. In October 1940, without consulting the German leadership, Mussolini had launched an attack on Greece from Albania, which the Italians had held since 1939. Strong Greek resistance to the Italian invasion and an anti-German rebellion in Yugoslavia led to German intervention in April 1941. From bases in Hungary, Romania, and Bulgaria, all allied with Germany by now, German forces conquered both Yugoslavia and Greece within three weeks. The Balkan campaign, however, delayed the start of "Operation Barbarossa," a delay that contributed to the failure of the Wehrmacht to vanquish the Red Army before the onset of severe winter weather in November 1941.

Hitler's letter to Mussolini on 21 June 1941, announcing the impending attack on the Soviet Union, provides some insight into his motives for launching the attack at this stage of the war. He believed that only elimination of the Soviet Union as a potential threat to Germany would persuade Britain to come to terms. If German victory in the east failed to bring Britain to the peace table, then control of the Soviet Union's vast territories and resources would put Germany in a favorable position for the inevitable global show-down with the Anglo-American powers. In his last paragraph Hitler also acknowledged his anti-communist motive. The decision to end the unnatural partnership with the USSR made him feel "spiritually free."

5.13 Hitler's letter to Mussolini, 21 June 1941

Duce!

I am writing this letter to you at a moment when months of anxious deliberations and continuous nerve-wracking waiting are ending in the hardest decision of my life.

The situation: England has lost this war. Like a drowning person, she grasps at every straw. Nevertheless, some of her hopes are naturally not without a certain logic ... The destruction of France ... has directed the glances of the British warmongers continually to the place from which they tried to start the war: to Soviet Russia.

Both countries, Soviet Russia and England, are equally interested in a Europe ... rendered prostrate by a long war. Behind these two countries stands the North American Union goading them on ...

Really, all available Russian forces are at our border ... If circumstances should give me cause to employ the German Air Force against England, there is danger that Russia will then begin its strategy of extortion, to which I would have to yield in silence simply from a feeling of air inferiority ... England will be all the less ready for peace, for it will be able to pin its hopes on the Russian partner. Indeed this hope must naturally grow with the progress in preparedness of the Russian armed forces. And behind this is the mass delivery of war material from America which they hope to get in 1942 ...

I have therefore, after constantly racking my brains, finally reached the decision to cut the noose before it can be drawn tight ... My overall view is now as follows:

1   *France* is, as ever, not to be trusted.
2   *North Africa* itself, insofar as your colonies, Duce, are concerned, is probably out of danger until fall.
3   *Spain* is irresolute and – I am afraid – will take sides only when the outcome of the war is decided ...
5   An attack on *Egypt* before August is out of the question ...
6   Whether or not *America* enters the war is a matter of indifference, inasmuch as she supports our enemy with all the power she is able to mobilize.
7   The situation in England itself is bad; the provision of food and raw materials is growing steadily more difficult. The martial spirit to make war, after all, lives only on hopes. These hopes are based solely on two assumptions: Russia and America. We have no chance of eliminating America. But it does lie in our power to exclude Russia. The elimination of Russia means, at the same time, a tremendous relief for Japan in East Asia, and thereby the possibility of a much stronger threat to American activities through Japanese intervention.

I have decided under these circumstances to put an end to the hypocritical performance in the Kremlin ...

So far as the air war on England is concerned, we shall, for a time, remain on the defensive ...

As for the war in the East, Duce, it will surely be difficult, but I do not entertain a second's doubt as to its great success. I hope, above all, that it will then be possible for us to secure a common food-supply base in the Ukraine which will furnish us such additional supplies as we may need in the future.

If I waited until this moment, Duce, to send you this information, it is because the final decision itself will not be made until 7 o'clock tonight ...

Whatever may come, Duce, our situation cannot become worse as a result of this step; it can only improve ... Should England nevertheless not draw any conclusions from the hard facts, then we can, with our rear secured, apply ourselves with increased strength to the dispatching of our enemy.

... Let me say one more thing, Duce. Since I struggled through to this decision, I again feel spiritually free. The partnership with the Soviet Union, in spite of the complete sincerity of our efforts to bring about a final conciliation, was nevertheless often very irksome to me, for in some way or other it seemed to me to be a break with my whole origin, my concepts, and my former obligations. I am happy now to be relieved of these mental agonies.

With hearty and comradely greetings.

Your
Adolf Hitler

Source: William L. Shirer, *The Rise and Fall of the Third Reich: A History of Nazi Germany* (New York: Simon & Schuster, 1960), pp. 849–51

The invasion of the Soviet Union

The selection below from Army Chief of Staff Franz Halder's war diary describes the success of the Germans in catching the Soviets by surprise. Stalin had ignored intelligence signals and British and American warnings, because he was convinced that the Western powers were attempting to provoke war with Germany. He did not believe that Hitler would risk an attack before a peace settlement had been reached with Britain. For Hitler and his generals, however, the German attack was intended to prevent a two-front war by knocking out Russia before the British and Americans could intervene. They believed that the success of Operation Barbarossa would induce Britain to sue for peace and would discourage the US from becoming involved in the war. Halder faithfully records Hitler's remarks on the effect of the invasion of Russia on Britain, Japan, and the US. Tensions between Hitler and Halder mounted after Hitler dismissed Army Commander Walter von Brauchitsch in December 1941 and assumed direct operational control of the army. Halder was dismissed from his post as Army Chief of Staff in late 1942. After the failure of the 20 July 1944 plot, Halder was arrested. He survived the war, however, as he had no direct links to the military resistance.

5.14 The Halder War Diary, 1941

22 JUNE 1941

The morning reports indicate that all Armies (except Eleventh) have started the offensive according to plan. Tactical *surprise* of the enemy has apparently been achieved along the entire line. All bridges across the Bug river, as on the entire river frontier, were undefended and are in our hands intact. That the enemy was taken by surprise is evident from the facts that troops were caught in their quarters, that planes on the airfields were covered up, and that enemy groups faced with the unexpected development at the front inquired at their headquarters in the rear what they should do. More effects of the surprise may be antici-pated from our armored assaults, which have been ordered in all sectors. The Navy reports that the enemy seems to have been taken by surprise in their zone of operation as well. His reactions to the measures of the last few days were of a purely passive nature, and he now is holding back his naval forces in ports, apparently in fear of mines.

[General Friedrich] *Paulus* communicates to me at 1100 Permanent Secretary [of the Foreign Office] von Weizsäcker's appraisal of the situation: Britain will at first feel relieved by the news of our attack on Russia and will rejoice at the "dispersal of our forces." But a rapid advance of German troops will soon bring disillusionment, for the defeat of Russia cannot but lead to a marked strengthening of our position in Europe.

As to Britain's readiness for an accord with us he has this to say: The propertied classes will strive for a settlement leaving us free hand in the East, but it would involve renunciation of our claims to Holland and Belgium. If these tendencies are to prevail, Churchill has to be overthrown, as he relies on the support of the Labor Party, which is not interested in a peace concluded by the propertied classes. Such a peace would bring the propertied interests back into power, whereas the Labor Party wants power for itself. The Labor Party therefore will continue the war until the propertied class is entirely excluded. Under what conditions it would eventually be willing to come to terms with Germany, cannot be predicted. Probably vehement opposition to National Socialism, because of strong Jewish influence on the Labor Party and Communist connections. For the time being, in any case, the Labor Party will not be disposed to put an end to the war.

In the Far East, an attack by Japan on Britain appears unlikely. Both Japan and the US will endeavor to keep from being drawn into the war. It is in Germany's interest to keep both out of the conflict; otherwise the war, both in duration and means, would become incalculable, and the making of an eventual peace would become extraordinarily complicated.

Source: Office of the Chief of Counsel for War Crimes, *The Halder Diaries:*
The Private War Journals of General Franz Halder
(Nuremberg: Office of the Military Government [US], 1948).
German version: Generaloberst Halder, *Kriegstagebuch*, Vol. 3,
Der Russlandfeldzug bis zum Marsch auf Stalingrad (22. 6. 1941–24. 9. 1942),
ed. by Hans-Adolf Jacobsen (Stuttgart: W. Kohlhammer Verlag, 1964), pp. 3–4

Germany urges Japan to enter the war

Increasing American involvement in the war in Europe induced the Germans to try to bring their Japanese ally into the war. This telegram from the German Foreign Minister Joachim von Ribbentrop to the German ambassador in Tokyo came three days after the United States had relieved British troops in Iceland despite the fact that Germany had declared the region a war zone. At this point Ribbentrop still hoped to persuade Japan to join in the attack on the Soviet Union, launched three weeks earlier. His main argument was that the rapid defeat of the USSR would leave the Tripartite powers (Germany, Japan, and Italy) in an optimal position to take on the Anglo-American powers. The one eventuality the Germans needed to prevent at all costs was a negotiated Japanese–American settlement, which would have left the US free to intervene in Europe.

The Japanese, however, having followed the German example of signing a non-aggression pact with the USSR in April 1941, opted to stay out of the war against Russia. It was the US, not the USSR, that stood in the way of Japanese expansion in East and South-East Asia. Having been informed by their agent Richard Sorge in the German embassy in Tokyo that the Japanese would not attack them, the Russians were able to withdraw troops from the Far East for the successful defense of Moscow in December 1941.

5.15 Telegram from Foreign Minister Ribbentrop to the German Ambassador to Japan, 10 July 1941

… Please take this opportunity to thank the Japanese Ambassador in Moscow for conveying the cable report. It would be convenient if we could keep on receiving news from Russia this way. In summing up, I would like to say: I have now, as in the past, full confidence in the Japanese policy, and in the Japanese foreign minister, first of all because the present Japanese government would really act inexcusably toward the future of its nation, if it did not take this unique opportunity to solve the Russian problem, as well as to secure for all times its expansion to the south and settle the Chinese matter. Since Russia, as reported by the Japanese Ambassador in Moscow, is in effect close to collapse, a report which coincides with our own observations as far as we are able to judge the present war situation, it is simply impossible that Japan does not solve the matter of Vladivostok and the Siberian area as soon as her military preparations are completed.

It is, of course, also in our interest that Japan wants to secure for herself further possessions in the South, Indo-China, etc., just as every measure of Japan directed toward expansion is in principle welcomed by us. I shall give you detailed instructions within the near future, relative to the consequences which might, and no doubt will, result from the occupation of Iceland by American military forces, and the attitude which we will take toward Japan in this connection. As a directive for talks we can advise you already today that the sending of American military forces to the support of England into a territory which has been officially announced by us as combat area, shows not only Roosevelt's aggressive intentions, but the fact of the intrusion of American military forces into the combat area in support of England is in itself an aggression against Germany and Europe. After all, one cannot enter a theater of war in which two armies are fighting, and join the army of one side without the intention of shooting and without actually doing so. I do not doubt for a moment that in case of the outbreak of hostilities between Germany and America, in which case today already it may be considered as an absolutely established fact that only America will be the aggressor, Japan will fulfill her obligations, as agreed upon in the Three-Power Pact. However, I ask you to employ all available means in further insisting upon Japan's entry into the war against Russia at the soonest possible date, as I have mentioned already in my note to [Foreign Minister Yosuke] Matsuoka. The sooner this entry is effected, the better. The natural objective still remains that we and Japan join hands on the Trans-Siberian railroad, before winter starts. After the collapse of Russia, however, the position of the Three-Power Pact states in the world will be so gigantic, that the question of England's collapse or the total destruction of the English islands will only be a matter of time. An America totally isolated from the rest of the world would then be faced with our taking possession of the remaining positions of the British Empire which are important for the Three-Power-Pact countries. I have the unshakeable conviction that a carrying through of the new order as desired by us will be a matter of course, and there will be no insurmountable difficulties if the countries of the Three-Power Pact stand close together and encounter every action of the Americans with the same weapons. I ask you to report in the near future as often as possible and in detail on the political situation there.

Ribbentrop

Transmitted to Embassy in Tokyo under No. 1018 Telegram Control, 10 July 1941

Source: Office of the Chief of Counsel for Prosecution of Axis Criminality, *Nazi Conspiracy and Aggression*, Vol. V (Washington DC: US Government Printing Office, 1946), pp. 564–5 [Doc. 2896-PS]

The Siege of Leningrad

The optimism of German war planners is reflected in Hitler's orders not to accept the surrenders of Moscow and Leningrad (formerly St. Petersburg), but rather to kill or drive out their populations and raze these cities to the ground. The first selection below is a letter transmitting the OKW orders to naval commanders. The second selection is an order by General Alfred Jodl, Chief of Staff at the OKW, to the operations section of the High Command, reiterating the Führer's wishes. Leningrad was surrounded by German and Finnish troops and cut off from all land access from September 1941 to January 1943. The city was, however, resupplied by the Soviets across Lake Ladoga, by a road over the ice in the winter. Despite more than a million civilian casualties, mostly from starvation, the city held out, until the blockade was definitively broken in January 1944. Moscow, too, on the brink of collapse in November 1941, was successfully defended by a Soviet counter-attack under harsh winter conditions in December 1941. Kiev had fallen to the Germans in mid-September after Hitler, over the objections of his generals, had diverted forces from the drive on Moscow.

5.16a Naval War Staff Book No. 1, letter on future of St. Petersburg

---

MOST SECRET   **Berlin, the 29th September 1941**

SUBJECT: FUTURE OF ST. PETERSBURG

1   In order to obtain a clear view of measures to be adopted by the Navy in case St. Petersburg should be occupied or should surrender, the question of further military operations against this city was made clear by the Chief of Staff, Naval War Staff to the Supreme Command of the Armed Forces. The result is reported as follows:

2   *The Führer has decided to have St. Petersburg wiped off the face of the earth.* The further existence of this large town is of no interest once Soviet Russia is overthrown. Finland has also similarly declared no interest in the continued existence of the city directly on her new frontier.

3   The original demands of the Navy: that the dockyard – harbor – and other installations important to the Navy be preserved, are known to the Supreme Command of the Armed Forces, but in view of the basic principles underlying the operation against St. Petersburg, it is not possible to comply with them.

4   The intention is to close in on the city and raze it to the ground by bombardments of artillery of all calibres and by continuous air attack.

Requests that the city may be handed over, arising from the situation within, will be turned down, for the *problem of the survival of the population and of supplying it with food is one which cannot and should not be solved by us.* In this war for existence, we have no interest in keeping even part of this great city's population. If necessary, a forced evacuation towards the Eastern territories of Russia may take place.

5   The consequences arising from the extinction of St. Petersburg and relating to the measures for organization and personnel, already carried out or held in readiness, will be worked out at Supreme Command and the corresponding guiding principles will then be made known. If any suggestions on this subject are to be made at Group Command, it is requested that they be forwarded at the earliest possible moment to Naval War Staff ...

Head of Naval War Staff

5.16b General Jodl's order, 7 October 1941

MOST SECRET

Supreme Command of the Armed Forces

Führer's Hq., 7 Oct. 41

To Army Supreme Command (Ops. Section)

The Führer has again decided that a *capitulation of Leningrad or later of Moscow* is not to be accepted even if offered by the enemy.

The moral justification for this measure is clear to the whole world. Just as in Kiev, our troops were subject to extreme danger through explosions with time-fuses, the same must be expected to a still greater degree in Moscow and Leningrad. The Soviet radio itself has broadcast that the foundations of Leningrad were mined and the city would be defended to the last man.

Extreme danger of epidemics is to be expected.

Therefore no German soldier is to enter these cities. Anyone who tries to leave the city through our lines is to be forced to return under fire.

The exodus of the population through the smaller, unguarded gaps towards the interior of Russia to be allowed. Before all other cities are taken, they are to be softened up by artillery fire and airraids and their population forced to flee.

We cannot take the responsibility of endangering our soldiers' lives by fire in order to save Russian cities, nor that of feeding the population of these cities at the expense of the German homeland ...

Chief of Supreme Command of the Armed Forces

By Order

[Signed:] Jodl

Source: Office of the US Chief of Counsel for Prosecution of Axis Criminality,
***Nazi Conspiracy and Aggression*, Vol. VI (Washington DC:**
US Government Printing Office, 1946), pp. 929–32 [Docs. C–123 and C–124]

The role of the Wehrmacht in Nazi atrocities

Under the guise of combatting partisans, the German Army gave official support to SS units (*Einsatzgruppen*) whose task it was to kill the Jewish population and suspect individuals behind the lines on the eastern front (see Doc. 6.6). The following order by Field Marshal Walter von Reichenau (1884–1942), at that time Commander of the German Sixth Army and later of Army Group South, received Hitler's full approval and was circulated as a model of its kind to other units in the east. The very need for such an order, however, suggests that many rank-and-file soldiers failed to sympathize with or see the need for atrocities against the civilian population. Reichenau's successor as commander of Sixth Army was General Friedrich Paulus (1890–1957), who led his army all the way to the outskirts of Stalingrad in late September 1942. Here, however, the Sixth Army was trapped by Soviet counter-offensives to the north and south of the city in November 1942 and forced to surrender on 1 February 1943.

5.17 Field Marshal Walter von Reichenau's order to his troops, 10 October 1941

SECRET!

Army H.Q., 10. 10. 41

SUBJECT: CONDUCT OF TROOPS IN EASTERN TERRITORIES

Regarding the conduct of troops towards the Bolshevistic system, vague ideas are still prevalent in many cases. The most essential aim of war against the Jewish–Bolshevistic system is a complete destruction of their means of power and the elimination of Asiatic influence from the European culture. In this connection the troops are facing tasks which exceed the one-sided routine of soldiering. The soldier in the eastern territories is not merely a fighter according to the rules of the art of war but also a bearer of ruthless national ideology and the avenger of bestialities which have been inflicted upon German and racially related nations.

Therefore, the soldier must have full understanding of the necessity of a severe but just revenge on subhuman Jewry. The Army has to aim at another purpose, i.e., the annihilation of revolts in hinterland which, as experience proves, have always been caused by Jews.

The combatting of the enemy behind the front line is still not being taken seriously enough. Treacherous, cruel partisans and unnatural women are still being made prisoners of war and guerilla fighters dressed partly in uniforms or plain clothes and vagabonds are still being treated as proper soldiers, and sent to prisoner-of-war camps. In fact, captured Russian officers talk even mockingly about Soviet agents moving openly about the roads and very often eating at German field kitchens. Such an attitude of the troops can only be explained by complete thoughtlessness, so it is now high time for the commanders to clarify the meaning of the present struggle.

The feeding of the natives and of prisoners of war who are not working for the Armed Forces from Army kitchens is an equally misunderstood humanitarian act as is the giving of cigarettes and bread. Things which the people at home can spare under great sacrifices and which are being brought by the Command to the front under great difficulties should not be given to the enemy by the soldier not even if they originate from booty. It is an important part of our supply.

When retreating, the Soviets have often set buildings on fire. The troops should be interested in extinguishing of fires only as far as it is necessary to secure sufficient numbers of billets. Otherwise the disappearance of symbols of the former bolshevistic rule even in the form of buildings is part of the struggle of destruction. Neither historic nor artistic considerations are of any importance in the eastern territories. The command issues the necessary directives for the securing of raw materials and plants, essential for war economy. The complete disarming of the civil population in the rear of the fighting troops is imperative considering the long and vulnerable lines of communications. Where possible, captured weapons and ammunition should be stored and guarded. Should this be impossible because of the situation of the battle, the weapons and ammunition will be rendered useless. If isolated partisans are found using firearm in the rear of the army, drastic measures are to be taken. These measures will be extended to that part of the male population who were in a position to hinder or report the attacks. The indifference of numerous apparently anti-Soviet elements, which originates from a "wait and see" attitude, must give way to a clear decision for active collaboration. If not, no one can complain about being judged and treated as a member of the Soviet System.

The fear of the German counter-measures must be stronger than the threats of the wandering Bolshevistic remnants. Being far from all political considerations of the future the soldier has to fulfill two tasks:

1   *Complete annihilation of the false Bolshevistic doctrine of the Soviet State and its armed forces.*
2   *The pitiless extermination of foreign treachery and cruelty and thus the protection of the lives of military personnel in Russia.*

This is the only way to fulfill our historic task to liberate the German people once and forever from the Asiatic–Jewish danger.

Commander in Chief
[Signed] von Reichenau Field Marshal

Source: Office of the US Chief of Counsel for Prosecution of Axis Criminality,
Nazi Conspiracy and Aggression,
Vol. VIII (Washington DC: US Government Printing Office, 1946), pp. 585–7 [Doc. UK–81]

Ribbentrop's reaction to the Japanese attack on Pearl Harbor

The failure of Japanese efforts to persuade the US to give up its opposition to Japanese expansion in China and Southeast Asia led to the Japanese decision to achieve its expansionist objectives through war. The Japanese attack on the American naval base at Pearl Harbor on 7 December 1941 occurred without a formal declaration of war. The news of the Japanese attack was welcomed by German leaders who had long sought to persuade Japan to enter the war. The following selection from Italian Foreign Minister Count Ciano's diary describes German Foreign Minister Joachim von Ribbentrop's enthusiastic reaction to the news of Pearl Harbor. The Japanese had previously sought and received assurance that Germany and Italy would stand by their commitments to Japan in the Tripartite Pact of September 1940 (Doc. 5.7). Ciano himself had his doubts about the advantages of the Japanese attack, doubts that would be borne out by later developments in the war.

5.18 Count Ciano's Diary, December 1941

5 DECEMBER 1941

A night interrupted by Ribbentrop's restlessness. After delaying two days, now he cannot wait a minute to answer the Japanese,[7] and at three in the morning he sent [Ambassador Hans Georg von] Mackensen to my house to submit a plan for a triple agreement relative to Japanese intervention and the pledge not to make a separate peace. He wanted me to awaken the Duce, but I did not do so, and the latter was very glad I didn't ...

7   The Japanese had requested a German and Italian commitment to declare war on the US in case of the outbreak of war in the Pacific.

8 DECEMBER 1941

A night telephone call from Ribbentrop; he is overjoyed about the Japanese attack on America. He is so happy about it that I am happy with him, though I am not too sure about the final advantages of what has happened. One thing is now certain: that America will enter the conflict, and that the conflict will be so long that she will be able to realize all her potential force. This morning I told this to the King who had been pleased about the event. He ended by admitting that in the "long run" I may be right. Mussolini was happy, too. For a long time he has favored a definite clarification of relations between America and the Axis ...

Source: Office of the US Chief of Counsel for Prosecution of Axis Criminality,
Nazi Conspiracy and Aggression, Vol. V
(Washington DC: US Government Printing Office, 1946), p. 692 [Doc. 2987-PS]

The German declaration of war on the US

On 7 December 1941 the Japanese attack on Pearl Harbor brought the United States into the war. On 11 December Hitler formally declared war on the US, thereby honoring Germany's commitment under the Tripartite Pact as well as the pledge given to Japan by Germany and Italy in late November 1941. Hoping to prevent a Japanese–American understanding that would leave the US free to intervene in Europe, the Germans had urged Japan to attack the US. Germany and the US had been waging a naval war in the Atlantic for many months before the Japanese attack on Pearl Harbor. From the German point of view a declaration of war only formalized an already existing conflict.

5.19 Declaration of war by Germany on USA, 11 December 1941

Note of the 11th December 1941 from the Reich Foreign Minister von Ribbentrop to the United States Chargé d'Affaires in Berlin, Legation Counsellor Morris.

Sir,

After the Government of the United States of America had from the very beginning of the European war brought about by the British Declaration of war on Germany on the 3rd September 1939, most flagrantly and to an ever increasing extent violated all the rules of neutrality in favor of Germany's enemies, and after it had been continuously guilty of the worst type of provocations against Germany, it has finally gone over to open military acts of aggression.

On the 11th September 1941, the President of the United States of America publicly announced that he had ordered the American fleet and air force to shoot at every German warship without hesitation. In his speech of the 27th October of this year he once again expressly confirmed that this order was now in operation.

On the strength of this order, American warships have been systematically attacking German naval forces since the beginning of September of this year. Thus, American destroyers, for instance the "Greer," the "Kearney," and the "Reuben James," have opened fire on German U-boats according to plan. The Secretary of State of the American Navy, Mr. Knox, himself confirmed that American destroyers had been attacking German U-boats.

Further, naval forces of the United States of America, acting upon the orders of their Government, have, in violation of international law, treated German merchant ships on the open seas as enemy ships, and have taken them as prizes.

The Government of the Reich therefore declares:

Although Germany for her part has always strictly observed the rules of international law in her dealings with the United States of America throughout the whole of the present war, the Government of the United States of America has finally gone over from breaches of neutrality in the beginning to open acts of war against Germany. It has, therefore, virtually created a state of war.

The Reich Government therefore breaks all diplomatic relations with the United States of America, and declares that under these circumstances brought about by President Roosevelt, Germany too considers herself to be at war with the United States of America as from today.

Source: Office of the US Chief of Counsel for Prosecution of Axis Criminality,
Nazi Conspiracy and Aggression, **Vol. VIII**
(Washington DC: US Government Printing Office, 1946), pp. 432–3 [Doc. TC–62]

The German reaction to the US entry into the war

The selections below from Joseph Goebbels' diary in December 1941 were only recently discovered in Soviet archives not previously accessible to Western scholars. They describe the very up-beat mood of German leaders following the Japanese attack on the US. Despite some apprehensions about what US entry into the war might bring, Goebbels confirms that the German leadership expected the US to have its hands full in Asia, forcing a curtailment of US aid to Britain and the Soviet Union. The news of the Japanese attack was particularly welcome as it came shortly after the Germans suffered some unexpected reversals in the campaign to capture Moscow before the onset of winter. Operation Barbarossa, predicated on the assumption that the Red Army would be defeated within four months, had failed to achieve its objectives. The news that Germany had gained a powerful new ally gave Hitler and his paladins a much-needed lift in morale. Hitler regarded the Japanese attack as a vindication of his policy, aimed at preventing a Japanese–American understanding. He also admired the Japanese method of launching the war without warning.

Goebbels' diary entry for 13 December 1941 also implies a possible connection between the German declaration of war on the US and the decision to implement the "Final Solution of the Jewish Question" (see Chapter 6). Although the "Final Solution," the decision to kill all the Jews under German control, was planned well in advance, its full implementation may have been delayed until the US entered the war. Now the Jews under German control had lost their potential value as hostages to deter American entry into the war or to otherwise affect American policy. On 12 December 1941, the day after the German declaration of war, Hitler informed his assembled *Gauleiter* (district leaders) that the "final solution" of physical annihilation was now in effect, thus fulfilling the prophecy he had made to the Reichstag in January 1939 (Doc. 4.15). Hitler also discussed his plans for a "New Order" in Europe, a plan that involved the displacement of millions of people in the East to make room for German settlement.

5.20 The Goebbels Diaries, December 1941

8 DECEMBER 1941

... Besides [the campaign in Russia] there has been a thrilling, breath-taking development in world and military affairs. Already in the morning one could tell that the crisis between the USA and Japan was intensifying by the hour. Roosevelt wrote another letter to the Tenno [the Japanese emperor], but it was so brazen and insolent that serious consequences could be expected. The demands made by the USA on Japan contain all the renunciations that Japan could possibly make to ensure the decline of its national life. If Japan accepted this, then it would abdicate its role as a world power in a silent and bloodless way. The dispute in their respective press organs escalated in vehemence. Already in the course of the day one got the impression that war was at hand. In the course of the afternoon the news grew more alarming almost every half hour and then, like a bolt of lightning out of a clear sky the news burst forth that Japan had attacked the United States. War is here. The Japanese fleet has apparently confronted the American fleet somewhere in the Pacific. Besides this the Japanese air force has undertaken attacks on Manila. Roosevelt himself declared that many were killed. The US president convened the government and the parties of Congress, and then late at night came the news that the United States and Japan were at war as of 6 a.m. I receive a call from the Führer, who is exceptionally happy about this development. He wants to convene the Reichstag on Wednesday afternoon to clearly state the German position. On the basis of the Tripartite Pact we will probably not get around a declaration of war on the United States. But now this isn't so bad anymore. We are now to a certain extent protected on our flanks. The United States will probably no longer make aircraft, weapons, and transport available to England so carelessly, as it can be assumed that they will need all these for their own war against Japan. The Japanese followed a very resolute tactic in unleashing this conflict. They simply pounced on the enemy that wanted to strangle them and attacked him. I trust that the Japanese still have a few things in reserve; for they generally pursue very cautious, tradition-ally conservative policies; they will not negligently risk their empire, and they surely have a whole series of military options, about which even we know nothing. They did not inform us in advance of their intention to attack suddenly, and this was also necessary to maintain the secrecy of their plans. All these events are still rather unclear for the time being. But the war is a fact. [General] Tojo was more dependable after all than we had assumed at first. The Führer and the whole headquarters are overjoyed at this development. We are now at least temporarily secure from a serious threat. In the coming weeks and months Roosevelt will no longer be as insolent as he has been in the past. Now this war has become a world war in the true sense of the word. Beginning for the slightest of reasons, it is now creating ramifications all over the globe. More even than before it offers us a great national opportunity. Now it all depends on our seeing the thing through and maintaining composure in every crisis that may come. If we win this conflict, then there is no more impediment to the realization of the German dream of world power. We want to venture everything to achieve this goal. The opportunities have never been as favorable as today. It is essential to take advantage of them.

10 DECEMBER 1941

Yesterday: ... The Führer has returned from his headquarters to Berlin. I have an extensive conversation with him in the early afternoon. He is full of joy about the advantageous development of the negotiations between USA and Japan and also about the outbreak of war. He rightly points out that he had always expected this development. That's true; for the Führer never doubted that Japan would act in the decisive hour and would also be forced to act. He has always expressed the view that when the time came the conciliators in Tokyo would have nothing to say any longer. Indeed, Japan had to act if it did not want to renounce its great power status altogether. There are certain situations in the life of a great power in which it must take up arms unless it wants to abdicate altogether. Such a situation had now come for Japan. The Führer maintains that the Japanese fleet in the Pacific is far superior to the Anglo-American fleet, especially after its early successes against the US fleet. The Japanese made a great start and can now dominate the Pacific Ocean almost without limit. There is scarcely a challenger in sight here any longer. The Japanese adopted an absolutely correct tactic by immediately mounting an attack and not getting involved in long preliminaries preceding the outbreak of war. Undoubtedly now the Japanese will take up the fight for the US bases in the Pacific first, and they will do this, judging by their whole character, very systematically, taking one base after another either by destroying or capturing it. Both the Americans and the English are thereby faced with the cruel fact that their influence in the Pacific will be lost altogether. Tojo, the Japanese prime minister, proves himself to be an extraordinarily realistic and astute politician, who, quite contrary to our view up to now, will not allow himself to be bluffed or browbeaten, while the Japanese foreign minister Togo [Shigenori], the former Japanese ambassador in Berlin, is regarded as the weaker one and the one more ready to back down. But this is not decisive now that war has actually broken out, and according to the current state of affairs there can be no more turning back for Tokyo. The Führer knew nothing beforehand about the outbreak of hostilities; he was completely surprised by this event and at first, like me, he did not want to believe it. According to the Führer Roosevelt gives the impression of having been severely weakened for the time being. Japan did the right thing by striking the first killing blow. That is always the case in conflicts, in athletic contests, for example, as well. A boxer who saves his killing blows for the fifth or sixth rounds can experience what [Max] Schmeling had to experience in his last fight with Joe Louis, namely that he is knocked out in the first round. Maybe the Japanese, too, have the opportunity to hit the Americans so lethally in their first strikes that the US will be significantly weakened in their naval capacity and will no longer be able to launch successful counter-strikes. The Führer rightly believes that in modern war the issuing of an ultimatum has to be seen as completely outmoded and medieval. If one intends to defeat the enemy one should strike immediately and not wait for him to prepare for the blow. That Japan has joined our side at this critical moment of the war is for the general public an essential guarantee of our victory; for as I have often emphasized, the Japanese pursue very conventional and cautious policies, and if in so precarious a situation they join the side of one party, it can be assumed that they have fully considered all the pros and cons and have come to the conclusion that victory will come to our side. ... By and large we have the impression that in the Japanese we have finally found a worthy ally. They do not wait for us to pull the chestnuts out of the fire for them but they attack and do their share to lead the war to a favorable end. They will undoubtedly use the opportunity offered to them. Nor do they lethargically remain on the defensive, but move to the offense with all the means at their disposal. They are indeed, as often used to be said, the Prussians of the Far East ...

Happiest about developments is the Japanese ambassador in Berlin, General [Hiroshi] Oshima. In the past weeks he telegraphed Tokyo again and again that Japan is lost if the policies pursued up to now were continued. He was a very strong and self-willed spokesman for an interventionist policy and he was able to prevail. He comes out of Tojo's circle and represents above all the interests of the Japanese army, which has always been known to be very aggressive and radical in its views. Oshima informed us that Japan intends to strike against Singapore and that presumably this British naval fortress will fall into Japanese hands in the foreseeable future. He is already drawing up plans for a joint attack on India. But we are not at that point yet. Then the Führer discusses the situation in the East extensively one more time. He says that the reverses of the last few days are only of an occasional nature, and above all that in a war one has to count not only on victories but also on reversals. In any case our position, especially after the entry of Japan into the war, is so favorable that there can be no doubt about the outcome of this mighty continental conflict. The Führer once again radiates optimism and confidence in victory. It feels good, after having to digest so much unpleasant news for many days, to come into direct contact with him again. ...

13 DECEMBER 1941

Yesterday: ... In the afternoon the Führer addresses the *Gauleiter*. ... The Führer is firmly resolved to conquer Soviet Russia at least as far as the Urals next year. Perhaps it will then already be possible to establish a kind of semi-peace in Europe, i.e., to make Europe self-sufficient and to take notice of the war effort of others only by arming correspondingly. ... In respect to the Jewish Question the Führer is firmly resolved to settle the matter entirely. He prophesied to the Jews that, if they once again brought about a world war, they would then be destroyed. That was not a mere phrase. The world war is here; the destruction of the Jews must be the necessary consequence. This question must be viewed without any sentimentality. We are not here to sympathize with the Jews, but only with the German people. If the German people have once again sacrificed close to 160,000 men in the eastern campaign, then the instigators of this bloody conflict will have to pay for this with their lives. In general the Führer sees in the East our future India. This is the colonial area that we want to settle. Here large farms for our peasant sons and the soldiers of our Wehrmacht must be created. This region, which has so often been conquered and settled by Germanics, is now to be annexed to the German Reich as the actual border region, but also as core territory, and in three or four generations it must be possible to view it as absolutely German. In the Crimea the Führer will create an "Eastern Gothic District" with the best racial stock from all Nordic nations. Such a doctrine does sound harsh in general, but in the light of the facts and of modern knowledge it is only logical and appropriate. If the Germans have to bleed for the New Order in Europe, then the other peoples will at least have to work for the New Order in Europe. It would be really too much if we had to bear both the sacrifice of blood and the burden of work while the other nations only gained the benefits of these. After all we do no one an injustice with the New Order that we are planning, for in the framework of the New Order everyone will be better off than before. Europe can not be viewed as an inorganic community of nations thrown together at random. Europe is always there, where it is defended; today, therefore, it lies in the German Reich. We are the vanguard of a coming better Europe and must therefore feel ourselves as its spokesmen and representatives. If we pave the way for the new Europe, it also falls to us to determine what form this new Europe is to take.

Source: *Die Tagebücher von Joseph Goebbels*, ed. by Elke Fröhlich, Pt. II, Vol. 2
(Munich: K. G. Saur, 1996), pp. 452–3, 463–5 468–9, 494, 497–9.
Translated by Rod Stackelberg

Starvation of Soviet prisoners of war

In the months following the invasion of the Soviet Union, the Wehrmacht leadership and the SS allowed millions of Soviet prisoners to die of starvation and exposure. This policy of deliberate, if gradual, liquidation was opposed by Nazi Party ideologue Alfred Rosenberg, whom Hitler had appointed to the newly-created post of Reich Minister of the Occupied Eastern Territories on 17 July 1941. As a Baltic German who had been forced to leave his homeland as a result of the Russian Revolution, Rosenberg was well aware of the widespread disaffection with Stalinist rule in the various satellite states of the Soviet Union. He hoped to exploit this disaffection to promote indigenous support for the German war effort in the east. He also deplored the waste of potentially useful manpower as a result of Nazi policies. In February 1942 he wrote to General Keitel, the Chief of the High Command of the Wehrmacht (OKW), to protest the maltreatment Soviet prisoners of war. German policy toward Soviet prisoners did indeed change in the later stages of the war as the need for manpower became more acute. Nonetheless, of about 5.7 million Soviet prisoners taken during the war, some 3.5 million died in German captivity. Rosenberg also failed to gain Hitler's approval for his proposal to establish independent anti-Communist states in the formerly Soviet territories under German occupation.

5.21 Letter from Alfred Rosenberg, Reich Minister for the Occupied Eastern Territories, to Field Marshal Wilhelm Keitel, Chief of the OKW, 28 February 1942

To the Chief of the Supreme Command of the Armed Forces (OKW):

SUBJECT: PRISONERS OF WAR

Since the beginning of its existence, the Reich Ministry for the Occupied Eastern Territories has taken the viewpoint that the large number of Soviet prisoners of war constitute highly valuable material for propaganda. The treatment of Soviet prisoners of war must be considered differently than the treatment of prisoners of war of other nations for various reasons:

1   The war in the East has not been concluded, and the treatment of the prisoners of war must have far-reaching effects on the will to desert of the Red Army soldier who is still fighting.

2   Germany intends to keep a large part of the former Soviet Union occupied, even after the end of the war, and to develop it industrially for our purposes. Therefore we depend on a far-reaching cooperation of the population.

3   Germany is conducting the fight against the Soviet Union because of ideological differences. Bolshevism must be overthrown and something better must be put in its place. Even the prisoners of war themselves must realize that National Socialism is willing and in a position to bring them a better future. They must return later to their homes from Germany with a feeling of admiration and esteem for Germany and German institutions, and thus become propagandists for the cause of Germany and National Socialism.

This attempted goal has not been attained so far. The fate of the Soviet prisoners of war in Germany is on the contrary a tragedy of the greatest extent. Of 3.6 million prisoners of war, only several hundred thousand are still able to work fully. A large part of them have starved, or died, because of the hazards of the weather. Thousands also died from typhus. It is understood, of course, that there are difficulties encountered in the feeding of such a large number of prisoners of war. Anyhow, with a certain amount of understanding for goals aimed at by German politics, dying and deterioration could have been avoided to the extent described. For instance, according to information on hand, the native population within the Soviet Union are absolutely willing to put food at the disposal of the prisoners of war. Several understanding camp commanders have successfully chosen this course. However, in the majority of cases, the camp commanders have forbidden the civilian population to put food at the disposal of the prisoners, and they have rather let them starve to death. Even on the march to the camps, the civilian population was not allowed to give the prisoners of war food. In many cases, when prisoners of war could no longer keep up on the march because of hunger and exhaustion, they were shot before the eyes of the horrified civilian population, and the corpses were left. In numerous camps no shelter for the prisoners of war was provided at all. They lay under the open sky during rain or snow. Even tools were not made available to dig holes or caves. A systematic delousing of the prisoners of war in the camps and of the camps themselves has apparently been missed. Utterances such as these have been heard: "The more of these prisoners die, the better it is for us." The consequence of this treatment now is that typhus is spreading due to the escape and discharge of prisoners and has claimed its victims among the Wehrmacht as well as among the civilian population, even in the old part of Germany.

Finally, the shooting of prisoners of war must be mentioned. These were partly carried out according to viewpoints that ignore all political understanding. For instance, in various camps, all the "Asiatics" were shot, although the inhabitants of the areas, considered belonging to Asia, of Transcaucasia and Turkestan especially, are among those people in the Soviet Union who are most strongly opposed to Russian subjugation and to Bolshevism. The Reich Ministry of the Occupied Eastern Territories has repeatedly emphasized these abuses. However, in November for instance, a detail (Kommando) appeared in a prisoner of war camp in Nikolajew, wanting to liquidate all Asiatics.

The treatment of prisoners of war appears to be founded for a great part on serious misconceptions about the people of the Soviet Union. One finds the opinion that the people become more inferior the further one goes east. If the Poles already were given harsh treatment, it is argued, even harsher treatment should be meted out to the Ukrainians, White Ruthenians, Russians, and finally the "Asiatics."

It was apparently completely ignored, in the treatment of prisoners of war, that Germany found – in contrast to the West (France, Belgium, the Netherlands, Norway) – a people who went through all the terror of Bolshevism, and who now, happy about their liberation, put themselves willingly at the disposal of Germany. A better gift could not come to Germany in this war, which requires every last man. But instead of accepting this gift, the people of the East are being treated more contemptibly and worse than the people of the West, who do not hide their enmity towards Germany ...

Source: Office of the US Chief of Counsel for Prosecution of Axis Criminality,
Nazi Conspiracy and Aggression, **Vol. III**
(Washington DC: US Government Printing Office, 1946), pp. 126–8 [Doc 081-PS]

Hitler's last great public speech

As the war turned against the Axis powers in late 1942, Hitler appeared in public less and less often. He gave his last major public speech to party faithful assembled in the Löwenbräukeller in Munich on 8 November 1942 to commemorate the nineteenth anniversary of the Beer Hall Putsch. This was the same day as the Anglo-American landings in North Africa and less than a week after the defeat of General Erwin Rommel's Africa Corps by the British at El Alamein in Egypt. In Stalingrad the battle for control of the city was raging. Only three weeks later the Russians would break through Axis lines and surround the German Sixth Army in the city. Hitler responded to these battlefield reverses with desperate optimism. He reminded his supporters that these battles were being waged hundreds and even thousands of miles from Germany's borders. Germany was far better off, he insisted, than in the First World War because of the unity of its people and the determination of its leadership. Hitler firmly believed that the Germans could make up in Nazi-inspired will and zeal what they lacked in material strength. Just as they had defeated the inner enemies they would prevail against the external enemies as well. A premonition of impending defeat does, however, seem to run through the speech, most clearly in his famous pronouncement that he would not stop fighting at quarter to twelve, as supposedly happened in the First World War, but rather at five past twelve. Hitler also openly acknowledged the ongoing Holocaust by repeating his 1939 prophecy that this war would end in the destruction of the European Jews (see Doc. 4.15).

5.22 Hitler's speech on the anniversary of the 1923 Putsch, 8 November 1942

Fellow Germans! Party Comrades!

I believe it is quite rare when a man can appear before his supporters after almost 20 years and in these 20 years did not need to make any changes whatsoever in his program ...

We are fighting on such distant fronts to protect our own homeland, to keep the war as far away as possible, and to forestall what would otherwise be the fate of the nation as a whole and what up to now only a few German cities have experienced or will have to experience. It is therefore better to hold a front 1,000 or if necessary 2,000 kilometers away from home than to have and have to hold a front on the borders of the Reich.

They are the same enemies as then, the same opponents as at that time, and it is no coincidence that the same state that in the [First] World War sent forward a man to break down Germany with a wave of mendacious propaganda is trying it again in the same way: At that

time the man was [Woodrow] Wilson, today it is Roosevelt. The Germany of that time –
without any state-sponsored national and political education, without any unity, without any
enlightenment about the Jewish problem and its effects – fell victim to this power. Our
enemies are making a great mistake to imagine that this will repeat itself a second time: for if
at that time we may have been the worst-organized nation in the world, then today we are
without a doubt the most disciplined peoples in the world. So if anyone in the other world
still imagines today that he can unnerve this people, then he doesn't know the heart of this
peoples today, nor the sustaining force that today is leading this peoples politically; he doesn't
know the National Socialist Party and its powerful organization!

... [In Germany] we wanted to eliminate this conspiracy of Jews, capitalists, and Bolsheviks,
and we finally did eliminate it. But hardly had they been toppled in Germany when the other
world once again as before 1914 began to encircle us. At that time it was Imperial Germany,
today it is National Socialist Germany. At that time it was the Kaiser, today it is me.

Only there is a difference: Germany at that time was Imperial in theory, in practice,
however, fully in inner decline. The Kaiser of that time was a man who lacked all strength of
resistance; but in me they have an opponent who doesn't even think of the word surrender!
Even when I was still a boy it was always my custom – at that time perhaps a vice, but all in all
maybe a virtue – to have the last word. And all our enemies can be sure: Germany at that time
laid down its arms at a quarter to twelve – in principle I always stop only at five past twelve!

My inner enemies got to know this ten years ago. They had all the power on their side, and
I was one man with a small group of supporters.

And today I must say that our external enemies' belief that they can crush us with their
power is almost ridiculous, for in reality we are today the stronger ones. When I count the
number of people who are today in our camp and who fight and work in our camp, then this
exceeds the number of those who have taken up positions against us. That cannot even
compare with the situation at the time [of the First World War] ...

You will remember, my old fellow fighters, how often I extended my hand to the inner opponents. How long I courted them, what efforts I made for them. What didn't I do to bring about a
reasonable understanding. Only after it proved to be in vain did I decide to use the means that
alone – when reason begins to fall silent – are capable of prevailing in this world. Those were our
SA and SS. And finally the hour came that we got the better of our opponents, and how! This
struggle at home perhaps only *seemed* easier than the struggle against the enemies outside.

In reality the men who once led the struggle inside [the Reich] were also the fighters
outside and are again today the fighters inside and outside ...

From us there will be no more offer of peace.

The last one was extended in the year 1940. There is only one thing now, and that is to
fight! Just as from a certain moment on I said to the inner opponent: one cannot come to a
peaceful understanding with you, you want force – hence you will now get force! And these
inner enemies, they have now been eliminated!

Another power, too, that once was present in Germany, has meanwhile learned that
National Socialist prophecies are not empty phrases. This is the main power to whom we
owe all our misfortune: international Jewry. You will remember the session of the Reichstag
at which I declared: If the Jews imagine that they can bring about an international world war
for the extermination of the European races, then the result will not be the extermination of
the European races, but the extermination of the Jews in Europe. My prophecies were always
laughed at. Of those who once laughed, countless numbers are no longer laughing, and those
who are still laughing today will soon perhaps no longer do so. This knowledge will spread

beyond Europe to the whole world. International Jewry will be recognized in all its demonic danger; we National Socialists will see to that. In Europe this danger has been recognized, and state after state has adopted our [anti-Jewish] laws ...

It is understandable that in such a world-wide conflict as is taking place today one cannot count on a new success every week. That is impossible. Nor is it decisive.

What is decisive is to gradually take up positions ... and to hold and reinforce them so that they can no longer be taken. And then one may believe me: What once we possess, we then also hold so firmly that wherever we stand in this war, no one will displace us ...

I am of the absolutely firm conviction that behind the leadership and the Wehrmacht there stands the German home front, and behind me the entire National Socialist Party as a dedicated community!

What distinguishes the present from the past is that at that time the people did not stand behind the Kaiser, whereas behind me there stands the greatest organization that has ever been established on earth. It represents the German people. And what further distinguishes the present from the past is that at the summit of this people stands a person who would never leave the country in perilous times, but rather someone who has always known only struggle and hence only one principle: fight, fight, and fight again!

And another thing distinguishes present-day Germany from the past: At that time it had a leadership without roots in the people; in the last analysis it was a class-based state. Today we are in the midst of completing what grew out of the last war. For when I returned from the war, I brought the experience of the front back home. From this experience of the front I built up the National Socialist people's community [*Volksgemeinschaft*]. Today the National Socialist people's community steps to the front, and you will see how the Wehrmacht will become more and more National Socialist month by month as it takes on the shape of the new Germany, as privileges, class prejudices, etc., are increasingly eliminated, as the German people's community asserts itself month by month; and at the end of this war the German people's community will perhaps have withstood its toughest test – that distinguishes the present Germany from the past. To this spirit we owe the boundless heroism at the front, the heroism of millions of individual soldiers, known and unknown, the heroism of tens and tens of thousands of brave officers, who today feel themselves more and more as a community with their men ...

Source: *Völkischer Beobachter*, 10 November 1942.
Translated by Rod Stackelberg

Mobilizing the nation for total war

On 18 February 1943 Propaganda Minister Joseph Goebbels, whom Hitler would appoint Reich Plenipotentiary for Total War in July 1944, gave one of his most infamous, but effective propaganda addresses. Less than three weeks after the surrender of the German Sixth Army at Stalingrad, he assembled a select audience of thousands of party loyalists from all walks of life in the largest indoor sports arena in Berlin to rally public morale after the disastrous setback on the eastern front. He needed to prepare the German people for greater sacrifices to come. His speech was also intended to convince the West of the unity and resolve of the German people. The speech is noteworthy for Goebbels' unusual candor in acknowledging the worsening of the military situation on the eastern front. But he portrayed the defeat at Stalingrad as a potentially

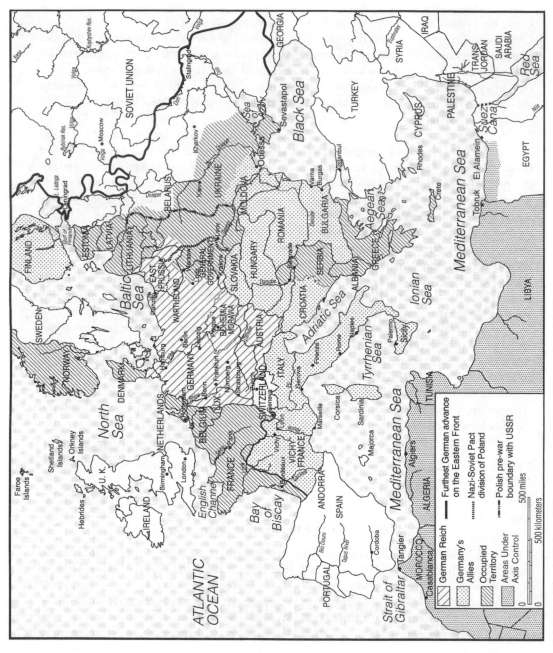

Map 3   The height of German expansion, November 1942

positive event that would make the German people aware of the growing danger and induce them to intensify their efforts for victory.

Goebbels announced the propaganda line that the Nazis would repeat for the rest of the war: Only Germany was capable of defending Western culture and civilization against the spread of communism. Germany's territorial ambitions in the East, a major motive for the attack on the Soviet Union, were never mentioned in public once the tide of war turned against the Germans. Goebbels' speech exemplifies the propagandistic use of the Führer myth – the myth of his genius and infallibility – to raise the confidence of the German people. In the end Goebbels resorted to the familiar Social Darwinist argument that any actions, no matter how destructive, were justified by a people's struggle for survival and dominance in a hostile world.

Only the beginning and end of Goebbels' long speech are excerpted in the selection below. The audience reaction, as published in the Nazi paper *Völkischer Beobachter*, is included to indicate the enthusiasm that Goebbels succeeded in arousing. When he asked, "Do you *want* total war?", he was almost drowned out by the exuberant assent of his audience. The Nazis were never able, however, to fully implement all the measures that Goebbels called for, particularly the mobilization of women, which contradicted the official Nazi precept that women's place was in the home (Doc. 5.25).

5.23 Goebbels' speech in the Berlin *Sportpalast*, 18 February 1943

My German national comrades!

Party comrades!

It is now barely three weeks ago, on the occasion of the Führer's proclamation on the tenth anniversary of our seizure of power, that I last spoke to you and the German people in this forum. The crisis we are currently facing on the eastern front was then at its height. Under the influence of the harsh setback that befell us in the battle for the Volga, we assembled on 30 January of this year [the tenth anniversary of the seizure of power] for a rally for unity and solidarity, but also with firm resolution to master the burdens that this war has imposed on us in its fourth year.

It was deeply moving to me and probably to all of you to learn several days later that the last heroic warriors of Stalingrad, joined to us by radio, took part in our uplifting *Sportpalast* rally. In their final report they wired that they had heard the Führer's proclamation and, perhaps for the last time in their lives, had sung the national anthem together with us with arms raised in the German salute. What German martial bearing at this great time! But what obligation this bearing also imposes on us, and especially on the German home front. Stalingrad was and is the great call of destiny to the German nation. A people that has the strength to bear such a setback and to overcome it, even to gain strength from it, is unconquerable. Remembrance of the heroes of Stalingrad must impose an obligation on me and on us all as I speak to you and to the German people today.

I do not know how many million people at the front and at home are participating in this rally by radio and are listening to me today. I would like to speak to all of them from the depths of my heart to the depths of their hearts. I believe that the entire German people is passionately involved in the cause that I will be speaking on today. I therefore want to give my remarks the gravity and candor that the times demand. The German people, reared, educated, and disciplined by National Socialism, can bear the *full truth*! [Shouts of "bravo," applause.] …

If I now again direct our focus from the recent past to what lies ahead, I do this purpose-fully. Time is pressing. There is no more time for fruitless debates. *We have to act*, and *without delay, rapidly, and thoroughly*, [shouts of "Heil," applause] as has always been the National Socialist way. From its beginning the movement has always acted thus in the many crises that it has had to endure and struggle through. And the National Socialist state, too, when a threat arose, hurled itself against that threat with resolute will! We are not like the *ostrich* that sticks its head in the sand in order not to *see* the danger. We are *courageous* enough to focus directly on the threat, to *boldly* and ruthlessly take its measure, and then to confront it with heads held high and with firm resolve! [Shouts of "Heil," applause.] Precisely at those times, as a movement and as a people, we always developed our *highest* virtues: namely, the furious and resolute will to destroy and banish the threat, a strength of character that overcomes *all* obstacles, a *dogged determination* to pursue our acknowledged goal, and an iron heart that is armored against all inner and outer challenges! [Shouts of "bravo," applause.]

So it is today as well. I have the task of giving you an unvarnished picture of the situation and to draw from it harsh conclusions for how the German leadership, but also the German people must now act.

We are currently going through harsh military difficulties in the East. These difficulties have temporarily taken on substantial dimensions and are similar in extent, if not in kind, to the difficulties of last winter.[8] We will have to talk about their causes at a later date. Today we have no choice but to acknowledge their existence and to examine the ways and means that we need to employ to bring about a remedy. There is therefore no use *at all* in denying these difficulties. It is beneath my dignity to give you an illusory picture of the situation; this could only lead to false conclusions and would give the German people a false sense of security in their lives and actions, which would be quite inappropriate in the current situation.

The assault of the steppe against our noble continent has broken out this winter with a force that exceeds all human and historical imagination. Against this the German Wehrmacht and its allies form the *only* possible protective wall. In his proclamation on 30 January in serious and incisive words the Führer already raised the question what would have become of Germany and Europe if on 30 January 1933 a liberal or democratic regime had come to power. What dangers would then have beset the Reich even more rapidly than even we could have suspected, and what defensive forces would *then* have been available to confront them? Ten years of National Socialism have sufficed to fully enlighten the German people about the seriousness of the fateful problems emerging out of eastern Bolshevism. It should now be easy to understand why we so often conducted our Nuremberg party rallies under the motto of the struggle against Bolshevism. We wanted to raise our warning voices to the German people and to the world in order to awaken Western humanity from an unprece-dented paralysis of will and spirit and to open their eyes to the gruesome historical dangers arising out of the existence of eastern Bolshevism, which had put a people of almost 200 million in the service of Jewish terror and was preparing a war of aggression against Europe.

When the Führer had the German Wehrmacht launch the attack in the east on 22 June 1941, we National Socialists were quite aware that thereby the *decisive* battle in this gigantic world struggle had broken out. We knew what dangers and difficulties it would bring for us. But we were also aware that if we had waited any longer, the dangers and difficulties would *only have grown*, but could never have diminished. It was *two minutes before twelve*! Further

8   The reference here is to the retreat of the German forces besieging Moscow in December 1941.

hesitation could easily have led to the destruction of the Reich and to the complete Bolshevization of the European continent.

In view of the large-scale tactics of deception and bluff of the Bolshevik regime, it is understandable that we did not correctly calculate the war-making potential of the Soviet Union. Only now it reveals itself to us in its whole fanatical dimensions. Accordingly, the fight that our soldiers have to endure in the East is hard, difficult, and dangerous *beyond* any human imagining. It requires mustering *all* of our national strength. This is a threat to the Reich and the European continent that exceeds *all* previous dangers to the West. If we fail in this fight, we would completely squander our historical mission! Everything that we have built up and achieved up to now pales in the face of the gigantic task that *directly* confronts the German Wehrmacht and *indirectly* the German people.

I turn in my remarks first to the world and proclaim to them the premises of our battle against the Bolshevik danger in the east. The first of these three premises is: If the German Wehrmacht were *not* able to *destroy* the danger from the East, the *Reich* and shortly thereafter *all of Europe* would fall to Bolshevism [applause]. The second of these premises is: The German Wehrmacht and the German people *alone* with their allies possess the strength to achieve a full-scale rescue of Europe from this threat [applause]. The third of these premises is: *Danger is imminent*; we must act *rapidly* and thoroughly, otherwise it will be too *late!* [Shouts of "bravo," applause.] ...

You, my listeners, represent the *nation* to the world at this moment! And I want to direct *ten questions* to you, which *you* along with the German people *must answer* before the whole world, especially our enemies, who are also listening to us on the radio at this hour! Do you want that? [Enthusiastic shouts: "Yes!"]

The English assert that the German people have lost their faith in victory [enthusiastic shouts: "No!" "Never!" "Nevermore!"]. I ask you: Do you, along with the Führer and with all of us, believe in the *final, total victory of German arms?* [Frenzied shouts: "Yes!" Loud applause, choruses of "Sieg Heil! Sieg Heil!"] I ask you: Are you determined to follow the Führer in fighting for victory through *thick and thin* and even under the *most difficult personal burdens?* [Enthusiastic shouts: "Yes!" Loud applause, choruses of "Sieg Heil! Sieg Heil!" "We salute our Führer!"]

Second, the English assert that the German people is *tired of fighting* [Shouts: "No!"]. I ask you: Are you ready, with the Führer, standing as the home phalanx behind the fighting Wehrmacht, to continue *this fight* with *furious determination* and *undeterred by any strokes of fate* until victory is in our hands? ["Yes!" Loud applause.]

Third: The English assert that the German people are no longer willing to undertake the increasing *war* efforts that the government demands. I ask you: Soldiers and workers, are you and the German people determined, *if* the Führer should command it in an *emergency*, to work *ten, twelve*, if necessary *fourteen and sixteen hours daily and to give your all for victory?* ["Yes!" Loud applause.]

Fourth: The English assert that the German people are rebelling against the government's measures to wage total war ["No!"]. The German people do not want *total war*, the English say, but rather *surrender!* ["No!"] I ask you: *Do you want total war?* ["Yes!" Strong applause.] Do you want it ["We want it!"], if necessary, *more total and radical than we can even imagine it today?* ["Yes!" Applause.]

Fifth: The English assert that the German people has lost its trust in the *Führer!* [Loud indignation.] I ask you [Choruses of "Führer command, we will follow!" "Heil!"], I ask you: *Do you trust the Führer?* ["Yes!"] Are you *absolutely and unconditionally* ready to *follow him on all his paths* and to do everything necessary to bring the war to a *victorious end?* ["Yes!"]

I ask you, sixth: Are you ready from now on to use all your strength *to supply the eastern front, our fighting fathers and brothers, all the men and weapons they need* in order *to conquer Bolshevism? Are you ready for this?* ["Yes!" Loud applause and acclamation.]

I ask you, seventh: Do you swear a sacred vow to the front that the home front stands behind the fighting front with *strong, unshakable morale* and will give the front *everything* it needs for victory? ["Yes!" Loud applause.]

I ask you, eighth: Do you, especially you women, want the government to ensure that women, too, make their work available to the war effort [feminine voices: "Yes!"] and that women *step in* wherever *possible to free up men for service on the front? Do you want this?* [Loud shouts, especially by women: "Yes!" Loud applause.]

I ask you, ninth: *Do you approve.* if necessary, the *most radical* measures against a small group of *malingerers and swindlers* ["Yes!" Loud applause], who in the middle of the war want to play at peace and try to use the needs of the people for selfish purposes? ["String them up!" Uproar.] *Do you agree* ["Yes!"] *that anyone who desecrates the war effort be beheaded?* ["Yes!" Loud applause.]

And now I ask you, tenth and last: Do you want, as prescribed in the National Socialist Party program, especially in wartime, that *equal rights* and *equal duties* prevail ["Yes!"] and that the home front take on the heaviest burdens of the war *in solidarity* and that these burdens be *equally* distributed among *high* and *low* and *poor* and *rich?* Do you want that? ["Yes!" Loud applause.]

I asked you and you did not withhold your answer. You are a cross-section of the nation. Through your voices the attitude of the people is manifested to the world. You have told our enemies what they need to know in order not to give in to illusions and false ideas. Thus, as from the first hour of our seizure of power on through all the past ten years, we are firmly and fraternally united with the German people! The mightiest ally there is in the world – the people themselves – stands behind us and is determined to fight for victory *with the Führer* – no matter what the cost or sacrifices ["Bravo!" Loud applause].

I stand before you not only as spokesman for the government, but also as the voice of the people. Seated around me are my old party friends, who hold high offices in the leadership of nation and state. Beside me is party comrade [Albert] Speer, to whom the Führer has entrusted the historical task [loud applause] of mobilizing the German war economy and of delivering weapons to the front *in abundance.* Beside me is party comrade Dr. [Robert] Ley ["Heil!" Applause] to whom the Führer has entrusted the task of leading German workers and of schooling and training them for the *tireless* performance of their wartime duties. We are joined with our party comrade [Fritz] Sauckel, to whom the Führer has entrusted the task of bringing *uncounted hundreds of thousands* [loud applause] *of workers into the Reich!* Beyond this we are united with all the leaders of the party, the Wehrmacht, and the state.

All of us, children of our nation, bound together with the people in this most fateful hour of our national history, – we vow to *you*, we *vow to the front*, and we *vow to the Führer* that we will fuse the home front into a *single bloc* on whom the *Führer* and his fighting soldiers can *unconditionally* and blindly rely! ["Bravo!" Loud applause.] In our lives and our work we pledge ourselves to do *everything* necessary for victory. We want to fill our hearts with the political passion that always burned inside us like an eternal flame in the great times of struggle of the party and the state! In this war we *never* want to fall into that false and hypocritical affectation of objectivity that has already brought the German nation *so much unhappiness* in its history!

When this war began, we directed our vision solely and exclusively to the *nation.* Whatever serves it and its struggle for existence is *good* and must be *sustained* and *nurtured.*

Whatever is injurious to it and its struggle for existence is *evil* and must be *removed* and *eliminated*. With a warm heart and a cool head we want to tackle the great problems of this phase of the war. We are thereby striding the path to ultimate victory. *It is grounded in faith in the Führer!* [Shouts of "Heil!" Loud applause.] He expects from us achievements that dwarf *everything* that has been achieved up to now! We do not want to refuse his demand; as we are proud of *him*, so he must be able to be proud of us. It is only in the *great* crises and shocks of national life that *true* men prove their worth, but also true women. Then one no longer has the right to speak of the "frail sex;" then *both* sexes show the *same* strength of spirit and fierce determination to fight. The nation is ready for this. The Führer has commanded, and we will follow!

If we have ever loyally and unwaveringly believed in victory, then it is in this hour of national reflection and inner restoration. We see victory *ready to grasp* in front of us, – we only have to *seize it*! We only have to generate the *resolve* to subordinate *everything* in its service; *that* is the commandment of the hour! And that is why from now on our adage is: *Now, Nation, rise – and storm, erupt!*[9] [Frenzied applause and shouts of "Sieg Heil! Sieg Heil! Sieg Heil! The national anthem is sung.]

Source: *Goebbels-Reden*, Vol. 2, *1939–1945*, ed. by Helmut Heiber (Düsseldorf: Droste Verlag, 1972), pp. 172–6, 204–8. Translated by Rod Stackelberg

Student resistance: leaflets of the White Rose

While the vast majority of Germans remained at least passively loyal to the regime until its collapse, there were also courageous acts of resistance among the general population. One of the most uncompromising resistance groups was the "White Rose," formed by students at the University of Munich in the summer of 1942, well before the military setbacks later that year. Four of the founding members, Hans Scholl, Alexander Schmorell, Christoph Probst, and Willi Graf, all in their early or mid-twenties, were members of the Wehrmacht on temporary duty to complete their medical studies. While serving on the eastern front they had been witnesses to Einsatzkommando killing of Jews. One of the most active members of the White Rose was Hans Scholl's 22-year old sister Sophie. Turning the language of Nazism ("subhumanity") back against the Nazi perpetrators, the White Rose composed and distributed a series of six leaflets, three of which are reproduced below. They contain not only a general exhortation to resistance, but specific suggestions for acts of sabotage. The last of the leaflets below was drawn up shortly before the surrender of the German Sixth Army at Stalingrad. In this leaflet the young dissidents turn to their vision of the future.

The leaflets, mimeographed in thousands of copies, were distributed mainly in Munich, but also disseminated through the mail. Individual copies turned up as far away as Vienna and Frankfurt. The group also painted slogans like "Down with Hitler" and "Hitler Mass Murderer" on buildings in Munich. Their efforts, however, failed to ignite the popular revolt they had hoped for. Apprehended by the Gestapo on 18 February 1943, they were tried and condemned by the notorious *Volksgerichtshof*

9　These lines refer to a well-known patriotic poem by Theodor Körner at the time of the Napoleonic wars.

(People's Court). Hans and Sophie Scholl and Christoph Probst were executed on 22 February 1943. Later that year Schmorell, Graf, and their mentor, the 50-year old philosophy professor Kurt Huber, were also executed.

5.24a The second leaflet, Fall 1942

It is impossible to engage in intellectual discourse with National Socialism because it is not an intellectually defensible program. It is false to speak of a National Socialist philosophy, for if there were such an entity, one would have to try by means of analysis and discussion either to prove its validity or to combat it. In actuality, however, we face a totally different situation. At its very inception this movement depended on the deception of one's fellow man; even at that time it was inwardly corrupt and could support itself only by constant lies. After all, Hitler states in an early edition of "his" book ... : "It is unbelievable, to what extent one must deceive a people in order to rule it." If at the start this cancerous growth in the nation was not particularly noticeable, it was only because there were still enough forces at work that operated for the good, so that it was kept under control. As it grew larger, however, and finally in a last sordid act of corruption attained ruling power, the tumor broke open, as it were, and infected the whole body. The majority of earlier opponents hid and German intellectuals fled to their cellars, there, like plants struggling in the dark, away from light and sun, gradually to choke to death. Now the end is at hand. Now it is our task to find one another again, to spread information from person to person, to keep a steady purpose, and to allow ourselves no rest until the last man is persuaded of the urgent need to struggle against this system. When thus a wave of unrest goes through the land, when "it is in the air," when many join the cause, then in a great final effort this system can be shaken off. After all, an end with terror is preferable to terror without end.

We are not in a position to draw up a final judgment about the meaning of our history. But if this catastrophe is to further the public welfare, it will be only by virtue of the fact that we are cleansed by suffering; that we yearn for the light in the midst of deepest night, summon our strength, and finally help in shaking off the yoke that oppresses our world.

We do not want to discuss here the question of the Jews, nor to compose a defense. No, only by way of example do we want to cite the fact that since the conquest of Poland *three hundred thousand* Jews have been murdered in this country in the most bestial way. Here we see the most frightful crime against human dignity, a crime that is unparalleled in the whole of history. For Jews, too, are human beings – no matter what position one may take with respect to the Jewish question – and this crime was perpetrated against human beings. ... Why tell you all these things, since you are fully aware of them – or if not of these, then of other equally grave crimes committed by this frightful sub-humanity? Because here we touch on a problem which involves us deeply and forces us all to take thought. Why do the German people behave so apathetically in the face of all these abominable crimes, crimes so unworthy of the human race? Hardly anyone thinks about that. It is accepted as fact and put out of mind. The German people slumber on in their dull, stupid sleep and encourage these fascist criminals; they give them the courage and opportunity to carry on their depredations; and of course they do so. Is this a sign that the Germans are brutalized in their simplest human feelings, that no chord within them cries out at the sight of such deeds, that they have sunk into a fatal sleep from which they will never, never awake? It seems so, and will certainly be so, if the German does not at last start up out of his stupor, if he does not protest wherever and whenever he can against this clique of criminals, if he shows no sympathy for these hundreds of thousands of victims. He must feel not only sympathy, no, much more: a sense of *complicity* in guilt. For through this apathetic behavior he gives these evil men the opportunity to act as they do; he tolerates this "government" which has taken upon itself such an infinitely great burden of guilt; indeed, he himself is to blame for the fact that it came about at all! Each man wants to be exonerated of a guilt of this kind, each one continues on his way with the best and most placid conscience. But he cannot be exonerated; he is *guilty, guilty, guilty!* It is not too late, however, to do away with this most reprehensible of all miscarriages of government, so as to avoid being burdened with even greater guilt. Now, when in recent years our eyes have been opened, when we know exactly who our adversary is, it is high time to root out this brown horde. Up until the outbreak of the war the larger part of the German people was blinded; the Nazis did not show themselves in their true aspect. But now, now that we have recognized them for what they are, it must be the sole and first duty, the holiest duty of every German to destroy these beasts. ...

Please make as many copies as possible of this leaflet and distribute them.

5.24b   The third leaflet, Fall 1942

"SALUS PUBLICA SUPREMA LEX."[10]

All ideal forms of government are utopias. A state cannot be constructed on a purely theoretical basis; rather, it must grow and ripen in the way an individual human being matures. ... Here we will not pass judgment on the many possible forms of the state – democracy, constitutional monarchy, monarchy, and so on. But one matter needs to be brought out clearly and unambiguously. Every individual human being has a claim to a useful and just state, a state which secures the freedom of the individual as well as the good of the whole. For, according to God's will, man is intended to pursue his natural goal, his earthly happiness, in self-reliance and self-chosen activity, freely and independently within the community of life and work of the nation.

But our present "state" is the dictatorship of evil. "Oh, we've known that for a long time," I hear you object, "and it isn't necessary to bring that to our attention again." But, I ask you, if you know that, why do you not bestir yourselves, why do you allow these men who are in power to rob you step by step, openly and in secret, of one of your rights after another, until one day nothing, nothing at all will be left but a mechanistic state system presided over by criminals and drunks? Is your spirit already so crushed by abuse that you forget it is your right – or rather, your *moral duty* – to eliminate this system? But if a person no longer can summon the strength to demand his right, then it is absolutely certain that he will perish. We would deserve to be dispersed through the earth like dust before the wind if we do not muster our powers at this late hour and finally find the courage that up to now we have lacked. Do not hide your cowardice behind a cloak of expediency, for with every new day that you hesitate, failing to oppose this offspring of Hell, your guilt, as in a parabolic curve, grows higher and higher.

Many, perhaps most, of the readers of these leaflets do not see clearly how they can practice effective resistance. They do not see any avenues open to them. We want to try to show them that everyone is in a position to contribute to the overthrow of this system. It is not possible through individual opposition, in the manner of embittered hermits, to prepare the ground for the overthrow of this "government" or to bring it about at the earliest possible

10   "The public health is the supreme law."

moment. No, it can be done only by the cooperation of many committed, energetic people – people who are agreed as to the means they must use to attain their goal. We have no great number of options as to these means. The only one available is *passive resistance*.

The meaning and the goal of passive resistance is to topple National Socialism, and in this struggle we must not recoil from any course, any action, whatever its nature. National Socialism must be attacked at every point, wherever it is open to attack. We must soon bring this rogue state to an end. A victory of fascist Germany in this war would have immeasurable, frightful consequences. Not military victory over Bolshevism must be the primary concern of Germans, but rather the defeat of the Nazis. This must be the *unconditional* first order of business. The greater necessity of this latter requirement will be discussed in one of our forthcoming leaflets.

And now every convinced opponent of National Socialism must ask himself: how can he fight against the present "state" in the most effective way, how can he strike the most telling blows. Through passive resistance, without a doubt. We cannot provide every individual with the guidelines for their acts, we can only suggest them in general terms, and everyone must find his own way of putting them into practice:

Sabotage in armament plants and war industries, sabotage at all gatherings, rallies, public cere-monies, and organizations of the National Socialist Party. Obstruction of the smooth functioning of the war machine (a machine for war that goes on *solely* to shore up and perpetuate the National Socialist Party and its dictatorship). *Sabotage* in all the areas of science and scholarship which further the continuation of the war – whether in universities, technical schools, laborato-ries, research institutes, or technical bureaus. *Sabotage* at all cultural events which could poten-tially enhance the "prestige" of the fascists among the people. *Sabotage* in all branches of the fine arts which have even the slightest connection with National Socialism or render it service. *Sabo-tage* in all publications, all newspapers, that are in the pay of the "government" and that defend its ideology and aid in disseminating the brown lie. Do not give a penny to public drives (even when they are conducted under the pretense of charity). For this is only a disguise. In reality the proceeds aid neither the Red Cross nor the needy. The government does not need this money; it is not financially interested in these money drives. After all, the presses run continuously to manufacture any desired amount of paper currency. But the populace must be kept constantly under tension, the pressure of the bit must not be allowed to slacken! Do not contribute to the collections of metal, textiles, and the like. Try to convince all your acquaintances, including those in the lower social classes, of the hopelessness and the senselessness of continuing this war; of our spiritual and economic enslavement at the hands of the National Socialists; of the destruction of all moral and religious values; and urge them to *passive resistance*!

Aristotle, *On Politics*: " … and further, it is part [of the nature of tyranny] to see to it that nothing is kept hidden of whatever any subject says or does, but that everywhere he will be spied upon, … and further, to set man against man and friend against friend, and the common people and the privileged and the wealthy against each other. Also it is part of these tyran-nical measures, to keep the subjects poor, in order to pay the bodyguards, and so that they will be occupied with earning their livelihood and will have neither leisure nor opportunity to engage in conspiratorial acts. … Also, the tyrant is inclined constantly to foment wars."

Please duplicate and distribute!

5.24c Resistance leaflet, January 1943

A CALL TO ALL GERMANS!

The war is approaching its certain end. As in the year 1918, the German government is trying to focus attention exclusively on the growing threat of submarine warfare, while in the East the armies are constantly in retreat and invasion is imminent in the West. Mobilization in the United States has not yet reached its pinnacle, but already it exceeds anything that the world has ever seen. It has become a mathematical certainty that Hitler is leading the German people into the abyss. *Hitler cannot win the war; he can only prolong it.* The guilt of Hitler and his minions has gone beyond all measure. Just retribution comes closer and closer!

But what are the German people doing? They will not see and they will not listen. Blindly they follow their seducers into ruin. Victory at any price! is inscribed on their banner. "I will fight to the last man," says Hitler – in the meantime the war has already been lost.

Germans! Do you and your children want to suffer the same fate that befell the Jews? Do you want to be judged by the same standards as your seducers? Are we to be forever the nation hated and rejected by all mankind? No! Therefore dissociate yourselves from the National Socialist subhumanity! Prove by your deeds that you think otherwise! A new war of liberation is about to begin. The better part of the nation is fighting on our side. Cast off the mantle of indifference you have wrapped around you! Make the decision *before it is too late*! Do not believe the National Socialist propaganda that has driven the fear of Bolshevism into your bones! Do not believe that Germany's welfare is linked to the victory of National Socialism for good or ill! A criminal regime cannot achieve a German victory. Separate yourselves in time from everything connected with National Socialism. In the aftermath a terrible but just judgment will be meted out to those who stayed in hiding, who were cowardly and hesitant.

What can we learn from the outcome of this war – this war that never was a national war?

The imperialist ideology of force, from whatever side it comes, must be shattered for all time. A one-sided Prussian militarism must never again gain power. Only in large-scale cooperation among the nations of Europe can the ground be prepared for reconstruction. Centralized hegemony, such as the Prussian state has tried to exercise in Germany and in Europe, must be cut down at its inception. The Germany of the future must be a federated state. At this juncture only a sound federative system can imbue a weakened Europe with new life. The workers must be liberated from their condition of down-trodden slavery by a reasonable type of socialism. The illusory notion of autarky must disappear in Europe. Every nation and each individual have a right to the resources of this world!

Freedom of speech, freedom of religion, the protection of individual citizens from the arbitrary will of criminal regimes of violence – these will be the bases of the New Europe.

Support the resistance. Distribute the leaflets!

Source: Inge Scholl, *Students Against Tyranny: The Resistance of the White Rose, Munich, 1942–1943*, trsl. by Arthur R. Schultz (Middletown CT: Wesleyan University Press, 1970), pp. 77–84, 89–90

Women in the Second World War

The official role of women in National Socialist society was as loyal, self-sacrificing wives and devoted mothers of numerous children to preserve and expand the German Volk. Although the Nazi ideal was already in conflict with reality in the 1930s, when millions of women served in the work-force, the conflict between ideal and reality became ever greater as Germany prepared for war. The Nazi ideology of confining women to the private sphere became a liability when women workers were needed to keep the war industries going. Greater participation of women in the public sphere became crucial to the survival of the Nazi state in the war. Despite a shift in policy and propaganda, however, the Germans were much less successful than the British or Americans in mobilizing women for the war economy. The Nazis were unwilling to make employment compulsory for all women for fear of losing popular support. They were never able to overcome the contradiction between their anti-feminist ideology and the practical exigencies of a militarized economy.

The following excerpts from a series of pamphlets for women members of the party issued by the office of Robert Ley (1890–1945), head of the German Labor Front, are typical of the Nazis' efforts to mobilize women for work, particularly after the tide of war turned against the Nazis in late 1942. The pamphlet also attests to the Nazis' growing concern about demoralization of the home front as a result of Allied bombing and military reversals. As suffering, shortages, and discontent intensified, the Nazis were increasingly forced to rely on the cooperation and complicity of women to sustain morale and keep the home front going in the face of impending defeat.

5.25 "The Women's Front and the Woman in the Party," 1943

For many women today increased educational and job-related duties are being added to their household responsibilities. In many cases the children have to do without their father, which requires the mother to double her care, prudence, and effort. But in other matters as well she often has to represent her husband and act independently. In the absence of the farmer, many a farmer's wife is running the farm with foreign workers and prisoners of war, i.e., under especially difficult conditions; many a businesswoman is managing the business under similar difficulties in the place of the husband who is serving in the army.

A certain degree of strength is called for in order to persevere in unaccustomed circumstances and not to become tired or frustrated. The party member does not allow herself to be outdone by anyone, for she knows: constancy leads to victory.

As a woman, the party member also participates in the most difficult aspects of war, worry about those at the front and pain for those who have fallen. *She feels a loss as deeply as everyone else, but she bears it with composure in the National Socialist manner.* In this way she can be a pillar and support for others and, because she herself knows the meaning of this war and the sacrifices connected with it, *she can help make sure that the great goal of our fight is not lost from sight because of personal misfortune.* A pronounced characteristic of total war is the *increased employment of women in the war economy.* As much as one would have liked to spare women this harsh situation – the necessities of war compel us. We cannot wage war against three great powers that are nearly the strongest industrially and richest in natural resources and at the same time allow our own economy to run at half speed. Realizing this, years ago many women party members voluntarily answered the call of the Führer and reported to work. This effort must now be expanded. It is a matter of honor for every woman party member not to shirk her duty under any circumstances, but rather to obey without protest the request issued to her, and, in cases where she is not included under the legal regulations, to make an effort on her own to be useful in the service of the common cause. ...

An important task falls to the woman party member with regard to the formulation of opinion and resolve. Not only the currency of national wealth passes through the hands of women, but also the currency of national morals. The current war has presented us with a completely new situation, it has created a front of women. That was not our intention, but rather the design of the enemy. He consciously included women in his calculations as a political factor in war. He directs his terror from the air against her in order to push back the whole front of the German people after wearing down women. This method is by no means new; the British already used it in the Boer war when they interned the Boer women in concentration camps and broke their resistance with the most primitive brutality. In the same way the enemy attempted to strike women and children in the First World War through the hunger blockade. The terror from the air in our time is without doubt the worst of all attacks directed against women up to this point. The physical and moral demands often reach the limits of what can be borne. Some are wounded, others lose family members, still others experience the loss of all their possessions. The horrors of bombing are followed by the difficulties of evacuation; one has to leave one's home, often also one's husband, and live as a guest in previously unfamiliar surroundings. These are misfortunes that require whole hearts and strong determination. In this front of women created by the force of circumstances the party member has her responsibility: she is the designated leader. The others look up to her; her psychological power of resistance comforts her companions; from her conviction they draw courage. Even in critical moments she keeps a clear head and maintains her determination, for she has so much political instinct and insight that she knows what's at stake.

She will demonstrate the necessary calm and steadfastness even in the face of legitimate human apprehensions. She understands the need and the longing of women for peace, but she knows that for us victory is crucial, not peace. She also represents this point of view with complete clarity and determination against the ideological groups among our people who always place only peace in the foreground, not victory. Those who speak only of peace and beg for it to appear undermine the people's will to fight; without saying a word against the war, they promote defeatism and undermine the heroic fight for justice and freedom.

The woman party member has a special responsibility with regard to *public opinion*. This is formed in wartime primarily by women, at least when it comes to spoken propaganda. Their more active imagination and the more emotional nature of their mental world make them more susceptible to sensational news, rumors, and exaggeration of facts. Here the party member has to be aware of her special responsibility. As a woman she is often in closer contact with her national comrades than a man, and she has the opportunity while shopping and on similar occasions to hear the conversations of larger or smaller groups. In the fourth year of the war it is understandable that not every word spoken will be pure joy. Malice, however, is involved only in the rarest cases. ... When the crudest complaints have spilled out of the soul, people are very receptive to enlightenment and correction. It is not necessary to give big speeches at this time; an appeal to feeling and resolve is more important than an appeal to reason. *The party member is most effective through her personality, her conviction, her calm and certainty, her trust in our army, and her belief in the Führer.* That makes a better impression than a debate – a woman often grasps a situation more with instinct than with reasoning, and holds to convictions thus achieved with tenacious, unshakable firmness, even in the face of setbacks. Precisely at times when the troops have difficult days, it is essential to oppose faint-heartedness and obsessive carping. Dissatisfaction with the events at the front is ingratitude towards our soldiers.

Source: *Die Front der Frauen*, issued by the Reichsorganisationsleiter der **NSDAP**, No. 14 (1943), pp. 5–8. Translated by Sally Winkle

D-Day: The Normandy Invasion, 6 June 1944

The long-expected Allied invasion of the mainland occurred at four major sites in Normandy on the northwestern coast of France on 6 June 1944. Although the Allies made slower headway than had been anticipated in their invasion plans, by the middle of July they were poised for the breakthrough that came two weeks later. In the following teletyped message, Field Marshal Erwin Rommel (1891–1944), commander in chief of Army Group B in the West, told Hitler in effect that the war was lost. Rommel graphically described the adverse conditions faced by the German army against growing Allied superiority in men and matériel. Hitler, however, insisted on a fight to the finish. Two days after sending this message Rommel was severely wounded by Allied aircraft at the front. Because he was designated, apparently without his knowledge, to become Army Commander in Chief by military conspirators planning to overthrow the Nazi regime, Rommel was given the choice between trial before the "People's Court" and suicide. On 14 October 1944 Rommel chose suicide.

5.26 Field Marshal Rommel's teletype message to Hitler, 15 July 1944

The situation on the Normandy front grows more difficult daily; it is approaching the proportions of a major crisis.

The fighting power of the divisions is steadily lessening, because of high losses that stem from the severity of the combat, from the enemy's bringing to bear of an overwhelming superiority of matériel, especially of artillery and armor, and from the activity of the enemy air force, which absolutely dominates the battle area. Replacements from home arrive only sparsely, and reach the front, because of the complicated transport situation, only after weeks. Up to now, 6,000 men have come as replacements for losses of some 97,000 men, among them 2,360 officers, including 28 generals and 354 commanders – that is to say, 2,500 to 3,000 men are lost as a daily average. Moreover the losses of matériel by the troops in action are extremely high. Up to now they have been replaced only to a slight extent; for instance, up to now 17 tanks to replace 225.

The new divisions are unaccustomed to combat, and with the shortage of equipment, including artillery, anti-tank weapons and weapons for tanks, they are unable in the long run to successfully parry large-scale enemy attacks and heavy, several-hour-long shelling. As combat experience has shown, the enemy employment of matériel smashes the best trained troops bit by bit. Supply conditions are so difficult, because of the destruction of the railway network, and the several attacks by the enemy air force on streets and highways as far as 150 kilometers behind the front, that only the most essential items can be moved up. Artillery and mortar ammunition in particular has to be rationed to the utmost.

It no longer is possible to bring to the front in Normandy any new forces worth mentioning. On the enemy side, new forces and new war matériel flow to the front day after day. The enemy's supply system is undisturbed by our air force. The enemy exerts stronger and stronger pressure.

Under these circumstances it must be assumed that the enemy in the foreseeable future – fourteen days to three weeks – will succeed in breaking through our own thin front, particularly in the 7th Army area, and in pushing into the broad expanse of France. The consequences will be incalculable.

Our troops everywhere are fighting heroically, but the unequal contest is drawing to an end. I must ask you to draw the consequences from this situation without delay. I feel bound as supreme commander of the army group to express this clearly.

Rommel, Field Marshal

Source: *Germans Against Hitler: July 20, 1944*, 5th edn., ed. by Hans-Adolf Jacobsen (Bonn: Press and Information Office of the Federal Government of Germany, 1969), p. 104

The military resistance

On 20 July 1944 Colonel Claus von Stauffenberg (1907–44), Chief of Staff of Germany's Reserve Army, detonated a bomb in the briefing room of the *Wolfsschanze* (Wolf's Lair), Hitler's East Prussian field headquarters. Although three persons were killed and several others severely wounded, Hitler escaped with minor injuries. The attempt to oust the Nazi government failed when news emerged that Hitler had survived the explosion. Stauffenberg and his leading co-conspirators, including General Ludwig Beck (1880–1944), Chief of the Army General Staff until his dismissal in October 1938 (see Doc. 4.12), were executed by a firing squad at army headquarters in Berlin that same night. Former mayor of Leipzig Carl Goerdeler (1884–1945), the leading civilian member of the conspiracy, went into hiding, but was arrested on 12 August 1944. After a sham trial by the *Volksgerichtshof* (People's Court), he was executed on 2 February 1945. Hundreds of other officers, enlisted men, and civilians fell victim to Hitler's demand for revenge.

The military resistance has been criticized by historians for failing to act until the war was lost and for pursuing unrealistic nationalist goals. The following selection from a Gestapo report lists Stauffenberg's conditions for a negotiated peace allegedly transmitted to England by unnamed emissaries in May 1944. They include restoration of Germany's 1914 borders, the retention of Austria and the Sudetenland, and continuation of the war, if necessary, in the east. The conspirators received no encouragement from the Western Allies, however. Having decided in January 1943 on a policy of unconditional surrender, the Western powers did not want to alienate their Soviet allies by entering into negotiations for a separate peace.

The conspirators may have acted late and more out of a desire to avert the total ruin of their country than out of principled opposition to National Socialism or its aims, but their courage is incontestable. Aware of the unlikelihood of success, many of the conspirators hoped at least to salvage German honor in the eyes of the world. The last words attributed to Major General Henning von Tresckow (1901–44) before his suicide on 21 July 1944 may serve as an example of this heroic attitude.

5.27a Gestapo report on Stauffenberg's relations with foreign countries, 2 August 1944

The recent interrogation of Captain [Hermann] Kaiser produces evidence that Stauffenberg had two contacts with the English, via two go-betweens. These contacts are now being investigated in detail. On May 25, Stauffenberg had already worked out a memo for Kaiser as to matters of negotiation with the enemy:

1 Immediate abandonment of aerial warfare.
2 Abandonment of invasion plans.
3 Avoidance of further bloodshed.
4 Continuing function of defense strength in the East. Evacuation of all occupied regions in the North, West, and South.
5 Renunciation of any occupation.
6 Free government, independent, self-chosen constitution.
7 Full cooperation in the carrying out of truce conditions and in peace preparations.
8 Reich border of 1914 in the east.
    Retention of Austria and the Sudetenland within the Reich.
    Autonomy of Alsace-Lorraine.
    Acquisition of the Tyrol as far as Bozen, Meran.
9 Vigorous reconstruction with joint efforts for European reconstruction.
10 Nations to deal with own criminals.
11 Restoration of honor, self-respect, and respect for others.

At the end of June 1944, Kaiser learned from [Carl Friedrich] Goerdeler that inquiries about the clique of conspirators had been made from highest English quarters. Stauffenberg transmitted:

(a) a list of individuals who were to be participants in future negotiations with England;
(b) the wish that Austria remain with the Reich;
(c) the request that a reckoning with the war criminals should be left to the future German government.

Kaiser's diary, which covered a period from May 9 to July 15, and which contains an abundance of clues, is being made use of at the moment.

5.27b General von Tresckow's Testament, as recorded by a fellow-officer, 21 July 1944

Now the whole world will leap at us and abuse us. But I remain, now as before, of the firm conviction that we have done the right thing. I consider Hitler not only the arch-enemy of Germany, but also the arch-enemy of the world. When I stand before God's judgement seat a few hours from now, to render an account of my actions and omissions, then I believe I shall be able to answer with clear conscience for what I have done in the fight against Hitler. As God once promised Abraham that he would not destroy Sodom if only ten righteous ones were found in it, so I hope that for our sake God will not destroy Germany. No one of us can complain about his death. He who entered our circle donned the poisoned garment of Nessus. The moral worth of a human being only begins where he is ready to give his life for his convictions!

Source: *Germans Against Hitler: July 20, 1944*, 5th edn., ed. by Hans-Adolf Jacobsen (Bonn: Press and Information Office of the Federal Republic of Germany, 1969), pp. 95–6, 292

Flight from East Prussia, 1945

After defeat in the Battle of Kursk in Russia in July 1943, the last great German offensive in the east, the Wehrmacht began the long retreat that brought the Red Army to the borders of the German Reich in late 1944. German defenses in the east had been weakened by the need to combat the Allied armies on the western front. After the invasion of Normandy in June 1944 (Doc. 5.26) it took the Allies only five months to advance to Germany's western borders. Hitler transferred additional forces from east to west in late 1944 to launch his last-ditch offensive in the Ardennes in December 1944, known in the West as the Battle of the Bulge. This opened the way for the rapid advance of Soviet forces into East Prussia and Poland in January 1945. Millions of Germans fled westward to escape the Soviet army.

The recollections below of one such escape by Countess Marion von Dönhoff (b. 1909), scion of an ancient aristocratic family that had settled in East Prussia more than 600 years ago, was published under the title, *Namen die keiner mehr nennt* ("Names That Nobody Knows Anymore") in 1962. Dönhoff had taken charge of the family's many estates, including her home of Quittainen, at the outbreak of war in 1939. Her account captures the chaos, panic, anger, and sense of loss that accompanied the German collapse at the end of the war. It also describes the ordeal of German refugees, who had been forbidden to leave their homes by the Nazis (to prevent "defeatism") until a day or two before the arrival of Soviet troops. Ethnic Germans who remained behind were forcibly expelled by the Soviets and Poles after the war. Approximately one-and-a-half million Germans died in the course of their flight or expulsion. Marion Dönhoff survived and gained renown as editor of Germany's most important liberal weekly, *Die Zeit*, after the war.

5.28 Marion Gräfin Dönhoff, *Names That Nobody Knows Anymore*

Two days later [after the activation of the *Volkssturm*],[11] it must have been January 21 or 22 [1945], I got on my way early in the morning. I rode from one farm to the other to make sure everything was all right. Everywhere there were problems: In Lägs the tractor driver had been conscripted, although he had been classified as indispensable for farming operations; in Skollmen

---

11   The *Volkssturm* (people's storm) was a military force created in September 1944 and made up of men between the ages of 16 and 60 who had not yet been conscripted into the Wehrmacht.

it was the inspector. On many farms horses were requisitioned indiscriminately, and everywhere the prisoners of war – the last available workers – began to get restless. The French were alarmed by the general disintegration and wondered how they were ever going to get home, and the Russians knew very well that the Soviet functionaries would treat them as saboteurs because they had survived and had worked for the enemy instead of cutting our throats.

Toward evening, when it was already dark, I called the district administration in [the town of] Prussian Holland, whose approval was needed for every train trip at that time. I asked them to issue me a ticket, since I wanted to go to Königsberg at 6 o'clock the next morning to make sure that everything was all right in Friedrichstein, the second set of properties that I had to look after. The voice on the other end was silent for several seconds; then I heard the words: "Don't you realize that the district has to be evacuated by midnight?"

"I had no idea," I answered without surprise, but taken aback; "so where are the Russians?"

"I have no idea," he answered.

"Well, where are we supposed to go and how are we supposed to get there?"

The voice of authority, which up to now had never tired of declaring that the authorities would take care of everything and that there was no cause for alarm, gave this answer to my question: "It's all the same to us. Go on land, by water, or through the air … "

I summoned the people to the estate inspector's office and explained what was in store for all of us now. They were completely flabbergasted. They had been told so much about victory at the end and that the "Führer" would never allow even a foot of East Prussian soil to be lost that they simply could not believe this news. I gave them exact directions how much, or rather how little, each one would be allowed to load on to the wagons, impressed on them the time we planned to meet at the Rogehner Street intersection that night, and delegated the responsibility for the whole business to the estate treasurer. …

In Quittainen Chief Inspector Klatt had just heard the news. I found him sitting in his office, staring gloomily into space while the local party leader stood in front of him talking furiously. It was about the refugees. We had taken in over 400 refugees from the Goldap region since the autumn. They had left their homes shortly before the Russians captured Goldap in October and journeyed westward. When the German troops succeeded in recapturing Goldap and Nemmersdorf in November, the refugees and their wagon train sought shelter with us. They have been waiting since then to see how it would turn out. …

So these Goldap refugees had spent the winter with us and had seriously reduced our feed stocks. That didn't worry me much, because I knew we wouldn't be able use them all up ourselves anyway. But it seemed to make the party leadership uneasy, and therefore one of these clever idiots came up with the idea of sending the men back with the horses to Goldap, 250 kilometers away, to use up the feed that was left there. It was the beginning of January, and we could already hear the thunder of artillery. So now here we were left with 380 women and children who packed up their wagons once again, but couldn't move them, because the men had been sent away with the horses and had probably long since been overrun by the Russian front.

To avoid this situation, made inevitable by the actions of the party leadership, I had suggested to the town officials of the region two days earlier that we should make our tractors available to the Goldap refugees, tie on their wagons, and send them away as quickly as possible, so they would at least be out of the way. But the officials had a thousand doubts: they said that we would need the tractors for the spring planting, and who knows whether they would be returned in working order … Therefore this plan was not carried out.

So now the local party leader stood before us and declared that his orders were to make sure we took the refugees with us – which was of course completely out of the question. He said that only over his dead body would we leave without them. Chief Inspector Klatt, a tall, heavy-set man with ruddy complexion and blond hair parted in the middle, was regarded in the whole region as an outstanding agricultural specialist. Everywhere his expertise was valued. The Nazis would have loved to be able to claim him as one of their own and make him District Farmers' Leader. Twice they had urged him in a flattering but determined way to join the party, but both times he had found a reason to refuse. His comment: "I want nothing to do with these scoundrels." Now he stood up, gave a withering look to the official, who in civilian life had run our local tavern, and did not deign to speak another word with him.

And then both of us took turns running around in the village at night and pleading with the people to take along only what was absolutely necessary. But our suggestions and instructions were overwhelmed by the general chaos that thwarted all my preparations as well. For months I had a kind of "flight plan" in my desk at home. It indicated exactly which of the men still left on each estate were to drive which wagon, the maximum number of possessions that each family was permitted to take, and the minimum that seemed absolutely necessary. I had secretly had copies made of surveyors' maps that indicated all the overland routes and ferries across the Nogat and Vistula rivers. Every estate was supposed to receive several of these maps to take along, because it would be difficult to get across the rivers whose bridges would probably have been destroyed by one side or the other by that time.

Now all these preparations were simply thrown out. The chaos was so great that it would have made absolutely no sense to even try to bring out these plans in view of the general panic and despair. Also it just was not possible anymore to contact the other estates in order to launch our trek together as planned. Would we meet the others on the way? Would we ever see them again at all? One more time – for the last time – I have to write down the names of the estates, so that they will at least be recorded somewhere, all these beautiful names that nobody knows anymore: Quittainen, Comthurhof, Pergusen, Weinings, Hartwigs, Mäken, Skollmen, Lägs, Amalienhof, Schönau, Big Thierbach, Little Thierbach, Nauten, Canditten, Einhöfen.

We had become so accustomed to living with the war and the absurdities of the Nazis that we thought and acted on two different levels without really noticing it: two levels that constantly merged, although the one actually excluded the other. Thus I had already known for years (not just since the outbreak of the war, but since I had been a student in Frankfurt, when that man seized power), that East Prussia would one day be lost. And yet we lived as if ... as if everything would keep on going, as if everything depended on passing on the properties in good condition and with improvements to the next generation. ...

But now back to our departure and the flight. I too had quickly packed a rucksack with items that seemed to me the most indispensable: some clothes and a few photographs and papers. A saddle bag with toiletries, bandage material, and my old Spanish crucifix was there as well, already packed, always handy. My cook Trudchen had quickly made supper, which we ate together, and the two secretaries joined us. Miss Markowski, the older one, who was very efficient, was an enthusiastic follower of the Führer. She had cheered every special announcement for years – now she was very quiet, but I am convinced that she was wondering if the non-believers and "traitors" were not really the ones to blame for this debacle. ...

We ate quickly together: Who knows, when we would get something to eat again ... Then we got up, left the food and silverware on the table, and for the last time went through the house door, which we didn't lock. It was midnight … In the meantime the wagons had gathered outside. I ran into the stall and got my saddle-horse ready, the one I knew would be able to handle all the strain. I instructed the driver to tie my beloved white Draulitter mare to his wagon. But the old man forgot these instructions in all the excitement, and she stayed behind with all the other animals.

It was only 11 kilometers from Quittainen to Prussian Holland. Normally we figured it would be a good hour's ride. On this day it took six hours. The streets were slick with ice, the horses could get no traction, and the coupé, in which we had loaded two sick people, constantly slipped sideways across the road. They came pouring out from all the side roads and clogged the intersections, and a kilometer outside of the town everything finally came to a standstill. We stood there over two hours without moving forward even a centimeter. At last I rode into the town just to see what was really happening there. Also I was very interested in what the Nazi functionaries were doing now, the same officials who three days earlier had condemned all preparations for escape as defeatism to be severely punished.

I wound my way through the profusion of wagons and people to the district office of the NSDAP. All the doors stood open, burnt paper swirled around in the air. Files were spread across the floor. All the rooms were empty. "Of course they were the first ones to leave, the pigs," said a peasant farmer, who was poking around there as I was. Yes, they were gone, and thank heavens they would all be gone soon. But at what a price! I had to think of how much we would have been spared if the attempt of 20 July – six months ago – had succeeded.

The town looked like a jammed turntable: the wagons had driven in from two sides and had clogged up the whole thing, and now there was no way to go either forward or backward. I went to the post office, and, lo and behold, the good old post office was still working. While on the outside the chaos grew and the "leaders" had taken to their heels, the old employees sat at their places.

I was even able to telephone Friedrichstein, which was 120 kilometers to the east, on the other side of Königsberg. The situation there was still normal, the kind of abnormal normality that had characterized our life for so long. At any rate they had not yet received an order to evacuate. They never did receive one. It was already too late for them. Just as I was calling, the Russian tank spearhead broke through 25 kilometers ahead of us from the south to Frisches Haff [a large lagoon on the Baltic Sea]. East Prussia was cut off, and for those who were not in the western border districts as we were, the order to evacuate was useless. The only way out left for them was across the frozen lagoon.

When I reached our wagons again two hours later, everyone was already frozen stiff and in despair. It was 20 below zero. Even Klatt thought the whole venture was absolutely pointless. "If we're going to fall to the Russians anyway, then better at home" – that was roughly the maxim on which all had agreed. And they had also decided something else among themselves in the meantime: that I should try to get through to the west with my horse, for the Russians would surely shoot me, while they, the workers, would just be milking the cows and cleaning the barns for the Russians in the future. Neither they nor I realized at the time what a misconception it was to think that nothing would happen to workers.

[Dönhoff decided to continue on alone, joining refugee columns from other areas of East Prussia and Pomerania along the way.]

Little by little, in slow motion – as if the images were to be impressed on our minds one last time – the beloved landscape passed by us like the background of a surrealistic film. Elbing, Marienburg, whose history was interwoven with my family in many ways, and then Dirschau. Dirschau looked like a gigantic open-air performance of *Wallenstein's Camp*: People everywhere in the most fantastic costumes.[12] Here and there a fire, where people were cooking. The roar of artillery was now very close; sometimes all the houses seemed to shake. We found shelter in a farm at the edge of the town. While one of us slept on a sofa, the other one had to stand watch over the horses in the stable – for a horse was worth a kingdom in these times. But it was no real sleep; people walked through the house all the time, taking a pillow or a towel or opening a jar of canned food. We, too, had eaten our first real meal here in the pantry.

Suddenly the whole misery of the human race crept upon me, and I started to regret not having returned home with our people. The thought of trying to change that decision, maybe to jump off this conveyor belt even now, seemed suddenly fascinating to me: If now and then full trains were still going west – were not perhaps other empty ones going east? Perhaps I could go to Königsberg and from there to Friedrichstein. I went to the train station. Here too there were thousands of people. Of course no open ticket window, no information, nothing. Finally I found a railroad employee: "What, to Königsberg?" He looked at me as if I wanted to go to the moon and shook his head. – No, there were no more trains going east. ...

The temperature had fallen even lower, and a blizzard-like east wind had begun blowing – which rarely happens when it is really cold. When we finally left the farmyard all bundled up and rode up a protected ravine, we saw once again across a field in the distance the great marching army of refugees on the road ahead of us. It was not snowing, but snow swept through the air. As if through a thick white veil we saw these unfortunate people creep forward slowly, very slowly, their coats whipped by the wind. The covers on many of the wagons had caved in. We joined this ghost train and saw the first dead people lying by the side of the road. No one had the strength, the time, or the opportunity to bury them.

And so it went for days – for weeks. More new vehicles, more and more people, joined in from the right and the left. And not only here in the northeast; the same images could be seen since last autumn in southeastern Germany: Wagon trains and more wagon trains. ...

Many of these images I will never forget. Somewhere on the way – I believe between Bütow and Berent – was a place where we had a view of the straight road 3 kilometers ahead and 3 kilometers back. On these 6 kilometers I did not see one square meter of street, only wagons, horses, people, and misery. No one spoke. All that could be heard was the grinding of wheels that were gradually drying out.

Another image: It was probably still in East Prussia. One day three tanks came by; they were laden with refugees – women and children, who had bags and suitcases with them. Civilian and military – this fusion of normal and abnormal, of wanting to destroy and wanting to survive, was something I had never seen before. It looked bizarre. For some reason they stopped for a minute. A farmer said: "It would be better if you stopped the Russians instead of pushing us off the street here." One of the soldiers, a rough fellow whose black, white, and red band dangled from his button hole, screamed at him: "We've had enough of this shit!"

And once – we had started to make some progress on our horses and had passed lots of wagons – suddenly all we saw were French prisoners. There were hundreds and hundreds, maybe thousands. Many had nailed two strips of wood like runners to their little cardboard suitcases and dragged their luggage on a string behind them. They did not say a word. Only the

---

12 *Wallenstein's Lager* (Wallenstein's Camp) is an eighteenth-century play by Friedrich Schiller about the Thirty Years War.

scratching, scraping sound of the boxes and suitcases could be heard. And all around endless snowbound solitude, like the retreat of [Napoleon's] Grande Armée 130 years ago. ...

Whereas east of the Vistula river all the houses and barns in which we found shelter for a few hours or a night had already been abandoned, it was the opposite in Pomerania, where everything was still intact – or what could be called "intact" in those days. But the people who lived there feared that one day what was happening to us could happen to them as well, although it seemed absolutely unimaginable to me that the people of Pomerania would have to flee too. ...

Many a person in Pomerania waved good-bye to us with just a trace of envy. Many of them would have liked to send at least the children, the young girls, and a few valuables away with us. But here, too, it was always the same: It was strictly forbidden. And there were people everywhere who informed on others out of misguided patriotism; therefore no one dared defy the prohibition. Never before had the leader of a nation done the enemy's business so efficiently, never before had a commander-in-chief driven his soldiers to their deaths by the hundreds of thousands through such amateurish leadership, never before had someone who claimed to be the father of the nation shackled his people to the executioner's block and prevented their escape. He who thought that German living space was too small and had set out to expand it – he had robbed millions of Germans of land that had been their home for many hundreds of years and had reduced Germany to a minimum. Long before the war broke out a joke circulated in Berlin in which Stalin talked about his *Gauleiter* Hitler. ...

I had seldom lived for a particular moment with such anticipation as I did for the reunion with my sister-in-law and her children. For weeks I had also been looking forward to being able to bathe and put on different clothes, as I had given up my rucksack on the second day after our departure because it was too unwieldy. But now it turned out that the family had already left three days earlier. Departed, fled. I could not believe that people had to flee in the region of Prenzlau. And where would all these people stay? From what would they live?

So we moved on again – "to arrive" – that was obviously a verb that we had to exclude from our vocabulary. We continued on through the Mark region, through Mecklenburg and Lower Saxony to Westphalia. I crossed three great rivers that at one time had given our eastern Germany its character: the Vistula, Oder, and Elbe. I had set off at the full moon; in the meantime there had been a new moon, a full moon again, and then another new moon.

I had ridden from my home on the estate in the deepest winter; when I finally arrived at the Metternichs in Vinsebeck, Westphalia, it was spring. The birds were singing. The dust rose behind the drilling machines in the dry fields. Everything was gearing up for a new beginning. Would life really go on – just as if nothing had happened?

> Source: **Marion Gräfin Dönhoff**, *Namen die keiner mehr nennt: Ostpreussen –*
> *Menschen und Geschichte* **(Munich: Deutscher Taschenbuch Verlag, 1964),**
> **pp. 16–18, 22–4, 26, 28–9, 31–3. Translated by Sally Winkle**

Hitler's Testament

Shortly before his suicide in the bunker of his chancellery on 30 April 1945, Hitler dictated the following self-serving political testament. He named Admiral Karl Dönitz (1891–1980) as his successor and urged him to continue the fight. Hitler showed no remorse for what he had done. To the bitter end he remained obsessed by the "Jewish Question," blaming the Jews for the start of the war and boasting that he had delivered on his promise of annihilation. His protestations of love for his own people ring hollow, however, in the light of his notorious "Nero Command" of several weeks earlier – the order to munitions chief Albert Speer (1905–81) to destroy the infrastructure necessary to the survival of the civilian population in areas vacated by the Wehrmacht. In his last days in the bunker Hitler was also quoted as saying that the German *Volk* deserved to perish inasmuch as it had shown itself weaker than the Slavic peoples. The suicidal and self-destructive impulse in National Socialist ideology was present from the start. Even now Hitler exhorted the German people to continue the struggle unto death. The trauma of surrender in 1918 remained deeply ingrained in Hitler's psyche. Many times he had vowed that it would never be repeated. Hitler bitterly denounced both Goering and Himmler, each of whom had separately sought to arrange a cease-fire in the west in order to continue the war in the east. Ironically, the destructive effects of the Nazis' fanatical fight to the finish may have contributed to the popular repudiation of Nazism after the war. But that same fanaticism continues to give pathological inspiration to right-wing racists and extremists today.

5.29 Adolf Hitler, "My Political Testament," 29 April 1945

More than thirty years have now passed since I in 1914 made my modest contribution as a volunteer in the First World War that was forced upon the Reich.

In these three decades I have been actuated solely by love and loyalty to my people in all my thoughts, acts, and life. They gave me the strength to make the most difficult decisions which have ever confronted mortal man. I have spent my time, my working strength, and my health in these three decades.

It is untrue that I or anyone else in Germany wanted the war in 1939. It was desired and instigated exclusively by those international statesmen who were either of Jewish descent or worked for Jewish interests. I have made too many offers for the control and limitation of armaments, which posterity will not for all time be able to disregard for the responsibility for the outbreak of this war to be laid on me. I have further never wished that after the first fatal world war a second against England, or even against America, should break out. Centuries will pass away, but out of the ruins of our towns and monuments the hatred against those finally responsible whom we have to thank for everything, international Jewry and its helpers, will grow.

Three days before the outbreak of the German–Polish war I again proposed to the British ambassador in Berlin a solution to the German–Polish problem – similar to that in the case of the Saar district, under international control. This offer also cannot be denied. It was only rejected because the leading circles in English politics wanted the war, partly on account of the business hoped for and partly under influence of propaganda organized by international Jewry.

I also made it quite plain that, if the nations of Europe are again to be regarded as mere shares to be bought and sold by these international conspirators in money and finance, then that race, Jewry, which is the real criminal of this murderous struggle, will be saddled with the responsibility. I further left no one in doubt that this time not only would millions of children of Europe's Aryan peoples die of hunger, not only would millions of grown men suffer death, and not only hundreds of thousands of women and children be burnt and bombed to death in the towns, without the real criminal having to atone for this guilt, even if by more humane means.

After six years of war, which in spite of all setbacks, will go down one day in history as the most glorious and valiant demonstration of a nation's life purpose, I cannot forsake the city which is the capital of this Reich. As the forces are too small to make any further stand against the enemy attack at this place and our resistance is gradually being weakened by men who are as deluded as they are lacking in initiative, I should like, by remaining in this town, to share my fate with those, the millions of others, who have also taken upon themselves to do so. Moreover I do not wish to fall into the hands of an enemy who requires a new spectacle organized by the Jews for the amusement of their hysterical masses.

I have decided therefore to remain in Berlin and there of my own free will to choose death at the moment when I believe the position of the Führer and Chancellor itself can no longer be held.

I die with a happy heart, aware of the immeasurable deeds and achievements of our soldiers at the front, our women at home, the achievements of our farmers and workers and the work, unique in history, of our youth who bear my name.

That from the bottom of my heart I express my thanks to you all, is just as self-evident as my wish that you should, because of that, on no account give up the struggle, but rather continue it against the enemies of the Fatherland, no matter where, true to the creed of a great Clausewitz.[13] From the sacrifice of our soldiers and from my own unity with them unto death, will in any case spring up in the history of Germany the seed of a radiant renaissance of the National Socialist movement and thus of the realization of a true community of nations.

Many of the most courageous men and women have decided to unite their lives with mine until the very last. I have begged and finally ordered them not to do this, but to take part in the further battle of the nation. I beg the heads of the Armies, the Navy, and the Air Force to strengthen by all possible means the spirit of resistance of our soldiers in the National Socialist sense, with special reference to the fact that also I myself, as founder and creator of this movement, have preferred death to cowardly abdication or even capitulation.

May it, at some future time, become part of the code of honor of the German officer – as is already the case in our Navy – that the surrender of a district or of a town is impossible, and that above all the leaders here must march ahead as shining examples, faithfully fulfilling their duty unto death.

SECOND PART OF THE POLITICAL TESTAMENT

Before my death I expel the former Reich Marshall Hermann Goering from the party and deprive him of all rights which he may enjoy by virtue of the decree of 29 June 1941, and also by virtue of my statement in the Reichstag on 1 September 1939.[14] I appoint in his place Grand Admiral Dönitz, President of the Reich and Supreme Commander of the Armed Forces.

Before my death I expel the former Reichsführer-SS and Minister of the Interior, Heinrich Himmler, from the party and from all offices of State. In his stead I appoint Gauleiter Karl Hanke as Reichsführer-SS and Chief of the German Police, and Gauleiter Paul Giesler as Reich Minister of the Interior.[15]

---

13   The Prussian general Karl von Clausewitz (1780–1831), author of *On War* (1833), advocated a policy of total war.

14   Hitler had previously named Goering as his successor in case of his death (see Doc. 5.1).

15   Karl Hanke (1903–45) and Paul Giesler (1895–1945) were Gauleiter of Silesia and Bavaria, respectively. Both died in the final days of the war.

Goering and Himmler, quite apart from their disloyalty to my person, have done immeasurable harm to the country and the whole nation by secret negotiations with the enemy, which they conducted without my knowledge and against my wishes, and by illegally attempting to seize power in the State for themselves. ...

... Our task, that of continuing the building of a National Socialist State, represents the work of the coming centuries, which places every single person under an obligation always to serve the common interest and to subordinate his own advantage to this end. I demand of all Germans, all National Socialists, men, women, and all the men of the Armed Forces, that they be faithful and obedient unto death to the new government and its President.

Above all I charge the leaders of the nation and those under them to scrupulous observance of the laws of race and to merciless opposition to the universal poisoner of all peoples, international Jewry.

Given in Berlin, this 29th day of April 1945. 4:00 a.m.

Adolf Hitler

Source: Office of the US Chief of Counsel for Prosecution of Axis Criminality,
Nazi Conspiracy and Aggression, **Vol. VI**
(Washington DC: US Government Printing Office, 1946), pp. 260–3 [Doc. 3569-PS]

German surrender

After the failure of the last desperate German offensive in the West, the Battle of the Bulge, in January 1945, the Allied armies made rapid headway in east and west. American and Soviet troops met at Torgau on the Elbe River on 25 April 1945. Hitler's suicide on 30 April created the conditions for German surrender, which was signed at Allied Commander-in-Chief General Eisenhower's headquarters at Rheims on 7 May and at Red Army Commander-in-Chief General Zhukov's headquarters in Berlin around midnight on 8 May 1945.

5.30 Act of Surrender by Germany, 8 May 1945

1   We the undersigned, acting by authority of the German High Command, hereby surrender unconditionally to the Supreme Commander, Allied Expeditionary Force and simultaneously to the Supreme High Command of the Red Army all forces on land, at sea, or in the air who are at this date under German control.

2   The German High Command will at once issue orders to all German military, naval, and air authorities and to all forces under German control to cease active operations at 2301 hours Central European time on 8th May 1945, to remain in the positions occupied at that time and to disarm completely, handing over the weapons and equipment to the local Allied commanders or officers designated by Representatives of the Allied Supreme Command. No ship, vessel, or aircraft is to be scuttled, or any damage done to their hull, machinery or equipment, and also to machines of all kinds, armament, apparatus, and all the technical means of prosecution of war in general.

3   The German High Command will at once issue to the appropriate commanders, and ensure the carrying out of any further orders issued by the Supreme Commander, Allied Expeditionary Force and by the Supreme High Command of the Red Army.

4   This act of military surrender is without prejudice to, and will be superseded by any
     general instrument of surrender imposed by, or on behalf of the United Nations and
     applicable to GERMANY and the German armed forces as a whole.

5   In the event of the German High Command or any of the forces under their control
     failing to act in accordance with this Act of Surrender, the Supreme Commander, Allied
     Expeditionary Force and the Supreme High Command of the Red Army will take such
     punitive or other action as they deem appropriate.

6   This Act is drawn up in the English, Russian and German languages. The English and
     Russian are the only authentic texts.

Signed at Berlin on the 8th day of May, 1945
FRIEDEBURG
KEITEL
STUMPF
On behalf of the German High Command

**Source: US Department of State Publication 9446, *Documents on Germany 1944–1985*
(Washington DC: US Government Printing Office, n.d.), p. 14**

Liberation

Not all Germans experienced defeat as a catastrophe. Those with left-wing political sympathies or connections experienced it as liberation, if they had the good
fortune to survive the war. The following selections from the personal diary of
"Erika S.," aged 18 at the end of the war, describe the last year of the war from a
disaffected and highly emotional teenager's point of view. Her father had been a
Social Democratic member of the municipal government in Hamburg when
Hitler came to power. He was arrested in 1934 and spent the next four years in
prison and in the Sachsenhausen concentration camp. After the failed attempt on
Hitler's life on 20 July 1944, he was arrested again. Erika thereupon wrote a letter
to Heinrich Himmler, assuring him of her family's loyalty to Nazism. After her
father was released again several weeks later, he was drafted into the *Volkssturm*,
the untrained and ill-equipped civil defense force of under- and over-aged men
formed in September 1944 to resist the Allied advance.

Not surprisingly, in view of Erika's youth, much of the diary is written in a spontaneous and intensely personal style. Her graphic confession of fear during an air-raid in
late 1944 leaves little to the imagination. In 1943–44 she was infatuated with a young
soldier, Benno, who hoped for a German victory. Her diary also provides evidence that
she knew of the killing of Jews by gas. Among the most interesting passages are those
that record the abrupt turnabout of Nazi sympathizers among her high school classmates in the last days of the war as they prepared for the coming occupation.

After the war Erika's father resumed a leadership role in the Hamburg SPD and
became the first chairman of the Social Democratic labor unions. Erika was also active
in the SPD and married a fellow member of the SPD youth group in 1946. Her diary lay
unpublished for more than 30 years until it was included in a collection of anonymous
wartime journals published in 1984.

5.31 Erika S., Diary, Hamburg, 1944–45

21 JULY 1944

Something incredible has happened! A group of officers carried out an assassination attempt on the Führer. The Führer is still alive; he is not injured. The assassins are all dead, either executed or suicide. It is now so dangerous for the Führer that he can't trust his own circle anymore! Anyone who says something about the Führer now will be shot …

24 JULY 1944

… Now we're in for it too. Last night I had the worst fear of my life. I was a terrible coward!

At 11:30 Pa, Ma, and Walli went to bed. I rolled up my hair (because I wanted to look pretty for Benno, if he comes tomorrow!) and then at midnight I listen to the aircraft situation report. There are solitary enemy aircraft over northwest Germany. Oh! So there is something there after all. Should I wake Pa? Better not. Before I get to sleep, the sirens are already sounding a preliminary warning. Right afterward the air-raid warning starts sounding. We drag our suitcases down into the cellar. The radio reports that one enemy formation is flying toward our city. Is it meant for us this time? My heart starts pounding a little, because I would like to live at least until Benno comes!

The radio reports: "In 4 minutes there may be an intermediate attack on our city. There are 100–150 enemy aircraft." Well, thanks a lot! That's enough for me. Now I would rather run to the air-raid shelter above ground, because I always feel terribly unsafe in the cellar, but I feel secure in the air-raid shelter. Ma and I lie on a shelter bed in the cellar. My head is turned to the wall. Tears are streaming down my face. Is it fear? Is it worry about waiting for Benno? Or don't I know myself, why I am crying? – Now there is anti-aircraft fire outside. I'm especially uneasy and anxious because Pa and Ma yelled at me for being afraid in the cellar. They are right, of course, whining does not make it any better. There's a thunderous noise outside, a hellish racket!! The first bombs start falling. But it's funny, when the bombs start falling the cowardly, pitiful fear that even I hate so much fades away. My whole body is trembling, but the fear is no longer caught in my throat. For the first time in my life I trembled with fear! A person can pull himself together, but this trembling, this awful trembling cannot be willed away, at least not by me. And it's a relief to me that Ma is trembling too! Pa has just told us that there are lots of fir trees above us, so that's where it will start!! In the very next moment the bombs are whistling; the anti-aircraft guns fire and bang. Our skirts fly up in the cellar, the floor seems to rise, and the door sways on its hinges. It is quite a while before the bombing dies down. The airplanes fly away. And we are alive! I can hardly believe it! Overjoyed, I drag our suitcases upstairs as the preliminary all clear signal sounds. At the all clear signal we go to bed. Suddenly an airplane drones outside; the droning is very strange, slower and slower, more muffled and then louder. I'm thinking, the night fighters are heading back from attacking the enemy. Suddenly I am wide awake; a deafening blast wrenches all of us out of our sleep. Could an airplane have gone down? I go up to the attic and look out the attic window at the city center. I can count nine fires; four of them are really big and bright. The flames lick greedily, hungrily, even eerily into the sky. The night is menacing. I sit on the ladder and look out the dormer window. Up here on my lonely seat the misery of it all really hits me.

What does the world look like, and how miserable all the people are today. Possessions have become ten times more valuable, but everything gets lost anyway. We are poor and naked and then every day over and over again we have to fear for the little, so beloved life that we have. Why? This word comes suddenly out of me without my wanting it to. I shout it one, two, three times! What am I doing? My behavior is ridiculous. Tears run down my face; I'm glad that no one can see me ... Slowly I climb down; the ladder wobbles and I almost fall down. Oh, this misery really has to end soon. What the people have to endure is just too much. – Benno, when are you coming? With this thought I fell asleep.

29 AUGUST 1944

The next to last day in Donauhof ... They arrested my father again! My dear Pa, who hasn't done anything! Ma wrote me about it yesterday, and now I'm leaving tomorrow, because I don't want to leave my Ma alone. I wrote the following lines to Himmler right away:

24 AUGUST 44

> To Reichsführer SS, Heinrich Himmler.
>
> Today during my stay in the KLV[16] the news reached me that my father, the worker Walter Sch., born 3 February 1901 in Hamburg, was arrested by the Gestapo on 23 August 1944.
>
> My father was already in custody from the beginning of '34 to October '38, because he belonged to the SPD before 1933 and was a member of the city council. – Our parents have raised me and my 14 year-old brother completely according to the goals of National Socialism. My mother is a member of the *Deutsches Frauenwerk* [German Women's Agency], my brother has been in the Hitler Youth for years, and I have been a leader and group song conductor of the League of German Girls since 1943. Before that I was a member of the Hitler Youth Orchestra of Hamburg for 1½ years. I rejoined the District Orchestra a few weeks ago, since we have gotten an apartment in Hamburg.
>
> I have been a member of the NSDAP since April '44 and up to now I have supported our ideas everywhere at all times.
>
> Herr Reichsführer SS Himmler, I am imploring you to order a review of the case, since the reasons for keeping my father in custody are totally unclear to me considering our conduct and views.
>
> Heil Hitler

---

16   KLV stood for *Kinderlandesverschickung* (Children's Evacuation), a program to send urban children to the country to escape the bombing and to relieve their parents of their care under the trying conditions of city life during the war. Thousands of camps were established throughout the country to care for evacuated children, to indoctrinate them, and to put them to useful work.

I'm not expecting Herr Himmler to show any mercy, but I mustn't overlook any chance to win the release of my Pa, because now I am big enough to fight together with Ma for my Pa. Back then I was still a child; now I can already be considered an adult. – ...

BACK IN HAMBURG, 10 SEPTEMBER 1944

Now I'm back here again and a lot, really a lot has happened. ... Pa was not here yet when I came. Ma and Walli and Uncle Arthur picked me up from the main train station and we got home without an air-raid alarm. At home there were two letters, from Paul and Benno. Thank heavens Paul has come back from France; now he is in Mannheim. On the first of September I didn't go back to school; instead I went to Prof. G. to ask to be excused. We told him about Pa, and he was very sympathetic. Then we went to the Gestapo. The men were all very nice, and they really raised our hopes. On Saturday we were back at the Gestapo, and this time the reception was cold. We had to run from one person to another; everyone had signed but the file could not be found. The department head, Senior Government Councillor B., dashed our hopes, because as the "chief" he did not want to sign the petition. Now Pa's file had to be sent to Berlin, and we have to wait to see what will happen. We don't have a single penny of income, but luckily we still have our savings accounts. Of course we feel worst for our dear Pa who is locked up now and can't even go to the cellar when the air-raid alarm sounds! Just like a dangerous criminal! It's just unbearable how people are treated in Germany. And we do everything so as not to attract attention. ...

9 NOVEMBER 1944

The 9th of November! Day of Remembrance for the Heroes![17] And now my Usch is dead too; I found out yesterday! I still can't believe it – my Usch dead? She was the victim of an attack by low-flying aircraft, along with several high-ranking leaders of the League of German Girls. Miraculously Lotti K. was not injured. Now it's a struggle between my head and my heart!! My heart mourns for Usch, my dear friend – my head says: "Usch was a victim of her ideas, she died willingly!" No, no, no, my head doesn't say that. I can only grieve; I don't think that Usch herself was guilty. I'm not a man; I'm not a politician. I *cannot* be as consistent as I would have to be to fully sustain our ideas. I see now that I am too soft to ever be able to take revenge. I couldn't – even if I wanted to. ...

Pa is not coming tonight; now Ma is worried. Ma is supposed to work, and of course there's a lot of fear now. And Pa has been ordered to the *Volkssturm*!![18] As if he could still be of any help! The English and Americans will most likely break through in the west in the next few days. The Russians are outside Budapest and will soon be 100 km inside of East Prussia!

V2 rockets have been underway since yesterday! There's talk of *Nebelgeschütze* [literally, "fog guns"] – the sailors are all running around here with gas masks on. – Uncle Willi is also writing about "getting gas masks ready", etc. Well, it will certainly come to an end soon ... If we can only live through it ... without injury, then every thing else doesn't matter.

17 The reference is to the Hitler Putsch on 9 November 1923.
18 The *Volkssturm*, created 25 September 1944, were units made up of previously non-conscripted men between the ages of 16 and 60 for the purpose of defending the homeland.

For today I would like to close, my friend, I'm tired. My heart is also tired and so hopeless, as if everything were going to end soon. Everything, happiness and also pain. Well, then let's get on with it! ...

4 MARCH 1945

It was a glorious Spring day, and things also went well in the morning at school. I gave my weekly report, and R. was very pleased with it. She said I had put a lot of work into the report, I had spoken well, and I also knew a lot about the map. It was just that I was too pessimistic!! I protested: "Excuse me, but I only presented the events." – R.: "But it depends on *how* you present the events and above all, the tone in which you present them!!!" I agreed, and gave her a friendly smile; she smiled back – Man, she really should know that my tone was intentionally pessimistic! Otherwise any other person could have given the report, but my "unique way" was to spell it all out so clearly, that even the most enthusiastic Nazi would notice that the war is lost. But they are so stupid and keep hoping for a miracle, because after all the Führer said (at the 25th anniversary of the Announcement of the Party Program): "Today I predict victory!" And whatever he says, must be true (... or so they think!)!! ...

And then the saddest thing I have heard in the last few weeks: They picked up Margot's mother, that is she had to go to a work unit outside the region. She is considered a full Jew, although it hasn't been proven, because she's an illegitimate child. She probably has to go to Theresienstadt. Margot told me that 10,000 women have already arrived there. 500 of them went to the work unit; the rest were sent to the gas chambers. – Such a thing only exists in Germany, the country where every speck of humanity has vanished! Hopefully Margot will actually see her mother again, because one can't expect much consideration from the Nazis. ...

20 APRIL 1945, THE FÜHRER'S BIRTHDAY

I've made you wait a long time – unduly long, and you probably thought that I didn't have any time, didn't you? It wasn't that I lacked time so much as the peace and quiet to be able to write. I'm so nervous, so restless inside. But shouldn't we be nervous, when the English are one kilometer away from Harburg?[19] Should we be calm, when we hear the noisy din of battle the whole day?

Yes, we *should* remain calm, if we can. For me it's impossible, though. But you don't have any idea what has happened! So very briefly the exciting events of the last four weeks:

Today Margot and I went to "Faust" Part 1. It was wonderful. I'm glad that I already knew the play, thanks to (Frau Dr.) R. and Fritz A. Who is Fritz A., you want to know? Listen and be amazed: An SS-man whom I met in the shelter and with whom I can have marvelous talks about literature. Clever mind. Too bad he's a Nazi. That's why I cannot like him and I'm afraid I have to despise him. I mean, can you like a Nazi if you're half-way normal? It's too bad. But as I said, the scoundrels should be sweating so much with fear that the "sweat is boiling in their innards." (That doesn't come from me, but from a doctor at the Albrecht Hospital.) (By the way, Ma is out of the hospital and back home. I should go back to the hospital and I will go as soon as the Tommys are here. Stomach and intestinal grippe again. I feel it, but what does

19   Harburg is an outlying suburb of Hamburg.

that help? One has to be *hard*. I'm not even telling Ma anymore how much the pains are bothering me, because then she would only worry needlessly and these days one should avoid unnecessary worries. Hopefully I won't get ulcers!) Enough of my medical problems, back to the situation at hand; back to politics, for it alone controls what happens today. Politics alone determines our lives, our happiness, and our well-being. Don't you know anything yet about the English and Americans' triumphant advance across Germany? It went extremely fast. First they crossed the Rhine River. Paratroop landings on the Lower Rhine supported the start of the offensive on the Middle Rhine. And then it all went fast. The liberators moved across Germany without meeting any serious resistance. Today they are in Nuremberg and in Czechoslovakia. In the meantime Vienna has fallen to the Russians. …

And now something else. The Nazi chieftains in my classes are behaving like shameful cowards. They have taken down the Adolf pictures and burned them and they are looking for something to replace the blank spaces on the wall … Isle-Marie G. said that she has song books in her house that her father got from house searches; Lisa K. is already burning all her party papers, documents of leadership service, etc., and she gets anxious whenever the girls under her still greet her with "Heil Hitler." And Gertrud B., who actually kept on believing in the good aspects of "Nazism," has woken up from her dreams and doesn't know what she should believe anymore. I stirred her up a bit by telling her a few things that could make her detest these criminals. In this way you can win over people we will need later.

Hopefully we will all survive the next few days. Things must be decided in any case. Boom, boom, boom … You can hear the front, it's moving closer – and we are waiting for what's going to happen. Waiting is the only thing that makes me nervous. – …

3 MAY 1945, 13:00

At this moment British troops are marching into the city! *At this moment* the first stage of freedom is beginning for us. *At this moment* the party is dead! *At this moment* the Nazis no longer have any power; the terror has stopped. Oh, I'm so excited.

First Secretary Ahrens [of the Hamburg city government] is speaking. He announces that Hamburg is an open city and that British troops are marching into the city at this moment.[20] Now he is saying goodbye to the citizens of Hamburg; he says that he will probably not be speaking to us again. That would be even better! But apparently these gentlemen thought they would be able to slip through the cracks.

One more announcement. The Reich radio station says goodbye to its listeners; it won't be broadcasting any more reports. – Pause –

Then the Coriolanus Overture begins. (So music is still allowed.) Beethoven Romanticism!

And there is droning outside … twelve British airplanes, probably Spitfires, drone in formation, very low, above our house and away!

I am so excited, tears of joy run down my face. This happiness is still so new and unimaginable to me that I can't quite grasp it yet. – And there is such beautiful music on the radio! The Nazi music is finally gone once and for all, and Goebbels' speeches, which always really got on my nerves, are over and done with forever.

Right now the population is under a curfew that will last until it is lifted by the British High Command. The people's conduct will determine how long the curfew stays in effect. But the

20   The term "open city" meant that the city would not be defended.

people are quiet. Almost everyone is happy and those who are not happy are the Nazi big shots and they're going to land in a concentration camp anyway! ...

And maybe tanks are driving through the streets of Hamburg right now! And our city has remained in pretty good shape. It's true that it was pretty much destroyed in 1943,[21] but that doesn't matter, because as compensation for the loss of our apartment they have freed us from the yoke of Nazism! – Even before 12:00 the Reich Radio Station in Hamburg broadcast the report several times that Hamburg was an "open city." Now our relatives in Bavaria will also have heard and will be glad that we are alive. Now I can also write letters again ...

I would so like to see Tommys! I would like to see tanks and soldiers so that we can experience something of the invasion too!! This silence on the streets is very peculiar. (I will write more later; in spite of all the happiness we mustn't forget to eat. What do you think??)

Source: Heinrich Breloer, ed., *Mein Tagebuch: Geschichten vom Überleben, 1939–1947* (Cologne: Verlagsgesellschaft Schulfernsehen, 1984), pp. 163–68, 175–76, 178–79, 183–84.

Translated by Sally Winkle

---

21   A massive Allied incendiary attack on the inner city in late July 1943 killed more than 40,000 people.

6

The Holocaust

The systematic murder of the Jews, the largest state-sponsored genocide in history, defies simple explanation. In its murderous excess the Holocaust remains the single greatest challenge to the explanatory powers of historiography. It is this event that epitomizes the unprecedented criminality of Nazism. The killing of defenseless civilians, including 1½ million children, far from serving a rational purpose, seemed if anything to impede the German war effort by diverting resources from the fighting fronts. Yet despite its apparent irrationality and historical contingency, the Holocaust marked the realization of two long-term Nazi aims. One of these was to expel all Jews from German society, and by logical extension from all German-controlled areas. The other aim was to "purify" the German race by both positive and negative eugenic selection. The debate about the "euthanasia" of "life unworthy of living" dated back to the early 1920s (see Doc. 2.9). The Nazis took advantage of the start of the war to launch the systematic killing of the mentally and physically handicapped under strict secrecy (Docs. 6.1 and 6.2). The technology of mass killing by gas in chambers disguised as shower rooms was first applied in the killing of the handicapped. In late summer 1941, just when the so-called "T-4" program was officially ended, in part because of protests by the churches (Doc. 6.1b), the SS personnel in charge were transferred to occupied Poland to supervise the construction of gas chambers at specially selected extermination sites for the "final solution of the Jewish Question" (see Table 6.1).

The war of extermination against the Jews was also a function of the barbaric methods the Nazis deliberately adopted in the invasion of the Soviet Union in June 1941 (see Doc. 5.11). Prior to this the Nazis had briefly considered the "territorial solution" of deporting Jews to the island of Madagascar, a plan based on the assumption that Britain would make peace and cooperate in the solution of the "world Jewish problem" (Doc. 6.3). War against the Soviet Union changed all that. The Nazis operated under the hallucinatory assumption that Jews had instigated and financed the Russian Revolution (see Doc. 2.3) to gain world domination through the spread of communism. According to this conspiratorial fantasy, finance capitalism and liberal democracy also served Jewish interests, but these typically Western institutions could not assure Jews as firm a grip on the masses as communism could. Although the Nazis also destroyed Gypsies, Jehovah's Witnesses, homosexuals, political opponents, Slavic elites, and Soviet prisoners of war (see Doc. 5.21), the Nazis viewed Jews as their principal enemies. The Social Darwinist notion that every race had the right to destroy its enemies in the struggle for existence served as the main rationale for the killing program. The "New Order" planned by the Nazis in the east required the elimination of whole population groups to create the conditions for future Germanization. The fact that German soldiers and civilians were dying in large numbers was also cited as a reason not to allow Jews to survive the war.

Special SS killing units (*Einsatzgruppen*) followed the front-line troops in June 1941 to kill Jews and partisans in conquered Soviet territory (Doc. 6.6). Just when the decision was made to expand the killing operations to include all European Jews has not been definitively determined, but the evidence suggests late summer 1941. Chief of the SS Security Services Reinhard Heydrich, who had already presided over forced emigration before the war and the ghettoization of Jews in the occupied territories, was put in charge of the "final solution" (Doc. 6.4). The practice of forcing Jews to wear identifying markers, already introduced in occupied areas in 1939 and 1940, was extended to Germany itself in September 1941. This eased the task of seizing Jews for deportation to the east, which soon thereafter began on a systematic basis. In October 1941 all emigration of Jews from areas under German control was prohibited. The day after the German declaration of war on the US on 11 December 1941, Hitler secretly informed Party leaders of the start of the "final solution" (Docs. 5.20 and 6.7).

The smooth execution of the extermination program required the cooperation of numerous government agencies, including the Economics Ministry, the Foreign Ministry, the Ministry of Justice, the Interior Ministry, and the Ministry for the Occupied Eastern Territories. To assure this cooperation was the purpose of the Wannsee Conference, originally convened by Heydrich for early December 1941, and finally held on 20 January 1942 (Doc. 6.8). Heydrich's main assistant for organizing the transports to the killing centers from all over Europe was SS-*Obersturmbannführer* (the equivalent of Lt. Col.) Adolf Eichmann (1906–62), the head of the "Jewish desk" in the Reich Security Main Office (RSHA).

At the request of officials of the General Government, the SS gave priority to killing the approximately 3 million Polish Jews under German control. Under the codename of "Operation Reinhardt," Polish Jews were killed, mainly by carbon monoxide gas, from March 1942 until October 1943 at three killing centers constructed near railway sidings in relatively remote areas of Poland: Belzec, Sobibor, and Treblinka. SS engineer Kurt Gerstein left a graphic eye-witness account of how the gassings were conducted (Doc. 6.9). Approximately 1¾ million Jews were killed at these camps. At least 150,000, most from the Lodz ghetto, were killed in mobile gas vans at Chelmo, and at least 60,000 Jews were killed at Majdanek, a suburb of the city of Lublin, where the SS had earlier planned to create a "Jewish reservation." Approximately one million Jews were murdered at Auschwitz-Birkenau, a huge holding camp for forced labor equipped with the latest technology for mass killing. Only persons deemed capable of work were temporarily exempted from the "selections" that were conducted on a daily basis (Docs. 6.15 and 6.16). At Auschwitz a lethal pesticide, Cyclon B, was used in combination gas chamber–crematories beginning in January 1942. Jews from all over Europe were killed here until the liberation of the camp by the Red Army on 27 January 1945.

Approximately 3 million victims of the Holocaust died in the six extermination camps in the east. Another 1½ million fell victim to the *Einsatzgruppen* and other killing units in shooting operations that continued throughout the war (Doc. 6.10). Perhaps as many as another 1½ million died of deprivation, disease, or abuse in the ghettos of eastern Europe, the concentration camps, and the literally hundreds of labor camps run by the SS all over occupied Europe. A fortunate few managed to hide or to escape, but even neutral countries like Switzerland put up barriers against refugees (see Doc. 6.11). The desperate anguish of the victims is recorded in fragments of letters, diaries, and drawings recovered after the war (see Doc. 6.12).

Deportations to the death camp at Treblinka from the Warsaw Ghetto, the largest ghetto in eastern Europe, began in July 1942. In April 1943 the surviving remnant of the ghetto population mounted a courageous armed revolt against their oppressors. It took hundreds of well-armed SS troops four full weeks to quell the desperate resistance (Doc. 6.13). The Warsaw Ghetto was reduced to rubble, and those captured alive were sent to their deaths at Treblinka.

"Operation Reinhardt" was formally ended in October 1943. Heinrich Himmler summoned SS leaders to a meeting in Poznán where he told them that the annihilation of the Jews was an unwritten and never-to-be-written page of glory in German history (Doc. 6.14). The killing centers at Belzec, Sobibor, and Treblinka were closed, the bodies of victims in mass graves exhumed and burnt, and the evidence of the killings removed. At Auschwitz, however, the killings by gas went on until November 1944, when Himmler ordered the gas chambers to be dismantled to conceal the evidence of murder. He hoped to use surviving Jews as bargaining chips in a futile effort to get the Western Allies to sign a separate peace. The dying, however, continued even beyond the end of the war. Thousands of Jewish and non-Jewish camp inmates were killed in the closing months of the war on death marches ordered by SS guards to evade the approaching Allied armies. Hundreds more died of their weakened physical state after the German surrender on 8 May 1945. The trauma of their camp experiences affected survivors for the rest of their lives. In public memory the Holocaust remains the signature event of a century of brutal ideological and ethnic conflicts, and a grim warning of the lethal consequences of radical-right racial supremacist doctrines and movements.

The killing of the handicapped

Shortly after the start of the war, Hitler signed an order, backdated to 1 September 1939, authorizing the systematic killing of mentally and physically handicapped adults and children. Authorization to direct the program was given on Hitler's personal stationary to Philipp Bouhler (1900–45), head of the Führer's Chancellery, and Dr. Karl Brandt (1904–48), Hitler's personal physician. The code-name of this secret program, "Aktion T-4," derived from the address of the building in Berlin, Tiergartenstrasse 4, from which the program was directed. Killings of deformed children had already started before the war. The killings, now extended to adults as well, were conducted by lethal injection or carbon monoxide gassing at several sites disguised as hospitals or nursing homes. These killings marked a further escalation of the eugenic practices that had begun with the Sterilization Law in 1933 (see Doc. 3.14). A precedent for such killings was the systematic starvation of tens of thousands of mental patients in the First World War to free up hospital space and preserve scarce food supplies for wounded soldiers. The need to end so-called "life unworthy of living" had long been part of the public discussion in Germany (see Doc. 2.9). Throughout the 1930s the Nazis sought to gain public approval for what was misleadingly called "euthanasia" or "mercy killing," for the Nazis' aim was not to release patients from suffering but to strengthen the *Volk* by eliminating "inferior" elements.

Despite the secrecy of the program, it was impossible to conceal killing on such a scale, as relatives demanded explanations for the sudden and unexpected deaths of their loved ones. Increasing numbers of complaints and demands for criminal investigations made it necessary to inform the Reich Ministry of Justice and the Ministry of the Interior of Hitler's secret order. Protests against the killings came from the both the Protestant and Catholic churches beginning in 1940 and reaching a crescendo in August 1941, when the Catholic Bishop of Limburg, Antonius Hilfrich, wrote a letter to the Reich Ministry of Justice containing (though in the attenuating context of a conditional sentence) the powerful phrase: "Germany cannot win the war, if there is still a just God." The Hadamar killing site outside of Limburg to which Hilfrich referred in his letter had opened in January 1941. Vigorous protest was also lodged by Bishop Clemens von Galen (1878–1946) of Münster, whose sermons against euthanasia in July and August 1941 received wide publicity. He also lodged a criminal complaint with the Reich Ministry of Justice, to which, however, he received no response.

Nonetheless, church criticism may have contributed to Hitler's decision to end the program on 24 August 1941 after more than 70,000 patients had been killed. Killings especially of handicapped children continued in secret, however, until the end of the war. Under the code-name "Aktion 14 f 13" the killing program was also extended to Jewish inmates of concentration camps in Germany. Many of the T-4 personnel were transferred to occupied Poland where they supplied the technical expertise for the systematic killing by gas of approximately three million Jews in the extermination camps set up for the "Final Solution of the Jewish Question." Except for isolated clerical leaders, such as the Berlin Catholic prior Bernhard Lichtenberg (1875–1943), there was no church protest against the killing of the Jews.

6.1a Hitler's authorization of the killing of the incurably ill

[On letterhead A. Hitler]   Berlin, 1 September 1939

Reichsleiter [Philipp] Bouhler and Dr. [Karl] Brandt, M.D. are charged with the responsibility of enlarging the authority of certain physicians to be designated by name in such a manner that persons who, according to human judgment, are incurable can, upon a most careful diagnosis of their condition, be accorded a mercy death.

[signed] A. Hitler

[Handwritten note]
Given to me by Bouhler on 27 August 1940

[signed] Dr. Gürtner

Source: Office of the US Chief of Counsel for Prosecution of Axis Crimiality,
***Nazi Conspiracy and Aggression*, Vol. III**
(Washington DC: US Government Printing Office, 1946), p. 451 [Doc 630-PS]

6.1b Letter from Bishop of Limburg to the Reich Minister of Justice, 13 August 1941

The Bishop of Limburg   Limburg/Lahn, 13 August 1941
To the Reich Minister of Justice, Berlin

Regarding the report submitted on July 16 by the Chairman of the Fulda Bishops' Conference, Cardinal Dr. [Adolf] Bertram, I consider it my duty to present the following as a concrete illustration of destruction of so-called "useless life."

About eight kilometers from Limburg in the little town of Hadamar, on a hill overlooking the town, there is an institution that had formerly served various purposes and of late had been used as a nursing home; this institution was renovated and furnished as a place in which, by consensus of opinion, the above-mentioned euthanasia has been systematically practiced for months – approximately since February 1941. The fact has become known beyond the administrative district of Wiesbaden, because death certificates from a Registry Hadamar-Mönchberg are sent to the home communities. (Mönchberg is the name of this institution because it was a Franciscan monastery prior to its secularization in 1803.)

Several times a week buses arrive in Hadamar with a considerable number of such victims. School children of the vicinity know this vehicle and say: "There comes the murder-box again." After the arrival of the vehicle, the citizens of Hadamar watch the smoke rise out of the chimney and are tortured with the ever-present thought of the miserable victims, especially when repulsive odors annoy them, depending on the direction of the wind.

The effect of the principles at work here are: Children call each other names and say, "You're crazy; you'll be sent to the baking oven in Hadamar." Those who do not want to marry, or find no opportunity, say, "Marry, never! Bring children into the world so they can be put into the bottling machine!" You hear old folks say, "Don't send me to a state hospital! After the feeble-minded have been finished off, the next useless eaters whose turn will come are the old people."

All God-fearing men consider this destruction of helpless beings as crass injustice. And if anybody says that Germany cannot win the war, if there is still a just God, these expressions are not the result of a lack of love of fatherland but of a deep concern for our people. The population cannot grasp that systematic actions are carried out which in accordance with Par. 211 of the German criminal code are punishable with death! High authority as a moral concept has suffered a severe shock as a result of these events. The official notice that N. N. had died of a contagious disease and that for that reason his body has to be burned no longer finds credence, and such official notices, which are no longer believed, have further undermined the ethical value of the concept of authority.

Officials of the Secret State Police, it is said, are trying to suppress discussion of the Hadamar occurrences by means of severe threats. But the knowledge and the conviction and the indignation of the population cannot be changed by it; the conviction will be increased with the bitter realization that discussion is prohibited with threats but that the actions themselves are not prosecuted under penal law.

Facta loquuntur.

I beg you most humbly, Herr Reich Minister, in the sense of the report of the Episcopate of July 16 of this year, to prevent further transgressions of the Fifth Commandment of God.

[signed] Dr. Hilfrich

I am submitting copies of this letter to the Reich Minister of the Interior and the Reich Minister for Church Affairs.

Source: Office of the US Chief of Counsel for Prosecution of Axis Criminality,
***Nazi Conspiracy and Aggression,* Vol. III**
(Washington DC: US Government Printing Office, 1946), pp. 449–51 [Doc. 615-PS]

Euthanasia of mentally and physically disabled and other "undesirables"

Euthanasia killings were carried out at various hospital sites by various means, including systematic starvation, over-medication, lethal injection, and gassing by carbon monoxide. The following selection is taken from the testimony of Berta Netz, a nurse at the institution for the mentally disabled at Meseritz-Obrawalde in the province of Posen, at the trial of euthanasia physicians and nurses in Munich in May 1962. More than 10,000 persons were killed on doctors' orders at Obrawalde during the war, most after the euthanasia program was officially halted in August 1941. Netz participated in the killings even though she knew it was wrong to do so. Her justification of her actions as motivated not by ideology but by her duty to follow orders was typical of the defense offered by most mid-level perpetrators after the war.

6.2 Testimony of Nurse Berta Netz, Munich, 1962

In our ward there were children of both sexes, from infants up to about 16 to 18 years of age. They were extremely deformed children, epileptics, and mentally-deficient children. They could only be kept busy with rudimentary games and by singing; the sick children could not be expected to do any real work. The adult patients also in our ward were women from the ages of 20 all the way to the elderly. The women were also mentally deficient, epileptic, etc., some of whom could be occupied with simple work such as darning socks or braiding rope.

In answer to the urgent charge and detailed discussions, I will now describe how I first became involved with the killing of a mentally ill patient and in what way the killings that came later were ordered and carried out.

I became aware for the first time around the Fall of 1942 that killings were being carried out on our station. The small room described earlier had been previously used as the so-called isolation room. For a very long time the room was occupied by a little girl who had diphtheria; she was long considered a carrier and was therefore isolated. After recovering from her illness this child was placed in foster care, and from this point on the isolation room was empty. I have to correct myself. For a short time a small boy was placed in this isolation room; he had been infected by the girl and later died. It was still in the fall of 1942 when a newly admitted patient came to our station. It was a mentally deficient girl, about 17 or 18 years old, and Frau Dr. Wernicke ordered her to be sent to the isolation room. Some time after the admittance Frau Dr. Wernicke ordered injections of 2 cc of Morphine-Scopolamin as the patient's treatment. The girl was then given daily injections of 2 cc of Morphine-Scopolamin for about 14 days. I was not present when the head physician gave the order in question. Therefore I cannot say whether the 14-day treatment of 2 cc MS daily was decided by Dr. Wernicke at the outset or whether she gave a new order every day for the administration of this dosage. The treatment was carried out mainly by head nurse Ratajczak. On the orders of Amanda Ratajczak I had to administer the aforementioned dosage of MS to one of the upper arms of the patient maybe two or three times during the time span mentioned above. I did not give any thought to this treatment at the time. But when the girl receiving this treatment died after 14 days, of course I came to the conclusion that her death had been caused solely by the injections given to her. Starting in that fall of 1942, adult patients and also children were often moved to the so-called isolation room. Of course in the meantime I realized the purpose of these transfers. But I could not bring myself to speak with anyone about it. On the one hand I was forbidden to do so by the pledge of secrecy, which was especially emphasized to me by the hospital director

Grabowski and the head physician Dr. Wernicke. On the other hand as a nurse previously stationed in Stralsund, I had hardly any contact with the other nurses from Treptow and Obrawalde. Our living arrangements were also determined accordingly, so that only nurses who knew each other from before and had previously worked together in other institutions came into contact with each other. The selection of patients slated to be killed was made by head physician Dr. Wernicke. Usually before her rounds she obtained the medical histories, which were kept in a cabinet in the doctors' room. During her rounds Dr. Wernicke examined the patient once more and then made decisions accordingly. Therefore about once or twice a week adult patients or children were transferred to the isolation room on orders from Frau Dr. Wernicke. The patients transferred there were undressed, dressed in a nightgown, and put to bed. Frau Dr. Wernicke ordered transfers to the isolation room only on workdays, not including Saturdays. At the same time as the transfer order, Frau Dr. Wernicke determined the medication to be administered according to the patient's age and constitution. So for example, usually five tablets of Veronal and 10 cc of morphine-scopolamin were ordered for adults. For children or weaker patients she ordered correspondingly smaller doses. In general, on the orders of Dr. Wernicke there was only one patient at a time sent to the isolation room. It was relatively rare that both beds were occupied in this room. Each time after the transferred patients had been put to bed, the five (or fewer) tablets of Veronal were mixed into a glass of sugar water. Either head nurse Ratajczak or I got the tablets from the medicine cabinet and administered them. Station nurse Jankow never prepared any medications herself. Generally, after some encouragement, the patients drank the dissolved tablets without further ado. After the patients had swallowed the Veronal preparation they were give a glass of clear water to wash it down.

I cannot for the life of me remember a time when the Veronal preparation was not effective. Always after about a half-hour the patients were either asleep or in a semiconscious state. In answer to further questions I declare that no other medication except Veronal in tablet form was administered. Also as far as I know, no one used stomach probes or enemas on our station. After the above-mentioned half-hour had elapsed, the adult patient or child who was in the isolation room at the time was injected with morphine-scopolamin. When I had to give these injections, I first made sure that the patient was really asleep. I tested this by speaking with the patient to find out whether or not she was responsive. It was never the case that a patient or child had not fallen asleep. Once I had clearly determined that the patient was asleep, I administered the Morphine-Scopolamin from a filled syringe into the upper left arm of the patient or child. The injection in the upper left arm was ordered by the physician, Dr. Wernicke, presumably because this part of the body was closer to the heart and the medication would therefore act faster. The injections on our station were only carried out by head nurse Ratajczak and me. After the patients were in a sleeping state, further assistance was not necessary.

The rounds were always made in the early morning hours. Right after that the patient was transferred to the isolation room, Veronal was administered, and a half hour later the injection of Morphine-Scopolamin was given. About noon or sometimes in the afternoon head physician Dr. Wernicke would confirm the death of the patient who had been sent to the isolation room. About two hours later, that would be in the late afternoon, the bodies were taken from our station to the morgue by male patients. The men who took the corpses away were able-bodied patients who were housed in the workers' quarters and probably belonged to the graveyard commando. A four-wheeled cart was used to transport the corpses. I myself never had anything to do with removing the corpses, nor did I ever entrust any of our nurses with that job. I also never went to the morgue. We wrapped the corpses in sheets and turned them over to the men from the graveyard commando. After cleaning, the sheets were returned to our station.

As a rule, Dr. Wernicke ordered the transfer of only one patient at a time to the isolation room. Now and then, however, two patients had to be transferred there.

When two patients were brought to the isolation room, they were usually put to bed at the same time. The tablets were also administered at almost the same time, that is, the drink was given first to one patient and then the other. I cannot recall any case in which one of the two patients ever struggled or resisted. Once they were encouraged, they always swallowed the medication diluted in sugar water. Afterwards they always fell asleep at the same time. Some time after the treatment of the 17- to 18-year old girl, which was described to me on page 8 of the interrogation, I was called to the office of administrative director Grabowski. I really can no longer specify the exact time when Grabowski sent for me. Nurse Wieczorek was also called with me to Grabowski's office, that is, we met there. Without being able to repeat Grabowski's exact words, I can still recall that he spoke to us about how it would be a relief for the patients of our institution if they were released from their terrible suffering. As the conversation continued, he admonished Fräulein Wieczorek and me to strictly follow all of Frau Dr. Wernicke's orders. Grabowski did not specifically mention the killings of mentally ill patients nor the way they were to be carried out, but based on his remarks we had no doubt that he was speaking to us about the killing of mentally ill patients. On this occasion Grabowski explicitly pledged us to secrecy and told us we were obligated to refuse to give evidence about this to anyone. Soon after this discussion in Grabowski's office, I was enjoined once again by Frau Dr. Wernicke in the doctors' room of our station not to say anything to anybody about my knowledge of the killing operation. For this reason I did not dare to speak with anyone at all about the incidents in Obrawalde. I was of course a member of the NSDAP and also a member of the National Socialist Women's Organization, but I never went to a meeting.

I did not feel at all obligated because of my membership in the NSDAP to carry out all the orders given to me. As a nurse in mental institutions for many years I really did see it in some respects as a relief that the most seriously ill patients were released from their suffering by inducing their deaths. I can also say with a clear conscience that only very seriously ill patients on our station were killed.

As I mentioned before, it was not my affiliation with the party, but my subordinate relationship as a nurse and especially as a civil servant that obligated and compelled me to follow all the orders that Frau Dr. Wernicke gave me.

To the question of whether a refusal was perhaps possible, I must say that I did not dare to refuse. I always believed that if I refused, I would have to count on being sent to a concentration camp or some similar place. In answer to a further question I declare that I am not actually aware of any concrete case in which a nurse who refused to cooperate with the killing action was in any way prosecuted afterwards. Without being able to offer proof, I do however vaguely remember that a Fräulein Seel, who was previously in Kückenmühle, was sent from Obrawalde to a concentration camp or someplace like that, because she resisted some kind of orders.

At that time in Obrawalde I was completely healthy physically and mentally. I had absolutely no personal motive or purpose in my involvement in the killings carried out in Obrawalde. As already mentioned, I acted only on the orders of the head physician Dr. Wernicke, and I was always under a certain obligation, which I really wanted to get out of, but was unable to. Of course I understood that what was happening in Obrawalde was wrong. But the assistance and the duties I had to perform there belonged to my profession, which I had pursued for many years, and which had become a part of me. I did not see any possibility of evading the orders of the head physician. As I performed each task, whether it was transferring patients or administering medication, I had certain inhibitions, and I really did not do anything willingly or on my own. The obligation and the duty to carry out everything as ordered was always hanging over me. The environment in which we lived as nurses was the world of the mentally ill. We hardly ever left the institution; we had a great deal of work to do and hardly had any contact with the outside world.

When I had free time I usually went to the woods to find peace and quiet. Due to the stress under which I suffered as a result of the incidents in the institution, I did not have the slightest interest in going to town or in meeting people in any other way.

I received a Christian upbringing as a child at home and also later. I could not at all reconcile the killing action in Obrawalde with my moral and Christian views. At that time I was very often alone, surrounded by my own thoughts; I stood face to face with myself as it were, and cried …

> **Source: Hilde Steppe, Franz Koch, Herbert Weisbrod-Frey, *Krankenpflege im Nationalsozialismus*, 3rd edn. (Frankfurt: Mabuse, 1986), pp. 118–121.**
> **Translated by Sally Winkle**

Rosenberg on the "World Jewish Problem"

Alfred Rosenberg, the Party ideologist who would be appointed Reich Minister for the Occupied Eastern Territories in July 1941, gave this speech over the radio on the occasion of the opening of the Institute for the Exploration of the Jewish Question in Frankfurt on 28 March 1941. At a time when the Nazi–Soviet Pact was still in effect (although plans for "Operation Barbarossa" were already well underway), Rosenberg omitted the usual Nazi denunciations of Jews as the carriers of communism (see Doc. 2.3), condemning them for "finance capitalism" and "financial dictatorship" instead. Prior to the invasion of the Soviet Union, the official Nazi policy was still to pursue a "territorial solution" to the "Jewish Question." Madagascar, a French colony, was briefly considered as a potential site for Jewish "resettlement" after the fall of France in June 1940. Although the Nazis supported Zionist efforts for increased immigration into British-ruled Palestine in the 1930s, Rosenberg made it clear that a Jewish state in Palestine was not acceptable. Instead, European Jews were to be confined to a "reservation" under German military rule.

A successful end to the war was the necessary precondition for the Madagascar Plan or any other "territorial solution." At the time of this speech secret preparations for the invasion of the Soviet Union were already in full swing (see Docs. 5.10 and 5.11). In the course of that barbarous campaign the Nazis implemented their "final solution of the Jewish question," the systematic killing of all European Jews. Physical annihilation was, however, already implicit in Rosenberg's plans for the establishment of a Jewish "reservation" under conditions that could never support the lives of millions of people.

6.3 Alfred Rosenberg, "The Jewish Question as a World Problem," 28 March 1941

The war which is being waged today by the German armed forces under the highest command of Adolf Hitler is a war of an immense reform. It does not only overcome the world of ideas of the French Revolution, but it also exterminates directly all those racially infecting germs of Jewry and its bastards, which now for over a hundred years could develop without check among the European nations. The Jewish question that for 2,000 years was an unsolved problem for the European nations will now find its solution through the National Socialist revolution for Germany and all of Europe.

And if one asks, in what form, then we have to say the following: During these decades a lot has been talked about a Jewish state as a solution, and Zionism appears to some people perhaps even today as an honest attempt on the part of the Jews to contribute something toward the solution of the Jewish question.

In reality there never was nor will there ever be a Jewish state.

Contrary to the other nations on this globe, Judaism is no vertical organization which comprises all professions, but has been always a horizontal class among the different nations, the class that carried on material and spiritual intermediate trade. Secondly, the space being considered in Palestine is in no way suitable for any Jewish state. It is too small to absorb what was formerly ten and is now fifteen million Jews; in other words, therefore impractical for solving the Jewish question. The purpose of Zionism, in reality, was not to solve the Jewish question in the sense of the coordination of the whole Jewish people, but lay in an entirely different direction.

It was intended to build in Palestine a purely Jewish center, a real legitimate Jewish state in order to be able, at first, to be represented at all diplomatic conferences with full rights as national Jew.

Secondly, it was intended to make Palestine into a huge, economic staging area against the entire Near East. Thirdly, this Jewish state should have been an asylum for all those Jewish adventurers in the world who were evicted from the countries in which they acted. And, finally, nobody was even thinking of limiting even in the slightest, the so-called state civil rights of the Jews in Germany, England, America, and also France. The Jews therefore would have maintained the rights of the Germans, Englishmen, Frenchmen, etc., and the spaceless Jewish world state would have come constantly closer toward its realization, that is, an all-Jewish center without any interference of non-Jews and the Jewish high finance at the state rudder in all other countries of the world.

This dream is now finished. Now, just the reverse, we have to think of how and where to put the Jews. This can, as mentioned, not be done in a Jewish state, but only in a way which I shall call the Jewish reservation.

It is to be hoped that future statesmen will get together in order to gradually create a settlement for Jews who, under experienced police supervision, should then do such useful work as they wanted to see done until now by non-Jews.

From an almost unlimited Jewish rule in all European countries to such a radical reversal – to an evacuation of this same Jewish race after 2,000 years of parasitism on the European continent – one can get from this an idea what an enormous philosophical and political revolution is in the making in Europe today.

Today the Jewish question is somewhat clear before our eyes. It is the problem of a simple national purity. It means the necessity for defense of national tradition for all nations which still value culture and the future. It is still an economic problem for all those who cannot solve their social questions under the Jewish financial dictatorship. It is a political problem of power, because in many states the will has not yet been found to break this financial dictatorship of Jewry. And, lastly, it is an ideological problem, given to the Europeans since the days when the first Jews immigrated to Rome. National Socialists have but one clear answer to all these questions:

For Germany the Jewish Question is only then solved when the last Jew has left the Greater German space.

Since Germany with its blood and its nationalism has now broken for always this Jewish dictatorship for all Europe, and has seen to it that Europe as a whole will become free from the Jewish parasitism once more, we may, I believe, also speak for all Europeans: For Europe the Jewish question is only then solved when the last Jew has left the European continent.

It does not matter whether such a program can be realized in five, ten, or twenty years. The transportation facilities in our time, if all nations join, would be strong enough to institute and to execute such a resettlement to a great extent. But the problem must and will one day be solved as we have visualized it from the first day of our fight – then accused as utopians – and now proclaim it as strict realistic politicians. All nations are interested in the solution of this question, and we must declare here with all passion:

In this cleaning-up even Mr. Roosevelt with his Baruchs[1] and his trophy film Jews will not be able to hinder us; quite to the contrary, their proclamation that the Jewish parasitical spirit represents today the freedom of the world will especially awaken all resistance of the German character, and the strongest military instrument which history has seen, the German Armed Forces of Adolf Hitler, will take care that this last furious attempt to have the white race once more march against Europe for the benefit of Jewish financial dominion will find an end for all times.

We are of the opinion that this great war constitutes also a cleansing biological world revolution and that also those nations which are still opposed to us will recognize at the end of the war that Germany's affair is today the affair of the whole European continent, the affair of the whole Jewish race, but also the affair of all other cultured races on this globe who fight for a safe national cultural and state life. Thus we hope that one day, in a reasonable distribution of the great living spaces of this globe the nations will find that peace, that work, and that prosperity which for decades have been harrassed by never-tiring parasitical activity. Thus we consider today the Jewish question as one of the most important problems among the total politics of Europe, as a problem which must be solved and will be solved, and we hope, yes, we know already today, that all nations of Europe will march behind this cleansing at the end.

Source: Office of the US Chief of Counsel for Prosecution of Axis Criminality,
Nazi Conspiracy and Aggression, **Vol. V**
(Washington DC: US Government Printing Office, 1946), pp. 554–7 [Doc. 2889-PS]

The "Final Solution"

Historians have long debated when the decision for the "Final Solution of the Jewish Question," the physical annihilation of the Jews, was made. The only written authorization that survived the war was the following directive issued by Hermann Goering to Reinhard Heydrich, head of the Reich Security Main Office (RSHA), the central bureau for all police functions formed on 27 September 1939. Heydrich had been put in charge of forced emigration in January 1939. After the start of the war, he issued instructions to newly-formed SS *Einsatzgruppen* to herd the two million Jews of occupied Poland into urban ghettos. In 1940 he headed efforts to find a "territorial solution," i.e., a plan for the permanent resettlement of Jews outside of Europe (see Doc. 6.3). Precisely when Hitler gave his authorization to put the "Final Solution" into effect may never be known with certainty. In October 1941 the first gassing facilities were constructed in occupied Poland, all emigration of Jews from areas under German control was prohibited, and deportations of Jews from Germany itself began. Adolf

---

1   The financier Bernard Baruch (1870–1965) was an economic adviser to Roosevelt and Churchill.

Eichmann (1906–62), the Gestapo's specialist on the Jewish Question (Office IV B 4 of the RSHA), was put in charge of organizing the deportations to the killing centers from all European countries to which the Nazis had access. On 12 December 1941 Hitler announced the commencement of the Final Solution to a meeting of Party *Gauleiter* (district leaders) in Berlin (see Docs. 5.20 and 6.7).

6.4 Goering's authorization to Heydrich, 31 July 1941

The Reich Marshal of the Greater German Reich
Commissioner for the Four-Year Plan
Chairman of the Ministerial Council for National Defense
Berlin, 31 July 1941
To: The Chief of the Security Police and the Security Service, SS-Gruppenführer Heydrich
    Complementing the task that was assigned to you on 24 January 1939, which dealt with a solution of the Jewish problem through emigration and evacuation as advantageously as possible, I hereby charge you with making all necessary preparations in regard to organizational and financial matters for bringing about a total solution of the Jewish question in the German sphere of influence in Europe.
    Wherever other governmental agencies are involved, these are to cooperate with you.
    I charge you furthermore to send me, before long, an overall plan concerning the organizational, factual, and material measures necessary for the accomplishment of the desired solution of the Jewish question.

[signed] Goering

Source: Office of the US Chief of Counsel for Prosecution of Axis Criminality,
Nazi Conspiracy and Aggression, Vol. III
(Washington DC: US Government Printing Office, 1946), pp. 525–6 [Doc. 710-PS]

The yellow star

The effort to define, identify, concentrate, and segregate Jews culminated in a decree forcing Jews in Germany to wear a yellow star attached to their clothing in September 1941. A similar decree had already been introduced in occupied Poland in late 1939 and in other occupied areas after they came under German control. This decree went into effect in Germany at a time when *Einsatzkommandos* were murdering Soviet Jews and preparations for the mass killings were already under way in Poland. A month later, as the decision for the "final solution" of physical annihilation was reached, emigration of Jews from all areas under German control was prohibited. The yellow star was designed to further segregate Jews from the general population and to minimize potential Jewish influence on popular attitudes toward the Nazis and the war. It was also intended to facilitate the rounding up of Jews for deportation. Mass deportation of German Jews to the killing sites in the east began in December 1941.

6.5 Police decree on identification of Jews, 1 September 1941

In agreement with the Reich Protector for Bohemia and Moravia the following law ... is herewith published:

ARTICLE 1

1   Jews over six years of age are prohibited to appear in public without wearing a Jewish star.
2   The Jewish star is a yellow piece of cloth with a black border in the form of a six-pointed star of the size of a hand of yellow material with the inscription "Jew." It has to be worn visible on the left side of chest, tightly sewed on to the garment.

ARTICLE 2

Jews are forbidden

(a)   to leave the boundary of their residential district without carrying a written permission of the local police authority.
(b)   to wear medals, decorations, and other insignia.

ARTICLE 3

Articles 1 and 2 will not apply

(a)   to a husband living in a Jewish mixed marriage, if there are children of the marriage who are not considered Jews. This also applies if the marriage has been dissolved or if the only son has been killed in the present war.
(b)   to the Jewish wife of a childless mixed marriage for the duration of the marriage.

ARTICLE 4

1   Whoever violates Articles 1 and 2 deliberately or carelessly will be punished with a penalty up to 150 Reichsmark or with imprisonment up to six weeks.
2   Further police security measures as well as penal provisions allowing more severe punishment remain unaffected.

ARTICLE 5

The police decree is also effective in the Protectorate Bohemia and Moravia with the provision that the Reichsprotektor in Bohemia and Moravia may adapt the instruction of Section 2 to the local conditions in the Protectorate Bohemia and Moravia.

ARTICLE 6

The police decree will be effective 14 days after its promulgation.
Berlin, 1 September 1941

For the Reich Minister of the Interior
Heydrich

Source: Office of the US Chief of Counsel for Prosecution of Axis Criminality,
***Nazi Conspiracy and Aggression* Vol. V,**
(Washington DC: US Government Printing Office, 1946), pp 541–2 [Doc. 2877-PS]

The Einsatzgruppen

Otto Ohlendorf (1907–51) was a well-educated economist who joined the SS in 1936 and advanced to the rank of *Gruppenführer* (the equivalent of general) in 1944. He had joined the Nazi party as a teenager in 1925. In June 1941 he was named chief of one of the four special killing units (*Einsatzgruppen*) whose assigned task it was to execute Jews, partisans, and communist functionaries in the sectors conquered by the Wehrmacht in the Soviet Union. Each killing unit was further subdivided into smaller detachments (*Sonderkommandos*). Between June 1941 and April 1942 the Einsatzgruppen murdered over a half-million people – men, women, and children. Most of the victims were killed by shooting, but in late 1941 mobile gas vans were used as well. Otto Ohlendorf's affidavit of November 1945 closely paralleled his testimony at the Nuremberg Trials in January 1946.

6.6 Affidavit of SS Gruppenführer Otto Ohlendorf

I, Otto Ohlendorf, being first duly sworn, declare:

I was chief of the Security Service (SD), Amt III of the Main Office of the chief of the Security Police and the SD (RSHA), from 1939 to 1945. In June 1941 I was designated by Himmler to lead one of the special commitment groups [*Einsatzgruppen*], which were then being formed, to accompany the German armies in the Russian campaign. I was the chief of the Einsatzgruppe D ... Himmler stated that an important part of our task consisted of the extermination of Jews – women, men, and children – and of communist functionaries. I was informed of the attack on Russia about four weeks in advance.

According to an agreement with the armed forces high command and army high command, the special commitment detachments [*Einsatzkommandos*] within the army group or the army were assigned to certain army corps and divisions. The army designated the areas in which the special commitment detachments had to operate. All operational directives and orders for the carrying out of executions were given through the chief of the SIPO [Security Police] and the SD (RSHA) in Berlin. Regular courier service and radio communications existed between the Einsatzgruppen and the chief of the SIPO and the SD.

The Einsatzgruppen and Einsatzkommandos were commanded by personnel of the Gestapo, the SD, or the criminal police. Additional men were detailed from the regular police [*Ordnungspolizei*] and the Waffen SS. *Einsatzgruppe* D consisted of approximately 400 to 500 men and had about 170 vehicles at its disposal.

When the German army invaded Russia, I was leader of the *Einsatzgruppe* D in the Southern sector, and in the course of the year, during which I was leader of Einsatzgruppe D, it liquidated approximately 90,000 men, women, and children. The majority of those liquidated were Jews, but there were among them some communist functionaries too.

In the implementation of this extermination program the special commitment groups were subdivided into special commitment detachments, and the *Einsatzkommandos* into still smaller units, the so-called Special Purpose Detachments [*Sonderkommandos*] and Unit Detachments [*Teilkommandos*]. Usually, the smaller units were led by a member of the SD, the Gestapo, or the criminal police. The unit selected for this task would enter a village or city and order the prominent Jewish citizens to call together all Jews for the purpose of resettlement. They were requested to hand over their valuables to the leaders of the unit, and shortly before the execution to surrender their outer clothing. The men, women, and children were led to a place of execution which in most cases was located next to a more deeply excavated anti-tank ditch. Then they were shot, kneeling or standing, and the corpses thrown into the ditch. I never permitted the shooting by individuals in group D, but ordered that several of the men would shoot at the same time in order to avoid direct, personal responsibility. The leaders of the unit or especially designated persons, however, had to fire the last bullet at those victims who were not dead immediately. I learned from conversations with other group leaders that some of them demanded that the victims lie down flat on the ground to be shot through the nape of the neck. I did not approve of these methods.

In the spring of 1942 we received gas vehicles from the chief of the Security Police and the SD in Berlin. These vehicles were made available by Amt II of the RSHA. The man who was responsible for the cars of my *Einsatzgruppe* was Becher. We had received orders to use the cars for the killing of women and children. Whenever a unit had collected a sufficient number of victims, a car was sent for their liquidation. We also had these gas vehicles stationed in the neighborhood of the transient camps into which the victims were brought. The victims were told that they would be resettled and had to climb into the vehicles for that purpose. Then the doors were closed and the gas streamed in through the starting of the vehicles. The victims died within 10 to 15 minutes. The cars were then driven to the burial place, where the corpses were taken out and buried ...

[signed] Ohlendorf
5 November 1945

Source: Office of the US Chief of Counsel for Prosecution of Axis Criminality,
***Nazi Conspiracy and Aggression*, Vol. V**
(Washington DC: US Government Printing Office, 1946), pp. 341–2 [Doc. 2620-PS]

Hans Frank's diary

Hans Frank (1900–46), a lawyer by training, was the leading Nazi official in the so-called Government General, the portion of Poland not directly annexed to the Reich after its conquest in 1939. Frank ruled the Government General from his headquarters in Krakow in southern Poland. At the time of this speech to his cabinet the decision for the "final solution" – the murder of all Jews under German control – had already been made, as Frank had been informed in Berlin earlier that week. Information on the means by which the SS intended to kill the Jews was not disseminated, however, in order to maintain the secrecy of the operation. At the upcoming Wannsee Conference (Doc. 6.8), to which Frank makes reference, agencies and officials whose cooperation would be needed were informed of the nature and scope of the program. The Jews of the General Government were the first large group of Jews to be liquidated by gas in an operation code-named "Aktion Reinhardt" in 1942–43. The name derived from Fritz Reinhardt (1895–1969), the official in the Finance Ministry responsible for administering the valuables, including dental gold, taken from the victims before or after their deaths.

6.7 Governor General Hans Frank's speech to his Cabinet, Krakow, 16 December 1941

As far as the Jews are concerned, I want to tell you quite frankly that they must be done away with in one way or another. The Führer said once: should united Jewry again succeed in provoking a world war, the blood of not only the nations, which have been forced into the war by them, will be shed, but the Jew will have found his end in Europe. I know that many of the measures carried out against the Jews in the Reich at present are being criticized. It is being tried intentionally, as is obvious from the reports on morale, to talk about cruelty, harshness, etc. Before I continue, I want to beg you to agree with me on the following formula: We will principally have pity on the German people only, and nobody else in the whole world. The others, too, had no pity on us. As an old National Socialist, I must say: This war would only be a partial success if the whole lot of Jewry should survive it, while we would have shed our best blood in order to save Europe. My attitude towards the Jews will, therefore, be based only on the expectation that they must disappear. They must be done away with. I have entered negotiations to have them deported to the East. A great discussion concerning that question will take place in Berlin in January to which I am going to delegate the State Secretary Dr. Bühler.[2] That discussion is to take place in the Reich Security Main Office with SS Lt. General Heydrich. A great Jewish migration will begin in any case.

But what should be done with the Jews? Do you think they will be settled down in the "Ostland," in villages? This is what we were told in Berlin: Why all the bother? We can do nothing with them either in the "Ostland" nor in the "Reichkommissariat."[3] So, liquidate them yourself.

Gentlemen, I must ask you to rid yourself of all feeling of pity. We must annihilate the Jews, wherever we find them and wherever it is possible, in order to maintain there the structure of the Reich as a whole. This will, naturally, be achieved by other methods than those pointed out by Bureau Chief Dr. Hummel. Nor can the judges of the Special Courts be made responsible for it, because of the limitations of the framework of the legal procedure. Such outdated views cannot be applied to such gigantic and unique events. We must find at any rate a way which leads to the goal, and my thoughts are working in that direction.

2   Frank is here referring to the Wannsee Conference held in January 1942 (see Doc. 6.8).
3   "Ostland" and "Reichkommissariat" refer to the conquered Soviet territories to the east. The "Reichkommissariat Ostland" under Gauleiter Heinrich Lohse (1896–1964) included the Baltic states and Belarus; the "Reichkommissariat Ukraine" under Gauleiter Erich Koch (1896–1986) included formerly Soviet-occupied eastern portion of Poland and the Ukraine.

The Jews represent for us also extraordinarily malignant gluttons. We have now approximately 2,500,000 of them in the General Government, perhaps with the Jewish mixtures and everything that goes with it, 3,500,000 Jews. We cannot shoot or poison those 3,500,000 Jews, but we shall nevertheless be able to take measures which will lead, somehow, to their annihilation, and this in connection with the gigantic measures to be determined in discussions in the Reich. The General Government must become free of Jews, the same as the Reich. Where and how this is to be achieved is a matter for the offices which we must appoint and create here. Their activities will be brought to your attention in due course.

Source: Office of the US Chief of Counsel for Prosecution of Axis Criminality,
Nazi Conspiracy and Aggression, **Vol. IV**
(Washington DC: US Government Printing Office, 1946), pp. 891–2 [Doc. 2233-D-PS]

The Wannsee Conference, January 1942

The Wannsee Conference, the minutes of which are given below, was convened on 20 January 1942 by the second-highest ranking SS leader Reinhard Heydrich (1904–42) in a luxurious villa taken over by the SS in the wealthy Berlin suburb of Wannsee. Its purpose was to announce the launching of the "final solution" of the Jewish question in Europe to leading government and party bureaucrats and to secure their cooperation in this project. Historians have not been able to determine with absolute certainty just when Hitler made the decision for systematic genocide. On 31 July 1941, six weeks after the SS *Einsatzgruppen* began murdering Soviet Jews in coordination with "Operation Barbarossa," Heydrich was delegated the task of drawing up plans for "a total solution of the Jewish question in the German sphere of influence in Europe" (see Doc. 6.4). It seems almost certain that he was given the green light to implement these plans by October 1941, when Jewish emigration was prohibited throughout Europe and preparations for the deportation of German Jews were put into place. Euthanasia "experts" had already been transferred to occupied Poland to set up the facilities for mass killings by poison gas. The ruthless racial and ideological war against the Soviet Union provided the conditions under which a systematic extermination program could be launched without generating wide publicity. Hitler announced the fulfillment of his 1939 promise to annihilate the Jews to a meeting of Nazi *Gauleiter* in Berlin on 12 December, one day after the German declaration of war on the United States (see Doc. 5.20).

The Wannsee Conference had originally been called for December 8 (the "invitations" had gone out in late November), but the Japanese attack on Pearl Harbor and the launching of the Soviet offensive against the German siege of Moscow forced a postponement of several weeks. The minutes of the conference do not openly describe the killing program, but none of the high-ranking participants from the various government ministries could have been in any doubt what Heydrich meant when he said that the remnant of Jews who survived forced labor would have to be "appropriately dealt with." Adolf Eichmann, the specialist on the "Jewish question" in the Reich Security Main Office run by Heydrich, provided the population statistics, which overstated the number of Jews in Europe by some two million. Much of the conference was taken up by the question of whether Jews of mixed ancestry (*Mischlinge*) and Jews in mixed marriages were to be included in the "final solution." The SS was forced by considerations of public morale to respect these distinctions in Germany itself. In the occupied areas, however, the Nazis made no exceptions for part-Jews or Jews in mixed marriages.

6.8 Minutes of the Wannsee Conference, 20 January 1942

I. Participants in the conference on the final solution of the Jewish question in Berlin, Am Grossen Wannsee 56–58, on 20 January 1942:

Gauleiter Dr. Meyer and Reich Office Director Dr. Leibbrandt	Reich Ministry for the Occupied Eastern Territories
Permanent Secretary Dr. Stuckart	Reich Interior Ministry
Permanent Secretary Neumann	Representative of the Four Year Plan
Permanent Secretary Dr. Freisler	Reich Ministry of Justice
Permanent Secretary Dr. Bühler	Office of the Governor General
Undersecretary Luther	Ministry of Foreign Affairs
SS Oberführer Klopfer	Party Chancellery
Ministry Director	Reich Chancellery
SS Gruppenführer Hofmann	Race and Settlement Main Office
SS Gruppenführer Müller	Reich Security Main Office
SS Obersturmbannführer Eichmann	
SS Oberführer Dr. Schöngarth, Commander of the Security Police and SD in the Generalgouvernement	Security Police and SD
SS Sturmbannführer Dr. Lange, Commander of the Security Police and SD in the District of Latvia, as representative of the Commander of the Security Police and SD for the Reich Commissariat for the Eastern Territories	Security Police and SD

II. At the beginning of the meeting the Chief of the Security Police and SD, SS Obergruppenführer Heydrich, announced his appointment as Plenipotentiary for the Preparation of the Final Solution of the European Jewish Question by the Reich Marshal and pointed out that this conference had been called to clear up fundamental questions. The Reich Marshal's request to have a draft sent to him on the organizational, substantive, and economic needs in regard to the final solution of the European Jewish question requires prior joint consideration by all central agencies directly concerned with these questions, with a view to keeping policy lines parallel.

Primary responsibility for the handling of the final solution of the Jewish question resides centrally, without consideration of geographic boundaries, with the Reichsführer SS and the Chief of the German Police (Chief of the Security Police and the SD).

The Chief of the Security Police and the SD then gave a brief review of the struggle up to now against this enemy. The most important aspects are

(a) forcing the Jews out of each sphere of the life of the German people;
(b) forcing the Jews out of the living space of the German people.

In carrying out these efforts, acceleration of the emigration of the Jews from Reich territory was undertaken in intensified and systematic fashion as the only feasible solution for the time being.

By decree of the Reich Marshal a Reich Central Office for Jewish Emigration was established in January 1939, and its direction was entrusted to the Chief of the Security Police and the SD. In particular, its tasks were

(a) to take all measures for the *preparation* of accelerated emigration of the Jews;
(b) to *direct* the flow of emigration;
(c) to expedite emigration *in individual cases.*

The objective of these tasks was to cleanse the German living space of Jews in a legal way.

The disadvantages entailed by such a forced emigration were clear to all the authorities. But in the absence of other feasible solutions they had to be accepted for the time being.

In the ensuing period, the emigration efforts were not merely a German problem, but also a problem with which the authorities of the countries of destination or immigration had to deal. Financial difficulties – such as increases on the part of various foreign governments in the funds which immigrants were required to have and in landing fees, lack of ship berths, and continually escalated restrictions or bans on immigration – made the emigration efforts much more difficult. Despite these difficulties, a total of approximately 537,000 Jews were induced to emigrate between the assumption of power and the date of 31 October 1941. Of these

since 30 January 1930 from Germany proper (*Altreich*) . . . . approximately 360,000
since 15 March 1938 from Austria (*Ostmark*) . . . . approximately 147,000
since 15 March 1939 from the Protectorate of Bohemia and Moravia
. . . . approximately 30,000

Financing of the emigration took place through the Jews or Jewish political organizations themselves. To avoid proletarianized Jews remaining behind, the principle was followed that well-to-do Jews had to finance the emigration of destitute Jews. To this end, a special assessment or emigration fee, assessed according to wealth, was levied, the proceeds being used to meet financial obligations in the course of the emigration of destitute Jews.

In addition to the funds raised in German marks, foreign exchange was needed for the funds which emigrants were required to have and for landing fees. To conserve the German supply of foreign exchange, Jewish financial institutions abroad were prompted by the Jewish organizations in this country to see to it that appropriate funds in foreign currencies were obtained. Through these foreign Jews a total of approximately $9,500,000 was made available in the form of gifts up to 30 October 1941.

In the meantime, in view of the dangers of emigration during wartime and in view of the possibilities in the East, the Reichsführer SS and Chief of the German Police has prohibited the emigration of Jews.

III. Emigration has now been replaced by evacuation of the Jews to the East as a further possible solution, in accordance with previous authorization by the Führer.

However, these actions are to be regarded only as provisional options; yet the practical experience is already being gathered here that is of major significance in respect to the coming final solution of the Jewish question.

In the course of this final solution of the European Jewish question approximately 11 million Jews are envisaged. They are distributed among the individual countries as follows:

Country	Number
A. Altreich	131,800
Ostmark	43,700
Eastern Territories	420,000
Generalgouvernement	2,284,000
Bialystok	400,000
Protectorate of Bohemia and Moravia	74,200
Estonia – free of Jews	
Latvia	3,500
Lithuania	34,000
Belgium	43,000
Denmark	5,600
France, Occupied Territory	165,000
Unoccupied Territory	700,000
Greece	69,600
The Netherlands	160,800
Norway	1,300
B. Bulgaria	48,000
England	330,000
Finland	2,300
Ireland	4,000
Italy, including Sardinia	58,000
Albania	200
Croatia	40,000
Portugal	3,000
Romania, including Bessarabia	342,000
Sweden	8,000
Switzerland	18,000
Serbia	10,000
Slovakia	88,000
Spain	6,000
Turkey (European part)	55,500
Hungary	742,800
USSR	5,000,000
Ukraine	2,994,684
White Russia, excluding Bialystok	446,484
Total:	over 11,000,000

However, the numbers of Jews given for the various foreign states reflect only those of Jewish faith, as definitions of Jews according to racial principles are still partly lacking there.

The handling of the problem in the individual countries, especially in Hungary and Romania, will meet with certain difficulties because of prevailing attitudes and ideas. To this day, for example, a Jew in Romania can for payment obtain appropriate documents officially certifying him to be of foreign citizenship.

The influence of the Jews on all areas in the USSR is well known. About five million live in the European area, a scant half-million in the Asian territory.

The occupational breakdown of Jews residing in the European area of the USSR was about as follows:

in agriculture 9.1%
urban workers. 14.8%
in commerce 20.0%
employed as government workers 23.4%
in the professions – medicine,
    press, theater, etc 32.7%

Under appropriate supervision, in the course of the final solution, the Jews are to be suitably assigned to labor in the East. In big labor gangs, with the sexes separated, Jews capable of work will be brought to these areas, employed in roadbuilding, whereby a large part will undoubtedly disappear through natural diminution.

The remnant that may eventually remain, being undoubtedly the part most capable of resistance, will have to be appropriately dealt with, since it represents a natural selection and in the event it is set free is to be regarded as the nucleus of a new Jewish revival. (Note the experience of history.)

In the course of the practical implementation of the final solution, Europe is to be combed through from west to east. The Reich area, including the Protectorate of Bohemia and Moravia, will have to be handled first, if only because of the housing problem and other socio-political necessities.

The evacuated Jews will first be brought, group by group, into so-called transit ghettos, to be transported from there farther to the East.

An important precondition for the implementation of the evacuation as a whole, SS Obergruppenführer Heydrich went on to explain, is the precise determination of the category of persons that may be affected.

The intent is not to evacuate Jews over 65 years of age, but to assign them to a ghetto for the aged. Theresienstadt is under consideration.

Along with these age groups (of the approximately 280,000 Jews who on 31 October 1941 were in the Altreich and the Ostmark, approximately 30 percent are over 65 years old), Jews with serious war injuries and Jews with war decorations (Iron Cross, First Class) will be admitted into the Jewish old-age ghettos. With this efficient solution, the many interventions [requests for exceptions] will be eliminated at one stroke.

The beginning of each of the large-scale evacuation operations will depend largely on military developments. As far as the handling of the final solution in the European areas occupied by us and under our influence is concerned, the proposal was made that the appropriate specialists in the Foreign Ministry confer with the competent official of the Security Police and the SD.

In Slovakia and Croatia the undertaking is no longer too difficult, as the most essential problems in this matter have already been resolved there. In Romania as well the government has by now appointed an official responsible for Jewish Affairs. To settle the problem in Hungary it will be necessary in the near future to impose upon the Hungarian government an adviser in Jewish problems.

With regard to launching preparations for the settling of the problem in Italy, SS Ober-gruppenführer Heydrich considers liaison with the Police Chief appropriate in these matters.

In occupied and unoccupied France the roundup of the Jews for evacuation can in all probability take place without great difficulties.

On this point, Undersecretary Luther stated that thorough resolution of this problem will occasion difficulties in a few countries, such as the Scandinavian states, and that it is therefore advisable to postpone these countries for the time being. In view of the small number of Jews presumably affected there, this postponement does not constitute an appreciable curtailment in any case. On the other hand, the Foreign Ministry sees no great difficulties in the south-east and the west of Europe.

SS Gruppenführer Hofmann intends to have a specialist of the Race and Settlement Main Office sent along to Hungary for general orientation when the matter is taken in hand there by the Chief of the Security Police and the SD. It was decided that this specialist of the Race and Settlement Main Office, who is not to be active, should temporarily be given the official designation of assistant to the Police Attaché.

IV. In the implementation of the final solution project the Nuremberg Laws are to form the basis, as it were; in this context a solution to the problems of mixed marriages and *Mischlinge* is a precondition for complete settlement of the problem.

In connection with a letter from the Chief of the Reich Chancellery the Chief of the Security Police and the SD discussed the following points – hypothetically, for the time being:

1 TREATMENT OF FIRST-DEGREE *MISCHLINGE*

As far as the final solution of the Jewish question is concerned, first-degree *Mischlinge* are deemed equivalent to Jews.

The following will be exempt from this treatment:

(a) First-degree *Mischlinge* married to persons of German blood from whose marriages children (second-degree *Mischlinge*) have been born. These second-degree *Mischlinge* are deemed essentially equivalent to Germans.

(b) First-degree *Mischlinge* for whom special dispensations in any area of life have been granted by the highest authorities of the Party and the State. Each individual case must be re-examined, and the possibility is not ruled out that the decision may again be to the *Mischling's* disadvantage.

The basis for granting an exception must always be the fundamental merits of the particular *Mischling* himself (not the merits of the parents or spouse of German blood).

The first-degree *Mischling* to be exempted from evacuation is to be sterilized in order to prevent any offspring and to resolve the *Mischling* problem once and for all. Sterilization takes place on a voluntary basis. It is, however, the condition for remaining in the Reich. The sterilized *Mischling* is thereafter freed from all restrictive regulations to which he was previously subject.

2 TREATMENT OF SECOND-DEGREE *MISCHLINGE*

Second-degree *Mischlinge* are in principle classed with persons of German blood, with the exception of the following cases, in which second-degree *Mischlinge* are deemed equivalent to Jews:

(a) Descent of the second-degree *Mischlinge* from a bastard marriage (both spouses being *Mischlinge*).
(b) Especially unfavorable appearance of the second-degree *Mischling* in racial terms, to the degree that by virtue of his exterior alone he is counted as a Jew.
(c) Especially adverse police and political evaluation of the second-degree *Mischling*, indicating that he feels and conducts himself like a Jew.

In these cases as well, however, exceptions are not to be made if the second-degree *Mischling* is married to a person of German blood.

3 MARRIAGES BETWEEN FULL JEWS AND PERSONS OF GERMAN BLOOD

It must be decided from case to case whether the Jewish spouse is to be evacuated or whether, taking into consideration the effect of such a measure on the German relatives of the mixed couple, he or she is to be assigned to an old-age ghetto.

4 MARRIAGES BETWEEN FIRST-DEGREE *MISCHLINGE* AND PERSONS OF GERMAN BLOOD

(a) Without children:
If no children have been born of the marriage, the first-degree *Mischling* is to be evacuated or assigned to an old-age ghetto. (The same treatment as in the case of marriages between full Jews and persons of German blood, item 3.)
(b) With children:
If children have been born of the marriage (second-degree *Mischlinge*), they are to be evacuated or assigned to a ghetto, together with the first-degree *Mischlinge*, provided they are deemed equivalent to Jews. Insofar as such children are deemed equivalent to Germans (normal cases), they are to be exempted from evacuation, and also therewith the first-degree *Mischling*.

5 MARRIAGES BETWEEN FIRST-DEGREE *MISCHLINGE* AND FIRST-DEGREE *MISCHLINGE* OR JEWS

In the case of such marriages (including children), all parties are to be treated like Jews and accordingly evacuated or assigned to an old-age ghetto.

6 MARRIAGES BETWEEN FIRST-DEGREE *MISCHLINGE* AND SECOND-DEGREE *MISCHLINGE*

Both spouses, regardless of whether there are children or not, are to be evacuated or assigned to an old-age ghetto, since any children of such marriages normally show a greater share of Jewish blood in their racial makeup than do second-degree Jewish *Mischlinge*.

SS Gruppenführer Hofmann takes the position that extensive use must be made of sterilization, especially since the *Mischling*, when confronted with the choice of being evacuated or sterilized, would prefer to submit to sterilization.

Permanent Secretary Dr. Stuckart stated that the practical implementation of the possible solutions just communicated for resolving the problems of mixed marriages and those of the *Mischlinge* would entail endless administrative work in their present form. Thus in order to take biological realities fully into consideration, Secretary Dr. Stuckart proposed undertaking compulsory sterilization.

To simplify the mixed marriage problem, further possibilities must be considered with the goal that the law-maker says something to the effect: "These marriages are dissolved."

As to the question of the effect the evacuation of Jews may have on economic life, Permanent Secretary Neumann declared that the Jews employed in essential war industries could not be evacuated at present as long as no replacements were available.

SS Obergruppenführer Heydrich pointed out that these Jews would not be evacuated anyway according to the directives approved by him for the implementation of current evacuation operations.

Permanent Secretary Dr. Bühler stated that the Generalgouvernement would welcome it if the final solution of this problem were begun in the Generalgouvernement, because here the transport problem plays no major role and considerations of labor supply would not hinder the course of this operation. Jews needed to be removed as quickly as possible from the territory of the Generalgouvernement, because here particularly the Jew constitutes a marked danger as a carrier of epidemics, and also because by his continuing black-market operations he throws the economic structure of the country into disorder. Furthermore, of the approximately two-and-one-half million Jews here in question the majority of cases were unfit for work.

Secretary Dr. Bühler added that the solution of the Jewish question in the Generalgouvernement is primarily the responsibility of the Chief of the Security Police and the SD and that his work would be supported by the agencies of the Generalgouvernement. He had only the one request that the Jewish question in this territory be solved as quickly as possible.

In conclusion, the various kinds of possible solutions were discussed, and here both Gauleiter Dr. Meyer and Secretary Dr. Bühler took the position that certain preparatory tasks connected with the final solution should be performed right in the territories concerned, in the course of which, however, any alarm among the population would have to be avoided.

The conference was concluded with a request by the Chief of the Security Police and the SD to the conference participants that they afford him appropriate support in carrying out the tasks connected with the solution efforts.

Source: Document NG–2586, Nuremberg Trial Record (Léon Poliakov and Josef Wulf, eds., *Das Dritte Reich und die Juden* [1955; rept. Munich: K.G. Saur, 1978], pp. 119–26)

The killing centers

SS engineer Kurt Gerstein (1905–45), whose responsibilities included distribution of chemical disinfectants and supervision of their use, was sent to the "Operation Reinhardt" camps at Belzec, Treblinka, and Sobibor in August 1942 to deliver to the SS officers in charge, Odilo Globocnik and Christian Wirth, the prussic acid (known under the trade name of Cyclon B) that Reich Security Main Office officials considered superior to diesel exhaust fumes for gassing of people. Cyclon B was used in what would become the largest of the six killing centers in Poland, at Oswiecim, known in German as Auschwitz (see Doc. 6.15). Gerstein, an enigmatic figure who claimed to have joined the SS to find out exactly what went on in the camps,

Table 6.1 Nazi concentration and extermination camps

Concentration camps	Date opened	Date evacuated or liberated	Satellite camps
Dachau	22 March 1933	29 April 1945	169
Sachsenhausen	August 1936	22 April 1945	61
Buchenwald	15 July 1937	11 April 1945	134
Flossenbürg	3 May 1938	23 April 1945	92
Mauthausen	June 1938	5 May 1945	56
Neuengamme	Fall 1938	29–30 April 1945	73
Ravensbrück	15 May 1939	30 April 1945	42
Stutthof (Danzig)	1 September 1939	after 27 January 1945	107
Auschwitz (I)	20 May 1940	27 January 1945	38
Groß-Rosen	2 August 1940	February 1945	99
Natzweiler-Struthof	1 May 1941	after September 1944	49
Lublin-Majdanek	October 1941	22–24 July 1944	10
Auschwitz II (Birkenau)	26 November 1941	27 January 1945	
Auschwitz III (Monowitz)	31 May 1942	27 January 1945	
Herzogenbusch-Vught	5 January 1943	5–6 September 1944	13
Riga (Latvia)	15 March 1943	after 6 August 1944	17
Bergen-Belsen	April 1943	15 April 1945	
Dora-Mittelbau	27 August 1943	9 April 1945	29
Warsaw	15 August 1943	after 24 July 1944	
Kauen (Lithuania)	15 September 1943	after 14 July 1944	8
Vaivara (Estonia)	15 September 1943	3 October 1944	10
Klooga (Estonia)	September 1943	19 September 1944	3
Krakau-Plaszow	11 January 1944	15 January 1945	

Extermination camps	Dates gas chambers or vans in operation	Number of victims (minimum numbers)
Kulmhof/Chelmno	8 December 1941– March 1943, Summer 1944	152,000
Auschwitz-Birkenau	January 1942–November 1944	over 1,000,000
Belzec	17 March 1942–Spring 1943	over 600,000
Sobibor	7 May 1942–Fall 1943	250,000
Treblinka	23 July 1942–October 1943	700,000–900,000
Lublin-Majdanek	Summer 1942–July 1944	200,000, including 60,000 Jews

reported to Swedish diplomats and high-ranking Catholic and Protestant church officials what he had seen at the camps. They failed, however, to act on his disquieting report, either because they doubted its credibility or because they wished to avoid friction with the German government. The selection below is excerpted from a deposition that Gerstein gave to Allied officers on 4 May 1945. Shortly thereafter he committed suicide in a French prison cell.

6.9 Kurt Gerstein's eye-witness account of gassings at Belzec and Treblinka

... In January 1942 I was appointed head of the Department of Sanitation Techniques and at the same time to the parallel position for the same sector of the SS and Police Medical Office. In this capacity I took over the entire technical service of disinfection, including disinfection with highly toxic gases. On 8 June 1942 SS Sturmbannführer Günther of the *Reichssicherheits-Hauptamt*, dressed in civilian clothes, walked into my office.[4] He was unknown to me. He ordered me to obtain for him, for a top secret mission, 100 kilos of prussic acid and to take it to a place known only to the truck driver. A few weeks later, we set out for the potash plant near Kolin (Prague).

I understood little of the nature of my mission. But I accepted. To this day I believe that it was luck, strangely resembling Providence, that gave me the opportunity to see what I was trying to find out. Out of hundreds of other possible assignments, I was put in charge of the post that was closest to the area that interested me ...

On the way to Kolin, we were accompanied by SS Obersturmbannführer Professor Pfannenstiel, Professor of Hygiene at the University of Marburg/Lahn.

From my deliberately bizarre technical questions, the people at the Kolin prussic acid plant could understand that the acid was going to be used to kill human beings. I did this in order to spread rumors among the population.

We then set off with the truck for Lublin (Poland). SS Gruppenführer Globocnik was waiting for us.[5] He told us: "This is one of our most secret matters, indeed the most secret. Anyone who talks about it will be shot. Only yesterday two babblers were shot." He then explained to us: "At present" – this was 17 August 1942 – "there are three installations:"

1   Belzec, on the Lublin-Lwów road. Maximum per day: 15,000 persons (seen)!
2   Sobibór, I don't know exactly where: not seen: 20,000 persons per day.
3   Treblinka, 120 km north-east of Warsaw: 25,000 persons per day; seen.
4   Majdanek, near Lublin; seen in preparation.

Except for the last one, I made a thorough inspection of all these camps, accompanied by Police Chief Wirth, the head of all three death factories.[6] Wirth was earlier put in charge by Hitler and Himmler of the murder of the insane at Hadamar, Grafeneck, and various other places.

---

4   Rolf Günther was Adolf Eichmann's deputy in Office IV B 4 of the *Reichssicherheits-Hauptamt*, the Reich Security Main Office (RSHA).
5   Odilo Globocnik (1904–45) was SS and Police Leader in the Lublin District of the *Generalgouvernement* (occupied Poland) from 1939–43 and as such was responsible for the death camps in the Lublin area.
6   Christian Wirth (1885–1944), a professional police officer who joined the SS in 1939, conducted the first gassings of disabled victims at the euthanasia institution Grafeneck after the start of the war. He became the first commandant of the Belzec death camp in December 1941 and was promoted to inspector of the three Operation Reinhardt death camps in August 1942.

Globocnik said: "You will have to disinfect large quantities of clothing ten or twenty times, the whole textile accumulation. It is only being done to conceal that the source of clothing is Jews, Poles, Czechs, etc. Your other duty will be to improve the service in our gas chambers, which function on diesel engine exhaust. We need gas which is more toxic and works faster, such as prussic acid. The Führer and Himmler – they were here on August 15, the day before yesterday – instructed me to accompany personally all those who have to see these installations." Then Professor Pfannenstiel: "But what did the Führer say?" Globocnik replied: "The Führer ordered all action speeded up! Dr. Herbert Lindner, who was with us yesterday, asked me: 'But wouldn't it be wiser to cremate the corpses instead of burying them? Another generation may perhaps judge these things differently!'[7] I replied: 'Gentlemen, if there were ever, after us, a generation so cowardly and so soft that they could not understand our work which is so good, so necessary, then gentlemen, all of National Socialism will have been in vain. We ought, on the contrary, to bury bronze tablets stating that it was we who had the courage to carry out this gigantic task!' The Führer then said: 'Yes, my good Globocnik, you are right!'"

Nevertheless, Dr. Lindner's opinion subsequently prevailed; even the corpses already buried were burned in gasoline or oil, on grates improvised on rails. The office for these factories is at the Julius Schreck barracks in Lublin. The following day I was introduced to the men who worked there.

We left for Belzec two days later. A small special station with two platforms was set up on a yellow sand hill, immediately to the north of the Lublin–Lwów railway. To the south, near the road, were some service buildings and a notice: "Sonderkommando of the Waffen-SS in Belzec." Globocnik presented me to SS Hauptsturmführer Obermeyer of Pirmasens, who showed great reserve when taking me over the installations. We saw no dead that day, but a pestilential odor blanketed the whole region and millions of flies were everywhere. Alongside the station was a large barrack marked "Cloak Room," with a ticket window inside marked "Valuables." Further on, a room with about a hundred chairs, "Barber." Then a passageway about 150 meters long, in the open, barbed wire on both sides, and notices: "To Baths and Inhalators." In front of us was a building of the bathhouse type, with large pots of geraniums and other flowers. Then stairs and then left and right 3 enclosures 5 meters square, 1.90 meters high, with wooden doors like garages. At the rear wall, not properly visible in the darkness, large wooden platform doors. On the roof, a copper Star of David. On the building, the inscription: "Heckenholt Foundation." That afternoon I saw nothing else.

Next morning, a few minutes before seven, I was told: "In ten minutes the first train will arrive!" Indeed, a few minutes later a train arrived from Lemberg, with 45 cars holding 6,700 people, of whom 1,450 were already dead on arrival. Behind the small barbed-wired window, children, young ones, frightened to death, women, men. The train pulled in: 200 Ukrainians detailed for the task wrenched open the doors and with their leather whips drove the Jews out of the cars. A loud-speaker issued instructions: to remove all clothing, even artificial limbs and eyeglasses; to tie their shoes together with small pieces of string handed out by a little Jewish boy; to turn in all valuables, all money at the ticket window "Valuables," without voucher, without receipt. Women and girls were to have their hair cut off in the "Barber's" barrack. (An SS sergeant on duty told me: "That's to make something special for submarine crews, for packaging or something like that.")

Then the march began. To the left and right, barbed wire; behind, two dozen Ukrainians, guns in hand.

---

7   Dr. Herbert Linden was a medical officer in the Ministry of Interior who played an active role in the euthanasia program.

They approached. Wirth and I, we were standing on the ramp in front of the death chambers. Completely nude, men, women, young girls, children, babies, cripples, filed by. At the corner stood a heavy SS man, who told the poor people, in a pastoral voice: "No harm will come to you! You just have to breathe very deeply, that strengthens the lungs, inhaling is a means of preventing contagious diseases. It's a good disinfection!" They asked what was going to happen to them. He told them: "The men will have to work, building roads and houses. But the women won't be obliged to do so; they'll do housework, cooking." For some of these poor creatures, this was a last small hope, enough to carry them, unresisting, as far as the death chambers. Most of them knew all, the odor confirmed it! They walked up the small wooden flight of stairs and entered the death chambers, most without a word, pushed forward by those behind them. One Jewish woman of about forty, her eyes flaming torches, cursed the murderers; after several whiplashes by Captain Wirth in person, she disappeared into the gas chamber. Many people pray, while others ask: "Who will give us water for washing the dead?"[8] ...

Inside the chambers, SS men crowd the people. "Fill them up well," Wirth had ordered, "700 to 800 of them every 25 square meters." The doors are shut. Meanwhile, the rest of the people from the train, naked, wait. I am told: "Naked even in winter!" "But they may catch their death!" "But that's what they're here for!" was the reply. At that moment, I understand the reason for the inscription "Heckenholt." Heckenholt was the driver of the diesel truck whose exhaust gases were to be used to kill these unfortunates. SS Unterscharführer Heckenholt was making great efforts to get the engine running. But it doesn't go. Captain Wirth comes up. I can see he is afraid because I am present at a disaster. Yes, I see it all and I wait. My stop watch showed it all, 50 minutes, 70 minutes, and the diesel did not start! The people wait inside the gas chambers. In vain. They can be heard weeping, "like in the synagogue," says Professor Pfannenstiel, his eyes glued to a window in the wooden door. Furious, Captain Wirth lashes the Ukrainian assisting Heckenholt 12, 13 times in the face. After two hours and 49 minutes – the stop watch recorded it all – the diesel started. Up to that moment, the people shut up in those four crowded chambers were still alive, four times 750 persons in four times 45 cubic meters! Another 25 minutes elapsed. Many were already dead; that could be seen through the small window when an electric lamp inside lit up the chamber for a few moments. After 28 minutes, only a few were still alive. Finally, after 32 minutes, all were dead.

On the far side members of the work commando opened the wooden doors. They – them- selves Jews – were promised their lives and a small percentage of the valuables and money collected for this terrible service. Like pillars of basalt, the dead were still erect, not having any space to fall, or to lean. Even in death, families could be seen still holding hands. It is hard to sepa- rate them as the chambers are emptied to make way for the next load; corpses were tossed out, blue, wet with sweat and urine, the legs covered with faeces and menstrual blood. Two dozen workers were busy checking the mouths of the dead, which they opened with iron hooks. "Gold to the left, without gold to the right!" Others inspected anuses and genital organs, searching for money, diamonds, gold, etc. Dentists hammered out gold teeth, bridges, and crowns. In the midst of them stood Captain Wirth. He was in his element, and showing me a large can full of teeth, he said: "See for yourself the weight of that gold! It's only from yesterday and the day before. You can't imagine what we find every day – dollars, diamonds, gold! You'll see yourself!" ...

Then the bodies were flung into large trenches, each $100 \times 20 \times 12$ meters, located near the gas chambers. After a few days the corpses swelled, because of the gases which formed inside them, and everything rose from two to three meters. A few days later, when the

---

8   A reference to *taharah*, the traditional Jewish rite of washing the dead body before burial.

swelling subsided, the bodies settled. Subsequently, I was told, the bodies were piled on train rails and burned in diesel oil so that they would disappear ...

The next day we drove in Captain Wirth's car to Treblinka, about 120 km north-east of Warsaw. The equipment in that place of death was almost the same as at Belzec, but even larger. Eight gas chambers and veritable mountains of clothing and underwear, about 35 to 40 meters high. Then, in our honor, a banquet was held for all those employed at the establishment. Obersturmbannführer Professor Doctor Pfannenstiel, Professor of Hygiene at the University of Marburg, made a speech: "Your work is a great work and a very useful and necessary duty." To me, he spoke of the establishment as "a kindness and a humanitarian thing." To all present, he said: "When one sees the bodies of the Jews, one understands the greatness of your work!"

Source: German text of Gerstein's deposition: *Vierteljahrshefte für Zeitgeschichte* 1 (April 1953), pp. 185–193. English text: Lucy S. Dawidowicz, ed., *A Holocaust Reader* (West Orange NJ: Behrman House, 1976), pp. 104–09

Open-air shooting of Jews, October 1942

Mass shootings of Jews, Communist commissars, and partisans were not conducted only by the Einsatzkommandos (see Doc. 6.6) but occurred throughout the war at the hands of the SS, units of the Order Police, and even auxiliary police units made up of East European collaborators. The following wrenching eye-witness report of a mass killing in the Ukraine in October 1942 is by a German engineer working for a construction firm with Wehrmacht contracts. It is estimated that as many as 1 and 1½ million Jews were killed by shooting in the Holocaust.

6.10 Affidavit of Hermann Friedrich Graebe

I, Hermann Friedrich Graebe, declare under oath:

From September 1941 until January 1944 I was manager and engineer-in-charge of a branch office in Zdolbunov, Ukraine, of the Solingen building firm of Josef Jung. In this capacity it was my job to visit the building sites of the firm. Under contract to an Army Construction Office, the firm had orders to erect grain storage buildings on the former airfield of Dubno, Ukraine.

On 5 October 1942, when I visited the building office at Dubno, my foreman Hubert Moennikes of 21 Aussenmühlenweg, Hamburg-Harburg, told me that in the vicinity of the site, Jews from Dubno had been shot in three large pits, each about 30 meters long and 3 meters deep. About 1500 persons had been killed daily. All of the 5,000 Jews who had still been living in Dubno before the pogrom were to be liquidated. As the shootings had taken place in his presence he was still much upset.

Thereupon I drove to the site, accompanied by Moennikes, and saw near it great mounds of earth, about 30 meters long and 2 meters high. Several trucks stood in front of the mounds. Armed Ukrainian militia drove the people off the trucks under the supervision of an SS man. The militia men acted as guards on the trucks and drove them to and from the pit. All these people had the regulation yellow patches on the front and back of their clothes, and thus could be recognized as Jews.

Moennikes and I went directly to the pits. Nobody bothered us. Now I heard rifle shots in quick succession, from behind one of the earth mounds. The people who had got off the trucks – men, women, and children of all ages – had to undress upon the order of an SS man, who carried a riding or dog whip. They had to put down their clothes in fixed places, sorted according to shoes, top clothing, and underclothing. I saw a heap of shoes of about 800 to 1,000 pairs, great piles of under-linen and clothing. Without screaming or weeping these people undressed, stood around in family groups, kissed each other, said farewells and waited for a sign from another SS man, who stood near the pit, also with a whip in his hand. During the 15 minutes that I stood near the pit I heard no complaint or plea for mercy. I watched a family of about 8 persons, a man and a woman, both about 50 with their children of about 1, 8, and 10, and two grown-up daughters of about 20 to 24. An old woman with snow-white hair was holding the one-year-old child in her arms and singing to it, and tickling it. The child was cooing with delight. The couple were looking on with tears in their eyes. The father was holding the hand of a boy about 10 years old and speaking to him softly; the boy was fighting his tears. The father pointed toward the sky, stroked his head, and seemed to explain something to him. At that moment the SS man at the pit shouted something to his comrade. The latter counted off about 20 persons and instructed them to go behind the earth mound. Among them was the family, which I have mentioned. I well remember a girl, slim and with black hair, who, as she passed close to me, pointed to herself and said, "23." I walked around the mound and found myself confronted by a tremendous grave. People were closely wedged together and lying on top of each other so that only their heads were visible. Nearly all had blood running over their shoulders from their heads. Some of the people shot were still moving. Some were lifting their arms and turning their heads to show that they were still alive. The pit was already ⅔ full. I esti- mated that it already contained about 1,000 people. I looked for the man who did the shooting. He was an SS man, who sat at the edge of the narrow end of the pit, his feet dangling into the pit. He had a tommy-gun on his knees and was smoking a cigarette. The people, completely naked, went down some steps which were cut in the clay wall of the pit and clambered over the heads of the people lying there, to the place to which the SS man directed them. They lay down in front of the dead or injured people; some caressed those who were still alive and spoke to them in a low voice. Then I heard a series of shots. I looked into the pit and saw that the bodies were twitching or the heads lying already motionless on top of the bodies that lay before them. Blood was running from their necks. I was surprised that I was not ordered away, but I saw that there were two or three postmen in uniform nearby. The next batch was approaching already. They went down into the pit, lined themselves up against the previous victims, and were shot. When I walked back, round the mound I noticed another truck-load of people which had just arrived. This time it included sick and infirm people. An old, very thin woman with terribly thin legs was undressed by others who were already naked, while two people held her up. The woman appeared to be paralyzed. The naked people carried the woman around the mound. I left with Moennikes and drove in my car back to Dubno.

On the morning of the next day, when I again visited the site, I saw about 30 naked people lying near the pit – about 30 to 50 meters away from it. Some of them were still alive; they looked straight in front of them with a fixed stare and seemed to notice neither the chilliness of the morning nor the workers of my firm who stood around. A girl of about 20 spoke to me and asked me to give her clothes, and help her escape. At that moment we heard a fast car approach and I noticed that it was an SS detail. I moved away to my site. 10 minutes later we hear shots from the vicinity of the pit. The Jews still alive had been ordered to throw the corpses into the pit – then they had themselves to lie down in this to be shot in the neck.

I make the above statement at Wiesbaden, Germany, on 10 November 1945. I swear before God that this is the absolute truth.

Hermann Friedrich Graebe

Subscribed and sworn before me at Wiesbaden, Germany, this 10 day of November 1945.

Homer B. Crawford, Major, AC

Investigator Examiner, War Crimes Branch

Source: Office of the US Chief of Counsel for Prosecution of Axis Criminality,
***Nazi Conspiracy and Aggression*, Vol. V**
(Washington DC: US Government Printing Office, 1946), pp. 696–8 [Doc. 2992-PS]

Escape from Germany

Elfriede Loew was born in Kattowitz in 1881, at that time a part of the Austro-Hungarian Empire. As a Jewish woman living in Berlin during the Third Reich she faced deportation and death. Loew fled from Germany to Switzerland with her foster daughter in October 1942 at the age of 61. By the 1940s it had become very difficult for Jews to leave Germany and even more difficult to find a country that would let them in. On 23 October 1941 all Jewish emigration from areas under German control was prohibited as the "Final Solution" went into effect.

Despite its reputation as a land of refuge, Swiss immigration policy did not include religious or racial persecution as a grounds for refugee status. Most Jewish refugees were not considered political refugees and were sent back to Germany by border guards without further action. Fearing a deluge of Jewish refugees following the Anschluss of Austria, Swiss officials requested the German authorities to identify Jews in their passports. The Germans were at first reluctant to do this because they wanted to encourage Jews to emigrate from Germany once they had deprived them of their property and assets. Faced by a Swiss refusal to accept any further immigrants, the Germans agreed in September 1938 to stamp the passports of Jews with a "J."

During the next few years Swiss authorities down-played reports of the increasing persecution of Jews. Government leaders compared Switzerland to a full lifeboat with little room for more occupants. In August 1942, months after the killing centers of the "Final Solution" had started operations, a number of Swiss citizens, especially members of refugee aid organizations, journalists, and clergy, began protesting the Draconian Swiss immigration policies. The public outcry resulted in the opening of the border in September 1942, although the official policy was not changed. Indeed, liberalized practices were applied inconsistently, and Elfriede Loew was very lucky that she and her foster daughter were not sent back. Swiss policy did not officially change until July 1944, when over five million Jews had already been killed.

About 28,000 Jews found refuge in Switzerland during the Second World War. The official number of those turned back between 1942 and 1945 is 9,747. There are no figures for those who were sent back from 1938 to 1942 and no way to tell how many Jews were discouraged by Swiss policies from attempting to enter the country. Many of the admitted refugees were sent to work camps or camps for illegal immigrants. Elfriede Loew spent three and a half years in a camp. She emigrated to England at the end of the war. In 1955, at the age of 74, she told the story of her escape for the Wiener Library Collection of Eyewitness Reports in London.

6.11 Elfriede Loew, "The Story of My Escape"

Beginning in the fall of 1941 all Jews in Berlin had to wear the star and later (1942) it had to be fastened to the apartment door also, right on the bell. Whenever the doorbell rang, we jumped with fright and no one dared to open the door. One evening about half past eight – we had to be at home by 8 p.m. – a policeman and a Gestapo man came to check whether all the tenants were in the house. Then they inspected the pantry to see whether they could find any forbidden goods like high-quality fruit or vegetables or sausage.

In February 1942 my husband died, and after that one by one my renters were deported. The rooms were sealed off, but I had to continue paying the whole rent. My foster daughter, Dr. Georgette Schüler, a former high school teacher, lived with me. She was nicknamed Go. In mid-August 1942 she was given "notice", that is, she was supposed to be picked up within three days. We knew that it would mean death. So on my advice Go left and hid at the house of a Christian friend, Luise Jonas, who was a piano teacher. There she heard from a Miss von Thadden that it would be possible to escape to Switzerland through Bavaria and the Tyrol. She gave Go the address of a friend, Mrs. Inge von Scherpenberg in Hubertushof near Weilheim in Bavaria. It wasn't until later that we discovered this was the daughter of Hjalmar Schacht. I had actually felt rather safe, because my friend Elisabeth Hoffer had introduced me to Mr. Bollert, a lawyer who had connections with the Gestapo. I gave him 300 Marks, and he told me that he had slipped the money to a Gestapo man, who had in return removed my card from the card file of the community. But one day my tenant Trude Feiertag, (formerly Kaputh), who worked in that department, came home and said "Mrs. Loew, you are in danger." Now we quickly got everything ready for our escape. Through her former pupil, Chief Administrative Advisor Dr. Franz Kaufmann, Go received a passport issued by the SS (at a cost 2000 Marks). This money and much more was made available to Go by two of her former colleagues. I did not have a photo-identity card, only ration cards without a "J" and a doctor's certificate stating that I should go to the Tyrol for recuperation following a serious illness. Miss Hoffer had gotten the certificate for me from an acquaintance, under whose name I then travelled. I was not sick, but I had lost about 50 pounds because of Go's problems. Everything had to go very quickly. We started in the beginning of October; by the middle of the month snow would already be falling in the mountains, and the escape could fail. On the 8th of October we were ready. Elisabeth Hoffer had taken care of the tickets; you had to show a passport to buy them, and Jews did not get any tickets. Elisabeth Hoffer and Edith Martens picked up our baggage. I left the house wearing the star of David and walked to the radio tower, where I pulled the star off my coat and threw it into the gully. Then on to the Anhalter Bahnhof, where the three ladies (Go and our two friends) waited. Both Go and I went separately on the night train to Munich. These two friends had risked their lives once again, as they always did when they visited me in my apartment. In Munich we took the risk of boarding the train to Weilheim together, and from there we went by narrow-gauge railway to Hohen-Peissenberg. Now in an icy wind we sought the way to the little estate Hubertushof. There a tall, slim blond woman opened the door. "We bring greetings from Miss von Thadden." "Oh, Jews?" Yes. "Come in." During our first conversation with Mrs. von Scherpenberg we found out that we would not be able to go across the border with a guide, as promised, but that we would have to risk it all alone. She showed us the location of the mountains with her hands: "You have to go from Nauders (in the Tyrol) over the Norbert Peak. Always go west, don't risk descending too early. The German border fortification at Martinsbrück must be far to the right behind you at all times." We rested for two nights in Hubertushof and traveled via Innsbruck to Landeck, from there by bus to Nauders. Frequent passport controls; Go's passport (Grete Schlüter is looking for vacation accommodations for Berlin children) was in order. I was repeatedly snarled at for not knowing that a real passport was necessary. But they let me through. In Nauders we found an inn with much difficulty and had to pay for eight days in advance. The very next morning we were looking for Norbert Peak and were just about to disappear into the woods when the German border guard appeared. Where do you want to go? Can't you read? Signs everywhere: *Verboten*! Go's passport was carefully examined, and then we asked him very innocently where there was a nice lookout point here; we had heard of one. He showed us the way. We sat there on a stone bench and saw the Promised Land before us, the Engadine, where we wanted to go, and we were being watched. The border guard waited until we started to leave, then he escorted us back to the village and – left us! "Practically dead already", said Go. We thought he would report us to the police. We were really determined to put an end to our lives. Many of our loved ones had already done it after all. But how? We brooded about it for two days and nights. On the third morning I found a Cologne newspaper at the inn and said to myself, if I find a name in this newspaper that's really familiar to me, we'll risk trying to escape again. I opened the paper and the first name I found was: Kattowitz! My home town! So let's go! Left everything there, only put on double underwear and warm coats. We had luck with the weather; no snow (on 16 October) and the sun was shining. We needed it because we didn't have a compass; instead we followed the shadows of the trees in the early morning. Over this mountain we have to go! All right, but there was barbed wire everywhere. Back onto the road. Barbed wire there, too. Suddenly there was one place where it was broken, a ravine-like cleft led upward, full of brushwood and dry branches. Up, quickly, quickly, up above was forest, there we would be safe. Now in the dense forest, through the trees, avoiding main tracks and paths, always following the shadows, heading west. Occasionally we saw the side of the mountain across from us, and we suspected that the headwaters of the Inn river flowed between us and the mountain. After several hours of hiking without stopping, we caught sight of the German border fortification at Martinsbrück already quite far to the right in the valley below. But we did not yet risk the descent. Finally toward evening we thought it was safe. Now down the mountain. That was difficult in street shoes. The slopes were covered with slippery fir needles; we slipped more than we walked. Then on the spur of the moment I sat down on the ground and slid from tree to tree. Finally Go stood below at the river Inn and I stood on a boulder, wanted to get to her, jumped and – felt a tear in my knee. In terrible pain I dragged myself on. A woman was working in a field. "Are we in the Tyrol or in Switzerland?" "In Switzerland!" We shouted for joy, but we had no idea where we had crossed the border. Just as we wanted to cross a small bridge to the other side, German soldiers whizzed by over there on motorcycles. We hid in the bushes and waited until they rode back to Martinsbrück. Then, slowly and laboriously, we walked across and went further into the country. We could already see the houses of the little village Strada when a Swiss border guard came toward us on his bicycle. "Where do you come from?" "From Germany. We escaped." "Passports!" Go showed them her National Socialist passport. "Well then, why are you fleeing?" "But these are false papers." – "So and where are your real ones?" Then we removed the identity cards with "J" which we had sewn into the collars of our coats and gave them to him. He was very suspicious, we could see that. He went with us to the little village post office, made us wait outside and went in. We saw him make a phone call. He was calling the canton police in Chur. We were trembling with fear. They had warned us in Berlin that the Swiss sent all refugees back to certain death. The man came out, but he didn't give us any information. What will happen us? "Go to the Post-Restaurant and wait for the bus!" We dragged ourselves there. A very nice girl gave us bread and milk and asked: What did the border guard say? – We're supposed to wait for the bus. – Well, there are two – one comes from Martinsbrück and goes to Schuls-Tarasp, the other comes from there and goes to the German border! – So we sat there for one and one-half hours and didn't know whether we were allowed to stay or would be sent back to Germany. That was the worst part of the whole escape. After one and one-half hours the young girl came in and said: "The bus to Martinsbrück is already gone!" And five minutes later the border guard called us to come out. The sign on the bus said: To *Schuls-Tarasp* – and off we went into the dark evening. Both of us still could not believe that we were saved. Saved from what? We could only guess. The police were waiting for us in Schuls-Tarasp and took us first to the doctor. After all, we could be carrying a disease. The very charming doctor bandaged my knee and said: "It's a torn ligament!" He told us: "Be glad you didn't come four weeks ago. At that time every refugee was sent back. The people rose up against that policy and expressed their outrage in the newspapers, so now each case is being examined one by one." We were then led to an inn where we received a good warm supper, the like of which we had not enjoyed for years, and a small room for the night. The next morning at six o'clock we met the police officer at the train station. He accompanied us to Chur. We could not really enjoy the beauty of the upper Engadine. We kept thinking: What will they do with us at the Canton Police Station in Chur? Well, several gentlemen interrogated us for hours. And not only about our personal experiences. They also wanted to know how the supplies were in Germany, what the German people thought, etc. Finally they brought us to the Rhätische Volkshaus, a simple, big hotel, and handed us over to the manager Anny Ackermann; she was to give us shelter and food for the time being. I was even sent a doctor, who treated my knee. We walked through the streets of Chur as if in a dream, amazed at the fully-stocked stores. We changed our smuggled 2000 marks into 200 Francs and sent telegrams to my daughter and my brother in London. On the third day the police picked us up, and again we continued on, this time to Zurich, and from there to Adliswil, to the camp. That was the flip side of the coin; it surpassed our worst fears. But still, we were saved. There would be much to tell about our three and one-half year stay in Switzerland, but that would be going too far. A few Jews and a few Christians tried to make our lives more pleasant. We are still in contact with them today.

Source: "Die Geschichte meiner Flucht." Bericht Elfriede Loew, Wiener Library Eyewitness Reports, PIIId No. 19. By permission of Wiener Library, London. This report is also available in "Testaments to the Holocaust." Series One: Archives of the Wiener Library, London. Microfilm collection. Ed. Ben Barkow. Publisher: Gale Group. Translated by Sally Winkle

The anguish of the victims

The fragments of the two anonymous unsent letters below were discovered among the clothes of victims of an SS extermination action against the last inhabitants of the Tarnopol ghetto in May 1943. Tarnopol, today a part of Ukraine, was the capital of the eastern-most district of the formerly Austro-Hungarian province of Galicia, incorporated into Poland after the First World War. Some 500,000 Jews residing in Galicia fell victim to the Holocaust. These heartrending letters give some indication of the depth of despair that the victims of Nazi genocide must have felt.

6.12 Farewell letters from Tarnopol, April 1943

TARNOPOL, 7 APRIL 1943

My beloved!
    Before I leave this world, I want to leave behind a few lines to you, my loved ones. When this letter reaches you one day, I myself will no longer be there, nor will any of us. Our end is drawing

near. One feels it, one knows it. Just like the innocent, defenseless Jews already executed, we are all condemned to death. In the very near future it will be our turn, as the small remainder left over from the mass murders. There is no way for us to escape this horrible, ghastly death.

At the very beginning (in June 1941) some 5,000 men were killed, among them my husband. After six weeks, following a five-day search between the corpses, I found his body … Since that day life has ceased for me. Not even in my girlish dreams could I once have wished for a better and more faithful companion. I was only granted two years and two months of happiness. And now? Tired from so much searching among the bodies, one was "glad" to have found his as well; are there words in which to express these torments?

TARNOPOL, 26 APRIL 1943

I am still alive and I want to describe to you what happened from the 7th to this day. Now then, it is told that everyone's turn comes up next. Galicia should be totally rid of Jews. Above all, the ghetto is to be liquidated by the 1st of May. During the last days thousands have again been shot. Meeting point was in our camp. Here the human victims were selected. In Petrikov it looks like this: before the grave one is stripped naked, then forced to kneel down and wait for the shot. The [other] victims stand in line and await their turn. Moreover, they have to sort the first, the executed, in the graves so that the space is used well and order prevails. The entire procedure does not take long. In half an hour the clothes of the executed return to the camp. After the actions the Jewish council received a bill for 30,000 Zloty to pay for used bullets … Why can we not cry, why can we not defend ourselves? How can one see so much innocent blood flowing and say nothing, do nothing and await the same death oneself? We are compelled to go under so miserably, so pitilessly … Do you think we want to end this way, die this way? No! No! Despite all these experiences. The urge for self-preservation has now often become greater, the will to live stronger, the closer death is. It is beyond comprehension.

> Source: Dick de Mildt, *In the Name of the People: Perpetrators of Genocide
> in the Reflection of Their Post-War Prosecution in West Germany:
> The "Euthanasia" and "Aktion Reinhard" Trial Cases*
> (The Hague: Martinus Nijhoff, 1996), pp. 1–2

The Warsaw Ghetto uprising, April 1943

Deportations from the Warsaw Ghetto to the killing center at Treblinka began on 22 July 1942. Of the more than 400,000 original residents of the ghetto, only a little more than 50,000 remained alive when SS and Higher Police Leader Jürgen Stroop (1895–1951) prepared to launch the final clearing of the ghetto on 19 April 1943. In the face of unexpected and tenacious resistance, however, troops of the Waffen SS (the military arm of the SS) required more than three weeks and the support of heavy artillery to complete the operation. The resistance was led by the so-called Jewish Combat Organization, using the armaments factories in the ghetto as their base of operations. On 23 April Himmler ordered the ghetto to be razed to the ground. On 16 May Stroop sent the following report of the operation to his superiors at the administrative center of the Government-General in Kracow. His report not only describes the heroic resistance struggle in detail, but also provides a brief history of the Warsaw ghetto from the German point of view. Even in official communications German authorities used a kind of code language, referring, for instance, to deportations as "resettlement" and suggesting that the reason for isolating the Jewish population was the danger of "epidemics."

6.13 SS General Jürgen Stroop, Report on the destruction of the Warsaw Ghetto, 16 May 1943

THE WARSAW GHETTO IS NO MORE

For the Führer and their country the following fell in the battle for the destruction of Jews and bandits in the former Ghetto of Warsaw:

[15 Names]

Furthermore, the Polish Police Sergeant Julian Zielinski, born 13 November 1891 ... fell on 19 April 1943 while fulfilling his duty ... They gave their utmost, their lives. We shall never forget them. The following were wounded:

[Names of

60 Waffen SS personnel;

11 "Watchmen" from Training Camps;

12 Security Police Officers in SS Units;

5 men of the Polish Police;

2 regular Army personnel engineers.] ...

The creation of special areas to be inhabited by Jews, and the restriction of the Jews with regard to residence and trading is nothing new in the history of the East. Such measures were first taken far back in the Middle Ages; they could be observed as recently as during the last few centuries. These restrictions were imposed with the intention of protecting the Aryan population against the Jews.

Identical considerations led us as early as February 1940 to conceive the project of creating a Jewish residential district in Warsaw. The initial intention was to establish as the Ghetto that part of the City of Warsaw which has the Vistula as its eastern frontier. The particular situation prevailing in Warsaw seemed at first to frustrate this plan. It was moreover opposed by several authorities particularly by the City Administration. They pointed out in particular that disturbances in industry and trade would ensue if a ghetto were founded in Warsaw, and that it would be impossible to provide the Jews with food if they were assembled in a closed area.

At a conference held in March 1940 it was decided to postpone the plan of creating a ghetto for the time being, owing to the above objections. At the same time a plan was considered to declare the District of Lublin the collecting area for all Jews within the Government General, especially for the evacuated or fugitive Jews arriving from the Reich. But as early as April 1940 the Higher SS and Police Leader, East, Kracow, issued a declaration that there was no intention of assembling the Jews within the Lublin District. In the meantime, the Jews had increasingly taken to crossing the frontiers without permission and illegally. This was noted especially at the limits of the Districts of Lowicz and Skierniewice. Conditions in the town of Lowicz became dangerous from the point of view of hygiene as well as from that of the Security Police, owing to these illegal migrations of Jews. The District President of Lowicz therefore began to install ghettos in his district in order to avoid these dangers.

The experiences in the district of Lowicz, after ghettos had been installed, showed that this method is the only one suitable for dispelling the dangers which emanate repeatedly from the Jews.

The necessity of erecting a ghetto in the city of Warsaw as well became more and more urgent in the summer of 1940, since more and more troops were being assembled in the district of Warsaw after termination of the French campaign. At that time the Department for Hygiene urged the speedy erection of a ghetto in the interest of preserving the health of the German Forces and of the native population as well. The original plan of establishing the ghetto in the suburb of Praga as intended in February 1940 would have taken at least 4 to 5 months, since almost 600,000 persons had to be moved. But since experience showed that greater outbreaks of epidemics might be expected in the winter months and since for this reason the District Medical Officer urged that the resettling action ought to be completed by 15 November 1940 at the latest, the plan of establishing a suburban ghetto in Praga was dropped; and instead, the area which hitherto had been used as a quarantine area for epidemics was selected for use as a Jewish residential area. In October 1940 the Governor[9] ordered the Commissioner of the District, President for the City of Warsaw, to complete the resettlement necessary for establishing the ghetto within the city of Warsaw by 15 November 1940.

The Ghetto established in Warsaw was inhabited by about 400,000 Jews. It contained 27,000 apartments with an average of 2½ rooms each. It was separated from the rest of the city by partition and other walls and by walling up of thoroughfares, windows, doors, open spaces, etc.

It was administered by the Jewish Board of Elders, who received their instructions from the Commissioner for the Ghetto, who was immediately subordinated to the Governor. The Jews were granted self-administration in which the German supervising authorities intervened only where German interests were touched. In order to enable the Jewish Board of Elders to execute its orders, a Jewish Police force was set up, identified by special arm-bands and a special beret and armed with rubber truncheons. This Jewish Police force was charged with maintaining order and security within the Ghetto and was subordinated to the German and Polish Police.

II

It soon became clear, however, that not all dangers had been removed by this confining the Jews to one place. Security considerations required removing the Jews from the city of Warsaw altogether. The first large resettlement action took place in the period from 22 July to 3 October 1942. In this action 310,322 Jews were removed. In January 1943 a second resettlement action was carried out by which altogether 6,500 Jews were affected.

When the Reichsführer SS visited Warsaw in January 1943 he ordered the SS and Police Leader for the District of Warsaw to *transfer to Lublin the armament factories and other enterprises of military importance which were installed within the Ghetto including their personnel and machines.* The execution of this transfer order proved to be very difficult, since the managers as well as the Jews resisted in every possible way. The SS and Police Leader thereupon decided to enforce the transfer of the enterprises in a large-scale action which he intended to carry out in three days. The necessary preparations had been taken by my predecessor, who also had given the order to start the large-scale action. I myself arrived in Warsaw on 17 April 1943 and took over the command of the action on 19 April 1943, 0800 hours, the action itself having started the same day at 0600 hours.

9   Governor General Hans Frank (see Doc. 6.7).

Before the large-scale action began, the limits of the former Ghetto had been blocked by an external barricade in order to prevent the Jews from breaking out. This barricade was maintained from the start to the end of the action and was especially reinforced at night.

When we invaded the Ghetto for the first time, the Jews and the Polish bandits succeeded in repelling the participating units, including tanks and armored cars, by a well-prepared concentration of fire. When I ordered a second attack, about 0800 hours, I distributed the units, separated from each other by indicated lines, and charged them with combing out the whole of the Ghetto, each unit for a certain part. Although firing commenced again, we now succeeded in combing out the blocks according to plan. The enemy was forced to retire from the roofs and elevated bases to the basements, dug-outs, and sewers. In order to prevent their escaping into the sewers, the sewerage system was dammed up below the Ghetto and filled with water, but the Jews frustrated this plan to a great extent by blowing up the turn-off valves. Late the first day we encountered rather heavy resistance, but it was quickly broken by a special raiding party. In the course of further operations we succeeded in expelling the Jews from their prepared resistance bases, sniper holes, and the like, and in occupying during 20 and 21 April the greater part of the so-called remainder of the Ghetto to such a degree that the resistance continued within these blocks could no longer be called considerable.

The main Jewish battle group, mixed with Polish bandits, had already retired during the first and second day to the so-called Muranowski Square. There, it was reinforced by a considerable number of Polish bandits. Its plan was to hold the Ghetto by every means in order to prevent us from invading it. The Jewish and Polish standards were hoisted at the top of a concrete building as a challenge to us. These two standards, however, were captured on the second day of the action by a special raiding party. SS Untersturmführer Dehmke fell in this skirmish with the bandits; he was holding in his hand a hand grenade which was hit by the enemy and exploded, injuring him fatally. After only a few days I realized that the original plan had no prospect of success, unless the armament factories and other enterprises of military importance distributed throughout the Ghetto were dissolved. It was therefore necessary to approach these firms and to give them appropriate time for being evacuated and immediately transferred. Thus these firms were dealt with one after the other, and we very soon deprived the Jews and bandits of their chance to take refuge time and again in these enterprises, which were under the supervision of the Armed Forces. In order to decide how much time was necessary to evacuate these enterprises thorough inspections were necessary. The conditions discovered there are indescribable. I cannot imagine a greater chaos than in the Ghetto of Warsaw. The Jews had control of everything, from the chemical substances used in manufacturing explosives to clothing and equipment for the Armed Forces. The managers knew so little of their own shops that the Jews were in a position to produce inside these shops arms of every kind, especially hand grenades, Molotov cocktails, and the like.

Moreover, the Jews had succeeded in fortifying some of these factories as centers of resistance. Such a center of resistance in an Army accommodation office had to be attacked as early as the second day of the action by an Engineer's Unit equipped with flame throwers and by artillery. The Jews were so firmly established in this shop that it proved to be impossible to induce them to leave voluntarily; I therefore resolved to destroy this shop the next day by fire.

The managers of these enterprises, which were generally also supervised by an officer of the Armed Forces, could in most cases make no specific statements on their stocks and the whereabouts of these stocks. The statements which they made on the number of Jews employed by them were in every case incorrect. Over and over again we discovered that these labyrinths of edifices belonging to the armament concerns as residential blocks contained rich Jews who had succeeded in finding accommodations for themselves and their families under the name of "armament workers" and were leading marvelous lives there. Despite all our orders to the managers to make the Jews leave those enterprises, we found out in several cases that managers simply concealed the Jews by shutting them in, because they expected that the action would be finished within a few days and that they then would be able to continue working with the remaining Jews. According to the statements of arrested Jews, women also seem to have played a prominent part. The Jews are said to have endeavored to keep up good relations with officers and men of the armed forces. Carousing is said to have been frequent, during the course of which business deals are said to have been concluded between Jews and Germans.

The number of Jews forcibly taken out of the buildings and arrested was relatively small during the first few days. The Jews had taken to hiding in the sewers and in especially erected dug-outs. Whereas we had assumed during the first days that there were only scattered dug-outs, we learned in the course of the large-scale action that the whole Ghetto was systematically equipped with cellars, dug-outs, and passages. In every case these passages and dug-outs were connected with the sewer system. Thus, the Jews were able to maintain undisturbed subterranean traffic. They also used this sewer network for escaping subterraneously into the Aryan part of the city of Warsaw. Continuously, we received reports of attempts of Jews to escape through the sewer holes. While pretending to build air-raid shelters they had been erecting dug-outs within the former Ghetto ever since the autumn of 1942. These were intended to conceal every Jew during the new evacuation action, which they had expected for quite a time, and to enable them to resist the invaders in a concerted action. Through posters, handbills, and whisper propaganda, the communist resistance movement actually brought it about that the Jews entered the dug-outs as soon as the new large-scale operation started. How far their precautions went can be seen from the fact that many of the dug-outs had been skillfully equipped with furnishings sufficient for entire families, washing and bathing facilities, toilets, arms and munition supplies, and food supplies sufficient for several months. There were differently equipped dug-outs for rich and for poor Jews. To discover the individual dug-outs was difficult for the units, as they had been efficiently camouflaged. In many cases, it was possible only through betrayal on the part of the Jews.

When only a few days had passed, it became apparent that the Jews no longer had any intention to resettle voluntarily, but were determined to resist evacuation with all their force and by using all the weapons at their disposal. So-called battle groups had been formed, led by Polish Bolsheviks; they were armed and paid any price asked for available arms.

During the large-scale action we succeeded in catching some Jews who had already been evacuated and resettled in Lublin or Treblinka, but had broken out from there and returned to the Ghetto, equipped with arms and ammunition. Time and again Polish bandits found refuge in the Ghetto and remained there undisturbed, since we had no forces at our disposal to comb out this maze. Whereas it had been possible during the first days to catch considerable numbers of Jews, who are cowards by nature, it became more and more difficult during the second half of the action to capture the bandits and Jews. Over and over again new battle groups consisting of 20 to 30 or more Jewish fellows, 18 to 25 years of age, accompanied by a corresponding number of women kindled new resistance. These battle groups were under orders to put up armed resistance to the last and if necessary to escape arrest by committing suicide. One such battle group succeeded in mounting a truck by ascending from a sewer in the so-called Prosta,[10] and in escaping with it (about 30 to 35 bandits). One bandit who had arrived with this truck exploded 2 hand grenades, which was the agreed signal for the bandits waiting in the sewer to climb out

10   The Prosta was a street running through the ghetto.

of it. The bandits and Jews – there were Polish bandits among these gangs armed with carbines, small arms, and in one case a light machine gun, mounted the truck and drove away in an unknown direction. The last member of this gang, who was on guard in the sewer and was detailed to close the lid of the sewer hole, was captured. It was he who gave the above information. The search for the truck was unfortunately without result.

During this armed resistance the women belonging to the battle groups were equipped the same as the men; some were members of the *halutzim* movement.[11] Not infrequently, these women fired pistols with both hands. It happened time and again that these women had pistols or hand grenades (Polish "pineapple" hand grenades) concealed in their underwear up to the last moment to use against the men of the Waffen SS, Police, or Wehrmacht.

The resistance put up by the Jews and bandits could be broken only by relentlessly using all our force and energy by day and night. *On 23 April 1943 the Reichsführer SS issued through the Higher SS and Police Führer East at Kracow his order to complete the combing-out of the Warsaw Ghetto with the greatest severity and relentless tenacity.* I therefore decided to destroy the entire Jewish residential area by setting every block on fire, including the blocks of residential buildings near the armament works. One concern after the other was systematically evacuated and subsequently destroyed by fire. The Jews then emerged from their hiding places and dug-outs in almost every case. Not infrequently, the Jews stayed in the burning buildings until, because of the heat and the fear of being burned alive they preferred to jump down from the upper stories after having thrown mattresses and other upholstered articles into the street from the burning buildings. With their bones broken, they still tried to crawl across the street into blocks of buildings which had not yet been set on fire or were only partly in flames. Often Jews changed their hiding places during the night, by moving into the ruins of burnt-out buildings, taking refuge there until they were found by our patrols. Their stay in the sewers also ceased to be pleasant after the first week. Frequently from the street, we could hear loud voices coming through the sewer shafts. Then the men of the Waffen SS, the Police or the Wehrmacht Engineers courageously climbed down the shafts to bring out the Jews, and not infrequently they then stumbled over Jews already dead, or were shot at. It was always necessary to use smoke candles to drive out the Jews. Thus one day we opened 183 sewer entrance holes and at a fixed time lowered smoke candles into them, with the result that the bandits fled from what they believed to be gas to the center of the former Ghetto, where they could then be pulled out of the sewer holes there. A great number of Jews, who could not be counted, were exterminated by blowing up sewers and dug-outs.

The longer the resistance lasted, the tougher the men of the Waffen SS, Police, and Wehrmacht became; they fulfilled their duty indefatigably in faithful comradeship and stood together as models and examples of soldiers. Their duty hours often lasted from early morning until late at night. At night, search patrols with rags wound round their feet remained at the heels of the Jews and gave them no respite. Not infrequently they caught and killed Jews who used the night hours for supplementing their stores from abandoned dug-outs and for contacting neighboring groups or exchanging news with them.

Considering that the greater part of the men of the Waffen SS had only been trained for three to four weeks before being assigned to this action, high credit should be given for the pluck, courage, and devotion to duty which they showed. It must be stated that

11   The halutz movement was a Zionist youth organization.

the Wehrmacht Engineers, too, executed the blowing up of dug-outs, sewers, and concrete buildings with indefatigability and great devotion to duty. Officers and men of the Police, a large part of whom had already been at the front, again excelled by their dashing spirit.

Only through the continuous and untiring work of all involved did we succeed in capturing or verifiably destroying a total of 56,065 Jews. To this should be added the number of Jews who lost their lives in explosions or fires but whose numbers could not be ascertained.

During the large-scale operation the Aryan population was informed by posters that it was strictly forbidden to enter the former Jewish Ghetto and that anybody caught within the former Ghetto without valid pass would be shot. At the same time these posters informed the Aryan population again that the death penalty would be imposed on anybody who intentionally gave refuge to a Jew, especially lodged, supported, or concealed a Jew outside the Jewish residential area.

Permission was granted to the Polish police to pay to any Polish policeman who arrested a Jew within the Aryan part of Warsaw one-third of the cash in the Jew's possession. This measure has already produced results.

The Polish population for the most part approved the measures taken against the Jews. Shortly before the end of the large-scale operation, the Governor issued a special proclamation which he submitted to the undersigned for approval before publication to the Polish population; in it he informed them of the reasons for destroying the former Jewish Ghetto by mentioning the assassinations carried out lately in the Warsaw area and the mass graves found in Katyn;[12] at the same time they were asked to assist us in our fight against communist agents and Jews.

The large-scale action was terminated on 16 May 1943 with the blowing up of the Warsaw synagogue at 2015 hours.

Now, there are no more factories in the former Ghetto. All the goods, raw materials, and machines there have been moved and stored somewhere else. All buildings, etc., have been destroyed. The only exception is the so-called Dzielna Prison of the Security Police, which was exempted from destruction ...

The SS and Police Führer in the District of Warsaw
[signed] Stroop
SS Brigadeführer and Major General of Police

Source: Office of the Chief of US Counsel for Prosecution of Axis Criminality,
Nazi Conspiracy and Aggression, **Vol. III**
(Washington DC: US Government Printing Office, 1946), pp. 718–727 [Doc. 1061-PS]

Himmler on the destruction of the Jews

Himmler gave this speech to SS leaders in the city of Poznán (formerly Posen) at the time of the official conclusion of "Operation Reinhardt," the program to kill the Jews of the Generalgouvernement. Himmler's main rationalization for the systematic killing of all Jews – men, women, and children – was that the first law of nature commanded

---

12   Katyn was the site of the massacre of Polish officers by the Soviet secret police in occupied Poland in 1940.

loyalty to one's own kind and lack of compassion for (perceived) rivals and enemies. But his admonition to maintain the secrecy of the program revealed some residual, deep-seated guilt and his realization that normal human beings would never accept the validity of the "law of the jungle" in human society. The best he could hope for was to ease the sense of guilt from which even hardened SS minions could not escape. Love for and service to one's own people was the moral principle that supposedly legitimated mass murder. The contrast between Himmler's defense of the killing of the Jews and his denunciation of petty theft provides a shocking view into the mental and moral world of Nazi leaders and the SS.

6.14 Speech of Reichsführer SS Heinrich Himmler at a meeting of senior SS officers in Posen, 4 October 1943

… I also want to talk to you quite frankly on a grave matter. Among ourselves it should be said quite frankly, and yet we will never speak about it publicly. Just as we did not hesitate on 30 June 1934 to do the duty we were bidden, and stand lapsed comrades up against the wall and shoot them, just so we have never spoken about this and will never speak of it. It was the natural tactfulness that is, thank God, inherent in us that made us never discuss it among ourselves, never speak of it. It appalled everyone, and yet everyone was certain that he would do it again the next time if such orders are issued and if it is necessary.

I mean the evacuation of the Jews, the extermination of the Jewish people. It is one of those things that is easily said – "the Jewish people are being eradicated" every party member says, "that's quite clear, it's in our program, elimination of the Jews, and that's what we're doing, wiping them out." And then they all come, the 80 million upright Germans, and each one has his decent Jew. Of course the others are pigs, but this one is a first-class Jew. Not one of those who talk in this way has witnessed it, not one of them has been through it. Most of *you* know what it means when 100 corpses are lying side by side, or 500 or 1,000. To have stuck it out and at the same time – apart from exceptions caused by human weakness – to have remained decent, that is what has made us hard. This is a page of glory that has never been written and is never to be written, for we know how difficult we would have made it for ourselves, if – with the bombing raids, the burdens, and deprivations of war – we still had Jews today in every town as secret saboteurs, agitators, and troublemakers. We would probably now have reached the 1916–1917 stage if the Jews were still in the German national body.

We have taken from them what wealth they had. I have issued a strict order, which SS General [Oswald] Pohl has carried out, that this wealth should as a matter of course be entirely handed over to the Reich. We have taken none of it for ourselves. Individuals who have lapsed will be punished in accordance with an order I issued at the beginning, which gave this warning: Whoever takes so much as a Mark of it is a dead man. A number of SS men – not very many – have fallen short, and they will die, without mercy. We had the moral right, we had the duty to our people, to kill this people which wanted to kill us. But we do not have the right to enrich ourselves with so much as a fur, a watch, a Mark, a cigarette, or anything else. We do not want in the end, as a result of exterminating a bacterium, to become infected by this bacterium and die of it. I will never stand by and watch even a small sepsis appear here or gain a hold. Wherever it may form, together we will cauterize it. All in all, however, we can say that we have fulfilled this most difficult task for the love of our people. And our spirit, our soul, our character has not suffered injury from it.

Source: Office of the US Chief of Counsel for Prosecution of Axis Criminality,
Nazi Conspiracy and Aggression, Vol. IV
(Washington DC: US Government Printing Office, 1946), pp. 563–4 [Doc. 1919-PS]

Auschwitz: the perpetrators

Auschwitz, which originated as a concentration camp for Polish internees in Spring 1940, was expanded in the course of the war to form both the largest holding camp for prison laborers and the largest killing center in the Third Reich. Prisoners fit to work provided much of the manpower for the industrial complex at Auschwitz-Monowitz. Those deemed unfit to work were killed in the gas chambers of the crematoria at Auschwitz-Birkenau. SS *Obersturmbannführer* (the equivalent of Lt. Colonel) Rudolf Höss (1900–47) was Commandant at Auschwitz from May 1940 to November 1943 before moving up to become deputy to Richard Glücks (1889–1945) as Inspector of Concentration Camps. A right-wing radical involved in assassinations of Jews and Social Democrats in the early 1920s, Höss moved up in the camp hierarchy after Hitler's accession to power.

In April 1946 Höss was called to testify at the Nuremberg trial of major war criminals by defense counsel Kurt Kauffmann, who hoped to use Höss' testimony to prove that his client Ernst Kaltenbrunner (1903–46), Heydrich's successor as head of the Reich Security Services (RSHA), had no role in the killings by gas at Auschwitz. Höss provided a chilling description of the killing process, but insisted that the operation was entirely secret. Lack of knowledge of what went on in the camps to which they consigned their prisoners became a favorite defense of Gestapo and other security personnel after the war. Although Höss estimated the number of victims at Auschwitz as 2 million, later historical research indicates that the actual toll was closer to 1 million. The discrepancy may be due to the fact that Höss kept no accurate records, and, in any case, all records were destroyed to prevent them from falling into the hands of the victor powers. After testifying at Nuremberg, Höss was extradited to Poland where he was tried and executed in April 1947.

6.15 Testimony of Rudolf Höss, 15 April 1946

DR. KAUFMANN: Witness, your statements will have far-reaching significance. You are perhaps the only one who can throw some light upon certain hidden aspects, and who can tell which people gave the orders for the destruction of European Jewry, and can further state how this order was carried out and to what degree the execution was kept a secret ... [*Turning to the witness.*] From 1940 to 1943 you were the Commander of the camp at Auschwitz. Is that true?

HÖSS: Yes.

DR. KAUFMANN: And during that time, hundreds of thousands of human beings were sent to their death there. Is that correct?

HÖSS: Yes.

DR. KAUFMANN: Is it true that you, yourself, have made no exact notes regarding the figures of the number of those victims because you were forbidden to make them?

HÖSS: Yes, that is correct.

DR. KAUFMANN: Is it furthermore correct that exclusively one man by the name of Eichmann had notes about this, the man who had the task of organizing and assembling these people?

HÖSS: Yes.

DR. KAUFMANN: Is it furthermore true that Eichmann stated to you that in Auschwitz a total sum of more than 2 million Jews had been destroyed?

HÖSS: Yes.

DR. KAUFMANN: Men, women, and children?

HÖSS: Yes.

DR. KAUFMANN: You were a participant in the World War?

HÖSS: Yes.

DR. KAUFMANN: And then in 1922 you entered the Party?

HÖSS: Yes.

DR. KAUFMANN: Were you a member of the SS?

HÖSS: Since 1934.

DR. KAUFMANN: Is it true that you, in the year 1924, were sentenced to a lengthy term of hard labor because you participated in a so-called political murder?

HÖSS: Yes.

DR. KAUFMANN: And then at the end of 1934 you went to the concentration camp of Dachau?

HÖSS: Yes.

DR. KAUFMANN: What task did you receive?

HÖSS: At first I was the leader of a block of prisoners and then I became clerk and finally, the administrator of the property of prisoners.

DR. KAUFMANN: And how long did you stay there?

HÖSS: Until 1938.

DR. KAUFMANN: What job did you have from 1938 on and where were you then?

HÖSS: In 1938 I went to the concentration camp at Sachsenhausen where, to begin with, I was adjutant to the commander and later on I became the head of the protective custody camp.

DR. KAUFMANN: When were you commander at Auschwitz?

HÖSS: I was commander at Auschwitz from May 1940 until December 1943.

DR. KAUFMANN: What was the highest number of human beings, prisoners, ever held at one time at Auschwitz?

HÖSS: The highest number of internees held at one time at Auschwitz was about 140,000 men and women.

DR. KAUFMANN: Is it true that in 1941 you were ordered to Berlin to see Himmler? Please state briefly what was discussed.

HÖSS: Yes. In the summer of 1941 I was summoned to Berlin to Reichsführer SS Himmler to receive personal orders. He told me something to the effect – I do not remember the exact words – that the Führer had given the order for a final solution of the Jewish question. We, the SS, must carry out that order. If it is not carried out now, then the Jews will later on destroy the German people. He had chosen Auschwitz on account of its easy access by rail and also because the extensive site offered space for measures ensuring isolation.

DR. KAUFMANN: During that conference did Himmler tell you that this planned action had to be treated as a secret Reich matter?

HÖSS: Yes. He stressed that point. He told me that I was not even allowed to say anything about it to my immediate superior Gruppenführer Glücks. This conference concerned the two of us only and I was to observe the strictest secrecy.

DR. KAUFMANN: What was the position held by Glücks whom you have just mentioned?

HÖSS: Gruppenführer Glücks was, so to speak, the inspector of concentration camps at that time and he was immediately subordinate to the Reichsführer.

DR. KAUFMANN: Does the expression "secret Reich matter" mean that no one was permitted to make even the slightest allusion to outsiders without endangering his own life?

HÖSS: Yes, "secret Reich matter" means that no one was allowed to speak about these matters with any person and that everyone promised upon his life to keep the utmost secrecy.

DR. KAUFMANN: Did you happen to break that promise?

HÖSS: No, not until the end of 1942.

DR. KAUFMANN: Why do you mention that date? Did you talk to outsiders after that date?

HÖSS: At the end of 1942 my wife's curiosity was aroused by remarks made by the then Gauleiter of Upper Silesia, regarding happenings in my camp. She asked me whether this was the truth and I admitted that it was. That was my only breach of the promise I had given to the Reichsführer. Otherwise I have never talked about it to anyone else.

DR. KAUFMANN: When did you meet Eichmann?

HÖSS: I met Eichmann about 4 weeks after having received that order from the Reichsführer. He came to Auschwitz to discuss the details with me on the carrying out of the given order. As the Reichsführer had told me during our discussion, he had instructed Eichmann to discuss the carrying out of the order with me and I was to receive all further instructions from him.

DR. KAUFMANN: Will you briefly tell whether it is correct that the camp of Auschwitz was completely isolated, describing the measures taken to ensure as far as possible the secrecy of carrying out of the task given to you.

HÖSS: The Auschwitz camp as such was about 3 kilometers away from the town. About 20,000 acres of the surrounding country had been cleared of all former inhabitants, and the entire area could be entered only by SS men or civilian employees who had special passes. The actual compound called "Birkenau," where later on the extermination camp was constructed, was situated 2 kilometers from the Auschwitz camp. The camp installations themselves, that is to say, the provisional installations used at first were deep in the woods and could from nowhere be detected by the eye. In addition to that, this area had been declared a prohibited area, and even members of the SS who did not have a special pass could not enter it. Thus, as far as one could judge, it was impossible for anyone except authorized persons to enter that area.

DR. KAUFMANN: And then the railway transports arrived. During what period did these transports arrive and about how many people, roughly, were in such a transport?

HÖSS: During the whole period up until 1944 certain operations were carried out at irregular intervals in the different countries, so that one cannot speak of a continuous flow of incoming transports. It was always a matter of 4 to 6 weeks. During those 4 to 6 weeks two to three trains, containing about 2,000 persons each, arrived daily. These trains were first of all shunted to a siding in the Birkenau region and the locomotives then went back. The guards who had accompanied the transport had to leave the area at once and the persons who had been brought in were taken over by guards belonging to the camp.

They were there examined by two SS medical officers as to their fitness for work. The internees capable of work at once marched to Auschwitz or to the camp at Birkenau and those incapable of work were at first taken to the provisional installations, then later to the newly constructed crematoria.

DR. KAUFMANN: During an interrogation I had with you the other day you told me that about 60 men were designated to receive these transports, and that these 60 persons, too, had been bound to the same secrecy described before. Do you still maintain that today?

HÖSS: Yes, these 60 men were always on hand to take the internees not capable of work to these provisional installations and later on to the other ones. This group, consisting of about ten leaders and subleaders, as well as doctors and medical personnel, had repeatedly been told, both in writing and verbally, that they were bound to the strictest secrecy as to all that went on in the camps.

DR. KAUFMANN: Were there any signs that might show an outsider who saw these transports arrive, that they would be destroyed or was that possibility so small because there was in Auschwitz an unusually large number of incoming transports, shipments of goods and so forth?

HÖSS: Yes, an observer who did not make special notes for that purpose could obtain no idea about that because to begin with not only transports arrived which were destined to be destroyed but also other transports arrived continuously, containing new internees who were needed in the camp. Furthermore, transports likewise left the camp in sufficiently large numbers with internees fit for work or exchanged prisoners.

The trains themselves were closed, that is to say, the doors of the freight cars were closed so that it was not possible, from the outside, to get a glimpse of the people inside. In addition to that, up to 100 cars of materials, rations, et cetera, were daily rolled into the camp or continuously left the workshops of the camp in which war material was being made.

DR. KAUFMANN: And after the arrival of the transports were the victims stripped of everything they had? Did they have to undress completely? Did they have to surrender their valuables? Is that true?

HÖSS: Yes.

DR. KAUFMANN: And then they immediately went to their death?

HÖSS: Yes.

DR. KAUFMANN: I ask you, according to your knowledge, did these people know what was in store for them?

HÖSS: The majority of them did not, for steps were taken to keep them in doubt about it and suspicion would not arise that they were to go to their death. For instance, all doors and all walls bore inscriptions to the effect that they were going to undergo a delousing operation or take a shower. This was made known in several languages to the internees by other internees who had come in with earlier transports and who were being used as auxiliary crews during the whole action.

DR. KAUFMANN: And then, you told me the other day that death by gassing set in within a period of 3 to 15 minutes. Is that correct?

HÖSS: Yes.

DR. KAUFMANN: You also told me that even before death finally set in, the victims fell into a state of unconsciousness.

HÖSS: Yes. From what I was able to find out myself or from what was told me by medical officers, the time necessary for reaching unconsciousness or death varied according to the temperature and the number of people present in the chambers. Loss of consciousness took place within a few seconds or a few minutes.

DR. KAUFMANN: Did you yourself ever feel pity with the victims, thinking of your own family and children?

HÖSS: Yes.

DR. KAUFMANN: How was it possible for you to carry out these actions in spite of this?

HÖSS: In view of all these doubts which I had, the only one and decisive argument was the strict order and the reason given for it by the Reichsführer Himmler …

Source: *Trial of the Major War Criminals Before the International Military Tribunal,*
Nuremberg, 14 November 1945 – 1 October 1946
(Nuremberg: International Military Tribunal, 1947), Vol. XI, pp. 396–401

Auschwitz: the victims

Lucie Begov was born to a Jewish family of academics and merchants in Vienna and educated in Vienna and Budapest. Begov and her two sisters successfully evaded the Nazis until 22 March 1944, when they were arrested by the Germans in previously Italian-controlled territory and transported to Auschwitz-Birkenau. They were young and healthy enough to be selected as capable of working. Their group was sent to a quarantine sector of Birkenau from where they were to be transferred to the main section of the camp. Lucie Begov wrote most of her memoir in 1945–46, while the details of her ordeal were still fresh in her mind. Over thirty-five years later, she reworked the rough draft of her manuscript and published it in Germany under the title *Through My Eyes* (*Mit meinen Augen*) in 1983.

The following excerpt describes Begov's and her sisters' initial inability to accept the reality of the gas chambers and the extermination program at Birkenau. Begov finally realized the awful truth when her sister disappeared from the infirmary during a selection that sent 500 women to the gas chambers. This excerpt also captures the surreal camp atmosphere in which inmates were often forced to compete for roles in the camp hierarchy as a way to enhance their chances of survival. By giving some inmates authority over others, the SS eased their own task of surveillance while at the same time pitting inmates against each other.

6.16 Lucie Begov, "A Ghost Emerges – The Gas Chambers – We Didn't Believe It"

In the evening, we new prisoners received a high honor that we were neither aware of nor fully appreciated, namely the opportunity to have an informative talk with our three inmate overseers, to ask them questions about the camp in general and above all about our prospects here. As we thought that we were in a work camp, we did not doubt that the quarantine was a transitional phase and that our situation had to get much better as soon as we had adjusted to the work process of the camp. And of course we immediately asked about the family camp, where we soon hoped to see our family and friends again.

Thoughts, hopes, as they had arisen again and again in every possible situation and variation since the beginning of our Nazi captivity: they proved how much we had remained attached to our "worldly" assumptions even in this hellish environment.

This evening conversation had to be seen as an honor because the inhumane demands that these female functionaries had to make on us and the methods they used in the course of their camp duties ruled out a normal relationship between us. The social difference between this kind of functionary in general and the ordinary prisoners who were in their charge was enormous and unbridgeable and cannot be compared with any work relationship in normal life. Only in very rare and isolated cases did an ordinary prisoner have normal, sometimes even friendly, relations with such superiors, a situation that always had a favorable effect on the fate of that individual.

We probably owed the talks with our three inmate functionaries on the first evening of our camp martyrdom to the interest that they, too, like all the other prisoners, had in new arrivals before they got lost in the masses, which happened very quickly. It probably also had to do with a childish desire to impress us ignorant newcomers with their camp knowledge and experience and in the process to reproach us, as it were, with their own past, as pioneering groups have always done toward those following them. Grotesque reproaches, however, if one considers that these girls were forced to be the pioneers of the largest extermination site in the history of humankind.

In any case it happened on that evening that Ruza, Frieda, and Judith set aside the "dignity" of their office for a while and granted our barrack "room" a personal visit. They strode back and forth by our rows of bunks and stopped here and there to engage us in conversation, so that something approaching a friendly dialogue could develop between us.

I watched with curiosity the three young things who one after another stopped in front of our bunks. They were simply and neatly dressed, were clean, and, with the exception of Ruza, they looked strikingly plump, an ideal condition that was passionately striven for in the camp. In the destructive comedy of the concentration camp, thinness counted as a life- threatening "infraction" and was considered an offense. Thus their outward appearance did not look different from that of many young girls in ordinary life. But their gaze seemed strange to me. In these three wide-open pairs of eyes, as in the eyes of all Jewish prisoners whom we met, there was the peculiar, hopeless, faraway Auschwitz look that did not become familiar to me until later. But also everything they said and how they said it as well as their silence in answer to some of our questions was strange and seemed as absurd to us as their manic zeal, which we could not comprehend.

In front of our bunks stood Judith, who, as we were later told, owed her survival up to that point to a daredevil act. Supposedly she had succeeded in the unique feat of escaping on the way from the camp to the crematorium. I remember the conversation between her and my bunk-mates in its entirety.

We heard from Judith that we were not in Auschwitz, but several kilometers away in Birkenau, and that there were several camps around Auschwitz. Then we asked her:

— Is it the same everywhere as it is here?

— I haven't been anywhere else yet, she replied.

Her answer to our next question was significant in that it contained the first fleeting hint of the reality in which we lived at Auschwitz and which seemed so absurd, so unbelievable to us that we were not able to grasp it for twenty-three more days. This next question pertained to something that concerned us most of all. The question was:

— And where is the family camp?

— The family camp! repeated Judith annoyed; apparently we were not the only ones who had asked her this. Her answer was short and blunt:

— There is no family camp.

Stunned and mistrustful we looked at her:

— Then where did our people go?

At that she shrugged her shoulders with the trace of an ominous smile and said nothing.

What sort of stupid self-importance is that, I thought to myself, and tried at once to refute Judith's information:

— But you just said yourself that there are several camps around Auschwitz that you haven't seen yet. How do you know that one of those is not the family camp?

Again she shrugged her shoulders ominously and said nothing.

As we thought we had to accept the fact that we were not going to get any sensible information about the family camp from her, we gave up and changed the subject …

We again asked her a question that revealed us to be total strangers to the camp:

— Will things get better for us when we are working?

At this she did not feel like chatting with us anymore. Shrugging her shoulders once more, she turned to honor another bunk with her visit.

For somewhat different reasons as our inmate overseers (*Stubowi*), several prisoners from nearby blocks came to visit us on the same evening. They did not belong to the "camp generation" but to the survivors – for the time being – of later transports who had hit the jackpot by somehow getting ahead in the camp. One had only occasional contact even with such harmless "parvenues" who had made it, and that was mainly if one was a relative or a friend from earlier times. Higher-ranking prisoners of all kinds formed their own cliques.

These visitors, too, like our block functionaries, seemed normal on the surface; but with regard to their whole personalities, their mannerisms, and their speech, they nonetheless made an odd impression. With their peculiar, weirdly distant way of looking and in an unnatural way they told us things, briefly and in fragments, from which we gathered mainly that these prisoners, too, knew nothing of a family camp. The things they told us were, if possible, even less credible, even more incomprehensible than Judith's previous remarks as well as her ominous silence on the subject.

Three of these visitors and our short dialogues with them remain etched in my memory. The first was a blond, robust young girl, a Yugoslavian Jew. She had heard that an Italian–Yugoslavian transport had arrived and she wanted to see us.

— I am the only one from my transport who is still alive, she said, and I thought I heard something like pride resonating in her voice.

— When did you arrive? We asked.

— A year ago.

— How many were there?

— 700 people – it was a small transport.

— And of 700 people you're the only one still alive today? was our next bewildered response.

— Yes, she nodded and it seemed to me she looked almost triumphant. Then she went on.

I believed these statements to be false, above all because of sentimental considerations.

— Can you imagine, I asked my bunk-mates, that she would talk about it in such a way, in such a tone, if it were really true? And is such a thing possible anyway?

The others argued along the same lines, but more objectively. They reflected: Let's say it were true, how did this girl know it? Since there are several camps, the prisoners could be separated from each other, they could lose contact. We finally agreed that such a high mortality rate was only understandable if there was an epidemic, and, besides, the Yugoslavian girl could not actually know who was still alive from her transport.

But the next ones were even more plain-spoken. And the plainer they were, the more vague and incomprehensible they became to us, so that finally, in the face of their brief, seemingly confused statements, we took refuge in the same kind of ominous silence as Judith had previously done toward us. For us it was certain that an *idée fixe*, a kind of camp psychosis, was rife here, something that we could not understand or cope with.

Especially suspect to us in this regard were the conduct and words of a very young girl; she was the second of this small group of visitors who remained vividly in my memory. At the railroad ramp she was selected for work and was lucky enough to become the protégée of a block leader here.

— Whom did you come here with? we asked her.

— With Mommy and a little brother and sister, she answered, but they went right away to the gas.

— Where? we asked.

— To the gas, she repeated.

Then we said nothing and merely looked at each other with glances that implied she was crazy.

Yet in spite of this uncomprehending and incredulous attitude, I began to get an uncanny feeling, under the impression of these odd apparitions who looked so strangely beyond us into the distance and at the same time told us outright cannibalistic stories from their lives in ordinary, everyday language.

My bunk-mates, too, in fact the inhabitants of our whole "room," seemed to have fallen under the spell of these visitors and their incomprehensible statements. There was now something eerily threatening in the air.

Then the last visitor of the evening came by, the third, whom I remember as the one whose words had a different effect on me than the others. This third visitor was a mature woman, and it seemed to me that one could carry on with her what we would consider a sensible conversation.

With the hint of a friendly smile she looked at us and was about to walk by our bunk. But I held on to her.

— Do you know where the family camp is? I asked bluntly, awaiting her answer hopefully but at the same time skeptically. She rested her hands on the edge of our bunk. The suggestion of a smile did not disappear from her lips as she calmly replied:

— There is no family camp.

— But where did our people go? I asked again – please tell us where they are.

— Then she raised her right hand and, with her forefinger and a corresponding movement of her eyes, she pointed upward.

— They are there, she said simply. And when she saw our incredulous horror she merely nodded and added:

— There, where all the others have gone.

With that she left us.

And again we exchanged meaningful glances with each other. Yet the serious, unambiguous words and gestures of this woman had made the first breach in my total ignorance, although I was still twenty-three days away from grasping this atrocity. A faint apprehension rose in me of something terrible happening in this camp that was totally foreign to me and threatened us all. An apprehension that gradually changed into a certainty that completely changed my view of the world. But at the same time a previously unknown feeling stirred in me, lurking, so to speak, like a wild animal ready to pounce on me and force me to the ground. It was the fear that the knowledge of our fate first unleashed in me in its full fury and that was completely different than anything called fear in normal life. A fear that ruled all Jewish prisoners and that was capable of causing completely unforeseeable reactions in every one of us.

Source: Lucie Begov, *Mit meinen Augen: Botschaft einer Auschwitz-Überlebenden* (Gerlingen: Bleicher Verlag, 1983), pp. 152–8. Translated by Sally Winkle

7

The aftermath of Nazism and the Historians' Debate

The Second World War was the most destructive war in history. Historians estimate total losses in the war at between 50 and 60 million killed. At least two thirds of these casualties were Soviet soldiers and civilians. German losses are estimated at between 5 and 6 million killed, including about 2 million civilian refugees who died on their westward treks (see Doc. 5.28) and more than half a million victims of aerial bombardment. Germany also lost considerable territory to Poland and the USSR (see map 4), although the final German borders were not to be fixed until the treaty of peace. Due to the growing rift among the victor powers, however, no such treaty was ever signed. In the international agreements that accompanied the reunification of Germany in 1990 the post-war border changes were formally recognized.

The "Big Three," Roosevelt, Churchill, and Stalin, met at the Crimean resort town of Yalta in February 1945 and again, after the German surrender, in the Berlin suburb of Potsdam in the summer of that year. Here they agreed to divide Germany into temporary occupation zones and the capital of Berlin into sectors. They also agreed on a punitive policy toward Germany that included, for the American occupying forces, an injunction against fraternization with Germans (Doc. 7.1). The Soviet Union was particularly committed to a policy that would make reparations available and at the same time prevent a revival of German power. The victor powers agreed to cooperate in the vigorous prosecution of war crimes, in the extraction of reparations, and in the elimination of all Nazi influence from German society.

But differences between the Soviet Union and the West soon emerged, mainly as the result of the imposition of communism in Poland, the country for whose independence Britain and France had gone to war in 1939. The Western powers abruptly terminated reparation shipments from the industrial Ruhr to the Soviet Union in early 1946. Fearful of the spread of communism, unable to gain Soviet acceptance of a market economy in Germany, and facing increasing economic problems as a result of the influx of Germans expelled from the eastern territories seized by Poland or the USSR, the Western powers decided to rebuild the economy in their zones and to establish a separate West German state (contrary to the stated aims of the Yalta and Potsdam conferences). The result was the division of Germany into two separate states until the collapse of the eastern German Democratic Republic (GDR) in 1989–90. Perhaps the greatest beneficiaries of the Cold War were former Nazis, for whose services both sides now competed. In the West, fixation on Nazi crimes came to be seen as abetting the communist cause.

Differences between the Soviet Union and the West already appeared during the Nuremberg trials of major war criminals from 14 November 1945 to 1 October 1946.

The Soviet Union vigorously dissented from the acquittal of the old conservatives, Franz von Papen and Hjalmar Schacht, as well as of three of the institutions under indictment: the Reich Cabinet, the SA, and the High Command of the Wehrmacht (Doc. 7.2). The denazification program, intended to permanently oust former Nazis from positions of power or influence, ground to a halt in 1948 in both the Soviet and Western zones, as the need for the skills and professional expertise of former Nazis were increasingly in demand in both east and west (see Docs. 7.3 and 7.5).

Rehabilitation of former Nazis, however, by no means meant the rehabilitation of Nazi ideology. In fact, paradoxically, repression of a thorough inquiry into personal complicity in Nazi institutions and activities went hand in hand with ever more insistent repudiation of Nazi ideology and Nazi crimes. Indeed, the right to claim greater difference and distance from Nazism became one of the means by which the ideological conflict between east and west was fought out. Interpretations of Nazism thus became weapons in the Cold War. Each side sought to discredit the other by linking it with Nazism. While East German leader Walter Ulbricht pointed out the institutional continuities between the Third Reich and post-war West German society (Doc. 7.3), West German leader Konrad Adenauer defined Nazism as the product of the same materialist, collectivist, and anti-religious mindset that produced communism (Doc. 7.4). In his inaugural speech as Chancellor of the newly-founded Federal Republic (FRG) in 1949, Adenauer shifted the focus from German responsibility for Nazism to German victimization at the hands of the Soviet Union (Doc. 7.5).

While in the East, Nazism was identified with capitalism and anti-communism, thus emphasizing the continuities in the FRG, in the West Nazism was defined primarily by its anti-Semitism and totalitarian suppression of liberal democracy. Against considerable opposition within his own party, the right-of-center Christian Democratic Union (CDU), Adenauer succeeded in gaining parliamentary approval for restitution payments to the state of Israel and to survivors of the Holocaust in 1952 (Doc. 7.6). The GDR, on the other hand, while criminalizing anti-Semitism, evaded restitution payments by refusing to acknowledge any responsibility for Nazi crimes. Both German states commemorated the Holocaust and paid tribute to the victims of Nazism, but in the FRG the special nature of Jewish victimhood was officially recognized (Doc. 7.7), while in the East Jews tended to be subsumed under the broader category of the anti-fascist resistance (Doc. 7.8).

The 1960s protests against the Vietnam War brought with them a general shift of the political climate to the left in the FRG. The student generation that had been born during or shortly after the war questioned their parents' Cold War anti-communism, which seemed closely related to the militant anti-communism of the Third Reich. The generation that reached adulthood in the 1960s challenged their parents to break the general silence of the Adenauer era about their involvement in the Nazi regime. The election of SPD leader Willy Brandt, an anti-Nazi emigré during the Third Reich, to the chancellorship in 1969 marked a changing of the guard. Brandt's *Ostpolitik*, a normaliza-tion of relations with the East bloc without renunciation of the goal of eventual German reunification, involved coming to terms with the results of the Second World War, including the existence of the GDR and the finality of the Polish–German border along the Oder and Neisse rivers. Brandt's spontaneous gesture of kneeling at the memorial to the victims of the Warsaw Ghetto uprising on his state visit to Poland in 1970 offered an eloquent symbol of German contrition for the atrocities of the Nazi era (Doc. 7.9).

Historiography of the Third Reich paralleled the political changes in the FRG. The emergence of a new critical social history marked the end of the conservative and nationalist historiographical tradition that had focused on high diplomacy and reason of state rather than on social structures and class conflict. The new critical history rejected the earlier conservative interpretations of Nazism as an accidental historical aberration or as the product of a small criminal clique. Instead, the younger generation of historians identified continuities in German history and analyzed the crucial role that Germany's economic and military elites played in the Nazi ascent to power (see Doc. 7.13). Totalitarianism theory, which emphasized the similarities between fascism and communism rather than the differences, gave way to historiographical approaches less governed by Cold War biases.

The political pendulum swung back to the right again with the return of the CDU to power under Chancellor Helmut Kohl in 1982. The Kohl government's elaborately-staged ceremony of conciliation with American President Ronald Reagan at the military cemetery in Bitburg (the site of graves of the Waffen-SS) on the 40th anniversary of the end of the Second World War symbolized the effort of conservatives to counteract the German "obsession with guilt" about the past in order to mobilize public support for the "New Cold War." Historiographical trends reflected the neo-conservatism of the 1980s (Doc. 7.10). The highly controversial views of historian Ernst Nolte, in particular, precipitated a fierce dispute among West German historians in 1986 known as the *Historikerstreit* (Docs. 7.11 and 7.12). Nolte's assertion that Nazism and the Holocaust were understandable (though excessive) reactions to the prior and greater crimes of communism found considerable resonance among Germany's "new right." Liberal and left-wing historians accused conservatives of seeking to revise the history of Nazism and expunge memory of its horrors to serve conservative political purposes. Conservatives countered by accusing the 1960s "new left" of undermining West German morale through their politically-motivated fixation on the horrors of the Nazi era and their obsession with *Vergangenheitsbewältigung* – atonement for the past.

The collapse of communism and the end of the Cold War in 1989–1991 seemingly validated the conservative interpretation of Nazism and led to a partial revival of the ideologically freighted totalitarianism theory that had been challenged by the 1960s generation. Nolte cited the historical failure of communism as proof of his contention that National Socialism was no worse than its left-wing counterpart. Reunification also led to renewed outbreaks of violence on the part of the radical right, mostly directed against African and Asian immigrants and Turkish and southern European guest workers recruited for the booming West German economy in the 1960s and 1970s. In the year 1992 seventeen deaths were officially attributed to *Ausländerfeindlichkeit* (hatred of foreigners) and right-wing violence (Doc. 7.14). While the political consensus in the new German Republic remained highly critical of right-wing extremism, and radical right-wing political parties have so far failed to gain enough votes to enter the Bundestag (the federal parliament), the continued activity of nationalist skinhead groups, particularly in the economically depressed areas of the former GDR, have given rise to growing concerns (Doc. 7.15). Nazism no longer represents a viable political movement in Germany, but invocation of its symbols and slogans continues to energize the intolerance and xenophobia of the radical right. Critics have also pointed out that police, courts, and the government have failed to react to right-wing violence with the same resolve they brought to the struggle against left-wing radicalism in the 1970s. Just how effective the Federal Republic is in controlling nationalist extremism in the years to come is widely viewed, both in Germany and abroad, as a test of the sincerity of the Federal Republic's official repudiation of its Nazi past.

Germany under military government

At the Yalta Conference in February 1945, the "Big Three" (US, Britain, and USSR) agreed on a punitive policy toward Germany at the end of the war. Such a policy was particularly favored by the Soviet Union, not only to insure that Germany could never again threaten the peace, but also to make reparations available to offset the terrible losses and devastation suffered by the Soviet Union during the war. American assent to a punitive policy is reflected in Joint Chiefs of Staff Directive 1067, portions of which with subsequent amendments are given below. The directive includes a non-fraternization policy, the disbarment of all Nazi party members and members of affiliated organizations from positions of influence in the public and private sectors, the punishment of war criminals, and a provision that the standard of living in Germany be no higher than in neighboring countries. There was, however, a loophole permitting the retention of officials whose services could be useful for US intelligence or the military. Under this provision many Nazis were recruited for covert operations against the Soviet Union after the start of the Cold War in 1946. Although the US shifted to a policy of economic reconstruction of the Western zones in 1946, JCS 1067 was not officially rescinded until 11 July 1947.

7.1 Directive to the Commander-in-Chief of the United States Forces of Occupation regarding the military government of Germany, 10 May 1945

BASIC OBJECTIVES OF MILITARY GOVERNMENT IN GERMANY

(a) It should be brought home to the Germans that Germany's ruthless warfare and the fanatical Nazi resistance have destroyed the German economy and made chaos and suffering inevitable and that the Germans cannot escape responsibility for what they have brought upon themselves.

(b) Germany will not be occupied for the purpose of liberation but as a defeated enemy nation. Your aim is not oppression but to occupy Germany for the purpose of realizing certain important Allied objectives. In the conduct of your occupation and administration you should be just but firm and aloof. You will strongly discourage fraternization with the German officials and population.

(c) The principal Allied objective is to prevent Germany from ever again becoming a threat to the peace of the world. Essential steps in the accomplishment of this objective are the elimination of Nazism and militarism in all their forms, the immediate apprehension of war criminals for punishment, the industrial disarmament and demilitarization of Germany, with continuing control over Germany's capacity to make war, and the preparation for an eventual reconstruction of German political life on a democratic basis.

(d) Other Allied objectives are to enforce the program of reparations and restitution, to provide relief for the benefit of countries devastated by Nazi aggression, and to ensure that prisoners of war and displaced persons of the United Nations are cared for and repatriated.

ECONOMIC CONTROLS

(a) As a member of the Control Council and as zone commander you will be guided by the principle that controls upon the German economy may be imposed to the extent that such controls may be necessary to achieve the objectives enumerated in paragraph 4 above and also as they may be essential to protect the safety and meet the needs of the occupying forces and assure the production and maintenance of goods and services required to prevent starvation or such disease and unrest as would endanger these forces. No action will be taken in execution of the reparations program or otherwise which would tend to support basic living conditions in Germany or in your zone on a higher level than that existing in any one of the neighboring United Nations …

DENAZIFICATION

(a) A Proclamation dissolving the Nazi Party, its formations, affiliated associations and supervised organizations, and all Nazi public institutions which were set up as instruments of Party domination, and prohibiting their revival in any form, should be promulgated by the Control Council. You will assure the prompt effectuation of that policy in your zone and will make every effort to prevent the reconstitution of any such organization in underground, disguised or secret form. Responsibility for continuing desirable non-political social services of dissolved party organizations may be transferred by the Control Council to appropriate central agencies and by you to appropriate local agencies.

(b) The laws purporting to establish the political structure of National Socialism and the basis of the Hitler regime and all laws, decrees and regulations which establish discriminations on grounds of race, nationality, creed or political opinions should be abrogated by the Control Council. You will render them inoperative in your zone.

(c) All members of the Nazi Party who have been more than nominal participants in its activities, all active supporters of Nazism or militarism and all other persons hostile to Allied purposes will be removed and excluded from public office and from positions of importance in quasi-public and private enterprises such as 1) civic, economic, and labor organizations, 2) corporations and other organizations in which the German government or subdivisions have a major financial interest, 3) industry, commerce, agriculture, and finance, 4) education, and 5) the press, publishing houses, and other agencies disseminating news and propaganda. Persons are to be treated as more than nominal participants in Party activities and as active supporters of Nazism or militarism when they have 1) held office or otherwise been active at any level from local to national in the party and its subordinate organizations, or in organizations which further militaristic doctrines, 2) authorized or participated affirmatively in any Nazi crimes, racial persecutions or discriminations, 3) been avowed believers in Nazism or racial and militaristic creeds, or 4) voluntarily given substantial moral or material support or political assistance of any kind to the Nazi Party or Nazi officials and leaders. No such persons shall be retained in any of the categories of employment listed above because of administrative necessity, convenience or expediency …

SUSPECTED WAR CRIMINALS AND SECURITY ARRESTS

(a) You will search out, arrest, and hold, pending receipt by you of further instructions as to their disposition, Adolf Hitler, his chief Nazi associates, other war criminals and all persons who have participated in planning or carrying out Nazi enterprises involving or resulting in atrocities or war crimes.

(b) All persons who, if permitted to remain at large would endanger the accomplishment of your objectives will also be arrested and held in custody until trial by an appropriate semi-judicial body to be established by you …

In no event shall any differentiation be made between or special consideration be accorded to persons arrested, either as to manner of arrest or conditions of detention, upon the basis of wealth or political, industrial, or other rank or position. In your discretion you may make such exceptions as you deem advisable for intelligence or other military reasons …

EDUCATION

(a) All educational institutions within your zone except those previously reestablished by Allied authority will be closed. The closure of Nazi educational institutions such as Adolf Hitler Schulen, Napolas and Ordensburgen, and of Nazi organizations within other educational institutions will be permanent.[1]

(b) A coordinated system of control over German education and an affirmative program of reorientation will be established designed completely to eliminate Nazi and militaristic doctrines and to encourage the development of democratic ideas.

(c) You will permit the reopening of elementary (*Volksschulen*), middle (*Mittelschulen*), and vocational (*Berufsschulen*) schools at the earliest possible date after Nazi personnel have been eliminated. Textbooks and curricula which are not free of Nazi and militaristic doctrine shall not be used. The Control Council should devise programs looking toward the reopening of secondary schools, universities, and other institutions of higher learning. After Nazi features and personnel have been eliminated and pending the formulation of such programs by the Control Council, you may formulate and put into effect an interim program within your zone and in any case may permit the reopening of such institutions and departments which offer training which you consider immediately essential or useful in the administration of military government and the purposes of the occupation.

(d) It is not intended that the military government will intervene in questions concerning denominational control of German schools, or in religious instruction in German schools, except insofar as may be necessary to insure that religious instruction and administration of such schools conform to such Allied regulations as are or may be established pertaining to purging of personnel and curricula …

Source: US Department of State Publication 9446, *Documents on Germany 1944–1985* (Washington DC: US Government Printing Office, 1985), pp. 15–23

---

1   NAPOLA stands for *Nationalpolitische Erziehungsanstalten* (National and Political Educational Institutions), which like the party-run Adolf Hitler schools were secondary schools for potential party and government functionaries. The three *Ordensburgen* (Order Fortresses) provided post-secondary training for future party leaders.

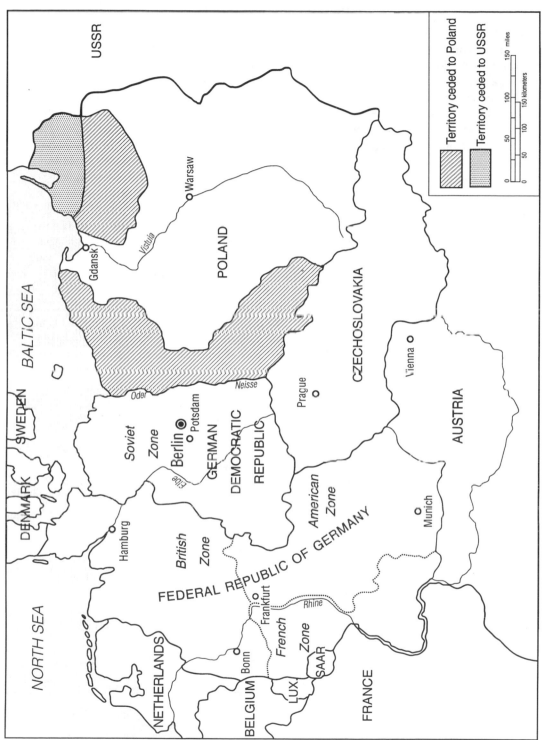

Map 4 Germany after 1945, showing territorial losses following the Second World War

Judgment at Nuremberg

On 1 October 1946 the International Military Tribunal at Nuremberg handed down its verdicts. The following high-ranking Nazis were sentenced to death: Hermann Goering, Joachim von Ribbentrop, Wilhelm Keitel, Ernst Kaltenbrunner, Alfred Rosenberg, Hans Frank, Wilhelm Frick, Julius Streicher, Fritz Sauckel, Alfred Jodl, Arthur Seyss-Inquart, and Martin Bormann (in absentia). Robert Ley had committed suicide before the start of the trial. Rudolf Hess, Erich Raeder, and Walter Funk were sentenced to life in prison (only Hess served his full term). Albert Speer and Baldur von Schirach received sentences of 20 years each, Konstantin von Neurath 15 years, and Karl Doenitz 10 years. Hjalmar Schacht, Franz von Papen, and Hans Fritzsche (the highest surviving official of the Propaganda Ministry) were acquitted. The Tribunal also declared the Nazi leadership and the SS (including SD and Gestapo) to be criminal organizations, while acquitting the SA (which declined in importance after the 1934 purge), the Reich Cabinet (which never met after 1938), and, most controversially, the High Command (OKW) and the General Staff of the Army (on the grounds that war crimes were the responsibility of individual officers, not of the institutions).

The Soviet Union lodged dissents against the acquittals. In the following excerpt from this dissent, the Soviet judge takes issue with the acquittal of the Wehrmacht leadership on the grounds of its close relationship with the SS *Einsatzgruppen* and other evidence submitted during the trials. (The Soviet Union, however, refused to take responsibility for the murder of Polish officers at Katyn in 1940 or to acknowledge the authenticity of the secret protocol of the Nazi–Soviet Pact of August 1939.) Differences in the victor powers' policies toward Germany, reflected in the far more punitive and "anti-fascist" Soviet attitude, contributed to the incipient Cold War and ultimately to the division of Germany. The question of Wehrmacht culpability, however, has remained in dispute. Historical research tended to bear out the Soviet view, most recently in a controversial exhibit on Wehrmacht crimes sponsored by the Hamburg Institute for Social Research in the late 1990s.

7.2 Soviet dissent, "Incorrect judgment with regard to the General Staff and the OKW"

The verdict incorrectly rejects the accusation of criminal activity directed against the General Staff and the OKW.

The rejection of the accusation of criminal activity of the General Staff and of the OKW contradicts both the actual situation and the evidence submitted in the course of the trial.

It has been established beyond doubt that the Leadership Corps of the Armed Forces of Nazi Germany together with the SS-Party machine, represented the most important agency in preparing and realizing the Nazis' aggressive and man-hating program. This was constantly and forcefully reiterated by the Hitlerites themselves in their official bulletins meant for the officer personnel of the armed forces. In the Nazi Party Bulletin called "Politics and the Officer in the Third Reich" it is quite clearly stated that the Nazi regime is founded on "two pillars: the Party and the Armed Forces." "Both are forms of expression of the same philosophy of life." "The tasks before the party and the armed forces are in an organic relationship to each other and each bears the same responsibility ... Both these agencies depend on each other's success or failure" (PS–4060, USA–928).

This organic interrelationship between the Nazi Party and the SS on the one hand and the Nazi Armed Forces on the other hand, was particularly evident among the upper circles of the military hierarchy, which the indictment groups together under the concept of criminal organization – that is, among the members of the General Staff and the OKW.

The very selection of members of the Supreme Command of the army in Nazi Germany was based on the criteria of their loyalty to the regime and their readiness not only to pursue aggressive militaristic policies but also to fulfill such special directives as related to treatment meted out to prisoners of war and to the civilian populations of occupied territories.

The leaders of the German Armed Forces were not merely officers who reached certain levels of the military hierarchy. They represented, first of all, a closely knit group which was entrusted with the most secret plans of the Nazi leadership. Evidence submitted to the Tribunal has fully confirmed the contention that the military leaders of Germany justified this trust completely and that they were the convinced followers and ardent executors of Hitler's plans.

It is not accidental that at the head of the Air Force stood the "second man" of the Nazi Reich, namely Goering; that the Commander in Chief of the Navy was Doenitz, subsequently designated by Hitler to be the latter's successor; that the command of the ground forces was concentrated in the hands of Keitel, who signed the major part of the decrees concerning the execution of the prisoners of war and of the civilians in occupied territories.

Thus the comparisons made with the organization of the supreme commands in Allied countries cannot be considered valid. In a democratic country, not one self-respecting military expert would agree to prepare plans for mass reprisals and merciless killings of prisoners of war side by side with plans of a purely military and strategic character.

Meanwhile it is precisely such matters that occupied the Supreme Command of the General Staff and the OKW in Nazi Germany. The commission by them of the heaviest crimes against peace, of the war crimes, and of the crimes against humanity is not denied but is particularly emphasized in the verdict of the Tribunal. And yet the commission of these crimes has not brought the logical conclusion. The verdict states:

> They have been a disgrace to the honorable profession of arms. Without their military guidance the aggressive ambitions of Hitler and his fellow Nazis would have been academic and sterile ...

And subsequently:

> Many of these men have made a mockery of the soldier's oath of obedience to military orders. When it suits their defense they say they had to obey; when confronted with Hitler's brutal crimes, which are shown to have been within their general knowledge, they say they disobeyed. The truth is they actively participated in all these crimes, or sat silent and acquiescent, witnessing the commission of crimes on a scale larger and more shocking than the world ever had the misfortune to know. This must be said.

All these assertions in the verdict are correct and are based on numerous and reliable depositions. It remains only incomprehensible why "these hundred or so higher officers" who have caused the world and their own country so much suffering should not be acknowledged a criminal organization.

The verdict advances the following reasons for the decision, reasons quite contradictory to the facts:

(a) That the crimes were committed by representatives of the General Staff and of the OKW as private individuals and not as members of a criminal conspiracy.
(b) That the General Staff and the OKW were merely weapons in the hands of the conspirators and interpreters or executors of the conspirators' will.

Considerable evidence disputes such conclusions.

(1) THE LEADING REPRESENTATIVES OF THE GENERAL STAFF AND OF THE OKW, ALONG WITH A SMALL CIRCLE OF THE HIGHER HITLERITE OFFICIALS, WERE CALLED UPON BY THE CONSPIRATORS TO PARTICIPATE IN THE DEVELOPMENT AND THE REALIZATION OF THE PLANS OF AGGRESSION, NOT AS PASSIVE FUNCTIONARIES, BUT AS ACTIVE PARTICIPANTS IN THE CONSPIRACY AGAINST PEACE AND HUMANITY

Without their advice and active cooperation, Hitler could not have solved these problems.

In the majority of cases their opinion was decisive. It is impossible to imagine how the aggressive plans of Hitler's Germany could have been realized had it not been for the full support given him by the leading staff members of the armed forces.

Least of all did Hitler conceal his criminal plans and motivations from the leaders of the High Command.

For instance, while preparing for the attack on Poland, as early as 29 May 1939, at a conference with the high military commanders of the new Reich Chancellery, he stated:

> For us the matter consists of the expansion of "Lebensraum" to the east.
> Thus the question of sparing Poland cannot be considered, and instead, we have to consider the decision to attack Poland at the first opportunity. (L–79)

Long before the seizure of Czechoslovakia, in a directive of 30 May 1938, Hitler, addressing the representatives of the High Command, cynically stated:

> From the military and political point of view, the most favorable time is a lightning attack on the basis of some incident, by which Germany will have been strongly provoked and which will morally justify the military measures to at least part of world opinion. (PS–388)

Prior to the invasion of Yugoslavia, in a directive dated 27 March 1941, addressing the representatives of the High Command, Hitler wrote:

> Even if Yugoslavia declares its loyalty, it must be considered an enemy and must, therefore, be smashed as soon as possible. (PS–1746)

While preparing for the invasion of the USSR, Hitler invited the representatives of the General Staff and the OKW to help him work out the related plans and directives not at all as simply military experts.

In the instructions to apply propaganda in the region "Barbarossa," issued by the OKW in June 1941, it is pointed out that:

> For the time we should not have propaganda directed at the dismemberment of the Soviet Union. (USSR–477)

As early as 13 May 1941, OKW ordered the troops to use any terrorist measures against the civilian populations of the temporarily occupied regions of the Soviet Union.

And the same order read: "To confirm only such sentences as are in accordance with the political intentions of the High Command" (G–50).

(2) OKW AND THE GENERAL STAFF ISSUED THE MOST BRUTAL DECREES AND ORDERS FOR RELENTLESS MEASURES AGAINST THE UNARMED PEACEFUL POPULATION AND THE PRISONERS OF WAR

In the "decree of special liability to punishment in the region of 'Barbarossa' while preparing for the attack upon the Soviet Union" the OKW abolished beforehand the jurisdiction of the military courts, granting the right of repression over the peaceful population to individual officers and soldiers.

It is particularly stated there that: "Crimes of hostile civilians are excluded from the jurisdiction of the court martials ... " "Suspected elements must be immediately delivered to the officer. The latter will decide whether they should be shot ... " "It is absolutely forbidden to hold suspects for the purpose of bringing them to trial." There are also provisions for "the most extreme measures, and, in particular, 'Measures for mass violence,' if circumstances do not permit the rapid detection of the guilty."

In the same decree of the OKW the guarantee of immunity was assured in advance to the military criminals from the service personnel of the German army. It is stated there as follows: "The bringing of suits of actions, committed by officials of the army and by the service personnel against hostile civilians, is not obligatory even in cases where such actions at the same time constitute military crimes or offenses ... "

In the course of the war the High Command consistently followed this policy, increasing its terroristic actions with regard to prisoners of war and the peaceful populations of occupied countries.

The OKW directive of 16 September 1941 states:

> At the same time, it must be borne in mind that a human life in the countries in question is frequently held to be of no account and that a warning example can be made only by measures of exceptional severity. (PS–389)

Addressing the commanders of the army groups on 23 July 1941, the OKW simply briefed them as follows: "It is not the demand for additional security detachments, but the application of appropriate draconic measures, that the commanding officers must use to keep order in the regions under their jurisdiction" (PS–459).

The OKW directive of 16 December 1941 states:

> The troops ... have the right and are obliged to apply ... any measures whatsoever *also against women and children* if this contributes to success ... .(USSR–16)

Among the most brutal OKW directives concerning the treatment of prisoners of war one must consider the order entitled "Kugel" (Bullet). The reasons for resorting to capital punishment for prisoners of war were offenses, which according to international conventions, generally should not carry any punishment; (for example, escape from the camp). Another order "Nacht und Nebel" (Night and Fog) states:

> Penalty for such offenses, consisting of loss of freedom and even a life sentence is a sign of weakness. Only death sentence or measures which entail ignorance of the

fate of the guilty by local population will achieve real effectiveness. (L–90, USA–224; Transcript, afternoon session 25 January 1946)

In the course of the present trial a great deal of evidence of application of the "Kugel" order has been submitted. One of the examples of this kind of crime is the murder of 50 officer pilots. The fact that this crime was inspired by the High Command cannot be doubted.

OKW also distributed an order for the destruction of the "Commando" units. The original order was submitted to the court (PS–498, USA–501). According to this order, officers and soldiers of the "Commando" units had to be shot, except in cases when they were to be questioned, after which they were shot in any case.

This order was unswervingly carried out by the commanding officers of army units. In June 1944 [General Gerd von] Rundstedt, the Commander in Chief of the German troops in the west, reported that Hitler's order in regard to "the treatment of the commando groups of the enemy is still being carried out" (PS–531, USA–550).

(3) THE HIGH COMMAND, ALONG WITH THE SS AND THE POLICE, IS GUILTY OF THE MOST BRUTAL POLICE ACTIONS IN THE OCCUPIED REGIONS

The instructions relating to special regions, issued by OKW on 13 March 1941, contemplated the necessity of synchronizing the activities in occupied territories between the army command and the Reichsführer of the SS. As is seen from the testimony of the chief of department III of RSHA and who was concurrently chief of the Einsatzgruppe "D," Otto Ohlendorf, and of the chief of department VI of RSHA, Walter Schellenberg, in accordance with OKW instructions there was an agreement made between the General Staff and the RSHA about the organization of special "operational groups" of the security police and SD "Einsatzgruppen," assigned to the appropriate army detachments.

Crimes committed by the Einsatzgruppen on the territory of the temporarily occupied regions are countless. The Einsatzgruppen were acting in close contact with the commanding officers of the appropriate army groups.

The following excerpt from the report of Einsatzgruppe "A" is extremely characteristic as evidence:

> ... Among our functions is the establishment of personal liaison with the commanding officer both at the front and in the rear. It must be pointed out that the relations with the army were of the best, in some cases very close, almost hearty, as, for instance, the commander of the tank group, General [Erich] Hoepner. (L–180)

(4) THE REPRESENTATIVES OF THE HIGH COMMAND ACTED IN ALL THE ECHELONS OF THE ARMY AS MEMBERS OF A CRIMINAL GROUP

The directives of the OKW and the General Staff, in spite of the manifest violations of international law and customs of warfare, not only did not provoke any protest on the part of the higher staff officers of the command of the various groups of the armies but were inflexibly applied and supplemented by still more cruel orders in the development of such directives.

In this connection it is characteristic to note the directive of Field Marshal [Walter] von Reichenau, army group commander, addressed to his soldiers: "The soldier in the eastern territories is not only a warrior skilled in the art of warfare but a bearer of merciless national ideology." And elsewhere, calling for the extermination of the Jews, von Reichenau wrote: "Thus the soldier must be in full cognizance of the necessity for harsh and just revenge on those subhumans, the Jews" (USA–556).

As another example the order of Field Marshal [Erich] von Manstein addressed to his soldiers can be referred to. On the basis of the "political aims of the war" the Field Marshal cynically appealed to his soldiers to wage the war in violation of the "recognized laws of warfare in Europe" (USA–927).

Thus, in the course of the hearing of evidence it has been proven beyond all doubt that the General Staff and the High Command of the Hitlerite army comprised a highly dangerous criminal organization.

I consider it my duty as a judge to draw up my dissenting opinion concerning those important questions on which I disagree with the decision adopted by the members of the Tribunal.

Soviet Member IMT, Major General Jurisprudence,

[signed] I. T. Nikitchenko

Source: Office of the US Chief of Counsel for Prosecution of Axis Criminality,
Nazi Conspiracy and Aggression: Opinion and Judgment
(Washington DC: US Government Printing Office, 1947), pp. 183–8

The end of denazification, 1948–49

In both East and West Germany denazification came to an end much sooner than the Allies had originally intended or anticipated. The main reason for this was the need for the technical and professional expertise of former Nazis both in rebuilding their shattered institutions and in strengthening their respective sides in the Cold War. East Germans sought to use the return of former Nazis to positions of influence in West Germany for propaganda purposes. In the following self-congratulatory article in the official Socialist Unity Party (SED) paper *Neues Deutschland* on 28 February 1948, the East German leader Walter Ulbricht (1893–1973) drew a distinction between denazification in the East, where all pre-war economic leaders were ousted in the course of the elimination of the capitalist economy, and in the West, where, according to Ulbricht, the main targets of denazification were not economic leaders but rank-and-file party members. In 1965 the East German regime issued a "Brown Book" listing hundreds of former Nazis who had returned to positions of influence after the war. The Cold War, however, enabled the persons affected to dismiss the list as communist propaganda and to escape public opprobrium.

7.3 Walter Ulbricht, "On disbanding the Denazification Commissions," 28 February 1948

We welcome the order by the Chief of Staff of the Soviet Military Government, Marshal Sokolowski, to disband the Denazification Commissions in the Soviet Occupation Zone of Germany. The content of the order is in agreement with the recommendations of the Socialist Unity Party (SED) and the bloc of anti-fascist democratic parties. At its last meeting of the party executive, the SED stated that following the establishment of the basic structures of the democratic system and at the beginning of the reconstruction period, the Denazification Commissions should conclude their activities, and the work of the sequestration commissions should now come to an end as well.

The disbanding of the Denazification Commissions in the Soviet Occupation Zone is possible because the purge of the administration has been completed, because the factories of the war criminals with or without Nazi Party membership and the banks have been turned over to the people, and because the property of the large landowners, who were among the major forces of militarism, have been transferred to the peasants. In this way the supporters of fascism have been stripped of their powerful economic positions.

In contrast to certain "politicians" in West Germany, we believe it was not the working people and the middle class who were the supporters of fascism; rather it was the corporate and bank bosses and the large landowners who brought the fascists to power in order to better exploit and repress their own people and other peoples. Therefore the fascist criminals were punished and expropriated in the Soviet Occupation Zone of Germany, in agreement with the anti-fascist and democratic parties, the unions, and other people's organizations. The ordinary Nazi party members were not called before the Denazification Commissions, however. On 21 February 1947, a year ago, the Chairman of the SED, Wilhelm Pieck, had already declared:

The majority of those, "who were taken in by the Nazi swindle and became members of the Nazi Party ... belong to the working population ... Of course their behavior must be judged by a different standard than that of the war criminals or the Nazi activists."

Wilhelm Pieck further demanded that everything be done to let these people know a new way must be taken in order to lead Germany out of misfortune:

> They are primarily the working masses, whom we do not want to push away; rather we want to draw them in as closely as possible and get them actively involved in the work of reconstruction. Real life shows us that there are tens of thousands of these people who are making an honest effort to get rid of the last bits of the Nazi spirit and who are already actively participating in the work of construction.

In the great movement for increasing production in recent months, many former members of Nazi organizations have proven themselves to be honest participants in reconstruction. Whether an individual is employed as a construction worker, or as a coal miner, in a government office, or as an engineer, he shows his true colors through his initiative and through his efforts to fulfill production goals. In this new period of reconstruction, previous organizational membership can no longer be the standard for judging the individual; instead the standard should be honest, self-sacrificing work. Nonetheless, former members of Nazi organizations have a special obligation to make up for their previous mistakes through honest work. The new aspect of this development was aptly expressed in a resolution of the recently held conference of the coal industry in the Soviet Zone of Occupation, which states:

> We recognize that many technicians and engineers who were formerly nominal members of Nazi organizations are aware that a new course must be charted, and they have consequently committed their energy to reconstruction and the creation of a better future.
>
> On behalf of the administrative agencies of the coal industry, every engineer and technician will be judged exclusively by their honest work. We are convinced that just like laborers and white-collar employees, they will make sure on their own that the actions of saboteurs, who are in the service of subversive forces, will be thwarted.

The discontinuation of the work of the Denazification Commissions in the Soviet Occupation Zone and the restoration of equal rights to former members of the Nazi party and its organizations are also signs of a changing situation. Wide circles of those who previously belonged to Nazi organizations are participating in the great struggle for the unity of our German fatherland. But some so-called opponents of Hitler from the ranks of monopoly capitalism are speaking in favor of tearing Germany apart. They are trying to make Germans compliant to the interests of Wall Street. The German people do not want to see the terrible rule of the German imperialistic authorities, the German corporate and bank bosses, replaced by the rule of US monopoly capital. The enemies of the German people are those who are forming a bizonal state in Frankfurt and who have restored the power of the corporations and big banks in West Germany. The major enemies are Zangen, Schacht, and Witzleben,[2] who are tearing apart Germany with the help of Wall Street in order to better exploit and suppress the German people. Their accomplices in the Soviet Occupation Zone are the Kaiser and Schwennicke groups and the delegates of the Schumacher group who carry out special orders of foreign powers.[3]

The fact that the Chief of Staff of the Soviet Military Government was able to order the disbanding of the Denazification Commissions indicates the progress of democratization in a third of Germany. The members of the Denazification Commissions ... have done great work in in the interests of democracy. Their work has helped the democratic forces in the world to regain trust in the democratic forces in the Soviet Occupation Zone, which have contributed to establishing a strong democratic foundation.

By contrast, in the Western Zones of Germany Hitler's arms industry leaders and other war criminals are in leading positions in the economy, the police and the courts. In a plainly absurd process, the nominal members of the Nazi party were called before the so-called denazification courts (*Spruchkammern*) and condemned, while the major war criminal [Wilhelm] Zangen, the Chairman of Hitler's Armaments Council, is already back at work once again. And war criminals like Dinkelbach, who belonged to the inner circle of Hitler's arms industry leaders, are now in control of West Germany's iron-producing industry.[4] *While in West Germany the period of great struggle has begun for the rights of the people, the punishment of war criminals, the expropriation of corporate and bank bosses, and for bread and wages for working people, in the Soviet occupation zone the period has begun of reconstruction and of the common struggle to increase production for a better life for the people.*

Now it all depends on following through with the restoration of equal rights for the former members of Nazi organizations and giving these forces the chance to develop their abilities through honest work. In this way we should actually achieve the great unity of all forces willing to participate in the construction and of all those who want the unity of Germany and who reject the Frankfurt resolutions and the Marshall Plan.[5] By working

---

2   Dr. Wilhelm Zangen (1891–1971) was head of the Reich Industrial Group and deputy leader of Reich Economic Chamber during the war and an executive with Mannesman A.G. after the war; Dr. Hjalmar Schacht (see Doc. 2.22) was a consultant to industry and co-owner of a bank in Düsseldorf after the war; Dr. Wolf-Dietrich von Witzleben, a relative of the resistance leader Erwin von Witzleben, was a member of the Siemens A.G. both before and after the war. All three former Nazis were on the original American list of war criminals.

3   Jakob Kaiser (1888–1961) was former leader of the CDU in the Soviet zone before his purge. He later served in Adenauer's cabinet. Kurt Schumacher (1895–1952), leader of the West German SPD, rejected any compromise with the Communists.

4   Dr. Heinrich Dinkelbach was a member of the board of United Steel Works before 1945 and a member of the board of Rhenish Steel Works after the war.

together on reconstruction and through friendly discussions at lecture evenings and in courses of the mass organizations, even those who still reveal many remnants of the old Nazi mentality will be deeply moved by the new spirit of democratic progress.

Source: Walter Ulbricht, *Zur Geschichte der deutschen Arbeiterbewegung:*
Aus Reden und Aufsätzen*, Vol. III, *1946–1950
(Berlin: Dietz Verlag, 1960), pp. 195–98. Translated by Sally Winkle

The Cold War and the official interpretation of National Socialism in West Germany

The inability of the victor powers to agree on governing institutions for Germany and on a final peace settlement led to the division of Germany beginning in 1947. The Western powers, particularly the US, were no longer willing to abide by the punitive policy of de-industrialization favored by the USSR and agreed to at Yalta and Potsdam. Instead they turned to a policy of economic reconstruction of their zones of occupation and establishment of a separate state. The Cold War provided the opportunity to reintegrate former Nazis in West German society on the basis of anti-communism. It also led to an official interpretation of Nazism as the result of the same godless, collectivist ideology that had produced socialism and communism. A good example of this kind of conservative interpretation is provided by the opening speech delivered by future chancellor Konrad Adenauer (1876–1967) at the second Christian Democratic Union (CDU) party convention in Recklinghausen in August 1948. Interpreting Nazism as the product of materialist, collectivist, and anti-Christian ideology served not only to discredit communism and the left, but it also exonerated Christians and conservatives from complicity in the Nazi debacle. The fact that the Nazis had made identical charges against socialism and communism did not deter West German conservatives, who could count on increasing Western support as the Cold War intensified. Some of Adenauer's language, particularly in respect to the "Asiatic" danger, resembled the vocabulary the Nazis had used in their war against the Soviet Union. In denouncing the Morgenthau Plan for the permanent partition of Germany, Adenauer also struck a tone of victimization that was sure to resonate favorably among his audience.

7.4 Konrad Adenauer, "Hope for Europe," 28 August 1948

... We want to re-create political life in Germany based on the spiritual principles developed by Western Christianity in the course of many centuries – and not only in Germany, but also in Europe and in the world. For this reason we call ourselves the Christian Democratic Union, not suggesting thereby that there are no Christians in the other parties; nothing could be further from our minds ... When I observe the situation as it is, I find that in Germany – and not only in

5   Frankfurt was the seat of the Economic Council of the British and American zones as well as of the *Länderrat*, the council representing the individual states of West Germany. It would also be the site of the Parliamentary Council that drew up the constitution for a separate West German state with its capital in Bonn in 1948–49.

Germany, as I will come back to – literally everything does have to be rebuilt from the bottom up. We find that it was not just National Socialism that had such a devastating spiritual effect in Germany. National Socialism was not the first to spread the ideas to the German people that might is more important than right and that the individual is nothing and the state is everything. These views were spread much earlier; they originated in the period in which the materialistic philosophy prevailed. In addition we find that with the rise of socialism a new false doctrine emerged, the *false doctrine of the collective*. This is a false doctrine that will yet cause mankind a tremendous amount of trouble in future decades. This doctrine is so destructive because, very much like the exaggerated nationalism of the recent past, it weakens the efforts of the individual to develop his own personality to the point that he feels almost happy to be a tiny part of the masses. Let us be clear that these views are diametrically opposed to the Christian view of the value and dignity of the individual as well as the Christian concept of personality and that this view of uniformity (*Vermassung*) and the collective is also diametrically opposed to every personal freedom.

Personal freedom is and continues to be the greatest good of mankind! (shouts: very good!) When we oppose dictatorship as the enemy of freedom, when we take issue with capital stifling the freedom of the individual in the economy and thus also in politics, when we oppose the state acquiring too much power and thus becoming an enemy of the individual, we thereby *oppose collectivism* in any form whatsoever now and also in the future, because it is as much an enemy of personal freedom as these other factors. This essential principle of Western Christianity on the value and dignity of every single human being and the freedom of the individual is one of the main premises of our political work. The worship of power, this modern idolatry, means the decline of personal freedom as well. In our time people in many countries are making sacrifices to the idol of power. *As the collectivist idea grows, it always leads to the worship of power.* Unhealthy spiritual views act like contagious diseases, they spread and infect. On the basis of our Christian philosophy we must stress that right is better than might, that power in itself is not evil, but that the temptation of power very easily leads a person to abuse it, and then it becomes evil. Because we stand for the freedom of the individual, we also have to do everything in our power in the social arena to enable each person to achieve a humane existence. A humane existence also in relation to material matters, including employment and the housing situation, is one of the essential prerequisites for the true freedom of the individual.

If in examining the question whether we are justified, even obligated, to conduct politics on the basis of a Christian philosophy we look beyond the German borders and see what the rest of world looks like, we find that in many places an *anti-Christian* spirit reigns which is fundamentally responsible for the current situation. A very large part of the world is ruled today by Soviet Russia: half of Germany, the Balkan states, Poland, Hungary, and Czechoslovakia. A thoroughly anti-Christian spirit reigns in this huge territory with several hundred million people – and furthermore the fight against Christianity is being undertaken there deliberately and systematically. The Communist Parties in Germany, France, Italy, and throughout the world get their political nourishment from the same power that is organizing and undertaking this fight, from Soviet Russia. In the rest of the world things are perhaps not as good as they should be, either, with regard to the Christian spirit. National Socialism committed terrible crimes, crimes that future historians will still recount with horror, but the *Morgenthau Plan*, which, thank heavens, was not implemented, but which was prepared and considered in great detail, represents an offense against humanity that is at least a worthy complement to the National Socialist crime. (Enthusiastic shouts: very true!) If it was planned in the enforcement decrees to let 30 or 40 million Germans die (Shouts: shame!) by choking them off economically, then the preparation and consideration of such a plan reveals such depths of cruelty and inhumanity that, by God, no one can speak of a Christian spirit any longer. (Shouts: very true!) This Morgenthau Plan is done for. The time will come when those who wrote it will be ashamed to talk about it. But I have the feeling that certain offshoots of this Morgenthau Plan have taken effect here. It is time to remove them. I am referring above all to this *insane policy of dismantling industries.* (Shouts: very true!)

No German believes that genuine war industries should be preserved. They should and must disappear. But why – recently with even greater enthusiasm – are more and more factories being dismantled that are not war factories? ... If in their renunciation of the Morgenthau Plan the Allies have finally accepted the notion that the reconstruction of Europe is only possible by fully utilizing German economic capacity, and if fear of competition is not the reason for dismantling, then it is sheer madness to so severely decrease and damage German economic capacity through this dismantlement. Then all those who are really serious about the restoration of Europe should order it to stop. We direct this demand and request especially to the Americans, who are financing the reconstruction of Europe with their dollars, and who should not allow a situation in which on the one hand they are following through with deliveries while on the other hand the reconstruction of Europe is being so severely damaged. (Shouts: very true!)

In many European countries there are active parties that have a Christian foundation and that conduct their politics based on a Christian foundation. That is true for Holland, Belgium, Luxembourg, Switzerland, France, and Italy ... In my opinion the connections we have with the Christian parties in these countries, who have accepted us with delight as equals at the meetings that have taken place, can never be too strong; for *only when all the forces that stand on the same principles as we do, when all the political forces in the whole of Europe come together, will it be possible to save not only Germany but Europe itself.*

Politics in these times – domestic and foreign policies – have to be viewed in the overall scheme of things. Thus we see, as I have already mentioned, that on one side there is the immense power of Asia, represented by Russia and her satellite states, strengthened by the vanguards of the Communist parties in various countries in the world, this immense power that is of a completely different spirit and way of thinking than we Western Europeans. In this sense South and North America also belong to the European, Western spirit, so that in reality over the whole earth two great fronts have formed or are in the process of being established. In spite of its small size, in spite of its military weakness, Europe plays a very great role in this struggle, because precisely in Europe lie the reservoir and source of the Christian and Western spirit; for in the last analysis what is involved in this struggle are spiritual conflicts of the greatest measure ...

Source: Konrad Adenauer, *Reden 1917–1967, Eine Auswahl*, ed. by Hans-Peter Schwarz (Stuttgart: Deutsche Verlags-Anstalt, 1975), pp. 124–127.
Translated by Sally Winkle

Repression of the past

Adenauer gave this speech in the Bundestag, the parliament of the Federal Republic of Germany, on 20 September 1949, shortly after he was elected the first Chancellor of West Germany (an office he would hold until 1963). Adenauer discussed what he deemed to be the most relevant issues facing the nascent Federal Republic in the aftermath of the war. The excerpts presented here include Adenauer's comments on denazification, which most

Germans heartily resented and which, because of the Cold War, the Allies no longer fully supported, either. Article 131 of the West German constitution reinstated without penalty all former civil servants who had been dismissed simply for membership in the Nazi Party or an affiliated organization. Adenauer was aware that most Germans did not want to confront the question of their own complicity with Nazism. Instead he focused on the plight of post-war Germans, prisoners of war still held by the Soviet Union, and Germans expelled from the east, and he forcefully rejected the finality of the territorial losses to Poland and the Soviet Union. Although the Communist Party (KPD) would remain legal in the FRG until 1956 and was well represented in the first Bundestag, Adenauer's speech signalled the government's enduring conviction that the major threat to stability came not from the radical right, but from the radical left. In contrast to Ulbricht and other GDR leaders, Adenauer rarely used the term "Nazi," preferring the more respectful "National Socialist." The speech is given here complete with parliamentary interjections to capture some of the differences between the parties of the left and the right.

7.5 Konrad Adenauer, inaugural speech in the Bundestag, 20 September 1949

... We will have to reform the civil service law. We are fundamentally and resolutely committed to the professional civil service. (Applause in the center and on the right.) A lot of unhappiness and damage has been caused by *denazification*. ("Very true!" from the center and on the right.) Those who are truly guilty of the crimes committed in the National Socialist period and in the war should be most severely punished. (Shouts from the KPD.) But as for the rest we must no longer distinguish between two classes of people in Germany: (agreement on the right) those who are politically beyond reproach and those who are reproachable. This distinction must disappear as soon as possible!

The war and the turmoil of the post-war period have been such a difficult trial for many and have brought such temptations that people must show understanding for a good many transgressions and misdemeanors. Therefore the federal government will consider the question of *amnesty*, ("bravo!") and furthermore it will consider applying to the High Commissioners for amnesty to be granted correspondingly for sentences imposed by the Allied military courts. (Applause on the right and in the center.)

If the federal government is determined to let bygones be bygones where it seems justified, convinced as it is that many have atoned for guilt that subjectively was not very great, the government is on the other hand absolutely determined to draw the necessary lessons from the past toward all those who undermine the existence of our state, ("bravo!" and "very good!") whether they belong to the *radical right* or the *radical left*. (Laughter and shouts from the KPD.)

— Oh, you really aren't that radical.

(Laughter. – Representative Renner [KPD]: You aren't as socially conscious, either, as you pretend to be here!)

Ladies and gentlemen, the fears that have been raised particularly in the foreign press about radical right activities in Germany are surely greatly exaggerated. ("Very true!" on the right.) I greatly regret that by circulating the offensive speeches of certain personalities, the news reports of German and foreign newspapers have attributed an importance to them that they have never had in Germany. (Applause in the center and on the right.) But ladies and gentlemen, I emphasize once again: even though we believe these reports are exaggerated, we are nonetheless in total agreement that we must devote our fullest attention to the emergence of right-wing and left-wing radical efforts that threaten the state. And I repeat once again: if necessary we will resolutely make use of the rights granted us under the law. (Applause in the center and on the right. – Interruption from the KPD: "We know all about that!")

Ladies and gentlemen! Let me offer a word in this context about the *anti-Semitic efforts* that have apparently turned up here and there. We most strongly condemn these efforts. We consider it shameful and really unbelievable that after everything that has happened in the National Socialist period there could still be people in Germany who persecute or despise Jews because they are Jews. (Approval from the KPD.)

Ladies and gentlemen! I am coming to an especially serious and important chapter. Due to its new organization as a state, Germany is now in a position to take up more vigorously than before the question of *German prisoners of war and deportees*. Millions of prisoners of war are still being detained in Russia. (Shout from the right: "Mr. Renner, listen!") We do not know the whereabouts of the 1.5 to 2 million German prisoners of war (Rep. Renner: "Ask Hitler!" – Laughter and shouts on the right) that could be calculated from Russian military reports beyond the number of war prisoners currently admitted by Russia. The same is likewise true for Yugoslavia. (Shout from the KPD: "And Indochina!" – Shout from the right: "Czechoslovakia!") The fate of these millions of Germans who have endured the bitter lot of captivity for years now is so cruel and the suffering of their relatives in Germany is so great that all peoples must help to finally return these prisoners and deportees to their homes and their families …

The fate of the *expellees*, ladies and gentlemen, is particularly harsh. The problem of their future destiny cannot be solved by Germany alone. ("Very true!" from the right) The solution to this problem can only be achieved through international channels. But it must be solved, if Germany is not to become a seed-bed of political and economic unrest for years to come.

Let me turn now to questions that are extremely important to us in Germany and that are vital issues for our entire people. It concerns the agreements of Yalta and Potsdam and the *Oder–Neisse border*. The Potsdam Agreement specifically states: The heads of the three governments – the United States, England, and Soviet Russia – have reaffirmed their view that the final determination of the Polish western border be postponed until the peace conference. ("Hear! hear!" from the right.) Therefore we cannot under any condition accept the separation of these territories which was later unilaterally carried out by Soviet Russia and Poland. ("Very true!" and enthusiastic applause from the right, the center and from the SPD.) This separation contradicts not only the Potsdam Agreement; it also contradicts the Atlantic Charter of 1941, which the Soviet Union specifically endorsed. (Agreement once again from the center and the right.) The provisions of the Atlantic Charter are completely unambiguous and clear. In its resolution of 3 November 1948 the General Assembly of the United Nations asked the great powers to conclude peace treaties according to these principles as soon as possible. We will not stop pursuing our claims to these territories in accord with orderly legal procedures. (Enthusiastic applause in the center and on the right. – Rep. Dr. Richter: "Please don't forget the Sudetenland here, Mr. Chancellor!") …

And now, ladies and gentlemen, let me say a word about our position in relation to the occupation statute! The occupation statute is far from ideal. It is an improvement over the status without rights in which we lived prior to the enactment of the occupation statute. But after the complete collapse that National Socialism bestowed on us there is no way for the German people to return to freedom and equality (Rep. Renner: "Peace treaty!") other than to climb back up together with the Allies. The only way to freedom is for us, in agreement with the High Allied Commission, to attempt to expand our freedoms and jurisdictions bit by bit. ("Very true!")

We have no doubt that according to our background and our way of thinking we belong to the *West-European world*. We want to maintain good relations with all countries, also on a personal level, and especially with our neighboring countries, the Benelux states, France, Italy, England, and the Nordic states. The German–French conflict, which dominated European politics for hundreds of years and gave rise to so many wars, so much destruction and bloodshed, must finally be eliminated. (Enthusiastic applause.) ...

I have just said that we wish to be included in the *European Union* as soon as possible. We will be eager and happy to help work on the great goal of this union. I would like to point out that in Article 24 of our Bonn constitution we have provided the chance for our federation to transfer sovereign rights to international organizations and to align with a system of mutual collective security for the preservation of peace ...

When I speak about peace in the world and in Europe, ladies and gentlemen, then I have to return to the *division of Germany*. It is our firm conviction that the division of Germany will one day disappear. (Enthusiastic applause.) I fear that if it does not disappear, peace will not come to Europe. ("Very true!") This division of Germany was caused by tensions which developed between the superpowers. These tensions, too, will pass. We hope that then nothing else will stand in the way of reunification with our brothers and sisters in the East Zone and in Berlin. (Rep. Dr. Richter: "Also with the Sudeten Germans!") ...

Ladies and gentlemen, allow me at this time to mention the *United States of America* with special appreciation. ("Bravo!") I do not believe that ever in history a victorious country has attempted to help the defeated country in this way and to contribute to its reconstruction and its recovery as the United States has done and is doing with regard to Germany. ("Bravo!" on the right, in the center, and in parts of the SPD.) We believe, ladies and gentlemen, that a future historiography will describe the post-war conduct of the United States as a greater deed than their efforts in the war. ("Very true!" – laughter from the KPD.) I know that in our most dire need, when hunger and hardship prevailed here, countless Americans helped us Germans in a stirring way out of genuine, personal sympathy and brotherly love. The German people must not forget what the American people have done and indeed they will not forget it. (Enthusiastic applause from the right, in the center, and from the SPD.)

Ladies and gentlemen! According to the Basic Law, *cultural affairs* fall under the jurisdiction of the states. But in the name of the entire federal government I can say this: all of our work will be supported by the spirit of Christian-Western culture and by respect for the law and for the dignity of man. ("Bravo!") We hope – that is our goal –, that with God's help we will succeed in leading the German people upwards and in contributing to peace in Europe and the world. (Long enthusiastic applause.)

Source: Konrad Adenauer, *Reden 1917–1967. Eine Auswahl*,
ed. by Hans-Peter Schwarz (Stuttgart: Deutsche Verlags-Anstalt, 1975), pp. 163–69.
(Original Source: Deutscher Bundestag. Stenographisches Protokoll der 5. Sitzung.
Bonn, Dienstag, den 20. September 1949, S. 22–30.) Translated by Sally Winkle

Restitution payments to Israel

The 1952 decision of the FRG to make restitution payments to Jewish victims of Nazism and to the state of Israel set it apart from the GDR, which disclaimed any responsibility for Nazi crimes. While the GDR, whose leadership had been active in the anti-Nazi resistance, encouraged its citizens to think of themselves as the innocent victims of Nazism, the West German government was prepared to make amends for the past. Ironically, most of the support for Adenauer's policy of *Wiedergutmachung* (restitution) came from the left, while many of his fellow conservatives in the CDU opposed it. In the address excerpted below, Adenauer sought to appeal to their self-interest to gain their support.

7.6 Konrad Adenauer, address to CDU Party Committee, Bonn, 6 September 1952

... Now I would like to say this to you about the agreement with Israel: It is absolutely true that Germany, the Federal Republic, does not have any legal obligations with regard to the Republic of Israel, but the Federal Republic does have great moral obligations. Even though we, and I am referring here to our circle, did not participate in the atrocities of National Socialism against the Jews, a considerable number of the German people did participate in them, and they not only actively participated, a certain percentage also got rich afterwards from their participation. We cannot ignore this fact. I consider it one of the most noble moral obligations of the German people to do, within their ability, whatever must be done to at least show that they do not agree with what was done to the Jews in the years of National Socialism, even if only by symbolic action. In unanimous resolutions the Bundestag has repeatedly expressed regret concerning the heinous crimes of the past against the Jews. Whoever speaks must also act. Words are cheap. But words must be followed by actions.

There is also a certain legal basis to the demands of the state of Israel, since it was after all due to measures taken by Germany that Israel had to accommodate so many refugees, especially old people from Germany and from countries that were occupied by Germany at the time; this resulted in serious financial burdens for Israel. It has been proposed that, following a cabinet meeting on Monday morning, I will go to Luxembourg, and in Luxembourg a kind of symbolic declaration will take place between me and the Minister of Foreign Affairs of Israel. This declaration is to express that from now on the past shall be past between the Jews and Germany. The representatives of the large Jewish world organization will also take part in this declaration.

I hope that the cabinet will not make things difficult for me. If the cabinet did cause problems, it would be a foreign policy disaster of the first order. It would not only be a political disaster, it would also strongly impede all our efforts to acquire foreign credit again. Let us be clear that now as before the power of the Jews in the economic sphere is extraordinarily strong, so that this – the term is perhaps a bit overstated – this reconciliation with the Jews is an absolute requirement for the Federal Republic from a moral standpoint and a political standpoint as well as an economic standpoint.

I have intentionally dwelled on this topic in somewhat more detail because I fear that afterwards all kinds of things will be said about this issue in Germany, and there will be difficulties. What I am telling you now does not have to be an absolute truth, but at one time I was told by a leading American authority: If the Federal Government succeeds in reaching this settlement with Israel and with the Jewish world organizations, it will be a political event for the Federal Republic of Germany comparable to the Germany treaty and the agreement on the European Defense Community. Therefore I ask you, if the matter turns out as I hope, and if opposition also arises in our own ranks, nonetheless to reflect on my words and to help people really appreciate that the settlement with the Jews is morally, politically, and economically an absolute necessity ...

Source: Konrad Adenauer, Reden 1917–1967. Eine Auswahl, ed. by Hans-Peter Schwarz (Stuttgart: Deutsche Verlags-Anstalt, 1975), pp. 266–267. (Original Source: Sitzung des Bundesparteiausschusses der CDU am 6. 9. 1952 in Bonn. Typewritten protocol [carbon copy]). Translated by Sally Winkle

Commemoration of the Holocaust in West Germany

Theodor Heuss (1884–1963), the first President of the Federal Republic from 1949 to 1959, gave the following talk at the dedication of a memorial to the victims of Bergen-Belsen concentration camp in northwestern Germany in 1952. Heuss, who had joined the tiny remnant of the former German Democratic Party (DDP) in voting for the Enabling Act in 1933 (Doc. 3.8), spent the Nazi years in "inner emigration," i.e., by withdrawing into private life. Like Adenauer (see Doc. 7.4), Heuss, a member of the liberal (in the European sense of *laissez-faire*) Free Democratic Party, stressed irreligion and biological naturalism as the sources of Nazi atrocities. Aimed at a German audience, his talk strikes a mildly apologetic tone with its references to German suffering and to German efforts for the surviving victims of Bergen-Belsen at the end of the war. He also could not resist a reference to prison camps in the GDR, still routinely called the "Soviet zone" at the time.

7.7 Theodor Heuss, speech at the Dedication of the Memorial for the Victims of Bergen-Belsen, November 1952

When I was asked if I would be willing to say a word here today on this occasion, I said yes without hesitation. For a refusal or an excuse would have seemed cowardly to me, and it seems to me that we Germans want to, should, and must learn to be courageous in the face of the truth, particularly on ground that was soaked and laid waste by the excesses of human cowardice. For pure brutality decked out with carbines, guns, and whips is somehow always cowardly when it struts around well-fed, threatening, and pitiless among defenseless poverty, illness, and hunger.

Anyone who speaks here as a German must trust in his inner freedom to recognize the full horror of the crimes committed here by Germans. Anyone who wanted to gloss over or trivialize these crimes or even justify them by referring to the misuse of so-called "reasons of state" would simply be insolent.

But now I want to say something that will surprise many of you here, but that I think you will believe, and that many a person listening on the radio will not believe: I heard the word Belsen for the first time in Spring 1945 from the BBC, and I know that it was the same for many people in this country. We knew of – or at least I knew of – Dachau, Buchenwald near Weimar, and Oranienburg, place names previously associated with cheerful memories that were now smeared a shade of dirty brown. Friends had been there, relatives had been there and had spoken about it.

And early on people learned the word Theresienstadt, which was prepared so to speak for visits by neutrals, and Ravensbrück. On a terrible day I heard the name Mauthausen, where they had "liquidated" my old friend Otto Hirsch, the noble and distinguished leader of the Reich Representation of German Jews.[6] I got word from his wife, whom I tried to support and counsel. Belsen was missing from my list of terror and shame and Auschwitz too.

This remark is not meant to be a crutch for those who like to say: We knew nothing about all that. We *did* know about these things. We also knew about the systematic murder of the inmates of German mental asylums from the letters by Protestant and Catholic bishops that found their way secretly to the people. This state, for whom human feeling was a ridiculous and expensive sentimentality, also wanted a *tabula rasa* here – a "clean slate" – and the clean slate had bloodstains and ash residue – what did that matter? Our imagination, nurtured by bourgeois and Christian tradition, did not comprehend the dimensions of this callous and grievous destruction.

This Belsen and this memorial are symbolic of a historical destiny. The memorial is for the sons and daughters of foreign nations, for the German and foreign Jews, for the German people and not only the Germans, who were also buried in this soil.

I know that some people think: Was this memorial necessary? Wouldn't it have been better if fields were planted here and the mercy of the earth's eternally rejuvenating fertility were to show forgiveness for what happened? After centuries a vague legend of sinister events might linger in this place. Well, we could reflect on this; and there are plenty of arguments, arguments of concern that this obelisk could be a thorn which will not allow wounds that time should heal to reach the goal of recovery.

We want to speak in all honesty about this. The peoples who know that the members of their people are in mass graves remember them, particularly the Jews who were practically forced by Hitler into a consciousness of their own ethnicity. They *will* never, they *can* never forget what was done to them; the Germans *must* never forget what was done by people of their nationality in these shameful years.

But I hear the objection: And the others? Do you know nothing of the internment camps in 1945–46 and their brutality, their injustice? Do you know nothing of the victims in foreign custody, nothing of the suffering of the legalistic and cruel justice to which people are still subject today? Do you know nothing of the continuing mistreatment in the camps, of the deaths in camps in the Soviet Zone, Waldheim, Torgau, and Bautzen? Only the insignias have changed there.

I know about that and I have never hesitated to speak of it. But to mention injustice and brutality of *others* in order to call attention to it are the methods of people without moral scruples, who exist among *all* peoples, among Americans as well as Germans or French and so on. No people is better than any other; in every people there are some good and some bad …

The relatives of many peoples lie here. The inscriptions are in multiple languages; they are a document of the tragic distortion of the fate of Europe. Many German victims of the terror lie here as well, and how many on the edge of other camps? But it is very significant that Nachum Goldmann spoke here for everyone.[7] For it was here in Belsen that particularly the Jews who could still be apprehended anywhere were supposed to starve to death or fall victim to the epidemics. Goldmann spoke about the painful journey of the Jewish people and about their strength to withstand historical catastrophes. Surely what happened between 1933 and 1945 is

---

6   The Reich Representation of German Jews (*Reichsvertretung deutscher Juden*) was founded in September 1933 under the presidency of Rabbi Leo Baeck (1873–1956). It was put under the control of the German Ministry of the Interior in 1939 and dissolved in 1943.

7   Nachum Goldmann was the President of the World Jewish Congress.

the most horrible thing that the Jews of the historical diaspora have experienced. Something quite novel happened. Goldmann spoke about that. Persecution of the Jews in many forms often occurred in the past. Heretofore they were caused in part by religious fanaticism and in part by feelings of socio-economic rivalry. One cannot speak of religious fanaticism after 1933. For to those who despised the holy scriptures of the Old *and* the New Testament, to the enemies of all religious commitments, metaphysical problems were completely foreign. And the socio-economic factor was not enough of a reason, if it does not merely refer to murder and robbery.

But that was not the only thing. Basically it was about something else. The breakthrough of the biological naturalism of the half-educated led to the pedantry of murder as a purely automatic process, without the modest need for a modest moral standard, as it were. Precisely this is the worst depravity of this time. And this is *our* shame, that such a thing came to pass in the history of a people from whose ranks Lessing, Kant, Goethe, and Schiller entered the world's consciousness. No one, no one, can relieve us of this shame.

My friend Albert Schweitzer reduced his cultural and ethical teachings to the formula: "Reverence for life." Presumably this formula is true, however paradoxical the recollection of this expression may seem in a place where it was mocked ten thousand times. But doesn't this formula need a complement, "Reverence for death"?

I want to tell a little story that may displease some Jews and some non-Jews. Both sides will say: but that isn't appropriate here! In the First World War 12,000 young men of Jewish faith died for the cause of their German fatherland. On the memorial in my home town their names too were entered in brass letters with the names of all the other fallen soldiers, one comrade next to the other, "as if he were a part of me".[8] The National Socialist District Leader had the names of the Jewish dead scratched out and filled in the gaps with the names of various battles. I am not telling you this because friends of my youth were erased in the process. My worst realization and horror was that the respect for death, for plain death in battle, was lost while new wars were already being planned.

Dying in war, because of war, then took on its most horrible forms. Here, too, in Belsen war raged, with hunger and epidemics as its unpaid assistants. A cynical lad, a vulgar fellow might say: For the most part they were only Jews, Poles, Russians, French, Belgians, Norwegians, Greeks and so on. Only? They were people like you and me; they had their parents, their children, their husbands, their wives! The pictures of the survivors are the most horrifying documents.

In April 1945 the war was over for this piece of land. But people continued to die from hunger and epidemics. British doctors lost their lives in the process. But in recent days I have been requested by distinguished Jewish persons to also say something precisely at this hour about this period after the war, when people who were dying were saved by *German* doctors, and by *German* attendants and nurses in the spring and early summer of 1945. I knew nothing of these things. But I was told how at that time, in the face of such misery, the wish to help grew to self-sacrifice, to awareness of a doctor's duty, to shame, lest one fail to carry out such a task, to Christian, sisterly devotion to the one in danger, who is always one's "neighbor." I am thankful that this was said to me and that this request was made. For there is after all some consolation in this test of unmitigated right and good.

Rousseau was mentioned in the speech of the English Land Commissioner. Rousseau begins one of his books with the apodictic statement: "Man is good." Oh, we have learned that the world is more complicated than the propositions of moralizing writers. But we also know this: *Man* and

---

8   The quoted phrase is a line from the traditional German dirge for soldiers killed in battle.

humankind are abstract concepts, statistical facts, often only noncommittal phrases; but *humanity* is individual conduct, a very simple test of one's behavior toward the other, no matter of what religion, what race, what social class, what profession he may be. That may be some consolation.

There is the obelisk, there is the wall with the inscriptions in many languages. They are stone, cold stone. *Saxa loquuntur*: stones can speak. It depends on the individual, it depends on you, to understand their language, their special language, for your own sake, for the sake of all of us!

Source: Theodor Heuss, *An und über Juden. Aus Schriften und Reden (1906–1963)*, ed. by Hans Lamm (Düsseldorf: Econ-Verlag, 1964), pp. 135–140. Translated by Sally Winkle

Anti-fascism in East Germany

After the creation of two separate states in Germany in 1949 both sides vied for the honor and status of having made the greatest break with the Nazi past. Both sides used Nazism as a negative foil to promote their respective political systems. They also made every effort to discredit the other side by linking it to the Nazi past. While publicists in the Federal Republic (FRG) pointed to the continuities in totalitarian repression in East Germany, publicists in the German Democratic Republic (GDR) emphasized the continuities in the economic system and the reemergence of former Nazis in positions of influence in West Germany.

The following speech by GDR Prime Minister Otto Grotewohl (1894–1964) at the dedication of a memorial at Buchenwald in 1958 provides a representative example of the rhetoric of official "anti-fascism," the main legitimating ideology of the GDR. East German communists drew their moral legitimacy from their active resistance to the Nazis and from the persecution they suffered in the Third Reich. Grotewohl used the occasion, however, not merely to commemorate the victims of Nazi crimes, but to launch a fierce attack on the alleged militarism and revanchism of leaders of the FRG. This was in keeping with Soviet policy, which had sought to prevent the creation of a separate West German state in the late 1940s and its rearmament and integration into NATO in the 1950s. For the East, accusations of fascist revival in West Germany were a major weapon in the Cold War arsenal.

In contrast to Theodor Heuss in his talk at Bergen-Belsen (Doc. 7.7), Grotewohl never specifically mentioned Jews in his recitation of concentration camp victims. Political resisters, many of them of course Jewish, always received pride of place in the Soviet and East German hierarchy of Nazi victims. Failure to single out Jewish victims for special acknowledgement was a symptom of growing anti-Zionism in the East, the rejection of Jewish nationalism as a threat to the communist system and Soviet interests. Grotewohl also failed to mention that Buchenwald was used as a detention camp for opponents of the communist regime in the late 1940s.

7.8 Otto Grotewohl, "Buchenwald admonishes us!" 14 September 1958

THE IDEA OF THE FALLEN ANTI-FASCISTS LIVES ON

In love and admiration we bow down to the fallen heroes of the anti-fascist resistance, to the millions of victims of fascist barbarity. Courageously they put their lives on the line against a dreadful, inhuman system of murder to fight for peace and for the happiness of peoples. We remember the brave sons and daughters from all the countries of Europe, who did not submit to terror and brutal force, whose courageous deaths were a terrible accusation against their murderers and a silent entreaty for the freedom and rights of the people. Steadfastly they fought and steadfastly they died. Their bodies were broken; they were battered, gassed, beaten, and tortured to death, but they did not submit. Unbowed and faithful to their great idea, they went to their deaths. Unbowed and with courage they took their last journey, like the Communist Thälmann, the Social Democrat Breitscheid, the pastor Schneider, the countless Soviet prisoners of war, the persecuted forced laborers from all countries, and the nameless thousands.

Glory and honor to their memory! Glory and honor to the heroic anti-fascist fighters, whom we shall never forget, for they are immortal.

Today for the first time the bells ring from the tower of the National Memorial, resonating far into the countryside and proclaiming the heroism of the European resistance fighters. They defied the dark, terrible night of Hitler-fascism; they gave their blood and their lives, their joy and their happiness in order to end the cruel fascist slavery. The voices of the dead and the living unite in the sound of the bells to utter a warning cry: Never again fascism and war! – " ... Peace be their first tidings!" They shall ring out to Moscow and Paris, to Prague and London, to Warsaw and Rome, to Berlin and everywhere, where people hate war and love peace as much as life.

The anti-fascist fighters who died gave us that mission. Their idea lives; it is risen out of war, misery, and ruins. Like a seed that has fallen on fertile ground, it has driven its roots deep into the hearts of the people. No one can tear it out again.

THE ANTI-FASCIST RESISTANCE STRUGGLE IS A PEOPLE'S STRUGGLE

The anti-fascist resistance fighters were outstanding sons and daughters of the European peoples. They loved life with every fiber of their beings and in the terrible darkness of the fascist prisons and concentration camps they knew that a newer, brighter morning would dawn.

It was incredibly difficult for them to sink into the world of eternal silence, for they all belonged to the future and to a new age. Their fight required courage and inner strength, boldness and willingness to make sacrifices, because they faced an enemy who brutally and ruthlessly destroyed all noble, humanistic feelings and persons in a horrendous system of terror and repression.

But whereever one fighter fell, new fighters emerged who were aware of the great sympathy and solidarity of the people for the anti-fascist fighters and who continued the struggle in the spirit of their dead comrades.

The anti-fascist resistance struggle was and is a people's struggle. It can only lead to success where the peoples rise up resolutely under the leadership of their working class to fight against fascist reaction. The resistance struggle against Hitler-fascism was also organized and led by the working class and their parties.

Fascist dictatorship is always inhuman, cruel, and criminal. Its methods of inciting people against each other, of terror, and of organized mass murder are the expression of a dying system on the decline. Nazi rule in Germany was a fascist dictatorship of the most reactionary circles of German imperialism. Its goal was the establishment of fascist world rule under German leadership. Its method was unrestrained terror and bloody mass murder. The

Hitler state was a totalitarian torture chamber, an executioners' state, whose protagonists waded without conscience in rivers of blood. Anyone who was ever caught in the wheels of its extermination machine was demeaned, maltreated, tormented to exhaustion, shot, poisoned, hanged, gassed, and tortured to death in a hundred ways.

More than 18 million people were deported to the extermination factories, the concentration camps. More than 11 million of them were murdered in the most brutal way. Here on this site, in the Buchenwald concentration camp, more than 56,000 people lost their lives.

But the catalog of crimes of Hitler-fascism does not end there. The Trial of the People in Nuremberg counted as victims 57 million people who died in the Second World War and in the resistance struggle against fascist slavery. What a horrific toll of death.

We thank first of all the heroic Soviet Union, the courageous sons and daughters of socialism, and the millions of nameless heroes of the anti-fascist resistance movement from many countries in Europe for the victory over this abominable system. They shed their blood and gave their lives to crush Hitler-fascism.

WARNING FOR ALL TIMES

For all who gave their best and noblest gift, their lives, we have established this memorial for all time here on blood-drenched soil in the heart of Germany. The memorial is not a lifeless stone. It shall proclaim to future generations the everlasting glory of the courageous fight against the tyrants, for peace, freedom, and human dignity. With this we want to cleanse the name of Germany before the world, a name that was sullied by Hitler-fascism.

This memorial shall be a place of friendship with the great Soviet people, who liberated our people and Europe from Hitler-fascism. The following words set the tone for this hour: "Glory and honor to the heroes of the resistance struggle and the victims of fascist terror!" We raise our voices from here in all directions and to all the people in Germany and beyond Germany's borders. We call the living to action; we admonish them not to grow weary in the fight against fascism and to continue to lead the people to success for world peace. With the cry: "People of all lands – defend the greatest good of humankind, peace!" this ceremony can become a protest demonstration against the preparation for an imperialistic atomic war, which, especially coming from West Germany today, threatens the German people and humankind.

Hitler-fascism was crushed militarily in 1945, but it was only destroyed at the roots in one part of Germany, in the German Democratic Republic. Here the militaristic and fascist soil was plowed up, here the cornerstone for a new Germany was laid, whose responsibility is the preservation of peace. Inciting people against each other and making propaganda for war are punishable offenses here. People are free from exploitation and repression, and they are establishing a joyful and happy life in their socialist society. The German Democratic Republic wants to live in peace and friendship with all peoples. Peace and humanism in Germany have found their home here.

In one part of Germany the great idea of the anti-fascist fighters has been realized and a peaceful state has been created, by which other peoples will never again be threatened. Today two German states stand before the world. One has learned from the mistakes of German history. It has learned good and right lessons. It is the German Democratic Republic – a state of peace and socialism.

But the West German state is a refuge of reactionaries in which militarists and fascists have attained power once again; the state's aggressive character is revealed in its reactionary actions.

In West Germany the Potsdam Agreement on the eradication of fascism has been betrayed and destroyed. Those who led Germany and Europe to ruin hid away in the tide of nameless people, only to emerge again at the first muted drum roll and march on in the old fascist spirit. They are all there once more, from the fascist generals … to the war criminals … to the mass murderers of the fascist prisons and concentration camps. They wear new uniforms and decorate themselves with the old medals for their terrible crimes. Once again they are inciting hatred in the same old way against the Soviet Union and other peace-loving countries. They hold in their blood-spattered hands the most horrendous weapons of mass destruction in human history, atomic bombs, in order to kill millions of people.

Fatefully involved in the politics of the NATO alliance, the forces of yesterday stand ready in West Germany to seek revenge for the defeat they suffered and to plunge the people into a new horrible war. Once again they rule the state and the economy; they are raising the youth for a new war, and they control the entire reactionary propaganda industry. They repress the democratic movement of the people and direct hate and persecution against all peace-loving people.

Thus the old fascist system in West Germany is currently becoming "socially acceptable" once again. It is high time to change the situation in West Germany. Threatening clouds darken the light of peace and freedom. All peace-loving people resolutely oppose America's and England's acts of aggression in the Near East against the Arab peoples and in the Far East against the Chinese people. The German people also oppose the auxiliary services provided in these cases by the Bonn government, which did not even recoil from direct military support. We must not allow the world to be plunged again into blood and misery and the people to be forced to the edge of catastrophe. The decision whether the nations follow the path toward peace or whether they steer toward the abyss of a third world war lies in the hands of peace-loving people.

PEACE-LOVING HUMANITY FIGHTS AND TRIUMPHS

The peace-loving people of the world are not defenseless in the face of the war-mongers. There is also a state representing peace in Germany – the German Democratic Republic. The German Democratic Republic is a state of workers and peasants; it is located firmly in the socialist camp and remains resolutely faithful to the world-wide peace movement. We stand united with millions of peace-loving people of all continents and nations on the side of world peace. The world is progressively developing and changing. The socialist states and the forces for peace in the whole world are stronger than the forces of war. They can force nations to agree and quickly extinguish any possible hot spots. The recent past has repeatedly provided proof of this fact.

Peace-loving people will continue to be successful in their fight against fascism and war. We are aware of the great responsibility that the German people have in this struggle. We must organize a unified people's movement of all Germans against the preparations for atomic war, because in this way we can promote the creation of an atomic weapon-free zone and peace in Europe. This people's movement would also facilitate a peaceful, democratic reunification through a confederation of both German states. With that the main source of danger for war in Europe would be eliminated.

The unity of the progressive and peace-loving people in Germany and in the whole world is the guarantee of a peaceful and happy future of humanity. This goal is also served by our meeting for the dedication of this memorial. It is a demonstration against war, for disarmament and the prohibition of atomic weapons, for the creation of an atomic weapons-free zone in Europe, and for friendship and understanding among all peoples.

The anti-fascist resistance fighters all over the world provide the example and model in this struggle. Their friendship to each other arose in misery and death and from common will to live. This staunch community of activists does not know any borders based on countries, languages, world views, or religious faiths.

The memorial at the former Buchenwald Concentration Camp proclaims the heroic struggle and the unspeakable suffering of the anti-fascists in all camps and in all countries of the world. People from all nations stood together here on this blood-drenched soil and vowed to keep the memory of the victims of Nazi barbarity alive. True to the unity born in suffering and in resistance against fascism, they vowed to dedicate themselves to the noble goal of achieving understanding among all peoples, in order to gain their security, their independence, peace, and freedom. Today we present to the German people and to the people of good will in other countries this National Memorial on the Ettersberg, which lies right in the heart of Germany. The tower and walls point far into the countryside. The flames from the sacrificial dishes are evidence of our love and respect for the dead. The bell in the tower shall echo far across the country. Its sound shall penetrate into the hearts of the people and bring them tidings of our irrevocable determination to fulfill the legacy of the heroes who died and not to rest until peace and freedom reign in the whole world and the peoples flourish in prosperity.

Source: Otto Grotewohl, *Im Kampf um die einige Deutsche Demokratische Republik: Reden und Aufsätze*, Vol. 6 (Berlin: Dietz Verlag, 1964), pp. 7–14. Translated by Sally Winkle

West German reconciliation with Poland, December 1970

The generational revolt of the 1960s, sparked mainly by resistance to the Vietnam War, brought with it a general reorientation of values to the left. Some historians even refer to this transformation as the second founding of the Federal Republic. In 1969 the SPD, which had formally cast off its Marxist ideology a decade earlier, took power for the first time under Chancellor Willy Brandt (1913–92), who had gone into exile in Sweden during the Third Reich. Brandt urged his countrymen to "dare to practice more democracy." He sought to normalize relations with the GDR and the Soviet bloc, a policy known as *Ostpolitik* (the West German version of the policy known in the US as "detente"). This new "opening to the left" brought with it a greater willingness to accept the territorial losses that followed the Second World War and a greater readiness to acknowledge German responsibility for Nazi crimes. One of the most dramatic gestures of German contrition occurred during Brandt's state visit to Poland in December 1970, when the German chancellor unexpectedly dropped to his knees at a wreath-laying ceremony at the memorial to the victims of the Warsaw Ghetto uprising in 1943 (see Doc. 6.13). For this *Kniefall*, as well as for his willingness to accept the finality of the post-war Polish–German border along the Oder and Neisse rivers, he was severely criticized by conservatives at home. In the following excerpt from his memoirs, Brandt describes the dramatic events in Warsaw in December 1970.

7.9 Willy Brandt, "Kneeling in Warsaw"

In 1970 and also later, I was asked why I did not give precedence over the treaty with the Soviet Union to the treaty to be concluded with the Poles, who had suffered so unspeakably. This was a purely academic question, and the Polish leaders shared my view. We had no choice; the key to normal relations lay in Moscow. Nor was Russia to be seen only as the seat of power; its own people had suffered terribly as well.

I will concede, though, that the Polish people and their leaders alike would have preferred our declaration on the Oder–Neisse border to be on the agenda in Warsaw first; as a "present from Russia" it seemed worth only half as much. The leaders, however, knew what the general public could not: a government I headed would be ready to accept the new western frontier of Poland contractually. I had signalled as much during the 1969 election campaign, before it was clear whether I would be able to form the new Government. In 1970 I accepted the Polish proposal to make the establishment of the border the prime concern in the Warsaw Treaty, and let non-aggression follow.

When I was talking to Wladyslav Gomulka, Polish Communist Party leader and de facto head of state, after the signing of the treaty, on the afternoon of 7 December 1970, the problem of the order of precedence surfaced again. Well-meaning Polish journalists had expressed a wish for us to ratify the Warsaw Treaty before the Moscow Treaty. [Party leader Wladyslaw] Gomulka asked me not to lose sight of the facts. Any attempt to pry Poland away from its alliance or even drive a wedge between Poland and its great neighbor to the east, he said, was bound to fail. Moreover, the Moscow Treaty had been concluded first; both should be ratified at the same time, or very close together …

Prime Minister Josef Cyrankiewicz, a survivor of Mauthausen and a member of the Social Democratic wing of the PVAP, the Communist Unity Party, said at the start of the Warsaw talks that our two governments should undergo a kind of psychoanalysis, digging up everything that was wrong first, and the therapeutic talking would follow. Various forms of cooperation would be a help, he said, and time, the great healer, would take care of the rest. On the eve of the signing of the treaty, Gomulka said that we should envisage taking at least a decade over the process of rapprochement. Even so, his estimate fell short.

The Warsaw Treaty clarified "the basis for normalizing relations" and showed on what thin ice we were skating. None the less, it was important for us to establish that, as with the other Eastern treaties, the validity of treaties concluded earlier was unaffected and that no international agreements were jeopardized. The Polish head of government did not hesitate to say that his side knew that the man signing in the name of the Federal Republic was one who "saw, as soon as the fascists seized power, the boundless misfortune it would bring upon the German people, the peoples of Europe and the peace of the world." In my reply I said I was aware that rifts brutally torn open could not be filled in by any paper, however important. Understanding, even reconciliation, could not be ushered in by governments but must come to maturity in the hearts of the people on both sides. I told my partners of talks I had with General de Gaulle about Germany and Poland. He and I, I said, had agreed that the nations of Europe must retain their own identities, and that indeed that would open up great prospects for the whole continent. I knew, I said, "that there are no answers in isolation, only European answers. That, too, has brought me here." In my speech on the signing of the treaty I said: "My government accepts the consequences of history: conscience and insight lead us to those conclusions without which we would not be here." But no one would expect me "to undertake more in political, legal, and moral respects than dictated by insight and conviction." Above all, I said, borders must "be less divisive and less hurtful."

It was a great burden I carried with me to Warsaw. Nowhere had a nation and its people suffered as they did in Poland. The routine extermination of Polish Jews took bloodlust to lengths no one would have thought possible. Who can name all the Jews from Poland, and other parts of Europe, who were annihilated in Auschwitz alone? The memory of six million murder victims lay along my road to Warsaw, and the memory of the fight to the death of the Warsaw ghetto, which I had followed from my observation post in Stockholm, and of which the governments fighting Hitler had taken hardly any more notice than they did of the heroic rising of the Polish capital itself a few months later.[9]

On the morning after my arrival, my Warsaw program contained two wreath-laying ceremonies, the first at the grave of the Unknown Soldier. There, I remembered the victims of violence and treachery. The screens and newspapers of the world featured a picture that showed me kneeling – before the memorial dedicated to the Jewish ghetto of the city and its dead. I have often been asked what the idea behind that gesture was: had it been planned in advance? No, it had not. My close colleagues were as surprised as the reporters and photographers with me, and as those who did not attend the ceremony because they could see no "story" in it.

I had not planned anything, but I had left Wilanow Castle, where I was staying, with a feeling that I must express the exceptional significance of the ghetto memorial. From the bottom of the abyss of German history, under the burden of millions of victims of murder, I did what human beings do when speech fails them.

Even twenty years later, I cannot say more than the reporter whose account ran: "Then he who does not need to kneel knelt, on behalf of all who do need to kneel but do not – because they dare not, or cannot, or cannot dare to kneel."

At home in the Federal Republic there was no lack of questions, either malicious or foolish, as to whether the gesture had not been "overdone." I noted embarrassment on the Polish side. The day after the incident none of my hosts referred to it. I concluded that others besides ourselves had not yet digested this chapter of history.[10] Carlo Schmid, who was with me in Warsaw, told me later that he had been asked why, at the grave of the Unknown Soldier, I only laid a wreath and did not kneel. Next morning, in the car on the way to the airport, Cyrankiewicz took my arm and told me that the gesture had in fact touched many people; his wife had telephoned a friend of hers in Vienna that evening, and both women shed bitter tears.

**Source: Willy Brandt, *My Life in Politics*, trsl. by Anthea Bell
(New York: Viking Penguin, 1992), pp. 196–200**

Neo-Conservatism in the 1980s

The accession of Christian Democrat Helmut Kohl (b. 1930) to the chancellorship in 1982 following thirteen years of SPD rule marked a swing of the pendulum back in a more conservative direction. This *Tendenzwende*, as it was called in Germany, paralleled similar changes in political climate in Britain and the United States, and left its mark on historiography as well. Conservatives challenged the critical historiography of the 1960s and 1970s that had singled out Germany's *Sonderweg* (special development), i.e., its failure to develop Western-style liberal and democratic institutions in the nineteenth and early twentieth centuries, as the

---

9   Brandt is here referring to the so-called Warsaw Uprising in August 1944, which, like the Warsaw Ghetto Uprising of April 1943, was brutally suppressed by German troops.

10 Brandt may here be referring to the fact that the Warsaw Ghetto fighters received virtually no support or encouragement from the Polish Home Army, the underground army that unsuccessfully sought to liberate Warsaw from the Germans in August 1944.

chief cause of the two world wars and the rise of National Socialism in Germany. Conservatives rejected the tendency of left-wing historians to view German history through the lens of
the Nazi experience. They feared that obsession with Nazi criminality and German guilt
would weaken German resolve in the new Cold War that had been revived in the early 1980s
under the leadership of President Ronald Reagan and Prime Minister Margaret Thatcher.

President Reagan's and Chancellor Kohl's official ceremony at the military cemetery
in Bitburg in May 1985 to mark the 40th anniversary of the end of the Second World War
symbolized a new willingness to downplay the Nazi past in favor of cementing the
Western Cold War alliance. Because the Bitburg cemetery contained the graves not only
of Wehrmacht soldiers but also of soldiers of the Waffen-SS, the choice of this site for an
official display of US–German friendship and reconciliation seemed like a deliberate
attempt to depreciate the horror and significance of the Nazi past.

One of Kohl's advisers was the outspoken neo-conservative historian Michael Stürmer,
who warned that the critical historiography of the 1960s jeopardized the FRG's chances of
winning the Cold War against the GDR. He published the following article in the conservative *Frankfurter Allgemeine Zeitung* on 25 April 1986 at the start of a bitterly contested election
campaign in which Kohl would be reelected by a narrow margin. Stürmer decried the
obsessive left-wing concern with the Nazi era, which he attributed to the dominant role of
the 1960s generation in forming public opinion. The task of historians, he maintained, was
to create a positive national identity, for "the future is controlled by those who fill the
content of memory, coin the concepts, and interpret the past." According to Stürmer,
obsession with Nazism undermined West German pride and self-confidence. Excessive
focus on this brief episode in German history threatened to help the other side in the Cold
War and diminish Germany's dependability as a NATO partner. Stürmer's insinuation that
the left was preparing the ground for communism was typical of the polemical style in
which the "Historians' Debate" was conducted.

7.10 Michael Stürmer, "History in a land without history"

In a country without memory anything is possible. Public opinion polls warn that among all
industrial countries the Federal Republic of Germany displays the greatest lack of communication between the generations, the least self-confidence among its people, and the greatest
shift in values. How will the Germans see their country tomorrow? How will they see the
West, how will they see themselves? Presumably continuity will prevail. But it is not certain.

Throughout the country the rediscovery of history is noted and commended. Museums
are flourishing. Flea markets live from nostalgia for the good old days. Historical exhibits
can't complain about a lack of interest, and historical literature, of only marginal interest
twenty years ago, is again being written and read.

There are two explanations for this search for a lost time. Some see in this a renewal of
historical consciousness, a return to cultural tradition, a promise of normality. Others
remind us that the viewer who finds no certainty in the future looks to the past for direction
and confirmation where the journey is going. Both factors explain the new search for the old
history: The loss of orientation and the search for identity are closely related. But anyone
who thinks that all this has no effect on politics or the future is ignoring the fact that in a
country without history the future is controlled by those who determine the content of
memory, define the concepts, and interpret the past.

That this insecurity only began in 1945 may be doubted. Hitler's ascent arose out of crises and catastrophes of a secularized civilization swerving from one new beginning to another. The hallmarks of these new starts were loss of orientation and a futile search for certainty. "There is nothing that is not questionable," Karl Jaspers said in a memorable lecture in Heidelberg in 1930. From 1914 to 1945 Germans were subjected to the torrents of modernity to such a degree that tradition was destroyed, the unthinkable made thinkable, and barbarism turned into a form of state. That's why Hitler was able to triumph; that's why he could capture and corrupt Prussia and patriotism, the state, and middle-class virtues.

But even before this epoch of wars and civil wars our history was a history of permanent upheaval. Anyone who laments the absence of revolutions in this history has understood little of the agricultural revolution, the demographic revolution, the industrial revolution, the partial revolution of 1848, and the revolution from above that triumphed with Bismarck. The horizon of hopes opened anew to each generation for 200 years, and in almost each generation these hopes collapsed. German history has worn out many constitutions, many value systems, many images of past and future.

For a long time the German dictatorship was the be-all and end-all of historiography – and how could it have been otherwise? Then more distant epochs opened up to our view again, the further the Federal Republic gained distance from its beginnings. Since 1973, when the price of oil shot up and *Tendenzwende* (the turn to conservatism) became the name of a new consciousness, the Germans have discovered that the Federal Republic and the world system of which it is a part are also subject to historical change. Today the history of the post-war system is the subject of political and scholarly studies.

The result has been to throw into clearer relief the achievement of Konrad Adenauer, who did everything to overcome the German *Sonderweg* (special development) of moral and political alienation from the West. But at the same time the notorious Stalin Note of 1952, which was intended to prevent this overcoming of alienation from the West, is being mythologized as the missed opportunity for reunification,[11] and the Russian tyrant is being presented as Santa Claus, to whom the Germans only needed to present their wishes to get what they wanted: Unity, freedom, prosperity, and security – in reality, however, what was offered were only foretokens of a Soviet Germany. And among the ghosts of the past anti-fascism is again becoming evident: The legend of the noble intentions of the Communists, of the failure of German Social Democrats, and of the blessings of the Popular Front. The fact that on the 40th anniversary of the German capitulation the party of Kurt Schumacher[12] was told by its leading thinkers that its main political task was to fight against the social foundations of fascism in the Federal Republic – this fact betrays hidden thoughts about the future.

Be that as it may: In observing the Germans *vis-à-vis* their history our neighbors must ask themselves where all this is leading. The Federal Republic has political and economic respon-

11 In 1952 the Western powers rejected Stalin's offer to allow the reunification of Germany on condition that a united Germany be neutralized (on the Austrian model). The offer was made in an effort to prevent the rearmament of West Germany and its integration into NATO (the North Atlantic Treaty Organization founded in 1949).

12 Kurt Schumacher (1895–1952), who lost his right arm in the First World War and was interned for ten years in Nazi concentration camps, was a lifelong Social Democrat and leader of the party when it was revived after 1945. He was critical of Adenauer's pro-Western policy, which he saw as a barrier to reunification.

sibilities in the world. It is the centerpiece of the European defense perimeter of the Atlantic system. But it is now becoming clear that each generation living in Germany today has different, even opposing, views of past and future. It is also becoming evident that the technocratic disparagement of history by the right and its progressive strangulation by the left have seriously damaged the political culture of our country. The search for the lost past is not some abstract striving for culture: it is morally legitimate and politically necessary. For it is about the inner continuity of the German Republic, and its predictability in foreign affairs. In a country without memory anything is possible.

> Source: Michael Stürmer, "Geschichte in geschichtslosem Land,"
> in "Historikerstreit". Die Dokumentation der Kontroverse um die
> Einzigartigkeit der nationalsozialistischen Judenvernichtung
> (Munich: Piper, 1987), pp. 36–8. Translated by Rod Stackelberg

The revisionism of the New Right

The most ambitious attempt at a conservative revision of the history of National Socialism was undertaken by the historian Ernst Nolte, whose critical study of fascist ideology, *Three Faces of Fascism: Action Francaise, Fascism, National Socialism*, had drawn favorable reviews in 1963. In the succeeding decades, however, partly in reaction to the protest movements of the 1960s, he moved to a steadily more positive interpretation of National Socialism. The following article in the *Frankfurter Allgemeine Zeitung* on 6 June 1986 outlined the provocative theses that informed his larger study, *The European Civil War, 1917–1945: National Socialism und Bolschevism*, published in 1987.[13] Nolte described National Socialism as a rational, though excessive, response to the greater evil of communism, on which National Socialism had modelled itself. He went so far as to suggest that the Holocaust was provoked by fear of communist atrocities, which, because they preceded Nazi atrocities, had to be considered the ultimate cause of the genocidal violence of the twentieth century.

Nolte thus went a step further than most of his conservative peers: He not only, like Stürmer, wished to end what he regarded as the unhealthy German obsession with Nazism and German guilt – an obsession that Nolte attributed to the desire of leftists to advance their political causes and the hope of survivors and the descendants of victims to maintain their "permanent privileged status" – but he also took issue with the notion of Nazism as absolute evil and sought to reinterpret it in a more favorable light. In his more extreme version of the totalitarianism interpretation of the Cold War, which only sought to tar communism with the Nazi brush (in the same way that communists sought to tar capitalism), Nolte defended Nazism as *less* iniquitous than communism. In the "European civil war" between extremists of left and right, Nolte found the latter more defensible. Nolte claimed that because his views were not "politically correct," an invitation to deliver this paper at a conference in Frankfurt was withdrawn, an account that the organizers of the conference denied (see Doc. 7.12).

13 *Der europäische Bürgerkrieg 1917–1945: Nationalsozialismus und Bolschewismus* (Berlin: Propyläen Verlag, 1987).

7.11 Ernst Nolte, "The past that will not pass: A speech that could be written but not delivered"

The "past that will not pass" can only mean the National Socialist past of the Germans or of Germany. This thesis implies that normally every past will pass and that this non-passing represents something quite exceptional. On the other hand the normal passing of the past cannot be understood as a disappearance. The era of the first Napoleon has again and again been portrayed in historical works, and the same is true of the age of Augustus. But these pasts have evidently lost the urgency they had for their contemporaries. Precisely for this reason they can be left to the historians. The National Socialist past on the other hand ... does not seem to be subject to this passing, this loss of urgency, but rather seems to be becoming ever more alive and vigorous, but not as a model, rather as a bugaboo – as a past that has established itself as the present or that is suspended over the present like an executioner's sword.

BLACK AND WHITE IMAGES

There are good reasons for this. The more definitively the Federal Republic of Germany and Western society as a whole evolve toward "full prosperity," the more foreign the picture of the Third Reich becomes, with its ideology of warlike self-sacrifice, its maxim of "guns instead of butter," its quotes from the *Edda*,[14] such as "our death will be a festival," which was declaimed in choruses at school celebrations. All people are pacifists by conviction today, but still they cannot view the bellicosity of National Socialism from a safe distance, for they know that the two superpowers spend far more on armaments every year than Hitler spent from 1933 to 1939. And thus there remains a deep insecurity that would rather condemn the enemy [of militarism] in its unambiguous form [under National Socialism] than in the confusions of the present.

Much the same is true of feminism: In National Socialism the "cult of masculinity" was still full of provocative self-confidence, while in the present it tends to deny and conceal itself – thus National Socialism is the present-day enemy in its last, still quite unambiguous form. Hitler's claim to "world domination" has to be seen as even more horrific the more it becomes obvious that the Federal Republic can at most play the part of a medium-sized state in world affairs. Despite this, however, "harmlessness" is not attributed to the Federal Republic, and in many places the fear still remains that the Federal Republic can be, not the cause, to be sure, but the precipitating factor of a third world war. More than anything, however, remembrance of the "Final Solution" has contributed to the non-passing of the past, for the horror of the industrial killing of several million people had to become even more incomprehensible the more the Federal Republic of Germany joined the vanguard of humanitarian states through its legislation. But doubts remained here, too, and numerous foreigners, like many Germans, have doubted and continue to doubt the identity of "*pays légal*" [the legal country] and "*pays réel*" [the real country].

But was it really only the stubbornness of the "*pays réel*" of ordinary people that fought against the non-passing of the past and wanted a "bottom line" to be drawn so that the German past would no longer differ fundamentally from other national pasts?

---

14   The *Edda* was a Norse saga much admired in the Third Reich.

Is there not a core of truth in many of the arguments and questions that have created something like a wall against the desire for continuously ongoing "examination" (*Auseinandersetzung*) of National Socialism? I am going to list some of these arguments and questions to conceptualize what I consider to be the decisive "failing" and to describe the kind of "examination" that is just as far from drawing a "bottom line" as it is from the ceaselessly invoked "overcoming of the past" (*Bewältigung*).

Precisely those people who speak of "interests" in the most negative way won't allow the question whether interests did and do not also play a role in the non-passing of the past – the interests, for example, of a new generation in the age-old struggle against "the fathers" or, too, the interests of the persecuted and their descendants in a permanent special and privileged status.

Talk of the "guilt of the Germans" all too easily overlooks the similarity to the talk of the "guilt of the Jews," a major argument of the National Socialists. All accusations of guilt against "the Germans" that come from Germans are disingenuous, as the accusers don't include themselves or the group they represent in this category, and basically only want to deliver a decisive blow against their old opponents.

The attention devoted to the "Final Solution" diverts attention from important facts about the National Socialist period, such as, for example, the killing of "life unworthy of living" and the treatment of Russian prisoners of war. But above all it diverts attention from crucial questions of the present – for example, questions about the existence of "unborn life" or the reality of "genocide" yesterday in Vietnam and today in Afghanistan.

The parallel existence of these two series of arguments, one of which is more prominent but has not yet fully won out, has led to a situation that can be described as paradoxical or even grotesque.

A hasty response of a Bundestag member to certain demands of the spokesman for Jewish organizations or the tasteless slip of the tongue by a municipal politician are blown up into symptoms of "anti-Semitism", as if all memory of the genuine and by no means already National Socialist anti-Semitism of the Weimar period had disappeared. At the same time the moving documentary *Shoah* by a Jewish director runs on television – a documentary that in some passages makes it seem probable that even the SS guards of the death camps might have been victims of a kind, and that on the other hand there was virulent anti-Semitism among the Polish victims of National Socialism.

The visit of the American president to the military cemetery at Bitburg provoked a very emotional discussion, but fear of being accused of "balancing one misdeed against another" or of making comparisons of any kind did not permit the simple question what it would have meant if in 1953 the Federal Chancellor had refused to visit the Arlington National Cemetery with the argument that there, too, men lay buried who had participated in terror attacks against the German civilian population.

For the historian precisely this is the most deplorable result of the "non-passing" of the past: that the most elementary rules that apply to every past seem to be suspended, namely, that every past has to become more and more recognizable in its complexity; that the context in which events occurred must become ever clearer; that black-and-white images of the contending contemporaries are corrected; and that earlier versions are subjected to revision.

Precisely this rule, however, appears to be "pedagogically dangerous" when applied to the Third Reich: Could it not lead to a justification of Hitler or at least to "exculpation of the Germans?" Doesn't it evoke the possibility that the Germans will again identify with the Third Reich, as a great majority did, at least in the years from 1935 to 1939, and that they will not learn the lesson that history has imposed on them?

These questions can be answered very briefly and apodictically: No German can have an interest in justifying Hitler, if only because of his destructive orders against the German people in March 1945.[15] That the Germans learn lessons from history is guaranteed not by historians and publicists but by the complete transformation of the conditions of power and by the obvious consequences of two great defeats. Of course, they can still learn the wrong lessons, but then in a way that is likely to be novel and certainly "anti-fascist."

It is true that there have been efforts to transcend the level of polemics and to draw a more objective picture of the Third Reich and its Führer; it will suffice to mention the names of Joachim Fest and Sebastian Haffner. But both authors focused first of all on the "German interior." In the following section I will try by means of several questions and key words to suggest the perspective in which this past should be seen, if it is to receive the "equality of treatment" that is a prime postulate of philosophy and historiography, but one that does not lead to sameness, but rather to the identification of differences.

KEY WORDS THAT ILLUMINATE

Max Erwin von Scheubner-Richter, who later became one of Hitler's closest associates and was then killed by a fatal bullet on the march to the *Feldherrnhalle* in November 1923, was the German consul in Erzurum in 1915. There he was witness to the deportations of the Armenian population that launched the first great genocide of the 20th century. He made every effort to confront the Turkish authorities, and in 1938 his biographer ends his description of these events with the following sentences: "But what could these few people do against the destructive will of the Turkish Porte, which did not even heed the most direct reproaches from Berlin; against the wolf-like savagery of the unleashed Kurds; against a catastrophe that unfolded with enormous rapidity, in which one Asian peoples dealt with another in an Asiatic way, far removed from European civilization?"

Nobody knows what Scheubner-Richter would have done or left undone if he instead of Alfred Rosenberg had been appointed the Minister of the Occupied Eastern Territories [in the Second World War]. But little speaks for the notion that there was a fundamental difference between him and Rosenberg and Himmler, or even between him and Hitler himself. But then one must ask: What could induce men who considered a genocide that they had witnessed at close quarters as "Asiatic" to initiate a genocide of an even more gruesome nature? There are some key words that provide some clarification. One of them is the following:

When Hitler received the news of the surrender of the Sixth Army at Stalingrad on 1 February 1943, he predicted at the briefing that some of the captured officers would actively participate in Soviet propaganda: "You have to bear in mind that (such an officer) is brought to Moscow, and then just imagine the 'rat cage.' He will sign anything. He will sign confessions, proclamations ... "

Commentators have offered the explanation that by "rat cage" the Lubjanka [prison] was meant. I think this is wrong.

George Orwell's *1984* describes how the hero Winston Smith, after torture by the "Big Brother's" secret police, is finally forced to deny his fiancé and thus to renounce his human dignity. A cage containing a rat half-crazed from hunger is placed in front of his head. The interrogator threatens to open the cage, and this is when Winston Smith breaks down.

---

15   According to Albert Speer, Hitler had ordered him to destroy the entire German infrastructure in advance of the Allied armies in March 1945.

George Orwell did not make up this story; it can be found in numerous passages of the anti-Bolshevik literature on the Russian civil war, among others in the work of the socialist Melgunov, who is considered reliable. It is attributed to the "Chinese Cheka."

GULAG ARCHIPELAGO AND AUSCHWITZ

It is a conspicuous shortcoming of the literature about National Socialism that it does not know or does not want to know to what extent everything the National Socialists later did, with the single exception of the technical procedure of gassing, was already described in the sizable literature of the early 1920s: mass deportations and shootings, torture, death camps, eradication of whole groups according to merely objective selection criteria, public demands for the destruction of millions of people who were innocent but were regarded as "enemies."

It is likely that many of these reports were exaggerated. It is certain that the "White terror," too, committed terrible deeds, although within its ideological framework there could be no analogy to the projected "eradication of the bourgeoisie." Nonetheless, the following question has to be permissible, yes, unavoidable: Did the National Socialists or Hitler perhaps commit an "Asiatic" deed merely because they and those like them considered themselves and their kind to be potential victims of an "Asiatic" deed? Was the "Gulag Archipelago" not prior to Auschwitz? Was the Bolshevik murder of an entire class not the logical and factual precedent for the "racial murder" of National Socialism? Cannot Hitler's most secret actions also be explained by the fact that he had *not* forgotten the "rat cage?" Did Auschwitz perhaps originate in a past that would not pass?

One does not have to have read Melgunov's forgotten pamphlet to ask such questions. But one is reluctant to ask them, and even I have long been reluctant to ask them. They are seen as anti-communist battle slogans or products of the Cold War. Nor do they adequately fit into the academic discipline, which must choose ever narrower research questions. But they are based on simple truths. There may be moral reasons to deliberately ignore truths, but to do so violates the ethos of scholarship.

Reservations would only be justified if historians left it at these facts and questions and did not place them in a wider context, namely the context of those qualitative ruptures in European history that began with the Industrial Revolution and precipitated an agitated search for the "guilty ones" or at least for the "originators" of a development regarded as baneful. Only in this context would it become quite clear that despite all of their comparability the biological extermination of National Socialism did differ qualitatively from the social extermination undertaken by Bolshevism. But just as a murder, especially a mass murder, cannot be "justified" by another murder, so, too, we will be led thoroughly astray by an attitude that only takes note of *one* murder and of *one* mass murder, and that does not want to take note of the other one, even though there is probably a causal connection between them.

Anyone who looks at this history not as a mythical story, but in its essential context will be driven to a fundamental conclusion: If history – in all its darkness and all its horrors, but also in its confusing novelty to the historical actors of the time – has had a meaning for succeeding generations, then that meaning must lie in the need to become free from the tyranny of collectivist thinking. At the same time this should mean the resolute turn to *all* the rules of a free system, a system that allows and encourages criticism, insofar as this criticism refers to deeds, attitudes, and traditions, thus also to governments and organizations of all kinds. But this system must stigmatize criticism of categories from which individuals cannot separate themselves, at least not without greatest efforts. Hence it must stigmatize criticism of "the" Jews, "the" Russians, "the" Germans, or "the" petty bourgeoisie. Insofar as the examination of National Socialism is marked by precisely this collectivist thinking, a bottom line should finally be drawn. It cannot be denied that then thoughtlessness and self-satisfaction could spread. But that does not *have* to be the case, and in any case truth must not be made dependent on utility. A comprehensive examination, which above all would have to consist in thinking about the history of the past two centuries, would, to be sure, also allow the past to "pass," as is appropriate for every past, but this is precisely the process that would lead to a genuine appropriation of the past.

> **Source: Ernst Nolte, "Vergangenheit, die nicht vergehen will: Eine Rede, die geschrieben, aber nicht gehalten werden konnte," in *"Historikerstreit:" Die Dokumentation der Kontroverse um die Einzigartigkeit der nationalsozialistischen Judenvernichtung* (Munich: Piper, 1987), pp. 39–47. Translated by Rod Stackelberg**

The *Historikerstreit* (Historians' debate)

The social philosopher Jürgen Habermas' incisive critique of Stürmer, Nolte, and neo-conservative revisionism in an article in the liberal weekly *Die Zeit* on 11 July 1986 set off the furious debate among German historians known as the *Historikerstreit*. The portions of Habermas' article that deal with Stürmer and Nolte are given below. Habermas also criticized the historian Andreas Hillgruber for a book in which he had sympathized with the perspective of German soldiers fighting to delay the advance of the Red Army in the closing stages of the war even though this resistance prolonged the war and meant that the killings in the camps and on the death marches would continue. Habermas also accused Hillgruber of attempting to pin all blame for the Holocaust on Hitler as a way of absolving the German elites of culpability for the crime. Habermas' central contention was that neo-conservative historians were engaged in an effort to normalize the history of the Third Reich and to "relativize" or trivialize its crimes in order to revive national pride and create a public consensus for conservative and illiberal policies. Habermas worried that the revival of German nationalism would weaken German commitment to democracy.

Habermas' article provoked a fierce reaction from conservative historians, while liberal historians came to his defense. Although the dispute was ostensibly about history, it was driven by politics. Both sides accused the other of instrumentalizing history for political purposes. It is no coincidence that this highly polemical debate occurred during an election campaign. The underlying issue was the "new Cold War" that had been set into motion by the elections of conservatives Margaret Thatcher in Britain, Ronald Reagan in the US, and Helmut Kohl in Germany. To understand the virulence of this debate it must be remembered that nobody at the time had the slightest expectation that within three years the Berlin Wall would come down, the GDR would collapse, Germany would be reunited, and the Cold War would end. While the differences between left and right in their interpretations of the Third Reich continued into the 1990s, the debate was no longer conducted in the strident tones of the *Historikerstreit*.

7.12 Jürgen Habermas, "A kind of damage control: Apologetic tendencies in contemporary German historiography"

It is a conspicuous shortcoming of the literature about National Socialism that it doesn't know or doesn't want to know to what extent everything the National Socialists later did – with the sole exception of the technical procedure of gassing – had already been described in the voluminous literature of the early 1920s ... Did the National Socialists and Hitler perhaps commit an "Asiatic" deed only because they saw themselves and their kind as potential or actual victims of an "Asiatic" deed?

Ernst Nolte in the *Frankfurter Allgemeine Zeitung*, 6 June 1986

I

The Erlangen historian Michael Stürmer prefers a functional interpretation of historical conscious-ness: "In a country without history, the future is controlled by those who determine the content of memory, define the concepts, and interpret the past." Stürmer's modernization processes present themselves as a form of damage control – in the spirit of the neo-conservative world view of Joachim Ritter that was brought up to date by his students in the 1970s. The individual has to be compensated for his unavoidable alienation as a "social molecule" in a commodified industrial society by the creation of a meaningful identity for him. Stürmer, to be sure, cares less about individual identity than about integration into the community. Pluralism of values and interests leads, "if it no longer finds common ground   sooner or later to social civil war." It requires "that higher creation of meaning (*Sinnstiftung*) that, aside from religion, only nation and patriotism have up to now been capable of." According to Stürmer, a politically responsible historical discipline will not ignore the summons to create and disseminate a view of history that will help promote a national consensus. Academic history is in any case "driven forward by collective and largely unconscious needs for the creation of inner meaning, but it has to create this meaning" – and Stürmer clearly regards this as a dilemma – "according to scholarly methods ... " Therefore historians must walk "a narrow path between creating meaning and demythologizing."

[In the remainder of Section I and Section II Habermas discusses the historian Andreas Hillgruber's book, *Two Kinds of Collapse: The Destruction of the German Reich and the End of European Jewry*, as an example of Stürmer's precepts in practice.][16]

...

III

In the *Historische Zeitschrift* (Vol. 242 [1986], pp. 465ff.) Hillgruber's colleague Klaus Hildebrand recommends a work by Ernst Nolte as "path-breaking" because it has the merit of removing from the history of the Third Reich its "seemingly unique quality" and of integrating "the destructive capacity of [Nazi] ideology and of the regime" in the overall historical develop-ment of totalitarianism. Nolte, who already gained wide acclaim with his book *Three Faces of Fascism* (1963), is indeed made of different mettle than Hillgruber.

16 Andreas Hillgruber, *Zweierlei Untergang: Die Zerschlagung des Deutschen Reiches und das Ende des europäischen Judentums* (Berlin: Siedler, 1986).

In his article, "Between Myth and Revisionism,"[17] he now justifies the need for revision by pointing out that the history of the Third Reich has largely been written by the victors and has become a "negative myth." To illustrate this Nolte invites us to perform the tasteful thought experiment of imagining how Israel would have been portrayed by a victorious PLO (Palestine Liberation Organization) *after* the complete destruction of Israel: "Then for decades and possibly for centuries no one would dare to trace the motivating origins of Zionism to the spirit of resistance against European anti-Semitism." Even the totalitarianism theory of the 1950s did not offer a different perspective [of the Third Reich], according to Nolte, but simply led to the inclusion of the Soviet Union in this negative image as well. A concept that lives to such an extent from its contrast to the democratic constitutional state is not enough for Nolte; for him it is a matter of the dialectic between reciprocal threats of destruction. Long before Auschwitz, he claims, Hitler had good reasons for his conviction that the enemy wanted to destroy him, too – "annihilate" is the word in the English version. As proof he offers the "declaration of war" that Chaim Weizmann expressed on behalf of the Jewish World Congress in September 1939 and that, according to Nolte, gave Hitler the *right* to treat German Jews as prisoners of war – and to deport them. Several weeks ago one could already have read in *Die Zeit* (without any names being mentioned, however) that Nolte served up this outlandish argument to his Jewish guest at dinner, his colleague Saul Friedländer from Tel Aviv – now I read this argument in print.

Nolte is not the officious and conservative narrator who gets worked up about the "identity problem." He solves Stürmer's dilemma between meaning-creation and scholarship with a forceful decision and chooses the terror of the Pol Pot regime in Cambodia as the point of reference for his discussion. From here he reconstructs a pre-history stretching back beyond the "Gulag," the expulsion of the Kulaks by Stalin, and the Bolshevik Revolution to Babeuf, the early socialists, and the English agrarian reformers of the early nineteenth century – a line of revolt against cultural and social modernization, driven by the delusory longing for the restoration of a manageable, self-sufficient world. In this context of terror the destruction of the Jews then appears only as the regrettable result of a nonetheless understandable reaction to what Hitler had to perceive as a threat of destruction: "The so-called destruction of the Jews during the Third Reich was a reaction or a distorted copy, but not a unique nor an original event."

In another essay Nolte tries to clarify the philosophical background to his "trilogy on the history of modern ideologies."[18] This work is not under discussion here. I am interested only in the "philosophical" aspect of what Nolte, the former student of [Martin] Heidegger, calls his "philosophical history."

In the early 1950s there was a debate in philosophical anthropology about the interrelationship of human beings' "openness to the world" and their "imprisonment in the environment" – a debate between A. Gehlen, H. Plessner, K. Lorenz, and E. Rothacker. Nolte's peculiar use of Heidegger's concept of "transcendence" reminds me of this. For with this expression he has, ever since 1963, been diverting the great change – the historical process of the break-up of the traditional way of life in the transition to modernity – into the anthropological realm of origins.

17   Ernst Nolte, "Between Myth and Revisionism: The Third Reich in the Perspective of the 1980s," in
     Aspects of the Third Reich, ed. by H. W. Koch (London: Macmillan, 1985), pp. 16ff.
18   This trilogy includes *Three Faces of Fascism* (1963), *Germany and the Cold War* (1974), and *Marxism and the
     Industrial Revolution* (1983).

In these depths, in which all cats are gray, he then asks for understanding for the anti-modernist impulse that opposes "an unreserved affirmation of practical transcendence." By "practical transcendence" Nolte means the supposedly ontologically-based "unity of world economy, technology, science, and emancipation." All this fits very well into climates of opinion that are dominant today – and into the colorful dance of California images of the world that sprout from them. More annoying is the failure to differentiate, which from this perspective makes "Marx and Maurras, Engels and Hitler, despite all their differences, into related figures."[19] Only when Marxism and fascism are seen as equally attempts to give an answer "to the frightening realities of modernity" can the true intention of National Socialism be cleanly separated from its unholy practice. "Its 'misdeed' was not contained in its ultimate intention, but in its attribution of guilt to a group of people who were themselves so greatly affected by the process of emancipation in liberal society that through their important representatives they declared themselves to be in mortal danger."

Now, one could ignore the scurrilous philosophy of an important, if eccentric mind if neo-conservative historians did not feel obliged to make use of just this form of revisionism.

As its contribution to this year's Römerberg Conference, which also included lectures by Hans and Wolfgang Mommsen on the topic "the past that will not pass," the *Frankfurter Allgemeine Zeitung* on 6 June 1986 bestowed on us a militant article by Ernst Nolte – incidentally, under a hypocritical pretext (I say this as someone familiar with the correspondence that the supposedly disinvited Nolte conducted with the conference organizers). On this occasion Stürmer, too, expressed solidarity with the newspaper article, in which Nolte reduces the singularity of the destruction of the Jews to "the technical procedure of gassing" and then documents his thesis that the Gulag Archipelago is "more original" than Auschwitz with a rather abstruse example from the Russian Civil War. All that Nolte gleans from the film *Shoah* by [Claude] Lanzmann is "that the SS guards in the death camps might also have been victims of National Socialism in their way, and that on the other hand there was virulent anti-Semitism among the Polish victims of National Socialism." These unsavory samples show that Nolte puts someone like Fassbinder in the shade by a wide margin.[20] If the *Frankfurter Allgemeine Zeitung* quite rightly campaigned against the planned performance of this play, why then does it publish Nolte's article?

I can only explain this by the fact that Nolte not only gets around the dilemma between meaning-creation and scholarship more elegantly than others, but also that he has a solution for another dilemma. Stürmer describes this dilemma with the sentence: "In the real world of a divided Germany the Germans have to find their identity, which can no longer be found in a nation state, but cannot be found without a nation, either." The planners of ideology want to create a consensus about reviving national consciousness, but at the same time they have to banish negative images of the [German] nation state from the NATO domain. For this manipulation Nolte's theory offers a great advantage. He kills two birds with one stone: Nazi crimes lose their singularity by being rendered at least understandable as a response to the (continuing) Bolshevik threats of destruction. The significance of Auschwitz shrinks to the level of a technological innovation and is explained on the basis of the "Asiatic" threat of an enemy that still stands at our gates.

19   Charles Maurras (1868-1952) was the founder and leader of the right-wing *Action française*.
20   The German filmmaker Rainer Werner Fassbinder (1946–1982) was accused of writing an anti-Semitic play about a Jewish landlord and developer in Frankfurt.

IV

When one looks at the composition of the commissions that have drawn up the concepts for the museums planned by the Federal Government, the German Historical Museum in Berlin and the Museum for the History of the Federal Republic in Bonn, one cannot wholly escape the impression that the ideas of the New Revisionism are to be translated into pedagogically effective displays and exhibit pieces. The expert reports do have a pluralistic face. But things will probably be no different in the case of the Museums than they were in the new Max Planck Institutes: The programmatic reports that regularly precede the founding of a new institution no longer have much to do with what the directors who are appointed to head them later make of them. [Historian] Jürgen Kocka, the token liberal member of the Berlin commission of experts, suspects the same: "In the end what will be decisive is which persons take the matter in hand ... here, too, the devil is in the details."

Who would want to oppose serious efforts to strengthen the historical consciousness of the population? There are also good reasons for gaining historical distance from a past that doesn't want to pass. [Historian] Martin Broszat has set them forth convincingly. The complex interrelationships between criminality and ambiguous normality in daily life under National Socialism – between destruction and vitality of achievement, between the dreadful perspective of the Nazi system and the inconspicuous and ambivalent close-up local perspective – could certainly use a healing and objective representation. The breathlessly didactic appropriation of the reductionistically moralized past of our fathers and grandfathers could then give way to a more detached understanding. Careful differentiation between understanding and condemning could also help take from a shocking past some of its hypnotic, paralyzing effect. But this kind of historicizing would not let itself be guided by the impulse to *shake off* the liabilities of a past happily freed from moral condemnation – as in the case of the revisionism of Hillgruber or Nolte, commended to us by Hildebrand and Stürmer. I do not want to impute evil intentions to anyone. There is a simple criterion on which the people in this dispute differ: Some take as their point of departure the assumption that the work of detached understanding will liberate the power of reflective memory and thereby expand the space for an autonomous treatment of ambivalent traditions; others want to put revisionist history at the service of a nationalist historical refurbishing of a conventional identity.

This formulation may not yet be unequivocal enough. Anyone who wants to revive an identity organically rooted in national consciousness, anyone who allows himself to be guided by functional imperatives of predictability, of consensus formation, and of social integration through meaning-creation (*Sinnstiftung*) has to shun the enlightening effect of historiography and must reject a widely effective pluralism of historical interpretations. One hardly does Michael Stürmer an injustice if one understands his articles in this sense: "In looking at the Germans *vis-à-vis* their history our neighbors are bound to ask where all this is leading. The Federal Republic ... is the centerpiece in the European defensive perimeter of the Atlantic system. But now we see that every generation living in Germany today has different, even contrasting images of the past and the future ... The search for the lost past is not an abstract striving for education: it is morally legitimate and politically necessary. For what is at stake is the inner continuity of the German Republic and its predictability in foreign affairs." Stürmer is pleading for a *unified* historical interpretation that can secure identity and social integration in place of the religious powers of belief that have drifted off into the private sphere.

Historical consciousness as a substitute for religion – is not this old dream of historicism asking too much of historiography? To be sure, German historians can look back to a tradition in which their discipline really did buttress the state. Recently Hans-Ulrich Wehler once again reminded us of the ideological contribution that historiography made to the stabilization of the "Prussian German" Empire and to the marginalization of inner "enemies of the Reich." Up to the late 1950s the mentality prevailed that had emerged after the failure of the Revolution of 1848/49 and the defeat of liberal historiography of the type of a [Georg Gottfried] Gervinus: "From then on for more than a hundred years liberal, enlightened historians could only be found in isolation or in small marginal groups. The majority of historians thought and argued in nationalist, statist, and power-political terms." The fact that after 1945 – at any rate in the generation of younger historians trained after 1945 – not just a different spirit, but a pluralism of interpretations and methodological approaches gained the upper hand is not just a breakdown that can simply be repaired. Rather, the old mentality was only the specifically historiographical expression of a mandarin consciousness that for good reason has not survived the Nazi period: By its proven impotence against or even complicity with the Nazi regime the lack of substance of this mandarin consciousness was revealed for all to see. This historically-compelled gain in the capacity to reflect has not just affected the ideological premises of German historiography; it has also sharpened methodological awareness of the dependence of *all* historiography on its historical context.

It is a misunderstanding of this hermeneutic insight, however, if the revisionists today assume that they can illuminate the present with the floodlights of arbitrarily constructed histories and can choose a particularly suitable historical interpretation from among these options. More incisive methodological awareness means, rather, the end of every historical interpretation that is closed, or, worse, decreed by government historians. The unavoidable pluralism of interpretations – by no means uncontrolled, but rather made transparent – only reflects the structure of open societies. Only now the chance is opened up to clarify one's own identity-forming traditions in their ambivalences. Precisely this is necessary for a critical appropriation of ambiguous traditions, that is, for the formation of a historical consciousness that is just as incompatible with closed and unreflective historical images as it is with every form of a conventional identity, namely one that is unanimous and shared without reflection.

What today is lamented as the "loss of history" does not only have the characteristics of displacement and repression, nor only of fixation on a past that is burdened and has therefore come to a standstill. If among younger people national symbols have lost their power, if naive identification with one's own origins have given way to a more tentative approach to history, if discontinuities are felt more strongly and continuities are not celebrated at all costs, if national pride and collective feelings of self-worth are filtered through universalistic value orientations – to the degree that this really is the case the signs of the emergence of a post-conventional identity are increasing. These signs are described by the Allensbach opinion poll in Cassandra-like terms; but unless they deceive, these signs reveal only one thing: that we have not entirely wasted the opportunity that the moral catastrophe could also mean to us.

The unreserved opening of the Federal Republic to the political culture of the West is the great intellectual achievement of our post-war time, which precisely my generation could be proud of. This result will not be stabilized by a NATO philosophy colored by German nationalism. After all, this opening was achieved by overcoming precisely that ideology of the center, which our revisionists are warming up again with their geopolitical palaver of "the old central location of the Germans in Europe" (Stürmer) and "the reconstruction of the destroyed European center" (Hillgruber). The only patriotism that will not alienate us from the West is a constitutional patriotism. A commitment to universalistic constitutional principles anchored in conviction unfortunately could not emerge in the national culture of the

Germans until after – and because of – Auschwitz. Anyone who wants to drive away our shame about this fact through a slogan like "obsession with guilt" (Stürmer and Oppenheimer) – anyone who wants to call the Germans back to a conventional form of their national identity – is destroying the only reliable foundation for our ties to the West.

Source: Jürgen Habermas, "Eine Art Schadensabwicklung: Die apologetischen Tendenzen in der deutschen Zeitgeschichtsschreibung" in *"Historikerstreit": Die Dokumentation der Kontroverse um die Einzigartigkeit der nationalsozialistischen Judenvernichtung* (Munich: Piper Verlag, 1987), pp. 62–3, 68–76. Translated by Rod Stackelberg

The historiography of the Third Reich in West Germany

The following brief review of post-war changes in the historical memory of Nazism and the Holocaust in West Germany by the prominent historian Hans Mommsen in 1987 places the *Historikerstreit* in its political context. Mommsen points out that the real purpose of the "new nationalism" was to combat the reorientation of values to the left that occurred as a result of the 1960s upheavals. Mommsen traces the shift in conservative historiography from its earlier stress on the singularity of Nazism – its unique, accidental, and aberrant nature outside of normal German history – to conservatives' more recent denial of the uniqueness and singularity of Nazism – its "normalization" as an admittedly extreme, but understandable response to the earlier and even greater destructiveness of communism. What is common to both approaches, however, is the effort to downplay the significance of the period from 1933 to 1945 and to reduce the stigma attached to it. Mommsen also provides an astute critique of the apologetic functions of totalitarianism theory and of interpretations that attribute all responsibility for Nazi crimes to Hitler or a small criminal band of top Nazi leaders.

7.13 Hans Mommsen, "Reappraisal and repression: The Third Reich in West German historical consciousness," 1987

I

As the recent controversy over the place of the National Socialist past in German self-understanding has shown, the long repression of this uncomfortable legacy postponed but could never eliminate the need for certain fundamental historical debates. The Federal government's attempt to lead West Germany back onto the path of "normalcy" via Bitburg and the Bonn war memorial backfired. So, too, did its desire to cover questions of individual and collective responsibility for Nazi crimes with a blanket of universal reconciliation. What basic lessons for its internal politics and international role should the Federal Republic derive from the experiences of Nazism and World War II? This issue is now being raised more insistently than ever before. At the same time, the widespread consensus concerning the thoroughly reprehensible nature of the National Socialist regime is dissolving. What was earlier an academic dispute over methodology within the historical profession has now gained immediate political relevance.

The fact that the past has suddenly regained a place in public discussion is a result of a gradual shift in national values, encouraged by forces within the West German government and lately dubbed *die Wende* (the turning point). The recent controversy over the relationship of the Federal Republic to National Socialism has produced no new arguments or research results. The Berlin historian Ernst Nolte has been expounding his provocative views for years without either the press or the academic community making much of them. The essence of Nolte's position is that Hitler's murder of 5 million Jews must be seen as a reaction to a well-founded fear of Bolshevism. The essays of Andreas Hillgruber, collected in the book *Zweierlei Untergang*, were also published previously. Michael Stürmer's theory of Germany's "middle position" [*Mittellage*] in Europe already occupied an established place in discussions of the German question.

The immediate cause of the Historians' Debate was Jürgen Habermas' vehement attack in the 11 July 1986 edition of *Die Zeit* on Nolte, Hillgruber, and Stürmer, as well as Klaus Hildebrand, who had supported Nolte in a review in the *Historische Zeitschrift*. The sharpness of the confrontation, as well as the extent of the publicity surrounding it, can be attributed principally to the *Frankfurter Allgemeine Zeitung*'s partisanship for Nolte and its condemnation of left-wing intellectuals for supposedly attempting to use the Nazi past for their own political purposes. The paper accused the Left of seeking to torpedo the long overdue historical normalization being championed by the Federal government. Habermas has called this, and similar attempts in the professional literature to relativize National Socialist crimes and to assign them a purely episodic character within German history, "neo-revisionism." But this neo-revisionism has in turn served to underwrite a broader revival of nationalist values among conservative groups both inside and outside the government camp, a revival that has gained wider attention as "the new nationalism."

Although it is the historical and political assessment of the Holocaust that stands at the center of the Historians' Debate, the Holocaust itself has functioned largely as a symbol for the totality of National Socialist policies. Still, an emphasis on the Final Solution as the true mark of Nazi violence and inhumanity remains significant precisely because the Holocaust was long neglected by researchers in West Germany. This new emphasis can perhaps be explained by the fact that with the changing of the generational guard in the Federal Republic, a preoccupation with the responsibility for the Nazi seizure of power has faded, while at the same time, consciousness of the long-term consequences of the National Socialist terror system and of the Second World War has increased. The real issue, however, remains the relative weight of the Nazi period within the broader continuity of both German and European history. The passage of time and the ensuing evolution of historical perspective have lent this problem a new dimension.

II

Over the past forty years, a number of identifiable concerns have inspired research on contemporary history. In response to Allied accusations of war guilt, Germans in the immediate post-war period did their best to highlight the terrorist nature of the Nazi dictatorship and the role of German resistance to Hitler's regime. Researchers accentuated the effect of the SS state, and the opposition to Hitler – a movement now christened "the other Germany" – came to stand for the nation as a whole. From this perspective, both the internal politics of the regime and the persecution of the Jews were pushed into the background. At first, an intellectual-history approach, linking National Socialism to the exaggerated nationalism of the imperial period, predominated. Slowly, however, the theory of totalitarian dictatorship established itself as *the* valid explanatory model. In this model, Nazi ideology was depicted primarily as a conscious instrument of manipulation.

Despite many variations in detail, theories of totalitarianism all assumed that the structure of the National Socialist system of domination was fundamentally monolithic, thus echoing the regime's own propagandistic self-interpretation. Later research, based primarily on documents impounded by the Allies and released after 1961, lent only partial support to the assumptions of the totalitarian model. This research revealed political fragmentation and instability in the institutions that the Nazis created as well as those they had inherited. In so doing, it contradicted the image of a totalitarian system organized down to the last detail in the service of power considerations. Yet the totalitarian image could still be maintained by interpreting the antagonisms within the regime as an attempt on Hitler's part to buttress his own unrestricted veto power through a strategy of divide-and-rule. Related to this was the tendency in the literature to regard Hitler, despite his obvious personal weaknesses, as the ultimate author of National Socialist policies and to emphasize the internal logic of his actions when seen in the light of his programmatic writings. Often this view went so far as to attribute to Hitler a coherent, ideologically motivated plan which he set about realizing in a methodical and gradual fashion.

The Hitler-centered interpretation of Nazism is so attractive as an explanatory model because it seems to lend consistency to a series of confusing and often contradictory actions. However, just because no one mounted effective opposition to Hitler, the symbol and embodiment of the Nazi regime, we should not necessarily conclude that he himself planned all Nazi politics and systematically put them into effect. It is only in the last decade that researchers have freed themselves from a preoccupation with Hitler as the sole center of decision-making. They have now discovered those areas of politics determined by the autonomous decisions of other leaders, areas where Hitler often exercised his (by no means systematic) influence only through haphazard intervention. The regime has begun to reveal itself as a political system that had a certain degree of openness, albeit within fixed ideological parameters.

Tim Mason has called the debate among historians over the personality and role of Hitler a clash between intentionalists and structuralists. The best way for scholars to decide between these two positions is to determine which explanatory model provides the best answers to specific important questions. Yet rather than resolve the intentionalist/structuralist controversy in a purely professional manner, historians in the Federal Republic have pursued it at a high emotional pitch. Perhaps this intensity can be explained in social–psychological terms: after the consolidation of power, Hitler became the very incarnation of German national identity, so it is logical that after 1945 he should become the central focus of blame for the German catastrophe. By personifying the events of National Socialism in the figure of Hitler and presenting the average German as the victim of a subtle mixture of propaganda, cynically exploited patriotism, and terroristic repression, historians could at least partially justify the conduct of the German people as a whole.

This perspective went hand in hand with the attempt to emphasize the break marked by 30 January 1933 and to excise the period between 1933 and 1945 from the continuity of German history. Accordingly, many historians sought to depict the foreign and domestic policies of the Nazis as a revolutionary break with all that had gone before them. This position found its culmination in Karl Dietrich Bracher's theory of the pseudo-legal totalitarian revolution, a revolution that distinguished itself from its bourgeois antecedents by its unscrupulous manipulation of power. In implicitly equating 1933 with the October Revolution, Bracher overlooked fundamental differences between the Bolsheviks' seizure of power and the transfer of power to the Nazis. This recasting of the formation of Hitler's "cabinet of national concentration," his coalition with the bourgeois parties in 1933, reflected a desire to impose a retrospective quarantine on those twelve years of Nazi rule – a period which, as Eberhard Jäckel recently put it, led out of German history and into a previously unimagined abyss.[21]

For these reasons the National Socialist period was assigned a place of historical "singularity" that was justified on the one hand by the destructive role of Hitler and on the other by the sheer magnitude of Nazi crimes, unparalleled even by those of other fascist or authoritarian systems. This emphasis on the singularity of Nazism was directed especially at those historians who had taken up Ernst Nolte's theory of comparative fascism but had replaced its phenomenological–ideological perspective with a Marxist one. While explanatory models based on economistic or agency theories have encountered widespread resistance, structuralist approaches that stress similarities in the styles and institutions of fascist politics have allowed a more nuanced picture of the NSDAP and its internal dynamics. The historiographic adherents of "Hitlerism" (Hans Buchheim's term) have criticized the comparative perspective for minimizing the horror of National Socialism. The real motive, however, behind the "Hitlerists'" rejection of any comparisons between Nazism and other fascist movements or regimes is that such an approach undercuts their own desire to equate National Socialism with communism.

Stressing the uniqueness of Nazism also served to negate the efforts of other researchers to uncover the historical roots of the movement and to identify links between National Socialism and various bourgeois nationalist, neo-conservative, and populist (*völkisch*) movements. These researchers naturally emphasized the strains of anti-communism, anti-socialism, anti-liberalism, and anti-parliamentarianism shared among a broad range of bourgeois groups in the period after World War I. Their opponents, the Hitlerists, have tried to discredit the claims of continuity between Nazism and various strains of bourgeois nationalism (claims admittedly often exaggerated) by focusing attention on the field of electoral analysis. They have sought to prove that the NSDAP attracted a considerable number of members and sympathizers from the proletariat and that an exchange of voters took place between the KPD (Communist Party of Germany) and the Nazis, especially after January 30, 1933. Linked to this claim is the argument that the parties of the republican center in the Weimar Republic were in fact strangled by extremists from both Right and Left. This claim is based on various episodes of cooperation between Nazis and Communists, normally the bitterest of enemies.

This argument, still a favorite in the popular media, corresponds to the denunciation of the Nazis during Weimar as "brown Bolsheviks." It has received only weak support from serious historical scholarship, although anti-Bolshevism certainly played an important role in the success of National Socialist propaganda. The equation between Nazis and Communists obscures the crucial role of the conservative elite in the events of 1933. Because of their opposition both to the "Marxist" SPD (the Social Democratic Party) and to the parliamentary system in general, the conservatives allowed Hitler's entry into the Cabinet – though they would have preferred a more purely authoritarian rule. In the wake of recent scholarly reevaluation of Heinrich Brüning's government, the literature now reflects a broad consensus concerning the strong continuity, both in personnel and in policies, between the earlier presidential cabinets and the "cabinet of national concentration." Nor does anyone dispute the fact that there was no significant purge of higher government functionaries (except for the generally applauded removal of Jews) after 1933, and that the regime owed its relative stability principally to the support it received from the army, the civil service, and the staff of the Foreign Office.

---

21   † Eberhard Jäckel, *Hitlers Herrschaft: Vollzug einer Weltanschauung* (Stuttgart, 1986), p. 146.

Meanwhile, there was a major convergence of political goals among the traditional elites and the inner circle of Nazi leaders after the Nazi seizure of power, even though each group differed in its choice of preferred methods and its degree of willingness to court risk. Ironically, it is research on foreign policy, once seen as the field *par excellence* for the systematic realization of Hitler's world vision, that now takes a non-Hitlerist approach, emphasizing strong historical continuities reaching back to the imperial period. This work has forced the intentionalists, who had previously concentrated mainly on domestic policies, to attempt to define those elements of the Nazi system that would most clearly distinguish it from its imperial predecessor. The elements they propose include the typically fascist reversal of the relationship between ends and means: the Nazis' desire to present the highly organized fascist party as a "movement;" and their avoidance of a specific program in favor of a purely propagandistic mobilization. This reversal of methodological positions, exemplified by the intentionalists' use of arguments drawn from the literature on comparative fascism, underscores the fact that the latest controversy over historical continuity has produced no new insights and has become largely counterproductive.

III

When viewed against this historiographic background, the "change of paradigm" now advocated by a prominent group of West German historians seems rather paradoxical. Klaus Hildebrand, who, like all intentionalists, has previously always insisted on the uniqueness of the Nazi regime, now joins Ernst Nolte in promoting a relativizing, world-historical perspective on this phenomenon. They no longer view National Socialism as an unfortunate accident coming at the end of the Weimar Republic, but rather as a complicated tangle of world-historical circumstances of tragic proportions. Stalin's dictum, "The Hitlers come and go, but the German people remain," has been taken up by conservatives in order to alleviate the traumatic psychological tensions which the Nazi experience has produced between the generations. Former United States ambassador Richard Burt also contributed to the "national rediscovery" sought by conservatives with his supportive comments.

In the case of Ernst Nolte, a relativist perspective leads directly to the anti-Bolshevism that has always been the hallmark of his approach to the past. It has motivated him to trace the development since the Industrial Revolution of what he calls an ideological "postulate of extermination" and its exemplification by the Bolsheviks, a phenomenon unparalleled in history. For Nolte the Holocaust is, in the final analysis, nothing more than a reaction to the class destruction committed by the Bolsheviks, crimes with which Hitler became obsessed.

Nolte's superficial approach, which associates things that do not belong together, substitutes tenuous analogies for causal arguments, and – thanks to his taste for exaggeration – produces a long outdated interpretation of the Third Reich as the result of a single factor. His claims are regarded in professional circles as a stimulating challenge at best, hardly as a convincing contribution to an understanding of the crisis of twentieth-century capitalist society in Europe. The fact that Nolte has found eloquent supporters both inside and outside the historical profession has little to do with the normal process of research and much to do with the political implications of the relativization of the Holocaust that he has insistently championed for so long.

Nolte argues that Hitler's "destruction of the Jews" was not in essence genocide, but rather "the most radical and at the same time most desperate form of anti-Marxism." He attempts in this way to provide a psychological explanation for the translation of the "extermination postulate" into actual biological reality. Such an enterprise provokes immediate objections. For Nolte, "anti-Marxism" always carries positive, freedom-preserving connotations; hence, in his view, Hitler merely fell victim to an unfortunate perceptual error while pursuing comprehensible aims. As far as their content is concerned, it is in fact not inaccurate to identify anti-Bolshevism with racial anti-Semitism, and Hitler was not alone in equating them. He merely radicalized the existing anti-Semitism of the early post-war years.

In Nolte's historical sketches, the Third Reich appears as an unfortunate response to the threat posed to German society by Bolshevism. According to him, this threat, although certainly exaggerated even with regard to the revolutionary period 1917–21, called forth a psychologically justified anxiety embodied most extremely and most tragically in the person of Hitler. The fundamentally apologetic character of Nolte's argument shines through most clearly when he concedes Hitler's right to deport, though not to exterminate, the Jews in response to the supposed "declaration of war" issued by the World Jewish Congress; or when he claims that the activities of the SS *Einsatzgruppen* can be justified, at least subjectively, as operations aimed against partisans fighting the German army.

IV

Ernst Nolte is not the real problem, however. As a nonconformist, in some respects pathbreaking, thinker, he obviously runs the risk of being identified with the ever more confident neo-fascist movement in the Federal Republic. More important is the fact that the new message of the Bolsheviks' responsibility for National Socialism has been eagerly taken up by groups that have for years lamented the absence of a healthy German national consciousness. They see the lack of nationalist sentiment as a regrettable weakness that may even pose a threat to the very survival of the German people, and they hope to respond by undoing the post-war reorientation of values and by fostering an aggressive national consciousness – one unashamed of the German performance during the Second World War. Ideas that just a few years ago still defined only a marginal neo-conservative position have now entered the political mainstream, thanks to the support provided by prominent CDU/CSU spokesmen. Whether the younger generation in the Federal Republic will be receptive to such views remains in doubt.

Historical writing has functioned above all as an indicator of the changed state of political consciousness regarding this reorientation of values. The fact that the fortieth anniversary of the German capitulation set off a lively public debate was due at least superficially to the failed spectacle of Bitburg, itself a reaction to the Allies' D-Day celebrations. The claim made at Bitburg that all republican forces in the FRG share a common anti-communist goal provoked a broad, totally unexpected historical-political response from the West German Left. As this response indicated, a reevaluation of the Federal Republic's relationship to National Socialism was long overdue. The Left's response was also a reaction to the quiet rejection of the antifascist consensus previously shared by all of West Germany's democratic parties. This rejection stemmed from the influence of German nationalist and revisionist groups in the government coalition, and had already been prepared by the far right and neo-conservative press.

The West German parliamentary system, which can no longer simply hearken back to the achievements of the democratic reconstruction period and has tended to distance itself from the electorate's primary political interests, is currently experiencing a growing crisis of legitimacy. As a result, the temptation to buttress a crumbling political consensus through recourse to a "national" view of the past has gained in strength. Questions of historical interpretation have become, as they were in the Weimar period, a battlefield for largely ossified political parties. In this situation, the totalitarian model of National Socialism, already increasingly undermined by the latest historical research, proved unable to stand up to accusations leveled from the Left that not enough was being done in either the political or the judicial sphere to confront the Nazi past. The peace movement has drawn analogies between certain structures in the Federal Republic and the Third Reich by reviving the notion of a "right to resistance" common in the 1950s. The violent and exaggerated criticisms provoked by this analogy demonstrated that such comparisons are extremely uncomfortable. At the same time, however, the government parties alluded freely to political conditions during the 1930s in order to denounce the Left.

What had until then been a fairly homogeneous picture of Weimar and the Third Reich thus began to fragment along party lines. Characteristic of this process was the tendency of historians closely associated with the government to depict the destruction of the bour-geoisie and the removal from power of the traditional upper classes as a central aim of the Nazis. In so doing, they recapitulated older conservative interpretations of National Socialism as the product of "mass democracy" and the unavoidable reaction to the threat of a left-wing dictatorship. Meanwhile, these same historians claimed that excessive wage demands made by the working class were primarily responsible for the collapse of Weimar. On the other side, historians who sympathized with the left republican positions of the 1920s and 1930s blamed heavy industry for destroying the socio-political compromise of the Republic's early years and thus bringing about the progressive breakdown of the parliamentary system. The decisive change in the almost canonical "totalitarian" view of the Third Reich occurred during the 1970s, when it became increasingly impossible to uphold the view that a small clique of fanatical Nazis were alone responsible for the criminal policies of the regime. Such a claim was no longer plausible given the evidence of broad involvement by higher army officers, diplomats, and industrialists in the plunder of Eastern Europe, the exploitation of prisoners of war, and forced laborers, and the extermination of the Jews.

Evidence for the political polarization of attitudes toward the Nazi past can be found in a speech delivered by Alfred Dregger, parliamentary leader of the CDU/CSU, on 11 November 1986 to mark West Germany's Memorial Day [Volkstrauertag]. In his address Dregger insisted that most German soldiers – and implicitly most of the general public as well – were ignorant of Nazi crimes. The only people in the know, according to Dregger, were "political functionaries," "a few higher army officers," and those in the support services behind the front lines, who were involved in activities that "violated every tradition of military honor." Dregger failed to mention that the war in the East, which aimed at the utter subjugation of the enemy, had from the begin-ning renounced all "military honor." Instead, he complained that the Allies had directed their demand for unconditional surrender at Germany as a whole rather than just at Hitler – thus echoing arguments previously formulated by Hillgruber. He described the dilemma imposed on the German soldiers, who indirectly facilitated Nazi crimes by defending their homeland. Dregger did not seem to realize that this bitter choice (defending the nation versus helping to end Nazi crimes) was a foreseeable consequence of policies that the military leadership, at least initially, unanimously approved. He preferred to regard the Third Reich as a system of domina-tion forced on Germany by Hitler and a small band of criminals.

Similarly, the word "seduction" [Verführung] appears in the plans for a Museum of German History in Berlin, again implying that the Third Reich was the result not of misguided long-term policies, but of deceptive propaganda. Nor can the cooperation of the army, bureaucracy, and industry in carrying out the regime's criminal domestic and foreign policy goals be made to disappear simply by invocations of the "dictated peace" [Diktatfrieden] of Versailles, or the misdeeds of other nations. Such attempts to rewrite the past understandably fulfill the need for self-justification felt by many older Germans, who would like to free themselves from the guilt heaped upon them from both inside and outside the country. These attitudes indicate that the past has been confronted on a moral, but not on a political or analytical, level; the result is a sense of painful surprise but not of accountability. One need not be an apologist to acknowledge that collaborators in German-occupied territories and ethnic minorities in the Soviet Union shared responsibility for Nazi crimes. But to claim that "the Germans are obsessed with guilt," or that Allied efforts at reeducation undermined national values, merely diverts attention from the Nazi destruction of traditional values – a process whose ultimate results were the complete corruption and then the disintegration of the very fabric of German society.

The representatives of the Right, including professional historians like Michael Stürmer, share the mistaken impression that their opponents seek to sustain collective feelings of guilt. This impression must be corrected. By reacting to National Socialism only with shock and moralizing self-criticism, as has so often been the case in the Federal Republic, Germans have managed to avoid the sensitive question of how far the general public and the elite functionaries were responsible for the Holocaust. The failure of the overwhelming majority of the German people to protest the abuse and deportation of the Jews can be only partially explained by their fear of the state's power. The point of studying the Third Reich cannot be simply to produce shock and sadness; rather, it must lead to guidelines for action aimed at preventing a recurrence of the constellation of circumstances that permitted the Holocaust. The task is to uncover the mechanisms that explain the growing moral indifference, especially among the upper classes, during the aftermath of World War I, and to identify the complex conditions under which genocide and a war of racial destruction could be conceived and carried out.

V

When [the historian] Martin Broszat called for a "historicization" of National Socialism, he sought to distance himself from contingent interpretations of the regime, such as the one that attributes the escalation of violence and terror solely to the conscious calculations of Hitler. Such interpretations overlook the conditions in which even people who did not belong to the hard core of the NSDAP and who were not greatly motivated by ideological concerns nonetheless participated (directly or indirectly) in the killing machine. Historicization means taking seriously the diversity, the relative openness, and the contradictory character of the Nazi system rather than simply rejecting it out of hand. It means analyzing both the destructive elements of the system and the features that appeared promising in the eyes of many contemporaries. Historicization will thereby allow us to explain how someone like Adolf Hitler, whose pathological refusal to face reality is uncontested, could come to enjoy such great (though never unlimited) popularity and, thanks to the systematic propagation of the Führer myth, could continue until well into the spring of 1945 to act as a symbol of national integration above and apart from the conflicts of state and party.

What is vexing is the understanding of the term "historicization" that takes it to mean merely relativization – that is, the acceptance of the Third Reich as historically inevitable, and the use of events and personalities from that period simply as metaphors. When this occurs, as with Helmut Kohl's comparison of Gorbachev to Goebbels, it indicates that the deep challenge that Nazism continues to pose for a society committed to individual freedom and the preservation of human dignity has not been understood and remains unmet. This applies equally to the particular way of settling accounts with the past that has recently found its way into the legislation of the

Federal Republic.[22] The fact that all manner of political claims have been and will be committed in no way alters the specific constellation of circumstances under which they occurred in Germany. The thinking of the regime's satraps, like Himmler and Goebbels, as well as of Hitler's conservative Cabinet colleagues, shows that they consciously sought the elimination (if only temporary and partial) of otherwise uncontested normative guidelines, and that they accepted a state of emergency as the normal condition for state action. The pretexts they used, such as the "threat" to national security, were clearly contrived and transparent. To the extent that psychotic compulsions drove the regime's henchmen to carry out their work, these were derived from self-created anxieties that had long been politically instrumentalized. A particular example is their hybrid anti-Bolshevism already formed by 1917, which bore no relation to the real threat posed to Germany by Lenin's program of world revolution.

Ernst Nolte therefore makes a fatal misrepresentation when he blames the anti-Bolshevism and racial anti-Semitism consciously fomented by the Pan-German Association and the right wing of the Conservative Party (DNVP) entirely on the Bolsheviks and their program of class murder, as if the hatred vented during the Russian Civil War had nothing to do with the tsarist autocracy and its methods of repression. Even more troublesome is the way in which Nolte identifies Hitler personally as a final cause. Some of Nolte's critics, including Eberhard Jäckel, have not taken sufficient notice of this. Nolte does not see that the road to the Final Solution was paved with a complex interaction of ideological motives and technocratic incentives. It can only be explained in close connection with the internal and external developments of the regime, a process in which Hitler's fanatical anti-Semitism was only one, and possibly not even the most important, factor.

One could simply disregard such prejudiced and intellectually esoteric explanations if it were not for the fact that they tend to cloud the lessons drawn by the overwhelming majority of Germans from the National Socialist experience. These lessons have taught a sober skepticism vis-à-vis nationalist slogans and the setting up of ideological enemies. Memories of the wartime air-raids and mass destruction have made the country unsympathetic to strategies of mass political mobilization and the use of military force. Germany today is ahead of its neighbors in its wariness of patriotic appeals and violent solutions to domestic conflicts. It is an illusion to believe that the moderation or absence of nationalism among the Germans makes them pathologically susceptible to antidemocratic slogans. Those who continually warn of the "German neurosis" completely overlook the fact that for the younger generation neither the Bismarckian nation-state nor the conflict of national loyalties under the Nazi regime retain any great importance.

The Historians' Debate is in many respects simply a proxy war fought along the fault lines of West German politics between adherents of authoritarian democracy and reformist republicanism. Behind it lies the problem of the unresolved political identity of the generation socialized under the Third Reich. When Alfred Dregger in his Memorial Day address uses a political slogan right out of the 1930s and ascribes the collapse of Weimar to "the Versailles Diktat," one is reminded of the 1928 election, when the DNVP made prominent use of Grand Admiral Tirpitz in its campaign even though less than a third of the electorate could remember his role during the pre-war period. The plans for a "House of History" in Bonn and a "German Historical Museum" in Berlin also raise the suspicion that their primary purpose is self-justification for the in-between generation raised under the Third Reich, rather than education about the

---

22   Mommsen is here referring to the so-called Auschwitz Law of 1985 that forbids insults to the victims of
        the National Socialist or other dictatorships.

German past for the younger generation. Michael Stürmer revealed the political intentions behind these museum projects when he stated that the future belongs to those who control the past and that the Germans must be made more "predictable" in both domestic and foreign affairs with the help of a balanced picture of the past. Yet the desire to use history to such manipulative ends is hardly compatible with the political maturity Germans have acquired through the bitter and sobering recognition of their complicity in the crimes of the Third Reich.

At the same time, the debate unleashed by the Historians' Debate concerning the historical place of the Nazi period is more than a mere episode. It should mark the end of efforts to counter neo- or post-fascist interpretations with legal sanctions or to render them socially taboo. For it will not be possible to prevent neo-fascist publications from drawing their own conclusions from the neo-revisionist relativization of the Holocaust or from Hillgruber's question about whether the attempt on Hitler's life of 20 July 1944 can still be seen as justified in light of the atrocities committed by the Red Army against the German people in 1944. There will be open disagreement over whether the overthrow of the regime and an end to the killings at Auschwitz deserved to take priority over the stabilization of Germany's eastern frontier.

Acknowledging that German soldiers were motivated by a desire to protect their homeland from Soviet invasion does not change the fact that their efforts objectively helped to prolong the Nazi rule of crime and destruction. If contemporary history has taught the German people anything, it is the ability to recognize this contradiction and to draw conclusions from it for their future political behavior. Margret Boveri has analyzed this state of affairs under the concept of "betrayal in the twentieth century," and in so doing has made it clear why it is psychologically impossible for Germans to use a broken and morally perverted tradition of the nation-state in order to find themselves. No exhortations of the "new nationalism," no matter what terminology it employs, can avoid this fact. Thus, neither a "reconstruction of the European center [europäische Mitte]" nor an exonerating theory of "Germany's middle position [deutsche Mittellage]" is necessary.

**Source: Hans Mommsen, "Reappraisal and Repression:
The Third Reich in West German Historical Consciousness," trsl. by Thomas Ertman,
in Reworking the Past: Hitler, the Holocaust, and the Historians' Debate,
ed. by Peter Baldwin (Boston: Beacon Press, 1990), pp. 173–184**

Right-wing extremism in the 1990s

Despite the strong official and unofficial repudiation of Nazi ideology and anti-Semitism after 1945 in the FRG (and even more so in the GDR, where all right-wing political activity was completely suppressed), Nazi organizations and activities never entirely disappeared in West Germany. Former Nazis formed political parties that professed allegiance to the parliamentary system in order to maintain their legal status. But neither the National Democratic Party (NPD), which enjoyed its greatest strength in the late 1960s by appealing to the backlash against the student movement, nor the equally misnamed Republicans, who exploited Ausländerfeindlichkeit (hostility to foreigners) in the 1980s, ever succeeded in gaining the 5 percent of the national vote necessary for representation in the Bundestag. Violence-prone neo-Nazi organizations outside the political process revived in the conservative climate of the 1980s, although to no greater extent than in other European countries or the US. The principal targets of right-wing violence were the Turkish population, now numbering more than 2 million, who had been recruited to meet the labor demands of West Germany's booming industrial economy in the 1960s and early 1970s.

The reunification of Germany in 1990, however, was accompanied by an unexpected and shocking outburst of radical right, neo-Nazi, and skinhead violence against African, Asian, and East European immigrants, particularly in the former GDR. This violence among youthful, underemployed, mostly male East Germans was fed by a backlash against the failed communist ideology on which they had been reared as well by the economic collapse that accompanied the sudden East German transition to a market economy. Violence reached a preliminary climax in four days of rioting against a refugee hostel in the East German city of Rostock in August 1992. It ended only after police authorities, who failed to restrain the rioters, transported the Vietnamese refugees to a different location. Across Germany, however, hundreds of thousands of people rallied to demonstrate their outrage against the violence.

The following report on right-wing violence in 1992 was published by the Ministry of the Interior on 6 February 1993. It is of note not only for its statistical evidence of the extent of the violence, but also for its defense of the adequacy of governmental measures to contain the violence. Critics had accused Helmut Kohl's CDU government of courting right-wing voters by failing to respond resolutely to the neo-Nazi threat and by downplaying its significance. Indeed, the major effect of the rioting was to strengthen the movement to curtail immigration by legal means. In 1993 the Federal government restricted the constitutionally guaranteed right to political asylum by accepting applicants for asylum only from countries whose human rights records had been officially certified as unsatisfactory. The result was a precipitous decline in the number of foreigners seeking asylum. Right-wing violence against foreigners, Jews, gays, left-wing activists, the poor, and other outsiders continued on a somewhat lesser scale throughout the 1990s.

7.14 "Right-wing acts of violence, 1992," Report of the Federal Ministry of the Interior, 6 February 1993

In 1992 the Federal Agency for Internal Security recorded 2285 acts of violence with proven or probable extreme right-wing motives. This is an increase of 54 percent in comparison to 1991 (1483 right-wing extremist acts of violence).

17 people – including 7 foreigners – were killed (1991: 3 deaths). Numerous people were injured, some seriously.

Arson and bombing attacks have risen most sharply among right-wing acts of violence, namely from 383 to 701. In 1992 bodily injury motivated by right-wing extremism increased to 598 (previous year: 449). An increase in property damage in conjunction with violent acts was also recorded, from 648 in the previous year to 969.

Again in 1992 foreigners were the major target of right-wing extremists, especially people applying for political asylum and the hostels in which asylum seekers reside. There were 1033 or 90 percent of the recorded right-wing extremist attacks and infractions, directed against these targets.

In the past year the internal security authorities were made aware of 77 cases of desecration of Jewish cemeteries, memorials, and other buildings. This is double the number of attacks of the previous year.

Juveniles and young people predominated among the violent perpetrators associated with right-wing extremism. Of 894 suspects investigated, about 70 percent were juveniles and young people. Only 2 percent were older than 30.

As far as security officials were able to determine, these violent acts were neither centrally controlled nor directly initiated by right-wing extremist organizations or associations in 1992. Most of the criminal acts were spontaneous and were committed by local offenders.

In the sphere of militant right-wing extremism the first signs of right-wing terrorism can be recognized.

Xenophobic or right-wing extremist violence reached its peak with 518 offenses in September – right after the Rostock riots.

Minister of Internal Affairs Rudolf Seiters made the following statement in regard to right-wing extremist crimes in 1992:

"Since the end of November 1992 there has been a decline in crimes directed against foreigners. This trend continued in January 1993 with 70 acts of violence, which is a significant decline in the monthly average compared to 1992. The decline in numbers can be attributed to the effects of a series of governmental and social measures taken to oppose hostility to foreigners. Nevertheless there is no reason to let down our guard. The most recent callous and brutal arson attacks on the houses in Cologne/Worringen prove that. Every one of these crimes is one too many. Therefore the state must not relax its efforts; it is essential to take swift and strong action against these repugnant extremist activities in the future as well.

The statistics presented above show the disgraceful tally of right-wing extremist acts of violence in the past year. These brutal attacks on defenseless people rank among the most bitter experiences of the present time.

Instigation of hate against foreigners and violence against the lives, health, or property of people living in our country, regardless of whether they are Germans or foreigners, must be resolutely condemned. We Germans know from the painful part of our history that extremism, hate, and violence have always led to disaster.

Our democracy has not passively accepted these despicable attacks. It has fought against its enemies with a variety of legal methods.

We Germans are not hostile to foreigners. Certainly the many hundreds of thousands of people who took to the streets and demonstrated impressively against hatred of foreigners with candlelight vigils provide persuasive proof of this. This is a convincing commitment to goodwill toward foreigners. The overwhelming majority of our population support our liberal constitution and condemn any form of extremism.

The significant decline in numbers can be attributed to the considerable symbolic and deterrent effect achieved by the measures taken.

I personally banned three right-wing extremist organizations at the end of last year: the 'Nationalist Front,' the 'German Alternative,' and the 'National Offensive.' These measures were necessary – above all because these organizations prepared a dangerous seedbed for militant right-wing extremism. The bans had an intensely unnerving and paralyzing effect on the right-wing extremist camp. Proceedings to deprive two leading neo-Nazis of basic rights are pending in the Federal Constitutional Court. Insofar as this is permitted by the results of current judicial reviews, I will utilize the opportunity to take further measures.

In order to improve the exchange of information a category, 'Criminal Offenses Against Foreigners,' will be included in the existing registry of offenses against state security. This should ensure a faster flow of information between the Federal Government and the states as a pre-condition for an effective common strategy to combat these crimes.

At the Federal Agency for Internal Security staff reductions that were originally planned have been dropped. At the same time the work unit responsible for the surveillance of right-wing extremism/terrorism has been appropriately expanded.

In the Federal Bureau of Criminal Investigation a new section (ST 2), responsible for combatting right-wing extremism/terrorism, has been set up in the Department of State Security.

Furthermore, on my initiative a Federal government/state government Information Team (IGR) was formed and began working last year to follow and combat right-wing extremist/ right-wing terrorist acts and especially acts of violence against foreigners.

Many measures have also been planned at the state level and some have already been implemented to prevent the fanatical actions of extreme right-wing perpetrators or to bring them swiftly to an end.

In 1991 police reacted immediately and comprehensively to the emergence of this new phenomenon of right-wing extremist crimes against foreigners. Special investigative squads and special commissions were formed in most states with hundreds of detectives who are trying to solve these crimes.

Thousands of police officers are on duty every day – some around the clock – to protect the homes of political asylum-seekers and foreigners.

Since Hoyerswerda,[23] integrated units and formations of the Federal Border Guards have also been called in more than 40 times to support regional police against right-wing extremists.

In relation to all the attacks on foreigners and other right-wing extremist crimes in 1992, a total of about 4000 suspects could be identified, of whom around 1500 were arrested. Cases of homicide were solved without exception.

The swift and complete investigation of these acts of violence against foreigners has led in many cases to the speedy prosecution and conviction of the criminals who were identified. This has increased the general deterrent effect of the sentences.

In conclusion I would like to emphasize: the Federal Government – together with other governmental authorities – will resolutely continue its measures against right-wing extremism, anti-Semitism, and hostility to foreigners.

All people in Germany – Germans and foreigners – must be able to feel safe and secure. Our democracy will also take advantage of all necessary legal possibilities and instruments in the future, so that the inner peace in our community will not be harmed. Anyone who attempts to violently confront our constitutional state will receive an unequivocal response."

Source: "Rechtsextremistische Gewalttaten 1992,"
Report of the Federal Ministry of the Interior, 6 February 1993.
Translated by Sally Winkle

Hostility to foreigners

The following article in *Die Zeit* on 6 July 2000 attests to the fact that right-wing activities and attitudes remain a problem, particularly in the economically depressed rural regions of the formerly communist East. Hostility to foreigners is proportionately no greater than in other European countries and certainly less politically significant, for instance, than in Austria, where Jörg Haider's anti-immigrant "Freedom Party" gained

---

23   Hoyerswerda is the town in the former GDR that was the site of a particularly vicious attack on asylum-seekers in 1991.

enough votes in national elections to join a coalition government with the conservative People's Party in February 2000. Nonetheless, because of the German past, signs of the revival of neo-Nazism provoke widespread concern both in Germany and abroad. The article reprinted here describes not only the pervasiveness of hostility to foreigners among young people in eastern Germany, but also provides eloquent testimony to efforts by some Germans to counter this trend through education and enlightenment.

7.15 Toralf Staud, "On a visit to schools in Saxony: Hostility toward foreigners remains unchallenged in many places"

Ronny is not right-wing. He says. Ronny just has something against foreigners. "Turks stink," he says. Ronny is 15. He lives in a village outside of Leipzig. Being hostile to foreigners, he thinks, is normal.

Jennifer, 14, is certain, that "the foreigners live at our expense." She lives in a small town in East Saxony. Her mother works in the supermarket. And there, according to Jennifer, the "foreigners" shoplift. That raises the prices, and "the Germans" end up having to pay more. Jennifer's 8th grade classmates agree with her. Also, when asked if Germany is overrun with foreigners, most of the students raise their hands.

Ronny and Jennifer are completely average youth. Ronny doesn't wear combat boots, but rather tennis shoes. Jennifer doesn't have a skinhead haircut, but rather long, beautiful hair. Nonetheless, right-wing prejudices have taken hold in their minds. When people from the Dresden Project "Show Courage for Democracy" show up at their schools to talk about racism, the students are baffled. It seems no one has ever contradicted them. Even with the simplest arguments the project leaders are able to throw the students off balance.

Paul, 13, from Ronny's class, says with conviction that all Poles steal. Jörn from the Project team asks, "How many Poles do you know?" – "None." – "How many Germans do you know who steal?" – Paul grins and says, "Many." – "Then it would be more justifiable to say that all Germans are thieves, wouldn't it?" Paul starts to stutter. Jörn probes further: "Do you just repeat everything you hear other people say?" – "No ... "

For the past year and a half, the workers from the Courage project – mostly college students barely older than the school children themselves and often dressed in the same brand name clothes – have been touring schools in Saxony. Paid by the DGB (German Federation of Labor), the project has visited more than 220 classes. For an entire day they show videos, pin colorful index cards on bulletin boards, and lead games utilizing group dynamics. Again and again the project workers realize that otherwise nothing would be said about right-wing extremism and violence. Most teachers shy away from taking a political stance, because when the GDR dissolved they had been accused – and rightly so – of having indoctrinated their students. Many teachers are not up to the job; they fight for authority. A girl from Jennifer's class is happy about the young project workers: "Finally someone who isn't yelling all the time." Ralf Hron, Youth Secretary of Saxony's DGB and coordinator of the Courage project, says: "We have come upon a need that is very big."

Every once in a while there is a boy with clean-shaven head wearing a t-shirt with an iron cross emblazoned in front who castigates the project worker as a "filthy Jewish pig." There is the teacher who for the life of her can't find anything wrong with the "Reich War Flag." It's hanging in her own son's bedroom. In a middle school there are the two boys who brag that they once attended an illegal skinhead concert, heard music forbidden at home, and that their big brothers were with the NPD. There is the student who was encouraged by the project workers to criticize neo-Nazis during class and was then beaten up during the next recess.

To be sure, there are also the classrooms – mainly in cities like Leipzig – in which, for example, Hip Hop fans set the tone; where a middle school student mentions in passing that he watched a documentary film on *Arte* [an educational TV channel], or where the students are proud of the fact that their school is named after an African-American civil rights leader. But these are exceptions. The norm is a classroom like Ronny's and Paul's. Nadine thinks foreigners bring all kinds of diseases to Germany. Robert thinks all of them work illegally. Ronny explains: "The foreigners take our jobs away."

Ronny is the heartthrob of the class. His baggy jeans hang to his knees. He has dark hair groomed with gel. Under the hairdo his big elephant ears stick out. Because he was held back once, Ronny is by far the oldest in his class. During the break he stands at the door and necks with his 9th grade girlfriend. What Ronny says is important to many in the class. And Ronny says there are so many foreigners here, pretty soon we will no longer know what land we are living in.

The project workers dig deeper. "How high do you think is the percentage of foreigners living in Saxony?" Jörn asks the students one after another. Ten percent is one answer, 12, 8, 25, 35 to 40. Paul picks 3 percent, Ronny guesses 30. "So you think on average about 20 percent?" asks Jörn. He counts off the class and has every fifth student stand up. "Each of you should be a foreigner." In reality, the percentage of foreigners living in Saxony is 2.3 percent. Among the 24 students there isn't a single foreigner. In the other 8th grade class there is one boy with dark hair and skin. He gets teased by everyone.

The Courage project workers calculate for the students just how much tax the foreigners living in Germany pay. They show them that after deducting all costs there is still money left over. They describe the living conditions in refugee hostels in Saxony and explain what is in the "survival kits" that the refugees receive and from which they must sometimes live for years. They give history lessons, explaining to the East German children when "our West German ancestors" brought Turks, Italians, and Yugoslavs into the country as guest workers. The Courage project seldom reaches dyed-in-the-wool right-wingers with this; its aim, anyway, is more geared toward strengthening the potential for resistance among normal kids.

In parts of East Germany, especially in rural areas, the slogans of right-wing extremists and right-wing populists shape the popular consensus and are widely accepted as plausible explanations for such problems as unemployment and crime. "Foreigners" are to blame – the fact that there are practically none living there merely leads to these prejudices not being challenged. In many places right-wing extremists dominate public life, are a constant part of the cityscape, and control the youth clubs. Thus their subculture soon becomes the only one available to adolescents. And when yet another political party offers the slogan "*Kinder statt Inder*" (children instead of Indians),[24] it is clear that the Courage project has lots of work to do.

"We wanted to offer the children something that would give them the chance to think in a different direction," says Petra Schlegel, teacher and counselor at Ronny's school. She finds the readiness for violence and the intolerance of many children shocking. And yet, her middle school has the best reputation far and wide. The teachers are known to be committed; there are, relatively speaking, lots of extra-curricular activities. On the other hand the town of Wurzen, only a few kilometers away, is a Nazi stronghold. Some parents from the city delib-

---

24   This is a reference to an initiative in 2000 to recruit trained technicians from India for the computer industry.

erately send their children to this school. Three years ago Paul moved from Wurzen to a village, because his parents built a house there. "Only then I noticed," he says, "how right-wing Wurzen is." It's not only there that Nazi gangs hang out at the school gates, passing out cigarettes and flyers.

Petra Schlegel speaks softly and very deliberately. She says her school sees to it that no one can practice incitement. Two years ago in Wurzen her son was beaten up by young Nazis. He ended up in the hospital with serious head injuries. After he reported the beating to the police the family received death threats. The case against the suspects is still being dragged out today.

Ronny thought the project day was "rather useless." The project workers had really only disparaged right-wingers. He isn't right-wing, he says once again, but his cousin is! His name is Lars; he repeated a year and is going to drop out now after the 9th grade. Out in the school-yard Ronny waves him over. Yes, says Lars proudly, he is a nationalist. Then he gripes about school. Not about stupid tests or some teacher. He complains about the principal, because he prohibited students from wearing combat boots to school.

Source: Toralf Staud, "Ganz normal rechts. Zu Besuch an sächsischen Schulen: Fremdenfeindlichkeit bleibt vielerorts unwidersprochen," *Die Zeit*, **6 July 2000. Translated by Jody Stewart-Strobelt**

Index